SPECIAL EDITION
USING

Microsoft®

Office
FrontPage®
2003

Jim Cheshire

Paul Colligan

TK
5105.8885
.M53
C43
2004

Pearson Education

800 E. 96th Street

Indianapolis, Indiana 46240

CONTENTS AT A GLANCE

SPECIAL EDITION USING MICROSOFT OFFICE FRONTPAGE 2003

Copyright © 2004 by Que Publishing

International Standard Book Number: 0-7897-2954-7

Library of Congress Catalog Card Number: 2003103663

Printed in the United States of America

First Printing: November 2003

06   05   04   7   6   5   4   3

Trademarks

Warning and Disclaimer

Bulk Sales

Que Publishing offers excellent discounts on this book when ordered in quantity for bulk purchases or special sales. For more information, please contact

> **U.S. Corporate and Government Sales**
> **1-800-382-3419**
> corpsales@pearsontechgroup.com

For sales outside of the U.S., please contact

> **International Sales**
> **1-317-428-3341**
> international@pearsontechgroup.com

Publisher
Paul Boger

Associate Publisher
Greg Wiegand

Acquisitions Editor
Stephanie J. McComb

Development Editor
Laura Norman

Managing Editor
Charlotte Clapp

Project Editor
Andy Beaster

Copy Editor
Rhonda Tinch-Mize

Indexer
Ginny Bess

Proofreader
Suzanne Thomas

Technical Editor
Jennifer Kettell

Team Coordinator
Sharry Lee Gregory

Interior Designer
Anne Jones

Cover Designer
Anne Jones

CONTENTS

II Creating and Editing Web Content

III Creating Web Sites with FrontPage

TROUBLESHOOTING TABLE OF CONTENTS

About the Authors

Jim Cheshire is the owner of Jimco Add-ins, the Internet's number one resource for FrontPage add-ins. Jim has been featured in numerous computer publications for his contribution to the FrontPage community, including *PC Magazine*. Jim has also been a contributor to the Microsoft Developer Network (MSDN) and has written an occasional newspaper column on computer topics.

Over the past five years, Jim has worked on the FrontPage team and the ASP.NET team at Microsoft, where he is currently employed. He has no official involvement in FrontPage, but still has a fond place for it in his heart.

You can contact Jim by visiting his Web site at
`http://www.jimcoaddins.com` or by emailing him at
`jcheshire@jimcoaddins.com`.

Paul Colligan is the Webmaster of FrontPage World, the Internet's most visited site about Microsoft FrontPage (`http://www.frontpageworld.com`). The traffic FrontPage World sees allows Paul to interact with tens of thousands of FrontPage users a month to understand their needs in working with the product. Paul writes a number of FrontPage-related newsletters and has coauthored numerous other books on FrontPage. Paul was awarded MVP status from Microsoft in 2002.

He is also a popular presenter on Internet technology topics and frequently speaks online, on the air, and before audiences about his passions. He has presented at events around the country that include Internet World, Linux World, Commission Junction University, and Microsoft Tech-Ed.

Mr. Colligan has played a key role in the launch of dozens of financially successful Web sites and Internet marketing strategies that have seen millions of visitors and millions of dollars in revenue. Previous clients have included InternetMCI, the Oregon Multimedia Alliance, Rubicon International, Microsoft, and the Electronic Boutique.

You can reach Paul in the FrontPageTalk Forum at
`http://www.frontpagetalk.com` or by email at `Paul@Colligan.com`.

DEDICATION

I have always chuckled when reading the dedications in technical books. After all, it's not as though a technical book is an important literary work along the lines of War and Peace. This book has changed my perspective. I now know the great deal of work that goes in to a project such as this and the sacrifice that loved ones make so that it might happen.

To my wife, Becky, thank you so much for your patience as I sat alone in my office for hours and days on end. I love you very much. To my two-year-old son, James, thank you for being so understanding while "Dadas writes chapters," and thanks to my editor for removing the "contributions" James made to them when I wasn't looking. Last, but not least, to my wonderful parents who have always shown their support and love.

—Jim Cheshire

Dearest Heidi, thanks for putting up with this whole project right after the birth of sweet Paige. Your patience and presence is heaven sent. I love you. Dearest Lord, thank you for giving me a wife with such patience, a job that lets me be me, and a promise of eternity with you. I love you as well.

—Paul Colligan

ACKNOWLEDGEMENTS

I owe a great deal of gratitude to Paul who brought me into this project. It has truly been an adventure, hasn't it? I hope we do it again. To Stephanie and Laura at Que Publishing, thank you for your patience and help while I learned the Que ropes. You made it a pleasure. To the developers of FrontPage, thank you for making such a great product and for making it so easy to add in all those cool features you left out. Thank God for the miracle of life and for blessing my life with such good fortune. All the glory is truly His.

—*Jim Cheshire*

Jim, thank you. This is a significantly better book because of your contributions. I've always known you were a pro, and I can't believe how right I was. *How about 100 more pages?* Stephanie, acquisitions editor extraordinaire—and we thought we'd never work together again? Laura, development editor with the patience of Mother Teresa—I can't believe you can edit while watching *American Idol*. (I can't even write with a fan on.) Ryan, Doug, Paul, and Erica, Support Team—thanks for freeing me up to make this happen. Randi, I blame this on you. Tom, Scott, Jason, Tina, Tiffany, Fran, Alex, Jonathan, Erik, Mike, Richard, and the rest—FrontPage World would be nothing without your help. And most importantly, to the FrontPage fans and to any customer who ever bought a template, tool, or training—Thanks for letting a guy like me make a living doing what he loves.

—*Paul Colligan*

WE WANT TO HEAR FROM YOU!

As the reader of this book, *you* are our most important critic and commentator. We value your opinion and want to know what we're doing right, what we could do better, what areas you'd like to see us publish in, and any other words of wisdom you're willing to pass our way.

As an associate publisher for Que, I welcome your comments. You can email or write me directly to let me know what you did or didn't like about this book—as well as what we can do to make our books better.

Please note that I cannot help you with technical problems related to the *topic* of this book. We do have a User Services group, however, where I will forward specific technical questions related to the book.

When you write, please be sure to include this book's title and author as well as your name, email address, and phone number. I will carefully review your comments and share them with the author and editors who worked on the book.

Email: feedback@quepublishing.com

Mail: Greg Wiegand
             Associate Publisher
             Que
             800 E. 96th Street
             Indianapolis, IN 46240 USA

For more information about this book or another Que title, visit our Web site at www.quepublishing.com. Type the ISBN (excluding hyphens) or the title of a book in the Search field to find the page you're looking for.

A Better FrontPage

WHY THIS IS THE ONLY FRONTPAGE 2003 BOOK YOU NEED

As the authors of this book, we consider FrontPage 2003 to be an incredible product. We are not technical writers hired to quickly produce a complementary text before a piece of software goes to market: We all have a long history with the product and are thrilled to share our passion as we examine why FrontPage 2003 is a *better* FrontPage than ever before and show you how to push it to its full potential.

We are thrilled to work on this project because it gives us the ability to both share our experiences with FrontPage and Web design while teaching others about the latest features that come with this new release. Expect *real-world* examples and teaching in this book from experts who have been working with FrontPage *in the real world* for a combined total of more than 20 years.

The goal of this short introduction is to quickly explain why FrontPage 2003 is such an important upgrade, examine where FrontPage came from, and touch on the competition and how FrontPage interacts with it. We'll also mention briefly where each of the authors come from so that you can understand what we bring to this project.

If you are a *straight to the facts* kind of person, go ahead and skip to Chapter 1, "What's New in FrontPge 2003," where we examine what's new in FrontPage 2003.

FRONTPAGE 2003: A MAJOR UPGRADE

In the software industry, there are different kinds of upgrades: There is the *incremental upgrade*, where only minor changes are made and *major upgrades* that result in major changes in form and functionality to the product. Previously, the only major upgrade for FrontPage was FrontPage 2000. FrontPage 2003 is only the second major upgrade to the popular Web design product.

While the release of FrontPage 2003 happens in parallel with the release of the entire Microsoft Office 2003 System, the differences between this version of the product and previous versions is considerably more significant than any of the other products introduced in this upgrade cycle.

To simply call FrontPage 2003 a major upgrade and to say that it is "better" than previous versions of the product is to understate the tremendous changes in form and functionality. Most of the complaints of existing users of FrontPage and other Web design products have been answered very well: Previous FrontPage users are responding to the 2003 release with "it's about time," and users of other products are simply saying "Wow!"

My History with FrontPage
I first created my Web site, FrontPageWorld.com on FrontPage 97 and have been updating it with new features as new versions of FrontPage were released. The goal of this site has always been to show users what FrontPage can do by showing them a site built and updated with FrontPage.

With this release I found that the old site couldn't reflect the power afforded to me by FrontPage 2003 and am completely redoing it based on what this new release finally makes possible. By the time this book is released, the new site will be in place. If you want to see where the site "came from," check out http://frontpageworldarchive.frontpagelink.com/.

You might want to consider what the new features provided by FrontPage 2003 mean to any existing Web sites you currently maintain.

In addition to the changes made to the product, FrontPage 2003 makes great strides in taking FrontPage toward to what Microsoft, and many others, consider to be the future of Web design.

A SHORT HISTORY OF FRONTPAGE

If you are new to FrontPage (and this version will be bringing a lot of new users), a short history of FrontPage and its reputation in the Web design industry are in order.

Unlike the other Office products, Microsoft didn't write or design FrontPage but bought FrontPage from the software startup Vermeer Technologies in 1995. The original version of FrontPage introduced a then radical approach to content design and management that is still seen in the product today.

After the acquisition, Microsoft quickly launched its version of the product (in just a few months) with a lot of code from the old Vermeer version and only recently began to truly make the product its own. Because it was purchased from a third party and released so quickly, FrontPage carried a lot of programmatic baggage that finally seems to be eliminated from the program with this release.

TIP

> If you want to read a *truly fascinating* book on the story behind Microsoft's purchase of FrontPage, I must recommend Charles H. Ferguson's *High Stakes, No Prisoners: A Winner's Tale of Greed and Glory in the Internet Wars*. FrontPage didn't come to Microsoft without a fight, and the cast of characters that made it all happen, and prevented other things from happening, makes for my favorite read from the dot-com gold rush that seems but a memory now.

FrontPage was, from the very beginning, a different kind of Web design product because it approached Web design from a management standpoint and saw things in terms of how the pages and content related and reacted to each other—not just how the pages were made. It also attempted to eliminate a lot of the more complicated server-side issues in Web design with the FrontPage Extension part of the product. The FrontPage Extensions interacted with different Web servers without requiring the developer to have skills in that area, allowing developers to perform server-side tasks (such as sending form data to email, a database, or another file).

The combination of a holistic approach to Web design and the ability for server-side capabilities without programming encouraged many Web designers to embrace FrontPage as their product of choice.

In order to maintain and manage the site on a server-wide basis, FrontPage previously edited Web page code in such a way that often frustrated users. This is no longer a problem because the HTML produced by FrontPage 2003 is as "clean" as can be and will satisfy even the most steadfast of the clean code club.

FRONTPAGE AND THE COMPETITION

Historically, competing Web design products seem to fall into different camps with different software groups under different software companies. The one thing that many of them had in common was the fact that previous versions of FrontPage didn't interact well with them at all.

More often than not, the multimedia enthusiast tends to work with the Macromedia line of products (Dreamweaver, Flash, and son on), those with an emphasis on graphics lean toward Adobe's offerings (PhotoShop, GoLive, and so on), and the open source movement regularly stays away from anything with a price tag.

It should be no surprise that those familiar and comfortable with the Microsoft product line often find themselves using FrontPage because it integrated so tightly with other Microsoft products. It should also be of no surprise that users looking to interact with other platforms looked other places for their Web development tools.

This division of users and allegiances is quickly going to change. FrontPage now integrates very tightly with non-Microsoft Web design products, multimedia and graphics systems, and any scripting language in existence, making it a much more compatible product with the competition. In addition, FrontPage 2003 also has a considerably smaller price tag than any of the products (with a price tag) mentioned previously.

In addition, FrontPage has historically been seen by many as a "beginners'" product that wasn't capable of doing serious Web design. "Real" developers used the other products and left amateurs to FrontPage.

Is FrontPage for "Professionals?"

I've always felt that the "pros" were the ones who got the job done the right way as quickly as possible, whatever the product. I have never been one for judging the quality of a product by how complicated it makes things.

This is why I've been such a big fan of FrontPage over the other products: *FrontPage allowed me do what I wanted to do faster than any other product ever did.* FrontPage 2003 is the same, only faster.

If you like the "under the hood" stuff or charge by the hour, FrontPage might not be the product for you. If you're looking to get the job done right, keep reading.

Historically, other Web design products have prided themselves in being powerful tools that didn't interfere with the code or content the developer might try to create. Fans of these products also frequently criticized FrontPage's legacy of bloated code and integration only with other Microsoft products. FrontPage 2003 now produces code as clean as any other product and integrates easily with its competitors.

FrontPage is not only in a place to meet the competition; it can also work with it in ways that will surprise many.

THE FUTURE OF WEB DESIGN

Web design is no longer simply about designing attractive Web pages that link to each other. Dynamic content, user collaboration, database integration, diverse content management, and server- and client-side scripting make up a world that can't be contained on a simple Web page or site. Web pages, sites, and users all communicate with each other in ways few could have guessed a few years back—let alone at the introduction of a piece of software from a company called Vermeer.

Microsoft obviously has some ideas about where things are heading. The press about its .NET focus continues, and a chunk of this book is dedicated to the integration of FrontPage with Windows SharePoint Services, a new server technology considered by Microsoft to be the future of Web content.

FrontPage 2003 is positioned to work with all these elements integrating tightly with the best Microsoft has to offer. In addition, it finally provides the tools to communicate with any other Internet authoring product or technology assisting you, the user, in the process of developing your most powerful Web site yet. We'll examine how to make that happen as well.

FrontPage 2003 is the future of Web design. We'll show you how—and why.

MEET YOUR AUTHORS

Before we tell you exactly what's new with FrontPage 2003, I wanted to introduce you to the authors of this book. We want you to know where we are coming from as we take you on this 1,200 page journey.

- **Jim Cheshire** is best known for founding and operating Jimco Add-ins, the most well-known source for FrontPage add-ins and utilities on the Internet. Jim is a regular contributor to Microsoft's MSDN Office Developer Web site and has been featured in other well-known publications such as *PC Magazine*. He remains a huge fan of FrontPage, and the authoring of this book has reminded him why. Expect to see new add-ins at his site based on what he uncovered as he wrote this book. You can visit his Web site at http://www.jimcoaddins.com.

- **Paul Colligan**'s site, FrontPage World, is the Internet's most visited site specifically about Microsoft FrontPage. The traffic FrontPage World sees enables Paul to interact with tens of thousands of FrontPage users a month to understand their needs in working with the product. Paul writes a number of FrontPage related newsletters and has coauthored numerous other books on FrontPage. Paul was awarded MVP status from Microsoft in 2002 and remains one of the world's biggest FrontPage fans. FrontPage is how Paul *makes his living*, so he brings a real-world element to this book you don't often see in tomes of this nature. Visit FrontPage World at `http://www. frontpageworld.com`.

HOW THIS BOOK IS ORGANIZED

The structure of this book was the result of a very well thought out process that came not only from our experience as authors but also through input from other professionals in the FrontPage community. We are certain that you'll find everything within FrontPage has been covered and even some things outside of FrontPage that are integral to the Web development process. Anytime we mention something that is beyond the scope of this book but is important for general knowledge, we've done our best to direct you to other sources for additional information if you find that you need it.

WHAT THIS BOOK COVERS

Here's a guide to the main sections of this book and the content covered in each section:

- **Part I, "FrontPage 2003: An Overview"**—Get an overview of the different elements of FrontPage 2003 and how they all come together to produce a complete Web design package. Learn what's new with FrontPage 2003 and take a tour of the different parts of the larger picture.

- **Part II, "Creating and Editing Web Content"**—This section is part tour of the most basic elements of FrontPage and part tutorial of how to design great Web content with FrontPage 2003. Learn about the different views that let you edit your site the way *you* want to, understand the interface for building Web content, see how an improved search and replace gives you more control than ever, and realize how the graphics and navigational tools integrate directly with your site. Integrate the use of layout tables and frames in Web design with FrontPage's toolset and reach the goal of an accessible Web site with FrontPage's new accessibility features.

- **Part III, "Creating Web Sites with FrontPage"**—A Web site is more than selections of Web content. Everything has to work together as an entire entity. In this section of the book, the entire process of Web site design is covered. The roles of FrontPage Templates, Wizards, and Packages in the design process are examined while creating, publishing, and editing an existing site are detailed. This section also presents the important issues surrounding the configuration and administration of a Web server should you choose to do this for yourself.

- **Part IV, "Advanced Page Design Concepts"**—FrontPage 2003 provides a number of tools that assist in areas commonly associated with advanced page design. The implementation and use of forms and style sheets are covered in detail with specific directions for using FrontPage 2003 to expedite the process considerably.

- **Part V, "Scripting, Dynamic HTML, and Dynamic Content"**—Dynamic templates and content are detailed in this part. The new FrontPage Behaviors tool that provides additional dynamic content is examined, as are the new interactive buttons. Client-side scripting and design-time layers are also covered with both an explanation of how FrontPage handles these technologies as well as their use in the Web design process.

- **Part VI, "Working with Code"**—FrontPage 2003 gives the user the ability to work with code directly in ways previously not possible with the product. Scripting languages not traditionally Microsoft (such as PHP, JSP, and so on) can be integrated into your FrontPage Web site with ease. The chapters in this part examine and explain the different views in FrontPage 2003 and how to maximize them in the code development process. You will also find out how the quick tag editor and code snippets functionality gives additional power in the Web design process. FrontPage's new HTML optimization tools and VBA integration tools are also examined.

- **Part VII, "Web Collaboration"**—Web design is no longer a solo process. Web sites are usually the results of the efforts of multiple people, and FrontPage provides a number of tools for making the Web design process a better and more efficient collaborative effort. Both the theory of designing with a team and the specifics of how FrontPage assists the process are covered here.

- **Part VIII, "Accessing Data with FrontPage 2003"**—FrontPage 2003 introduces a new level of data capability that is covered in detail in this part. The types of data used with FrontPage, FrontPage's data access technologies and toolsets, and how FrontPage works with other data sources (such as XML) are all covered in this part of the book.

- **Part IX, "Integrating FrontPage 2003 with Office 2003"**—As part of the Microsoft Office System, FrontPage integrates easily and directly with other products in the suite. Part IX covers how Microsoft Office Word, Excel, PowerPoint, and Publisher can be used in the creation of Web content. Tricks and shortcuts for getting the most out of each of the programs are also covered.

- **Part X, "Creating and Adapting Graphics for the Web"**—Developers often need to create Web graphics for their projects. In Part X, we cover both the theory and practical nature of developing Web graphics while giving specific direction for doing so with some of the most popular graphics programs available today.

Four appendixes are also included in this book. They help FrontPage users further extend the product by giving detailed directions on how to find additional FrontPage and Web design information on the Web, how to use FrontPage to transact online commerce, how to integrate FrontPage into a Windows SharePoint Services site, and how to make personalized Web components:

- Appendix A, "FrontPage Resources Online"
- Appendix B, "FrontPage and E-Commerce"
- Appendix C, "Windows SharePoint Services 2.0"
- Appendix D, "Creating Your Own Web Components"

SPECIAL ELEMENTS

Various elements exist in each chapter that have been crafted to make your reading experience as easy and useful as possible and also to make this book truly serve as the only reference you need for FrontPage 2003.

Terms that appear in *italics* are new or unusual and will be defined in the same section of text. Items that you are to type as part of a stepped exercise will appear in **bold**. We've also included a hotkey indicator so that those of you who are non-mousers can quickly access a command by pressing Alt and the underlined letter of a command.

 You will find that we've included a "new" icon so that you can easily locate information that is new to FrontPage 2003. It will appear next to a section of text where the new item is being discussed.

CROSS REFERENCES

Cross references lead you to specific information in other chapters that relates to the topic you are reading. Whenever possible, they direct you to a specific section of a chapter to help you quickly and easily find what you need.

→ You will find cross references sprinkled throughout the chapters that will redirect you to related information should you need to learn more about a specific topic.

NOTES, TIPS, CAUTIONS, AND SIDEBARS

These elements provide you with useful little tidbits of information that relates to the discussion of the text.

NOTE

> Notes will give you additional information that you might want to make note of as you are working in FrontPage.

TIP

> A tip can contain special insight from the authors about their professional experience in using FrontPage 2003, as well as items of particular interest to you that you would not find elsewhere.

CAUTION

> Although you'll miss out on some good information, you can skip over Notes and Tips as you are reading, but definitely make sure to read Cautions. This element will caution you on pitfalls or problems before you get into them.

Sidebars Can Be Goldmines

Just because its in a sidebar doesn't mean that you won't find something new. Be sure to watch for these elements that bring in outside content that is an aside to go along with the discussion in the text.

TROUBLESHOOTING

The second to last section of just about every chapter is called "Troubleshooting" and contains a series of question/answer type of issues that are designed to help you troubleshoot some of the common problems that you might run into when working with the topic covered in that chapter. You'll find that within the chapter text itself, special notes refer you to the "Troubleshooting" section, where you will find issues specific to the topic being discussed.

 This is a Troubleshooting note like you will see in the chapters of this book. It will then direct you to a specific title of an issue in that chapter's "Troubleshooting" section.

In order for this element to be truly useful, we've also compiled a list of all the Troubleshooting items from the entire book. You will find this Troubleshooting table of contents following the full table of contents in the front of the book. This way, if you are having a specific problem, you can flip to this table and find just the item you are looking for help with.

FRONT AND CENTER

Although we expect the readers of this book will learn how to maximize their investment in FrontPage 2003, we also hope that they'll have a great time with the product.

At the end of each chapter, we'll include a section called "Front and Center" that will assist you in putting the pieces together as you develop a solid understanding of how FrontPage 2003 relates to the modern Web design process.

We'll use this area of each chapter to interject our real-world experiences and provide that extra piece of knowledge that will help you see the whole picture. We'll also attempt to have a little "fun" in this section, showing the personal side to the product we have spent so much time with.

We also have worked on too many products to know that the dynamic nature of the Web means that any URL we publish in this text could be obsolete before you are able to use it. As a result, we've made it possible for all links in this book to have the format `http://x.frontpagelink.com`. These links will dynamically redirect you to the page we wanted you to see. Go ahead and try out `http://frontpageatmicrosoft.frontpagelink.com` to understand the power of this valuable tool.

Enjoy the book, enjoy FrontPage 2003, and enjoy the process of taking your Web sites in the most amazing directions! We promise that we'll enjoy going there with you as well.

Jim and Paul

FrontPage 2003: An Overview

1

WHAT'S NEW IN FRONTPAGE 2003

In this chapter

THREE AREAS OF FOCUS: DESIGNING, CODING, AND EXTENDING

The changes made to FrontPage 2003 focus on three specific areas: *designing*, *coding*, and *extending*. Each of these elements is vital to good Web design and finds considerable attention in this release.

IMPROVEMENTS FOR DESIGNING

In the area of design, FrontPage 2003 has provided tools to make it easier for users to create the site they want. Developers now have tools that enable precise layout and easy integration with graphics and multimedia from other products. With FrontPage 2003, you have more control of the layout of your Web site, you have the ability to use the design and graphics tools you want to use, and you now have a suite of additional tools within the product that help make your site more accessible to the outside world.

IMPROVEMENTS FOR CODING

Whereas FrontPage 2003 has many new design and layout features, the product also takes a strong emphasis in creating the best code possible. Not only is the code developed by FrontPage 2003 cleaner than previous versions, but also the capability to optimize the HTML adds a new element to the process. Unlike previous releases, the HTML code created by FrontPage 2003 easily competes with that of any existing Web design product.

In addition, Microsoft has added a number of new features in dealing with code from within the FrontPage interface that will make most experienced coders incredibly happy. New built-in scripting and coding tools make it a much more powerful tool for coding Web sites.

IMPROVEMENTS FOR EXTENDING FRONTPAGE

An additional major focus in FrontPage 2003 is the ability to extend the product to work with XML data-driven Web sites and Windows SharePoint Services. Users are now able to produce powerful data-driven sites significantly faster than ever before with this new toolset and direction.

DESIGN CHANGES

FrontPage has always excelled as a WYSIWYG (what you see is what you get) Web page development product. The changes in this release continue in that proud tradition by providing additional layout tools that give you more specific design capabilities, graphics tools that let you use whatever elements you want to use (Microsoft or not), and compatibility tools that make sure your site can be seen by whoever is looking at it.

LAYOUT TOOLS

An impressive number of layout tools are introduced in FrontPage 2003 that provide a number of features that assist considerably in the design process. They are brand new to FrontPage 2003 and not just improvements on previous features.

Layout Tables and Cells provide a means and paradigm for producing Web content with a more traditional layout process that is closer in approach to traditional print. Integration into FrontPage is done through a new Layout Tables and Cells task pane.

The new *Dynamic Web Templates* introduce a Web template format that enables certain sections or areas to be "locked" from editing by the end user. When used properly, this approach can force a set look and feel through a Web site.

FrontPage 2003 also provides *Page Ruler* and *Layout Grids* options that assist considerably when the pixel layout is being developed.

A new *Image Tracing* tool can help a developer trace Web layout (usually in the form of layout tables and cells) up against a graphic superimposed on the FrontPage workspace. This graphic is never seen by the end user, but simply provides another means for layout and design down to the pixel level.

FrontPage 2003 uses and implements Themes differently than in previous versions. Because they affect the layout of a Web page, they are also discussed in this section.

THE LAYOUT TABLES AND CELLS TASK PANE

You are now able to take considerably more control over your page layout through a new Layout Tables and Cells task pane (see Figure 1.1). To open it, select Table, Layout Tables and Cells while in Design view. You can also access it using the dropdown menu in the task pane itself.

With this tool, you can choose from a preset page layout or use the Layout Tool to define exactly how your page is to be laid out.

→ For more detailed information on designing with tables and the use of Layout Tables and Cells, **see** "Using Tables," **p. 189**.

DYNAMIC WEB TEMPLATES

Dynamic Web Templates are Web templates with additional design and layout capabilities. A Dynamic Web Template lets you create multiple pages on a site that shares the same layout and gives you the power to lock areas of a Web page from being edited by others in your design team. This gives you the ability to broaden the amount of people who can assist you in the Web design process because the fear of a beginner deleting something can quickly be erased by his simple inability to do so.

→ For more detailed information on using dynamic Web templates, **see** "Dynamic Web Templates," **p. 411**.

Figure 1.1
The Layout Tables and Cells task pane provides new tools for enabling a specific layout on your Web page.

PAGE RULERS AND LAYOUT GRIDS

FrontPage 2003 adds the option for page rulers and layout grids to assist in page layout (see Figure 1.2).

Figure 1.2
The Page Rulers and Layout Grids provide assistance with exact layout requirements.

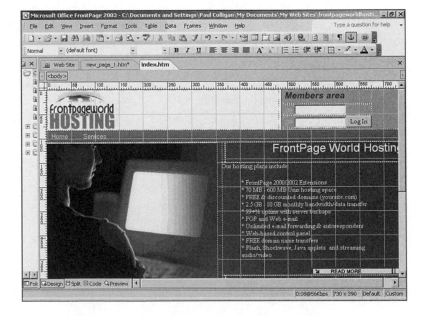

IMAGE TRACING

This new tool enables a developer to develop a site by tracing elements of a graphic while working in Design view (see Figure 1.3). This enables developers to produce sites from artist renditions.

Figure 1.3
FrontPage 2003 will let you place graphics behind your page that can be "traced" into your Web design.

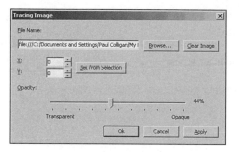

NEW AND IMPROVED THEMES

FrontPage Themes were previously contained and published via HTML, adding a considerable amount of additional content to a Web site. In FrontPage 2003, they are applied using CSS, giving a much smaller footprint to their use than before.

→ For more information on themes, **see** "Using Themes," **p. 133**.

ADDITIONAL LAYOUT TOOLS

In addition to the specifics mentioned previously, FrontPage 2003 provides the following additional Layout Tools:

- *Design Time layers* make it easier to work with multiple pieces of content activated through included DHTML scripting tools.
- *Layout detection* makes it easier to work with layout tables because you can toggle the ability to lay out a table based on table contents.
- Through the new views and streamlining of the desktop interface, FrontPage 2003 also provides a *potentially bigger design area*. If desired and set accordingly, the product gives more space than previously providing for an improved working environment.

GRAPHICS TOOLS

The Internet holds many different file types and graphics standards. Microsoft has realized this and introduced a considerably more advanced level of graphics support to the product. When bringing graphics from another program, Smart Tags are attached to give you more configuration capabilities.

Macromedia Flash has quickly become an industry standard for multimedia. Flash content is now added to a FrontPage Web site by simply dragging it into the work area. Double-clicking a Flash element in design view will allow you to set specific movie properties.

In addition, you can now configure a different editor for every graphic type with FrontPage 2003's multiple editor configuration option. You can set this feature through the Configure Editors tab of the Options dialog box.

TIP

> Editor configuration is not just specific to graphics. It also works with all file types. If you have a specific product you use to edit certain script or data types, be sure to include it through the Configure Editors tab of the Options dialog box.

COMPATIBILITY TOOLS

FrontPage 2003 provides a considerably more complex browser and resolution compatibility toolset. The following list outlines some of the improvements you will find:

- FrontPage 2003 lets you set the page size you are designing for in a new page size option.
- The Preview in Browser option has been updated to included screen resolution.
- Browser compatibility features are enhanced with the new Browser Compatibility tool (see Figure 1.4).

Figure 1.4
The Browser Compatibility tool provides considerably more power to make sure that your site can be viewed on the platforms you choose.

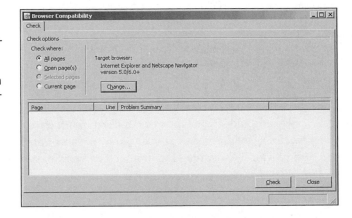

In addition, FrontPage 2003 has a new accessibility checker that will let you know how well your site follows accessibility guidelines and will make recommendations for making your site more accessible.

→ For more information on FrontPage's new accessibility features, **see** "FrontPage's Accessibility Features," **p. 235**.

CODING CHANGES

FrontPage 2003 has a number of new coding tools that not only enhance your abilities to work with HTML, but also provide additional options for working with various other coding languages.

HTML TOOLS

The following additions to FrontPage will assist in your development of cleaner HTML code than before in far less time.

SPLIT VIEW

 New to this release is the Split view—a very powerful way of working on your Web site (see Figure 1.5).

Figure 1.5
The new Split view allows you to see both the design of your site and the code behind it.

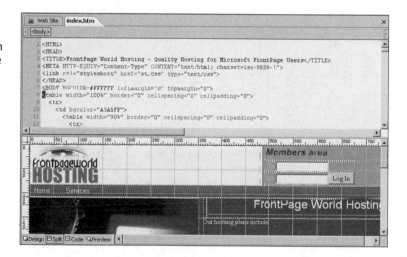

By having both elements on the screen at the same time, you can make sure that the site you are designing has the code you require behind it.

> **TIP**
>
> Don't know HTML? Design your site in the Split view, and you can see the code you are "creating" as you design your site. At its core, HTML isn't that complicated, and learning as you are creating might be the perfect teacher for you.

QUICK TAG SELECTOR AND EDITOR

When working in Design view, a Quick Tag Selector is provided at the top of the page that quickly lets you jump to the area of the site handled by those tags.

In addition, a dropdown menu is provided for each tag that lets you quickly change specifics of the tag without having to edit the HTML (see Figure 1.6).

SMART FIND AND REPLACE

The Find and Replace option provided with FrontPage 2003 is significantly more powerful than before. It enables site-wide updates for both content and HTML.

Figure 1.6
The Quick Tag Selector and dropdown editor options make it easy to quickly edit the specific element of HTML you are looking for.

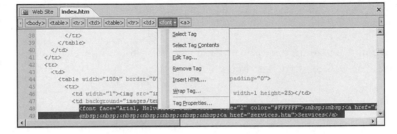

→ For more information on this new feature, **see** "The Improved Find and Replace," **p. 101**.

EDITING OF TEXT FILES

You can now edit any text file (JavaScript, XML, XSLT, and so on) from within the FrontPage editor without have to worry that FrontPage will mangle the code.

> **NOTE**
>
> Just because you can edit different file types in FrontPage 2003, it doesn't mean that you can render them from within FrontPage 2003. For example, FrontPage 2003 will completely support the development of an entire PHP-based Web site, but will require viewing the site content on a Web server that supports PHP.

CLEANING UP HTML

It is no doubt that the number one complaint about FrontPage, from friend and foe alike, was the product's production of bloated HTML code. FrontPage 2003 introduces two options for producing cleaner HTML when working with FrontPage.

The first option comes in an Optimize HTML tool that can be invoked on a page by page basis. See Figure 1.7 for a listing of the options provided by this new tool.

The second option enables FrontPage 2003 to optimize HTML during the publishing process. When working with Remote Web Site view, the option is made available to only Optimize Remote HTML (see Figure 1.8).

> **TIP**
>
> Consider using the second option when working with Web sites because it lets you keep the data where you need it (on your local copy) while optimizing only what the public sees. Fishing through condensed HTML is never fun, and there is no need to do this with the optimize at publish approach.

Figure 1.7
The Optimize HTML tool lets you quickly clean up the HTML on any page in your FrontPage Web site following your exact directions.

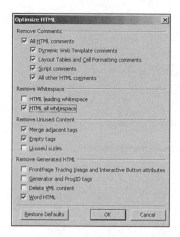

Figure 1.8
You can also choose to only Optimize Remote HTML while in the Remote Web Site view.

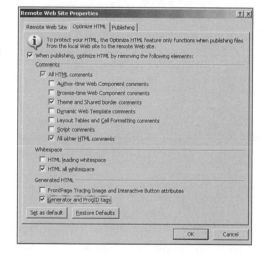

NOTE

The importance of this new focus cannot be overstated. Having FrontPage produce clean HTML quickly pushes the product into the role of direct competitor with the industry's other Web design products.

SCRIPTING TOOLS

Although this was seen in the Visual Studio products for some time, FrontPage 2003 provides IntelliSense for authoring both JScript and VBScript in Code view.

In addition to IntelliSense integration, FrontPage 2003 also provides two additional tools that aid in the use and implementation of scripting.

One of the most common uses for scripting in a Web page was to support rollover affects for Web page buttons. FrontPage 2003 introduces a new Interactive Buttons maker that not only eliminates the need for script, but also generates the graphics for the buttons (see Figure 1.9).

Figure 1.9
The new Interactive Buttons maker quickly produces rollover buttons (effect and graphics).

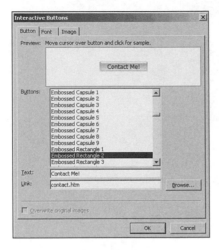

→ For more information on this new feature, **see** "Using Interactive Buttons," **p. 441**.

FrontPage 2003 also introduces "behaviors"—snippets of JScript code that can be integrated into your site with the click of a button.

→ For more information on this new feature, **see** "Using Behaviors," **p. 449**.

THE CODER'S TOOLBOX

In addition to the integration of IntelliSense in Code view, FrontPage 2003 also introduces the following powerful elements to the toolbox:

- Preview of ASP.NET controls is now supported in FrontPage Preview view.
- Word wrap, line numbering, auto indentation, matching tags, and temporary shortcuts are all supported in Code view.
- FrontPage 2003 also provides the capability to store blocks of code for quick integration into your site with the Code Snippets feature.

Not a Coder?
Don't worry about the emphasis FrontPage 2003 puts on the coding elements. You still don't need to know any HTML to make a great site with FrontPage; the product now simply makes the option available for those who require, or are interested in, the capability.

Again, don't be scared by this product's power. If you aren't a coder and don't want to learn the skill, skip to the next section of this chapter and simply ignore the sections on coding throughout this book. You will see that FrontPage 2003 more than meets your design and layout needs.

EXTENDING FRONTPAGE 2003

Microsoft is betting a lot of its future on data-driven Web sites through the Windows SharePoint Services product line. It should be of no surprise that FrontPage integrates tightly with SharePoint.

DATA-DRIVEN WEB SITES WITH WINDOWS SHAREPOINT SERVICES

The combination of FrontPage 2003, Windows Server 2003, and Windows SharePoint Services 2.0 provides a surprisingly powerful platform for developing Web sites that closely integrate XML data into site content.

FrontPage 2003 integrates tightly with Windows SharePoint Services, part of the recently released Windows Server 2003. It can be used as a tool for both designing SharePoint pages and Web Parts but can also leverage the data capabilities of a SharePoint Team Services site to create data-driven Web sites.

Features include a data source catalog that provides easy data view integration into your Web pages, the creation of XSLTs, and the introduction of Web Package Templates that provide complete XML solutions.

TIP

> If you are going to do a lot of work with XML and FrontPage, the integration and tools provided by a Windows SharePoint Services hosting platform is going to be well worth your time and efforts.

As with the data-driven Web sites already discussed, support for XML is limited when you are not working in conjunction with a Windows 2003 Server that has Windows SharePoint Services installed. You are still able to author and code pages that can interact with any data source (XML or otherwise) but will not be able to leverage the XML toolset that comes with FrontPage 2003.

NOTE

> This is a book about FrontPage, not SharePoint. We'll touch on the issue of SharePoint throughout this book—but only in terms of how it integrates with FrontPage. Check out Appendix A, "FrontPage Resources on the Web," for additional Web sites covering this topic.

In short, if you want to develop powerful data-driven Web sites leveraging key Microsoft technologies, you'll need the integration of Windows SharePoint Services on the server you are publishing to.

This is not to say that you can't create data-driven sites with FrontPage. As mentioned previously, you can use FrontPage 2003 to write whatever code you want to integrate with whatever scripting language and databases you want. Windows SharePoint Services represents a client/server combination that works quickly and easily and has the added benefit of being tightly integrated with FrontPage 2003.

NEW WAYS TO PUBLISH AND NEW PUBLISHING TOOLS

Despite the Microsoft marketing machine, it was very hard to publish a FrontPage Web site to anything other than a Web site with FrontPage Extensions installed. The FTP publish option in FrontPage 2002 was a step in the right direction, but FrontPage 2003 finally opens up the entire world of Web publishing options to the FrontPage environment (see Figure 1.10).

Figure 1.10
FrontPage 2003 provides four different options for publishing your site.

Also new is the Remote Site view, which lets you view the contents of a remote site and compare them with your local copy of a Web site. It is important to note that you don't need FrontPage Server Extensions to utilize this feature.

TIP

> Many FrontPage users found themselves working with hosting partners who supported FrontPage Extensions in order to make publishing as smooth and as easy as possible. Often, this support came at a higher price.
>
> If you are not going to be using any of the scripting or database options provided to you by a Microsoft Hosting platform and don't require the benefits of FrontPage Extensions, you are free to publish your site *anywhere*. FrontPage 2003 will make that very easy to do. This simple realization might save you a great deal of money and headache when choosing (or changing) your Web host.

ALSO WORTH NOTING

As hinted at already, FrontPage is no longer just a product for simply creating Web sites. It integrates so tightly with other products and services (Microsoft and otherwise) that it should no longer be viewed as a standalone tool. Tight integration with SharePoint and XML bring FrontPage to the next level of Web publishing and integration. In addition, new Web Site Management capabilities make the product even more solid.

WEB SITE MANAGEMENT

FrontPage has always excelled as a Web site management tool, and the new features brought with 2003 only strengthen the product's position as such.

In addition to the management offerings traditionally provided by FrontPage, its new publishing features provide additional powerful management functionality.

The Remote Site view supports a two directional publishing process that allows for different users to edit the same master site while syncing their version with whatever changes have been made. By supporting file locking through WebDAV and the use of .lck files (made popular by Dreamweaver), you'll be able to work with other users on the same Web server without accidentally stepping on each others changes.

WHAT HAPPENED TO FRONTPAGE EXTENSIONS?

With the new publishing options and the tight integration with SharePoint, there is a great deal of confusion about what "happened" to FrontPage Extensions.

Historically, FrontPage Extensions were both friend and foe to the Web developer (and the greater Web development community). While they added great functionality to the Web site and the Web design experience, they were often perceived as unstable and insecure and frustrated many users in the process. Many Web hosts opted out of the provision of FrontPage Extensions as a result. This resulted in FrontPage users having to limit their choices for hosting providers.

In short, FrontPage Extensions are not dead—they are simply no longer a focus by Microsoft. Microsoft decided to "create a new and radically more powerful server story" with SharePoint and eliminate the need for FrontPage Extensions with 2003.

FrontPage Server Extensions 2002 will still be supported by Microsoft, but no new growth in this product should be expected.

> **TIP**
>
> Despite the buzz surrounding the *"death"* of FrontPage Extensions, a great deal of power is still afforded by servers with this option (be they UNIX or Microsoft at the core).
>
> The ability to directly edit content at a remote site is the functionality that simply can't be replicated through any technology other than FrontPage Extensions. Quick site-wide changes at the click of a button without the need to re-publish a site still requires FrontPage Extensions.

What does this "really" mean? If your single purpose for using FrontPage Extensions was to make the publishing process easier, don't worry about that anymore. If you've been shying away from using FrontPage Extensions because of the server issue, don't.

If you used the non-publishing tools provided by FrontPage Extensions, stay with a server that provides them. You won't see any new functionality from Microsoft, but FrontPage Server Extensions certainly aren't dead.

→ For more a basic examination of how the different server options and tools work in to the Web development process, **see** "Creating a Web Site," **p. 251**.

→ For more detailed information on the administration of these different server technologies, **see** "Security and Administration of a Web Site," **p. 323**.

COMPARISONS TO DREAMWEAVER MX

Some of the new functionality introduced in FrontPage 2003 certainly resembles some of the functionality found in Macromedia's Dreamweaver MX product. There are different ways to approach these similarities, and we'll suggest the least political of them here.

TIP

> Frank Johnson of ExtremeFrontPage.com does a great job of following the "politics" of the Web design world that we won't discuss here. You can find his site at
> `http://extremefrontpage.frontpagelink.com`.

It is my opinion that these new features should be standard to any professional Web development product, and I am thrilled to see FrontPage embrace them in this latest release. Developers are now free to choose their development package based on both functionality and overall approach to the Web design process.

In the second area, FrontPage and Dreamweaver still remain considerably different. It is up to the developer to choose which product he wants to use to accomplish the task at hand.

But now, and perhaps most importantly, FrontPage and Dreamweaver play nicely with each other, and any Web development project can (if and when necessary) integrate both tools side by side.

FRONT AND CENTER: A BETTER PRODUCT PROVIDES BETTER RESULTS

FrontPage 2003 keeps the strength that FrontPage has always brought to Web design while introducing powerful new elements to help in the design, coding, and product extension that make it as powerful as any other product on the market today.

It would be easy to get overwhelmed by the new features and power enabled by FrontPage 2003. In short, don't. Perhaps the most powerful element of FrontPage is that its power is integrated into a common interface and paradigm that most users can easily understand.

It is a better product that provides better results through the considerably larger toolset offered in this release.

No one ever uses every single element provided by any product, and FrontPage 2003 is no different. Use the items you want to use and know that the rest is there if you need them one day.

Note that the rest are *pretty powerful*, and we wrote this book to help you harness that power.

In the next chapter, we'll take a complete tour of the FrontPage 2003 package showing how each of the tools discussed here integrate with each other.

CHAPTER 2

FRONTPAGE 2003—A COMPLETE TOUR

ABOUT THE "TOUR"

The power of FrontPage 2003 is in how the product covers the *entire* process of Web design. Although the different elements of FrontPage are as powerful as their competitive counterparts, the combination of the elements through a simple paradigm is what makes FrontPage so exciting, so powerful, and so easy to use.

Based on the experience of this book's authors, we've found that very few people understand completely how the different FrontPage elements work together. It is also our belief that many don't realize how simple it is to use *all* the elements in any Web design product—no matter what your skill or programming knowledge level.

In this chapter, we are going to take you on a "tour" of FrontPage 2003 and show you how these different elements work together to provide a complete Web design product. We cross reference each part of our tour with the more complete chapters dedicated to these elements and present numerous screenshots that add the visual component to providing a solid understanding of what this product offers to anyone who picks it up.

We recommend that you read this chapter in its entirety, even if you are familiar with previous versions of FrontPage. The new tools provided in this release and a solid understanding of how they all fit together will place you in a position of competitive advantage.

THE ELEMENTS

All the elements of any Web design program can be found in FrontPage 2003:

- **Creating and Editing Web Content.** FrontPage 2003 provides a robust and powerful Web content editor that can be quickly mastered by anyone comfortable in front of a computer. Because the product looks and feels like other products in the Microsoft Office system, millions of users are instantly comfortable and experienced with the interface.

- **Creating Web Sites.** You will seldom see a single self-sustaining piece of Web content anywhere on the Internet. The power of the Web is in how everything links to everything else. FrontPage provides a powerful tool for creating and managing Web sites.

- **Advanced Page Design.** Where traditionally standard HTML will meet most needs of the Web developer, options for advanced page design are tightly integrated in to FrontPage 2003. Interactive forms and style sheets can quickly be integrated in to your site through FrontPage.

- **Scripting, DHTML, and Dynamic Content.** A few years ago, HTML made up the most significant percentage of Web content. This continues to change, and the role of scripting, DHTML, and dynamic content continues to rise in importance and penetration. FrontPage 2003 provides the necessary tools to integrate such content into your Web product.

- **Coding.** Some elements of Web design simply can't be done through a WYSIWYG interface. The new coding tools integrated in to FrontPage 2003 make it a powerful tool for coding Web site content.

- **Collaboration.** Web design is seldom ever a solitary job. In most Web design projects, teams work together to develop the final product. The collaboration tools offered by FrontPage 2003 make this process considerably easier and provides a platform for collaboration that, when leveraged correctly, can assist the design process considerably.

- **Data.** Web sites and content no longer come solely from static sources of data and information. Data comes from sources as varied as a database to dynamically generation XML streams. The tools for integration with multiple data sources are provided with FrontPage 2003.

- **Office Integration.** The market penetration and impact of the Microsoft Office System is undeniable. Knowledge workers around the world use Office to generate considerable amounts of content, and FrontPage integrates tightly with all elements of Office to port the content from other Office products to a Web friendly presentation.

- **FrontPage and Web Graphics.** FrontPage 2003 provides a basic set of tools for managing and integrating Web graphics but also works well with popular graphic design products.

- **Integrating FrontPage with Other Systems and Products.** As powerful as FrontPage is, it would be downright silly to claim that it is the only product you will ever need when designing a Web site. The more complex any Web product becomes, the better the chance that you will need to integrate or use a third-party product. FrontPage integrates closely with many third-party products and server systems to provide the needed power when FrontPage doesn't provide it.

THE INTERFACE

Web design doesn't have to be a complicated effort. Many companies and products have made the process of building Web content considerably more complex than it needs to be. You can see this in popular Internet design products that have complicated interfaces and terminology either all their own or industry specific.

Because FrontPage 2003 comes from Microsoft, it utilizes the Office and Windows interface and paradigms understood by anyone using the Office products. As a result, considerable elements of the product don't need to be learned.

THE OFFICE INTERFACE

As seen in Figure 2.1, the basic Design view of FrontPage looks almost identical to other Office products and most Windows programs. Not only are these elements provided to enable most users the chance to quickly jump in and work on the product, but also they use *the exact same code* as seen in the other Microsoft Office products in most cases.

In short, if you are familiar with the interface of any other Office product, you are familiar with the FrontPage 2003 interface.

Figure 2.1
The blank FrontPage design screen resembles a blank Microsoft Word 2003 screen and offers the same interface for quickly entering and modifying content.

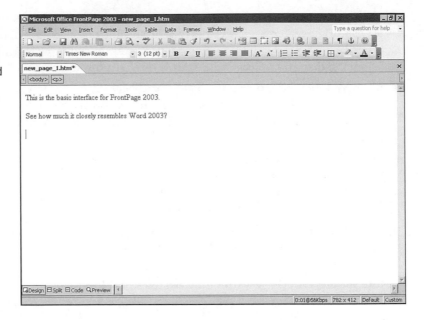

The Windows Interface

When FrontPage doesn't mimic the Office interface, it often mimics the Windows interface. As seen in Figure 2.2, the Folders view in FrontPage 2003 looks a lot like Windows Explorer and offers the user the chance to navigate (and manage) site content through the same toolset he uses to navigate (and manage) his hard drive or corporate network.

Figure 2.2
The FrontPage 2003 Folders view mimics closely many elements of Windows Explorer allowing another familiar interface.

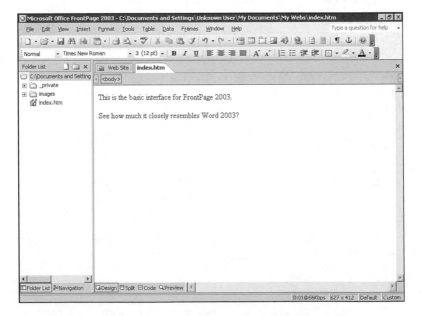

In addition to the familiar Folders view, FrontPage 2003 takes many other elements of Windows into consideration when assisting in the Web design process. Elements as standard as Find and Replace are part of FrontPage. Sites can be sent to your Web server as easily and as quickly as you send a Word document to your printer, as seen in Figure 2.3.

Figure 2.3
The File menu in FrontPage 2003 offers a Publish Site option in addition to the Print option.

NOTE

If you are familiar and comfortable with Web publishing concepts and terminology and will always prefer FTPing to publishing, don't worry. FrontPage 2003 provides for all the Internet standards but also provides a Windows interface and paradigm because it is considerably less complicated and enables a considerably larger audience the ability to make use of the tool.

You can drag and drop files between folders in the Folders view. If you move content linked elsewhere in the site, FrontPage will rewrite the HTML to prevent broken files.

TIP

Make sure that you understand the power of site organization through drag and drop. A site with thousands of pieces of content can quickly be organized with FrontPage instantly editing the appropriate HTML that most coders would take weeks to clean up.

CREATING AND EDITING WEB CONTENT

At the most basic level, the Web developer needs to create and edit Web content. FrontPage provides the tools and interface to make this approach as easy as possible.

THE DIFFERENT VIEWS

Different elements of the Web design process require different ways of interfacing with your content and Web site. Instead of using a single interface that attempts to meet all needs, FrontPage 2003 provides a series of views that present the necessary data in a format advantageous to the specific instance:

- **Design View**—The most basic of views as seen previously in Figure 2.1. Design view is the WYSIWYG (what you see is what you get) interface for FrontPage most similar to other Microsoft Office products. Most users will find that most of their work is done in Design view.

- **Code View**—When you need to interface directly with the code behind your HTML pages, Code view provides an interface for doing just that.

- **Split View**—A much requested feature new to FrontPage 2003 is a Split view that allows the user to see both the Design and Code views and how they interface with each other. Selecting elements in one panel will highlight the corresponding elements in the other pane, as shown in Figure 2.4.

Figure 2.4
The Split View new to FrontPage 2003 gives the ability to see both the code and the Design view that the code will produce.

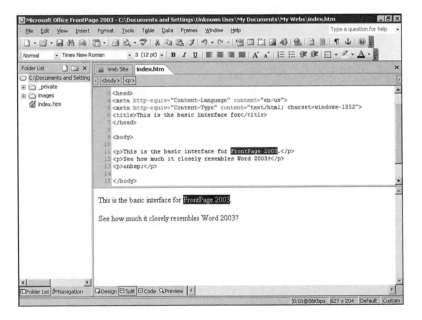

- **Preview View**—During the development process, most users want to see how their product would be presented in a browser window. This is most often a request of users developing in Code view, but it is also often to test the functionality of page that can't be tested in Design view. Viewing the content in Preview is different from viewing the content in a browser because the content is rendered much quicker as it is part of the FrontPage 2003 interface.

NOTE

Preview view should never be used as a replacement for viewing site content in a browser. Preview view is a way to quickly see how your content is most likely to be presented in the version of Internet Explorer installed on your system.

Because Preview view is contained in the FrontPage interface, it typically won't show you your site content in the proportions of the traditional Web browser. Viewing the content in a browser is the only way to get that perspective.

Because the content is shown through Internet Explorer's engine, you will need to remember that same content might look considerably different in other browsers such as Netscape and Opera.

- **Folder View**—When a user needs to see the entirety of his site content and how it is organized, Folder view (shown previously in Figure 2.2) provides a view of your site similar to the Windows Explorer interface. Like Windows Explorer, content can be moved from one folder to another through the familiar drag-and-drop interface.

- **Navigation View**—If desired, you can maintain a site's navigation structure through FrontPage 2003. The Navigation view will provide an overview of your site in terms of site navigation.

- **Reports View**—FrontPage provides numerous reports of site health and content in addition to traffic reporting (when made available through server extensions). The Reports view lets you examine such reports.

→ For more detailed information on FrontPage views, **see** "FrontPage's Views," **p. 61**.

DEVELOPING THE BASIC PAGE

There should be no hesitance when using FrontPage to design basic site content. The interface is easy, self-explanatory, and provides most of the tools needed to add most types of content to your Web site.

A basic Web page can quickly be developed through the Design view. The interface is familiar to most users enabling the quick entry of text, lists, and tables. In Figure 2.5, the user quickly developed some basic Web content with a hyperlink and basic formatting.

→ For more on basic page and content development with FrontPage 2003, **see** "Developing the Basic Page: Text, Lists, and Hyperlinks," **p. 77**.

Figure 2.5
Design view makes it
easy to design Web
content.

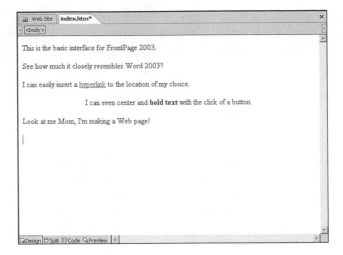

ADVANCED FIND AND REPLACE

Beginning Web masters are often surprised how quickly their site grows in size. What was a simple five page information site a few months back can explode to a site of hundreds of pages or more.

No developer should be expected to memorize and track every element of every page in an exhaustive Web site. In addition, the Advanced Search and Replace features in FrontPage 2003 make such a requirement pointless. As can be seen in Figure 2.6, a site-wide search for the smallest of terms can be made through a single interface.

NOTE

If you were put off by the Find and Replace feature of previous versions of FrontPage, take another look. The tool in considerably more powerful this time.

Figure 2.6
The Find and Replace
dialog box lets you
search an entire site
for a specific word or
phrase and replace it
with the content of
your choice.

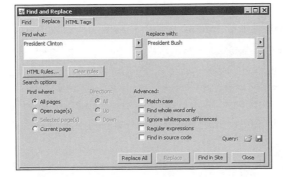

The use of Find and Replace is not limited to site content. Source code and HTML tags can be run through the same tool to fix mistakes made on a site-wide basis. In Figure 2.7, the developer mistakenly referenced the wrong URL throughout his entire site and was able to fix it with a single click.

Figure 2.7
The Find and Replace dialog box enabled the site developer to change all references to a specific site.

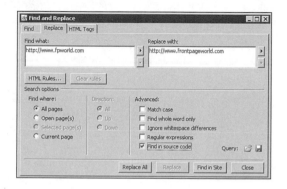

NOTE

Frequently used queries can be saved through the Find and Replace interface for reuse later.

→ For more on FrontPage 2003's expanded search and replace feature, **see** "The Improved Find and Replace," **p. 101**.

GRAPHICS AND MULTIMEDIA

Obviously, a Web site needs more than text. The graphics and multimedia tools offered by FrontPage 2003 make the integration of such content quite easy.

Only a small percentage of FrontPage users realize that the purchase of FrontPage 2003 includes the ability to use an *extensive* online library of clip art and multimedia. The library continues to grow in size and is a considerable resource for those who use the feature. An example of an obscure search can be seen in Figure 2.8.

In addition to the Clip Art library, is easy to add pictures from external sources as wide-ranging as other Web sites, other devices (you can pull a digital photo from a camera and place it directly on your Web page), or other content sources such as clip art CDs.

The addition of Flash content is much easier with FrontPage 2003 and no longer requires a plug-in or tool (or careful HTML manipulation) to accomplish. Video and audio can also be added quickly to your site.

→ For more on integrating graphics and multimedia with your site, **see** "Enhancing Pages with Graphics and Multimedia," **p. 113**.

Figure 2.8
The online Microsoft Clip Art library contains more content than most people would guess.

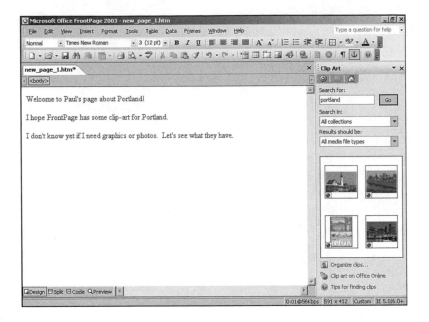

THEMES

Not everyone has the ability to design a great looking site out of the box. FrontPage provides the ability to give a site a uniform look and feel using themes. In Figure 2.9, the resume page created earlier in this chapter looks a lot better with the application of a FrontPage Theme.

Figure 2.9
The example page from Figure 2.5 looks a lot better with a FrontPage Theme applied to it. The total transformation happened in two seconds.

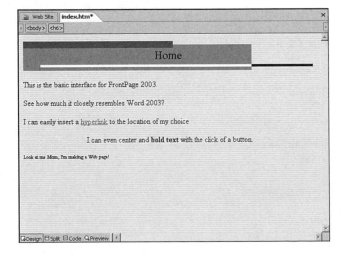

NOTE

The Themes process has not seen any major improvements since they were first introduced, and many prefer the use of FrontPage templates.

→ For more on using Themes with your site (as well as some of the potential problems of using this tool), **see** "Using Themes," **p. 133**.

NAVIGATION TOOLS

As sites get bigger and bigger, the flow of a site becomes harder to manage and visualize. At the same time, the addition of content to a site navigational structure requires updating other pages in the site to reflect changes made. FrontPage 2003 comes with a set of navigational tools that can be used to both design the site navigation and manage corresponding links throughout the site as needed.

In Figure 2.10, the developer has linked his site pages together in a layout that makes design and navigational sense. This was done by moving the files from within the Navigation view.

Figure 2.10
Navigation view allows the developer to put together a site in a logical design and navigational fashion.

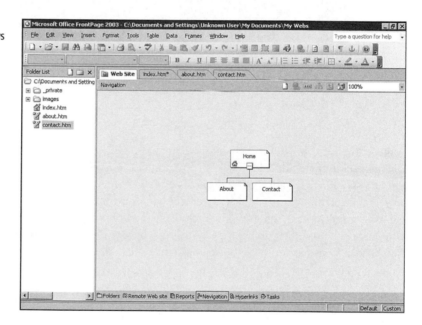

Once a site's navigation has been set, FrontPage navigational elements can be inserted that are dynamically updated as needed as new content is added to the site.

→ For more on using FrontPage's Navigation tools, **see** "FrontPage's Navigation Tools and Elements," **p. 147**.

WEB COMPONENTS

Web sites often require more complicated content than traditional HTML can provide. Although in some cases this requires special coding or scripting, in other cases FrontPage Web Components can be used to bring content to the site without the need for any additional programming. Web components are additions to FrontPage built for the specific purpose of integrating such code in to a FrontPage Web site without requiring additional programming.

Although Web components can be specifically built to meet specific needs, a number of Web components come built in to FrontPage 2003, including a component that integrates a map in to your Web site from Microsoft's Expedia Web Services. An example of this Web component can be seen in Figure 2.11.

Figure 2.11
The FrontPage Expedia static map plug-in lets you place a map from the Expedia Web Server in to your site without entering a single line of code.

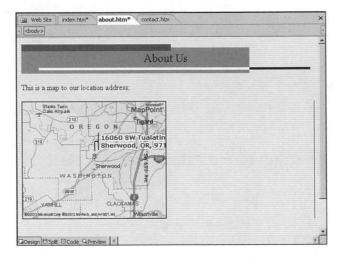

Some of the most powerful Web components in FrontPage are the included content components that let you add additional HTML content to a Web page. This can be set to happen at a specific time, allowing you to update your site without having to be there. Another powerful implementation of this component comes from creating specific site elements such as headers and footers and using the included content components to insert these elements in to your site's pages. If done properly, a single header file could be updated, resulting in a new header information throughout your entire site.

→ For more on the Web components that come with FrontPage and their use in the Web design process, **see** "Using Web Components, Shared Borders, and Link Bars," **p. 167**.

→ For more on making your own FrontPage Web components, **see** "Making Your Own Web Components," **p. 965**.

TABLES AND FRAMES

Some of the more detailed HTML layout effects popular on the Internet are done with HTML Tables and Frames. FrontPage 2003 provides solid tools for integrating both of these in to your Web design process.

 The table features in FrontPage 2003 have been considerably enhanced. In addition to the new Tables toolbar seen in Figure 2.12, a new Layout Tables and Cells task pane (seen in Figure 2.13) provides table layout options that can be added to your site with the click of a mouse.

Figure 2.12
The new Tables toolbar provides considerable options for table development within the Design view.

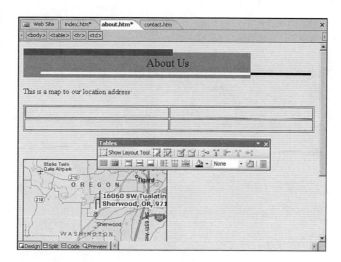

Figure 2.13
The New Layout Tables and Cells task pane provides additional options for table devclopment within the Design view, including several pre-design table layouts for easy insertion.

Although the use of Frames in Web design is a stylistically and functionally debated feature, FrontPage provides a solid toolset for working with frames, including a series of premade framesets that can be easily edited from within FrontPage.

→ For more on the new Table tools in FrontPage 2003 and the use of Tables in Web design, **see** "Using Tables," **p. 189**.

→ For more on the Frames tools provided by FrontPage 2003 and the examination of the problems they present, **see** "Enhancing Web Sites with Frames," **p. 219**.

ACCESSIBILITY FEATURES

The development of an accessible Web site is becoming an important legal and design issue for many. FrontPage 2003 introduces an Accessibility Checker, seen in Figure 2.14, that can compare your site with the latest accessibility standards and suggest areas of improvement.

Now you can develop your site with accessibility standards in mind and make sure that your project meets industry standards.

Figure 2.14
The new FrontPage 2003 Accessibility Checker will quickly show you how your site rates in terms of current accessibility standards.

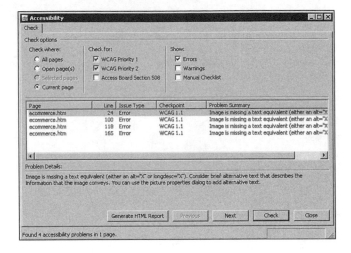

→ For more on accessible Web design and using the FrontPage 2003 Accessibility Checker, **see** "FrontPage's Accessibility Features," **p. 235**.

WEB SITE CREATION TOOLS

Up to this point, we've examined FrontPage's capability to create Web content, touching only slightly on the tools provided that assist in the Web Site design and maintenance process. You will find that FrontPage 2003 makes it very easy to create a Web site, provides templates, wizards, and packages to make the process even easier, lets you work with existing Web sites, and provides for a simpler Web site configuration process than you might expect.

CREATING A WEB SITE

You can create a new FrontPage Web site through the same interface that you use to create a new page. The New task pane (seen in Figure 2.15) lets you create new pages or Web sites from scratch or from templates.

NOTE

> Although the Web site templates in FrontPage 2003 are no different from those in FrontPage 2000 or 2002, new features discussed later add exciting new elements to the Web design process.

→ For more on creating a Web site with FrontPage 2003, **see** "Creating a Web Site," **p. 251**.

Figure 2.15
Choose between new pages or sites from scratch or from templates.

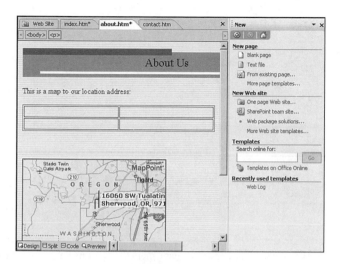

FRONTPAGE'S WEB TEMPLATES, WIZARDS, AND PACKAGES

FrontPage comes with a number of Web (site and page) templates and wizards that will help you create a site or page from scratch. Although the content of these templates have not changed in this version, they still provide a quick way to develop a Web page or site.

 New to FrontPage 2003 is the introduction of Web Packages—collections of files that come together to provide new levels of site functionality and power. They integrate with Windows SharePoint Services to provide complete Web-based solutions that can be modified and updated with FrontPage 2003.

> **NOTE**
>
> You can only use Web Packages on a Windows SharePoint Services Web site.
>
> Because they contain executable script and content that could be used maliciously, Web packages are digitally signed (a digital code attached to a file to identify the source of the file).

An existing SharePoint Team Services site can easily be exported to a FrontPage Web Package and transferred to another site through FrontPage 2003.

→ For more on the templates, wizards, and Web packages that come with FrontPage 2003, **see** "FrontPage's Web Templates, Wizards, and Packages," **p. 267**.

OPENING AND WORKING WITH EXISTING WEB SITES

One of FrontPage's greatest strengths has always been the user's ability to open a site anywhere on the Internet and create (or edit) site content directly on the Web server (see Figure 2.16). This includes sites open to the public or sites under development that currently aren't available on your local network.

Figure 2.16
You can open a site
directly in FrontPage
2003 and edit site
content as if it were
on your desktop.

TIP

> Working live on a site for anything more than a simple or quick fix is seldom recommended because a mistake could quickly impact your entire site.

Previous to FrontPage 2003, this required a server with FrontPage Extensions installed and simply "didn't work" with any products that used other publishing methods such as the industry standard FTP. Now, FrontPage can work with external sites through multiple connection options including FTP, WebDAV, or an internal file systems, as seen in Figure 2.17.

Figure 2.17
You are no longer lim-
ited to connecting to
remote sites with
FrontPage Server
Extensions in
FrontPage 2003.

→ For more on opening and working with an existing Web site, **see** "Opening and Working with Existing Web Sites," **p. 283**.

PUBLISHING A FRONTPAGE WEB SITE

As mentioned previously, you are no longer limited to publishing to sites with FrontPage Server Extensions installed. As seen in Figure 2.17, you now have multiple options for publishing your Web site.

 In addition to multiple publishing options, FrontPage 2003 offers you the ability to optimize HTML at publishing time. Figure 2.18 shows the Optimize HTML tab of the Remote Web Site Properties dialog box.

Figure 2.18
You can optimize most elements of your site's code at publishing time.

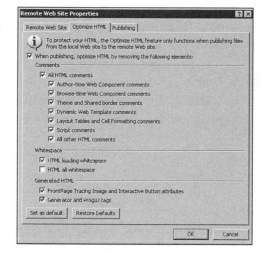

By waiting until publishing time to optimize your code, you can benefit from a richer, more commented code base full of metadata useful to you but unnecessary to the end user.

→ For more on publishing FrontPage Web site and the different options provided with this new release, **see** "Publishing a FrontPage Web Site," **p. 299**.

→ For more on the HTML optimization options that are provided with FrontPage 2003, **see** "Optimizing FrontPage's HTML," **p. 549**.

CONFIGURATION AND ADMINISTRATION OF A WEB SITE

As with previous versions of FrontPage, you can configure servers with FrontPage Extensions directly through the FrontPage interface.

→ For more on the configuration and administration of your Web site, **see** "Security and Administration of a Web Site," **p. 325**.

ADVANCED PAGE DESIGN

HTML is a markup language for text. Once you start integrating interactivity in to your Web sites, you are going to need more complex code. FrontPage has great support for forms and CSS, as you will see in this section.

FORMS AND INTERACTIVE PAGE TEMPLATES

The first part of a form is in designing the form elements. FrontPage 2003 lets you quickly build forms through the Design view.

The second part is in handling the form content. If FrontPage Extensions are installed on the server your site is hosted on, FrontPage gives you the ability to send the form content directly to a file, email address, or database. If you are working with form handlers external to those provided with FrontPage Extensions, you can call any custom script. All this is possible through the Form Properties dialog box seen in Figure 2.19.

Figure 2.19
Build your form quickly with FrontPage 2003 and send the data to a file, email address, database, or external script.

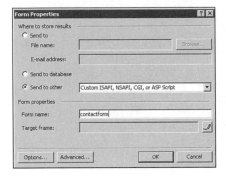

→ For more on the use of forms in Web design, **see** "Using Forms," **p. 359**.

STYLE SHEETS

The use of style sheets in Web design has grown considerably in the last few years. FrontPage 2003 embraces the technology and introduces a new set of tools to help integrate them in to your Web design process.

FrontPage 2003 now uses CSS to apply FrontPage Themes. This makes their implementation smaller, more transparent, and easier to control.

In addition to direct support for the development of CSS, FrontPage also provides several CSS templates, as seen in Figure 2.20. Use them as the basis for any CSS files you might use in the Web design process.

→ For more on the use of style sheets in Web design and how FrontPage handles them, **see** "Using Style Sheets to Format Web Pages," **p. 385**.

Figure 2.20
You can jump-start your CSS development with the CSS templates provided by FrontPage 2003.

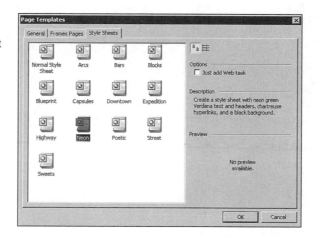

SCRIPTING, DHTML, AND DYNAMIC CONTENT

In addition to the built-in handling of forms examined previously, FrontPage provides a number of tools integrated in to FrontPage 2003 that enable the rapid development (and management) of dynamic content elements.

DYNAMIC WEB TEMPLATES

New to FrontPage 2003 are *Dynamic Web Templates*. This powerful new feature allows you to create multiple pages in the same site that have the same layout, look, and feel but enable the user to prevent certain regions of the page from being edited.

Users can make any page in their site a Dynamic Web Template and use the technology to enlist project help that might have shied away from Web development because of their fear of making disastrous layout mistakes.

→ For more on the use of Dynamic Web Templates and their implementation, **see** "Dynamic Web Templates," **p. 411**.

ADDING DYNAMIC ELEMENTS TO YOUR SITE

DHTML (Dynamic HTML) has added numerous stylish options to the Web design process. Whereas you can use FrontPage 2003 to code the DHTML behind collapsible outlines, page transitions, and layers, FrontPage provides the tools to build these elements directly in to your site.

As an example, Figure 2.21 shows a check box in the List Properties dialog box that results in a DHTML collapsible outline without a single line of code being written by the developer.

→ For additional information on adding dynamic elements to your site and how FrontPage adds them easily, **see** "Making Your Pages and Sites More Dynamic," **p. 425**.

Figure 2.21
When possible, FrontPage 2003 integrates DHTML options directly in to the design interface.

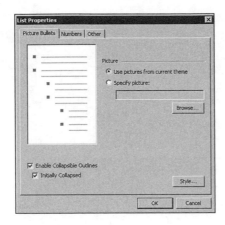

INTERACTIVE BUTTONS

Another exiting addition to the FrontPage 2003 is the addition of Interactive Buttons. Interactive Buttons are a Web component that adds a traditional (and attractive) mouseover button to your Web design. Unlike the "hover buttons" in previous versions of FrontPage that used Java to produce the effect, the new Interactive Buttons use JScript (created on-the-fly by FrontPage 2003) and work considerably better.

TIP

> If you are using the older hover buttons on any of your Web sites, do yourself and your site visitors a favor and redo them with FrontPage Interactive Buttons.

FrontPage 2003 holds the button content as metadata allowing the developer to quickly edit a button without having to reproduce the three different button elements each time an edit is required.

Figure 2.22 shows the Interactive Buttons dialog box. By simply double-clicking the button in Design view, the user can edit the text of the button right in FrontPage.

→ For more on FrontPage's new Interactive Button feature, **see** "Using Interactive Buttons," **p. 441**.

BEHAVIORS

Behaviors, new to FrontPage 2003, are small scripts elements that give you the ability to quickly (and easily) add functional elements to your Web page. Behaviors will write the necessary scripting to your page with the click of a button. In Figure 2.23, the Check Browser behavior is used to direct the user to a specific page based on browser type.

→ For more on using behaviors and the ones that come with FrontPage 2003, **see** "Using Behaviors," **p. 449**.

Figure 2.22
The Interactive Buttons tools makes the production of mouseover buttons considerably easier.

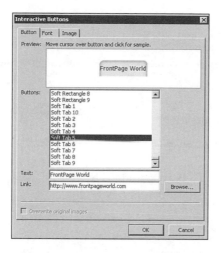

Figure 2.23
Behavior checks the browser type and sends them to the appropriate page.

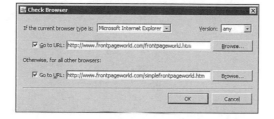

CLIENT-SIDE SCRIPTING

Because FrontPage 2003 handles all code types through the Code view, the design and implementation of client-side scripting directly through the FrontPage interface is supported. There is no need to use a third-party product to develop such solutions, and all scripting languages are supported—not just Microsoft-specific languages.

→ For more on how FrontPage handles client-side scripting and suggestions on how to maximize the technology, **see** "Client-side Scripting," **p. 475**.

→ For a detailed look on the coding tools provided with FrontPage 2003, **see** "Working with Code," **p. 517**.

DESIGN-TIME LAYERS

CSS and modern design elements utilize design-time layers in the Web design process. FrontPage 2003 not only supports design-time layers, but also provides a set of tools to implement them quickly and easily in the design process.

→ For a detailed look at design-time layers, **see** "Using Layers," **p. 499**.

CODING

Although FrontPage 2003 provides a number of tools that keep you from having to code elements of your site, the product also provides a solid toolset for the times when direct hand coding is required.

Essentially with FrontPage 2003, it is totally up to you to choose whether you want to code your Web site or let FrontPage do the work.

WORKING WITH CODE VIEW AND SPLIT VIEW

The Code view in FrontPage 2003 has been considerably enhanced with additional formatting and tool options that are examined further in this section.

New to FrontPage 2003 is the Split view, seen in Figure 2.24. This view splits the screen in to both the WYSIWYG Design view and the Code view, allowing the user to see how code directly affects the HTML design and vice versa.

Figure 2.24
Split view shows the direct relationship between HTML code and content created in the FrontPage design view.

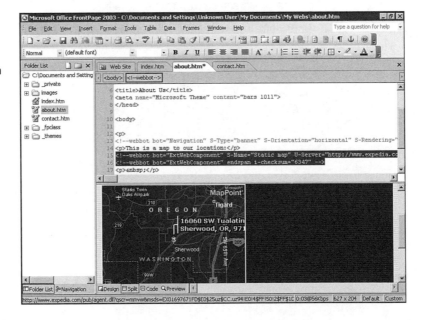

→ For a more detailed look at Code and Split views, **see** "Working in Code View and Split View," **p. 519**.

THE QUICK TAG EDITOR AND CODE SNIPPETS

Two additional tools that assist the coder in FrontPage 2003 is a Quick Tag Editor, seen in Figure 2.25 and the Code Snippets tool, seen in Figure 2.26. The Quick Tag Editor allows the developer to edit specific elements of a tag, and the Code Snippets tool provides the developer a means to insert predefined code elements in to the Web site through a simple interface.

Figure 2.25
You can quickly edit the contents of any tag while in Design, Code, or Split view using the dropdown options associated with it.

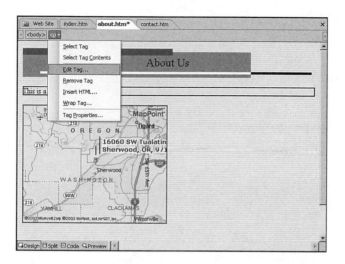

Figure 2.26
The Code Snippets tool lets you quickly insert elements of code in to your Web site.

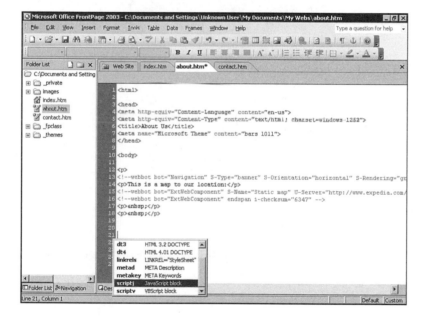

→ For a detailed look at the Quick Tag Editor, **see** "Editing Code with Quick Tag Tools," **p. 529**.

→ For a more significant examination of code snippets, **see** "Using Code Snippets," **p. 543**.

OPTIMIZING FRONTPAGE'S HTML

The combination of code produced by FrontPage and edited or inserted by a Web developer can produce interesting results. Most developers want to provide the cleanest possible HTML at their Web site, and FrontPage 2003 provides a series of HTML optimization tools to provide this feature set. One of the most powerful tools, the Optimize HTML tool seen in Figure 2.27 provides a means to quickly optimize the HTML on any page in your site with the click of a button.

This is different from the optimize at publish feature discussed earlier because it gives you the ability to go in and update already existing pages directly through the FrontPage interface. This is ideal for the user with an already existing Web site or for someone who updates (or builds) his site directly, bypassing the publishing process. Unnecessary comments and whitespace, as well as unused content and FrontPage generated HTML, can be removed quickly and easily.

Figure 2.27
The Optimize HTML tool lets you decide which elements of the HTML you would like cleaned.

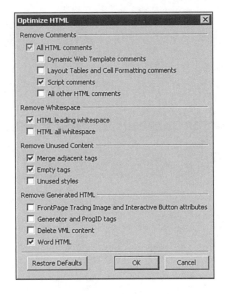

→ For information on the other tools provided for cleaning and streamlining FrontPage HTML, **see** "Optimizing FrontPage's HTML," **p. 549**.

WORKING WITH VBA AND FRONTPAGE

Coding is not just limited to the Web server or site content. Microsoft's Visual Basic for Applications language is ideally suited to adding capabilities directly to the FrontPage product.

If you need to extend the power of FrontPage to perform specific tasks for you on a regular basis, you can write such functionality in VBA and quickly integrate it into FrontPage.

A quick Google search will find numerous sites around the Net that offer FrontPage Macros written in VBA that complete simple tasks such as removal of FrontPage meta tags or transferring FrontPage content to Outlook for easy emailing.

→ For more on working with FrontPage and VBA, **see** "Working with VBA and FrontPage," **p. 567**.

COLLABORATION

Web development is no longer a solo task. Entire teams need to be brought together to produce the average Web site, and FrontPage provides the tools to make such collaboration possible.

The most powerful tool in collaboration is the Tasks view, which allows a central location for everyone involved in the site design to view and interact with tasks specifically assigned to them. An example of the task screen can be seen in Figure 2.28.

Figure 2.28
The Tasks view allows a quick peek at all tasks assigned to a specific Web project.

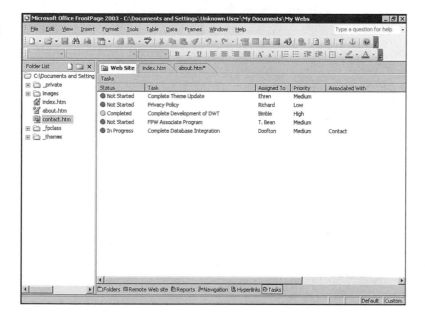

In addition to the Tasks view, FrontPage 2003 allows individual files to be tagged with project specific information such as workgroup, users, and review status. An example of this can be seen in Figure 2.29.

→ For a detailed examination of the collaboration features provided by FrontPage 2003 and an examination of the bigger issues associated with the collaborative authoring environment, **see** "Web Collaboration," **p. 595**.

Figure 2.29
Every file can be assigned category, assignment, and review status information through the Workgroup tab of any file's Properties dialog box.

WORKING WITH DATABASES AND XML

HTML, DHTML, and scripting languages are all supported in FrontPage 2003. Using these technologies to interact with data sources, such as databases and XML feeds, brings a new level of power to the Web design process. In addition to the coding tools of FrontPage 2003 that you can bring to the design, the product also comes with several tools for interacting with data sources without the necessity for coding a line.

→ For a better understanding of the different types of data used by FrontPage and how the product interacts with them, **see** "Types of Data Used with FrontPage: An Overview," **p. 663**.

→ For information on the programming languages used for accessing data, **see** "Data Access Technologies," **p. 679**.

→ For detailed directions for the tools provided by FrontPage 2003 for integrating with databases, **see** "FrontPage's Data Toolset," **p. 689**.

→ For information on the FrontPage 2003 wizards that integrate with databases, **see** "FrontPage and Databases," **p. 705**.

→ For a look at how FrontPage interacts with other sources of data such as XML, **see** "FrontPage and Web Parts," **p. 735**.

INTEGRATION WITH OFFICE 2003

As could be expected, Microsoft FrontPage 2003 integrates tightly with other products in the Microsoft Office System. Microsoft Word documents can quickly be converted in to Web content, Excel can be used to both format and present Web data, PowerPoint slideshows can be translated in to a Web friendly format quicker than ever before, and Publisher files and content can be updated and edited to port to the Web. Part IX of this book specifically covers the integration of FrontPage with these products.

→ For more on the integration of FrontPage with Word 2003, **see** "Working with Microsoft Word," **p. 765**.

→ For more on the integration of FrontPage with Excel 2003, **see** "Working with Microsoft Excel and FrontPage," **p. 777**.

➔ For more on the integration of FrontPage with PowerPoint 2003, **see** "Working with Microsoft PowerPoint 2003," **p. 799**.

➔ For more on the integration of FrontPage with Publisher 2003, **see** "Working with Microsoft Publisher," **p. 811**.

N O T E

> Although Microsoft Access is a Microsoft Office System product, specific issues of data integration are covered in Part VIII of this book.

FRONTPAGE AND WEB GRAPHICS

Prior to FrontPage 2003, Microsoft tried to position the combination of FrontPage with other Microsoft products as capable of providing the necessary Web graphic and multimedia solutions for Web design. With the introduction of FrontPage 2003 comes a change in strategy.

No specific Microsoft product is available for the purpose of Web graphic design. The Image Composer and PhotoDraw products packaged with previous versions of FrontPage are no longer available to the public, and no products have been introduced to replace them.

 FrontPage 2003 now works tightly and easily with other graphic design products and prevents no barrier to working with any standard Web graphic format or product. For example, a tool for inserting Macromedia Flash Movies is built right in to FrontPage 2003.

Part X of this book covers the creation and adaptation of Web graphics for use in a FrontPage Web site. Chapter 46, "Using FrontPage's Tracing Image Feature," gives a detailed examination of the new image tracing tool. The dialog box for the tool is shown in Figure 2.30.

Figure 2.30
The FrontPage 2003 image tracing feature lets you develop a Web site around an image designed specifically to have a site design traced around it.

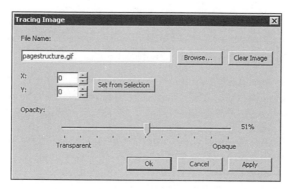

➡ For more on color concepts and FrontPage 2003, **see** "Color Concepts and Web Design," **p. 825**.

➡ For a detailed examination of the different Web graphics formats and how they are handled by FrontPage 2003, **see** "Web Graphic Formats," **p. 847**.

➡ For more on the creation of professional Web graphics, **see** "Creating Professional Web Graphics," **p. 865**.

➡ For directions on the use of FrontPage's image tracing feature, **see** "Using FrontPage's Image Tracing Feature," **p. 879**.

➡ For more on the direct integration of FrontPage with other graphic design tools, **see** "FrontPage and Graphic Tools," **p. 887**.

INTEGRATING FRONTPAGE WITH OTHER SYSTEMS AND PRODUCTS

FrontPage 2003 supports the insertion and integration of third-party systems and products. From the ability to edit PHP within the FrontPage interface to the simple insertion of a Macromedia Flash file from the Insert menu, FrontPage works better with other products than it ever has before.

Because FrontPage supports 100% HTML preservation, no longer requires server extensions for full functionality, and can interact with other Web development control systems such as WebDAV, the ability to use FrontPage 2003 in conjunction with other design products becomes quite clear.

You can use FrontPage in ways you were never able to before. As always, a little planning should be done when you integrate any two products together, but FrontPage finally makes it possible.

FRONT AND CENTER: A SUM FAR GREATER THAN THE PARTS

You won't find a chapter like this in many manuals of this type. Most books try to tell you how a product works, but we truly believe that the *real* power of FrontPage 2003 is in how it all *works together*. We hope you've seen that here.

You can use FrontPage to quickly design Web content through the WYSIWYG interface, use FrontPage Wizards to develop code that might be used within the page, use FrontPage to edit that code or script (or create your own), and use FrontPage to manage how all the files are maintained and stored in your site.

In addition, you can use FrontPage to publish (or synchronize) your site to any server with publishing capabilities and use third-party graphic and multimedia development products to enhance your site. You can also make use of Microsoft's full line of additional server-based technologies to produce the best Web development experience possible.

As the site is being developed, the Task view can be used to keep everyone on "the same page" while development occurs and keep track of the site through complex reports and file assignments.

It isn't the only program you will ever use, but a solid understanding of the product will keep it at the front (pun intended) of any Web development project you might find yourself involved in.

Enjoy the rest of this book as we delve deeply into the features we only briefly discuss here.

2

CREATING AND EDITING WEB CONTENT

CHAPTER 3

FRONTPAGE'S VIEWS

In this chapter

ABOUT FRONTPAGE VIEWS

One of FrontPage's most powerful features has always been its capability to give you multiple ways to look at your Web site during the many stages of the design process. Many of these options also provide a means for editing site content that might be more advantageous than another. This is done through the different views provided by FrontPage.

Specifically new to FrontPage 2003 is the Split view, but many of the others have been updated to provide more power to the end user.

The views are either *page* or *site* related and are grouped accordingly. In this chapter, we'll look at the different FrontPage views and show how to maximize the unique development angle they provide in the Web design process.

FrontPage 2003 provides the following views:

- **Design.** The WYSIWYG (what you see is what you get) interface to the development process similar to the look and feel of most Microsoft Office System products. Most users will find that a considerable amount of their work is done in Design view.

- **Code.** The means for direct coding of HTML or other scripting languages. FrontPage provides a number of tools that assist in entering code through this view.

- **Split.** A new option that splits the screen between Design and Code view. This allows the developer a means to instantly see how her HTML will be rendered.

- **Preview.** Lets you see a quick preview of your site as you are designing it. Because it is integrated in to the FrontPage interface, there is often no need to open an additional browser window.

- **Folders.** A look at your entire site through an interface similar to Windows Explorer. Folder view supports drag and drop and most other Windows Explorer related features. Folders view should not be confused with the Folder list described later in this chapter.

- **Remote Web Site.** Similar to Folder view but shows your site as compared to the remote Web site. Enables you to examine the two sites side by side.

- **Navigation.** If you want to have FrontPage maintain the site navigation structure, this view both presents the structure as well as provides simple manipulation options.

- **Reports.** FrontPage provides a number of reports about site status and traffic that can be accessed directly through FrontPage. These reports give the developer both a high-level view of the site and the means to quickly fix whatever problems the reports identify.

- **Hyperlinks.** This unique tool gives you a bird's eye view of how your Web site links to files that are internal and external. How every file relates to every other one can be examined, and broken links are clearly identified.

- **Tasks.** If you use the task management system built in to FrontPage, you can access it directly through the FrontPage interface using the Tasks view.

ACCESSING THE VIEWS

Unfortunately, there is no simple interface to choose between all the views in FrontPage 2003. Depending on where you are in the FrontPage interface, selecting certain views will make other views available directly through an icon on the FrontPage interface.

The page development related Design, Code, Split and Preview views are available through the button bar at the bottom of these screens, as seen in Figure 3.1. Selecting any of the icons will toggle the appropriate view.

Figure 3.1
When working in Design view, the Design, Split, Code, and Preview views are available via icons at the bottom of the interface.

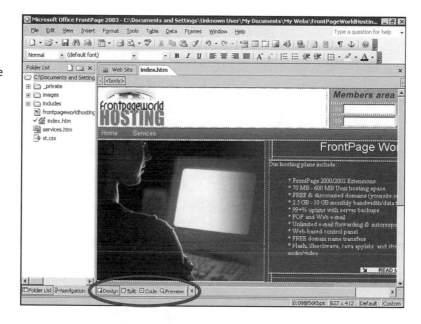

The *site specific* Folders, Remote Web Site, Reports, Navigation, Hyperlinks and Tasks views are available through the button bar at the bottom of these screens, as seen in Figure 3.2. Selecting any of the icons will bring up the appropriate view.

NOTE

> If you do not have a Web site open in FrontPage 2003 and are working on a single file, the site specific Folders, Remote Web Site, Reports, Navigation, Hyperlinks, and Tasks views will not be available.

USING THE FOLDER LIST

In Figures 3.1 and 3.2, a Folder list to the left of the screen provides a simple view of the site files with navigation similar to both Folders view. Folders can be opened with the click of a mouse, and the entire list can be toggled on/off through the Folder List option in the View menu or by selecting Alt+F1.

Figure 3.2
When working in Folders view, the Folders, Remote Web site, Reports, Navigation, Hyperlinks, and Tasks views are available via icons at the bottom of the interface.

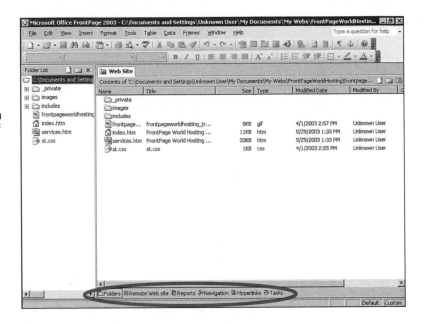

NOTE

If you are designing or coding a single page and don't have a site open, the Folder list will not be an option in the interface.

WORKING WITH PAGE RELATED VIEWS

The first groups of views are all page related because they deal with the specific design and editing of individual Web pages. They provide a means to directly develop site content or edit what already exists. Design view provides a means to edit a page in a WYSIWYG interface, Code view enables for direct entry and HTML of Web page code, and Split view offers a split-screen option that shows the other views at the same time.

DESIGN VIEW

The view most users will spend the most significant amount of their time in is Design view. It mimics the interface of most Microsoft Office System products and provides a WYSIWYG interface for designing most of your Web site content. Figure 3.3 shows another site in Design view.

Design view combines the ability to see what you are building as you build it with the tools in the FrontPage interface and the standard Microsoft and Office keyboard shortcuts. It is also the best interface for building your vision as quickly as possible.

Figure 3.3
If you are working on
a site, the Folder list
appears to the left of
the Design view.

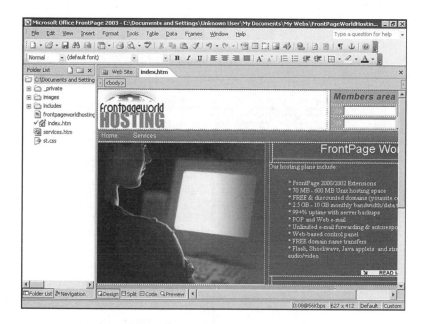

NOTE

Although Design view is a WYSIWG environment, the nature of such an approach requires that some elements appear on the screen that won't appear on your site and vice versa. Make sure to examine your work in Preview view and on various browsers to determine if you are getting the exact effect you are looking for.

➔ For more detailed information on developing site content through Design view, **see** "Developing the Basic Page: Text, Lists, and Hyperlinks," **p. 77**.

CODE VIEW

Code view offers an interface for entering and editing code directly through the FrontPage interface.

Code view does not limit you to only working in HTML or with simple client-side scripting elements. ASP, JSP, PHP, and other scripting languages can be edited in Code view.

NOTE

If you are programming in a scripting language that FrontPage can't render in the Preview view such as PHP, FrontPage will not allow a jump to Design or Split view.

➔ For more on developing code through the FrontPage interface, **see** "Working in Code View and Split View," **p. 519**.

SPLIT VIEW

FrontPage 2003 introduces a Split view option that offers a full-screen look at both the Design and Code views. As seen in Figure 3.4, editing the content in one panel will automatically update the other panel's content accordingly.

Figure 3.4
Split view presents both Design and Code views, allowing editing in either panel.

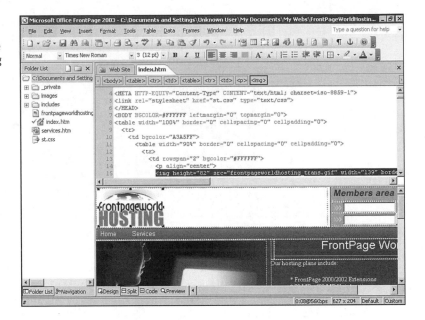

Split view provides a unique opportunity for Web design because it allows the developer to edit site HTML or site content and instantly see how the information is presented in the other panel. This view is ideally suited for times when a slight nudge or editing of HTML is needed and you want to see exactly how it will be rendered.

NOTE

Split view will only work when developing HTML Web pages. Because FrontPage can't render scripting languages such as PHP and ASP, these can't be edited through Split view.

One way around this issue is to work on the ASP or PHP files as HTML files and then save them accordingly as the last step in the design process. FrontPage won't be able to render any of the active content but can still be used for a considerable part of the design process.

TIP

Want to learn HTML? Consider developing several pages in the Design part of the Split view and watch how FrontPage writes the HTML as you do. It is a fascinating way to learn HTML through deconstruction.

PREVIEW VIEW

Preview view gives the developer the chance to view site content in a browser interface without having to open an additional window. As seen in Figure 3.5, Preview view not only shows site content, but also shows effects such as hyperlink rollovers. It is the same screen as Figure 3.3 but demonstrates the added hyperlink rollover effect. Note the location of the cursor.

Figure 3.5
Preview view shows you how the page you are working on will look in a browser window. Compare to Figure 3.3.

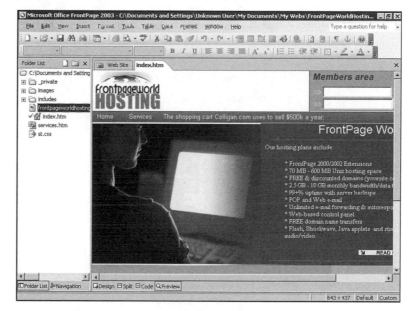

> **TIP**
>
> Because Preview view will accept a form field entry and will link to other sites within the Preview window, you can do a considerable amount of basic functional testing in Preview view without having to open a browser.

> **NOTE**
>
> FrontPage uses the version of Internet Explorer installed on your system to provide the rendering engine for Preview view. As a result, it will present a pretty solid view of how your site will look in Internet Explorer, but won't be as predictable with other browser types.

→ For more on viewing site content in a browser (as opposed to Preview view), **see** "Developing the Basic Page: Text, Lists, and Hyperlinks," **p. 77**.

USING SITE RELATED VIEWS

Although the WYSIWYG and supporting coding environments are considerable assets to the development of the basic page, the true power of the different FrontPage views comes from the site related viewing options.

In addition to the views mentioned previously, FrontPage 2003 offers the ability to view your site in terms of folders, a way to both view and develop site navigational elements, a solid site reporting engine, a means for examining how hyperlinks relate to each other, and a direct access to the task management system built right in to FrontPage. All of these are offered through the additional site related views discussed next.

FOLDERS VIEW

As shown in Figure 3.6, Folders view presents in a familiar Windows Explorer type interface. As in Windows Explorer, elements can be renamed and copied with a right-click and dragged and dropped in to other folders via the mouse. Considerable site management and control can be established and maintained through the Folders view.

Figure 3.6
Folders view presents your site as a series of folders and files similar to the familiar Windows Explorer interface.

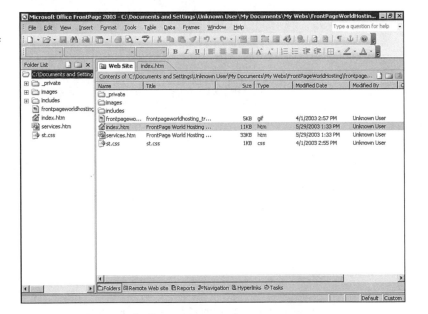

If you change the filename or path of any files from within Folders view, FrontPage automatically updates all the necessary HTML with the appropriate naming or paths.

TIP

Use the ease of management offered by Folders view to maintain control of your site. Simple housekeeping tasks such as grouping all images and placing them in an images folder can be done with a few clicks of the mouse and can make it much easier to find things when needed.

TIP

> If you rename or move more than a few files between folders, select <u>R</u>ecalculate Hyperlinks from the <u>T</u>ools menu. This will make sure that all changes are caught throughout the Web site. FrontPage *should* catch all these changes, but this is a quick and easy way to make sure that it does.

REMOTE WEB SITE VIEW

If you are working on site content that is published to another location, the Remote Web Site view gives you a chance to compare your content with the content at the other site. You can then make appropriate publishing decisions from a position of strength because you are able to examine both versions of your site side by side.

→ For more detailed information on the Remote Web Site view and on publishing a FrontPage Web site, **see** "Publishing a FrontPage Web Site," **p. 299**.

NAVIGATION VIEW

If you want FrontPage to manage the navigation of your site, Navigation view provides a means to both manage and view site navigation. Navigation view, seen in Figure 3.7, acts as both a representation of the site navigational structure as well as the means to change it.

NOTE

> Navigation View "works" only if you built your Web site navigation using the FrontPage navigational tools. If you didn't, the view will show nothing other than your home page and will not accurately reflect your site.

Figure 3.7
You can move elements of your site navigation around to redevelop the site navigational structure. FrontPage will make all changes as needed.

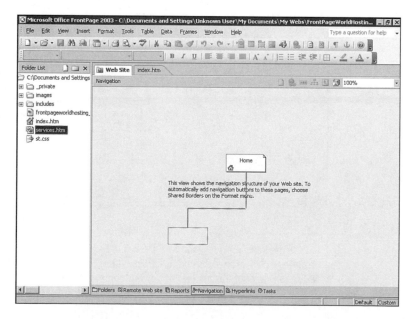

Dragging any element of the Navigation view to another location will automatically change the navigation accordingly. In addition, the deletion of a file through that view will also delete it from the navigational structure of the site.

Site navigational structure is most effectively used when FrontPage is expected to maintain site navigational across FrontPage bars and links. Because FrontPage can update such links across the site as they are added to any individual page, it provides a powerful site management tool. By simply dragging a new page into the site navigational structure, FrontPage will update the rest of the site as needed automatically.

→ For more on the way FrontPage handles site navigation, **see** "FrontPage's Navigation Tools and Elements," **p. 147**.

REPORTS VIEW

FrontPage provides a number of reports that help you assess both the status and health of your Web site. These are all simply and quickly accessed directly from the Reports view in FrontPage 2003.

As seen in Figure 3.8, when the Reports view is selected, FrontPage presents the Site Summary Report by default. You can choose between the different FrontPage reports by selecting the Site Summary dropdown menu.

Figure 3.8
The Site Summary report shows a detailed overview of the site you are working on.

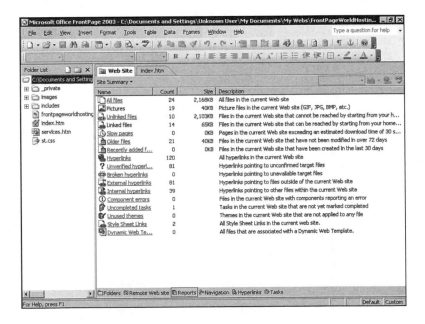

NOTE

To use the traffic reports, your Web site has to be hosted at a server that provides both FrontPage 2002 extensions and has activated this reporting feature. Many hosts offer the extensions without this feature, so do your homework accordingly.

FrontPage Server Extensions can be installed on multiple server types (Unix, Linux, and so on) and don't require Microsoft Server Technologies such as Windows Server 2003.

NOTE

The new HTML Compatibility and Accessibility reports generated through FrontPage are presented as new HTML pages in the FrontPage design view—not through the Reports view.

→ For more on FrontPage's reporting, **see** the chapters in Part VII, "Web Collaboration," **p. 595**.

 If you aren't getting all the reports you think you should be getting, see "Reports View Shows Nothing" in the "Troubleshooting" section at the end of this chapter.

HYPERLINKS VIEW

Hyperlinks view provides a fascinating look at your Web site in terms of how every file on your site relates to every other file linked within it. As seen in Figure 3.9, a file in Hyperlinks view is shown in terms of which files link to it and which files it links to. FrontPage will report on any external links called from your site but won't show external sites that call a file within yours.

Figure 3.9
In Hyperlinks view, files are shown in terms of hyperlinks to and from the file.

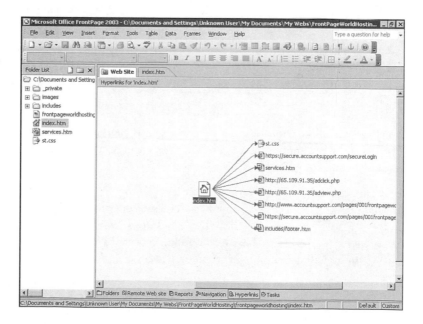

NOTE

Hyperlinks view is not just limited to items with hyperlinks. All items in your site (images, CSS files, scripting, and so on) are all included in this view.

Hyperlinks can call files external to your Web site as easily as they can call internal files, but link types are shown in this report.

Any HTML file in the view can be expanded to show how other files link to that file. Simply click the "+" symbol in the file to activate this. Figure 3.10 shows an expanded view from Figure 3.9 utilizing this feature.

Figure 3.10
By clicking the "+" icon in any file, the Hyperlinks view will show the links that relate to that file.

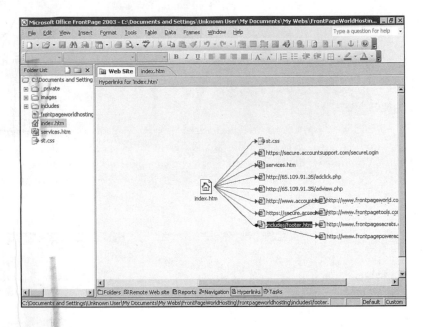

FrontPage will allow you to continue to expand this view as many times as possible. If the view passes the confines of the screen, FrontPage will provide scrollbars to let you view the area you are interested in.

Right-clicking within the Hyperlinks view lets you toggle several options for viewing the information. The first option, Show Page Titles, toggles the display between the filename and the file title. The second option, Hyperlinks to *Pictures*, toggles the showing of hyperlinks to pictures on and off. The third option, Repeated Hyperlinks, toggles the option for showing multiple links to the same item on and off.

As seen in Figure 3.11, broken and external hyperlinks are symbolized by a broken line and alternate colors with a dot next to the page. A quick glance of the view can let you quickly distinguish between internal and external links.

Figure 3.11
In Hyperlinks view, broken hyperlinks are presented with a broken line and external hyperlinks are shown with a dot symbol. Note the broken link to stt.css in this example.

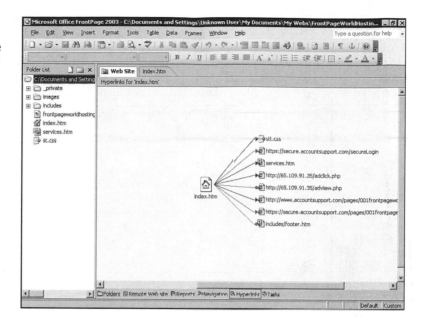

 If you looking for a way to get around the fact that you can't print Hyperlinks view, see "Print Hyperlinks View" in the "Troubleshooting" section at the end of this chapter.

TASKS VIEW

FrontPage 2003 provides a simple task management system that can be used by everyone developing the site. Individual tasks can be assigned independently of individual pages or assigned to a specific file. As seen in Figure 3.12, the Tasks view gives a reporting of site tasks at their different stages of completion.

NOTE

> Tasks view can be used with any server option and does not require a Windows server or FrontPage extensions for use.

→ For more on working with the Tasks tools, **see** "Collaboration with FrontPage 2003," **p. 615**.

Figure 3.12
The Tasks view shows the current status of all assigned tasks in a specific Web site.

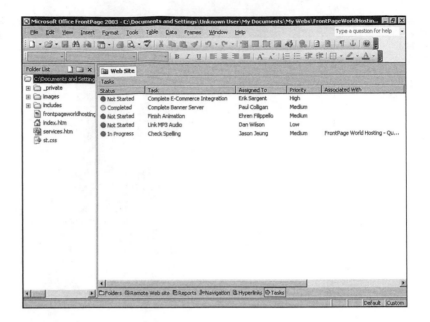

TROUBLESHOOTING

NAVIGATION VIEW SHOWS NOTHING

I switched over to Navigation view, and FrontPage shows me nothing. Where is my site navigation?

Navigation view only shows what you have told FrontPage about your site. If your initial template didn't contain navigation and you didn't build one as you built the site, there is simply no navigation to view.

REPORTS VIEW SHOWS NOTHING

My host has FrontPage 2002 Extensions installed, but I'm unable to view any of the site usage reports.

Site usage reports can be toggled on/off by your Web host. Many discount Web hosting providers don't offer this feature or require an additional fee to do so. Contact your Web host directly to see if this option is available to you.

WANT TO PRINT HYPERLINKS VIEW

I love the Hyperlinks view of my site and would like to print it for later reference. The option is greyed out—what do I do?

FrontPage 2003 does not provide an option to print Hyperlinks view. The only workaround is to do a screen grab of FrontPage and print the resulting graphic.

FRONT AND CENTER: VIEWS MATTER

I've received email and heard a number of FrontPage users tell me proudly that they only work in a single view and don't make use of the others. They tell me they are more "comfortable" looking at their site one way over another. Some only work in Design view, whereas others prefer to stay with the Code view to keep "pure."

This is as intelligent as only typing in caps because you aren't comfortable with the Caps Lock key. It is not a matter of *preference*; it is a matter of *power*.

FrontPage provides multiple views to your Web site project because you need to look at (and interact with) your site in different ways as you work through a project. Each view is used at different parts of the project to provide the best possible design toolset.

It should be of no surprise that most users will spend most of their time in Design view. The view is by far the easiest to use and the most comfortable to work in. Design view uses an interface most users are familiar with and empowers them with the ability to design the Web site they are looking to develop.

Spend more than a few weeks working on a Web site, and you will realize that there is no way around occasionally jumping in to Code view. There will be times when you will need to tweak your HTML—this isn't an issue of FrontPage; this is an issue of designing a Web site. When you work in Code view, remember that most of the buttons in the toolbar also work in this view. Need to build a table? Use the Insert Table button. Need to underline text or insert a picture? Do this from the interface as well.

After you've spent some time in Code view, you will realize the need to regularly examine how your HTML affects your Web content. Sure, you can jump to the Preview view or look at the site in a browser, but the Split view gives you an instant presentation of how your code will perform. Make use of it.

Obviously, you will need to examine your work in a browser on a regular basis. Despite the WYSIWYG element provided through Design view, there are still items that can confuse the process. Some preview issues require a browser: "Does this work on Netscape 3?" Some issues simply don't: "Does this table look right?" Most users preview a site in their browser when Preview view actually provides the information they need.

Web sites are just that, sites. True design isn't about any one single page; it is about the entirety of your site content and how it all fits together. Folders view lets you view your site as if it were your hard drive. Need to sort your files? Click on the header column. Need to move a batch of GIFs to the images directory? Drag and drop.

If you are working with a remote Web site, Remote Web Site view gives you the same power as Folder view.

Many FrontPage users like to develop their site navigation using a simple flowchart-like diagramming process. It should be of no surprise that the Navigation view uses that approach. Need to quickly redirect how everything connects to everything else or need to explain your

site layout to someone who is "uncomfortable" with Internet programs? Use this view navigation and manipulate these sites issues.

The reports FrontPage provides the end user are incredibly valuable. Even if you aren't hosted on a server that provides the traffic reports, the look in to the health of your site provided through this view is significant. If you aren't examining Reports view on a regular basis, you are missing out.

This is the World Wide Web—every page in your site usually interacts with other pages internal and external to your project. The Hyperlinks view gives you the only way to really see how these hyperlinks interact with each other—there is no other way to visualize this status. It also provides the ability to view broken links and quickly fix them with a few clicks of the mouse.

Tasks view is obviously only of benefit if you are using the tasks management feature built in to FrontPage. If you are, you will find that the power of not having to work with an additional system joined with the ability to have a task automatically open the corresponding page is a solid combination.

Make use of the different views in FrontPage. Independently, they provide different needs for different situations. Combined, they provide an ability to understand and control your site that puts you in a considerable place of power.

CHAPTER 4

Developing the Basic Page: Page Properties, Text, Lists, and Hyperlinks

In this chapter

ELEMENTS OF GOOD PAGE DESIGN

Before we start the process of developing text on a Web page, a few moments should be spent on the topic of good page design.

In this chapter we'll examine the interfaces and tools for entering text, lists and hyperlink in the FrontPage interface. In addition, we'll show you how to view your content in different browsers to make sure that they appear as you'd like them to.

As with any product used in the design of anything, you are given the full ability to design whatever you want with FrontPage 2003. Nothing will prevent you from making bad design decisions other than your style and taste when approaching a project.

Take a few minutes to ask yourself the following questions before you start any design process:

- *Will your audience find what they are looking for on your page?* Most developers forget this simple fact and create dozens and dozens of pages for no other purpose than because they thought the content should be there.

- *Will anything on your page cause them to leave?* You've got your audience at your site on the page you want them on—is there anything that might make them leave? Are there too many fancy graphics and special effects? Is the page laid out nicely? Does it load quickly? Is there anything on the page that doesn't need to be there or that might be offensive?

- *Is your content any good?* Most people think that having a Web page is enough. It isn't—it is only the first step. Much like a poorly painted office with no place to sit and trash on the ground won't do well to anyone who visits your company, a Web site without good content causes people to leave quickly, wondering why they came in the first place.

- *Are you trying to squeeze too much on a single page?* Are you overwhelming your audience? If the content is *good*, is there too much of it on any given page?

TIP

> Although you don't *have* to think in terms of physical pages in Web design, you also don't have to destroy the paradigm that most of the world is still used to and still using. Is your page too long? Divide it in to a number of other pages.

- *Is there too much technology and too little content?* FrontPage provides great effects and great multimedia elements at the click of a button. The desire to use these tools often is understandable but needs to be controlled.

- *Is your content truly accessible?* Your site looks great on the computer you designed it on, but how will it look to someone using another browser, another computer platform, or another device such as a cell phone? What if your audience is visually impaired and uses a screen reader to "surf" the Net? Will your content work for them as well?

→ For more on building accessible Web sites and the tools provided by FrontPage for doing so, **see** "FrontPage's Accessibility Features," **p. 235**.

Have these elements in mind at *the very first moment* you start developing your Web site. These issues are true for the tools and technologies discussed throughout this book, but are equally important from step one, setting your page properties, discussed next.

CONFIGURING PAGE PROPERTIES

By default, FrontPage presents you with a white screen on which you develop your site. Internet Explorer defaults to a white screen where your Web content appears.

The problem is that *a good chunk of the world doesn't work in default mode*. Many browsers use different background colors, don't have the same fonts you do, often can't view graphics (or multimedia), and many times purposely present content in an as "non-Microsoft" a way as possible. You will need to be aware of this throughout the Web design process, but the issue is also vital when entering the basic elements of text, hyperlinks, and lists.

NOTE

I do a considerable amount of Web surfing on my HipTop phone with black and white browsing up against a grey background. I love being wireless, and the world is quickly going the same way.

But numbers are numbers: According to my most recent stats, more than 96% of the visitors to my sites are using some form of Internet Explorer, so you need to run the numbers and make the decisions accordingly.

4

As seen in Figures 4.1 through 4.5, you can set *some* issues of the Web page through the Page Properties dialog box, accessible through the File menu. *Many* of the elements set through the dialog box set how you would like elements of page content to be presented. The term "like" is used because many browser types will override these variables either from a technical necessity or from the preference of the user. We examine that issue throughout this chapter.

NOTE

The Properties dialog box sets the *page* properties for the page you are working on and doesn't make changes on a site-wide basis.

THE GENERAL TAB

The General tab, seen in Figure 4.1, is where you set the title, description, keywords, base location, default target frame, and the background sound for the page.

Figure 4.1
The General tab of the Page Properties dialog box lets you set descriptive information, frame handling data, and a background sound (if desired).

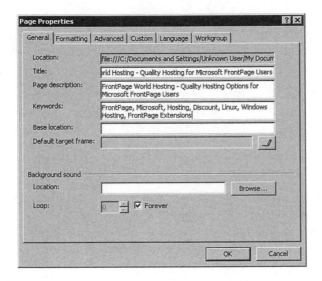

Title, page description, and keywords are vital content for each page and help search engines identify what each of the pages in your site are about. They add the information directly to the HTML that can be edited at any time (through this interface or in the HTML).

Base location and target frame set defaults for links when working with frames.

→ For more on working with frames, base locations, and target frames, **see** "Enhancing Web Sites with Frames," **p. 219**.

TIP

A large percentage of Internet users consider background sounds to be a considerable nuisance. The concept of "background music" for a Web page (not selected by the user) is just too much for most. I recommend simply not using this feature unless some element of the page specifically requires it.

If you must add music into your Web site, several plug-in options can give the end user control over the sound (including the ability to turn the sound off) that you should consider using.

THE FORMATTING TAB

On the Formatting tab of the Page Properties dialog box, you can set background and color variables for the page (see Figure 4.2).

If you want to place a background image at your site, you can easily add it through this interface. You can select the file through the Browse button and then decide whether you would like it positioned as a watermark. The watermark effect keeps the image in place while the visitor scrolls up and down through the content on the page.

Figure 4.2
The Formatting tab of
the Page Properties
dialog box lets you set
a background picture
and the color scheme
you'd like followed.

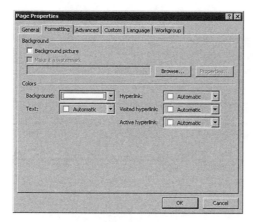

TIP

It is my strong held belief that 99.999% of all background images distract from the Web site design.

I won't say 100% because I saw one site that integrated the image in perfectly—but only one.

The Colors area of the Formatting tab is where you set the Background, Text, Hyperlink, Visited Hyperlink, and Active Hyperlink colors for the page.

TIP

If you want to prevent yourself from ever assuming that the world surfs with a white background, default your personal Web browser of choice to have a page background color of bright yellow. When you view your sites in this way, you will never forget to set your pages accordingly.

One thing to keep in mind is that every element of this tab can be overwritten by the browser used by the person viewing site content. Some browsers don't allow background pictures. Some browsers only present text in a single color. As a result, all of the page properties set here should be decorative only and not an integral part of your site.

The second issue worth mentioning is that the practice of managing site and page colors through this method is a considerably older method for accomplishing such a task. The use of FrontPage themes and the implementation of cascading style sheets (CSS) accomplish the same goals with a considerably easier implementation process.

→ For more on working with FrontPage themes, **see** "Using Themes," **p. 133**.

→ For more on working with style sheets, **see** "Using Style Sheets to Format Web Pages," **p. 385**.

THE ADVANCED TAB

The Advanced tab of the Page Properties dialog box, seen in Figure 4.3, enables you to set page margins down to the specific pixel, assign styles for your page, and set design-time control scripting elements for the page you are working on.

Figure 4.3
Set page margins, styles, and design-time control scripting on the Advanced tab of the Page Properties dialog box.

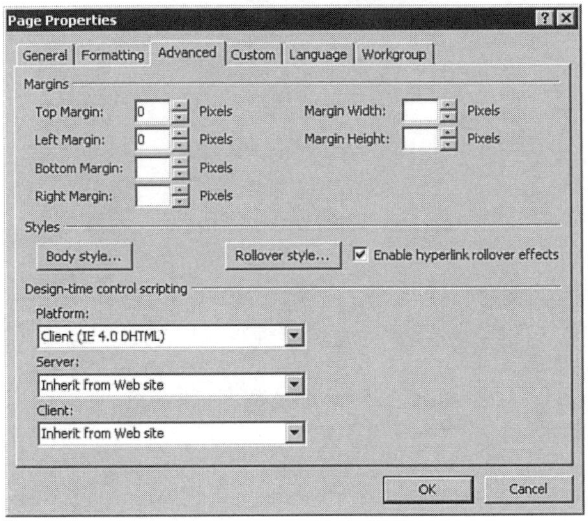

The Margins options in the Advanced tab are self-explanatory: Top, left, bottom, and right margins can be set, as well as a specific assignment of margin width and heights. This effect, usually used in traditional page layout, can be used to produce specific effects when laying out your text. You can create Web documents that have layout specifications that can be used to mimic the traditional printing world.

> **NOTE**
> Never assume that your page layout will be exactly the same on every screen. Not all browser types support page margins. You should design your sites accordingly. In the case of page margins, make sure that your page will also look fine without them.

You can also set any Body Style for your page through this interface. In addition, Rollover styles can be set directly through this tab in an easy-to-use interface, as seen in Figure 4.4. Rollover styles are the basic effect seen when the user rolls her mouse over a hyperlink and the link changes form in one way or another.

> **NOTE**
> The Font dialog box is used to select the Font type for the rollover. When you set rollover text through this interface, you set how the text will be seen when the curser passes over the hyperlinks.

Figure 4.4
FrontPage 2003 lets you set rollover styles down to the font used in the rollover and any text effects you might want to attribute to it.

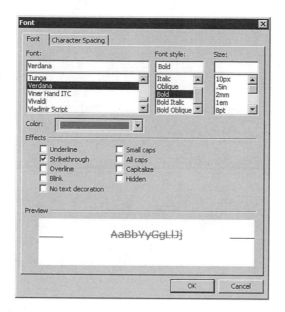

→ For more on the use of styles in Web design and how they are handled by FrontPage, **see** "Using Style Sheets to Format Web Pages," **p. 385**.

The Design-time control scripting area of the Advanced tab lets you set the Platform, Server, and Client for any design-time controls that might be implemented on that page.

4

NOTE

Design-time controls are components that expose certain properties and methods inside a design-time only interface enabling the control to generate code to implement certain functionality at runtime. No design-time controls come with FrontPage—this option is for the more advanced user who is implementing such controls in a FrontPage Web site.

A great MSDN article on design-time controls can be found at http://dtcarticle.frontpagelink.com.

NOTE

It is important to point out that not all design-time controls will be affected by this setting. If any Design-time control specifies any execution parameters, the settings in the control will override anything set in this tab.

THE CUSTOM TAB

The Custom tab of the Page Properties dialog box, seen in Figure 4.5, controls the system or user variables for the page. These are assigned as metatags within your page's HTML.

System variables are set with the *HTTP-EQUIV* attribute and are used for page-specific variable information related to the page content such as *Content-Type* or *Expires.*

Figure 4.5
System and User variables are set through the Custom tag of the Page Properties dialog box.

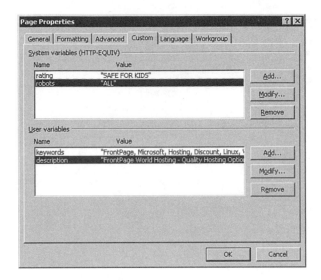

User variables are set with a *Name* and *Content* variable that are often used for site information notation such as designer name, department responsible, and so on.

> **NOTE**
>
> The most common meta tags are <META NAME="Keywords" CONTENT="*insert site keywords here*"> and <META NAME="Description" CONTENT="*insert description of Web site here*"> used to identify page content for certain search engine technologies.
>
> A great resource on meta tags can be found at http://metatags.frontpagelink.com.

THE LANGUAGE TAB

The Language tab of the Page Properties dialog box, seen in Figure 4.6, lets you set page language and HTML encoding variables for the page you are developing.

> **NOTE**
>
> The language settings don't do translate page content; they just change the encoding of the text to the required character set. People are working on accurate translation tools, but the technology simply isn't "there" yet.

 If you having problems with your formatting choices being accurately reflected on the screen, *see "My Choices Aren't Showing Up" in the "Troubleshooting" section at the end of this chapter.*

 If you don't quite get the formatting right on content from included files, *see "Included Content Page Properties Don't Work" in the "Troubleshooting" section at the end of this chapter.*

Figure 4.6
Page language and HTML encoding variables are set in the Language tab.

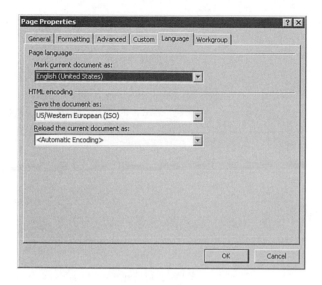

ENTERING AND FORMATTING TEXT

As seen in Figure 4.7, the basic Design view of FrontPage 2003 looks like many other interfaces in the Microsoft Office System, such as Microsoft Word or PowerPoint.

Figure 4.7
The Design view enables page entry and design much like other traditional Windows products.

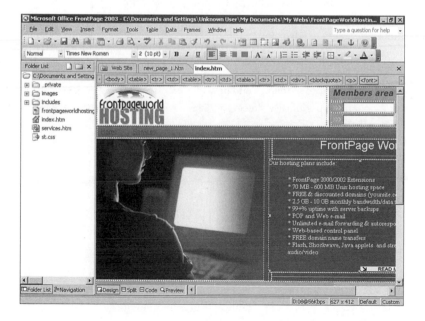

The importance of this should be understood: *The majority of the Web page design process through FrontPage 2003 is no different from the design process for any other text-related*

information in any other Windows product. There is no special interface to learn, there are no new keyboard shortcuts, and the average user can quickly start developing HTML content in little to no time.

It would be pointless in this level of book to go over items such as what the bold icon does or how to center your text. Instead, we'll examine the HTML specific issues of format headings, how the Web handles paragraph breaks, character formatting, fonts on the Web, the use of horizontal lines, and how Office's unique tools for cutting and pasting content are specially suited for Web design with FrontPage 2003.

Format Headings

HTML formatting is different from traditional text formatting. In many ways, it is more of a "recommendation" than it is an actual format command. Like other programs in the Microsoft Office System, FrontPage 2003 contains a format headings dropdown box in Design mode. The implications of this need to be understood.

If you are using themes or CSS in your Web design, format headings are vital; it is the way for you to tell FrontPage how to format a specific area of text. Simply select the text you want to format and choose the appropriate formatting from the dropdown list.

In addition to support theme or CSS work, the Format headings that come default with FrontPage 2003 represent the traditional HTML markup associated with the original HTML specifications of almost 10 years ago. Format elements, such as bulleted lists, simply insert the list tags in to the page. Different browsers interpret tags differently (many ignore them), and this needs to be taken into consideration during the Web design process. Never assume that because you assigned text to a specific format heading that it will look a certain way—always test it in multiple browsers.

→ For more on the use of themes and how they are used in FrontPage, **see** "Using Themes," **p. 133**.

→ For more on the use of style sheets and CSS in Web design, **see** "Using Style Sheets to Format Web Pages," **p. 385**.

Line Breaks Versus Paragraph Breaks

When you press the Enter key in FrontPage, you will note that it drops two lines down, not a single line as it would in most other text editing products.

This happens because, by default, the HTML tag used in this case is the paragraph tag (the <p> tag). In short, FrontPage assumes that you mean to start a new paragraph and formats any tags accordingly.

If you don't want to start a new paragraph and simply want to move to the next line, press the Shift key when pressing Enter and FrontPage will accommodate; then place a <br> tag instead of a paragraph tag, resulting in a single line break.

TIP

> If you want to see a paragraph break and a simple line break, toggle the Show All button in the Standard toolbar. (It's the one that looks like a backward P.)

FONTS AND THE WEB

The Font dropdown menu in the FrontPage Design view needs to be thoroughly understood before it is used in the design process. Yes, you can select whatever font you'd like to see on your Web site, but in order to work as desired, it requires two things: 1) the user must have that font installed on her system and 2) the user must have a browser that actually shows fonts.

Whereas a good percentage of Internet surfers are Windows users with the standard font install, a good percentage of them aren't. If your Web site says use font "x" and the surfers don't have the font installed, they typically won't install it for your page. Although it is possible to embed a font into a Web page (as you would a PDF or Word document), such practice is considered a Web "no-no" and isn't a standard Web practice. In addition, some browsers (such as the one on my phone) have only one font and one font size.

The same is true for the font size dropdown capabilities and even options as "simple" as bold and italics. Some browsers don't support these options because, simply, they can't.

To make things even more interesting, you need to remember that some users won't even read your Web page at all. Assisted surfing devices for the handicapped user might read a page to her or offer site content in Braille. You need to plan your site accordingly.

With all these warnings about making your site work well on all browsers, someone could take my comments as meaning that you shouldn't use a wide font selection or even bold text. This couldn't be further from the truth. Use the technology you have at your finger tips to produce the best looking sites possible—just make sure that you remember your entire audience and develop accordingly. This is the delicate "art" of Web design that makes it, for many, so exciting.

→ For more on using FrontPage to make an accessible Web site, **see** "FrontPage's Accessibility Features," **p. 235**.

So, in short, you can "suggest" font types and sizes, but you can't be sure that your user will be able to support them. *Never* design a site that requires the specific use of fonts because you can never be guaranteed their installation on the reader's browser.

TIP

> If, for branding purposes, you *must* have a specific font somewhere in your site, you have two options: design graphics using the font on your system and place them in the site or design the content in Flash.
>
> Obviously, this will require the user who can support images or Flash but does put you in a position of control—if it is needed.

4

ADDING HORIZONTAL LINES

Although many elements of the FrontPage interface have counterparts similar in the publishing world, there is an element to Web design offered by FrontPage (and other Web development products) that simply doesn't have a counterpart elsewhere. This element is the horizontal line, or the <hr> tag.

Horizontal lines are used to break up text in a simple way. Using a basic horizontal line is browser friendly because it gives no specific directions other than insert the line however the browser sees fit. Figure 4.8 shows a page with horizontal lines used to divide text.

Figure 4.8
Horizontal lines used to divide key sections of a privacy policy text.

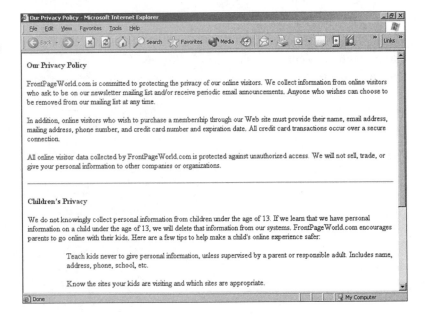

Double-clicking a horizontal line in FrontPage will open the Horizontal Line Properties dialog box, allowing you to set specific features for your horizontal line. As seen in Figure 4.9, you can edit elements of the horizontal line to better achieve the look you are striving for. As with all design elements described in this chapter, remember that your additional formatting might be ignored by certain browsers.

Figure 4.9
You can choose properties such as a width, height, and color for the horizontal line inserted with the <hr> tag.

CUTTING AND PASTING TEXT

It might seem that cutting and pasting text should be a simple process in a WYSIWYG design environment such as FrontPage 2003. This is not the case because a number of elements must be taken into consideration: not only is there the issue of the source font style and size, but also there is the addition of any metadata that might be included in the original content.

For example, a simple paragraph cut and paste from Microsoft Word might be the same font and size as the destination page, but the Word content might also include metadata such as original spacing and formatting. You don't want this additional content in your final HTML because it does little more than slow down the loading speed of the page.

As seen in Figure 4.10, when you paste content from another source into FrontPage, a paste options button appears next to the text that gives you choices of what to do with the content. Most of the time, the two choices are Keep Source Formatting or Keep Text Only. The first option will insert *all* cut content in to your page, whereas the second will eliminate all metadata associated with the content. The second option will also format the data in the same format as the area that the content was pasted on to.

Figure 4.10
Content pasted directly in to FrontPage is met with a paste options button that offers the ability to either keep the source formatting or only transfer the text content contained in the clipboard.

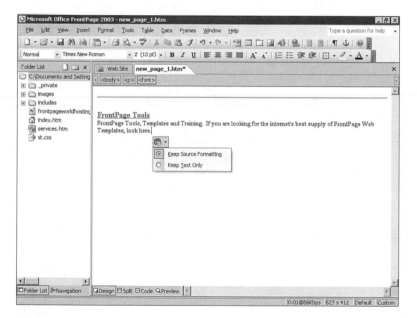

This feature was not available in previous versions of FrontPage and was a frustrating element for a number of previous users. If you were frustrated by the cut-and-paste features of earlier versions of FrontPage, you will enjoy this new element tremendously.

TIP

> The options provided by FrontPage 2003 when pasting content in to your site make it very easy to paste content from pretty much anywhere in to your Web page. Because FrontPage will take the extra step of stripping all metadata from the content, there is no need to worry about it being sent to your page. In addition, because no style content is sent with the paste, content will conform to the font choice already in the area where content is being pasted.

NUMBERED AND BULLETED LISTS

Content on a Web page is often presented in a list format. This format lends itself well to the brevity normally associated with Web content and provides a way to present content in an orderly fashion.

As with most other Windows programs, the Number and Bullets buttons in the Formatting Toolbar, shown in Figure 4.11, will let you present content in list format. You can either press the button and enter the content or select the content and press the appropriate button to format accordingly.

→ For more on building collapsible outlines, a cool list option, **see** "Making Your Pages and Sites More Dynamic," **p. 425**.

OTHER LIST STYLES

You are not stuck with the standard list formatting with FrontPage (or with HTML). FrontPage 2003 provides options for adding a bit of flair to your lists.

Right-clicking any list in FrontPage will allow the selection of the List Properties dialog box. Each tab in the box provides for considerable list formatting options.

The first tab, Picture Bullets (seen in Figure 4.11), lets you substitute the bullets in your list with either the bullet image associated with the current page theme or with another defined item. You can use this feature to create a stylistic list in your site.

The second tab, Plain Bullets, lets you pick the type of bullet you'd like presented in your list. You are given options that include the elimination of bullets (but still allowing for list formatting), bullet outlines, or square bullets.

On the third tab, Numbers (seen in Figure 4.12), you can set the kind of list you'd like (number, roman numerals, letters, and so on) and tell FrontPage where you'd like to start the numbering. If your list is broken in to a number of sections, you can set them to appear as one succinct list with this option.

Figure 4.11
The Picture Bullets tab lets you substitute list bullets with a graphic—either from the page's theme or selected from another source.

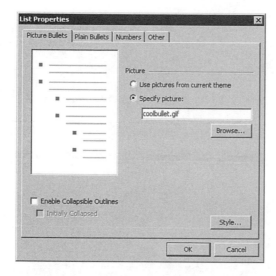

Figure 4.12
The Numbers tab lets you set whether the list is number or letter defined and lets you set the starting number.

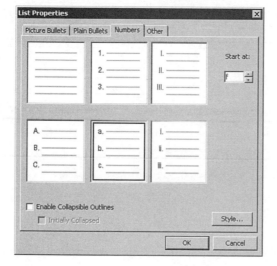

The fourth tab, Other (seen in Figure 4.13), lets you set the style of the list. Figure 4.14 shows you each of the list types and what they are used for.

NOTE

Each tab in the List Properties dialog box lets you select the option of making the list a collapsible outline. If this is selected, DHTML will be inserted in to the page content to allow the list items to be collapsible. The nice thing about this effect is that if the browsers support the feature, it will be presented accordingly. If they don't, the DHTML will be ignored and the list will be provided in full. As a result, you can usually use this feature without fear of browser compatibility issues.

Figure 4.13
The Other tab lets you define a list style.

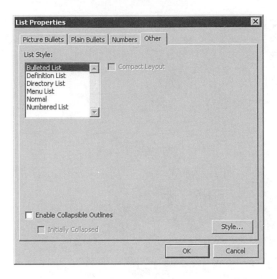

Figure 4.14
Each of the formatting types.

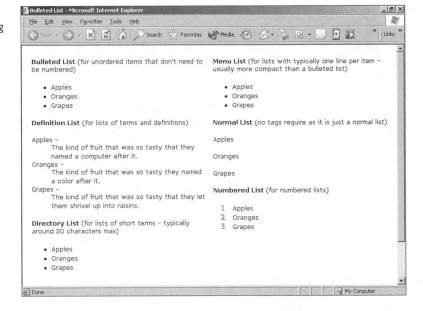

Inserting and Formatting Hyperlinks

The standard Hyperlink button works in FrontPage as it does in most other Windows programs. It is seen in Figure 4.15 and opens the Insert Hyperlink dialog box shown in Figure 4.16.

Figure 4.15
The Hyperlink button (in the standard tool-bar) opens the Insert Hyperlink dialog box, shown in Figure 4.16.

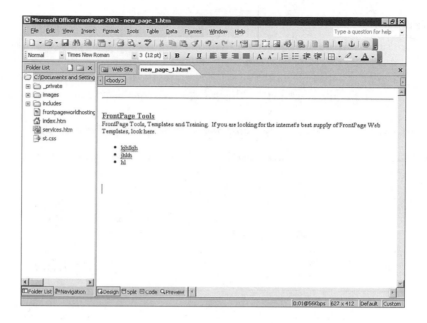

Figure 4.16
The Insert Hyperlink dialog box provides the interface for creating any kind of hyperlink.

HYPERLINKS TO EXISTING FILES

In the Insert Hyperlink dialog box shown in Figure 4.16, you will notice a number of files contained in the list. These are other files located in the folder where the file you are working on is located. Often, the files you want to link to are right there, which can help expedite the linking process.

You can pick within the interface between the current folder, browsed pages, and recent files and find most of the files you are looking for. You can also insert an address directly in to the Address field or select the Look In dropdown field to locate the desired file. Most, if not all, of your potentials for adding hyperlinks are a button click away through this interface.

HYPERLINKS TO NEW FILES

Often in the initial stages of the design process, you want to create a link to a file that doesn't yet exist. Obviously the next step is to create the file. By selecting the Create a New Document button, FrontPage will both create the link and the new file. You can then edit and save the file accordingly. The initial screen for this process can be seen in Figure 4.17.

Figure 4.17
By selecting Create a New Document, FrontPage will let you create a link and the page you want to link to.

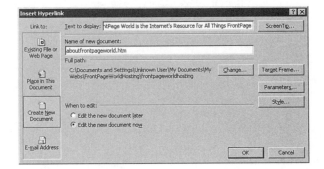

Simply edit the file created by FrontPage. Don't worry if the file is misnamed or if it isn't quite what you wanted it to be. You can always change the filename or content later and FrontPage will update the HTML accordingly.

HYPERLINKS WITHIN DOCUMENTS (BOOKMARKS)

Links to a certain area within a document (or within the same document) are called *bookmark* links and can also easily be created and linked to from within FrontPage 2003. These are a powerful option because they give you the ability to jump to longer areas within texts—no longer requiring the user to scroll through a long page to get to what she is looking for.

The first step is to create the bookmark within the Web page. This is done by selecting the text or item you'd like to bookmark and selecting Insert, Bookmark. It will open the Bookmark dialog box, seen in Figure 4.18.

> **NOTE**
>
> For those familiar with other Web design products such as Dreamweaver, the term bookmark and anchor are interchangeable.

> **NOTE**
>
> You will need to save the file with the bookmark before FrontPage will recognize it.

Figure 4.18
The Bookmark dialog box lets you quickly set up bookmarks within a Web page.

Once the bookmark has been created, the second step is to link to the desired file and then the bookmark within the file. By selecting Place in This Document from the Hyperlink dialog box, all bookmarks within the selected file will be available to choose from. In Figure 4.19, the bookmarks seen previously in Figure 4.18 are reflected in the choices.

Figure 4.19
Use the Select Place in Document dialog box to select the Bookmark within the page that you'd like to link to.

LINKING TO AN EMAIL ADDRESS

Instead of linking to other Web addresses, you can also link to an email address, called a *mailto* link. Typically this results in opening up the user's email program with a blank email with the address defined in the link already entered as the To address. As with most browser functionality, this is handled on a browser-by-browser basis but is most often the standard. To insert a mailto link of this type, select the E-mail Address button in the lower left side of the Insert Hyperlink dialog box and insert the desired address in the E-mail Address field. You can also insert a subject for the email, as seen in Figure 4.20. When the blank email opens, the items inserted in this screen will be pre-populated on the mail form.

Figure 4.20
The E-mail Address option in the Hyperlinks dialog box lets you insert email address and subject.

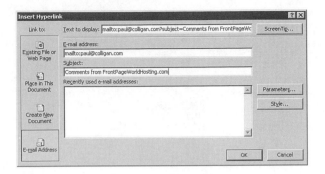

SPELL CHECK AND OTHER TEXT TOOLS

As with all other Office System products, FrontPage provides a complete spell check and thesaurus. If you have other Office System products installed, the products will share the Office system dictionary.

You can also check spelling on a single page or throughout the entire site. FrontPage 2003 even gives you the option of creating new tasks for each page where misspellings are found.

In Figure 4.21, the interface for spell checking is shown. Note that you can choose to check your spelling on a single page, multiple page, or site-wide basis. If you choose to have FrontPage add a task for each page with misspellings, the window expands to show the needed corrections, as seen in Figure 4.22.

Figure 4.21
The fist panel of the Spell Check tool asks you how deep into your site you want to check.

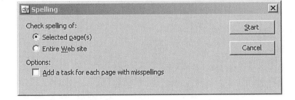

Figure 4.22
An easy task list for fixing your site-wide spelling mistakes.

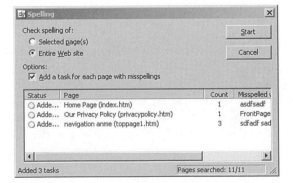

NOTE

The task list of misspelled words is also placed in the site-wide task list.

When you select a misspelling from the list, FrontPage will open the Office System Spelling dialog box, shown in Figure 4.23. You can choose to ignore the instance of the spelling, ignore it throughout your site, change to the recommended spelling, or add it to your Office System dictionary.

Figure 4.23
The Microsoft Office System Spelling tool is the same on all Office products.

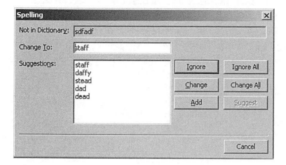

PREVIEWING SITE CONTENT IN A BROWSER

Although the Preview view discussed in Chapter 3, "FrontPage's Views," is a solid option for viewing a considerable amount of your design elements, you will sometimes need to check your site in a browser. FrontPage makes this process easier than would be expected.

 The Preview in <u>B</u>rowser option in the <u>F</u>ile menu lets you preview the open page on any browser installed on your system in any desired screen size (see Figure 4.24). This menu also contains the <u>E</u>dit Browser List command, which enables you to select which browser and screen sizes you'd like pre-populated in the list (see Figure 4.25). You are not limited to the pre-populated choices; they are simply provided for you to place your common testing elements within.

 If you aren't seeing the fonts you think you should seeing when you preview your sites on another browser, *see "Where Did the Fonts Go?" in the "Troubleshooting" section at the end of this chapter.*

TIP

The Preview in Browser option is automatically prepopulated with all the installed browsers on your system. You won't need to set them up, but you should consider the addition of different screen sizes.

To view the page open in the browser of your choice, select the browser type and screen size. FrontPage will launch the browser and send the file to it for preview.

Figure 4.24
The Preview on Browser option will let you view your site in any browser installed on your system on the screen size of your choice.

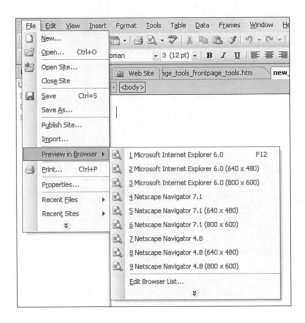

Figure 4.25
The Edit Browser list lets you choose which browser types and screen sizes you'd like set by default in the preview in browser tool.

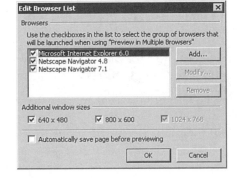

NOTE

Whereas Microsoft will only let you install one version of its browser on your computer, you can install multiple versions of Netscape on the same Windows installation.

Can't see your edits when you preview your content in the browser, *see "My Edits Aren't There" in the "Troubleshooting" section at the end of this chapter.*

TROUBLESHOOTING

MY CHOICES AREN'T SHOWING UP

I set specific hyperlink coloring preferences on several pages in my site through the Page Properties dialog box, and they aren't being reflected when I view the content. I'm using the latest version of Windows and Internet Explorer, so I know that isn't the problem.

Many browsers (including Internet Explorer) allow the user to set how hyperlinks are presented when viewing a Web page. If the browser is set to present hyperlinks a certain way, it will override whatever was placed in the HTML.

INCLUDED CONTENT PAGE PROPERTIES DON'T WORK

I set some specific page properties for some included content in my site, and the content is not reflecting my selection.

Content added to a page through an included content Web component won't take any of the style formatting data from the original source. Included content conforms to the styles set for the page in which the content is placed. There is no way around this.

MY EDITS AREN'T THERE

I made some changes and am looking at them in the browser. They don't appear; what's wrong?

If you haven't saved you most recent changes to the page, FrontPage won't be able to read them from the file. Save the page you made the changes to and select Refresh in your browser. Your new content will appear then.

WHERE DID THE FONTS GO?

I was looking at my Web site on another browser on another computer, and my font choices weren't reflected on the page.

If the browser you are viewing the site content on doesn't have the font choices you selected for your page, the browser will not be able to present the content in those fonts. Unlike other documents that can transfer fonts in the file type (Word, PDF, and so on), there is no way to embed a font in to a Web page.

As a result, if multiple fonts are necessary, it is a good idea to use standard fonts found on most computer systems.

FRONT AND CENTER: LEARNING FROM FRONTPAGE

If you haven't realized it yet, realize it here: *developing for the Web is very different than developing in any other medium.* You simply don't have the control that you'd like to think you have.

Despite your best efforts, users and browsers can set or change font types, colors, just how much "fancy stuff" will be allowed, and more. You simply aren't able to control every aspect of what your audience will see. This requires an approach to design different than any of the other traditional design mediums because you need to understand what the possibilities are and how that affects *everything* you do.

This book isn't about this issue. It's about FrontPage 2003 and how to use it to create the site you want to create. Knowing what kind of site you want to create and what your limitations are is key, and we hope that we've made that clear.

I'd like to make one suggestion as a means for better understanding the HTML you are creating with FrontPage 2003:

One of the more unique new elements in FrontPage 2003 is the Split view that shows both site HTML and the content it is creating in WYSIWYG mode. It is discussed in detail in Chapter 3.

Many will use the tool to fine-tune their designs, "nudging" HTML when and where needed. In many ways, that's what the tool was built for. Many will update to the latest version just for this part of the product.

However, another element associated with this tool shouldn't be overlooked.

Want to learn HTML? Want to get a greater understanding of the elements discussed in this chapter? Design in Split view. As you develop your page, FrontPage will show you the *exact* HTML it is using to create your page and you can see (and learn) the efforts of your development *as you are doing it*. You will be surprised how quickly you will learn the basics of HTML through this approach. Use this tool to understand what happens when you set the properties for your pages and content through the FrontPage interface.

Just how much HTML do you have to know to build a Web page—especially when products such as FrontPage 2003 make the design process so easy? In some cases, you can get by without learning a single tag. In other cases, there won't be a page in your site where you won't have to "nudge" the code to get the effect you are looking for.

You will have to figure out yourself where you stand on this one. Using the Split view will give you a unique peek into what FrontPage is creating on your behalf.

Welcome to the wonderful world of Web design.

CHAPTER 5

THE IMPROVED FIND AND REPLACE

In this chapter

IMPROVEMENTS IN FIND AND REPLACE

FrontPage users have been asking for a better Find and Replace feature for years, and with the release of FrontPage 2003, Microsoft delivers in a big way. The Find and Replace feature (shown in Figure 5.1) in FrontPage 2003 is such an advancement over past versions that we have devoted an entire chapter to getting the most out of this useful FrontPage feature.

Figure 5.1
The Find and Replace feature in FrontPage 2003 offers significant enhancements over previous versions.

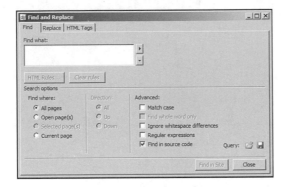

In addition to the usual find and replace functionality, you can also search for particular HTML tags and perform advanced editing that includes everything from removing the tag altogether to changing, removing, or adding an attribute.

FINDING AND REPLACING TEXT

In its simplest form, the Find and Replace feature allows you to search for text by entering the text you're looking for and clicking the Find button. The real power comes into play when you are doing complex searches and searching inside of HTML code.

 If you are searching for text in HTML code and you are unable to click the Find in Source Code check box, see "Unable to Select Find in Source Code Radio Button" in the "Troubleshooting" section of this chapter.

Suppose that you have just created a new Web site for a client. The Web site contains a couple of hundred pages, and each page has several telephone numbers listed as static text. The phone numbers are entered in the format (###)-###-####. Your client is very particular about the site and wants all phone numbers changed to the format ###.###.####.

In previous versions of FrontPage, you'd be stuck with hours of tedious work to change all these entries. With the new Find and Replace feature, the task is quick and easy because for the first time in FrontPage, you can use *regular expressions* to find and replace text.

NOTE

> Regular expressions are special codes that allow for detailed control over text searches and replacements. For a great reference on regular expressions, read *Sams Teach Yourself Regular Expressions in 10 Minutes*.

DEVELOPING REGULAR EXPRESSIONS FOR FIND AND REPLACE

To access the Find and Replace dialog box, open your Web site in FrontPage and select Edit, Find to open the dialog box with the Find tab selected, or Edit, Replace to open the dialog box with the Replace tab selected.

The first thing you will need to do is develop a regular expressions statement that will locate all instances of the incorrectly formatted phone number. You can build regular expressions from either the Find tab or the Replace tab. When building a regular expression that will replace text in your Web pages, it's often a good idea to build it in the Replace tab so that you can easily reference both the Find and the Replace regular expression. However, if you do build it in the Find tab and then click the Replace tab, your regular expression will still exist inside the Find What text box.

In the phone number example, you need to find one digit between 1 and 9, followed by two digits between 0 and 9. These three digits should be enclosed in parenthesis and followed by a dash and three digits between 0 and 9. To complete the phone number, you will find three more digits, followed by another dash and four digits between 0 and 9. Here's the regular expression that will match your search:

`\({[1-9][0-9]^2}\)\-{[0-9]^3}\-{[0-9]^4}`

Table 5.1 lists the regular expression characters used in the phone number regular expression.

TABLE 5.1 REGULAR EXPRESSION CHARACTERS	
Regular Expression Character	**Purpose**
\	The escape character. Specifies that the character immediately following is part of the text to find and not part of the regular expression syntax.
[]	Square brackets indicate that any character within the brackets will produce a match.
{}	Marks the enclosed expression as a tagged expression that can be reused later.
^n	Repeat expression character. Indicates that the expression preceding it should be repeated n times.

The first character you want to find is the open parenthesis. The open parenthesis is represented in the regular expression as \(. Because parentheses are special characters that are actually used in regular expressions, you want to make sure that FrontPage knows that you are literally looking for the parenthesis character and not simply using the parenthesis to enclose a part of the regular expression. To indicate that a character is part of the text you want to find and not simply part of the regular expression itself, you precede the character with a backslash. This is known as *escaping* the character, and the backslash character is known as the *escape* character.

The first character in the area code must be from 1 to 9, so the next part of the regular expression is {[1-9]. When characters are enclosed in square brackets, it means that if any of those characters are found, it will produce a match. The opening curly bracket will be explained later.

To finish the area code portion of your regular expression, you want to search for a set of two numerals, both from 1 to 9, followed by a closing parenthesis. The regular expression syntax for this search string is [1-9]^2\)}. The ^ character is the repeat expression character, and followed by a 2, it means that the [1-9] expression should be repeated two times. Finally, the closing parenthesis is escaped with the backslash. Once again, I'll explain the curly brackets shortly, so ignore them for now.

Next you need to search for a dash, followed by three characters of any digit from 0 to 9, followed by another dash. The regular expression for this is \-{[0-9]^3}\-. The dash, just as the parentheses, is a special character that must be escaped with a backslash.

The final search is for four characters from 0 to 9. The regular expression for this is {[0-9]^4}. You now have a regular expression that will find any phone number in the format (###)-###-####.

If you can't remember what all the regular expressions characters are, the Find tab provides a regular expressions menu that allows you to insert them easily and provides a description of each (see Figure 5.2). To access the regular expressions menu, click the top arrow button to the right of the Find What text box.

Figure 5.2
The regular expressions menu in the Find tab makes creating regular expressions easier.

Notice that each of the three sets of numbers in the regular expression are each enclosed in curly brackets. Expressions enclosed in curly brackets are called *tagged expressions*. Any text that is matched by a tagged expression can be reused in your replace expression. For example, in the phone number find and replace operation, the parentheses and dashes in the phone number will be removed or replaced, but the phone number itself will remain the same. In order to use the phone number that was found with the find expression, you will store it temporarily in tagged expressions and then use those tagged expressions to insert the phone number into your replace expression.

Your replace regular expression will replace any phone numbers that are found with the same phone number in the format ###.###.####. Here is the syntax for that regular expression:

\1\.\2\.\3

The first two characters, \1, represent the first tagged expression. This means that the characters returned by the search string that was within the first set of curly brackets will be inserted in place of the \1. Inserting tagged expressions is made easy with the regular expressions menu in the Replace dialog box (see Figure 5.3), which is accessible by clicking the top arrow button next to the Replace With text box.

Figure 5.3
The regular expressions menu in the Replace dialog box allows you to easily use regular expressions to replace text.

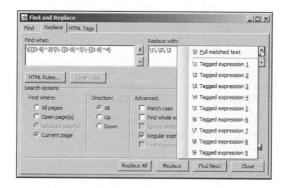

Next a period is inserted, and because a period is a special character, it is escaped with a backslash. This is followed by the second tagged expression, another period, and the third tagged expression. You can now run the search and locate and replace your incorrectly formatted phone numbers.

In this example, you'll likely want to search through all files in the site. To do that, select the All Pages radio button in the Find Where section of the Find and Replace dialog. After selecting that, you'll notice that a Find in Site button appears. By clicking this button, FrontPage will search through all files in your site and will display all files with one or more matching results in the bottom of the dialog as shown in Figure 5.4.

Double-clicking a file in the list will open that file and take you to the first occurrence of the search string. After you've made your change, click the Return to List button in the Find and Replace dialog to return to the list of files. The red dot changes to a yellow dot, and the file's status is marked as *Edited* as seen in Figure 5.4.

If a Find and Replace operation changes text on a page that is currently opened in FrontPage, the changes will not be automatically saved. However, if a Find and Replace operation is performed against a page that is not opened in FrontPage, any changes will be automatically saved by FrontPage and cannot be undone.

5

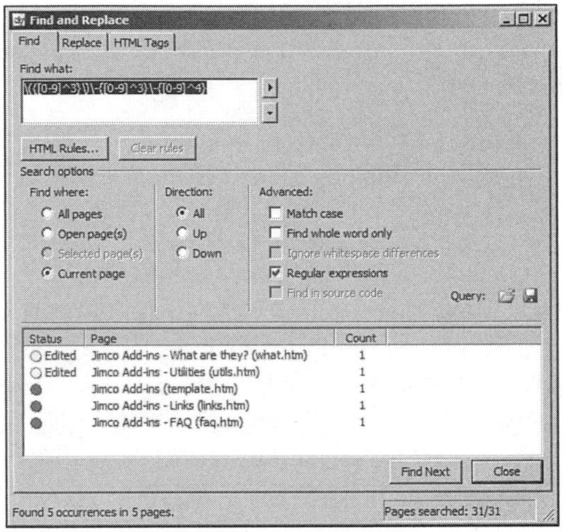

Figure 5.4
The Find in Site feature makes it easy to make replacements in multiple files.

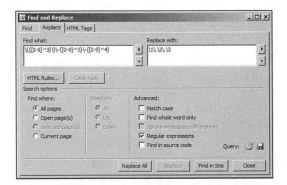

HTML RULES

HTML Rules add another level of power to the Find and Replace feature. Suppose your requirements in the previous phone number example are that you replace the phone number format everywhere in the Web site except when the phone number appears inside of a `<div>` tag. In cases where the phone number is located inside of a `<div>` tag, you want to leave it alone. HTML Rules allow you to accomplish this easily.

Enter the search expression in the Find What text area and the replace expression in the Replace With text area as seen in Figure 5.5.

Figure 5.5
The Find and Replace dialog with the regular expressions ready for your phone number replacement.

Click the HTML Rules button to open the HTML Rules dialog. Click New Rule and select Not Inside Tag from the dropdown. Another dropdown will appear with a list of HTML tags. Select `div` from the second dropdown (see Figure 5.6) and click OK. The Find and Replace dialog should now indicate that an HTML rule is in effect. Now when you run a replace, FrontPage will only replace those phone numbers that are not inside a `<div>` tag.

Figure 5.6
HTML Rules are an
extremely powerful
tool for searching and
replacing in a Web
site.

You can take HTML Rules as far as you want to go, and with each level, more options are available to you. For example, you can easily search for all instances of text inside an <a> tag not containing a target attribute.

 If you are having touble with FrontPage not finding your search text inside an HTML tag, see "Expression Not Found When Searching HTML" in the "Troubleshooting" section of this chapter.

FIND AND REPLACE IN HTML TAGS

The HTML Tags tab in the Find and Replace dialog is the perfect tool for complex searches inside HTML code. The HTML Tags tab should not be confused with the same functionality provided by HTML Rules. HTML Rules allow you to precisely control which HTML tags are returned in a Find or Replace operation and can be used in conjunction with settings on the HTML Tags tab. The HTML Tags tab allows you to specify how HTML tags are modified during a Find and Replace operation.

Suppose you have created a Web site that serves as an HTML reference. You have set most of your hyperlinks with a target of _self, but you haven't set these by setting a base target. Instead, you have set the target on each individual hyperlink. After the site is complete, you decide that you would like to replace the target of these hyperlinks to _blank so that they will open in a new window.

Because this is a site about HTML, you have several occurrences of *target=_self* in tutorials throughout the site that is actual text in the site and not HTML code. You don't want these to be replaced. You only want to replace the text if it is actually part of the HTML code itself. This is a common scenario, and in past versions of FrontPage, this type of complex replacement would have been impossible. However, now it is not only possible, but quite easy to do.

Open the Find and Replace dialog by selecting Edit, Replace and click the HTML Tags tab. Because you want to find only those incidents of your text that are inside of the <a> tag, select a from the Find Tag dropdown box. In the Replace Action dropdown, select Set Attribute Value. In the Attribute dropdown, select target, and in the To attribute dropdown, select _blank (see Figure 5.7).

Figure 5.7
Complex replace functions are made easy with the HTML Tags feature.

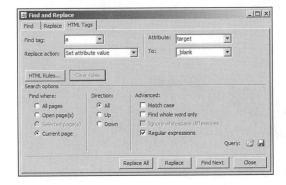

If you run the replace as it's currently configured, it will set the target attribute on every hyperlink to _blank. Because you only want to change those tags with a current target attribute of _self, you will need to configure an HTML Rule to control the Replace operation.

Click the HTML Rules button. You'll see that HTML Rules currently has one rule labeled Find tag: <a>. Click the New rule entry and select With Attribute in the New Rule dropdown. In the [any attribute] dropdown, select target and in the [any value] dropdown, select _self (see Figure 5.8).

5

Figure 5.8
HTML Rules allow you to carefully control what text is found and replaced.

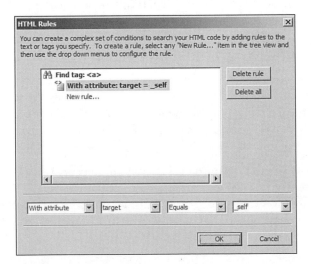

Your Find and Replace dialog should now indicate that an HTML Rule is in place by displaying *With attribute: target = _self*. You now have a query defined that will search for all `<a>` tags with a `target` attribute equal to `_self`. When it finds them, it will change the `target` attribute to `_blank`.

SAVING FIND AND REPLACE QUERIES

As you can probably tell by now, it is quite easy to develop very complex queries with the new Find and Replace feature. Fortunately, FrontPage allows you to save your queries so that they can be retrieved and used later. You can also share your queries with other FrontPage users to implement in their Web sites.

FrontPage Query files are XML files that contain all the information contained in the query. To save a query, click the diskette icon in the Find and Replace dialog and enter a name for your query. Click the Save button to complete the process.

TIP

> FrontPage Query files are saved by default in the `C:\Documents and Settings\<user>\Application Data\Microsoft\FrontPage\Queries` folder.

To share a query with another FrontPage 2003 user, copy the `.fpq` file to their computer and open it from the Find and Replace dialog by clicking the folder button next to the Query: label as seen in Figure 5.9.

Figure 5.9
The ability to save and share Find and Replace queries makes it easy to reuse your queries or to share them with others.

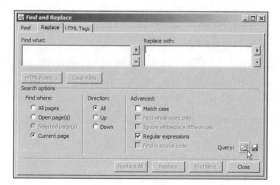

TROUBLESHOOTING

UNABLE TO SELECT FIND IN SOURCE CODE RADIO BUTTON

I am trying to find text in my source code, but the Find in Source Code radio button is disabled and I can't click it.

If you currently have Current page selected in the Find Where section of the dialog, the Find in Source Code radio button will be disabled. In this case, the button is checked or unchecked automatically depending on whether you are in a view that displays code. If you open the Find dialog box while in a view that displays code, FrontPage will automatically search in your code.

TEXT NOT FOUND WHEN SEARCHING HTML USING HTML RULE

When I search for my text in HTML code and I'm using an HTML Rule, my text is not found. What's wrong?

There's a trick to searching in HTML text when you have an HTML Rule enabled. If you are setting an HTML Rule to search for something contained inside a particular tag, FrontPage will not find that text if the text is part of the tag itself, such as an attribute of the tag.

The following example shows a link to the Jimco Add-ins Web site:

```
<a href="http://www.jimcoaddins.com">Jimco Add-ins</a>
```

In this example, if you are searching for `Jimco Add-ins` using an HTML Rule configured to find text inside the <a> tag, it will produce a match. However, if you are searching for `http://www.jimcoaddins.com` with the same HTML Rule applied, a match will not be produced. This is because `http://www.jimcoaddins.com` is an attribute of the <a> tag and not considered to be inside it. `Jimco Add-ins` is considered to be inside the <a> tag because it appears between the opening <a> tag and the closing </a> tag.

FRONT AND CENTER: REUSABLE QUERIES

FrontPage Query files are a convenient way to save queries for later use and to share them with other users. But just what do these files contain?

FrontPage Query files are actually XML files that contain description information necessary to rebuild the options in the Find and Replace dialog. The FrontPage Query file for the phone number query you created in this chapter is shown in the following code. I've stripped off the XML header line to make the code more readable.

```
<fpquery version="1.0">
  <queryparams regexp="true" />
  <find text="\({[0-9]^3}\)\-{[0-9]^3}\-{[0-9]^4}">
    <rule type="insideTag" tag="div" negate="true" />
  </find>
  <replace text="\1\.\2\.\3" />
</fpquery>
```

Look at the <queryparams> tag. You'll notice that the attribute `regexp` is set to `true`. This tells you that the Regular expressions check box was checked and that the `text` attribute in the <find> tag on the next line represents a regular expression.

Within the <find> tag, you can see the HTML Rule that you applied so that FrontPage would only replace phone numbers not in a <div> tag. You then have the <replace> tag and the replace text, which is also a regular expression because the `regexp` attribute for this query is set to `true`.

Now that you know how to analyze and take apart a FrontPage Query file, you'll be able to take advantage of any regular expressions gurus that you know who might not have FrontPage. Just send your query file to them and have them write a regular expression for you that performs your desired task. Open the edited file in the Find and Replace dialog box in FrontPage, and you're on your way.

5

CHAPTER 6

ENHANCING PAGES WITH GRAPHICS AND MULTIMEDIA

In this chapter

ADDING GRAPHIC AND MULTIMEDIA ELEMENTS USING FRONTPAGE 2003

Once you've created your Web page, the next step is to add multimedia files to enhance both the content and the presentation. This can be something as simple as a basic piece of clip art or as complicated as a streaming video file. Multimedia is what makes the Web so exciting.

FrontPage 2003 makes it very easy to add multimedia content to your site and provides a considerable library of such content as part of your product purchase. In this chapter, we'll walk through the process of adding graphic and multimedia content to your site and examine the limited toolset for modifying these files within the FrontPage interface.

NOTE

Microsoft considers photographs, movies, and sounds to all be "clip art." As a result, this content can also be accessed through the Clip Art task pane.

All multimedia elements are inserted using the Insert, Picture command as seen in Figure 6.1.

Figure 6.1
The Insert, Picture menu item enables the insertion of a lot more than pictures.

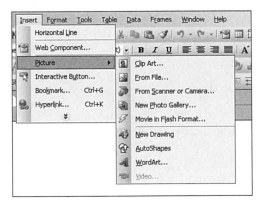

THE CLIP ART COLLECTION INCLUDED WITH FRONTPAGE

All products in the Office System come with a significant clip art collection. If chosen during the installation process, the content is usually added to your hard drive for quick and easy access. You can search the collection that came with FrontPage without having to be online.

ACCESSING CLIP ART ONLINE

Your FrontPage license includes the ability to both search and use content from Microsoft's exhaustive clip art library in your Web site. Selecting Microsoft Office Online from the

Web Collections option in the Clip Art task pane will automatically search this content for you.

Obviously an Internet connection is required to access this content, and you are responsible for any related connection fees.

TIP

> Microsoft's clip art collection is tremendous and sadly underutilized by most customers. Spend some time hunting around this collection, and you'll discover a considerable resource available to you at no extra charge.
>
> Microsoft adds new content to its collection on a weekly basis, so make sure to frequent this resource often.

INSERTING PHOTO GALLERIES

Photo Galleries can be inserted directly in a Web page without the requirement for the Photo Gallery Web component.

→ For more on the Photo Gallery Web component, **see** "Using Web Components, Shared Borders, and Link Bars," **p. 167**.

DRAWINGS, AUTOSHAPES, AND WORD ART

Drawings, AutoShapes, and Word art are legacy tools from previous versions of Office that can all be quickly inserted into a FrontPage Web site the same way they would be placed on a Word document or PowerPoint slide.

To use these tools, select the New Drawing option from the Picture option in the Insert menu.

WORKING WITH CLIP ART

The clip art offerings provided with FrontPage 2003 and the standard Office install are all managed in the Clip Art task pane. To access the task pane, select Clip Art from the Insert, Picture menu option. The Clip Art task pane is illustrated in Figure 6.2.

USING THE CLIP ART TASK PANE

To search for images, photographs, or multimedia, in the Clip Art task pane, you'll follow the same basic process:

1. Enter your search term in the text entry field under Search For.
2. Decide where you would like to search from the Search in the dropdown menu.
3. Define which kinds of media you are searching for in the Results Should Be list.

After you click the Go button, FrontPage will show thumbnails in the results area of the items it has found based on the criteria you chose (see Figure 6.3).

6

Figure 6.2
The Clip Art task pane neatly docks to the right side of the screen, allowing you to search for media types without having to open another program.

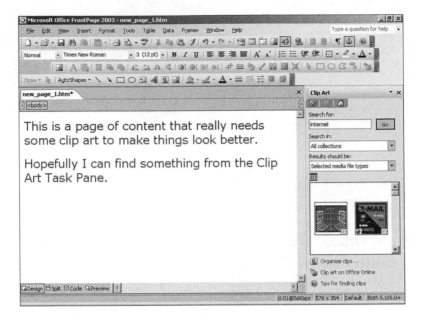

Figure 6.3
A search from the Clip Art task pane can provide multiple clip art types from different sources.

TIP

> If you don't find what you are looking for in your online search, redo your search with similar words and terms. The resource is tremendous and will, more often than not, provide you with what you are looking for.

Right-clicking any of the clip art pieces in the Clip Art task pane opens a menu of options. Included in this list is the powerful option to Find Similar Style. The clip art provided by

Microsoft (both online and off) is usually offered in stylistic groupings that might give you an image collection with a similar look and feel. Selecting the option will fill the Clip Art task pane with pieces of clip art similar to the style you collected.

TIP

If you are going to make considerable use of clip art in your Web design process, consider using the Clip Art task pane's Organize Clips option to make sense of your collection.

INSERTING GRAPHICS FILES

If you don't find what you are looking for in the Microsoft clip art collection, you are free to insert a graphics file of your choice from the source of your choice. This is done by selecting Insert, Picture, From File. When this option is selected, the Picture dialog box will open, allowing you to pull your content from anywhere on your computer or network (see Figure 6.4).

Figure 6.4
The Picture dialog box lets you insert any picture type from any location accessible from your computer.

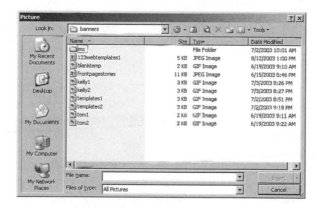

NOTE

Just because FrontPage lets you enter a graphic on a Web page doesn't mean that it can be read by all browser types.

6

→ For more on which graphics types work on the Web, **see** "Web Graphic Formats," **p. 847**.

ADJUSTING IMAGE PROPERTIES

Double-clicking on any image in FrontPage will open the Picture Properties dialog box (see Figure 6.5).

The Appearance tab of the dialog box lets you choose the layout and size of the image so that it works specifically in the format you want it to. Keeping the aspect ratio is vital if you don't want your image to appear distorted when reduced or enlarged on a Web page.

Figure 6.5
The Appearance tab of the Picture Properties dialog box lets you set the appearance of the image.

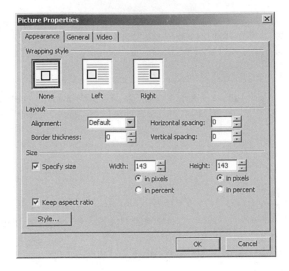

TIP

If you are placing one or more pictures next to each other, a nice effect is often achieved by setting a horizontal and vertical spacing of 5 or so pixels.

The General tab lets you change the picture file type and set, if desired, a low-res, alternative text and long description representations (see Figure 6.6). If used on certain browsers, a low-res image will load first as a placeholder, allowing a more detailed graphic to load later. Alternative text is shown in browsers that are unable to parse graphics. The option to provide a long description for an image file works with certain browser types for the visually impaired and presents the longer description accordingly.

Figure 6.6
The General tab of the Picture Properties dialog box sets specific elements related to file type, alternative representations, and hyperlinks.

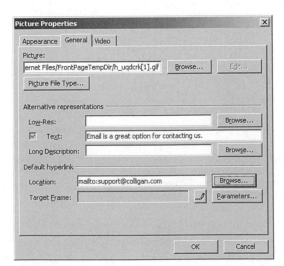

Is Alternative Text Necessary?

Good Web design dictates that you set an alternative text description for all of your graphics files so that readers without the ability to view graphics will know what you meant with the placement of the graphic.

In many high-end browsers, alternative text will also provide the cool effect of description balloons when you mouse over a graphic.

In addition, image files with text descriptions give search engines a better idea of what is on the page, often resulting in higher positions on valuable keywords.

You can also change the file type of the graphic by selecting the Picture File Type button in the General Tab of the Picture Properties Dialog Box, shown previously in Figure 6.6. Doing so will open the Picture File Type dialog box, shown in Figure 6.7, that will let you switch between file types as well as quality settings.

Figure 6.7
The Picture File Type dialog box will let you pick the file type that you'd like your picture to be saved as.

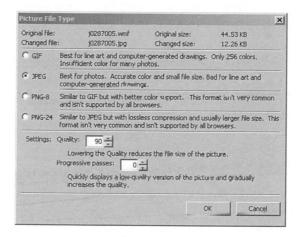

The Video tab is specifically related to video files, which are discussed later in this chapter.

MANIPULATING CLIP ART USING THE PICTURES TOOLBAR

FrontPage provides basic image manipulation capabilities from within FrontPage through the Pictures toolbar. If you don't see the toolbar on your screen, it can be invoked by selecting Pictures from the Insert toolbar. We'll examine each of these capabilities of the toolbar here.

NOTE

The capabilities provided through this toolbar are similar throughout the Office System and haven't changed for the last two versions of FrontPage (or Office). If you are familiar with this toolset, you can jump ahead to the next section of this chapter.

TIP

> By no means is the Pictures Toolbar everything you'll ever need for graphic and image manipulation. It is, however, a very powerful collection of tools. Mastery of this toolset will prevent you from having to round-trip your image to the graphics program of your choice for many common image manipulation tasks.

You need to first select a graphic in order to use the tools on the Pictures toolbar (see Figure 6.8).

Figure 6.8
The Pictures toolbar provides 27 tools for modifying your graphics.

INSERTING PICTURES

Use the Insert Picture from File button to bring another file to your Web page.

TEXT

FrontPage allows you to add text to any graphic on the screen through the Text button. FrontPage requires that the file be a GIF formatted file and will offer to change the file accordingly if it is not already so.

TIP

> Adding text to GIF files is a quick way to produce graphic banners for your Web site.

AUTO THUMBNAIL

If the image you are working with is oversized, FrontPage can create a thumbnail of the graphic and see that the graphic is loaded when the thumbnail is clicked on. FrontPage will insert the required HTML in to your Web page and create the necessary additional graphics files.

POSITION ABSOLUTELY

The button assigns the style attribute of *position: absolute* to the image. If you are using CSS in your page, you can then set a specific x, y location of your image.

→ For more on formatting Web page with CSS, **see** "Using Style Sheets to Format Web Pages," **p. 385**.

BRINGING FORWARD OR SENDING BACKWARDS

If two items are located on the same place on the screen, this option will let you bring one item to the top or send it to the bottom. If several items are located in the same place, it will sort them accordingly.

BRIGHTNESS AND CONTRAST

The brightness and contrast of an image can be manipulated through the More and Less Brightness and Contrast buttons.

FLIPPING AND ROTATING

You can easily flip or rotate a graphic through the Rotate and Flip buttons.

CROP

The Crop tool can easily be used to crop a graphic you have brought into your Web page (see Figure 6.9).

Figure 6.9
The Crop tool lets you easily crop a file from within FrontPage.

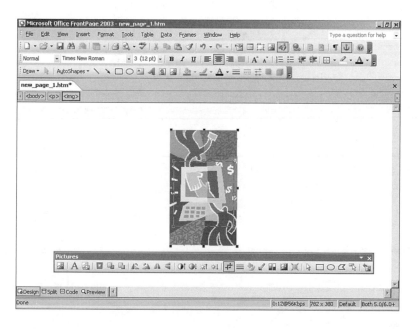

When the option is selected, sizing corners will be shown on the image. Drag the corners to define the area of the image you want to crop, and then click the crop button again.

LINE STYLE AND FORMAT PICTURE

These elements are used in the Drawing tool, which is described later in this chapter.

SET TRANSPARENT COLOR

One of the unique capabilities of the GIF image format is the capability to make a single color in the GIF "transparent." This effect provides for a significant blending element that helps give many pages a flowing look they couldn't get elsewhere.

To set a transparent color on any graphic, select the tool and point to the color you would like to make transparent. If the graphic is not a GIF, FrontPage will translate it to a GIF for you (see Figure 6.10).

Figure 6.10
A transparent GIF flows nicely on a Web page.

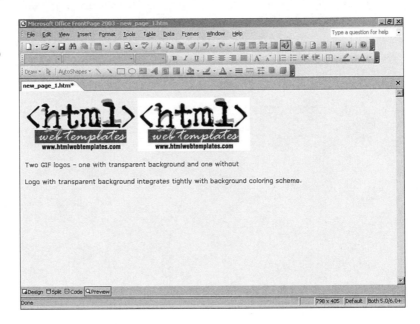

COLOR

You can quickly produce a grayscale, washed out, or black and white image of any graphic with this tool.

> **TIP**
>
> Want a quick and easy attractive background for your Web page? Pick a photographic image from the Clip Art task pane, wash out the image with this tool, and set it as the background.

BEVEL

Beveling takes a graphic and produces an outline around the image to give the effect of a button or bevel around the graphic (see Figure 6.11).

Figure 6.11
The Bevel button will quickly change any graphic to a simple button.

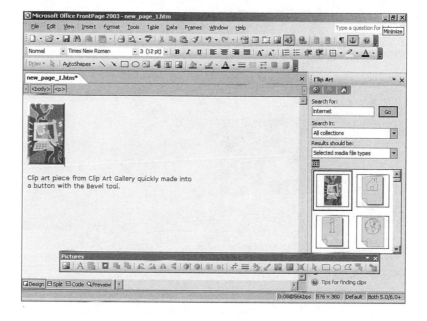

TIP

Beveling produces impressive buttons that can quickly produce navigational components for your site, but the new FrontPage Interactive Buttons are considerably more impressive and can produce similar functionality. Consider their use as well.

RESAMPLE

The Resampling tool is used in conjunction with resizing an image. If you have made an image smaller, FrontPage maintains the original image size (in case you want to undo your changes, and so on). Clicking the Resample button will shrink the graphic down to the stated size, decreasing the file size considerably. Figure 6.12 shows how the resampling tool is used with before and after pictures.

NOTE

The Resampling button does not always produce the ideal graphic. Make sure that its final results are what you are looking for. If they are not, you might have to manipulate your graphic in a different graphics program and roundtrip it back into FrontPage.

6

Figure 6.12
Two photos made smaller by FrontPage— one resized and the other left at the original size. Note the considerable size difference without the loss of graphic quality.

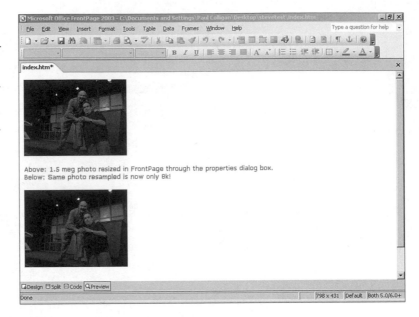

SELECT AND HOTSPOT BUTTONS

The Select and Hotspot buttons are used to make image maps, as discussed in the "Creating Image Maps" section of this chapter.

RESTORE

The Restore button returns an image you are manipulating to the state it was in before it was previously saved.

SAVING YOUR NEW IMAGE

Saving your Web page will automatically save any images (or other files) found on the page. It will allow you to choose what you want to do with these files in the Save Embedded Files dialog box that will appear after you save the page (see Figure 6.13).

You can select any image in the list and rename the file or change the folder that the file will be saved to. You can also set whether FrontPage saves the file or reverts to the source HTML through the Set Action button. You can also change the file type of every image saved through this powerful dialog box.

Figure 6.13
The Save Embedded Files dialog box lets you set the name, folder, and picture type for every image you save on your Web page.

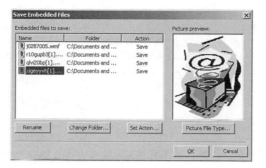

Making good use of the Embedded Files dialog box can save you a lot of heartache in the future. From the very beginning, consider saving all your image files to an image directory and giving them names that will clearly define what they are. Nothing is more frustrating than trying to sort through a huge Web site of graphic images with the naming convention given to them when they were pulled from the Microsoft Office Online Clip Art library.

CREATING IMAGE MAPS

An image map is a graphic with a number of hyperlinks associated with the graphic that lead to different places within a Web site. Image maps are usually used for navigational purposes and are quite time-consuming to code by hand. In Figure 16.14, a Web page with a map of Oregon is used to determine the location the user is interested in.

Figure 6.14
The Oregon graphic is divided into four hotspots—each leading to a different URL.

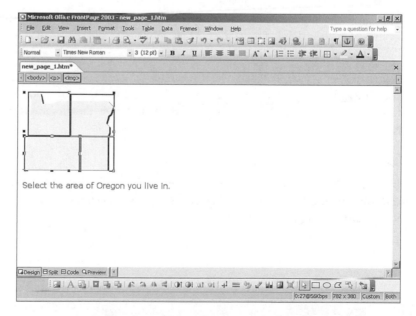

6

TIP

> Image maps are also pretty much pointless for any browser that can't support images and image maps. If you are going to use image maps as a navigational element, remember to also include a navigational option for browsers that won't support the technology.

FrontPage makes the development of image maps very easy through the Select and Hotspot buttons found on the Pictures toolbar. Use these tools to define an image as an image map and then draw the area with the hotspot drawing tools. Once the hotspot is drawn, FrontPage will open the Insert Hyperlink dialog box, providing the means to embed the hyperlink into that area of the graphic. If you need to edit an existing hyperlink or hotspot, double-click the area with the Select tool. In the Oregon image map (seen previously in Figure 6.14), the image was divided into four hotspots.

NOTE

> Image maps are a considerably older technology seldom used now because of accessibility and browser compatibility issues. FrontPage's support for the technology and endorsement for its use should not be considered.

IMAGES FROM OTHER SOURCES

You aren't limited to only images from the Microsoft Clip-Art database. You can also easily insert items from external devices (such as digital cameras or scanners) or even bring in images from other Internet sources.

INSERTING IMAGES FROM AN EXTERNAL DEVICE

You can insert any image from an external device, such as a scanner or camera, directly from within FrontPage. FrontPage will let you choose the source of the file and will pull it directly from the device.

If you are using a scanner, you will also be able to activate your specific scanning software as you would from any other program that utilizes the scanner. After you have selected From Camera or Scanner from the Pictures menu item, follow the directions specific to your camera or scanner.

INSERTING IMAGES FROM OTHER INTERNET SOURCES

It is possible to call any graphic from any file source, including other Web sites. Instead of selecting the file location in the Picture dialog box, you simply enter the URL of the picture as seen in Figure 6.15.

Figure 6.15
You can insert a picture in to your Web site from any available online location.

INSERTING AND CONFIGURING FLASH MOVIES

Macromedia's Flash file format has quickly become the Internet's unofficial default standard for multimedia implementation. The considerable compression capabilities and broad spectrum of player options have made it a preferred choice for many multimedia developers and Web designers.

Previously, inserting Flash movies in to FrontPage required editing the HTML directly. New to FrontPage 2003 is the ability to insert a Flash movie directly in to your FrontPage Web site.

Flash movies (SWF files) can be dragged directly into a FrontPage site. FrontPage will recognize the file and write the appropriate HTML code. The other option is to insert the file through the Insert, Picture, Movie in Flash Format option. The Movie in Flash Format Properties dialog opens, where you can choose the settings for the Flash movie (see Figure 6.16). Figure 6.17 shows how FrontPage Design view presents the Flash movie.

The Movie area of the dialog box lets you set the quality, scale, background color, and alignment for the movie file. In most cases, you'll want to use the default settings. The layout area of the movie will let you set alignment, border thickness, and any horizontal or vertical spacing. The size area will let you set how you prefer the movie to be presented if the size of the movie needs to be changed. The General tab establishes the source and base URL (set when you inserted the movie) and any playback variables you want to change.

6

Figure 6.16
The Movie in Flash Format Properties dialog box lets you set the variables for inserting a Flash Movie without the need for editing any HTML.

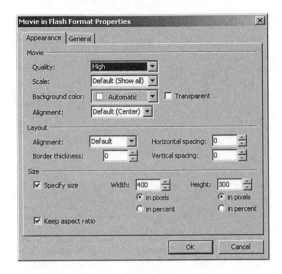

Figure 6.17
FrontPage shows the insertion of a Flash file with an appropriate graphic.

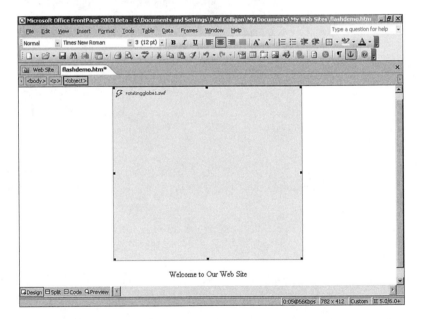

TIP

> If you insert a third-party Flash movie in your site, you will probably want to keep the variables as they were set by FrontPage.

INSERTING AND CONFIGURING VIDEO AND AUDIO FILES

FrontPage 2003 directly supports the integration of several video and audio file types. You can either place the file directly into your Web page or provide a link to the file in your Web page.

TIP

> If a video or audio file isn't essential to your Web page, consider offering a link to the file so that your audience has the choice of whether to view the file. Users will appreciate the fact that you gave them the choice.

FrontPage will also let you set playback options for these files by right-clicking the icon in the page and selecting Set Properties from the list of options.

Supported file types include

- **Windows Video files (*.avi)**—Audio and video files for use with the Microsoft Windows Media Player. These are standard for the Windows system desktop application but usually aren't compressed, so they take a great deal of time to download. Compressed AVI files most often require an advanced codec that won't be standard on all user systems. Even when compressed, AVI files are considerably larger than ASF files examined next.

- **Windows Media files (*.asf)**—Compressed streaming file format used with Windows Media Player. These files are compressed, providing for a quicker download option. In addition, the file can be streamed (if supported by the Web server), enabling the user to listen or view the file as it is being downloaded.

 If you can't get your video file to stream, *see "Video File Doesn't Stream" in the "Troubleshooting" section at the end of this chapter.*

- **RealAudio files (*.ram; *.ra)**—The compressed streaming file format used with Real Networks RealPlayer product. Streaming services are provided by the Web server. If the server doesn't provide streaming capabilities, the files are downloaded completely and then played.

- **Moving Picture Experts Group (*.mpeg)**—File format used for movies, video, and music in a digitally compressed format. MPEG files are generally compressed and much smaller than most other video formats. ASF and RA files are typically smaller than MPEG files, but usually sacrifice quality accordingly.

- **Apple QuickTime (*.mov; *.qt)**—QuickTime is Apple's audio and video compression technology. Windows users can view or play QuickTime files with the QuickTime plug-in available from Apple.

When a video or audio file is inserted in a Web page, FrontPage will place a graphic in the page to show the location of the file.

6

If you can't get your video file to play, *see "Video File Doesn't Play" in the "Troubleshooting" section at the end of this chapter.*

VIDEO AND AUDIO FILE PROPERTIES

Double-clicking any video or audio file in a Web page will open the Picture Properties dialog box. The third tab in the dialog box lets the user pick file looping details and if she wants the file to load when the page is opened or when she mouses over the file.

Figure 6.18
The third tab in the Picture Properties dialog box sets specific multimedia elements.

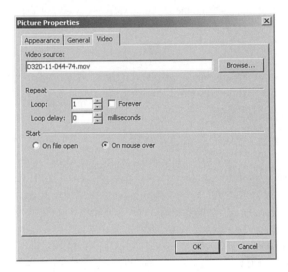

TROUBLESHOOTING

VIDEO FILE DOESN'T STREAM

I inserted a video file to my Web site and it doesn't "stream the content"—it makes the user download the entire file first.

On a Web server, files are first downloaded and then implemented by default. In order to stream video (or audio) content, you'll need a Web server capable of providing this service. See your streaming content server directions for details on how to implement a streaming download.

VIDEO FILE DOESN'T PLAY

I inserted a video file to my Web site, and it looks great on my system. A friend tried to view the video file and said that she wasn't able to do so. What do I do?

Each video file requires a different player to view the file type. If your friend doesn't have the appropriate media viewer installed, she will not be able to view the movie.

Make mention of the viewing or listening software requirements for any media you might place on a Web page. Offer links to the download sites for the players to make it as easy as possible for your audience to view your content.

FRONT AND CENTER: GRAPHICS, MULTIMEDIA, AND THE WEB

The introduction of graphics and multimedia to the Web was what caused its initial exponential growth curve. People had been accessing text content online for years through bulletin boards and online services, but the introduction of images to the online presentation made all the difference in the world.

One day after the introduction of multimedia to the Web came the introduction of *multimedia abuse to the Web*. Graphics were suddenly placed everywhere regardless of whether they belonged and pages suddenly got bigger and messier. Sound and effects were added to bring attention to pages that did little more than cause headaches to the viewer.

My mom once told me, "Just because you can doesn't mean you should," and her advice rings true to this day. The desire to fill Web content with as many graphics moving as many directions as possible needs to be overcome with a strong desire to produce content that does what it is supposed to do—without leaning on technology to "make it cool."

When you design for the Web, certainly make use of everything it has to offer. If graphics or multimedia can be used to explain or emphasize, certainly use them and use FrontPage to make the most of them.

However, if you find yourself looking at a Web page, hoping to "add some zip" to it, ask yourself if it is really necessary.

In addition to this call for basic common sense, consider the following other issues:

Not everyone can view the multimedia elements you have placed on your Web site. There are thousands of potential causes of these restrictions, ranging from a browser that doesn't support it (you trying to watch flash files on your cell phone) to people who don't have the time or bandwidth to view it.

In addition, despite the marketing machines behind many popular multimedia options for the Web, not everyone has all the plug-ins installed on their browsers and don't intend on ever waiting for the download. They will, instead, simply pass over your site, causing you to have jumped from trying to impress to losing a customer.

This is also the simple issue of Web site accessibility. For some, it isn't a question of which plug-in is installed, it is the reality of a disability that might prevent them from viewing or hearing your content as you originally designed it.

Adding a link with information on how to download the appropriate player is not enough: Some users won't, some users are prevented by technology from doing so, and others simply are unable to do so. Make sure that you design for them as well.

→ For more on FrontPage's accessibility features and how you can make sure that your site can be seen by everyone, **see** "FrontPage's Accessibility Features," **p. 235**.

6

USING THEMES

In this chapter

WHY USE THEMES?

The basic idea behind FrontPage themes is a good one—provide a means to easily give a Web site a consistent look and feel. It is easy for a Web site to look more like a collection of hundreds of different pages than a single entity when you have pages without a similar look and feel (see Figure 7.1).

Figure 7.1
A simple Web page designed in FrontPage 2003.

A *theme* is a group of graphics, formatting, and color schemes that can be applied to one or more Web pages to produce a consistent and professional look and feel (see Figure 7.2). Themes are a technology that have been part of FrontPage since version 98 and are not available on other Web development products.

Themes can be applied on a page-by-page basis or to an entire site with the click of a button. Sites can also be set with a default theme so that all newly created pages in the site have the theme information already embedded in them.

N O T E

Historically, FrontPage themes have received a bad reputation in the Web development community. They were hard to use, were hard to implement, were Microsoft specific, and just didn't look very good. Some changes have been made to FrontPage 2003's integration of themes, but this issue should also be examined before arbitrarily applying a theme to a page or site.

7

Figure 7.2
The same page with the Evergreen theme applied to it.

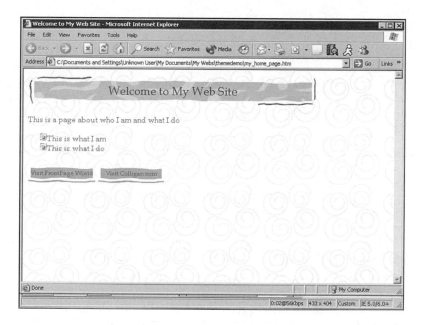

 If you are having problems with themes and have multiple Web development tools being used on your project, see "My Themes Got Killed" in the "Troubleshooting" section at the end of this chapter.

THEMES VERSUS TEMPLATES

Themes are only made up of specific graphics, formatting, and color scheme elements. The only graphics contained in a theme are bullets or are related to navigational and title buttons and bars. Themes do not contain any content or functionality.

Templates contain one or more specific Web pages that might be formatted with a theme. In short, a template can contain a theme, but a theme doesn't always contain a template. Many FrontPage specific templates use a theme to provide the formatting structure for a site.

After an explanation like that, I'm sure that you are wondering "*When should I use a theme, and when should I use a template?*" Whereas a decision like that is certainly up to the designer, you can follow this simple rule: *If you are going to need more than simple formatting elements, you will need to use a template.*

→ For more information on FrontPage Templates, **see** "FrontPage's Web Templates, Wizards, and Packages" **p. 267**.

WHAT'S NEW WITH FRONTPAGE 2003 THEMES?

There is really only one change in the way FrontPage 2003 handles themes over previous version of FrontPage, but it is a big one: *FrontPage 2003 uses CSS instead of HTML to apply themes.* As a result, the process is faster, smaller, and easier to control and modify.

7

Other than that, themes are the same product as in FrontPage 2000 and 2002. This "thinning" of the theme process is significant and needs to be understood.

NOTE

Pages with themes from previous versions of FrontPage will still work in FrontPage 2003, but you might want to consider reinstalling the themes with FrontPage 2003 so that you can take advantage of CSS application over the previous approach.

At one point, themes slowed down both the Web development process with FrontPage and the loading of the page in the Web browser. The cumbersome method that the content was integrated into a Web site slowed down anything that it worked with. Now that the content is applied via CSS, it is retrieved and edited easily.

In theory, integration with other Web design products (through the CSS application) is somewhat more plausible because of an industry standard of implementation. However, FrontPage 2003 themes still use FrontPage specific elements, so sharing the development of a site with themes isn't recommended when working with other users on sites not using FrontPage. In short, if you are going to use FrontPage in conjunction with a number of other programmers who are using other Web development tools such as Dreamweaver, it would a best practice to shy away from the use of themes.

THEMES VERSUS CSS

There is a technology called CSS, or *Cascading Style Sheets*, that provides many of the same features provided by FrontPage themes. They are described in detail later in this book. FrontPage themes are applied with CSS, but the two technologies are not completely interchangeable with each other.

→ For more information on styles in the Web design process, **see** "Using Style Sheets to Format Web Pages," **p. 385**.

It is important to point out that themes in FrontPage closely mimic what other Web development programs usually call "design templates." Design templates contain graphics and CSS for the most common parts of a Web site. This gives developers the freedom to focus on their content instead of worrying about their design. This is the same goal as the FrontPage template; the implementation is the same.

TIP

Because style sheets are a universal standard and are easily integrated into a FrontPage Web site, it is my opinion that in most cases, style sheets should be the technology of choice.

APPLYING AN EXISTING THEME

By default, FrontPage 2003 comes with 78 themes. These can be applied on a per page, multiple page, or per site basis.

You can either apply a theme to a single document by selecting the document in Web Site view and choosing Format, Theme or open the page in FrontPage and select the same. This will open the Theme task pane (see Figure 7.3).

Figure 7.3
The Theme task pane lets you scroll through the theme options currently installed on your computer.

You can then select the theme you want to apply. To apply a theme to a number of pages, select all the pages in Web Site view and choose Format, Theme. Then select a theme from the Theme task pane list that you want to apply to all the selected pages.

NOTE

> You are not limited to single theme per Web site. You can use as many themes as you want. Each theme does carry supporting files in your Web site, so excessive use can lead to considerably increasing your site size.

To apply a theme to an entire site, select the entire site from the folder list and select the theme to apply from the Theme task pane. When you apply a theme to a Web site, all the information regarding that theme is saved in the site. As a result, anyone who opens the site from another machine has instant access to the theme information and elements.

7

To remove a theme from any group of pages, follow the directions for applying a theme and select the No Theme option from the list of available themes.

TIP

> If you are going to develop your site to use different themes for specific areas, consider making each area a subsite so that you can quickly update the Web with the theme decision of your choice.

THEME ELEMENTS

Themes are made up of colors, graphics, and style information. Colors relate specifically to hyperlinks, body and heading text, banner text, link bar labels, table borders, and the background color for the page. Theme graphics include a page background, a page banner, bullets, and navigation buttons. Styles relate to all issues traditionally covered in CSS. This includes font styles and formatting.

 If the theme hyperlink colors set are the hyperlink colors you see, see "Different Hyperlink Colors" in the "Troubleshooting" section at the end of this chapter.

TIP

> Interestingly enough, all Microsoft Office products support the implementation of themes. As a result, you can, *in theory*, apply the theme used for your Web site to a Word document or Excel spreadsheet for visual continuity.
>
> The term "in theory" is used here because in some cases, the Microsoft Office System allows you to only use certain themes in certain applications. If you want to use themes across applications, double check that Office allows you to do so.

→ For more information on CSS, **see** "Using Style Sheets to Format Web Pages," **p. 385**.

VIVID COLORS, ACTIVE GRAPHICS, AND THE BACKGROUND PICTURE

You will notice that a check box option for Vivid Colors and Active Graphics is available for each Theme at the bottom of the Theme task pane. These options can be toggled on and off for each theme.

The Vivid Colors option adds a more vivid color scheme to the theme. Turn this option off for a more traditional looking site.

Active Graphics indicate the use of small animated elements in the theme. Turn them off if the animation is a bit distracting. The toggle also applies to rollover buttons and text if they are used in the theme.

Background picture is a toggle for the use of a background image that relates to each theme. Not using the background picture won't always result in white background because many themes have a background color in addition to the background picture.

CREATING NEW THEMES

There are two ways to create a theme: from scratch or by editing an existing one. To create a new theme from scratch, select the Create a New Theme option at the bottom of the Theme task pane. To edit an existing theme, right-click the theme in the list and choose Customize. Both paths will open the Customize Theme dialog box (see Figure 7.4).

Figure 7.4
Be sure that a theme is selected before opening the Customize Theme dialog box; otherwise, you will be editing a blank theme.

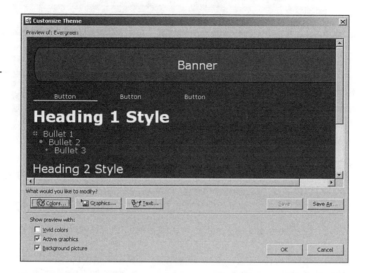

At the bottom of the Customize Theme dialog box are three buttons for the different elements of the theme that you can edit: Colors, Graphics, or Text.

NOTE

What you are actually editing with the Text button are the various styles for text, not the text of your page.

MODIFYING COLORS

Clicking the Color button in the Customize Theme dialog box will open a new screen in the box as shown in Figure 7.5.

The first tab lists all the themes installed on the machine you are working on and shows a graphical representation of the color schemes applied by each. You can select any option in the list to see what the elements look like in the preview pane to the right of the list. Use this tab of the dialog box if you want to copy the scheme of another theme or to modify an existing theme.

The second tab shows the elements in a color wheel format. You can adjust the colors of the scheme through the color wheel format to get a better matching of colors through this design technique.

7

Figure 7.5
The first of three tabs in the Colors section of the Customize Theme dialog box lets you quickly pick the color scheme of any theme installed.

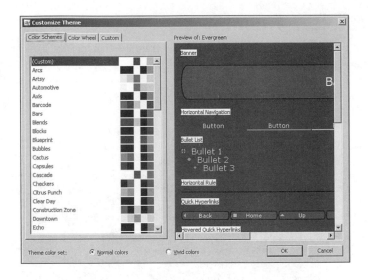

NOTE

> Clicking on a color in the wheel affects all the colors in that scheme.

→ For more information on Web design and color concepts, **see** "Color Concepts and Web Design," **p. 825**.

The third tab allows you to pick a custom color for each element in a theme (see Figure 7.6). Simply select the item you want to edit from the dropdown menu and choose the desired color from the color dropdown menu.

Figure 7.6
The third tab in the Colors section of the Customize Theme dialog box lets you specifically define any element in a theme.

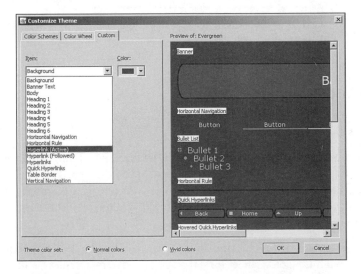

When you select the color dropdown menu, FrontPage will suggest a number of options from the existing theme. If you select the more colors option from that menu, FrontPage will open the More Colors dialog box (see Figure 7.7).

Figure 7.7
The More Colors dialog box lets you find the exact color you are looking for.

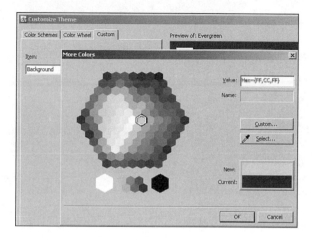

In the More Colors dialog box, you can select a specific color from the image to the left. If you are still not satisfied, you can select the eyedropper icon on the screen to lift the specific color from any graphic on the screen.

TIP

Too many people spend way too much time trying to find the specific color they are looking for by cross referencing color wheels and charts. The eyedropper element is your best friend because you can use it to lift the color you want. You can use the eyedropper on any graphic on the screen (inside or outside of FrontPage), so if you need a color from something else, size the screen accordingly and you are good to go.

Clicking the OK button at the bottom of any tab on the color screens brings you back to the original Customize Theme dialog box.

MODIFYING GRAPHIC ELEMENTS

Clicking the Graphics button in the Customize Theme dialog box will open a new screen in the dialog as shown in Figure 7.8.

In this screen, you choose the graphic element you want to modify from the Item dropdown box. FrontPage will show you a preview of the item in the preview area to the right of the screen.

The Picture tab lists the specific graphic that is currently used for that element. If you'd like to load a new graphic, you can load one in directly from this interface—simply click the Browse button and load the graphic from your computer.

7

Figure 7.8
The Picture tab in the Graphics section of the Customize Theme dialog box lets you modify any graphic element of any theme installed.

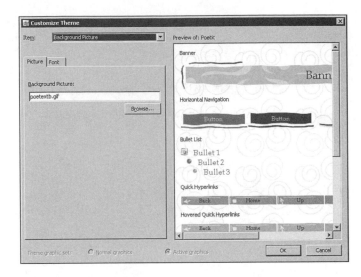

The Font tab shows the font that will be used, if needed in that graphic element. You can set the style, size, and alignment for the font here as well.

MODIFYING STYLES

Clicking the <u>T</u>ext button in the Customize Theme dialog box will open a new screen in the dialog box as shown in Figure 7.9.

Figure 7.9
The Text section of the Customize Theme dialog box lets you modify any text element of any theme installed.

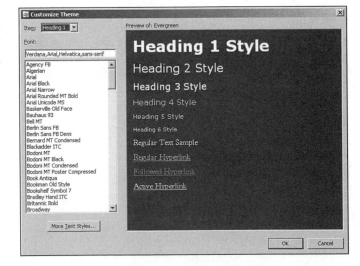

To modify a text element, select the Style from the Item dropdown list and choose the font you want to use from the Font list. The change to your theme will be immediately reflected in the preview screen on the right.

NOTE

For a user to see a certain font in her Web browser, that font must be installed on her system and her browser must be capable of using different fonts. If neither case is true, her choice in the theme will not be seen. What will be seen is the font standard for that system.

SAVING YOUR NEW (OR MODIFIED) THEME

Once you are done creating or modifying a theme, a click of the Save As button in the Customize Theme dialog box will save the theme with the name you give it.

TIP

If you are modifying an existing theme, consider changing the name to something that will remind you that it is a modified version of an existing theme. In addition, if you use the naming protocol *Theme Name (Modification #)*, the modified versions of the themes will appear in the theme task pane right under their original source.

If you modify a theme, FrontPage will save the theme to the installation of FrontPage you are working on. If you would like the theme data to be moved to the site you are working on, apply the new theme to any page in the site.

TROUBLESHOOTING

MY THEMES GOT KILLED

I'm working with a team of developers on my site. Some of them don't use FrontPage 2003. Someone edited something somewhere, and now all my theme elements are seriously tweaked. I thought FrontPage 2003 themes used CSS. Why did this happen? What can I do?

FrontPage uses CSS to apply themes, but some elements of themes are still very much FrontPage specific (such as the graphical title bars). The good news is that you can easily reapply your theme to any page in your site and that should undo whatever problems you've found.

DIFFERENT HYPERLINK COLORS

Visitors don't see the same hyperlink colors that I set in my theme.

It is important to remember that anything set in a theme is merely a *recommendation* of how you'd suggest that your site be viewed. Most higher-end browsers allow the user to set hyperlink colors and choose fonts, and the decision of the user overrides anything you set in a theme.

The same is true for graphics. If your user sets her browser to not show graphics (or the browser is incapable of showing them), these theme elements obviously won't show up as well.

FRONT AND CENTER: SHOULD YOU USE THEMES?

When they were first introduced to the FrontPage, themes seemed like a good idea. How nice and how easy to be able to change a site's look and feel with the click of a button! The integration with other Office products also provided a potential synergistic element because developers could apply a theme across their work—despite the application.

Themes were born with a number of significant problems. The most important of which was the fact that all the themes that came with FrontPage were downright ugly. Some companies were formed for the purpose of creating better looking themes than what came with the CD. Although a small cottage industry was born of third-party theme developers, most users didn't think that was enough and shied away from them altogether.

Microsoft could develop an attractive theme, but the limitations to what could and couldn't be done in this format prevented themes from having a significant impact on Web design. They kind of came and went quickly and are seldom used anymore by the professional developer.

NOTE

> One developer's unique answer to the limitations of a FrontPage theme produced a FrontPage product called SuperThemes. You can read more about this product at `http://superthemes.frontpagelink.com`.

Instead, developers worked with FrontPage Templates (often supplemented with themes) to provide the professional out-of-the-box look-and-feel element others were hoping to accomplish with the use of themes. You weren't able to apply a template to an existing project, but many felt the trade-off was worth it.

In most cases, the template content supplemented with theme information could easily also be supplemented with CSS. Because themes are still so tightly integrated into the FrontPage interface, many template developers chose to take that path to make the support process somewhat easier.

If you look around the Net, you will find that most template developers have a "FrontPage version" with themes and another version with CSS providing the same. The second is usually marketed as a generic template or focused toward the Dreamweaver or GoLive user. You can really use both with FrontPage 2003, but the marketing angle of using themes in packaging is still chosen by many.

→ For more information on FrontPage Templates, **see** "FrontPage's Web Templates, Wizards, and Packages," **p. 267**.

In addition, the metadata associated with theme use added a considerable amount of information to any Web site (especially when more than one theme was used) and could slow down both the publishing and editing process.

With Microsoft's push to move theme elements to CSS, the size and slowness issue has been somewhat answered. However, the limitations of what can be accomplished in a theme simply prevent most template developers from suggesting that they are the best alternative for offering presentation options to a FrontPage Web site.

In addition, if all theme elements are published and supported through CSS, many more experienced FrontPage users wonder why themes aren't eliminated completely for this more industry standard technology.

NOTE

A great CSS resource can be found at http://csshelp.frontpagelink.com.

It is still my feeling that themes as a standalone style tool simply aren't enough. When integrated with a FrontPage Template, they can be a powerful tool, but they seldom provide more than a good CSS file does to the Web design process.

7

FRONTPAGE'S NAVIGATION TOOLS AND ELEMENTS

In this chapter

THE BIG PICTURE

If you've ever built a site on your own, you know what a pain it is to keep track of all of your pages and what links to what. Navigation can also quickly get out of hand if you don't keep the "big picture" in mind. As new pages are added to your site, even the best efforts to keep everything linked to everything else can still result in several missed links.

Understanding how a Web site works on larger level is also vital to anyone who is charged with maintaining a Web site.

Adding a page to a Web site is never as easy as simply adding the page. Where should it link to? What should the links look like? Where should it be linked from? Where does it belong in the flow of your site?

If you've never built a site on your own, you're going to learn the wonders of keeping navigation under control. The wonder of the Web is not the individual Web page, but the way everything works and links together. If your site doesn't work and link together well, you will have problems.

FrontPage has a batch of navigational tools that are both easy to use and powerful to implement. By building a site with these tools in place (and in mind), you will find that adding and removing pages and links is easy because FrontPage manages the process as needed.

In this chapter, we'll look at FrontPage's navigational tools, how to build and maintain a site with the tools, how to manage the dynamically generated navigational elements and examine how FrontPage's new publishing options require a number of considerations when working with this toolset. We'll also take a look at how FrontPage Page Banners relate to the FrontPage navigational elements.

As always, we'll take a deeper look at the human side of using these tools in the "Front and Center: Navigation Power and Building a Site in Navigation View First" section at the end of this chapter.

UNDERSTANDING FRONTPAGE NAVIGATION ELEMENTS

The FrontPage navigational elements have been part of FrontPage since the very beginning. They are part of what separates the product from the others and are often misunderstood by the average FrontPage user. When implemented correctly, they are a powerful tool; when implemented incorrectly, they become an unmanageable beast.

THE NAVIGATION STRUCTURE

If the FrontPage navigation tools were used in the development of a FrontPage Web site, the site's navigational structure can be seen from the FrontPage Navigation view, seen in Figure 8.1.

Figure 8.1
The FrontPage
Navigation view
shows how each of
the pages in your site
are connected to
each other.

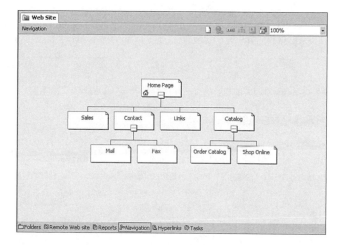

Pages can be added, edited, and removed through this interface with a simple drag-and-drop operation.

> **NOTE**
>
> Navigation view is a means to view your site in terms of how pages relate to one another. They have nothing directly to do with the design of each page other than providing the linking data for any link or menu bars. However, paying attention to where and how the pages are related to each other can have a great effect on the final design of your site.

→ For more about FrontPage Navigation view, **see** "FrontPage's Views," **p. 61**.

HOW FRONTPAGE HANDLES SITE NAVIGATION

FrontPage handles site navigation based only on what the user tells FrontPage is part of the site navigation. For example, in Figure 8.2, a 10 page site only has 3 pages listed in the Navigation. As a result, only 3 links would be seen on any link bar.

Figure 8.2
In this example, a 10
page site only has 3
pages defined in the
site navigation.

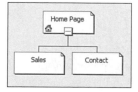

Because FrontPage navigation is based on user definition and not site content, the developer is free to develop a site based on both elements. Site navigation can be modified without requiring a page-to-page correspondence.

TIP

> You don't have to put *every* page in your site in Navigation view. You only have to include the ones you want FrontPage to generate navigational elements for.

→ For more on adding pages in Navigation view, **see** "FrontPage's Views," **p. 61**.

THE NAVIGATION BARS AND MENUS

Once FrontPage has pages assigned to the site navigation, it can dynamically generate navigational elements to the site in the form of link bars and menus. In Figure 8.3, a simple menu bar created from the navigational structure in Figure 8.2 is shown.

Figure 8.3
This simple menu bar was created from the site navigational structure shown in Figure 8.2.

→ For more on the creation of link and navigation bars, **see** "Using Web Components, Shared Borders, and Link Bars," **p. 167**.

Best Uses

FrontPage navigational elements make the addition of pages to a Web site simple and easy. Once the page is created, the developer can drag the page to the desired area of the FrontPage navigation and let FrontPage develop the menu and navigational bars as needed. The developer gets the additional benefit of being able to see the entire site in terms of how each page relates to every other page.

In addition, running all pages through the FrontPage navigational elements makes the generation of tables of contents and sitemaps just a click away.

It should be of no surprise that a number of professional FrontPage Web templates utilize FrontPage navigational structures. A user can quickly take a page from a template and drop it in to the right place, letting FrontPage do the rest of the work.

WORKING WITH A SITE IN NAVIGATION VIEW

There are two elements to building a site in FrontPage navigational view. The first is in developing a navigational structure; the second is in naming the pages and files accordingly.

BUILDING NAVIGATION USING DRAG AND DROP

Adding navigation to a FrontPage Web site is as simple as dragging the file from the Folder List and aligning it with the desired page in the navigational structure, as seen in Figure 8.4.

Figure 8.4
The About page is being dragged into the site navigation.

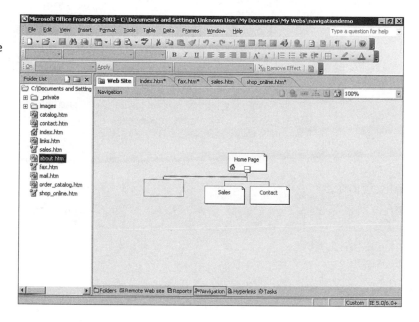

USING NAVIGATION VIEW BUTTONS TO BUILD SITE NAVIGATION

The Navigation view buttons (seen in Figure 8.5) at the top right corner of the screen are, left to right, as follows:

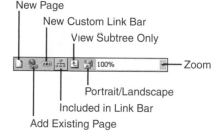

Figure 8.5
The buttons seen in Navigation view.

- **New Page**. Adds a new page to your Web site and places the page in the Navigational structure without attaching the page to any other.
- **Add Existing Page**. Adds an already existing page to the site navigation without attaching the page to any other.
- **New Custom Link Bar**. Lets you create a new custom link bar, based on the links of your choice (not site navigation).
- **Included in Link Bar.** Allows you to define files that are included in a link bar.
- **View Subtree Only.** Allows viewers to see site navigation in terms of subtrees.

- **Portrait/Landscape.** Lets you toggle between viewing the site navigation in portrait and landscape mode.
- **Zoom.** Lets you zoom in to or away from the entire site navigation.

NOTE

Initially, FrontPage will show pages in the Navigation view using the original HTML file names for each file. If the title is changed in Navigation view, FrontPage will change the title of the page accordingly.

VIEWING SUBTREES

Every page in a site navigation is noted with a "-" icon, as seen in Figure 8.6. Selecting the - icon will collapse the files below the selected file in navigational view, as seen in Figure 8.7.

Figure 8.6
Each item in the site navigation is noted with a "-" icon that can be selected to collapse part of the view of the site navigation.

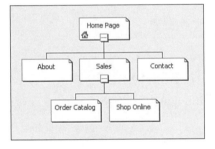

Figure 8.7
By selecting the "-" icon in Navigation view, only part of the site shown in Figure 8.6 is now available. A "+" sign indicates that there is more content below the sales page.

TIP

Use subtrees to get smaller views of a larger site. Looking at an entire site in Navigation view can overwhelm many (and often can't fit on a single page). Looking at a subtree can provide needed information without being overwhelming.

DELETING PAGES FROM NAVIGATION VIEW

Delete a page from Navigation view by selecting the page and pressing the Delete key. When a page is deleted from Navigation view, FrontPage asks the user if the page is to be entirely deleted from the FrontPage site or only from site navigation. The message displayed is shown in Figure 8.8.

Figure 8.8
When a file is deleted from site navigation view, FrontPage checks what kind of deletion is required.

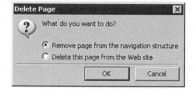

PRINTING THE NAVIGATION VIEW

 In previous versions of FrontPage, you were unable to print your site structure in Navigation view. That has changed with FrontPage 2003. To print your site structure in Navigation View, simply select the Print button while in Navigation view and FrontPage will print a very basic and simple representation of your site Navigation. You can also select Print from the File menu.

CREATING LINK BARS

Once your site has a navigational structure, the true power comes in the ability to dynamically build a link bar based on site navigation. Link bars are dynamically generated HTML content menu bars based on the developer's preference and site navigation information set in the Navigation view. In addition, link bars can be customized to meet the look and feel of your Web site as needed.

Link bars are added either through the Web Component menu or Navigation option under the Insert menu. FrontPage provides three options for building link bars, as seen in Figure 8.9.

Figure 8.9
You can build link bars with custom links, back and next links, or a bar based on the navigational structure of your site.

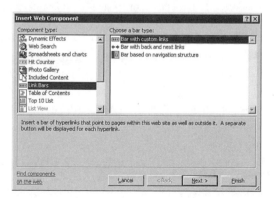

You can set link bars to follow whatever navigational pattern you'd like, as can be seen in Figure 8.10. You can also create a link bar with no pattern other than a specific set of links chosen by you.

Figure 8.10
The General tab of the Link Bar Properties dialog box gives you a number of navigation approaches.

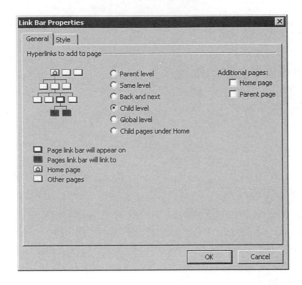

 If you are using back and forth buttons and the site doesn't present the pages in the order you think they should, *see "Back and Forth Buttons Out of Order" in the "Troubleshooting" section at the end of this chapter.*

A number of the FrontPage templates that come with FrontPage (and available from other third-party vendors) place link bars directly in to a Web site. With this feature, a new page can be added to the site (and navigation) and FrontPage will update all the necessary link bars accordingly. You are not limited to placing link bars within your HTML pages. Link bars can be placed in included files and in Shared Borders.

TIP

> You can use multiple link bars on the same page and aren't required to use the same type. Many users will find that they want multiple link bar options placed in different locations on the page.

→ For specific information on building and editing link bars through FrontPage or on Shared Borders, **see** "Using Web Components, Shared Borders, and Link Bars," **p. 167**.

 If your link bars are only showing some, but not all the pages in your site, *see "Odd Link Bars" in the "Troubleshooting" section at the end of this chapter.*

NAVIGATIONAL ELEMENTS: BUILDING BARS AND MENUS

This section takes a more specific look at the navigational bars and menus that can be produced through FrontPage. You will see the specifics of building bars and menus based on site navigation and walk through the process of building custom bars and menus. At the end of this section, the process of editing look and feel of your navigational elements (or creating your own) will also be examined.

Automatic navigation elements can only be created if you have assigned your site navigation through the Navigation view, discussed previously in this chapter.

Insert the cursor where you would like the navigational element to be created. Select Navigation from the Insert menu. FrontPage will open the Web Component dialog box with the Link Bar option preselected. The next part of this chapter walks you through the process of adding the navigational elements you want.

 If you want link bars in your site but don't want to go through the process of putting your entire site through the Navigation view interface, see "Link Bars Without Navigation View" in the "Troubleshooting" section at the end of this chapter.

CHOOSING A BAR STYLE AND ORIENTATION

The first step of menu or bar creation requires selecting a bar style. The interface for selecting a style is shown in Figure 8.11. You get from one step to the next by clicking the Next button.

Figure 8.11
The options for choosing a bar style lets you pick button styles from any theme installed on your copy of FrontPage.

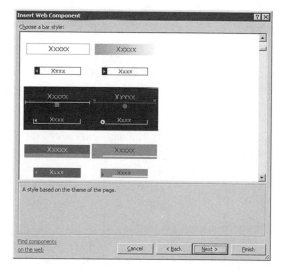

The selections offered by FrontPage come from all themes currently installed your copy of FrontPage. This includes Themes that came with the product, modified themes created by the user, and themes that were either directly purchased by a third-party directly or came as part of a FrontPage template purchase. At the end of the list are a number of text-only HTML styles that aren't associated with any themes.

The second step in the process is in selecting orientation. Your options are left to right or top to bottom.

8

Bars Based on Site Navigation

If you are building a bar based on site navigation, FrontPage will then ask you which pages you'd like added to the navigational element through the interface shown in Figure 8.10.

You can select each option in the interface to see which pages they effect. The options are as follows:

- **Parent Level**—Links files one level above the existing file. This effect is good for pages that want to show where you came from.
- **Same Level**—Links files on the same level. Used for showing all pages on certain levels without overwhelming with complete site content.
- **Back and Next**—Links files to the right and left of the file as seen in Navigation view. If you want to specifically lead people through pages of your site, this link bar is perfect.
- **Child Level**—Links files under the level of the existing file. Great for showing all "next step" options.
- **Global Level**—Links all files in the Web. Perfect for making sure that the visitor knows every option.
- **Child Pages Under Home**—Links all pages below the Home page. This approach produces the common top-level link bar approach that defines the areas of your site without getting too detailed.

Two toggle buttons also let you choose if you'd like FrontPage to include the home page and the parent page in the link bar.

> **NOTE**
>
> Selecting the Design tab in the Link Bar Properties dialog box will let you edit the style of the link bar if desired.

Back and Next Links

Back and Next links (the second link bar component option from Figure 8.9) only present links to the page immediately to the left and right of the page that the bar is added to. Back and Next are the only text associated with the buttons, not the specific page names.

This effect is most often used to walk a user through specific areas of a Web site. Back and Next links can also be used to effectively direct people through your site a page at a time, directing them to look at the pages you want them to in the order you specify.

Custom Bars and Menus

More often than not, developers will want to create link bars without a specific pattern (at least one that can be defined by selecting from a list). The third choice for creating custom link bars, Bar with Custom Links, allows you to create a custom bar and actually keeps these bars maintained on the system so that you can call them back and use them in different projects or pages if desired.

If you are selecting a custom bar or menu, FrontPage will prompt you to name the link bar. Then the final screen, shown in Figure 8.12, lets you create and edit custom bars at will. Note that the dialog box is the same as in the other link bars, but the options are different.

NOTE

> You can also make your own navigational structure without the component or use the new FrontPage Interactive Buttons to generate a custom navigation system.
>
> If you do so, you'll have considerably more control over the look and feel of your navigation, but you'll also have to update them accordingly each time you make a site navigation change.

Figure 8.12
You can create as many link bars as you'd like through this interface.

You can create a new link bar by selecting the Create New button or select a bar from the dropdown list. Links can be added, removed, modified, or moved by selecting the appropriate button in the interface. You can add as many links and as many custom bars as you'd like.

When you add a link, FrontPage opens the Add to Link Bar dialog box, shown in Figure 8.13. You can use the interface to quickly find and link to any file in your Web. You can also use the interface to link to a third-party site as shown in this example.

In addition, FrontPage gives you the opportunity to have your custom link bar link to the home page of your site or parent page from which the link is located. You can also link to an email address if desired.

Figure 8.13
The Add to Link Bar dialog box lets you combine internal and external links to your bar. In this example, a link to FrontPage World is shown.

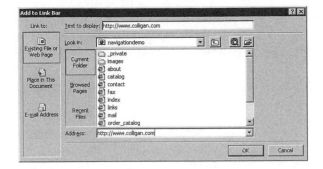

Once your link bar is created, you can modify it easily by right-clicking the bar and selecting Link Bar Properties. FrontPage will also append an add link option to any custom link bar in FrontPage Design view, providing a means to quickly add a link to your bar as seen in Figure 8.14.

Figure 8.14
A custom link bar will show an add link option in Design view. Selecting this will let you quickly add another link.

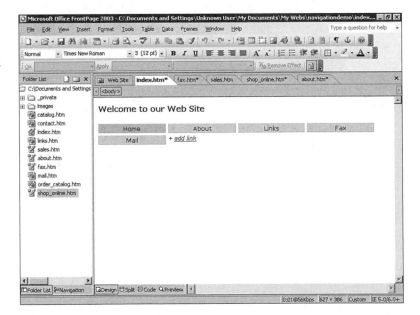

BARS AND MENU LOOK AND FEEL

Although FrontPage provides numerous options for menu bar look and feel, developers also have the ability to edit them to create the exact look desired. This is done by modifying a Theme file or selecting a different font choice for simple text bars.

As mentioned previously, bar elements are taken from Themes currently installed on your system. If you'd like to modify the buttons in your bar, you will need to modify the Theme accordingly. If you'd like to create a new look and feel for a bar from scratch, you will need to create a new Theme and install it on your system first.

➔ For specific information on the use and modification of FrontPage Themes, **see** "Using Themes," **p. 133**.

TIP

> A number of great free themes (and therefore Link bar buttons) can be found at
> `http://freethemes.frontpagelinks.com`.

By default, FrontPage will make a text link bar the font style and size of the page's default font. If you'd like to change either font or size, right-click the text bar and select Font from the menu options.

MODIFYING LINK BAR PROPERTIES

To edit the properties of any link bar, double-click the link bar from within Design view. FrontPage will open the Link Bar Properties dialog box, shown previously in Figure 8.10, and will allow you to modify any element of the link bar.

By default, the General tab will open, allowing you to set the type of hyperlink to be added to the bar. If you'd like to go into the style of the bar, select the Style tab and make your changes to formatting accordingly.

 If you need more link options from your link bars than what is provided through the link bar interface, see "Link Bar Options Don't Meet My Needs" in the "Troubleshooting" section at the end of this chapter.

CONSIDERATIONS

Anyone should take a number of considerations into account if they use FrontPage to manage their site navigational structure. On the simple level, there are a number of publishing issues you will want to consider. Things also get a bit more complicated if you are developing your site with others who are using different Web development products. Developers should also make sure to take a long term view of the use of navigational elements and be aware of the product's limitations throughout the design and maintenance of a site.

If everyone in your Web development team isn't using FrontPage, you might want to shy away from using the FrontPage navigational tools. Because the FrontPage navigational tools are FrontPage specific, other products won't recognize them and won't know how to write to, or edit the information. This is true for any product-specific tool on any Web development product.

You also might refrain from the tool if your site doesn't contain enough pages to necessitate any dynamically generated navigational elements. A good chunk of the Web is made up of sites four or five pages in size, and the navigational tools described in this chapter would simply be overkill in such an effort.

8

Another reason not to use the toolset is if you plan on developing a navigational system of your own. There is no need or reason to use two systems at the same time. FrontPage does not require that you use these tools to build your site; they are only there for your use if desired.

The final reason for not using these tools comes from the desire to maintain a free-flowing site linking strategy that simply can't be managed through FrontPage's toolset.

ISSUES TO CONSIDER WHEN MAKING YOUR OWN NAVIGATIONAL STRUCTURE

There are times when the navigation features provided by FrontPage are more than enough for your need. There will also be times when you'll want to bypass FrontPage and make your own.

First of all, the Navigation options discussed in this chapter are FrontPage specific. As a result, any other development product, from Dreamweaver to Notepad, could easily modify navigation specific content (unintentionally), causing damage to the structure and navigational elements.

As a result, great care should be taken if other development products are used to edit a site with FrontPage navigational options used. In this case, alternative navigation options should also be examined.

The biggest issue worth examining is the *time issue*. When you create your own navigational structure, *you are in charge of every element of the project* and won't have FrontPage to do the updating for you. Every change (to navigation and page title) will require you updating your site accordingly. If that time, which can and will add up quickly, is worth the benefits obtained, create your own.

The next section of this chapter, "Alternatives to Using FrontPage Navigation," offers a number of choices.

PUBLISHING ISSUES

If you use publishing through FrontPage server extensions or always FTP your entire site over whenever a page change is made, this does not concern you and you can jump to the next section.

If you tend to ftp, publish, or synchronize pages as they are built and updated, remember that navigational elements will update pages in your site even without your editing. As a result, every time a navigational or link bar change is made to the site, you will need to publish or synchronize *every* page affected by this issue—not just the new pages added to your site.

LIMITATIONS OF FRONTPAGE

The FrontPage navigational elements can only map specific files within your Web site taking the title for the page (if any) from the HTML or script file. Any dynamically driven content or multi-function pages can't be mapped appropriately through this interface. In addition, you can't add any scripting or logic to link bars, so no dynamic content can be added to a link bar through the add link option.

NOTE

> You can't combine link bars with FrontPage behaviors.

LONG TERM VIEW

If you build a site with FrontPage Navigation elements, realize that you will always need to utilize the features for the life of the site.

FrontPage's navigation system works great on smaller sites, but once your site pages pass 20 or so, it is pretty hard to contain everything within the FrontPage Navigation option.

In addition, you will quickly find that you will quickly need special navigation options that can be produced through the custom link option. But once FrontPage stops doing the hard work for you, you might want to consider the options discussed in the next section of this chapter.

SPEED ISSUES

The bigger your FrontPage Web site, the more information FrontPage has to keep together and keep in mind. The more FrontPage specific elements added to your site multiplied by the number of pages in your site could result in FrontPage having to track potentially thousands of page changes, navigational bars, and the like.

If your site exceeds a few hundred pages and makes considerable use of FrontPage navigational features, you will find that the design and saving process can slow down as FrontPage attempts to catch up with the work done. Developers with slower machines might find this issue quite frustrating.

One way around this issue is to divide your site into a number of subsites as it increases in size.

NOTE

> If you create a site made up of subsites, the only way you'll be able to use links bars to do navigation from one subsite to another is to create custom bars with absolute URLs.
>
> If you change a link in one subsite, FrontPage will not automatically update your custom bars—you'll need to do that yourself.

→ For more on creating subsites from FrontPage sites, **see** "Opening and Working with Existing Web Sites," **p. 283**.

ALTERNATIVES TO USING FRONTPAGE NAVIGATION

The benefit of a dynamically updated menu bar can be obtained through means other than FrontPage navigational components. Many FrontPage sites use the FrontPage Included File Web component to manage their navigational elements, and others make use of a dynamically generated database drive site to manage all content as necessary.

The benefits of placing navigational elements in an included file are obvious. You have complete control over content and look and feel, and you can add and remove whatever elements are desired. In addition, you can build an unlimited amount of included files for whatever navigation elements you might need. The negatives to building your own navigational elements through included content comes from the simple fact that FrontPage can't keep content up-to-date for you and you will have to update such content accordingly every time a new page is added.

Scripting navigational elements so that they render link bars and buttons from content within a database is a powerful option for anyone developing data driven Web sites and should certainly be considered by anyone attempting to do so.

CREATING PAGE BANNERS

Link bars are not the only benefit offered by FrontPage's navigational tools. Once you have named your pages through FrontPage's navigational system, FrontPage can also generate dynamic page banners for each of your pages as desired. Figure 8.15 shows a page with a dynamic page banner generated from FrontPage.

Figure 8.15
The Page Banner was automatically generated by FrontPage.

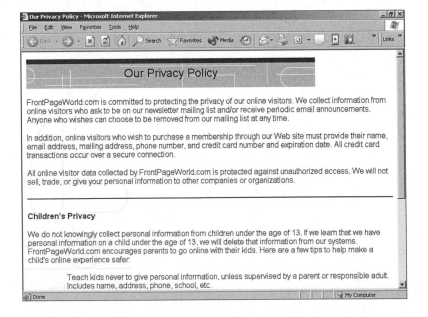

Page banners are dynamically generated elements that state the name of the page set in Navigation view. They are added to a Web page through the Insert, Page Banner option. Selecting this choice will open the Page Banner Properties dialog box, shown in Figure 8.16.

Figure 8.16
The Page Banner Properties dialog box lets you set if the banner should be text or picture.

If Picture is selected, FrontPage will generate a graphical banner for the page based on the page's Theme with the title set in page navigation mode. If Text is selected, FrontPage will generate a text banner based on the title set in page navigation mode. The text option also allows for different text input.

It is important to note that if a page banner is inserted on a page not part of the established FrontPage navigation, FrontPage will require entering the page into the Navigation view in order to create the banner (text or graphic). An example of this is seen in Figure 8.17.

Figure 8.17
If your page isn't in the navigation structure, FrontPage will tell you.

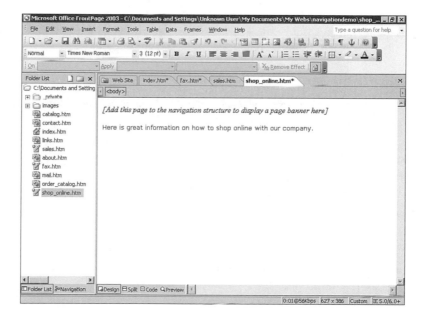

TROUBLESHOOTING

BACK AND FORTH BUTTONS OUT OF ORDER

I'm using back and forth link bars in my site, and the pages aren't ordered as I'd like them to be. What can I do?

Back and forth buttons order the page as they appear in Navigation view. If you'd like FrontPage to present them in a specific order, order the pages accordingly in Navigation view.

ODD LINK BARS

My dynamic link bars only show some of the pages in my site. What am I doing wrong?

FrontPage only shows dynamic link bars based on the navigational structure you set in Navigation view. If you created a page and didn't position it in Navigation view, it won't show up in a dynamic link bar. Return to Navigation view and add the appropriate pages as needed. FrontPage will automatically update your link bars accordingly.

LINK BAR OPTIONS DON'T MEET MY NEEDS

I need link bars with some child pages, as well as some pages higher up the navigational structure. What can I do?

If your needs can't be met through the bar based on navigation options, you can set a custom bar to meet your needs. If you do, make sure to update the bar accordingly when you add a new page that should be in the navigation.

LINK BARS WITHOUT NAVIGATION VIEW

I don't want to have to spend hours developing a Navigational view for my site because the only link bar I intend on using will be a custom bar.

If you are only going to use FrontPage to create custom link bars and menus, there is no need to create a Navigational view of the site for FrontPage to pull content from.

LINK BARS FROM FRONTPAGE INTERACTIVE BUTTONS

How do I build my link bars from FrontPage Interactive Buttons? I love to power of link bars and would love to combine them with the great new look and feel of interactive buttons.

You are not able to build link bars from interactive buttons in this release of FrontPage. The only option is to build your navigational elements from included files that are made up of interactive buttons.

FRONT AND CENTER: NAVIGATION POWER AND BUILDING A SITE IN NAVIGATION VIEW FIRST

The navigation elements built in to FrontPage 2003 are quite possibly the most underutilized feature of the product. They make the development process considerably easier because you can, in short, produce navigation with the simple drag and drop of the mouse. Personally, I have saved countless hours letting FrontPage write navigation bars for me.

The continually popular FrontPage Template industry also makes great use of these features. The fact that the top selling templates make use of FrontPage's navigational features shows how powerful and attractive these features are for FrontPage users.

As was hinted at in this chapter, there are a few potential problems that anyone—who is developing a site in FrontPage and wants to use these features—needs to take into consideration. In short, once you've committed to using this feature, there is pretty much no way to go back without considerable time and effort to redo all that has been done. Make sure that you understand these issues. I've received too many emails from folks whose sites have gone out of control, so I can't emphasize this fact enough.

Obviously, this is an issue of site size. A more traditional "brochure ware" site of eight or so pages should certainly make use of these features. I would say that concern for anything mentioned in this chapter should only be voiced after a site exceeds 50 or so pages.

The *other* option of building site navigational elements from an included file cannot be overemphasized either. Although it doesn't give you the element of dynamically generated menu bars that you get from FrontPage, it can speed up the design process considerably because editing a single file can update all necessary pages. Consider this option as well.

It is also important to note that the custom link bar is not based on site navigational properties and can be used on any project to produce link bars at the click of a mouse. Some users will find that they'll ignore every element of FrontPage's navigational system and bars based on them, but will embrace this very cool and very functional feature.

One of the things I like most about Navigation view is how it forces you to look at your site in terms of hierarchy and position—how one page not only connects, but relates with another. I would bet money that a number of people would never be able to produce such a map of their "simple" sites. These are the same people who complain that people can't figure their way around their sites.

If you have the luxury of building a site from scratch, consider building the site first entirely in Navigation view, having FrontPage force you to think of your site the way you should. Once you have created a navigational view of your site, you will be many steps ahead of anyone who hasn't.

You will be very surprised at what happens when you "build" a site this way. Suddenly, the importance of certain pages will come into question, whereas pages buried deep inside your site will suddenly find a new position because no one realized how buried the content was.

8

Must you use the link bars that come with FrontPage if you decide to take my recommendation? *Of course not*. The other thing I love so much about FrontPage is how it lets you take the parts you want and lets you do what you want with them. Just make sure that you are taking advantage of the best that FrontPage offers to you.

CHAPTER 9

Using Web Components, Shared Borders, and Link Bars

In this chapter

USING WEB COMPONENTS

FrontPage provides a very strong environment for designing and coding Web pages. In the previous chapters, we've examined how to use FrontPage to develop the exact pages you want to make.

Another part of FrontPage's strength and complexity is in the toolset that it provides to users for producing content rich Web sites with a low maintenance overhead. Included in these tools are the Web components, shared borders, and link bars.

Although FrontPage 2003 introduces no new elements to these tools, their role in the Web design process is considerable and needs to be examined here. Many of the tools provide benefits that can be replicated using other elements or design approaches. Take care to find which of these tools work best for your specific implementation.

We examine each of the Web component groupings installed with the standard install of FrontPage 2003, link bars and shared borders, in this chapter.

One of the more powerful elements of FrontPage is the Web component. A Web component is a FrontPage plug-in made available through the Insert Web Component dialog box (under the Tool menu) that adds HTML content to the FrontPage document. As a result, specific detailed code can be integrated into a Web page without requiring the developer to produce any HTML. This brings a new level of power to users uncomfortable with writing and implementing code of their own.

NOTE

> Many Web components require either FrontPage Server Extensions or Windows SharePoint Services. If you are using one of these Web components, be sure that the server has the necessary extensions or WSS installed or the component will not work as intended.

Sometimes the HTML inserted is little more than code that pulls information or content from another source. Examples of this include a MSNBC component that lets you insert news headlines into your site. Other times, it inserts more complex code that interacts with a Web server to produce additional content (see Figure 9.1). Examples of this approach include search pages and SharePoint Web Parts.

→ For a fascinating option on creating your own Web components, **see** "Making Your Own Web Components," **p. 965**.

Once a Web component is placed on your page, you can double-click the component to bring up its properties and edit or change the component as you want.

If you want to delete the component from your site, you can delete it with one click and not be worried that any code associated with the component will be left in your page.

Figure 9.1
A Web page with the MSNBC Web components pulls impressive content from a top 100 Web site without the need to enter a line of code in your Web site.

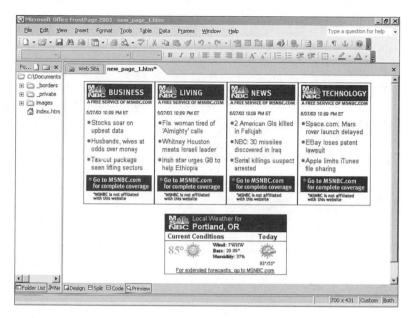

The Web Component dialog box, mentioned throughout this chapter, is found by selecting Web Component from the Insert menu (see Figure 9.2). This will open the Web Components dialog box, which allows you to select from a number of Web components for insertion in your site.

Figure 9.2
The Internet Web Component dialog box.

If you having problems making your Web Component work on your Web page, see "It Doesn't Work" in the "Troubleshooting" section at the end of this chapter.

DYNAMIC EFFECTS

Two options for dynamic effects are provided through this component type: the Marquee and the Interactive button.

The marquee is a simple tag that will cause text to scroll horizontally across the screen. You can control many of the elements of the effect through this component. The marquee tag is only supported in Internet Explorer and will not produce scrolling text if invoked from any other browser type.

The Interactive button is a new powerful feature of FrontPage 2003 and is examined in detail elsewhere in this book.

→ A full chapter is given to the Interactive button toolset in, "Using Interactive Buttons," **p. 441**.

WEB SEARCH

Two options for Web search are provided as a Web component: Current Web and Full Text Search.

Current Web requires a server with FrontPage Extensions in order to run and adds limited search functionality to your Web site. The results of this feature are limited in nature but can be used to provide out-of-the-box search functionality.

Full Text Search is a considerably more complex search feature, but it is only supported on servers running Windows SharePoint Services.

SPREADSHEETS AND CHARTS

This component type provides the ability to add Microsoft Office spreadsheets, charts, or pivot tables to a site. In order to view this type of content on your site, the site visitor will need a copy of Microsoft Excel (version 2000 or higher) installed on his system (see Figure 9.3) and will need to be browsing the content with Internet Explorer version 4 or higher.

NOTE

> The licensing issues with these Web components prevent their general use in public Web sites, but they are powerful assets to intranet development when all users have Microsoft Office installed.

→ For more information on how Excel content is published to the Web, **see** "Working with Microsoft Excel and FrontPage," **p. 771**.

HIT COUNTER

Hit counters provide a simple way for users to see how many times their page has been *hit* (visited by another computer system).

The hit counter provided in this Web component is easy to use; however, it requires a server with FrontPage Extensions to run. You can choose from five counter type faces.

Figure 9.3
With the Chart Web component, specific charting and spreadsheet data can be quickly integrated into a FrontPage Web site.

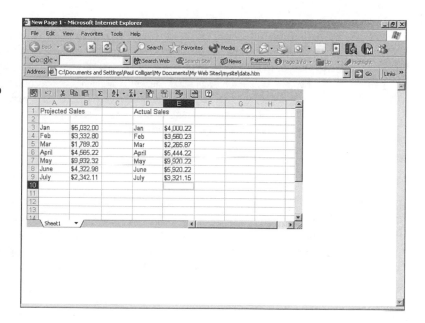

To insert a counter, simply select the Web component. FrontPage asks you which counter style you want to use, what number you want the counter to "start" at, and if you'd like your counter to be of fixed digit spacing. Simply select the appropriate options and check boxes and click OK (see Figure 9.4). You can create your own character set for your hit counter by selecting the Custom Picture option and entering the path of the graphics file.

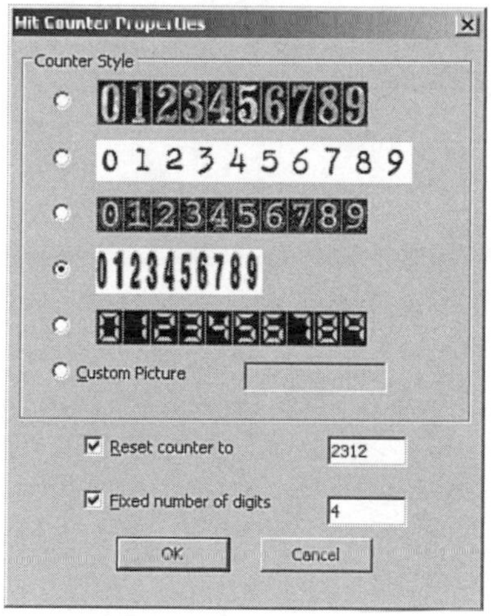

Figure 9.4
The Hit Counter options are all accessible from this simple dialog box.

TIP

> Hit counters do nothing more than tell you how many times a page has been hit. A Webmaster needs much more data than that and should be referencing server logs for this kind of information. Hit counters simply don't provide enough information.
>
> If you must have a hit counter at your site, you might want to consider using one of the many free Internet services that provide attractive counter options, which also provide better statistics for your personal reference. One great free counter service can be found at `http://counteroption.frontpagelink.com`.

PHOTO GALLERY

The Photo Gallery Web Component provides four different options for placing pages of images (usually photographs) in an attractive layout with thumbnails on a single page that directly click to the larger image files. One of the layout options, Slideshow, provides a slideshow type functionality that requires only JavaScript to use. Selecting any of the Photo Gallery options opens the Photo Gallery dialog box, seen in Figure 9.5.

Figure 9.5
The first tab of the Photo Gallery dialog box is used to add the pictures to the gallery, set the thumbnail size, and enter the desired content.

The first tab of the Photo Gallery dialog box will help you collect the photos you want to see in the gallery and define the order in which you'd like to see the images presented. The lower half of the screen is used to enter captions and descriptions for each of the images, if supported by your chosen layout.

The second tab lets you quickly switch between layout types and set the number of pictures per row (see Figure 9.6).

→ For more information on the Photo Gallery and how to use it to integrate photos into your site, **see** "Enhancing Pages with Graphics and Multimedia," **p. 113**.

Figure 9.6
The second tab of the Photo Gallery dialog box lets you jump back and forth between the different Photo Gallery layout options.

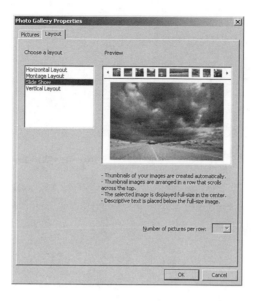

INCLUDED CONTENT

The most powerful of the Web components are the included content options. They enable the user to include various types of external content throughout the Web site with ease. By using the included content options found through this Web component, automatic updates of a page or Web site can be done quickly and easily. In addition, changes made to included content can automatically update later throughout a Web site without having to touch all the pages the content is contained in.

THE SUBSTITUTION COMPONENT

The Substitution component lets you quickly enter a page configuration variable into your FrontPage Web site. Options for this include author, page modifier, URL, description, or any freeform text you want to insert.

THE PAGE COMPONENT

The Page component lets you insert the entirety of another Web page inside an existing one. When content from an inserted page is updated, FrontPage automatically updates all pages in the FrontPage Web that have inserted the page content. When used and implemented correctly, inserted pages can be used to dynamically update an entire site by simply updating a single page.

Pages included through this process are usually smaller pages specifically designed to be elements of a larger site. Popular included page options contain headers, footers, menu bars, advertising zones, and the like.

When this option is selected, FrontPage opens a simple Include Page Properties dialog box that lets you find the page you want to include in your site (see Figure 9.7). Once selected,

FrontPage integrates the included page content at the page location chosen when the component was inserted.

Figure 9.7
The Include Page Properties dialog box lets you select the page that will be inserted into your Web page.

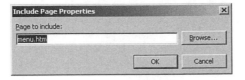

NOTE

FrontPage strips the header content from an included file before it is inserted into a Web page.

TIP

It is important to remember that when you use an included file to update an entire site, every page updated will be changed, regardless of the content on that page. For instance, a two year old press release will be updated with new menu content if it includes a recently updated menu bar or new copyright information if a footer with copyright information has been updated.

If you are working on a site that uses included content, make sure that you publish or synchronize any page in your site that might be updated by such use.

THE PAGE BASED ON SCHEDULE COMPONENT

The Page Based on Schedule Component ads a twist to the included page concept by allowing you to have content added to your site at a specific time. This approach can be used to offer specific content at specific times such as a "good morning" or "closed for the weekend" notice, without having to be there to change the content when needed. Figure 9.8 shows how easy it is to program this information.

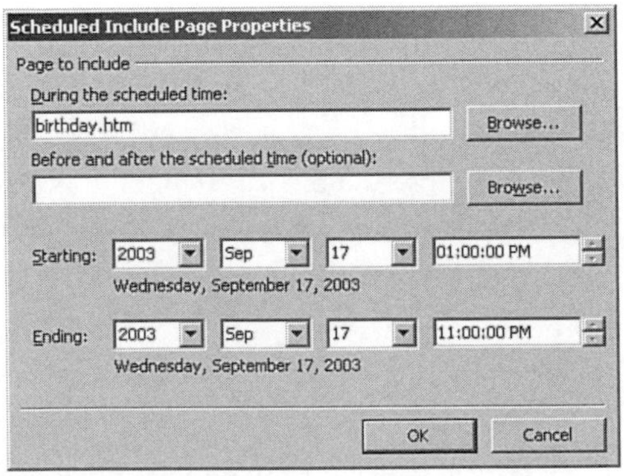

Figure 9.8
The Scheduled Include Page Properties dialog box lets you set the time for the included content and offer alternative content (if desired).

NOTE

Because this feature relies on the Web server to serve the content when needed, it only works on servers with FrontPage Extensions installed.

The Scheduled Include Page Properties dialog box asks for the location of the content, the start and finishing times for when the content should be presented, and the location of optional content to be shown when the scheduled content is not displayed.

TIP

You can have all sorts of fun with this component. Consider using it to add special holiday or birthday messages to your Web site.

THE PICTURE BASED ON SCHEDULE COMPONENT

The Picture Based on Schedule component follows the same concept as the Page Based on Schedule component, but it uses graphics instead of content files.

There are a number of ways this could be used. Examples included a "special offer" graphic that only appears at certain times in your site or holiday imagery that not only appears on your site on certain holidays, but also updates your site when you are (hopefully) out of the office.

TIP

The Scheduled Picture option will only show an image at the requested time. If you need anything else from the image, such as a hyperlink or accompanying text, you might want to consider using the Scheduled Content Include to include an HTML file with your image and whatever additional content you desire.

THE PAGE BANNER COMPONENT

Page banners are dynamically generated content that place a "banner" on the page based on the title of the page in the FrontPage Web site. Whenever the name of the page is updated anywhere, FrontPage will automatically update the page banner without the need for any additional effort on your side.

Page banners are part of the FrontPage theme engine and will create a banner graphic or will format the banner text based on the page theme. If no theme is select on the page with the page banner, no banner will be created.

To add a banner to a page, use the Page Banner component and choose either text or graphics for the banner. FrontPage will do the rest.

→ For more information on page banners and how Themes are integrated into a FrontPage Web site, **see** "Using Themes," **p. 133**.

9

LINK BARS

Link bars are hyperlinked navigational elements for a Web site. They can be generated specifically for a single purpose, or they can pull data from an existing FrontPage navigational structure. In addition, if desired, link bars can pull elements from installed themes to produce a consistent look and feel that matches your Web site.

→ For more information on building site navigational structure and link bars and the Navigation view, **see** "FrontPage's Navigation Tools and Elements," **p. 147**.

Link bars help the Web design process because they provide a means to quickly manage and produce navigation elements without having to enter every hyperlink on every page. Link bars can be created and cut and pasted to as many pages as desired. When using the Link Bars component, you can save even more time by adding new pages using the site navigation structure, which results in the new pages automatically being reflected in the appropriate link bars throughout your entire Web site.

Three options are available for the Link Bar component: Bar with Custom Links, Bar with Back and Next Links, and Bar Based on Navigational Structure, which are covered in the sections that follow. Each of the options provides considerable variables resulting in the ability of the FrontPage user to produce the link bar navigational element of her choice.

Once a bar is inserted into a Web page, double-clicking the bar will bring up the Link Bar Property dialog box and allow you to edit the bar and its content (see Figure 9.9). You can also switch between bar types with this interface.

Figure 9.9
The Link Bar Properties dialog box lets you set, modify, and move links, as well as edit the style of the link bar if desired.

 If your link bars don't contain all the content you think they should, *see "Where's That Page?" in the "Troubleshooting" section at the end of this chapter.*

BAR WITH CUSTOM LINKS

The bar with Custom Links option lets you choose the style of the bar from the list of installed themes or lets you produce one of eight different text only bars that don't have a corresponding theme. Once this element is chosen, you can select a horizontal or vertical alignment and then a Link Bar Property dialog box opens that lets you build the link bar with the specific link and text elements that you require.

BAR WITH BACK AND NEXT LINKS

This bar option blends the Bar with Custom Links option discussed previously with the ability to add links to pages within your FrontPage navigational structure that are on the same level as the page to which the link bar is added. FrontPage will take the links you added and automatically produce additional links to any pages on the same level.

BAR BASED ON NAVIGATIONAL STRUCTURE

A bar based on navigational structure pulls the pages to be linked in the bar from the existing site navigational structure. The dialog box will show the different options for your bar and present a graphical representation of your options for quick selection. The Link Bar Properties dialog box, shown in Figure 9.10, shows the options for which links can be added.

Figure 9.10
When associated with a navigational structure, the Link Bar Properties dialog box doesn't allow you to add links but takes link information from your existing site.

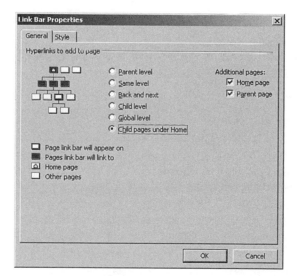

TABLE OF CONTENTS

The Table of Contents Web component will produce, on-the-fly, a table of contents for your Web site. You can choose to have FrontPage create the contents for your entire Web site or only choose to catalog certain pages. You can also tell FrontPage to regenerate the table of contents if any page in your site is edited. FrontPage generates the table of contents file based on links to and from the files in your Web site.

The first of the two options in the Insert Web Component dialog box, For this Web Site, will open the Table of Contents Properties dialog box seen in Figure 9.11.

Figure 9.11
The Table of Contents Properties dialog box lets you set how you'd like the table of contents to appear.

You can control the following options from this dialog box:

- **Page URL for starting point of the table**—Most users will select the home page, but if you want to start from a different area, this option will enable you to do so.

- **Heading font size**—You can choose how large or small you want your table of contents to be.

- **Show each page only once**—Because the table of contents is generated based on links, a page can be listed multiple times. Toggle this option on or off as desired.

- **Show pages with no incoming hyperlinks**—If you'd like pages with no incoming links to be listed in the table of contents, check this box.

- **Recompute table of contents when any other page is edited**—If you want FrontPage regenerating your table of contents on a regular basis, select this option.

TIP

> The table of contents developed through this component is based only on what is contained in your site. Pages designed only to be used as included content and private pages will show up in your table of contents unless you specifically tell FrontPage that you don't want this to happen.
>
> Be careful with an automatically generated table of contents. It is seldom what users are looking for and often requires a great deal of editing to get "just right."

TOP 10 LIST

The Top 10 List Web component works in conjunction with FrontPage 2002 Server Extensions to provide quick top ten reports of elements related to your server traffic reporting. The Top 10 List options are as follows:

- **Visited Pages**—Presents the top ten most popular pages on your Web site.

- **Referring Domains**—Shows the top ten domains that are sending traffic to your site.

- **Referring URLs**—Lists the top ten specific Web addresses that are directing traffic to your site.

- **Search Strings**—Reports the top ten search entries in the search engines that were used to find your Web site.

- **Visiting Users**—Offers whatever information is available on the top ten visiting users. If the users are registered with the site and not anonymous visitors, the information is significantly more useful.

- **Operating Systems**—Records the top ten operating systems used by visitors at your site.

- **Browser**—Gives details on the top ten browser types used by your audience.

Going Public wwith Top 10 Results

Making your site's traffic details public is always an interesting endeavor. It is great to be able to share content such as this with your audience, but before implementation, ask yourself if your competitors would benefit from these facts. If they will, or even possibly might, are they worth publishing for the world to see?

In addition, some data might give hackers the information they are looking for. If you have internal pages or elements that make it to the top ten lists, do you want to broadcast them to the world—even if they are password protected?

If you want to make this information available to only certain people (such as employees, partners, and so on), consider placing the entire report behind a password protected area.

You need FrontPage 2002 server extensions installed for any of the Top 10 lists to work.

Double-clicking on any of these lists will let you format how they are presented on your Web page and will let you specify the time span represented in each of these reports. Figure 9.12 shows the options for formatting each list.

Figure 9.12
Top 10 List properties can be formatted a number of different ways.

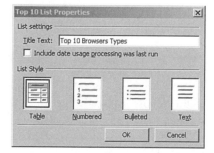

 If your Top 10 list contains now content, see "Top 10 List Shows Nothing" in the "Troubleshooting" section at the end of this chapter.

LIST VIEW AND DOCUMENT LIBRARY VIEW

Windows SharePoint Services provides a number of powerful Web Parts that can be added to a Web page to provided extended functionality to that page. Two of the most popular

Web Parts, the List View and Document Library View can be added to the site through FrontPage directly. List View provides a means to view data from a data source in a list view. Document Library View generates a dynamic list of files in a document library.

Through the Web Component dialog box, you can add a Windows SharePoint Services List View or Document Library View Web Part to a Web page. You can then directly edit the Web Part and the look and feel of the content in FrontPage to make sure that it matches the rest of your site.

→ For more information on working with Web parts in Windows SharePoint Services, **see** "FrontPage and Web Parts," **p. 735**.

→ For more on Windows SharePoint Services, **see** "Windows SharePoint Services 2.0," **p. 943**.

EXPEDIA COMPONENTS

These Web components let you add map information to your Web site (see Figure 9.13). You can either choose to develop a link to Expedia that presents the map on the Expedia servers or place the map on your site directly.

Figure 9.13
The Static Map Properties dialog box lets you enter the very address of the map you'd like integrated into your Web site.

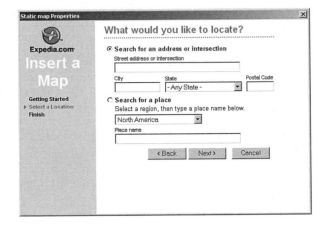

MSN COMPONENTS

The MSN Web components provide two search box items for your site that either search the MSN search engine or provide a stock quote from MSN's Money Central Web site. There are no variables for these components; they simply insert the HTML that integrates with the MSN sites. Figure 9.14 shows both of these elements placed on a basic Web page.

MSNBC COMPONENTS

The MSNBC components write code that pulls a news headline graphic from MSNBC and presents it at your Web site (see Figure 9.15). The Weather Forecast component enables you to place a weather update for the location of your choice at the site of your choice.

Figure 9.14
The MSN search engine and MSN Money Central MSN Components.

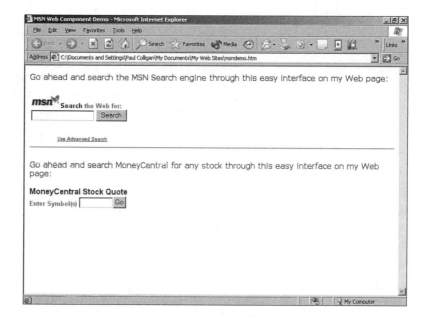

Figure 9.15
The MSNBC components provide basic dynamically updated content to your Web site with the simple insertion from FrontPage.

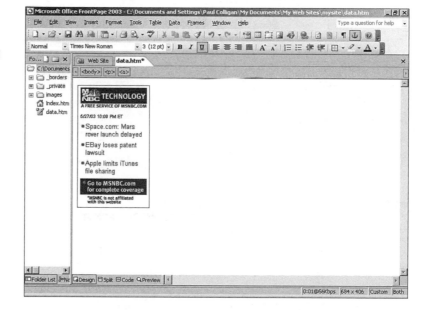

NOTE

The MSNBC components pull a graphic of the information you select and places that graphic in your Web page. As a result, there is no way for you to edit the size, color, or content of this component.

In addition, if your audience is unable to view graphics, the component offers nothing other than the recommendation to visit MSNBC.com to find news information.

9

NOTE

> The MSN and MSNBC components only provide the initial information at your site and then direct the user to additional information at their sites once the graphic is clicked. Before choosing to use these components, determine whether the value of providing the data at your site outweighs the loss of your audience being redirected to another site.
>
> A large percentage of Web developers consider items that direct traffic away from their site to seldom be worth the (usually limited) benefits.

ADDITIONAL COMPONENTS

The Additional Components option will let you choose from any third-party Web components installed on your system. Until an additional component is installed, the option is empty.

No additional components are installed in a standard FrontPage 2003 installation.

NOTE

> Most third-party components (free and otherwise) come with their own installer program that will usually add the tool directly to FrontPage (often through the Tools menu). The additional components option is only for the (very limited) instances when a component needs to be added without an installer.

ADVANCED CONTROLS

The Advanced Controls options give you a way to add content to your site that would otherwise have to be entered using Code view. These options provide an alternative way for those uneasy with editing HTML code in any way to add elements such as Java Applets and Flash movies.

The available controls are shown in Figure 9.16 and are as follows:

Figure 9.16
Enter the Advanced Control of your choice through this easy interface.

- **HTML**—Lets you directly insert HTML into your FrontPage site. To prevent you from modifying HTML inserted in this manner, FrontPage will not allow you to edit or show the HTML from within Design view. This element is meant for times when a user has been given a piece of HTML to put in her site and is uneasy with Code view and the implications of being able to edit code directly.

- **Java Applet**—This option enables you to insert a Java Applet into your Web site without requiring the editing of the page's HTML code. The Java Applet Properties dialog box makes it simple for you to be sure that appropriate information is associated with the insertion of the Applet (see Figure 9.17).

Figure 9.17
The Java Applet Properties dialog box lets you enter parameters and layout information for your Java Applet.

- **Plug-In**—If you need to insert a browser plug-in into your Web site, this control will make insertion easy.

- **Confirmation Field**—This control is used to present confirmation field information to a site visitor for pages delivered after a form is filled out. These are also called "thank you" pages.

- **ActiveX Control**—The functionality of this control is similar to the Plug-In and Java Applet control capabilities. You are presented with a dialog box in which you can make sure that the data needed to support your ActiveX control is also included in your Web page without coding it by hand.

- **Design Time Control**—Using this control lets you install any design-time control available in your system. If none are installed on your system, you will not be able to use this feature. *Design-time controls* are controls specifically built for the developer that are never seen on a client system. In contrast, *runtime controls* are controls seen at run-time, or on the side of the client.

- **Movie in Flash Format**—Walks you through the process of inserting a Flash movie into your Web site.

WORKING WITH SHARED BORDERS

Shared borders provide an option for site-wide navigation and consistent appearance. Shared borders "share" borders of a Web page with other pages in the site so that when one change is made to one border, the rest of the site is updated accordingly.

In many ways, shared borders are the same technology as included files, described earlier in this section, and are often used for the same reason. When one shared border on one page is edited, all pages that contain the shared border are also automatically updated by FrontPage.

NOTE

In order to use Shared Borders in a FrontPage Web site, the option must be selected in the Authoring tab of the Page Options dialog box, accessed by selecting Page Options from the Tools menu.

To create shared borders in a Web site, simply select the Shared Borders option from the Format menu. FrontPage will open the Shared Borders dialog box, allowing you to choose which borders you would like to add. You can add borders to the entire site or only to selected pages. You can only have one shared border set per Web site. Figure 9.18 shows the Shared Border dialog box.

Figure 9.18
The Shared Borders dialog box lets you set which borders you would like to share within your site and if you'd like to update all pages in the Web accordingly.

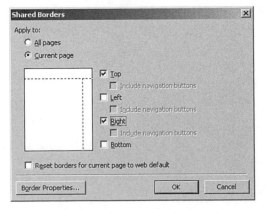

Shared border content is indicated with a dotted line separating the border from the rest of the page and at first use contains a prewritten comment from FrontPage to indicate its presence.

NOTE

> Because shared border content is edited or deleted in the Web page, you can only remove shared borders through the Shared Borders dialog box.

Once the comment inserted by FrontPage is replaced with content from the user, the content becomes the site-wide shared border content. Shared border content can contain any element desired including Link Bar navigation or other HTML elements.

If shared border content is changed on any page within the Web, all pages containing the same border are automatically updated with FrontPage.

TIP

> Shared Borders is a technology that has been made obsolete by effective use of included content, as seen in this chapter, or through Dynamic Web Templates, seen elsewhere in this book. If you need the functionality shared borders provides, I strongly recommend considering these alternative options.

→ For more on the use an integration of Dynamic Web Templates in the Web design process, **see** "Dynamic Web Templates," **p. 411**.

 If your shared borders are getting out of control, *see "Shared Border Chaos" in the "Troubleshooting" section at the end of this chapter.*

TROUBLESHOOTING

IT DOESN'T WORK

I inserted the Web component in my Web site, and it doesn't work when I view it on the Web site.

Some components require FrontPage Server Extensions or Windows SharePoint Services. If you must use the component, you'll need to publish to a Web server that can meet these requirements.

For a list of which features require Server Extensions (and which versions), see http://extensionsneeded.frontpagelink.com.

TOP 10 LIST SHOWS NOTHING

My host provides FrontPage 2002 extensions but the Top 10 List components don't show what I think they should.

Some Web hosts have FrontPage 2002 extensions installed but cripple the server logging features associated with the extensions because of the stress they put on the system. If your host has taken this approach, the Top 10 List component won't work on your Web site.

WHERE'S THAT PAGE?

I don't see my pages where they should be in a link bar.

Link bars pull their content from the navigational structure used during the design of the site. If your link bar isn't showing a page that should be there, you need to make sure FrontPage knows that the page belongs in the corresponding navigational structure. This is easily fixed by dragging the structure where it belongs in Navigation view.

SHARED BORDER CHAOS

Something went crazy somewhere on some page, and now all my shared borders are out of whack.

First of all, don't feel bad—this is a common problem with shared borders. Because anyone on any of the pages can edit the borders, they can also easily make a mistake that propagates through your entire Web site with the click of the Save button.

The solution is as simple as the cause. Simply re-create the correct Shared Border format and let FrontPage update your site accordingly.

FRONT AND CENTER: CHOOSING THE RIGHT TOOL FOR THE JOB

It was the Included Content Web component that initially drew me to FrontPage as my Web design product of choice. The ability to create a single element that could easily be replicated throughout my Web site with the click of a button was the very tool that I knew would help me speed up the rate at which I designed Web sites. At the same time, the tool simultaneously increases my site's quality and navigability while speeding up the process at which I develop Web pages. I will continue to use this tool as long as I use FrontPage.

It is also, for me, the one tool that separates FrontPage from the others.

The link bar capabilities in FrontPage are an interesting beast. They require the use of the Navigation view when developing your FrontPage Web site, but when used properly, they can quickly produce a navigational structure for a site that is easily updated as you add new content. The benefit, however, is easily replicated with a solid included content navigational element and doesn't require you to check every page in your site in Navigation view. Which path you pick is up to you. I recommend the former.

If you spend any time online with other FrontPage users, you'll find that almost all of them fall into two categories: (1) those who used shared borders at one point in time and swear they will never do it again, and (2) those who think better options exist than what shared borders provides and wish Microsoft would simply remove the option from FrontPage. I'm sure that I'll get some email on this issue, but I simply recommend that you stay away from them. The benefit is easily reproduced using other elements without the (all too often) heartbreak associated with shared borders.

Many of the tools included in FrontPage provides similar benefits as other tools within the product. One example is the ability to add navigational elements through link bars, included menu content, or shared borders. This is partially because of the old cliché that "there's more than one way to skin a cat" and partially because some legacy elements (such as shared borders) have been made obsolete with other technologies (such as included content) without Microsoft eliminating the older set from the FrontPage program.

You can use this fact to your advantage. FrontPage comes with a solid toolset that can be used many different ways to produce many different results. Be sure to explore all the available options and then choose the toolset and approach that makes the most sense to you.

9

CHAPTER 10

USING TABLES

In this chapter

TABLES AND FRONTPAGE 2003

Tables are the design cornerstone of the basic page layout process. Their use in HTML allows for page layout capabilities that are compliant to all browser types and more like the page layout capabilities similar to other desktop applications.

Tables are different from other forms of page layout (such as layers) because they don't require x, y positioning or CSS and enable a greater flexibility in implementation. With tables, you can still provide layout elements to your site but let the elements be flexible in relation to the screen size your site is being presented on.

 FrontPage 2003 introduces the concept of layout tables and cells. Layout tables and cells are HTML tables and cells with a few extra tags to provide additional layout and markup capabilities. The effects provided by the use of layout tables and cells are considerable and can result in a very attractive look and feel.

Pages can be made entirely of layout tables and cells or contain a combination of traditional HTML tables and cells with the newer layout tables and cells. Both options will be discussed side by side throughout this chapter.

FrontPage has always excelled in working with tables, and FrontPage 2003 includes a new Tables toolbar and the layout tables and cells task pane that can guide you through the process of developing a site with this technology.

This chapter starts by looking at the process of designing page content with tables and how the tools provided by FrontPage 2003 enable the developer to quickly implement tables in their site design process. After that, we'll look at the new layout tables and cells tools and how they are used and implemented. Once that is done, we'll look at the pros and cons of using both technologies in the Web design process.

USING TABLES IN DESIGN

Without the use of some form of design layout, site content runs from the left to the right of the screen without anyone having control over layout capabilities. In Figure 10.1, a paragraph and piece of clip art are simply placed on the page. In Figure 10.2, the same content is placed in a table to provide a more attractive design.

Layout tables and cells provide additional layout design capabilities, as can be seen in Figure 10.3 where the content from Figure 10.2 is formatted with a layout table with some additional flourishes.

On the most basic level, tables are used to contain content as was seen in the previous figures. Tables and cells can be placed as deep as desired within tables and cells to provide the layout effect the developer is looking for. In Figure 10.4, an almost desktop publishing effect is produced by placing tables within tables.

Figure 10.1
A paragraph of text and a piece of clip art are placed on a Web page without the use of tables.

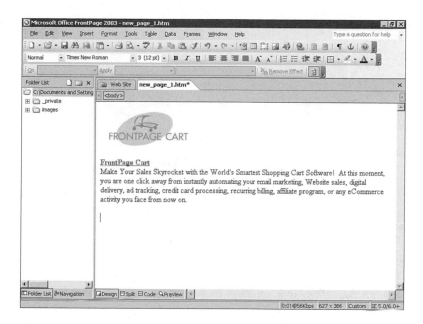

Figure 10.2
The same content shown in Figure 10.1 is placed inside a two-celled table to provide a cleaner layout.

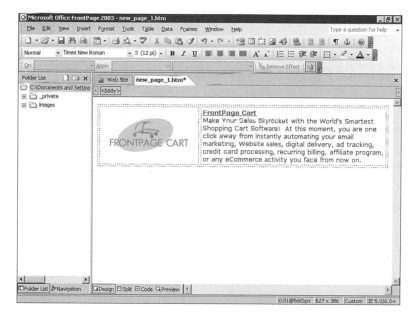

10

Figure 10.3
The content shown in Figure 10.2 is instead placed in a layout table with a few additional flourishes such as a colored border on the corners.

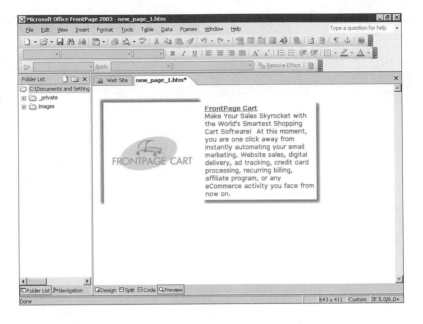

Figure 10.4
The page content shown here is a traditional 770 pixel table with a number of sub tables and cells within.

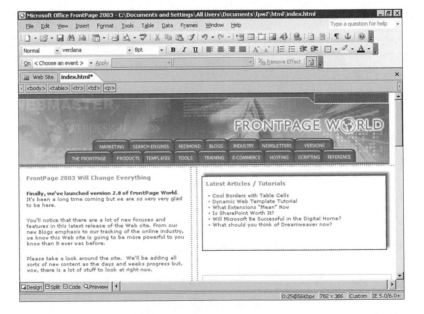

→ The use of tables in Web design does not automatically mean that site content is accessible. To learn more about this issue and see how FrontPage can assist in designing a truly accessible site, **see** "FrontPage's Accessibility Features," **p. 235**.

 If you are having problems making your tables print correctly, *see "Tables Don't Print" in the "Troubleshooting" section at the end of this chapter.*

How Tables Work in FrontPage

The Insert Table button in the Standard toolbar, seen in Figure 10.5, lets you create a table x cells across by y cells down similar to other products in the Microsoft Office System. Table properties can be set through the Table Properties dialog box, shown in Figure 10.6. The Table Properties dialog box can be invoked by right-clicking anywhere within the table and selecting the Table Properties option from the menu.

NOTE

You can also insert tables through the Table toolbar or the Layout Tables and Cells task pane, both discussed later in this chapter.

Figure 10.5
A 7 by 7 table is selected from the Insert Table button in the Standard toolbar.

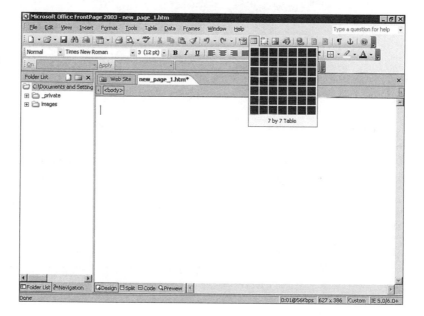

TIP

The Insert Tables button in the Standard toolbar can also be called in Code or Split view. If you insist on hand-coding your Web site, allow FrontPage to do the tedious work of writing the tags associated with a complete table.

Tables are sized either by pixel or by percentage of screen size. When a specific pixel size is set, the browser will usually show the table in the desired size. If a percentage is set, the table will be presented as a percentage of screen size.

 If you are frustrated that your table text seems to line right up against your table borders producing an awkward affect, see "Text Touching Borders" in the "Troubleshooting" section at the end of this chapter.

Figure 10.6
The Table Properties dialog box lets you set almost all options of any table in your site.

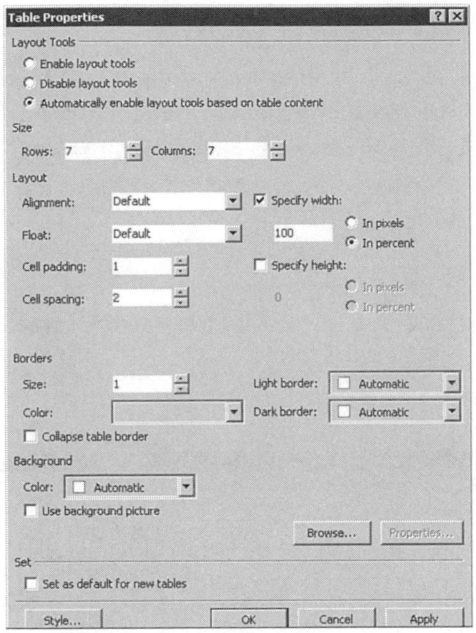

> **NOTE**
>
> If a picture is placed in a table larger than the selected pixel size or percentage, most browsers will present the entire graphic, ignoring the table size definitions.

All content that can be placed on a Web page can be placed within a table. In addition, tables and cells can have separate background images and colors.

> **TIP**
>
> Mastery of tables is mastery of Web design. Spend some time in this chapter and practice layout processes and approaches using tables.

There are no limits to the cells that can be placed within a table. In addition, tables can be placed within tables for additional design power and flexibility.

If you notice that FrontPage seems to be overriding your cell specifications, see "Cell Content Is Bigger Than Defined" in the "Troubleshooting" section at the end of this chapter.

In Figure 10.6, the Table Properties dialog box was shown. In Figure 10.7, the Cell Properties dialog box is shown. Notice the difference in variables between the two. Where the Table Properties dialog box sets issues that will affect the entire table, the Cell Properties dialog box can be used to better define specific areas of the table.

> **NOTE**
>
> If you tell a table to do one thing and a cell to do another (such as show background color), the cell will win.

Figure 10.7
Cells have fewer variables for design than tables do, as seen in the Cell Properties dialog box.

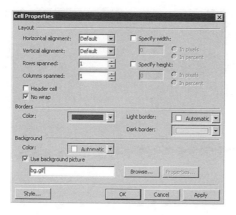

CELL PROPERTIES

You are not confined to table modification in FrontPage. You can also edit numerous cell properties. The Cell Properties dialog box shown in Figure 10.7 lets you set the following options for each cell:

- **Horizontal** and **Vertical Alignment**—Relates to the content within the cell and how it is aligned.

- **Rows** and **Columns Spanned**—This option will force the cell to expand to the number of rows and columns selected pushing the existing cells outward into the table. This will not delete any other cells in the table; it will simply push them out in the directions supplied through this option. Figure 10.8 shows a 5 by 5 table. Figure 10.9 shows the same table with the highlighted cell spanned two cells in each direction.

Figure 10.8
A simple 5 by 5 table.

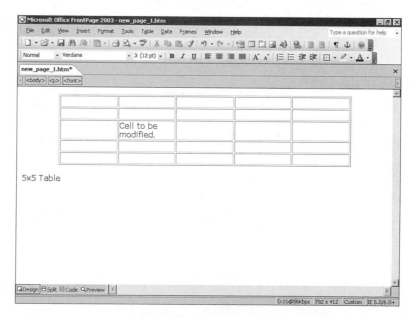

Figure 10.9
The table from Figure 10.10 with a cell pushed out to span two cells in each direction.

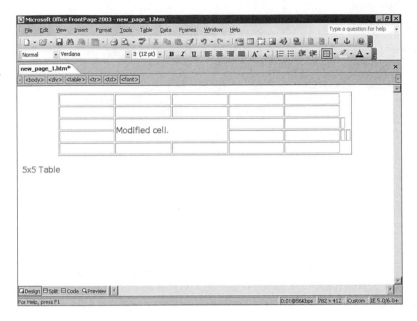

- **Header Cell**—This check box lets you set a cell as a header cell. This option has no direct effect in page layout, but will send the metadata to any element that might read the content accordingly, such as Microsoft Excel. If the **No Wrap** check box is set, cell content will not be allowed to wrap, resulting in an expanded cell if content exceeds the cell size.

- **Specify Height** or **Width**—Similar to the Tables Properties dialog box, these variables are set as either pixel or percentage specific.

- **Borders** and **Background**—These areas are the same as the Tables Properties dialog box.

PIXELS VERSUS PERCENTAGES

When tables are used in the Web page layout process, basic layout effects can be produced by setting table and cell sizes as percentages of page or table layout. This has the additional benefit of providing page content that "works" despite browser screen size. In Figure 10.10, a three-celled table is used to produce a two-column effect by giving the columns 45% of the table size and giving the middle spacer area a 10% setting.

NOTE

If you are going to assign cells based on a percentage of screen size, make sure that the total percentage adds up to 100%.

Tables can also be sized by pixel, providing an exact sizing element for page design. Although it gives the ability to provide a specific design specification, odd effects can result when a browser sized differently than the page views the page content. Pixel-specific page design should be used with this issue in mind.

Figure 10.10
A three-celled table is used to provide a two-column effect that will work on any screen size.

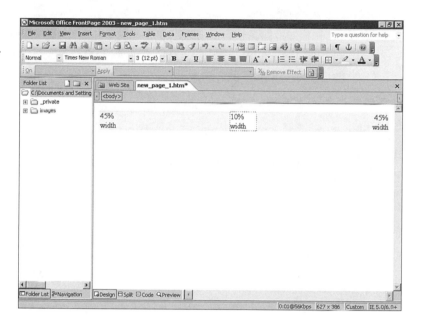

Effective page design can be accomplished with a careful combination of pixel and percentage specific sized cells. In Figure 10.11, such a combination is used to set the menu bar to a specific pixel size while allowing the rest of the page to fix the browser window.

Figure 10.11
The menu bar to the left of this table has a specific pixel size. Content to the right of the menu bar will expand as the page does because the table is set to 100%.

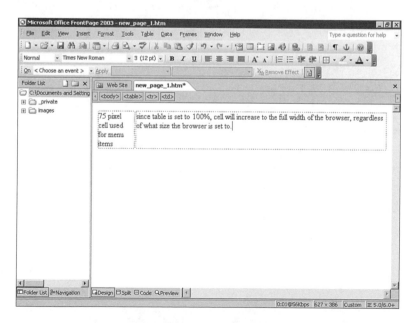

10

TABLE PROPERTIES

The Table Properties dialog box shown previously in Figure 10.6 enables you to set the following options for each table:

- **Layout Tools**—This area lets you toggle between the automatic enabling or disabling of layout tools. Layout tools are discussed later in this chapter but are the means to place tables and cells at precise pixel locations in a paradigm similar to traditional page layout. Also provides an option to enable tools based on site content.

- **Size**—Sets rows and columns for each table.

- **Alignment**—Sets specific alignment properties for the table. If a table is less than 100% the size of the screen, the Alignment variable will determine whether the table is aligned to the left, right, or center of the screen. If default is set, the table will align with the content surrounding it.

- **Float**—This dropdown menu lets you set how the content within the page floats. The Float option sets the way that table elements flow around the table (if the table is not as wide as the Web page). In the Float box, click the float setting you want.

- **Cell Padding and Spacing**—Represent the pixel separation between the borders of the table and the content within it. When set to 0, table content will line up directly against any table border.

- **Specify Width and/or Height**—Provides the means to set table width and height (either in pixel or percentage).

- **Borders**—This area lets you set the size and color of the table border. You can also choose from light and dark border options through the two dropdown menus. A check box lets you decide if you'd like to collapse the table border. A collapsed border is a border with a single line, not two lines with spaces between them.

- **Background**—Lets you choose a background color or picture for the table. Use the Browse button to locate an image file for use as a background.

The last check box in the Table Properties dialog box enables you to request that FrontPage set all tables on that page with the same variables.

THE TABLES TOOLBAR

In some cases, most table and cell requirements can be set through the Insert Table button and modification of the table and cell properties as described previously. FrontPage also provides additional table and cell modification and creation through the Tables toolbar, shown in Figure 10.12.

Figure 10.12
The Tables toolbar provides numerous options for table creation and modification.

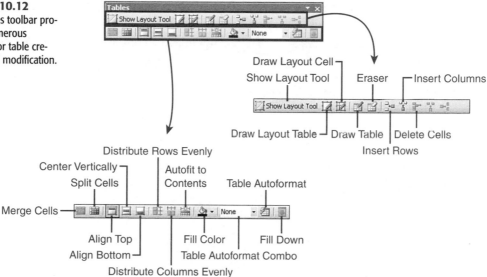

Each of the buttons in the Tables Tools bar are as follows (from left to right):

- **Show Layout Tool**—Toggles the layout tool on and off.
- **Draw Layout Table** and **Draw Layout Cell**—Give you the tools to develop layout tables and cells. These tools are discussed later in this chapter.
- **Draw Table**—This tool gives you the ability to draw a single celled table anywhere on your Web page.
- **Eraser**—This tool lets you erase a table's sides or cell borders within a table.
- **Insert Rows** and **Insert Columns**—Add the desired elements to an existing table.
- **Delete Cells**, **Merge Cells** and **Split Cells**—Additional cell management tools that act as their titles describe.
- **Align Top**, **Center Vertically**, and **Align Bottom**—All position text within a single cell.
- **Distribute Rows Evenly** and **Distribute Columns Evenly**—Can take a table of multisized cells and clean them up.
- **Autofit to Contents**—Sizes a cell based on contents over the developer's original input.
- **Fill Color**—Sets the fill color for the cell you are working in.
- **Table Autoformat Combo**—Tells FrontPage to autoformat your table based on the style selected from the combo box.

- **Table Autoformat**—This button activates the Table Autoformat tool.
- **Fill Down** and **Fill Right**—These buttons tell FrontPage to fill content down the cell or to the right of the cell accordingly. The Fill Right button only appears if multiple cells (side by side) are selected.

Another option for modification and creation is in the Layout Tables and Cells task pane, described later in this chapter.

USING THE DRAWING AND ERASE TOOLS

Selecting the Drawing tool (table and cells) replaces your pointer with a pencil-like icon. You can use this tool to "draw" a table or cell on your screen, as can be seen in Figure 10.13.

Figure 10.13
The drawing tool can be used to quickly draw a table of any size in Design view.

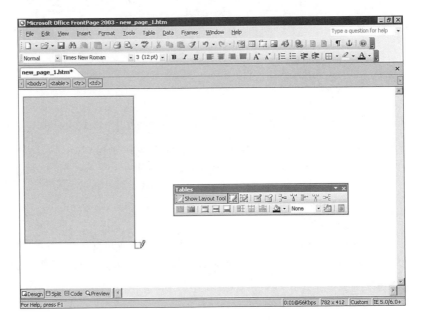

When the Erase tool is selected, the pointer is replaced with an eraser icon that can be used to "erase" cell and table borders. This results in two tables or cells merging with each other and is used to produce additional layout effects. An example of this can be seen in Figure 10.14. It is essentially the same as merging cells.

Figure 10.14
The Erase tool is used to erase the fourth cell border in a table, producing a single cell in that area of the table.

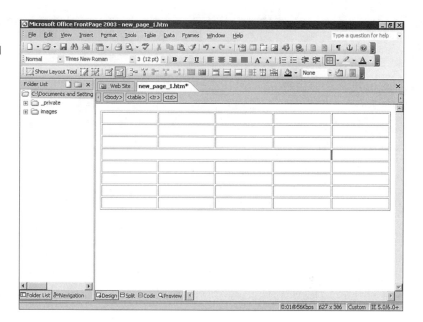

USING LAYOUT TABLES

With FrontPage 2003, Microsoft introduces the concept of the layout table and layout cell. In short, they are tools for doing pixel specific layout from within FrontPage. This approach to Web design was standard in several other Web development products, and it is great to see this toolset added to FrontPage 2003.

The Layout Table is the framework for a specific page layout made up of different regions made up of layout cells. As a result, FrontPage doesn't handle them the same way it handles traditional tables. At the core, a layout table is the same as a regular one-celled table, but FrontPage ads a `<!-- MSTableType="layout" -->` tag to identify it as such. You can edit the properties of layout tables the same way regular tables are updated. The tag has no effect on the rendering of your site, and it is there so that FrontPage can identify it as a layout table and offer the appropriate program support.

The layout tool shows the exact pixel size of all layout tables and cells. Figure 10.15 shows a layout table with the tool turned on. Use the table tool to get an exact view of your site down to the pixel level and make additional layout decisions accordingly.

Layout cells are the building block to a layout table. They can either be drawn with the draw layout cell tool or inserted automatically when the Layout Tables and Cell task pane is used.

Height and width is set in a layout table cell, regardless of whether you set one specifically. The implications of this issue are discussed later in this chapter.

Figure 10.15
The Layout Tool shows the exact pixel size of each element in a layout table. Clicking any of the numbers attached to the table will let you further set table elements.

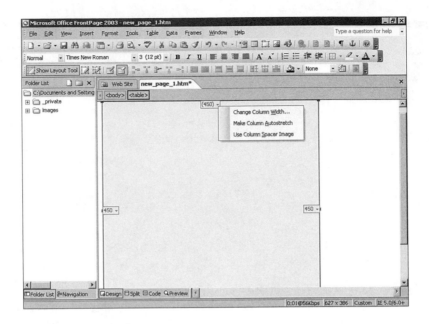

LAYOUT TABLES AND CELLS TASK PANE

The Layout Tables and Cells task pane, seen in Figure 10.16, provide the tools and means to develop an entire layout table.

Figure 10.16
The Layout Tables and Cells task pane provides the tools needed to create right layout tables.

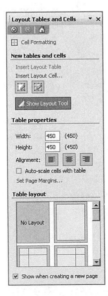

The three areas of the pane and what they do are described below.

INSERTING NEW TABLES AND CELLS

The Insert Layout Table text link in the New Tables and Cells area of the Layout Tables and Cells task pane will add a layout table to the page your are working in.

> You can edit the table size through the Table Properties dialog box.

The Insert Layout Cell text link opens the Insert Layout Cell dialog box, seen in Figure 10.17. You can set all aspects of a layout cell through this interface.

Figure 10.17
The Insert Layout Cell dialog box lets you insert layout cells into your layout table through an easy text interface.

The Draw Layout Table or Draw Layout Cell buttons let you create layout elements with a simple drawing interface. These are the same tools as found in the Tables toolbar described earlier in this chapter.

The Show Layout Tool button toggles the Layout Tool on and off.

TABLE PROPERTIES

The Width and Height boxes in the Table properties area of the Layout Tables and Cells task pane let you modify the size of the table through a simple text interface.

The alignment buttons let you set the alignment of the table against the page it is located on.

TABLE LAYOUT

The Table layout area of the Layout Tables and Cells task pane lets you select a page layout template from a number of preset options. You aren't forced to use these layout options, but they do provide a great starting point for most table layout designs.

TIP

> The table layout templates provided by FrontPage are actually quite good and provide a number of solid options for page design through this method. Consider using them in the design process. (They are considerably better than the other templates provided by Microsoft.)

CELL FORMATTING TASK PANE

The Cell Formatting task pane, seen in Figure 10.18, contains most of the tools that make layout tables so powerful. It is actually made up of three different parts, all accessible through the first three text links in the task pane. It is accessed by clicking the Cell Formatting option on the Layout task pane.

Figure 10.18
The Cell Formatting task pane lets you set all aspects of any layout cell in a layout table.

EDITING AND CONFIGURING LAYOUT TABLES

As with most elements of a FrontPage Web site, a right-click of a layout table or cell will let you open one or more dialog boxes for properties associated with the area right-clicked. Tables, layout tables, cells, and layout cells are no different. To edit or configure any element of a table or cell (regular or layout), right-click the element and make the appropriate selection from the menu.

CELL PROPERTIES AND BORDERS

The Cell Properties and Borders page of the Cell Formatting task pane, seen in Figure 10.19 lets you set a number of cell-specific options.

The Layout Cell Properties area lets you set traditional cell formatting:

Option	Action
Width, Height, Padding	Let you set exact cell specifications.
VAlign	Sets the vertical alignment of the cell's content.
BGcolor	Lets you set the background color of the cell.

Figure 10.19
The Cell Properties and Borders page lets you set some new features to your layout cell.

The Borders area is new to FrontPage 2003 and lets you set cell borders similar to what is traditionally seen in other products such as Microsoft Excel, PowerPoint, and Word. You can set the width and color of each border and toggle on/off which locations of the cell you would like to place the borders on. Figures 10.20 and 10.21 show a simple cell set with a left and right border and how that effect looks in Internet Explorer.

CAUTION

At publication time, this feature was still a bit "buggy." We hope everything was fixed at final release, but don't say that we didn't warn you.

NOTE

Each of the images in this section is very simple in nature to show you the specific elements that can be accomplished through these tools. In Figure 10.28 at the end of this section, we show the type of effects these tools can accomplish.

The Margins area lets you set the margins for a cell.

NOTE

Borders are done *external* to the cell in new cells. If you placed padding on the cell, it will pad from the newly created cells that hold the borders.

Figure 10.20
A cell in Design view is given two borders with the Cell Formatting dialog box. Compare this with Figure 10.21.

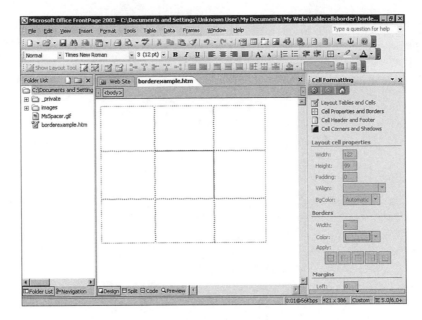

Figure 10.21
The page seen in Figure 10.20 as displayed in Internet Explorer.

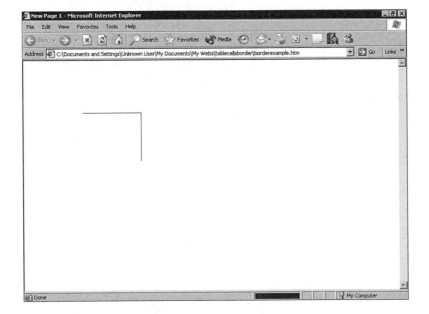

 If you find getting your layout cell effects to "take" is harder than expected, *see "Layout Cell Effects" in the "Troubleshooting" section at the end of this chapter.*

 If you find your shadow effects are skewed after editing them, *see "Shadow Effects Went Bad" in the "Troubleshooting" section at the end of this chapter.*

CELL HEADER AND FOOTER

The Cell Header and Footer page of the Cell Formatting task pane, seen in Figure 10.22, lets you add header and footer information to any layout cell.

Figure 10.22
You can add Cell Header and Footer information to a cell.

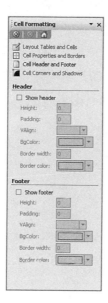

Any content can be added to a cell header or footer, and the background color and border can also be set through this interface. In Figure 10.23, a cell with a footer using a grey background is set.

Figure 10.23
A small footer for the cell is set with a grey background by using the Cell Header and Footer page of the Cell Formatting task pane.

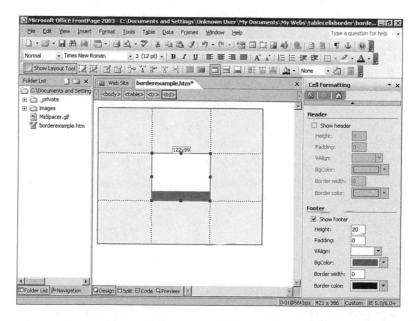

CELL CORNERS AND SHADOWS

The most interesting effects that can be added to a layout cell are a corner or shadow. Both effects are visually impressive and can easily be added with the Cell Corners and Shadows page of the Cell Formatting task pane (see Figure 10.24).

Figure 10.24
The Cell Corners and Shadows page of the Cell Formatting Task Pane lets you add shadows and corners to any layout table cell.

The Corners effect adds one or more curved corners to a cell element. This helps reduce the impact of the normally squared corners of any table or cell. This effect can be seen in Figure 10.25.

NOTE
In addition to the corner graphics, you can use a custom corner image through this interface.

The other effect provided via the Cell Corners and Shadows page is the Shadows effect. The Shadows effect places a number images around the cell as specified, producing an impressive basic 3D effect. An example of this can be seen in Figure 10.26.

In addition to the application and color of the shadow effect, the width and softness of the shadow can be set through this interface.

Figure 10.25
A curved corner is added to a layout cell.

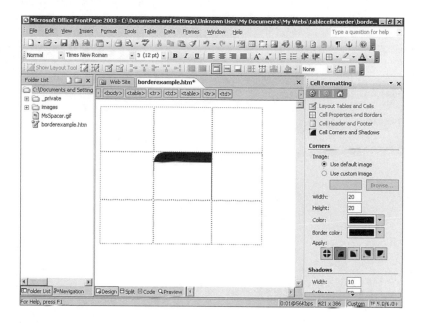

Figure 10.26
A shadow placed against a layout cell produces a simple 3D effect.

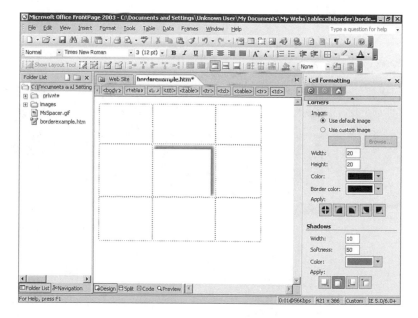

It is important to note that shadows and borders can be used together for an interesting effect. An example of this is seen in Figure 10.27.

Figure 10.27
A shadow and border are used together to provide an artistic effect.

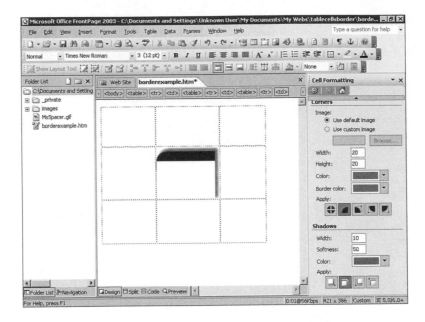

PUTTING IT ALL TOGETHER

In Figure 10.28, a Web page is shown in Internet Explorer that uses a number of the previously shown effects to produce an impressive three-dimensional frame that stands out.

Figure 10.28
Multiple cell border and shadow effects were used to produce the advertising cell to the right.

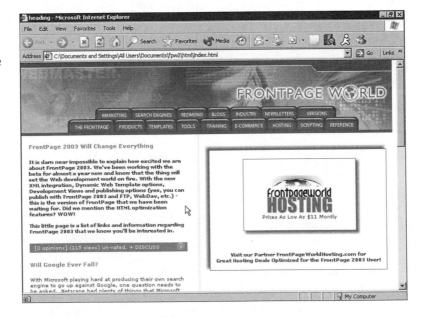

The combination of all these tools can produce the look and effect your are aiming for. Spend some time practicing each of these effects individually, and you will find that you are producing rich layout effects in no time at all. For reference purposes, Figure 10.29 shows the HTML behind the effect shown in Figure 10.28.

Figure 10.29
The HTML behind the layout table effect shown in Figure 10.28.

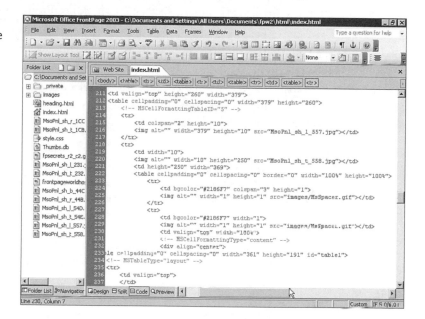

10

Table Layouts for Dynamic Web Templates

Because FrontPage layout tables and cells provide a powerful controlled environment for developing Web pages, they also make great tools for the design and implementation of FrontPage Dynamic Web Templates.

This is exactly what Microsoft created them for—so go ahead and take advantage of this powerful combo.

You can set each cell as an editable region right in FrontPage and quickly save your work as a new Dynamic Web Template.

→ For more on FrontPage 2003's Dynamic Web Templates, **see** "Dynamic Web Templates," **p. 411**.

CONSIDERATIONS FOR USING LAYOUT TABLES AND CELLS

Any developer who uses layout tables and cells needs to be aware of, and consider, the following issues in the Web design process.

The layout cell effects demonstrated in this chapter aren't simple shadow and border images similar to a PowerPoint or Excel document. FrontPage adds a great deal of additional HTML to create more table and cell elements where these effects are added as graphic files. It is an impressive piece of programming, but the implications of such an approach need to be considered.

A number of nontraditional browsers present table content in different ways. Because this effect results in multiple cells, the potential for distortion needs to be taken into consideration. In addition, the accessibility issues for such an approach need to be examined as well.

→ For more on the accessibility issues and Web design, **see** "FrontPage's Accessibility Features," **p. 235**.

The second issue, although not specific to layout tables and cells, is in the forcing of the pixel size of a screen layout. When a browser sets content to be delivered at a screen resolution larger than is capable on the viewing device, the browser must either shrink the content or require left-right scrolling. Both effects are most often less than desirable and should be considered during the development process.

TIP

> When a layout table is implemented and a specific size for your content is set, your pages are presented how the browser "thinks" you'd like them presented, and not in your original vision. Keep this in mind throughout the design process.

The final consideration relates to the simple concept of font types and sizes. Because layout cells are set both x and y, they don't expand (as traditional cells do) when the content is more than can be contained in the cell. If a user sets her browser for a different font type or sets her screen for a bigger font size, some content won't be contained in the cell as specified. A number of users set their screen to show fonts in a larger size that can't be tracked through traditional server log files, so the impact of this can't be completely understood.

→ For more on the use of fonts in Web design, **see** "Developing the Basic Page: Page Properties, Text, Lists, and Hyperlinks," **p. 77**.

FUN WITH TABLES AND CELLS

For the new user of any Web development package, the fuss made about tables and cells in this chapter might seem a bit overkill. Why should you care? How does this really help the Web development process (instead of making it more complicated)? We'll answer those questions here.

The first issue is simply one of layout. Although you can set text and picture to appear next to each other through a slight massaging of HTML, the most basic of layout capabilities require tables to provide the desired effects. Because tables and cells can (and more times than not, most often do) contain pixel-less borders, only the developer knows they exist.

As you dive deeper into these layout issues, you will realize the simple fact that tables and cells let you do some pretty fun things with your site—hence the name of this section.

We'll look at how included content and tables provide a very simple, yet powerful, content management system. We'll also look at fun background image and color effects. We'll even examine some border effects that don't require the more complicated layout tables.

USING INCLUDED CONTENT

The Included Content Web component lets you pull HTML files from within your Web site and place them within your Web page. Popular uses for this feature include, but are not limited to, navigational elements and page headers/footers. By producing a single version of these included content files and then reusing the content throughout your site, a simple change to the original source files can result in the automatic updating of an entire site.

→ For more on the Included Content Web component, **see** "Using Web Components, Shared Borders, and Link Bars," **p. 167**.

In some instances, included content needs no layout because it contains layout content of its own. Examples of this might be a header or footer included file. A simple include at the top and bottom of the page can result in the desired effect.

Sometimes, you will want to place the content in a specific area of the page and have specific requirements for size, position, and so on. This is done by placing content in, or around, tables.

In Figure 10.30, a simple table with four cells is shown. A user could quickly insert header, footer, and menu included content. Not that this isn't a layout table (or layout cells), but the same approach could be used for these as well.

Figure 10.30
A simple table with four cells is used to contain header, footer, menu, and content information.

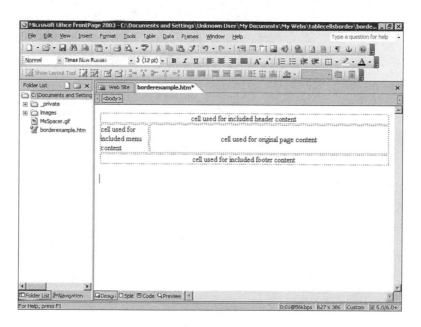

TIP

> The power provided by included text in tables and cells can't be overemphasized. Instead of having to create content one page at a time, you can create content used on multiple pages while maintaining a site-wide look and feel.

ADDING BACKGROUND IMAGES AND COLORS

Both tables and cells (layout and regular) can contain their own background colors or images. This can be used to produce additional effects on your page that can't be done any other way. In addition, the ability to put a background color in a table or cell enables a certain emphasis effect as the eye is drawn to color. Place important content in a color table or cell, and the user has a much better chance of viewing it. Figure 10.31 shows the Cell Properties dialog box with the option to add a background image to a cell selected, and Figure 10.32 shows the editing of a table to include a yellow background in the Table Properties dialog box.

Figure 10.31
The Cell Properties dialog box lets you set either a background color or image. In this example, a background image is set.

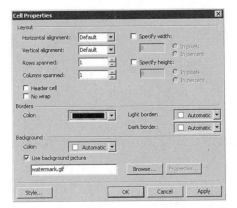

NOTE

> Not all browsers support table (or cell) background color or images.

BORDER EFFECTS

Layout cells, although impressive, aren't the only option for border effects. If you know that your audience is going to be viewing your content on machines that can quickly render these effects, go ahead and use them (and impress your audience with the effects). If your audience is using older machines or simpler browsers (or you are creating alternate content for them), consider alternative options.

If you'd like to produce some border effects that are more HTML related than graphic intensive, there are a number of ways to do so:

Figure 10.32
Set a background color or image through the Table Properties dialog box.

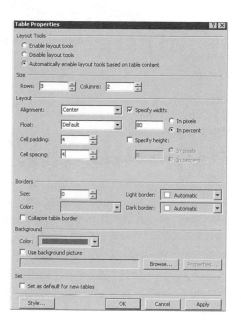

On the most basic level, any table or cell can have a border that helps separate content elements away from others. The properties dialog boxes for both tables and cells will let you add border thickness and color with a few clicks of the mouse.

As shown previously, the border size and coloring can be set in any table. Cells can be placed within a table and given their own border and color options. This effect can be repeated over and over again to give the effect desired. Although the black and white nature of this book can't show the subtlety of such an effect, simple experimentation by the user will quickly provide interesting results.

The other added benefit of producing border effects this way is that browsers will have little to no problem rendering the HTML on any screen type. If needed, they'll simply ignore the border-related HTML and present the content without the GIF images produced through the other approach.

TROUBLESHOOTING

TABLES DON'T PRINT

I used tables to design a site that looks great on any screen—including 800¥600, but when I print the page, the printer cuts it off at the right. How can I fix this?

Just because a Web page can be viewed on a screen without left-right scroll doesn't automatically mean that it can be printed off on a printer with no problems. Just like Web browsers, printers have their own limitations that have to be taken into account as well. In addition, different Web browsers print Web pages differently. Surprisingly, there is still no industry standard for printing Web pages yet.

You can see how many pixels your printer will print and set your pages to match that specific size. Realize that this approach will only work with the paper size and orientation you test again, but it is a good place to start.

CELL CONTENT IS BIGGER THAN DEFINED

I set a layout cell for a specific size and made sure that the text included in the cell fit the cell on the browser systems installed on my computer. I added a shadow effect for extra emphasis. A friend's browser shows the content as desired, but the cell is extended and the shadow effect is only shown on part of the cell. It looks terrible—what do I do?

If the user sets her browser to show fonts larger than normal and there is no "free" space in the cell to expand to, most browsers will increase the cell size to fit the additional content. Because the shadow effects were set for the smaller cell size, the extended size won't have the coverage resulting in the effect you are describing. Sorry, there is no way around this issue, and it is one of the limitations of using borders with set sizes.

One way around this is to produce your own shadow effect graphic to the specific size you want and place that as the background image in your cell.

TEXT TOUCHING BORDERS

The text in my cells and tables is shown right up against the border of my tables and cells. The effect is less than attractive. What can I do?

The padding variable for both tables and cells sets a pixel distance between the border of any cell or table and the content contained in it. Set your padding number to a desirable pixel size, and the browser will render the content accordingly.

LAYOUT CELL EFFECTS

In an attempt to produce a nice layout effect, I set the spacing for a cell in my table to only be 100 pixels. The content in that same cell takes more than 50% of my screen. Why won't FrontPage accept my sizing request?

If the content in a cell exceeds the set size of the cell, the cell will stretch to contain all the content. This is an HTML issue, not a FrontPage one. Any image or collection of letters without a space (such as very long URL) will cause this to happen.

SHADOW EFFECTS WENT BAD

I placed a shadow effect on a layout cell, and it looks great. Now that I added additional content to the cell, the shadow is broken up and looks terrible. How can I fix this.

When a shadow is placed on a cell, it is based around the exact size of the cell with the existing content within it. If the size of that cell is increased, you will need to redraw the shadow to keep the effect.

FRONT AND CENTER: SHOULD YOU TABLE THE LAYOUT TABLE?

I love tables. I always have. It was the realization of table's powers (paired with included content files) that let me move Web development from a page-a-day process to a site-a-week method. Tables are part of the reason I am such a fan of FrontPage—the product makes it so easy to add and edit table content as needed.

I love fancy graphics and sites that look like a million bucks. A picture does speak a thousand words, and the Web is still king at delivering such content. Look at the screenshots again in this chapter…wow, impressive stuff.

When I surf the Internet on anything other than my desktop, I'm always amazed at the ways "other" browsers handle tables and the like. There is the Pocket PC method of trying to successfully re-create the browsing experience on a much smaller window; there is the Eudora Web approach on the Palm pilots of just taking the text; and there is the HipTop approach to ignoring tables and presenting data as one long scroll without the annoying left-right issues that plague the Pocket PC approach. I won't even mention WAP browsers or assistive browsing devices and how they might handle these effects.

Layout tables help you produce gorgeous results. There is no denying that. They trump some of the other Web development products with their effects, and that is going to make a lot of FrontPage users very happy. When used in conjunction with the new dynamic Web template features, FrontPage now offers a very powerful page layout system unlike anything else out there.

The problem is simple: Layout tables assume a world where people are surfing the Internet on the screen size associated with a desktop or laptop computer. They just play havoc with the nontraditional browsers, and, well, those nontraditional browsers are seeing their numbers inch up every day.

I'm not quite sure what to do about these issues. All the great new technologies seem to come with their reality-set limitations. Why can't we have the good without the bad?

First of all, I'll admit, I am going to use layout tables and cells in Web design. They are just too impressive and too powerful not to do so. You will see at lot of them at FrontPage World very soon.

But, and I say this with hesitance, I'm also going to examine what I need to do with users who are using browsers and fonts in which such effects will be more of a nuisance than a help.

I have been looking at the Check Browser behavior as a means to make sure my traffic goes to the pages that work best for them.

I suggest that you do the same.

10

CHAPTER **11**

Enhancing Web Sites with Frames

In this chapter

USE OF FRAMES IN WEB DESIGN

Frames were a technology introduced by Netscape in version 2 of its browser. This fairly old technology caught on quickly and has been steadily declining in use since introduction (and some dare say abuse). Numerous pros and cons exist for using frames in Web design, and we'll examine them here. We'll also take a look at how FrontPage handles frames and examine the newer technology of inline frames, as well as how to add them to your Web.

Navigation in a Web site is never an easy task. Giving users a means to quickly find their way through your site is the dream of every Webmaster and a simple requirement of good Web design. What is the point of a non-linear communication tool if people have to start from the beginning and work their way through?

WHAT ARE FRAMES AND WHY WOULD YOU USE THEM?

Frames enable the developer to divide a Web site into different sections, each with its own scrollbars and navigational capabilities (see Figure 11.1). Each section is called a frame because it "frames" a separate Web page. The total of the framed pages is called the *frameset*. A frameset allows for an easy navigation because each section (frame) behaves independently from the others.

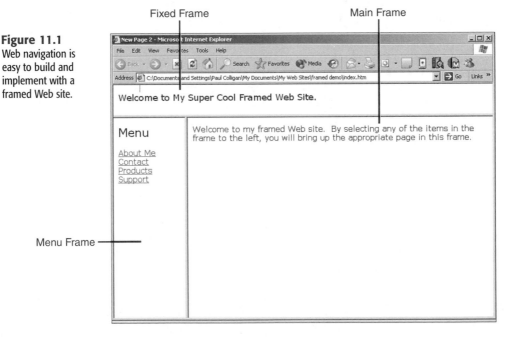

Figure 11.1
Web navigation is easy to build and implement with a framed Web site.

It is common for a developer to develop a manageable frameset for a site and then quickly produce a series of content pages for the main frame. Not having to focus on navigational elements for every page of a site can expedite the Web design process and provide an easy model for navigation.

You'll find that a frameset is very easy to create and implement in a Web site. No coding or scripting is required because FrontPage does everything needed through the FrontPage interface.

Why use frames in Web design?

- *They are very easy to design and implement.* Once a frameset is implemented, the developer can quickly create the rest of a site by simply adding links to pages as needed in the menu frame.

- *They are very easy for the user to navigate.* A framed Web page design is very easy for the user and leaves little room for mistake on the part of the reader.

WHEN NOT TO USE FRAMES

There are numerous reasons not to use frames in Web design:

- *Not all browsers support them.* Some browsers simply don't support frames. In addition, as the rise of browsers on smaller forms (such as cell phones) continues, there is simply no way to implement frames, and therefore they don't. Nothing is more frustrating than designing a Web page or site that isn't available to all of your readers.

- *They wreak havoc with the search engines.* Because framed pages are all individual pages, many search engines will index each of these pages individually and might not put them together the "right way" if someone comes through their index.

- *They are very hard to print.* The idea of a paperless society is nice but is simply not reality. People print Web pages that they can later reference; and printing framed pages is not only very complicated, but also hard to put together in a way that makes sense in a printed paradigm.

- *Hyper linking within Frames is much more complicated than the traditional hyperlink.* If implemented incorrectly, you can link to a framed site within a framed site, producing a never-ending spiral known by some as "frame hell."

- *Technologies now exist that make frames unnecessary.* This is the most important reason to shy away from frames. The benefits afforded by frames can be easily replicated through intelligent Web design. We'll examine this issue in more detail later in this chapter.

TIP

My *strong* opinion is that frames should not be part of modern Web design. The hassles considerably outweigh the disadvantages. Although I understand the benefits provided by frames, I am thoroughly convinced that you can get them through other means. You should still read this chapter through to fully understand the implications of using frames.

If that argument doesn't convince you, look at the top 100 sites in any list anywhere and tell me how many of them use frames.

11

CONSIDERATIONS WHEN USING FRAMES

If you must use frames, remember the following:

■ *You'll need to provide an alternative for browsers that don't support frames.* Telling users to update their Web browser to something that supports frames is not an option for many users (see Figure 11.2). If there is any option that your site might attract users with unsupportive browsers, you'll need to design your site in such a way that you can serve the information to them as well. If you find yourself designing for a project in which only one browser option is available (often the case in an intranet project), frames might be a viable option for you.

Figure 11.2
A frameset provides a default message for users unable to use frames. FrontPage's default message is shown here.

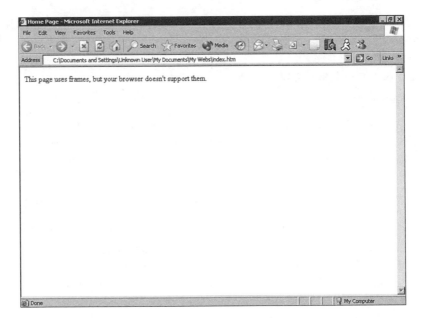

■ *You'll need to provide for search engines that won't provide for your site structure.* This can either be done with client-side scripting or a disclaimer on each of your content pages.

■ *You should provide printing directions.* If you might think that any of your users will print your site, you'll need to give them directions for doing so.

■ *Be careful to use the correct linking options when linking within frames.* You don't want to catch your users in "frame hell."

■ *You'll need to keep screen size in consideration.* Plenty of people are still surfing the Internet with 15-inch monitors. A frameset that might look perfect on your desktop might be unreadable on older display technology. Make sure to test your framesets for screen size compatibility.

 If you are having problems with your links opening the right content in the wrong frame, *see "Links within My Frames Are All Tweaked" in the "Troubleshooting" section at the end of this chapter.*

CREATING AND MANAGING FRAMES AND FRAMESETS

Framed pages are managed in a frameset. You can either create a frameset from scratch or edit an existing one. FrontPage 2003 provides a number of frameset templates that can easily be integrated into your site without having to design one of your own.

Content is added to a framed page the same way it is added to a normal page, directly through Design or Code view. Each frame has an independent page of content to edit through the FrontPage view of choice.

FrontPage handles frames in the same Design view environment it tries to handle most everything else. The only additions are the new buttons at the bottom of the Design view relating to the multiple sets of HTML (see Figure 11.3).

Figure 11.3
Designing with frames in FrontPage is easy because the Design view simply places each page you are editing within the frames.

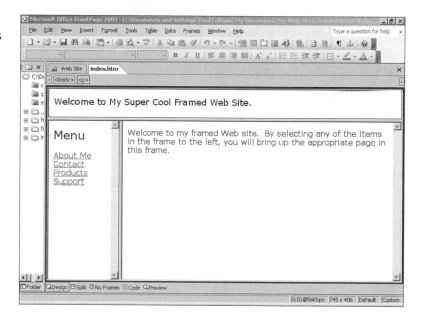

A frameset can be created using the Frames Pages tab in the Page Templates dialog box. Framesets are edited either through Design View interface or through the coding for the specific set. Content in the frameset is edited just like a normal page in FrontPage.

CREATING A FRAMESET

To create a frameset from within FrontPage 2003, open the Page Templates dialog box by selecting File, New, and selecting More Page Templates from the New Task Pane. Select the Frames Pages tab within the dialog box to view your options (see Figure 11.4). You will have 10 frameset options from which to work.

Figure 11.4
A series of predefined
framesets are made
available through the
Page Templates dialog
box. Pointing to any of
the options will give
you an estimate of the
layout.

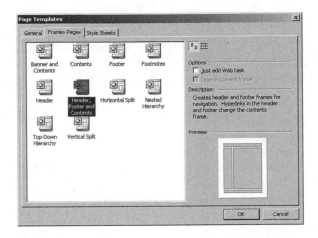

Select any of the framesets in the dialog box, and it will open in Design view. The framesets
provided in a standard install are as follows:

- **Banner and Contents**—Ideal for a framed site with a banner, a contents section (or
  menu), and a large main frame.

- **Contents**—Similar to Banner and Contents in purpose and functionality, but it doesn't
  include the Banner frame.

- **Footer**—Creates a large text frame with a footer frame below it. All links in the footer
  frame automatically affect the main frame.

- **Footnotes**—Contains a main frame with a small frame for footnotes beneath it. It is
  preset so that hyperlinks in the main page change the Footnotes frame.

- **Header**—Creates a simple navigation header over a larger framed main page. Links in
  the navigation header affect content in the main page.

- **Header, Footer and Contents**—Creates the four different described frames.
  Hyperlinks in the header and footer are preset to affect the contents frame.

- **Horizontal Split**—Splits the screen horizontally into two equal sized frames.

- **Nested Hierarchy**—Used for a nested information hierarchy. A left frame affects content in a footer frame that affects content in the main frame.

- **Top-Down Hierarchy**—Similar to the Nested Hierarchy frame, but works from a
  top-down approach.

- **Vertical Split**—Splits the screen vertically into two equal sized frames.

Microsoft has done a great job of figuring out pretty much any frameset requirement you
might have in these 10 options. There are very few reasons that anyone would need to create a frameset of their own.

 Once you've created your frames, if you find that they don't appear in the browser the way you
think they should, *see "My Frames Don't Look Right Online" in the "Troubleshooting" section at
the end of this chapter.*

EDITING A FRAMESET

You can edit the proportions of your frameset by placing your cursor over any of the elements, clicking and dragging the border of the frame to where you would like it to be. This is fine for an approximation of how the frameset should look.

You can also edit the specific numbers behind the frameset (either the pixel size of each frame or the screen percentage the frame will take) by selecting Code view. It will show the HTML behind the frameset, and you can adjust the numbers to your specific requirements. Another option is to select the Frame Properties option from the Frames Menu or right-click the frame you want to modify and select Frame Properties.

EDITING CONTENT WITHIN A FRAMESET

You'll note that when the initial frameset is developed, each frame has two buttons—Set Initial Page and New Page.

Set Initial Page will let you choose a previously existing Web page for that frame. Once entered, FrontPage will load that content into the page.

NOTE

> You can enter *any* address you want when setting the initial page, including sites not under your control. FrontPage will import that page into your frame. If you attempt to make any changes to the content, it will ask you to save the page. If you do not, it will call the page from the external source.
>
> If the content is behind a password protected site, you'll need to enter the login and password for FrontPage to access and import the content.

The New Page button will simply fill the frame with a blank page in Design view. You can then edit content in the frame the exact same way you would add the content to an unframed page. Each page in a frameset acts independently of the other pages.

Once you save your frameset, FrontPage will also prompt you to save any pages within the set.

ABOUT LINKING TO EXTERNAL CONTENT IN A FRAME

If you link to external content in a frame, you won't be able to edit that content in FrontPage and save your changes to the external site. If you make changes to external content in a frame, FrontPage will assume that you would like to save the changed content to your Web and treat the page as if you were selecting Save As from the File menu.

THE NO FRAMES VIEW

Selecting the No Frames view from FrontPage 2003 will, by default, show the message that will be presented to users who can't view frames on their browsers.

11

Figure 11.5
The No Frames view enables communication with a browser that doesn't support frames.

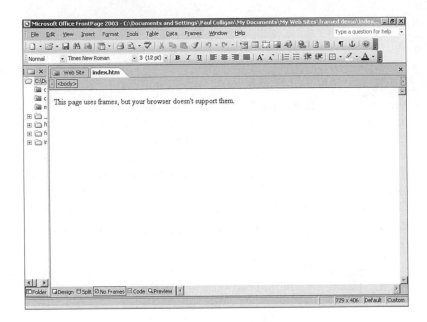

Consider editing the page to say something a little less sharp and give directions on how the visitor can access your content without frames.

SPLITTING FRAMES

Don't worry if you haven't created the perfect frameset before starting the design of your page. While in Design view, you can press and hold down the Ctrl key and drag any frame border. This will split that frame in two. You can repeat this as many times as needed.

To split a frame in two evenly divided columns or rows, select Split Frame from the Frames Menu.

LOCKING FRAMES

In some instances, you might want the user to be able to change the frames in your site based on his preferences. By default, the Frames pages product by FrontPage allows for this.

If you do not want the user to be able to change the way he views the frames on your site, you will need to lock those particular frames. Right-click from within a frame, select the Frames Properties dialog box and uncheck the Resizable in Browser option (see Figure 11.6).

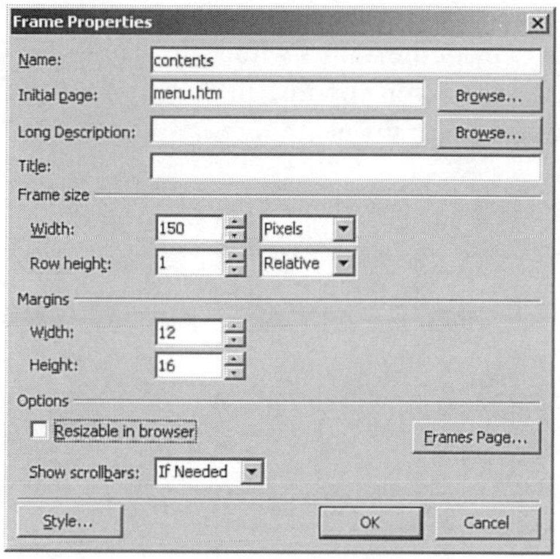

Figure 11.6
Unchecking the Resizable in Browser option in the Frame Properties dialog box will result in the frame being locked.

HYPERLINKING FROM WITHIN FRAMES

Hyperlinking within frames is not as easy as it is from one single-framed document to another. You insert the hyperlink either through the hyperlink button on the Standard toolbar or by selecting Insert, Hyperlink (Ctrl+K).

When hyperlinking within frames, you need to tell the browser which page to open up, but also you need to tell it where to put the page in the frameset. You can also tell the browser to instead open a frameless page or to generate opening a new window for the link.

Destinations within framed pages are called *targets*. All these options can be chosen from within the Target Frame dialog box (see Figure 11.7). To open the Target Frame dialog box, select the Target Frame button in the Insert Hyperlink dialog box.

Figure 11.7
The Target Frame dialog box lets you choose which frame a hyperlink will open in or if the link should open a new window.

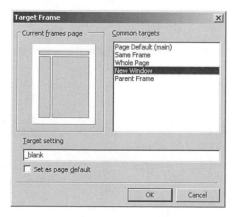

→ For more on hyperlink targets, **see** "Developing the Basic Page: Page Properties, Text, Lists, and Hyperlinks," **p. 77**.

Under the Current Frames Page area of the dialog box, you will note a diagram of your existing frames page. Selecting any of the frames within the dialog box will show you the name of that frame with the Target Setting option. In the example seen in Figure 11.8, the central frame on the site has been given the name *main*.

Figure 11.8
The frame selected in the Target Frame dialog box has been named "main" by default. You can change the name of the frame through this interface.

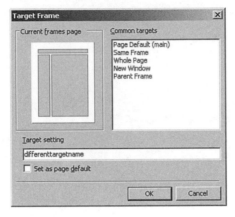

NOTE
"Page Default" and "main" are interchangeable in FrontPage when working with targets.

The Common targets area on the right side of the Target Frame dialog box lists the most common targets in that frameset. You can choose a target from the list, select one from the image of the framed page, or insert one of your own in the Target Setting field.

You can change the name of any frame through the Frame Properties dialog box or in the frameset HTML code using Code view.

NOTE
The Set as Page Default option in the dialog box will set all links to default to your selected option. This will speed up time if you need to enter a lot of hyperlinks into a single page.

If you want the Target Frame to be a blank new page, select New Window in the Common target list. If you want it to forgo the frameset and link to a window without frames, select Whole Page.

DELETING A FRAMESET

Because framesets are simply Web pages, they can be deleted as any other page. Find the page in Folder list or Web Site view and delete accordingly.

Remember that a frameset might have multiple pages associated with it that need to be deleted as well.

WORKING WITH INLINE FRAMES

Inline frames keep much of the same look and feel to traditional framed pages but are actually embedded in an existing page instead of being locked in a frame. They provide a great effect to Web design and solve some of the problems introduced by frames, but they still require considerations of their own. Inline frames are sometimes also called "floating frames" because of the way they seem to float over the page they are embedded in. Figures 11.9 and 11.10 show a regular frame versus an inline frame.

Figure 11.9
A traditionally framed page separates the content into two distinct sections.

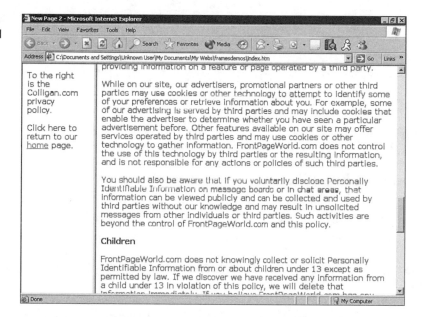

CAUTION

As with normal frames, not all browsers support inline frames. Take this into consideration when using them. In addition, most of the disadvantages of frames remain disadvantages in the inline frame option.

Inline frames are a very attractive design option, but they should be used with caution for these very reasons.

TIP

It is a popular practice for some to use inline (or regular) frames to frame content from another Web site within their own. If you are going to do so, it is a good idea to make it clear that the content you are framing comes from another site.

Figure 11.10
An inline framed page places the content directly into the Web page.

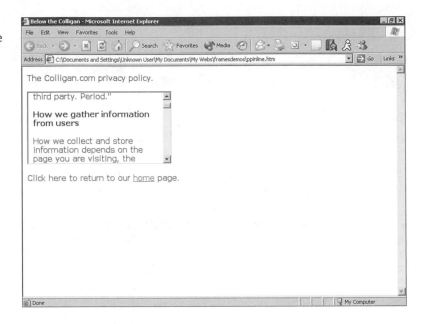

 If you can't see your inline frames in your browser, *see "Inline Frames Don't Work for Me" in the "Troubleshooting" section at the end of this chapter.*

CREATING AN INLINE FRAME

To create an inline frame, select where you would like to place the frame and choose Insert, Inline Frame. FrontPage will then place a holder for the inline frame on your page (see Figure 11.11).

Figure 11.11
An inline frame embeds directly onto an existing Web page. Note the Set Initial Page and New Page options are the same as in a regular frame.

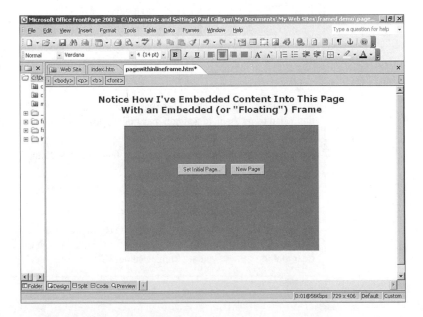

FrontPage offers two initial options when working with an inline frame: Set Initial Page and New Page. If you select the Set Initial Page option, FrontPage will ask you for the source of the page. The New Page option will let you create the content for the new frame directly in the FrontPage interface.

EDITING INLINE FRAME PROPERTIES

You can easily drag and drop the borders of an inline frame when working in Design view to get an approximation of how the frame will look on your Web page. You can also double-click on the inline frame to open the Inline Frame Properties dialog box to modify the frame more precisely (see Figure 11.12).

Figure 11.12
The Inline Frame Properties dialog box lets you edit every aspect of your inline frame.

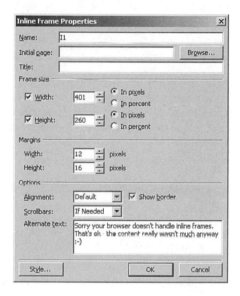

You can also modify the HTML for an inline frame in Code view.

ALTERNATIVES TO FRAMES

There is no arguing that frames provide easy menu options and a quick way to develop a multipage Web site with an easy to understand navigational structure. A similar effect can be accomplished a number of other ways, and FrontPage makes it considerably easy to do so:

- *Use a FrontPage Link bar to provide navigation through your site.* You can easily add the link bar to every page of content and then, as you update the options on the link bar, allow FrontPage to update the rest of the site accordingly.

- *Use an Included Page to provide a navigational element.* As you want to introduce new navigational options to your site, you can update the included file when needed and have the site navigational element update accordingly.

- *Use a Shared Border option to provide a navigational element.* As with the first two options, an update of the Shared Frame will update the site navigation as needed.

> **TIP**
>
> The Shared Border option mentioned here is one of the historically old FrontPage technologies that many believe should have been eliminated with this release of the product. The FrontPage Link bar and Included Page options mentioned previously are easier to implement, more powerful, and produce fewer options for error.

→ For more information on FrontPage Link bar, Included Page, or Shared Border options, **see** "Using Web Components, Shared Borders, and Link Bars," **p. 167**.

> **TIP**
>
> If you are using any of the options to provide an alternative navigational structure, don't feel limited with the location of the element. You can easily place the navigational tool to the left or right of any piece of content with the use of tables giving much the same effect offered by frames.

All three of these options are easy to integrate with FrontPage and don't carry the problems associate with designing with frames.

COMPREHENSIVE NAVIGATION WITHOUT FRAMES: AN EXAMPLE

In previous versions of FrontPageWorld.com, we used FrontPage Link bars to provide site navigation. They were placed in included files that updated the site as needed. This method of navigation was part of the site since we launched it. The "old" version of FrontPage World can be seen online at `http://oldfpw.frontpagelink.com`.

In Figure 11.13, you see the latest version of the FrontPage World Web site. Note the comprehensive navigation option at the top of the page. Again, no frames are used.

The top navigation for the site is accomplished through an included file called header.htm that can be easily updated in FrontPage and used to update the entire site. As new areas are added, the appropriate button will be added and the site will be updated.

In the future, we plan to update the site to use several Dynamic Web Templates for navigation options. When changes are made, we'll simply reapply the template to the necessary pages as needed. The end result is the same (and you won't be able to see any difference from the browser), but the additional options provided by DWTs make them very attractive.

All three of these approaches demonstrate how site navigation can be done without frames.

Figure 11.13
The new
FrontPageWorld.com
Web site provides an
easy to navigate inter-
face without the use of
frames.

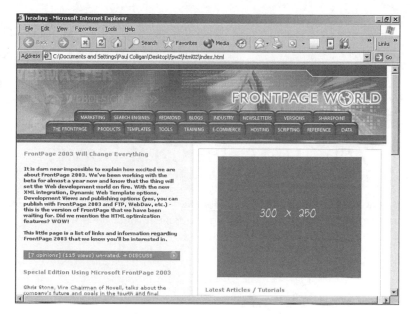

TROUBLESHOOTING

LINKS WITHIN MY FRAMES ARE ALL TWEAKED

When hyperlinks are clicked, pages show up in the wrong frame or new frames open up within other frames.

You need more than a traditional hyperlink when dealing with links from within frame pages. You have to be careful when entering links into framed pages because there are a number of options you need to consider. Review the "Hyperlinking from Within Frames" section of this chapter for more specific information.

INLINE FRAMES DON'T WORK FOR ME

I try to preview my page with an inline frame, and I get the alternate text instead of the inline frame.

Inline frames are not supported by all browsers, and some browsers and security programs will turn off inline frames by default. If your browser is giving the alternate text, something is either telling it not to accept inline frames or it simply isn't capable of doing so.

MY FRAMES DON'T LOOK RIGHT ONLINE

When I view my frames in FrontPage, the proportion is exactly how I want it to be. When I view it on a Web browser, everything is askew.

Although the FrontPage Design view is a close to WYSIWYG as possible, it is not always an accurate representation of what the user is going to see.

Many different issues affect how a user will view frames. These include screen resolution, font resolution, screen size, and if he has moved the borders to better suit his needs.

You should always preview your work on as many browsers as possible to make sure that what you've developed will work on different platforms.

→ For more information on viewing your site on different browser types, **see** "Developing the Basic Page: Page Properties, Text, Lists, and Hyperlinks," **p. 77**.

FRONT AND CENTER: THE GREAT FRAMES "CONTROVERSY"

It is probably obvious that I am not a big fan of frames, but I hope I have presented a clear picture of their implementation in FrontPage. FrontPage does provide a solid platform for designing with frames should the need ever arise.

The frames "controversy" is actually part of a larger dialog that every Web developer should consider: *At what point do I sacrifice technologies for my audience?*

In short, if you are going to use frames (inline or otherwise), you are going to need to either answer the issues the use of frames surfaces, ignore the issues, or come up with another option altogether. In the "Comprehensive Navigation Without Frames: An Example" section of this chapter, you can see a solid site navigational structure that provides all the navigation of frames without any of the problems.

I believe that there are alternatives for every benefit afforded by frames, making their implementation no longer an issue. I also feel strongly that time spent answering questions asked by the implementation of an obsolete technology is pointless.

You'll have to decide if you agree with me or not.

CHAPTER 12

FRONTPAGE'S ACCESSIBILITY FEATURES

In this chapter

ACCESSIBILITY ON THE WEB

Making Web sites accessible is big business. Some project that the cost of making the Internet accessible is more than was spent on the Y2K issue a few years back. With a societal and governmental push behind this issue, we can only assume that it will continue to remain an important issue for Web developers.

Legal issues are also associated with this topic. In some cases, inaccessible content created by a governmental agency is *against the law* and in almost all other cases, it just makes poor business sense. Accessibility is a big issue in Web design, and it is only going to get bigger as time progresses.

WHY CREATE AN ACCESSIBLE SITE?

The issue of making a Web site as accessible as possible is a desire of every Web developer—regardless of the design product they use. An important rising trend in Web design is an accessibility movement that hopes to ensure that all users, even those differently abled, can access online content. This movement has numerous big names behind it and has already seen one piece of federal legislation pass as a result. As the Internet continues to become more integrated into every aspect of our lives, this issue will only rise in importance.

Accessibility in Web design is an issue that developers should not ignore. In addition to the good neighbor benefits of making sure that your site can be viewed by everyone, legal issues are quickly rising to the front as well.

What makes a site accessible? A site is accessible when it can be accessed by anyone, regardless of their abilities. For instance, a visually challenged surfer might have his Web content read to him by a screen reader that requires specific layout approaches to be effective. Another example is making text versions of multimedia content available for the hearing impaired.

In the context of this chapter, the term "accessibility" in Web design regards making content accessible to people with disabilities.

 If you are worried that an accessible site translates as a "boring" site, see "Accessible Sites Are Boring" in the "Troubleshooting" section at the end of this chapter.

CREATING ACCESSIBLE SITES WITH FRONTPAGE

Until this release, FrontPage contained no tool related to creating accessible Web content, placing you on your own to develop pages the right way. New to FrontPage 2003 is an accessibility checker that will tell you how your page (or site) compares to the established accessibility guidelines. The checker will also produce an HTML report that provides specifics about how your site might be out of compliance with accessibility standards. The accessibility checker won't help you create an accessible Web page; it will only tell you if you have accomplished the task.

The task of, and responsibility behind, creating an accessible Web site still belongs to the developer.

TIP

> It will *always* be easier for a developer to create accessible Web pages during the design process than it will be to edit or update existing pages to make them accessible. Consider that fact when starting any Web design project.

NOTE

> We provide several links in this chapter to additional online content that will show you what you need to think about when trying to develop an accessible Web site.

In this chapter, we'll explain some basic issues of Web accessibility, show you how to use the accessibility checker and generate reports with it.

WHAT MAKES A SITE ACCESSIBLE?

No steadfast definition of what makes content accessible exists because the very definition of Internet content changes on a daily basis.

In short, there are two things a developer can do to make sure that his site is as accessible as possible:

- Verify that his site is W3C compliant.
- Verify that his site is Section 508 compliant.

TIP

> Although the accessibility movement loves to use acronyms and complicated standards to make its point, it is important to stress that the most important element of making an accessible Web page is *common sense*. If you are creating anything on the Web that requires any specific technology, screen size, or plug-in, it simply isn't accessible to those who don't have it. Certainly use the tools provided by FrontPage: Just remember to use your head as well.

W3C STANDARDS

W3C is short for the *World Wide Web Consortium*. The W3C is an international group of educational institutions and organizations that work with the Internet hoping to contribute in the process of making it a better place for all involved. Its goal is to guide the public into the use of standards ensuring that the Internet grows in a single inclusively beneficial direction rather than being splintered among competing technologies, standards, and companies.

How effective is the W3C? Is it necessary? Is it accomplishing its goals? These questions are hotly debated topics online, and we won't go into them here.

The W3C has provided the world a standard for making Web sites compliant. Because it is the only such standard available, many use it for determining the true accessibility of a Web site.

> **NOTE**
>
> The W3C's Web site can be accessed at `http://w3c.frontpagelink.com` and contains a lot of additional information on this topic.
>
> Archives of all the W3C-related mailing lists are also available online and can be found at `http://w3clists.frontpagelink.com`.

SECTION 508

Section 508 is a federal law requiring that federal agencies' electronic and information technology be accessible to people with disabilities. Under Section 508, all federal agencies are required by law to give the disabled public access to information that is comparable to the access available to all others. Because almost all publicly available information is provided through the Internet and on Web pages, the implication of Section 508 is obvious.

The impact of Section 508 is clear to any federal agency—its Web sites and Internet content must be accessible. States and large companies are quickly following suit with similar laws and regulations. It will only be a matter of time before most significant Internet publishers have specific requirements regarding accessible content.

Section 508 specifically covers the U.S. government accessibility standards for a wide range of technologies and informational sources. Section 508 resulted in the development of Web Content Accessibility Guidelines (WCAG). WCAG outlines specific priorities for making Web sites accessible to people with disabilities so that the process of making a Web site accessible can be prioritized.

WCAG issues are rated on a priority basis: Priority 1 issues *must* be addressed, Priority 2 issues *should* be addressed, and Priority 3 issues *may* be addressed.

> **NOTE**
>
> An article that discusses the prioritization issue in greater detail can be found at the W3C's Web site at `http://w3cpriorities.frontpagelink.com`.

COMMON ACCESSIBILITY PROBLEMS

The following is a short list of some of the most common accessibility problems in some of the most common elements of Web design. It is by no means an attempt at a comprehensive list but was created to help you understand the common issues surrounding building an accessible site.

- **Images and Multimedia**—If you don't have alternatives to your site images and multimedia, your site is inaccessible. You need to be able to communicate your media to people who might not be able to see it.

12

- **Frames**—If your site only uses frames, screen readers that can't read frames won't be able to view your site.

- **Tables**—If your content in your tables don't make sense to screen readers, it also won't make sense to the people reading your content with screen readers.

- **Scripts**—If you are using scripts to provide any form of functionality on your site (content generation), you will need to make sure that they work everywhere or provide options if they don't.

This list (and the implications of it) could continue for the remainder of this book and into dozens of others. At the end of this chapter, a significant resource list is included.

CHECKING A SITE FOR ACCESSIBILITY PROBLEMS

So, how does your site match up to the W3C standards? Would you be able to design pages for a federal agency if so contracted? The accessibility checker in FrontPage 2003 will help you figure out the answer to these questions.

USING THE ACCESSIBILITY CHECKER

Microsoft Office FrontPage 2003 features a new accessibility checker for Web pages (see Figure 12.1). By running the accessibility checker, you can discover issues that are identified as being in conflict with the WCAG (priority 1 or 2) and check for specific section 508 compliance.

Figure 12.1
The new Accessibility Checker can check pages for accessibility on a site-wide or page-at-a-time basis. This example shows the findings from the current page.

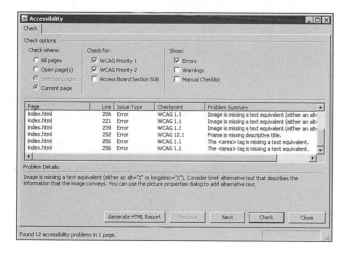

CHECKING FOR ACCESSIBILITY

To open the Accessibility dialog box, select Tools, Accessibility (or press F8).

CHECKING A SINGLE PAGE

To run the report from the page you are working on, open the dialog box and select Current Page. Choose what you want to check for and what you want the report to show.

Figure 12.2
You can choose to run the check on the current page you are working on, the pages currently open in FrontPage, a group of selected pages, or the entire open site.

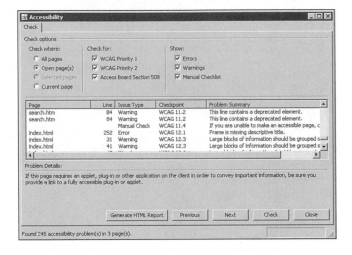

After you have chosen the option for your report, press the Check button. FrontPage will list everything it found in the search in the dialog box (see Figure 12.3).

Figure 12.3
Selecting a problem from the list will give you more information about that specific problem.

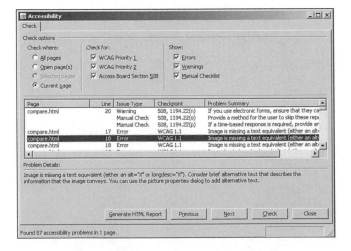

To see specifics about any of the findings of the report, select the item from the list. The checker will give you more details about the problem and, if possible, suggest solutions.

TIP

The checker can contain a great deal of content after a run. The checker is a separate element that you can enlarge or minimize as you would any other running program.

You can press any of the column headers in the report to sort by that column.

Note that when you select an issue from the list, FrontPage 2003 shows the site in Split view and highlights both the problem code and the specific area of the page the issue affects (see Figure 12.4).

Figure 12.4
When you select a problem from the list, FrontPage 2003 shows the affected areas in FrontPage.

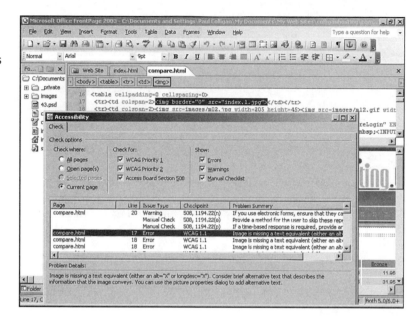

The Next and Previous buttons can be used to work your way through the entire list while highlighting the issues in the Web site.

> **NOTE**
> Many of the issues raised in the checker are Warnings that don't necessarily require a "fix" but are notations for issues and trends that you might need to pay attention to.

CHECKING A SERIES OF PAGES OR AN ENTIRE WEB

You are not stuck with checking your site a page at a time. You can use the accessibility checker to check as many or as few pages as you want (see Figure 12.5).

> **NOTE**
> Checking an entire site can take a great deal of time—especially if you are connecting to the site over the Internet.

12

Figure 12.5
You can choose to check all pages in a site, all open pages, all selected pages, or the page currently open. In this example, 200 problems were found in a 2-page Web site.

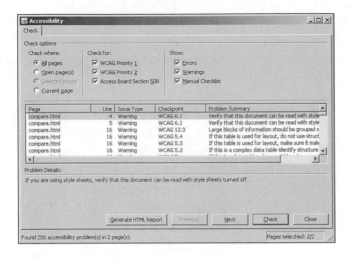

TIP

Running an entire site through the checker could result in some overwhelming results. Consider taking any task of making your Web site more accessible one page at a time.

If you are working with multiple pages, the checker will bring whatever page you are examining to the front after you click on any problem in the list.

GENERATING A REPORT

After the first check is run in the accessibility checker, the option to create a report is made available. If selected, a report is generated as a new page as seen in Figure 12.6.

12

Figure 12.6
The report generated by the Accessibility Checker is generated as a Web page from within FrontPage. Note the hyperlinks to supporting online documentation.

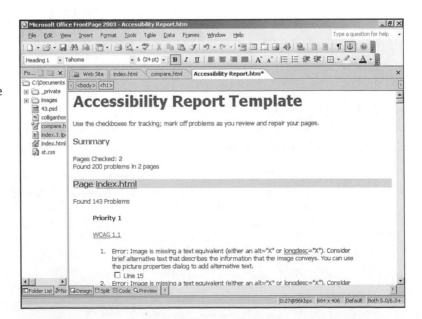

NOTE

You can easily run through the issues raised by the checker on an element-by-element basis without ever having to run a report. The Accessibility Checker can be run side-by-side with FrontPage as you take on each issue one at a time.

The report can then be saved to your site, sent via email, or printed off for easy reference.

TIP

The report created by the checker is downright boring and unattractive. Consider editing it slightly for great impact before passing it on to the people who need to see it. Nothing gets people to act faster than an official looking report.

After you have the report, you can use the content within to begin updating and repairing your Web site accordingly. The HTML version of the report actually hyperlinks to the Web documents that hold the standards the page is being checked against.

UPDATING YOUR SITE BASED ON THE REPORT

An aggressive user might want to run the report for an entire Web site and immediately start the process of going through the checklist that comes from the resulting report. This is not the recommended course of action.

TIP

There is no need to run reports on a site-wide basis. Starting with small strategic chunks will help divide up the process and result in stronger efforts.

In many cases, walking through the site on an issue-by-issue basis while running the checker (as described in the previous section) will let you fix each issue as it comes up.

A Web site is often made up of elements that are used throughout a site. Items, such as included files and menu bars, might be single files replicated thousands of times. Because a report looks at sites on a page-by-page basis, it won't recognize that fixing a single file might eliminate hundreds of items from the report.

→ For more on included files and shared borders, **see** "Using Web Components, Shared Borders, and Link Bars," **p. 167**.

TIP

A solid understanding of how your site is put together and a strategic approach to answering the issues raised in the report will assist greatly in a strategic response to report findings.

continues

continued

> One way to start such a project is by running the checker on your most commonly used pages. From there you can go deeper into your site and fine-tune your efforts. The 80/20 rule is certainly applicable here.
>
> Taking large projects like this one page or problem at a time will help speed up the process.

TIP

> Be careful with handing over a report to someone who doesn't understand the difference between warnings and errors. It would be easy for someone to misread a series of warnings as specific problems with a site resulting in unnecessary headaches.

 If you need a report that contains only errors, not warnings, see "Reports Without Warnings" in the "Troubleshooting" section at the end of this chapter.

WHERE TO GO FOR ADDITIONAL INFORMATION AND SUPPORT

The Internet is abuzz with great accessibility information and also contains solid examples of how sites can be made accessible while still maintaining an exciting look and feel.

TIP

> The accessibility issue is one of the hottest topics on the Internet right now. Even if you don't consider the accessibility issue to be something that specifically concerns your products or sites, bringing yourself up-to-date with the latest issues can only make you a better developer.

MICROSOFT ARTICLES

Microsoft has issued an article that contains specific design suggestions for using FrontPage to make a Web site more accessible. It was written for FrontPage 2002, but it contains information valuable to the FrontPage 2003 user. When Microsoft publishes a FrontPage 2003 version of the article, we'll update this link accordingly.

```
http://accessibilityarticle.frontpagelink.com
```

SECTION 508 RESOURCES

The U.S. government maintains the following (accessible) Web site about Section 508. The site contains information on the law, options for training, and links to a program for vendors who provide Section 508 related products and services.

```
http://section508.frontpagelink.com
```

AccVerify

HiSoftware, of Concord, New Hampshire, has a very powerful product called AccVerify that works with your Web site to verify and repair Web site issues relating to accessibility, site quality, and searchability. It has a plug-in for the product that works with FrontPage and should be considered when taking on any large scale compliance project.

```
http://accverify.frontpagelink.com
```

Web Site Accessibility Resource Center

This regularly updated site contains important links and information regarding the latest issues in Web site accessibility. Because it is run by a FrontPage MVP, you know that the content will remain FrontPage friendly.

```
http://wsarc.frontpagelink.com
```

Accessibility Resources at Microsoft

The Microsoft Accessibility area contains constantly updated content on making information accessible. It also stands as a good example for making an accessible Web site. Sign up for the free newsletter to be kept up-to-date with the latest issues in accessibility across all Microsoft products.

```
http://microsoftaccessibility.frontpagelink.com
```

Accessibility Resources at MSDN

MSDN contains a continually growing reference area of code and content specific to making products accessible. Although the content isn't always Web specific, it is a valuable resource that shouldn't be overlooked.

```
http://msdnaccessibility.frontpagelink.com
```

12

Web Accessibility Initiative (WAI)

The WAI is the project name of the efforts behind the W3C's push for accessibility. The following URL takes you to the project Web site and provides solid information on the topic. The site obviously contains specific guidelines, but it also provides techniques and checklists for creating specific Web sites that should be used by any developer who considers this topic important.

```
http://wai.frontpagelink.com
```

INTERNATIONAL ACCESSIBILITY ISSUES

It should be of no surprise that there are a number of international issues related to accessibility and Web design. This resource will start you on the process of understanding these needs and requirements as well.

```
http://internationalaccessibilityissues.frontpagelink.com
```

BOBBY ONLINE FREE PORTAL

Long before the FrontPage accessibility checker, the free Bobby Online portal was in existence. The site has checked millions of pages on-the-fly and has become a standard in many a developer's toolbox. The free version can only check one page at a time (and requires that they be online) but is always worth a look.

Figure 12.7
The Bobby Online Free Portal (`http://bobby.frontpagelink.com`) will take any page on the Web and check it against either standard on-the-fly.

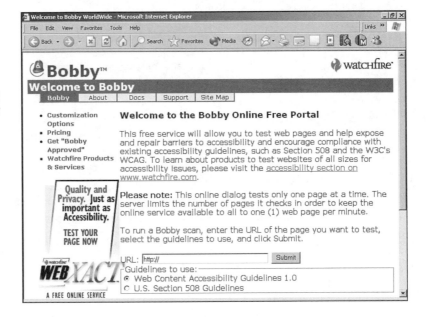

12

TIP

It never hurts to get a second opinion. Even with the addition of the accessibility checker to FrontPage 2003, still consider using Bobby with your sites as a second layer of protection.

HOW PEOPLE WITH DISABILITIES USE THE WEB

You'd be surprised by the large amount of users with disabilities who surf the Internet on a regular basis. Wonder how they do it? Looking for a better understanding of how people with disabilities use the Web? This article provides a fascinating look into this very topic.

```
http://disabilityweb.frontpagelink.com
```

TROUBLESHOOTING

REPORTS WITHOUT WARNINGS

I need to be able to show my boss a report that only shows site errors—not the warnings and checklist elements currently on the report.

You can select which items the checker looks for under the Show header. Deselect <u>W</u>arnings and <u>M</u>anual Checklist and generate a new report.

ACCESSIBLE SITES ARE BORING

With all the stuff I can't do on a site in order to make it accessible, I can't create the cool sites I used to.

Not true.

Consider this a challenge. Can you create an exciting and accessible Web page at the same time? Millions of designers can make pages that look good—what about making a page that looks good to someone unable to read?

Surf the Net for examples of accessible sites and see what they've done to liven up their efforts. You'll not only learn how to make your site accessible, but you'll also pick up on some techniques for Web design that will make you a better developer. One such example can be found at `http://gorgeousandaccessible.frontpagelink.com`.

FRONT AND CENTER: WHY IS ACCESSIBILITY SUCH A BIG DEAL?

Most Web developers are attracted to the Web because of its universal accessibility: We can connect to the Internet from pretty much anywhere and view it on pretty much anything.

But what about those who can't view? Developers are usually willing to create non-framed pages for those who can't use frames in their Web sites or will put alternative text options in their sites to do well in the search engines. Should at least the same effort be placed on making your site readable by someone who simply might not be able to read it?

Another angle on the accessibility issue is the seldom mentioned fact that a *truly accessible Web page needs to be developed once* and will result in content that every individual and product can view. Many Web developers take great effort to produce multiple versions of their sites and content for the different technologies that might view the site.

If that same effort were used in creating accessible pages, the need for multiple versions would be erased and the site could be viewed by not just all browser technologies—but by anyone who might care to look.

CREATING WEB SITES WITH FRONTPAGE

CHAPTER 13

CREATING A WEB SITE

In this chapter

WHAT IS A WEB SITE?

FrontPage is designed to work with *Web sites* and not just Web pages. A Web site (called a Web in previous versions of FrontPage) is a collection of files and folders that are all related to each other. A FrontPage Web site is also defined as a group of related files and folders, but it also shares other elements that specifically make it a FrontPage Web site.

The following FrontPage features apply to a Web site. If you need to change one of these settings for a section of your site, you should create a new subsite from that section.

- Setting up permission for specific users to access a site (Some hosting companies and ISPs don't allow this.)
- Shared border content
- Themes applied to the site instead of to a specific page
- Navigation structure defined in Navigation view
- Web site tasks defined in Tasks view
- Parameters for use with the Substitution Web component
- The ability to publish all or part of the Web site to a remote Web server

NOTE

Not all hosting companies will allow you to control permissions on your FrontPage Web site. If they don't allow you to control permissions, your Permissions menu might be disabled or you might receive an error message informing you that you do not have sufficient privileges when you try and change permissions.

→ For more information on parameters and the Substitution Web component, **see** "Using Web Components, Shared Borders, and Link Bars," **p. 167**.

NOTE

Shared border content is listed for those who are still using the feature from Web sites created in previous versions of FrontPage. Beginning with FrontPage 2003, the Dynamic Web Template feature is preferred over shared borders.

13

ANATOMY OF A FRONTPAGE WEB SITE

When you create a FrontPage Web site, FrontPage adds special folders and files that describe the Web site to FrontPage. Each one of the folders begins with _vti and contains a specific type of information called *metadata*.

NOTE

The vti in FrontPage's configuration folders stands for Vermeer Technologies, Inc., the company from which Microsoft purchased FrontPage version 1. The FrontPage you use today bears no resemblance to that early version.

A FrontPage Web site contains the following special _vti folders.

- **_vti_cnf**—Contains information on each file in the Web site such as when the file was last saved, who saved it, the size of the file, and so on.

- **_vti_log**—This folder is only added to the root Web site and contains log files if logging is enabled on the Web site.

- **_vti_pvt**—Contains numerous files that describe the Web site itself. In the root Web site, this folder also contains a file with a list of all subsites.

- **_vti_script**—Contains the files generated by *Microsoft Index Services* when the Web site is configured to use Index Services to perform site searches.

- **_vti_txt**—Contains the text indices when the FrontPage search engine is used to perform site searches instead of Index Services.

 If you can't see some of the _vti folders, see "FrontPage Metadata Folders Not Visible" in the "Troubleshooting" section of this chapter.

CAUTION

> Don't modify the content in any of the _vti folders yourself unless you are absolutely sure that you know what you are doing. FrontPage relies on these files to correctly open and display your Web site.

WHY USE SUBSITES

The top-level Web site on the Web server is called the *root Web site*. All Web sites created under the root Web site are known as *subsites*. (Subsites were known as subwebs in previous versions of FrontPage.) There are many reasons to separate specific Web site content into its own subsite.

Some FrontPage features are designed to be applied to a Web site only and not to individual pages. If you want different settings for these features on some pages, those pages must exist in a separate Web site. You might also want to restrict access to certain pages so that only specific people can access them. In order to do that, you must separate those pages into their own Web site so that you can apply the appropriate permissions to that Web site.

CREATING A DISK-BASED WEB SITE

When FrontPage is first started, a blank page is available for editing. However, because FrontPage is designed to work with Web sites and not just individual pages, you should create a FrontPage Web site that will contain all the files and folders for your Web site.

13

There are two types of FrontPage Web sites—*disk-based* and *server-based*. A disk-based Web site is created at a disk location such as C:\Documents and Settings\User\My Documents\My Web Sites. A server-based Web site is created on a Web server and has a location such as http://localhost/MySite. Although FrontPage can create both, not all operating systems support both.

TIP

> The location http://localhost points to the local machine. If you are creating Web sites on a Web server installed on your local machine, you can use http://localhost, your IP address, or your machine name. All three mean exactly the same thing.

Windows 2000, Windows XP Professional Edition, and Windows Server 2003 all ship with *Microsoft Internet Information Services*, or *IIS*. IIS also ships with the *FrontPage Server Extensions*, which allow you to create FrontPage Web sites directly on the Web server. We'll talk about creating Web sites on a Web server in the section "Creating a Server-based Web Site" later in this chapter.

 If you can't find IIS on your machine and you want to find out if it's installed and working, see "How to Tell if You Have a Web Server Installed" in the "Troubleshooting" section of this chapter.

→ For more information on the FrontPage Server Extensions, **see** the "Creating a Server-based Web Site," **p. 258**.

Windows XP Home Edition does not ship with a Web server and does not support having a Web server installed. Therefore, users of Windows XP Home Edition will need to create disk-based Web sites and then transfer them to a Web server—a process known as *publishing*.

→ For more information on publishing Web sites with FrontPage, **see** "Publishing a FrontPage Web Site," **p. 299**.

To create a new disk-based Web site:

1. Select File, New. The New task pane is displayed as seen in Figure 13.1.

2. In the New Web Site section of the New task pane, choose a Web site template or click the More Web Site Templates option. The Web Site Templates dialog box is displayed as seen in Figure 13.2.

3. Enter a disk location for your new Web site or accept the default location. By default, FrontPage places your Web site at C:\Documents and Settings\<User>\My Documents\My Web Sites, where <User> is your user ID on the machine. Use the Browse button to easily locate a particular directory.

4. Click OK and FrontPage will create the Web site at the location you specified.

13

The New task pane

Figure 13.1
The New task pane provides easy links to creating new Web sites and new Web pages.

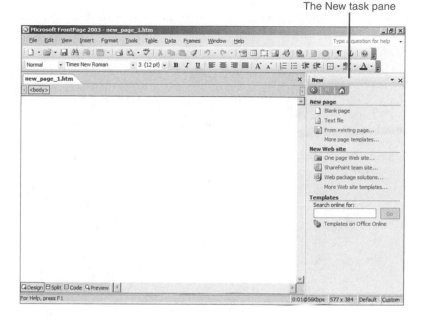

Figure 13.2
The Web Sites Templates dialog box allows you to specify the location where you want your new Web site created.

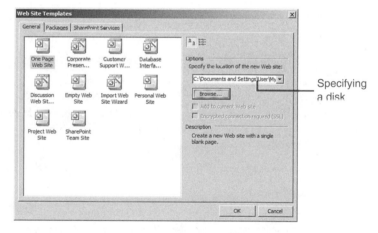

Specifying a disk

CAUTION

Whatever you do, don't ever create a FrontPage Web site on the root of your hard drive! Doing so makes it all too easy to accidentally delete that Web site, thereby deleting your entire hard drive.

FrontPage doesn't have a Recycle Bin. If you delete something from within FrontPage, it's gone for good. I've seen more than one person create a new Web site at C:\ and then later delete it only to find to their horror that their computer had just been made inoperable.

13

If a Web site is already opened in FrontPage, the Add to Current Web Site check box will be available, as shown in Figure 13.3. Checking this box will cause FrontPage to add the Web site you are currently creating to the Web site open in FrontPage. You will not be able to select a location for the new Web site because the new Web site will automatically be created at the same location as the existing Web site.

Figure 13.3
By checking the Add to Current Web Site check box, you can easily add features to an existing Web site.

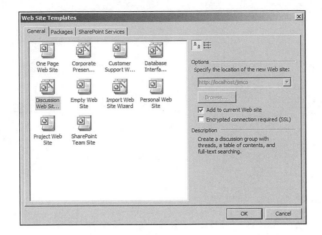

Adding a new Web site to an existing Web site is convenient if you want to add some specific functionality to an existing Web site by using a FrontPage template. For example, if you want to add a discussion board to an existing Web site, you can choose the Discussion Web Site Wizard and add it the current Web site.

After FrontPage creates the Web site, the new Web site will be opened automatically for you so that you can begin creating and editing your Web pages (see Figure 13.4). This new Web site is a disk-based Web site because FrontPage accesses it by using a path on your disk drive.

→ For more information on creating and editing Web pages, **see** "Developing the Basic Page: Text, Lists, and Hyperlinks," **p. 77**.

> **TIP**
>
> The home page for a disk-based Web site is index.htm. This might not be the home page that you want after your site is finished and you've published it to the Internet, but don't worry about it at this point. FrontPage will take care of renaming the page automatically when the Web site is published.

Some FrontPage components will not work correctly on a disk-based Web site because they require a Web server. *Active Server Pages (ASP)* and *ASP.NET* pages will also not work in a disk-based Web site. In order for these features to work, you must first publish your Web site to a Web server.

Figure 13.4
Your new Web site has been created, and you are now ready to get to work on your Web pages.

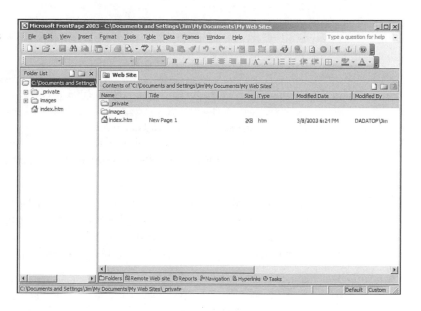

→ For more information on ASP and ASP.NET pages, **see** "Data Access Technologies," **p. 679**.

FRONTPAGE SERVER EXTENSIONS AND WINDOWS SHAREPOINT SERVICES

The *FrontPage Server Extensions* are a collection of executable files and scripts that are installed on a Web server to allow FrontPage to talk directly to the Web server and to provide enhanced content in a FrontPage Web site. Each new version of FrontPage (except FrontPage 2003, as you will see later) has provided a new version of the FrontPage Server Extensions for Microsoft Windows Web servers, as well as Web servers running on other operating systems.

Checking for FrontPage Extensions on a Server

If you want to check to see if a Web server has the FrontPage Server Extensions installed, you can use the form located at http://www.dnswiz.com/fptype.asp. By entering in the Web site location, this form will tell you if the FrontPage Server Extensions are installed as well as the version number that is installed.

If the version number starts with a 3, the FrontPage 98 Server Extensions are installed. Version 4 indicates that the FrontPage 2000 Server Extensions are installed, and version 5 indicates that the FrontPage 2002 Server Extensions are installed.

There will be no FrontPage 2003 Server Extensions because no new features in FrontPage 2003 require the use of the FrontPage Server Extensions.

The FrontPage Server Extensions (sometimes simply referred to as Server Extensions) provide for extended Web page functionality in the form of Web components. Although some components only require the FrontPage Server Extensions when the site is being created (known as *save-time* or *author-time* components), other components (known as *browse-time* components) rely on the FrontPage Server Extensions when the site is being browsed.

→ For more information on FrontPage Web Components, **see** "Using Web Components, Shared Borders, and Link Bars," **p. 167**.

For example, the Photo Gallery introduced in FrontPage 2003 uses some of the components in the FrontPage Server Extensions when you are creating galleries. However, after the Photo Gallery component has been inserted and configured, the FrontPage Server Extensions are no longer required. A page containing a Photo Gallery component will work correctly regardless of whether the Web server hosting it has the FrontPage Server Extensions installed.

The Hit Counter component, on the other hand, requires the FrontPage Server Extensions when the page is being created, but it also requires them when the page is being browsed. The Hit Counter, therefore, is a browse-time component. The Hit Counter is not visible if the FrontPage Server Extensions are not installed on the Web server.

One of the other major capabilities that the FrontPage Server Extensions provide is the ability for you to create Web sites and open Web sites directly on the Web server. As long as the Web server has the FrontPage Server Extensions installed and the host has given you sufficient access, you can open a Web site live, make changes to your Web pages, and those changes are immediately viewable by people browsing to your Web site.

→ For more information on opening Web sites with FrontPage, **see** "Opening and Working with Existing Web Sites," **p. 283**.

Beginning with FrontPage 2003, Microsoft has replaced the functionality of the FrontPage Server Extensions with *Windows SharePoint Services*. Windows SharePoint Services not only provide for the ability to create and open Web sites directly on the server with FrontPage, but they also provide many other features that are not otherwise available. Web components such as the Hit Counter, however, still require the FrontPage Server Extensions.

TIP

Windows SharePoint Services will only install on Windows Server 2003. You cannot install them on Windows XP or Windows 2000.

→ For more information on Windows SharePoint Services, **see** Appendix C, "Windows SharePoint Services 2.0," **p. 943**.

CREATING A SERVER-BASED WEB SITE

Creating a server-based Web site is accomplished following almost the same steps used when creating a disk-based Web site. To create a server-based Web site

1. Select File, New. The New task pane is displayed.
2. In the New Web Site section of the New task pane, choose a Web site template. The Web Site Templates dialog box is displayed, as seen previously in Figure 13.2.

3. Enter a server location for your new Web site, as seen in Figure 13.5. You will use this URL to browse to the site once it has been created. For example, `http://localhost/mysite` will create a new server-based site called `mysite` on the local Web server.

Figure 13.5
By entering an `http://` location for your new Web site, you are creating a server-based Web site.

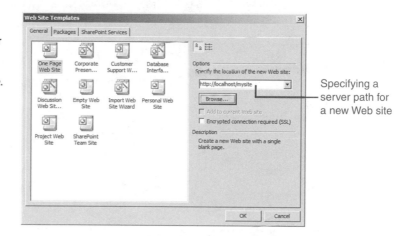

Specifying a server path for a new Web site

4. Click OK and FrontPage will create the new Web site at the location you specified.

 If you encounter an error message telling you that the FrontPage Server Extensions are not installed when creating your Web site, see "Server Extensions Don't Appear to Be Installed" in the "Troubleshooting" section of this chapter.

This new Web site is a server-based site because it has been created at a server location and not a disk location. FrontPage Web components will work correctly in this Web site, as will ASP pages and ASP.NET pages if the server supports them.

→ For more information on Active Server Pages and ASP.NET, **see** "Data Access Technologies," **p. 679**.

In this example, the new Web site is created on the local Web server. You can also create a new server-based Web site on a remote Web server, but doing so requires that the remote server be configured to allow for the creation of new Web sites. In some cases, server administrators will either not give you sufficient permissions necessary to create a new Web site on their server, or they will configure the FrontPage Server Extensions so that new sub-sites are not allowed on the server. In these cases, your hosting company will have to create the Web site for you. After the site has been created, you can publish your local Web site to the remote Web server.

When you open a server-based Web site, FrontPage will most likely create a Web Folder that points to that Web site. A Web Folder is a special shortcut to a Web server location. Web Folders use FrontPage Server Extensions to show you the files on the Web server, and they are located in My Network Places. Figure 13.6 shows a Web site opened in FrontPage, and Figure 13.7 shows the Web site's Web Folder in My Network Places. Double-clicking on the Web Folder displays all the files in the Web site (see Figure 13.8).

13

Figure 13.6
A server-based Web site opened in FrontPage. When this site was opened, FrontPage created a Web Folder for it.

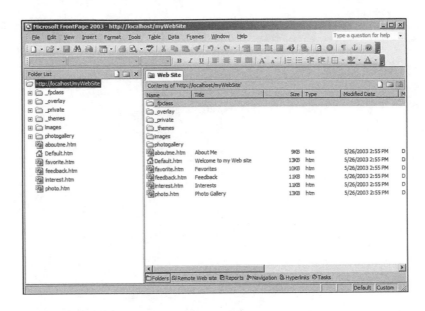

Figure 13.7
This Web Folder was created when the site was opened in FrontPage.

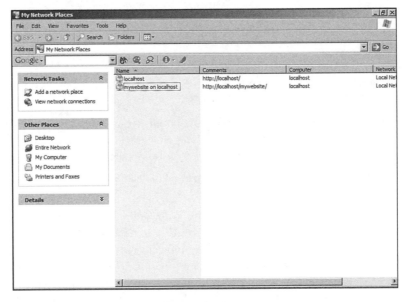

 If you get an error message when attempting to open a Web Folder, or if you open the Web Folder and none of the files within it are visible, see "Web Folders Aren't Working" in the "Troubleshooting" section of this chapter.

 If you don't see a Web Folder for your Web site in My Network Places, see "I Don't See My Web Folder" in the "Troubleshooting" section of this chapter.

Figure 13.8
This Web Folder displays all the files in the Web site just as they are seen in FrontPage.

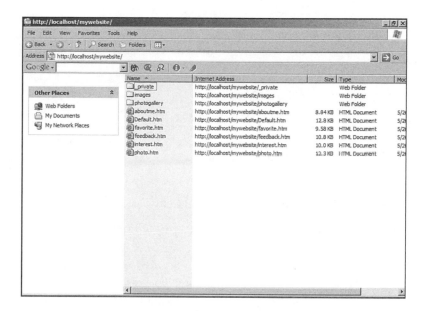

If your Web server has Secure Sockets Layer (SSL) enabled, FrontPage will allow you to create a Web site using SSL by checking the Encrypted Connection Required (SSL) check box. Doing so will change the location from an http:// address to an https:// address (see Figure 13.9)—the required format for a Web site on an SSL-enabled Web server.

Figure 13.9
This Web site will be created on an SSL server, allowing it to be encrypted for higher security.

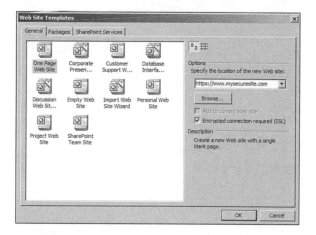

13

NOTE

> *Secure Sockets Layer*, or *SSL*, is a technology developed by Netscape Communications that enables information transferred over the Internet to be encrypted for a higher level of security. SSL is commonly used to provide a high level of security in e-commerce applications.

NOTE

For more information on Secure Sockets Layer, read Sams Publishing's *HTTP Developer's Handbook*. It's an excellent resource for anyone seeking a better understanding of Web development.

SERVER-BASED OR DISK-BASED?

Many FrontPage developers ask which is better, a disk-based Web site or a server-based Web site? No answer to that question works for all scenarios. It simply depends on what you are doing with your Web site and what you need to test as you are developing your site.

Some of the benefits to a server-based Web site are

- FrontPage Web components that require the FrontPage Server Extensions at browse-time will run.
- If running on a Windows SharePoint Services enabled Web server, many more features are available to you that cannot be used on a disk-based Web site.
- You can test your ASP and ASP.NET pages during development as long as the Web server supports ASP and ASP.NET.
- If connected to the Internet, others may be able to browse to your Web site. However, bear in mind that this also means that they can see your Web site as you are developing it.
- You can create Web sites on computers that are not accessible from a disk path such as computers on other networks.

In comparison, the only benefit to a disk-based Web site is that no Web server software is required, so setup and administration of the Web site is much easier.

As mentioned previously, if you are using Windows XP Home Edition, you cannot install a Web server on your machine. Therefore, if you are going to create a server-based Web site from a Windows XP Home Edition machine, you must create it on a remote Web server.

WHERE ARE YOUR FILES CREATED ON A SERVER-BASED SITE?

When you create a disk-based Web site, it is easy to know exactly where your files are being created because you are specifying the exact location when the Web site is created. It might not, however, be quite so easy to tell when you are creating a server-based Web site.

If you are creating your Web site on a hosting company's Web server or on your ISP's Web server, you might not have access to the files outside of FrontPage. However, some hosting companies will provide access to your files via FTP. If your hosting company or ISP does not have the FrontPage Server Extensions installed, using FTP to access your Web site is perfectly fine. However, if they do have the FrontPage Server Extensions installed, using FTP to access your files is not a good idea.

When you change, add, or remove a file on an extended Web server using FTP, the FrontPage Server Extensions are not aware of that change. Therefore, the FrontPage metadata are not updated and get out of sync with the Web site. In some cases, this can be corrected by opening the Web site in FrontPage and selecting Tools, Recalculate Hyperlinks, but that won't always do the trick. In worst-case scenarios, things get so badly out of sync that the only way to correct them is to reinstall the FrontPage Server Extensions on the Web server.

TIP

> The Recalculate Hyperlinks option in FrontPage does more than its name implies. When you run this command, FrontPage checks through all of its metadata files to make sure that they are synchronized with the Web site. It will also check all FrontPage form handlers and other Web components to make sure that their connection to the FrontPage Server Extensions is in working order.
>
> In many cases in which Web components are not working correctly or FrontPage isn't displaying files or folders correctly, running the Recalculate Hyperlinks option will correct the problem.

If you are creating your server-based Web site on your local Web server, your content will be stored in `C:\inetpub\wwwroot` by default. Therefore, if you create a Web site at `http://localhost/mysite`, the physical location for the files is `C:\inetpub\wwwroot\mysite` by default.

TIP

> If you are creating a disk-based Web site and you forget where you created the Web site, it's simple to find again. By selecting File, Recent Sites, you can find the last Web site that was opened. If you have just created a new Web site, it will appear first on this list, and you will be able to see exactly where it is stored on your hard drive.

TROUBLESHOOTING

FRONTPAGE METADATA FOLDERS NOT VISIBLE

When I look in the folder that contains my FrontPage Web site, I don't see some of the `_vti` folders in there. Is my Web site broken?

Your Web site's not broken. Some of the `_vti` folders are hidden folders, and if your operating system settings are using the default configuration, you won't be able to see them.

To show hidden files and folders:

1. Double-click the My Computer icon on your Desktop.
2. Select Tools, Folder Options in the My Computer window.

3. Click the View tab.

4. Select the Show Hidden Files and Folders option.

5. Click OK.

You should now be able to see all the _vti folders.

HOW TO TELL IF YOU HAVE A WEB SERVER INSTALLED

I'm not running Windows XP Home Edition, but I don't know whether I have a Web server installed on my machine. How can I tell, and what do I do if I don't have one?

If you have a Web server installed and running correctly, you should be able to open your Web browser and browse to http://localhost. If a Web page is displayed, your Web server is installed and functioning.

If you get an error indicating that your Web browser could not find the server, you might now have IIS installed. You can install IIS from the Add/Remove Programs applet in Control Panel. Make sure that you have your Windows CD handy and then complete the following steps:

1. Open Control Panel and double-click on Add/Remove Programs.

2. In the Add/Remove Programs applet, click the Add/Remove Windows Components button.

3. In the Windows Components Wizard dialog box, check the Internet Information Services check box and click Next.

4. If you are prompted to enter a path to any files, point Windows to the i386 folder on the Windows CD.

5. Click Finish when the Wizard finishes.

The installation of IIS includes the FrontPage 2000 Server Extensions by default.

SERVER EXTENSIONS DON'T APPEAR TO BE INSTALLED

I am trying to create a new server-based Web site on my local machine, and I keep getting an error that says my server doesn't appear to have the FrontPage Server Extensions installed.

It is possible that you have not installed the FrontPage Server Extensions on your Web server. To ensure that they are installed:

1. Open Control Panel and double-click the Add/Remove Programs applet.

2. Click the Add/Remove Windows Components button.

3. Scroll down until you see Internet Information Services and select it by clicking on it once.

4. Click the Details button.

5. Make sure that the FrontPage 2000 Server Extensions check box is checked and click OK.

6. Click Next.

7. Click Finish when prompted.

If the FrontPage 2000 Server Extensions check box was already checked, remove the check and complete an uninstall of them. Then complete the preceding steps again and install the FrontPage 2000 Server extensions by checking the FrontPage 2000 Server Extensions check box.

WEB FOLDERS AREN'T WORKING

When I try to look at my FrontPage files using a Web Folder, I get an error message telling me that the files are unavailable. I have been able to open these Web Folders in the past, but even then, they were empty even when I knew files were there.

Web Folders are sometimes problematic, and when they get broken, they are often difficult to get working again. Fortunately, Microsoft has done a very good job of documenting all the known troubleshooting steps to correct problems with Web Folders.

You can access Microsoft's Knowledge Base article entitled "Troubleshooting Web Folders" at the following URL:

```
http://support.microsoft.com/default.aspx?scid=kb;en-us;287402
```

I DON'T SEE MY WEB FOLDER

I opened my Web site in FrontPage, but I don't see my Web Folder.

FrontPage doesn't always create a Web Folder when a Web site is opened. It will only create the Web Folder if it needs it to access the site.

FrontPage will not create a Web Folder under the following conditions:

- When the site is opened automatically by FrontPage immediately after it's created
- When the site being opened appears on the Recent Webs List on the File menu
- If the Web site being opened is a disk-based Web site
- If another Web Folder already exists for the Web site

FRONT AND CENTER: USER RIGHTS AND FRONTPAGE SERVER EXTENSIONS

Many people developing a FrontPage Web site don't have any access to the Web server where the Web site lives. They are at the mercy of a Web hosting company or an ISP, and when problems occur, they aren't exactly sure how to diagnose the problem.

When creating Web sites on a remote Web server, you can run into many problems if things don't work right. The most common problem is permissions related. This problem can manifest itself in many different ways, but the most common symptom is a dialog box informing you that you don't have the necessary permissions to create the Web site.

The FrontPage Server Extensions control access to a FrontPage Web site. There are several roles to which any particular user can belong, and each of these roles has particular rights that define what users of that role can do. The roles for a FrontPage 2000 or earlier Web site are *Administrator*, *Author*, and *Browser*. FrontPage 2002 Server Extensions introduced the *Advanced Author* role, which is the same as an Author in FrontPage 2000 and earlier.

An Author or Advanced Author has the right to open the Web site in FrontPage, make changes to pages, and save those changes. However, an Author or Advanced Author cannot change the permissions on a Web site, and they cannot create new Web sites. Only an Administrator can create new Web sites.

Most hosting companies and ISPs give FrontPage users Author or Advanced Author access, and because of that, when you try to create a new Web site in FrontPage, you are informed that you do not have permission to perform that operation. In order to correct this problem, your hosting company or ISP has to either make you an Administrator, or they have to create the Web site for you and then you can open it in FrontPage and add content to the existing site.

FrontPage 2002 introduced SharePoint Team Services 1.0, which allows you to create FrontPage Web sites that are designed to allow teams to collaborate and share information. SharePoint Team Services 1.0 shares FrontPage's security scheme, so if your host is running SharePoint Team Services, you are bound by the same security restrictions as you are when using the FrontPage Server Extensions.

FrontPage 2003 introduces Windows SharePoint Services, the next product in the SharePoint line. Windows SharePoint Services introduces new roles, but you still must be an Administrator to create new Web sites.

13

CHAPTER **14**

FrontPage's Web Templates, Wizards, and Packages

In this chapter

COMPARISON OF WEB TEMPLATES, WIZARDS, AND PACKAGES

You are not alone in your quest to develop the perfect looking (and working) Web site. FrontPage provides for design (and technology) assistance through the use of Web templates, wizards, and Web packages. These tools are part of what makes FrontPage such a powerful product.

Templates are wonderful tools in Web design because they not only assist in layout for a site, but also they can help point you in the right direction for navigation and functional elements.

FrontPage has always come with Web page and site templates that assist in the design process. New to FrontPage 2003 is the introduction of the Web package.

Templates, wizards, and packages are each different in their use and implementation:

- *A page template is a predeveloped Web page made up of page settings, formatting, and page elements.* Page templates are often used when another has already developed a look and feel for a site, allowing the developer to simply enter the needed content.

- *A Web template is made up of more than one page template and often contains navigation elements that connect the pages to each other.* A Web template often contains all the needed elements of a complete Web site, allowing the developer to quickly focus on content instead of layout and design.

- *A wizard takes you step by step through a series of questions to produce the required results in a Web page or site.* The technology is similar to the wizards seen throughout other Microsoft technologies, such as the Resume Wizard in Microsoft Word or a Microsoft PowerPoint Presentation Wizard. Wizards are found in Page Templates and Web Site Templates dialog boxes and lead to the eventual creation of FrontPage Web pages and Web sites.

 - *Web packages are a group of files that can contain, but are not limited to templates, components, themes, graphics, style sheets, scripting, and other elements.* The difference between a Web package and a Web template is in the complexity of the additional files and that a Web package requires Windows SharePoint Services version 2.0 or higher to implement.

WHERE DOES THE DYNAMIC WEB TEMPLATE COME IN?

Dynamic Web Templates are Web templates with additional design and layout capabilities that simply can't be contained within the confines of HTML. A Dynamic Web Template lets you create multiple pages on a site that shares the same layout.

The implications for this technology in Web design are exciting. Whereas a Web page template defines how a single page looks (and could have any part edited by anyone with FrontPage), a dynamic Web template can be used to define as many pages as desired and can be locked to prevent others from changing the developer's original view. In short, Web page templates are limited in scope and can be altered by anyone (by accident or on

14

purpose), whereas Dynamic Web Templates can be used to format an entire site and can't be edited through the normal FrontPage interface. Make sure to read the chapter on this topic in the book.

Dynamic Web Templates also give you the power to lock areas of a Web page from being edited. This broadens the amount of people who can assist you in the Web design process because the beginner's fear of deleting something can quickly be erased by his inability to "mess up."

TIP

If you aren't quaking in your boots with the thought of this kind of power, reread this section again.

Dynamic Web Templates greatly increase the power of the Web designer because he can let those not familiar with the design process into that very process and they will no longer be able to do the damage they were once so capable of doing.

In addition, Dynamic Web Templates give you a powerful new way to make sure that your site keeps the specific look and feel you've been striving for.

There is no limit to the amount of Dynamic Web Templates that can be used in any site. In addition, the creation of a Dynamic Web Template is as simple as saving a Web page as a Dynamic Web Template (see Figure 14.1). No other tools are needed.

Figure 14.1
Dynamic Web Templates are saved with the .dwt file suffix.

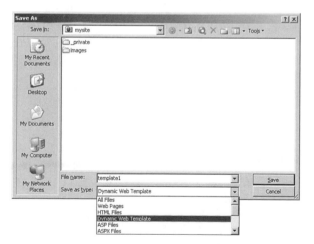

TIP

The earlier FrontPage technology of shared borders was once used as a quasi-crutch to provide some of the power now afforded by Dynamic Web Templates. If you are using shared borders on any project, consider this as a much more powerful, and server-friendly, solution.

14

→ For more on the use of an integration of Dynamic Web Templates in the Web design process, **see** "Dynamic Web Templates," **p. 411**.

SOURCES FOR OBTAINING TEMPLATES

Historically, design elements and templates provided by Microsoft often carried a certain "designed by Microsoft" look that many designers wanted to shy away from.

The rise of the third-party Web template industry is in many ways a response to that very issue. If you don't like the options that came with your copy of FrontPage, a simple search of the Internet for Web templates will provide many additional options.

TIP

> It is obviously buyer beware when working with third-party providers for Web site or page templates and similar technologies. A Web template and a FrontPage Web template are not the same technology—although you can use both with FrontPage 2003.

→ For more information on recommended sources of third-party templates, **see** "FrontPage Resources Online," **p. 911**.

USING FRONTPAGE 2003 WEB SITE TEMPLATES

To open or use any of the Web Templates that come with FrontPage 2003, select <u>N</u>ew from the <u>F</u>ile menu and then select More Web Site Templates from the New task pane (see Figure 14.2).

Figure 14.2
The New task pane will let you choose from Page or Site templates in addition to searching Office Online for additional template options.

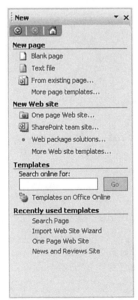

Microsoft has not updated any of the Web Site Templates in this release. Here we will describe, briefly, each of the Web templates that come with the full install of FrontPage 2003:

- **One Page Web Site**—Just as it sounds, this template provides nothing more than a single page Web site. This is provided to offer a quick and easy way to create a new Web from which you can start a site from scratch.

- **Corporate Presence Wizard**—This wizard takes you through a series of questions that helps you create a corporate Web site quickly and easily (see Figure 14.3).

Figure 14.3
The Corporate Presence Wizard walks you through the process of building a corporate Web site unique to your situation.

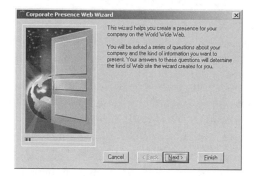

- **Corporate Support Wizard**—This wizard walks you through the process of getting a limited support site up quickly.

TIP

> If you have access to a Windows SharePoint SharePoint Services Server, the options provided by the Corporate Support, Discussion Web, or Project Web Site Wizards listed later have considerably better options built right in to SharePoint.

→ For more on FrontPage and SharePoint Team Services, **see** "Windows SharePoint Services 2.0," **p. 943**.

- **Database Interface Wizard**—This wizard has been updated to provide the most powerful wizard of the bunch. This wizard walks you through the process of interfacing with a database for dynamic data and content integration (see Figure 14.4).

14

Figure 14.4
The updated Database Interface Wizard writes the code needed to integrate with the latest database technology.

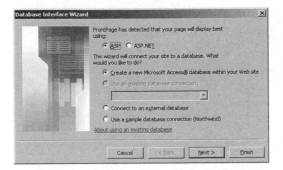

→ For more help in the implementation and use of this wizard, **see** "FrontPage's Data Toolset," **p. 689**.

- **Discussion Web Site Wizard**—Provides a simple discussion Web site.

- **Empty Web Site**—Sets up all the files necessary for a Web site, but it doesn't even create the first page. This template is used by those who intend on building a site in any scripting language and don't want HTML in their sites.

- **Import Web Site Wizard**—This is probably the most powerful wizard that comes with FrontPage. The Import Web Site Wizard helps you grab an existing Web site (either on your network or elsewhere on the Web) and import it into a new Web site that you have control over.

NOTE

> Could you use the Import Web Site Wizard to pull Web content from a site that isn't yours? Yes.
>
> You don't need this book to tell you that grabbing someone else's content without their permission isn't legal or ethical.

- **Personal Web Site**—This template helps you develop a simple personal Web site. Serves as a decent jumping off point for creating a site to tell others about you and your services.

- **Project Web Site**—With this template, you can put together a Web site that tracks a project.

- **SharePoint Team Site**—Build a basic SharePoint Team Site using this Wizard.

If you can't get your template to provide you with the functionality you expect it to, *see "The Template Doesn't Work" in the "Troubleshooting" section at the end of this chapter.*

14

After the Web template is selected and the appropriate information (if any) is entered, FrontPage will create the entire Web site and place it in your FrontPage Web.

When the new Web is created, you can edit any element of the new site with FrontPage as you would anything created on your own.

USING WEB PAGE TEMPLATES IN FRONTPAGE 2003

To open or use any of the Web Page Templates that come with FrontPage 2003, select File, New and then select More Web Page Templates from the New task pane.

As with the Web templates mentioned previously in this chapter, Microsoft has not updated any of the Web Page Templates in this release. Here we will describe, briefly, each of the templates that come with the full install of FrontPage 2003.

GENERAL PAGE TEMPLATES

A number of basic page templates come with FrontPage 2003. The following list describes the templates and their use.

NOTE

> The page templates that come with FrontPage 2003 haven't been updated for the last two revisions of the product.

- **Normal Page**—Creates a normal page with no mark-up or formatting.
- **Bibliography**—Provides a simple start to developing a bibliography page at your Web site (see Figure 14.5).

Figure 14.5
The Web page offered by the Bibliography template is simple but provides an easy jumping off point for creating the necessary content.

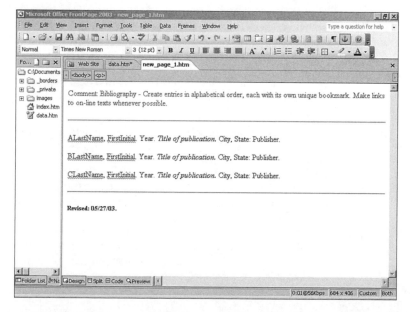

- **Confirmation Form**—Template for acknowledging receipt of a completed form element from within your FrontPage site.

- **Feedback Form**—Provides a template and the functionality for offering a feedback form on your site.

- **Form Page Wizard**—Walks you through the process of building a form on your site (see Figure 14.6).

Figure 14.6
You don't need to add form elements one at a time. Use the From Page Wizard to create the form you need.

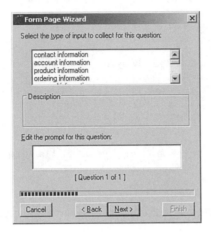

- **Frequently Asked Questions**—This quick template is used for producing frequently asked questions.

- **Guest Book**—Provides traditional guest book functionality to any Web site.

- **Photo Gallery**—Uses the Photo Gallery Web component to provide a simple Photo Gallery page.

→ For more on the Photo Gallery Web component, **see** "Using Web Components, Shared Borders, and Link Bars," **p. 167**.

- **Search Page**—Provides a basic template for a Search page at your Web site with directions for the end user. By default the page supports FrontPage Extensions and Windows Server enabled Web searches, but the code can be quickly modified to work with other search engines.

- **Table of Contents**—Uses the Web's FrontPage navigation database to provide a table of contents for the site.

- **User Registration**—Provides a basic user registration element to your site. Only provides the interface for communicating with the registration element and does not provide any functionality for creating or distributing id or password information.

NOTE

All the page templates listed previously, with the exception of Normal Page, Bibliography and Frequently Asked Questions, require either FrontPage Extensions or hosting on a Microsoft platform to work correctly.

If you like the idea of FrontPage templates but don't care for the style of templates that come with the product, *see "Don't Like Microsoft Templates" in the "Troubleshooting" section at the end of this chapter.*

FRAMES PAGE TEMPLATES

The Frames Pages tab in the Page Templates dialog box provides for a number of frameset options, keeping you from having to design one of your own (see Figure 14.7).

Figure 14.7
You don't need to create a frameset; FrontPage offers any option you might need with the Frames Page Templates option.

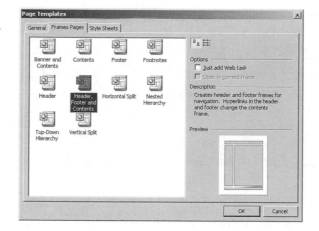

→ For more help on the frames page templates, **see** "Enhancing Web Sites with Frames," **p. 219**.

STYLE SHEETS

Perhaps the most powerful of the templates provided in FrontPage 2003 are found in the Style Sheets tab of the Page Templates dialog box (see Figure 14.8). Because these style sheets use the industry standard CSS format and no Microsoft specific proprietary formats, they can easily be interchanged with other Web development packages and systems.

Figure 14.8
The 12 style sheets (and one blank one) provided by FrontPage 2003 provide a simple jumping off point for creating style sheets of your own.

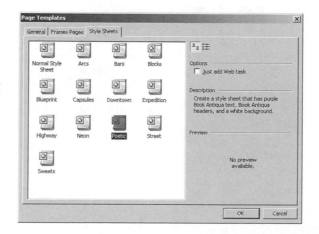

14

Because there is no need to create a Web page from scratch, there is also no need to create a style sheet from scratch. Find a style sheet closest to the look and feel you are interested in and update/edit the style accordingly.

→ For more help on the use of style sheets or CSS in Web design, **see** "Using Style Sheets to Format Web Pages," **p. 385**.

WORKING WITH WEB PACKAGES IN FRONTPAGE 2003

NEW Web packages are new to FrontPage 2003 and as mentioned previously, provide an entire package of Web design features. The Web Packages options are accessed through the Packages tab of the Web Site Templates dialog box.

CAUTION

> It is important to stress that Web packages will only work in the SharePoint hosting environment.

By default, FrontPage 2003 comes with two Web Packages: News and Reviews Site and Web Log.

TIP

> I have no doubt that the introduction of Web packages will quickly bring a number of third-party packages. At the time of writing, these were the only two available, but you can check the Office Marketplace for more at http://officemarketplace. frontpagelink.com.

If you are installing a Web package not available through the Packages tab (for instance, a third-party package), select Tools, Packages, Import. The Import Web Package dialog box, seen in Figure 14.9, will walk you through the process.

Figure 14.9
The first step of the Web package installation process requires telling FrontPage which parts of the Web package you would like to install or import.

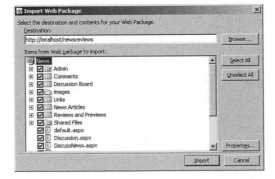

The install process will first ask you which elements of the Web package you would like installed. By default, all options are selected. Refer to your specific Web Package documentation for which package elements are right for you.

NOTE

> Because they can contain scripting and database information, a Web package could do considerable damage if it contained malicious content. Any Web package you use should be digitally signed to ensure that it comes from a trustworthy source. The News and Reviews and Web Log packages are digitally signed by Microsoft.

 If you aren't able to import your Web package into your Web site, see "Can't Import a Web Package" in the "Troubleshooting" section at the end of this chapter.

NEWS AND REVIEWS WEB PACKAGE

The News and Reviews Web package provides a complete News and Reviews Web site that allows you to share news and information with others through a Windows SharePoint Service enabled Web site. Participants in the site can post News information directly through the Web interface if they have the appropriate permissions to do so. The initial home page is seen in Figure 14.10.

Figure 14.10
The Web site produced by the News and Reviews Web Package instantly enables powerful online interaction without any additional coding or development work.

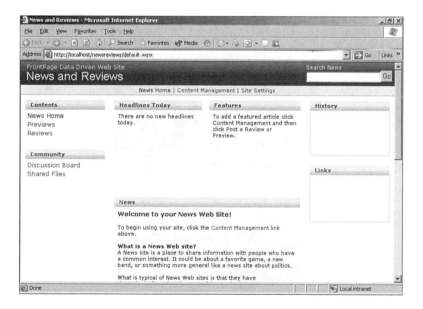

The Web package provides content management, headline generation, and dynamic historical updating generated from content as it is entered into the Web site.

As will all SharePoint site content, look and feel for the News and Reviews Web site can be edited and updated through FrontPage (see Figure 14.11).

14

Figure 14.11
Any page in the News and Reviews Web site can be edited for content and look and feel through FrontPage.

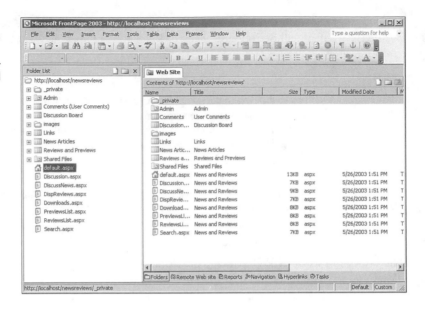

 If you can't get your Web package to install on your site, *see "Web Package Doesn't Install" in the "Troubleshooting" section at the end of this chapter.*

WEB LOG WEB PACKAGE

Web Logs (or *blogs*) are a popular Internet technology used for everything from "stream of consciousness" rantings to legitimate vehicles for news and information dissemination. A quick search of the term "blog" on the Internet will show that they are a fascinating element of the Internet landscape and have key players and providers behind them. The interactive nature of blogs and their low barrier to entry has caused an exponential growth rate.

The Microsoft Web Log Web package hopes to provide a blogging solution to both the FrontPage and SharePoint user. The Web Log Web package provides the ability to post a Web log from browser and lets readers of your blog comment on content written. In addition, the site presents your Web log online, provides search capabilities, and offers a historical archive of content added to the site. The initial home page is seen in Figure 14.12.

The Web package provides everything you need to run a personal Web log. As with all SharePoint site content, look and feel for the News and Reviews Web site can be edited and updated through FrontPage (see Figure 14.13).

EXPORTING A WEB PACKAGE

Creating a Web Package is as simple as placing all the content in a single FrontPage Web and selecting Export from the Packages option in the Tools menu (see Figure 14.14).

Figure 14.12
The Web site produced by the Blog Web Package instantly provides an online blogging system with remote content management and historical content archiving capabilities.

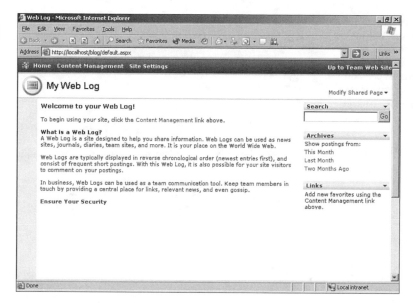

Figure 14.13
Any page in the Web Log Web site can be edited for content and look and feel in FrontPage.

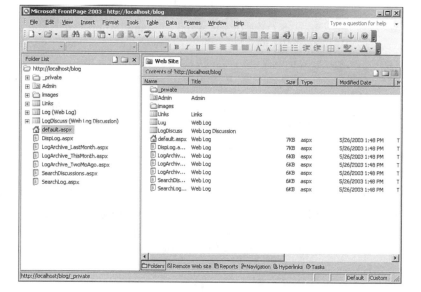

14

Figure 14.14
The Export Web Package dialog box will walk you through the process of exporting your package into a single Web package file.

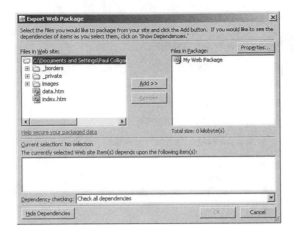

TROUBLESHOOTING

THE TEMPLATE DOESN'T "WORK"

The funtionality implied by my template doesn't work on my Web site.

Many of the templates (Web or page) and packages require Microsoft specific technologies to work completely. Because FrontPage allows you to open/edit these templates external to a Microsoft server, things can get a bit confusing.

> **TIP**
>
> For a continuously updated chart of which FrontPage features are support on which server implementations, visit http://serverfeatures.frontpagelink.com.

CAN'T IMPORT A WEB PACKAGE

When I try to import a Web package through the Tools menu, the Packages item is greyed out.

You can't use or import Web packages on disk-based Webs or on Web sites hosted on a SharePoint Team Services 1.0 server. You can only import a Web package to a SharePoint Team Services Server running version 2.0 or higher.

WEB PACKAGE DOESN'T INSTALL

I go through the entire process of installing a Web package, and after the process is completed, my Web site shows nothing new.

There was a bug in the earlier releases of Windows SharePoint Web Server version 2.0 that are still being used by a number of Web hosts. You'll need a recent version to use the Web packages as described.

DON'T LIKE MICROSOFT TEMPLATES

I'd love to use a Microsoft template, but I don't like the look or feel of anything that came with FrontPage 2003.

As mentioned earlier, there is an entire industry based around Web templates. Some are Microsoft specific, whereas others are not. If you like the idea but don't like your existing options, plenty of additional choices are out there.

One of the often overlooked features of a Web template is the simple fact that you can use it as a "starting point" in your Web design process. Sometimes a Web template will do little more than point you in a color scheme direction or layout structure that you build into your own. Your Web site doesn't have to look anything like the template it started as.

FRONTPAGE CENTER: SHOULD YOU USE WEB TEMPLATES?

Some in Web design would say that using a Web template (or package) in the design process is "cheating." This is a silly notion that should be dismissed immediately.

For many, templates provide a great jumping off point that allows the users to get their hands around a design concept and form the site they really are looking for from that skeleton. For others, the deconstruction of a template provides a training process they couldn't have received anywhere else. For others, the simple reality is that they don't need (and often can't afford) a custom design all their own. Templates provide a great path for any of these situations.

Templates in Web design are no more cheating than is the use of templates in desktop layout or even in database design. If at all possible, let someone else do the hard work for you ahead of time.

Just because Microsoft hasn't updated the FrontPage templates for many revisions of the product, it doesn't mean that they are no longer a viable option. Plenty of great developers are all over the Net who would love to sell you a template of their design.

One of the most powerful implications of the changes introduced in FrontPage 2003 and the minimization of server extensions is that a FrontPage user can easily integrate a third-party template into his Web design. Obviously, a FrontPage-friendly template will always integrate quicker, but the option to branch out is now available to the FrontPage 2003 user.

→ For recommendations of third-party template options, **see** "FrontPage Resources Online," **p. 911**.

The third-party Web template industry is thriving by providing templates to people who don't have time to design them for themselves. The new options provided by FrontPage 2003 allow you to use what it has to offer.

I've seen too many people get so trapped in the process of developing the look and feel of their Web site that they never actually get to the process of publishing their Web and actually doing business online.

Don't let this happen to you. If you need help, certainly consider using a template. You now have more choices and better tools than ever before.

CHAPTER **15**

OPENING AND WORKING WITH EXISTING WEB SITES

In this chapter

15

FRONTPAGE 2003 AND WEB SITE MANAGEMENT: AN OVERVIEW

FrontPage doesn't think in terms of pages; it thinks in terms of entire Web sites. That is what makes the product so powerful and moves it from a simple maker of Web pages to the site management system that it is. Because of the product's focus on site management and design, FrontPage opens a site and is then capable of maintaining and modifying elements on a site-wide basis.

Many in Web development will build their site on their hard drive and publish directly to a live server. This is a simple process that is described carefully in the next chapter. Others will need to remotely access a development site along with other team members and on a regular basis publish site content to a live server. Others will find that at times they need to work directly on a live Web site.

In this chapter, we'll examine the process of opening and working with existing Web sites (both on the desktop and on the remote server). Direct connections to servers through FrontPage Extensions will be compared with other options made available with the most recent release of FrontPage. We'll also take a short look at the role of subsites in the development (and publishing) process and how those are handled.

There will be times when a developer will be working with a local site that publishes to a Microsoft Server installed with FrontPage Extensions. There will be times when a developer finds themselves the only Microsoft user in an entire development team. Because FrontPage supports multiple design and publishing protocols and approaches, FrontPage works well in both environments.

In addition to the traditional Web design and site management features previously associated with the product, FrontPage 2003 is now also a powerful product for connecting to, presenting, and editing data from numerous data sources through Windows SharePoint Services. Unlike the other models described here, this approach requires a remote updating and editing process to capture the power of these two tools working in conjunction with each other.

→ For more on publishing a FrontPage Web site, **see** "Publishing a FrontPage Web Site," **p. 299**.

→ For more on FrontPage and SharePoint Team Services, **see** "SharePoint Team Services 2.0," **p. 943**.

WORKING WITH LOCAL WEB SITES

Unlike most Office System products, FrontPage offers the ability to open both individual files as well as entire Web sites, as seen in Figure 15.1. When the user wants to edit a single page, there is no need to open the entire site. If the management of hyperlinks and navigational elements is required, you will need to open the site, even if you only want to edit a single page.

Figure 15.1
The File menu option in FrontPage provides the option to open both individual files and entire sites.

Reasons for only opening a single page of HTML can range from the editing of an HTML email piece (which FrontPage designs and develops very well) to editing or modifying a single page of content, where someone else is in control of site-wide issues. A developer will not want to introduce site-wide elements to these types of projects because that might be the job of the Webmaster.

Previous versions of FrontPage required that the user run a copy of Personal Web Server (or a more powerful Web server) on his site for any serious development process. With FrontPage's introduction of the disk-based Web, sites can be opened from any folder anywhere on your hard drive. This makes the Web design and maintenance process with FrontPage considerably easier than ever before.

A majority of users will simply access and edit site content on their computer with FrontPage 2003 and publish to their Web sites as needed. This approach requires an understanding of how FrontPage handles and manages sites based on a local hard drive.

NOTE

> Previous versions of FrontPage used the term *Webs* to describe a Web site. With the increase in Web technology, Microsoft now refers to them as *sites* instead of Webs. If you read documentation that makes mention of previous versions of FrontPage, you will need to keep this issue in mind. You also shouldn't be surprised if FrontPage mixes the terms in this most recent release.

The first time you open a folder as a site, FrontPage will need to add a number of elements to the folder content to enable FrontPage's site-wide maintenance capabilities, as seen in Figure 15.2.

Figure 15.2
If you open a folder with FrontPage 2003 as a site, FrontPage will require you to make the folder a site.

There is no way around this process. If you are going to view content on a site-wide basis, FrontPage must build a site of your folder and add the appropriate metadata.

> **TIP**
>
> Don't let FrontPage's conversion of folders into sites concern you too much. For all intents and purposes, no content is changed and you can still access the folder as you would any other folder on your computer with any other application. FrontPage merely adds the meta information required to manage that folder content as if it were an entire Web site. Without this content, site-specific data such as navigational elements, included files, and search capabilities would be impossible.

Opening Versus Importing

Some might mistake FrontPage's Import Web Wizard (discussed in Chapter 14) with opening an existing site. They are completely different issues, and we'll discuss them both here.

FrontPage can only work with an existing FrontPage Web site. As shown previously in this chapter, if you use it to open nonFrontPage content, it will wrap a FrontPage Web site around the content and then allow you to edit it.

If the site you want to edit isn't directly accessible, you can use the FrontPage Import Web Wizard to import the site content into a FrontPage Web site that you can then update, edit, and publish at will.

It is very important to point out that just because you *can* import (most content from) any publicly accessible Web site using this tool, *it doesn't mean* that you have permission to do so. Make sure that you have permission before using this tool.

UNDERSTANDING SUBSITES

As mentioned previously, when a site is created, FrontPage places site-specific content within hidden folders in the site (and in the folder holding the site). These folders hold security and access permissions, Web data, navigational elements, theme information, and the like.

Web design traditionally sorts site content into various folders within a site. This enables the developer to prevent a site from getting too overrun with content and provides a simple way to sort site content. An example of this can be seen in Figure 15.3.

Figure 15.3
Image, script, and ordering information in this site are stored in their own appropriately titled folders.

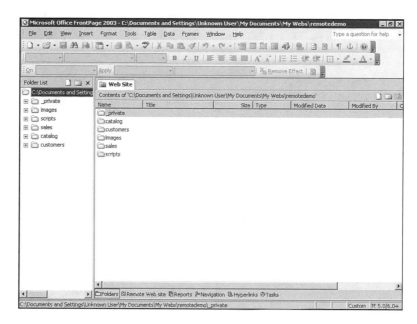

If the developer prefers, any folder within a site can be converted to its own site, creating what is called a subsite. In Figure 15.4, the Web site shown in Figure 15.3 has converted the Sales folder into its own subsite.

Figure 15.4
The folder called Sales from Figure 15.3 has now been converted to a subsite.

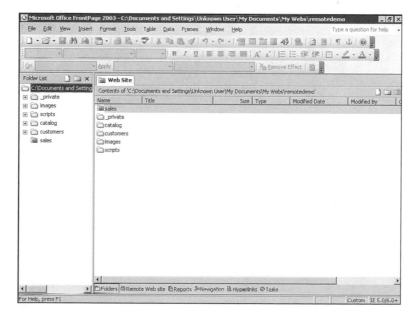

Unless security issues are set differently, visitors to a Web site won't know that they are in a subsite. To the visitor, the URL will make it appear as though he has just entered a new folder.

→ For more on subsites, **see** "Creating a Web Site," **p. 251**.

→ For more on setting access permissions to a site or subsite, **see** "Security and Administration of a Web Site," **p. 323**.

When you double-click any subsite from within FrontPage, the subsite will open in a new instance of FrontPage. If security settings require a different login and password than used to access the root site, FrontPage will require that they be entered before the site is opened.

> **NOTE**
>
> Because subsites are treated by FrontPage as their own entity, each subsite needs to be published on its own. Publishing a site that contains numerous subsites will not publish any subsite data—each subsite will need to be individually published.

CONVERTING FOLDERS TO SITES AND VICE VERSA

Converting a folder to a site is as simple as selecting the folder, right-clicking the folder, and selecting the Convert to Web option. FrontPage will confirm that this is the action you'd like to take and will warn you about its implications, as seen in Figure 15.2.

Any subsite can be right-clicked and converted back to a folder through the Convert to Web option. As per Figure 15.5, FrontPage will again warn you of the effects of this action.

Figure 15.5
When you convert a subsite back to a folder, FrontPage will warn you of the action's implications.

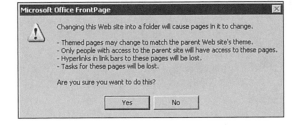

WHEN TO CREATE A SUBSITE VERSUS USING A FOLDER

At first, it might seem desirable to create a great number of subsites or to keep everything sorted by folders only. The most effective Web design strategy is a strategic mix of both. Because a developer can quickly change a folder back into a site and vice versa, a developer should feel free to make the changes as many times as needed.

Link Bars and Themes in Transition

If you convert a folder to a subsite or convert a subsite back to a folder, theme and link bar content will get "lost" in the translation.

If you convert a subsite back to a folder and the site containing that folder has a site-wide theme, the folder pages will also inherit that theme. If you convert a folder with theme content to a subsite, the subsite will not inherit the theme.

15

If you convert a subsite back to a folder that contains link bars, the nature of the bars will change considerably because there are new home and parent page structures throughout the entire site. FrontPage will handle each instance differently, so you will need to check that the site maintains the structure you were looking for.

In short, if you do change between one and the other and use either of these FrontPage technologies, never assume that FrontPage will be capable of sorting things out for you. Always double check your pages.

In short, the main reasons for creating subsites are if you need or desire separate access information to a certain area of the site or need site-wide content to be limited to a specific area. If a better organization of site content is all that's desired, folders work wonderfully.

TIP

> If you are going to use any of the FrontPage site-wide capabilities, such as navigational elements, table of contents, and search, FrontPage will only navigate and present content from within that existing site. If you site is made up of multiple subsites, you won't be able to use this technology across them.

My Documents and My Web Sites

Windows 2000 and Windows XP place a My Web Sites folder within each user's My Documents folder when FrontPage 2003 is installed. The "My Web Sites" title can be a little misleading because it contains not just *your* Web sites, but the sites you have control over or are keeping a copy of.

By default, FrontPage will attempt to place sites within this folder. You aren't required to place them there; it only provides one standard for where sites might be located on your computer system.

This approach can create problems in Web design because if multiple people are working on the same site, they might not have access to your personal Web folders and therefore won't be able to do the work assigned to them.

Because FrontPage 2003 no longer requires a Web server for serious Web development capabilities, site content can be placed in any location on your hard drive(s) and is not required by FrontPage to be located in any specific area.

Place your Web sites in an area that makes sense to you and that can be accessed by everyone on your team.

Working with Remote Web Sites

There are a number of reasons why you might want to access and modify content located on a remote server. From tasks as simple as correcting a simple typo to integrated solutions such as third-party security analysis, there will be times when you will want such access and capabilities.

When a site isn't on your system and you want to access it remotely, you have a number of options available that are examined in this section. Included is the simple access of sites with FrontPage extensions installed, remote access via FTP and WebDAV, and the seldom considered option of remote access through Web folders and file shares.

→ For more on collaborating with other authors in the Web development process, **see** Part VII, "Web Collaboration," **p. 595**.

EDITING LIVE WITH FRONTPAGE EXTENSIONS

The easiest way to access and work with remote Web content with FrontPage is to open a site with FrontPage extensions installed and work on the site as if it were on your hard drive. When the development process is approached this way, FrontPage works directly with the server to provide a seamless editing experience, as can be seen in Figure 15.6. Quick (or complex) edits to a site can quickly be made with updates happening the second the developer clicks the Save button. With this approach, there are no steps to publish site content and the results are seen instantly.

Figure 15.6
This site is being edited at a server thousand of miles away from the developer using the Internet as transport.

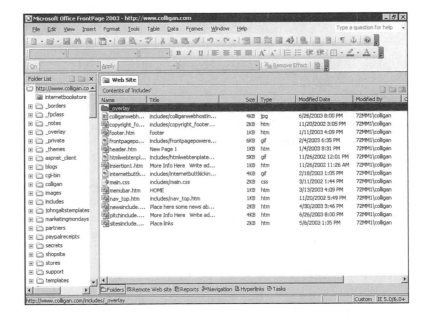

 If you are having problems opening up your FrontPage Web site, see "Can't Open Site" in the "Troubleshooting" section at the end of this chapter.

Sites with FrontPage Extensions installed or Windows SharePoint Services sites enable simple access through this method.

CAUTION

> If you open a live site and make changes on it directly, take extra precautions to keep from making a mistake that your readers will be able to access instantly. The wrong click of a button could delete files (or entire subsites) while your customers are surfing them. An file rename or move could result in file not found errors for anyone surfing without the most recent path links.
>
> Editing live is essentially walking a tightrope without a net, but in this case, you have nothing to win by not having a net below you.
>
> Although editing a site live might save you a few minutes of time from the publishing process, it could also steal a week of your life as you try to re-create what you killed with the Delete button.
>
> Consider the potential costs of editing a site live and certainly review additional backup requirements and strategies if you intend on using this updating method.

→ For more on FrontPage and SharePoint Team Services, **see** "Windows SharePoint Services 2.0," **p. 943**.

OTHER REMOTE ACCESS OPTIONS

With the introduction of FrontPage 2003, site publishing through FTP, Web Folders, and WebDAV (Web-based Distributed Authoring and Versioning) is now possible. These methods can also be used to access remote content and edit accordingly. This is done through the Web site synchronization process. You must create a "local" version of the site, and then open the remote version of the site and make changes accordingly. This is done by transferring the file from the remote site to your local version, editing the content, and then publishing it back to the remote site.

CONNECTING TO A REMOTE SITE

You can't connect to a remote site without opening a local site to compare with the remote version. If desired, you can create a new empty site through FrontPage 2003 and then connect to the desired remote site.

→ For more on creating a new Web site, **see** "Creating a Web Site," **p. 251**.

After the local version of a site has been created, you can access the remote Web site by selecting the Remote Web Site option from the View menu.

NOTE

> The local version of your site can be completely blank and set up in a temporary site for the purpose of making a few minor changes. FrontPage merely needs to create a site for the synchronization process to work.

If a Remote Web Site has not previously been associated with the local Web site, FrontPage will present you with a blank interface, seen in Figure 15.7. You set the Remote Web Site

Properties using the Remote Web Site Properties button seen along the top edge of the screen. This will open the Remote Web Site Properties dialog box. You will then be looking at the options on the Remote Web Site tab seen in Figure 15.8.

Figure 15.7
If no remote Web site is set, you will need to set the Remote Web Site Properties.

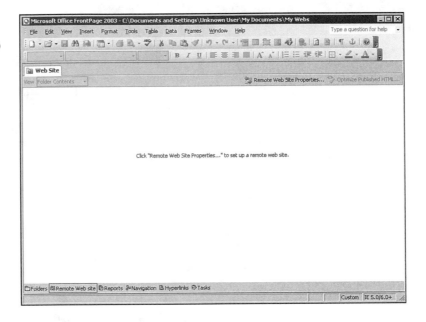

Figure 15.8
The Remote Web Site Properties dialog box lets you set the means by which the Remote Web Site will be accessed.

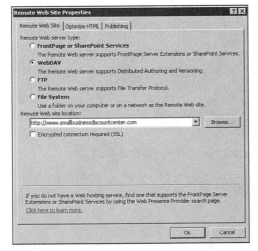

The options are as follows:

- **FrontPage or SharePoint Services**—Produces a synchronization option for accessing remote content in addition to the options described earlier in this chapter.

> **NOTE**
>
> If you are concerned about making mistakes while working on a live site, using the remote access and synchronization options in this section is a great way to prevent making big mistakes.

- **WebDAV**—Helps you connect to sites that use a Web-based Distributed Authoring and Versioning (WebDAV) system on the back end. WebDAV is a popular standard that adds additional information through HTTP that can be used to produce a collaborative authoring environment where multiple users can edit and manage files on a remote Web site. The most powerful aspect of WebDAV is the ability to add properties on site metadata that can lock files and provide additional remote file management capabilities.

> **TIP**
>
> A great online resource for WebDAV can be found at http://webdav.frontpagelink.com. You can use a site that uses WebDAV as your remote site with FrontPage 2003 and utilize all the Web development features and capabilities a WebDAV site has to offer.

> **NOTE**
>
> At publication time, the future of WebDAV features of FrontPage 2003 were still being decided. It is quite possible you won't see them in the release of FrontPage 2003 that you are using right now.

- **FTP**—Short for *File Transfer Protocol*, is the Internet's oldest standard for moving files across the Internet. Most other Web development programs use FTP to move files from the desktop to the server, and FrontPage only provided limited support in previous versions of the product.

 If you are having a hard time getting FrontPage Server Extensions to work "nicely" with FTP, see "FrontPage Server Extensions and FTP" in the "Troubleshooting" section at the end of this chapter.

- **File System**—Web folders are file shares accessible over the Internet that provide file sharing functionality that works as if the content were located on a file share on a local network. Web folders can be saved and accessed through drive letters, and content can be dragged and dropped between folders.

15

TIP

A great article on Web folder behaviors can be found online at `http://webfolderarticle.frontpagelink.com`. There are several third-party providers of Web Folder services, such as MyDocsOnline (`http://mydocsonline.frontpagelink.com`).

Because Web folder technology already uses a navigational paradigm embraced by most Windows users, the use of Web folders as a means to store Web content is obvious. Although it might seem that Web Folders and network shares would react with FrontPage the same way that a local drive does, this is not the case. If your Web site is located on a Web or network folder, you will need to follow the process explained next.

→ For more on Web folders and FrontPage 2003, **see** "Creating a Web Site," **p. 251**.

REMOTE CONTENT MODIFICATION THROUGH THE SYNCHRONIZATION PROCESS

Although the specifics of site synchronization are discussed in the next chapter, the process of modifying and working with site content through the synchronization is discussed here.

The process of modifying files on remote process is a simple four step process:

1. Connect to the remote site.
2. Synchronize the desired file.
3. Edit the synchronized file on the local site.
4. Re-synchronize the updated document to the remote Web site.

A basic example of this process in action can be seen in Figure 15.9. In it, you will see that a blank Web has synchronized a single file for editing on the local computer.

→ For more about publishing and synchronizing site content with FrontPage 2003, **see** "Publishing a FrontPage Web Site," **p. 299**.

Once a file is synchronized to a local computer and edited accordingly, the file can then be synchronized back to the remote site.

WORKING WITH WINDOWS SHAREPOINT SERVICES

Windows SharePoint Services is a powerful tool that gives users the ability to organize and access information, manage documents online, and provide online collaboration tools in a simple to use browser-based environment. It is part of the Windows 2003 Server system and is one of the more exciting technologies to come out of Microsoft. It represents the future of Web sites and Web services and (I predict) will quickly be embraced by the business workforce and information worker.

15

Figure 15.9
A blank Web accesses a remote Web site via FTP. A single file has been synchronized between the two sites for later editing.

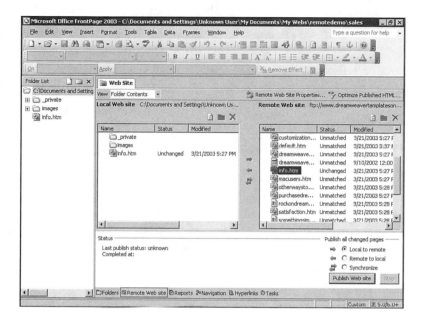

Whereas Windows SharePoint Services provides a powerful means to run a next generation Web site completely, independent of any Web development package, the teaming of Windows SharePoint Services with FrontPage 2003 needs to be understood and explained.

The traditional Web site model allows for the approach of editing content on a development server and publishing to a live site described previously in this chapter. The dynamic and constantly changing nature of a Windows SharePoint Services Web site simply prevents such an approach. FrontPage 2003 was built with this fact in mind.

You can open a Windows SharePoint Services Web site directly from FrontPage 2003 as you can another Web site with FrontPage extensions. FrontPage 2003 allows you to work directly with site data and both edit and produce data-driven pages at the site.

Appendix C of this book goes into great deal about how these two products work with each other.

NOTE

> More information about Windows SharePoint Services can be found online at http://sharepointatmicrosoft.frontpagelink.com.

→ For detailed directions on using FrontPage to edit/update content on a Windows SharePoint Services Web site, **see** "Windows SharePoint Services 2.0," **p. 943**.

TROUBLESHOOTING

CAN'T OPEN SITE

I'm trying to open an existing Web site, and I enter the Web address into the Open Site option. FrontPage says that FrontPage Server Extensions aren't installed, but I know for a fact that they are. What can I do?

FrontPage will report that FrontPage Server Extensions aren't installed if they don't respond. Many times, the actual problem is that the server is down or the server extensions aren't responding.

If you are getting such a message on a server that you know has FrontPage Server Extensions installed, first check to make sure that the site is actually up. If the site is live, something is wrong with the server extensions, so ask you server administrator to look into it. Sometimes FrontPage Server Extensions will need to be reinstalled.

FRONTPAGE SERVER EXTENSIONS AND FTP

I update my site with FrontPage Server Extensions. Other people on my team use other products and want to update site content via FTP. It seems that FrontPage Extensions "break" on a regular basis after this happens. Why is this the case, and what can I do to fix it?

In all honesty, FrontPage Server Extensions and FTP never worked nicely together. Although some will claim that they can make them work together in harmony, I have never been able to make it work. Because Microsoft is no longer updating the FrontPage Extensions product, there is no reason to expect that this issue will be fixed.

The answer is simply picking one protocol and sticking with it. Either require that everyone on your team access site content through FrontPage and the Server Extensions, or embrace FrontPage's new handling of FTP and join the others in your team accordingly.

FRONT AND CENTER: THE POWER OF OPEN SITES AND DEAD EXTENSIONS

I've been a big fan of FrontPage since the very beginning. That should be of no surprise to anyone reading this book.

One of the things I always loved about the product was the ability to go in live to a server and update certain elements directly on the site (and yes, those previous warnings about doing so come from personal experience). Obviously, solid development work needs to be done on a development machine and perfected before published, but, on occasion, there are reasons to edit on the server side.

Being able to enter the URL in to FrontPage, open the site live, and make a small change here and there has saved me countless hours. If you've used FrontPage for any amount of time, I'm sure that you feel the same way.

But, this approach has always required FrontPage Extensions. Now that FrontPage Extensions are, if not dead, well on their way out, the options discussed in this chapter make things even more powerful than before.

Although you aren't updating and modifying a page directly as is possible with a server with FrontPage Extensions, the other methods described in this chapter provide a quick and easy means to edit and modify content at a remote site. No one should be worried about making sure that they have a copy of an entire site at their disposal in order to get any work done.

The true power of FrontPage is how it speeds up the Web design process. Embrace every aspect of the product that lets you do just that.

CHAPTER 16

PUBLISHING A FRONTPAGE WEB SITE

In this chapter

A BIRDSEYE VIEW OF PUBLISHING

Publishing is easily one of the most troublesome aspects of FrontPage for many users. When you publish a FrontPage Web site, you rely on not only your own machine being configured correctly, but you also rely on the machine to which you are publishing the Web site to be configured correctly. In addition to that, you have to contend with any machines that lie between you and the destination server. Quite simply, plenty can go wrong when you're publishing a Web site.

WHERE THE INFORMATION GOES

When you request a page from your Web site on the Internet, you aren't sending and receiving information directly to and from the Web server your site is hosted on. Instead, you are sending and receiving information through many machines on the Internet. For example, I traced a browsing session between my machine and a Web server that I know to be just across town. The information being exchanged between my machine and that Web server went through 13 other machines on the Internet before it reached the remote Web server.

NOTE

> If you are curious about how information is exchanged between computers on the Internet, read *Special Edition Using TCP/IP*.

Tracing Your Data

Each time information you transmit moves from one computer to another, it's called a *hop*. Microsoft Windows ships with a utility called `tracert` that will allow you to see how many hops there are between you and another computer on the Internet.

You can run `tracert` from a command window by running the command as follows:

```
tracert www.mysite.com
```

Change `www.mysite.com` to the URL that you want to trace. The output will show you each computer along the route between you and the site you enter as well as the amount of time it took for the round-trip between you and each computer along the route. Three time periods are listed for each hop, each one in milliseconds, because `tracert` sends three separate requests to each computer along the way and it times the round-trip for each. Here is sample output from running `tracert` from my computer to `www.microsoft.com`.

```
Tracing route to www.microsoft.akadns.net [207.46.249.222]
over a maximum of 30 hops:

  1     3 ms     3 ms     3 ms   192.168.0.1
  2    20 ms    20 ms    20 ms   66.140.45.254
  3    20 ms    21 ms    20 ms   151.164.162.130
  4    21 ms    19 ms    21 ms   151.164.1.143
  5    19 ms    20 ms    20 ms   151.164.240.233
  6    22 ms    19 ms    21 ms   151.164.240.82
  7    54 ms    54 ms    52 ms   151.164.243.218
  8    53 ms    54 ms    54 ms   151.164.242.70
  9    53 ms    54 ms    55 ms   151.164.241.26
 10    54 ms    55 ms    55 ms   151.164.89.194
```

```
11    53 ms    55 ms    54 ms   207.46.33.117
12    55 ms    55 ms    52 ms   207.46.34.22
13    53 ms    55 ms    54 ms   207.46.34.25
14   111 ms   111 ms   110 ms   207.46.33.61
15   110 ms   111 ms   110 ms   207.46.36.78
16   112 ms   112 ms   111 ms   207.46.155.13
17     *        *        *      Request timed out.
```

Notice that after 16 hops, you see asterisks in place of the time value and a message that the request timed out. This happens when you hit a *firewall*, a special computer that is designed to prevent unauthorized access into a network. Most firewalls are configured not to respond to utilities such as tracert.

If you'd prefer to see a map of each hop in your request, you can purchase an application called Visual Trace from McAfee Security. Visual Trace is available from the McAfee Security Web site at http://www.mcafee.com/myapps/antihacker.asp.

16

When you are simply browsing to Web sites, information will usually travel to and from your machine without any problems. However, when you are publishing a Web site, it is a bit more complicated. In addition to the normal information exchanged, you will also be passing login credentials, and you will be passing much larger amounts of information than you do when you request a single page. Because of these differences in the way you are communicating with the remote Web server, problems are sometimes encountered that can be difficult to diagnose.

THE PUBLISHING PROCESS

Publishing will be discussed in detail in this chapter, but it's important that you understand how the publishing process works before we go into detail. Therefore, let's look at a very high-level view of what happens when you publish a Web site with FrontPage.

1. FrontPage connects to the remote Web server and requests access to publish the site.

2. The Web server checks to see if the request coming in should be allowed to publish. At this initial point, access will always fail and the Web server will usually send a request for you to enter a username and password.

3. You enter your username and password and submit it to the Web server.

4. The Web server takes the username and password you entered and verifies them. Assuming that the login is successful, publishing proceeds with the next step.

5. The Web server checks to see if you have sufficient permissions to publish. If you do, publishing proceeds with the next step. If you do not, you are prompted again for the correct username and password.

6. Assuming that you are successfully authenticated, FrontPage generates a list of files on the remote Web server and a list of files on the local Web server. It does this by checking its metadata.

7. FrontPage displays which files it intends to publish depending on the current settings.

8. If you accept the current publish settings, FrontPage begins the transfer of all files to be published.

9. After the files have been transferred, FrontPage completes the process by recalculating hyperlinks on the remote Web site.

Failures in publishing with FrontPage almost always occur at step 4 or 8.

→ For more information on FrontPage metadata, **see** "What Is a Web Site," **p. 252**.

COMMON REASONS FOR PUBLISHING PROBLEMS

At step 4, your username and password are verified by the Web server. Many times a failure at this point is caused by incorrect entries on the part of the user. However, there are cases in which authentication will fail because of server configuration.

Microsoft Web servers can use a type of authentication known as *Windows Integrated authentication*. (This type of authentication is commonly referred to as *NTLM authentication*, but Microsoft no longer uses that terminology.) Windows Integrated authentication was designed to be used on a Windows network. It allows users to log in to a network only one time, and that single login is used for other network resources that are requested during that login session. When the user requests another network resource that requires a username and password, the credentials used when he initially logged on are passed automatically instead of the user being prompted again.

Windows Integrated authentication is extremely beneficial in a Windows network environment, but it was never designed to be used on the Internet. Even so, many hosting companies and ISPs will enable Windows Integrated authentication because it is a very secure method of authentication. This can cause problems because on the Internet, your username and password are often not passed directly from your machine to the remote Web server. Many times, another computer will pass your username and password on your behalf. Windows Integrated authentication is designed to fail when this happens, and when it does, you will be continuously prompted for a username and password. After three attempts, you will be denied access. The solution to this problem is to have your host enable Basic authentication on the Web server.

> **NOTE**
>
> For more information on authentication types in Microsoft Web servers, read *Internet Information Services Administration* from Que Publishing.

The other common cause of problems when publishing is caused by the remote Web server timing out because of a lengthy file copy process. Occasionally, the hosting company or ISP can increase the timeout period on the Web server to correct this problem, but you are often better off breaking up a large site into smaller subsites. By breaking up your Web site into smaller subsites, smaller portions of the entire site are transferred when publishing and you stand a lesser chance of timeout problems.

Publishing is easily one of the toughest problems to troubleshoot with FrontPage because problems that you encounter are often not isolated to your machine. You also often have to rely on the support of your hosting company to assist in troubleshooting. Unfortunately, many hosting companies don't offer the level of service they should when publishing problems occur. Choosing a reliable host is essential in order to avoid unnecessary frustrations when problems occur.

WHERE TO HOST YOUR SITE

16

Once you've finished your Web site, you'll want to make it available for everyone to see on the Internet. Many hosting options are available to you that will allow you to share your site with the world.

HOSTING YOUR OWN WEB SITE

Broadband Internet has experienced tremendous growth over the past couple of years, and many Internet users are now connected to the Internet over a high-speed connection. Hosting your Web site on your own computer is a real possibility, but check with your service provider first. Many Internet service providers do not allow users to host Web sites over their connection, and doing so might put you at risk for losing your service.

Assuming that your service provider will allow you to host your site on your own computer, you'll need

- An operating system that supports installation of a Web server.
- Web server software. (Windows 2000, Windows XP Professional, and Windows Server 2003 ship with IIS.)

When you make your Web site available to the world, you are drawing a bull's eye on your computer and challenging hackers to shoot for the center. You'll want to make sure that you stay up-to-date on all operating system and Web server updates, and make sure that you are running a firewall of some type. You can purchase a broadband router from your local computer store for very little money, and most of these have a hardware firewall that, when properly configured, can make your Web server quite secure.

Several personal firewall software products are also available that offer a secure environment. Regardless of whether you are hosting a Web site on your computer, if you are connect to the Internet, you should look into some degree of firewall protection.

NOTE

> For more information on personal firewalls, read *Absolute Beginner's Guide to Personal Firewalls* from Que Publishing. It teaches how to configure personal firewalls and how to test them for reliability.

Your computer is identified on the Internet using an *IP address*. Most service providers will provide you with an IP address that changes at preset intervals. This make it difficult to host your own Web site because the identifier for your computer on the Internet keeps changing.

One answer to this problem is a service known as *Dynamic DNS*, or *DDNS*. Using DDNS, you can create a name for your computer on the Internet, and when your IP address is changed by your service provider, the DDNS service gets updated and continues to redirect the name you choose to your new IP address.

Many DDNS service providers are available, but one of the most popular (probably because it is free) is DynDNS.org. Once you set up an account with DynDNS.org, you simply update your account when your IP address changes. DynDNS.org will give you a name to use (such as `mySite.homeip.net`) to access your computer.

Another great benefit of configuring DDNS on your computer, even if you aren't going to host you Web site on your own machine, is that you can use it to access your computer from anywhere on the Internet. Using either Terminal Services for Windows 2000 or Remote Desktop Connections for Windows XP Professional and Windows Server 2003, you can remotely control your home computer from any other computer on the Internet. If you configure this on your computer, make sure that you follow directions for your firewall to keep your computer as secure as possible.

TIP

> Many broadband routers will support the configuration of DDNS. Those that do will automatically update your DDNS record whenever your IP address changes. This allows you to set up the account with your DDNS provider and then forget about it.
>
> Because of the way the Internet works, there is always a short delay between the time your IP address changes and the time that your DDNS redirects your name to the new IP address.

HOSTING YOUR SITE WITH YOUR ISP

Many Internet service providers provide free Web space where you can place your Web site. Although the cost for such Web space is certainly attractive, the downside of hosting your Web site with your ISP is that you don't get to use your own domain name. In other words, instead of using `http://www.mysite.com` to get to your Web site, people will have to enter in a hard to remember Web address assigned by your ISP.

If you simply need a Web site to share pictures with family members or if you feel that you might not be up to maintaining a Web site forever, hosting with your ISP might be the perfect solution. The cost of the Web space it provides is built into what you pay for your Internet service, so you might as well put it to good use.

HOSTING WITH A FREE SERVICE

Many free hosting services are available, and some of them even offer support for FrontPage Server Extensions. Tina Clarke, owner of the AccessFP Web site, provides an exhaustive list of free FrontPage hosting sites. You can access Tina's list at `http://accessfp.net/freefp.htm`. I don't classify these free hosts as real hosting companies because they don't host your domain name. Instead, you get a URL that they assign to you.

Free hosts usually run servers that are overloaded and a bit slow. Additionally, you might have to contend with banner and popup ads. If you can't live with those inconveniences, a hosting company might be just what you need.

TIP

> Even if you don't want to host your site with a free service, these companies are still great for testing out your site. You can create as many accounts as you'd like, and it provides you with a free real-world environment to use for testing.
>
> FrontPage 2003 also ships with coupons for limited-time free hosting on Web servers that provide Windows SharePoint Services. By using these free trials, you have the opportunity to check out some of the very cool features that are added when you host against Windows SharePoint Services.

HOSTING YOUR SITE WITH A HOSTING COMPANY

If you are going to share your Web site with more than just a few people, hosting it with a hosting company is your best option. Most hosting companies offer a full range of services and can register your domain for you and host your site.

Prices vary widely depending on what services you need. When choosing a hosting company, pay careful attention to what services are offered and what services you require. For example, if your Web site uses FrontPage's Database Results Wizard, you will need a Web server that supports ASP. If you are using features from the Data menu in FrontPage, you will need a host that supports Windows SharePoint Services. Careful review of a host will prevent you from paying for more than you need to.

→ For more information on using the Data menu in FrontPage, see "FrontPage and Web Parts," **p. 735**.

Most hosting companies will offer both dedicated hosting plans and shared hosting plans. Dedicated hosting plans consist of a dedicated computer just for your Web site, and they are typically very expensive. Unless you are operating a very high volume Web site or a Web site that requires a high level of security, a shared hosting environment is usually a better option. You can find shared hosting options with full-featured hosting for very little money.

NOTE

> Your initial choice of hosting might not be your last. It's common for Web sites that offer enticing content (such as Web sites with popular forums) to grow beyond the original expectations of the designer.

Most hosting companies provide you with a guaranteed level of service. Most hosting companies guarantee uptime (typically 99% uptime) on their Web servers, which means that they guarantee that your Web site will almost always be available. The hosting company will also take care of backing up your Web site on a regular schedule.

Another advantage to a hosting company is that it typically provides you with many email addresses that are all personalized with your domain name. For example, you can have an email address for webmaster@*mydomain*.com, suggestions@*mydomain*.com, and so on. If you want to provide an image of professionalism, a hosting company is the only way to go.

To find a hosting company that meets requirements for your Web site, click the Click here to learn more link in the Remote Web Site Properties dialog.

PREPARING TO PUBLISH YOUR WEB SITE

Now that you've got a place to put your Web site on the Internet, you'll need to configure FrontPage to publish to the remote Web server. FrontPage 2003 offers major advancements in publishing over previous versions, and one of those enhancements is the Remote Web Site view. Using this view, you can set publish options and once you have configured a remote Web site for your local Web site, you can see at a glance what files will be published the next time you publish the local site.

The terminology used when publishing a FrontPage Web site can be misleading. It would have been better had Microsoft used the term "destination Web site" rather than "remote Web site" because the remote Web site need not be remote. For example, you might open up your Web site on your hosting company's Web server and configure it to publish down to your local machine. In this scenario, the local Web site is the site on your hosting company's remote Web server, whereas the remote Web site is the Web site on your local machine. To keep it all straight, it's best to just remember that the local Web site is always the Web site that is open in FrontPage.

> **TIP**
>
> The Remote Web Site view actually works just like the Folder List in FrontPage, and the options available to you are the same. You can right-click on files and rename them, rearrange the files according to specific attributes, delete files, and so on.

To see the Remote Web Site view in action, perform these steps:

1. Create a new FrontPage Web site. It can be a disk-based Web site or a server-based Web site.

→ For more information on creating a new disk-based FrontPage Web site, **see** "Creating a Disk-based Web Site," **p. 253**.

→ For more information on creating a new server-based FrontPage Web site, **see** "Creating a Server-based Web Site," **p. 258**.

2. Select <u>V</u>iew, Remote <u>W</u>eb Site. The Remote Web Site view is displayed as seen in Figure 16.1.

Figure 16.1
The Remote Web Site view is empty until a remote Web site is configured by clicking the Remote Web Site Properties button.

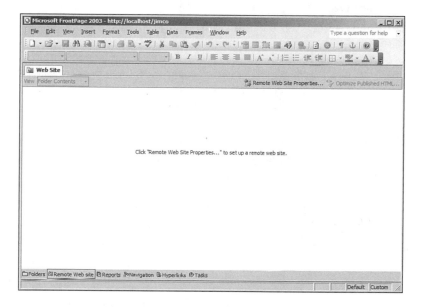

3. Click the Remote Web Site Properties Button as seen in Figure 16.1.

4. The Remote Web Site Properties dialog box is displayed as seen in Figure 16.2.

Figure 16.2
The Remote Web Site Properties dialog box is a vast improvement over the Publish dialog box in previous versions of FrontPage.

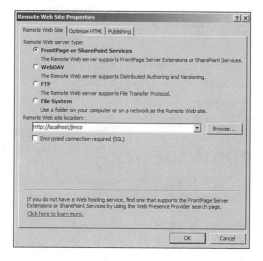

5. Choose a server type applicable to the server to which you will be publishing this Web site.

6. Enter the location for the remote Web site in the Remote Web site location box. The Web site location you enter here does not need to be an existing Web site.

7. If the remote Web server is using Secure Sockets Layer, check the Encrypted connection required (SSL) check box.

8. Click OK.

9. If the remote Web site doesn't exist and FrontPage prompts you to create it, click Yes.

> **NOTE**
>
> For more information on Secure Sockets Layer, check out Sams Publishing's *HTTP Developer's Handbook*.

Once FrontPage finishes creating the remote Web site (if necessary), Remote Web Site view displays a side-by-side view of the local and remote Web site as shown in Figure 16.3. From here you can copy files, synchronize files, or publish your Web site.

Figure 16.3
The Remote Web Site view provides easy access to the local and remote Web site.

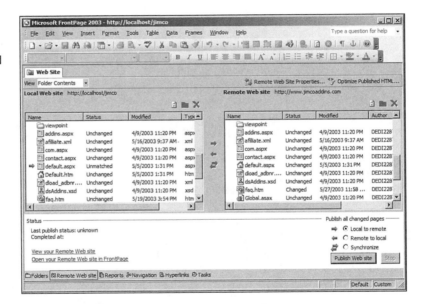

SERVER TYPES IN FRONTPAGE 2003

Before you proceed further with the Remote Web Site view, we should first discuss the server types that are available when publishing a FrontPage Web site.

Previous versions of FrontPage provided publishing functionality using either the FrontPage Server Extensions or FTP. FrontPage 2000 and FrontPage 2002 also allow for publishing to a SharePoint Team Services 1.0 Web server. FrontPage 2003 supports all those options, but also adds Distributed Authoring and Versioning (WebDAV), as seen in Figure 16.3. Choosing which option is best for you is, more often than not, a matter of what your host or ISP offers.

The following is a list of server types you can publish a Web site to using FrontPage 2003:

- **Server Extensions/Windows SharePoint Services**—Publishes to the server using FrontPage Server Extensions 2002 or earlier, or by using Windows SharePoint Services.

- **WebDAV**—Publishes to the Web server using Distributed Authoring and Versioning, also known as WebDAV or DAV.

- **FTP**—Publishes to the Web server using the *File Transfer Protocol*, commonly referred to as FTP.

- **File System**—Allows you to publish a FrontPage Web site to a file location. A Web server is not used when using this option.

> **NOTE**
>
> For more information on SharePoint Team Services v1.0, read *Special Edition Using Microsoft FrontPage 2002*. For more information on WebDAV and FTP, check out Sams Publishing's *Microsoft IIS 5 Administration*.

SERVER EXTENSIONS OR SHAREPOINT SERVICES

FrontPage no longer ships with the FrontPage Server Extensions, but FrontPage 2003 can publish to a Web server running the 2002 or earlier Server Extensions. If the Server Extensions are installed on the remote Web server, you should always choose the FrontPage or SharePoint Services option.

> **NOTE**
>
> A Web server can have the FrontPage Server Extensions or SharePoint Services installed, but not both. FrontPage can connect to either one in exactly the same way.

FrontPage is designed to always give precedence to FrontPage Server Extensions. If you connect to a Web server to open a Web site, the first thing that happens is a check for the FrontPage Server Extensions. Only when the server finds that they are not installed will FrontPage resort to other methods such as FTP or WebDAV. FrontPage's Web Folders work the same way. If the FrontPage Server Extensions are present, Web Folders will use them. If they are not, they will use WebDAV if it's available.

> **TIP**
>
> You can create a My Network Places shortcut to an FTP location, but it's not considered a Web Folder. A Web Folder uses either the FrontPage Server Extensions or WebDAV to communicate with the Web server.

CAUTION

Some Web components require the use of the FrontPage Server Extensions. If you are using one of these components, make sure that you choose the Server Extensions server type when setting remote Web site properties in FrontPage.

WebDAV

 WebDAV is a new publish option in FrontPage 2003. WebDAV is a protocol that allows for creating and editing files on a Web server. WebDAV also provides a means for storing information about each file and for file locking so that multiple people cannot overwrite a single file at one time. This makes WebDAV a good option for those who do not need FrontPage Server Extensions or Windows SharePoint Services.

You cannot publish to a remote Web server using WebDAV if the FrontPage Server Extensions, Windows SharePoint Services, or SharePoint Team Services are installed. If they are installed, FrontPage will inform you that you cannot publish to the server using WebDAV, as seen in Figure 16.4.

Figure 16.4
FrontPage will not allow you to publish using WebDAV if Server Extensions or SharePoint Services are installed.

 If you attempt to configure a remote Web site running WebDAV and you receive an error that the FrontPage Server Extensions aren't installed, see "WebDAV Tries to Use Server Extensions" in the "Troubleshooting" section of this chapter.

FILE TRANSFER PROTOCOL (FTP)

If Server Extensions, SharePoint Services, SharePoint Team Services 1.0, or WebDAV are not available to you, FTP will likely be your only other option. Even when Server Extensions are installed, many FrontPage users will resort to publishing using FTP if something goes wrong when publishing using the Server Extensions. This is not a good idea because FrontPage does not update its metadata when you publish using FTP. If you are using FrontPage and not a third-party FTP package, you can usually correct any problems by recalculating hyperlinks after publishing. Even so, if the remote server has the Server Extensions installed on it, you should use Server Extensions and not FTP when publishing. Any problems you do cause that can't be corrected by recalculating hyperlinks will have to be corrected by your host, who might not get the site fixed as speedily as you might like.

TIP

You will hear many people say that publishing using FTP corrupts the Server Extensions. Although not entirely true, it can cause problems when you publish to a Server Extensions Web server using FTP if you use a third-party FTP package.

FrontPage itself is smart enough to not publish any of the _vti folders when you publish using FTP. Third-party FTP products know nothing about the _vti folders, so they transfer them with the rest of the site. If you copy the _vti folders from one Web server to another, it can cause serious problems with the Server Extensions.

16

When you choose the FTP option, you are provided with a box to enter the FTP path as seen in Figure 16.5. If you are unsure of what directory to use, check with your hosting company or ISP.

Figure 16.5
When using FTP as your publish option, you must specify an FTP server name and a directory.

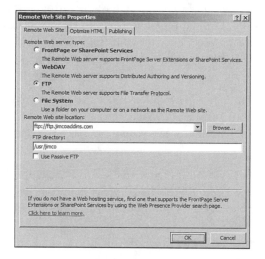

FrontPage 2003 also adds the ability to publish to an FTP server in passive mode by checking the Use Passive FTP check box. Passive FTP is a mode of FTP in which the client initiates all communication. Prior to passive FTP, all FTP communication was accomplished using active FTP. When using active FTP, the FTP server is responsible for initiating some of the communication. Because many computers block communication being initiated from an outside source, passive FTP is a better method to use in most cases.

Previous versions of FrontPage did not support passive FTP, and this addition is a welcome one to many FrontPage users. If you aren't sure whether you should use passive FTP, check with your host or Internet service provider.

 If publishing using FTP appears to succeed, but you can't see your Web site on the Internet, see "FTP Publish Isn't Working" in the "Troubleshooting" section of this chapter.

FILE SYSTEM

If you are publishing your Web site to a machine on your own network or to your local machine, you can choose to publish to the file system instead of to a Web server. Using this method, you can back up your Web site to another hard drive or to a removable device for archival purposes.

You can publish both to your local machine or to any other computer that is on your network. However, you will need to make sure that you have sufficient permissions to save files to any remote computers. Check with your network administrator if you're not sure about your level of access.

OPTIMIZING HTML

Another exciting new enhancement to FrontPage publishing introduced in FrontPage 2003 is the Optimize HTML feature. Using this feature, you can reduce the size of your files, thereby creating a faster browsing experience for your site visitors. Don't expect a huge increase though. Unless you have used a very large number of FrontPage components in your site, you won't be removing enough code to make a significant difference.

When using this feature, FrontPage will optimize the HTML of your Web pages before transferring them to the remote Web server. What types of optimization FrontPage performs depend on how you have configured the optimizations in the Remote Web Site Properties dialog.

The Optimize HTML settings (shown in Figure 16.6) are available by selecting View, Remote Web Site, clicking the Remote Web Site Properties button, and then clicking the Optimize HTML tab, or by clicking the Optimize Published HTML button.

Figure 16.6
FrontPage 2003 offers a wide assortment of HTML optimizations that can be applied when publishing your Web site.

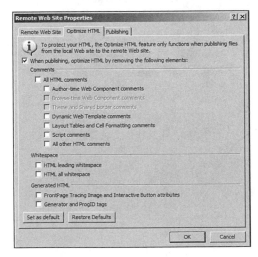

NOTE

> FrontPage will only apply the HTML optimizations when publishing from a local Web server to a remote Web server. This prevents any changes to the original source files.

By checking the When Publishing, Optimize HTML by Removing the Following Elements: check box, the following optimization settings are available:

- **All HTML Comments**—Selects all the check boxes in the Comments section, thereby removing all comments from your Web pages when publishing.

- **Author-time Web Component comments**—Removes all comments for author-time Web components. Removing these comments will make it impossible to edit the FrontPage Web component on the remote Web server.

- **Browse-time Web Component comments**—Removes the comments for browse-time Web components. This option is unavailable if the FrontPage or SharePoint Services option is chosen on the Remote Web Site tab because removing these comments in that situation would break the Web components.

- **Theme and Shared Border comments**—Removes the comments for themes and shared borders. This option is unavailable if the FrontPage or SharePoint Services option is chosen on the Remote Web Site tab because removing these comments in that situation would break the themes and shared borders.

- **Dynamic Web Template comments**—Removes comments from Dynamic Web Templates and the pages to which they are attached. Removing these comments essentially detaches the Web pages on the remote Web server from the Dynamic Web Template and converts the Dynamic Web Template on the remote server into a regular page.

- **Layout Tables and Cell Formatting comments**—Removes comments for FrontPage Layout Tables and Cells. Although this does convert the table in the Web page on the remote Web server back into a regular table, layout tools can be re-enabled on the remote server if needed.

- **Script comments**—Removes comments from client-side scripts.

- **All other HTML comments**—Removes all HTML comments not covered in any of the preceding options.

- **HTML leading whitespace**—Removes any tab characters or spaces at the beginning of all lines of code.

- **HTML all whitespace**—Removes all whitespace in HTML code. This includes any line breaks in the code, but does not include any whitespace inside scripts.

- **FrontPage Tracing Image and Interactive Button attributes**—Removes the attributes from Tracing Images and Interactive Buttons. These attributes allow you to see Tracing Images and edit Interactive Buttons in the local Web site.

- **Generator and ProgID tags**—Removes the FrontPage Generator and ProgID meta tags from your pages when the Web site is published.

16

By clicking the Set as Default button, you can save the current optimization settings as the default settings for your Web site so that they can be restored easily by clicking the Restore Defaults button. This change only applies to the site currently open in FrontPage and not to other Web sites.

 If you copy your files to the remote Web server, and the optimization settings don't seem to work, see "HTML Optimization Doesn't Change Anything" in the "Troubleshooting" section of this chapter.

CONFIGURING THE PUBLISH SETTINGS

By clicking the Publishing tab in the Remote Web Site Properties dialog, you can configure the settings that FrontPage uses to determine which files to automatically transfer and you can enable and disable logging while publishing (see Figure 16.7).

Figure 16.7
The publishing options allow you to configure how FrontPage chooses which files to publish.

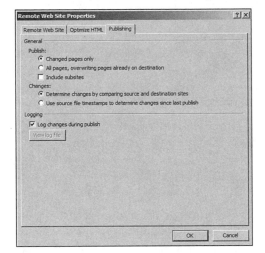

FrontPage essentially has two options for publishing your Web site; publish only those pages that have changed since the last time the Web site was published and publish all pages regardless of whether or not they have changed. The latter overwrites all pages that currently exist on the remote Web site, so use it only when you are sure that it's what you need to do.

By selecting the Changed Pages Only option, FrontPage will publish only those pages that have changed since the last successful publish of the Web site. To determine whether a change has taken place, FrontPage uses the option you have selected in the Changes section.

- **Determine Changes by Comparing Source and Destination Sites**—If this option is selected, FrontPage will use its metadata to determine which files have changed since the last successful publish.

- **Use Source File Timestamps to Determine Changes Since Last Publish**—This setting causes FrontPage to compare timestamps on the local server with those on the remote server to determine if a change has taken place.

By default, only files in the local Web site are published. Any subsites of the local Web site are not published unless the Include Subsites check box is checked.

 If your files aren't copied even though changes have been made, see "Changed Files Aren't Published" in the "Troubleshooting" section of this article.

TIP

> If you tend to publish your Web site from more than one computer, you should always choose the first option because you will not be able to rely on timestamps on the local server to indicate which files have changed.

If you would like for FrontPage to log all activity during the publish process, check the Log Changes During Publish check box. Publish logs can be viewed in your Web browser by clicking the View Log File button.

 If you receive errors when attempting to view the publish log, see "Unable to View Publish Log" in the "Troubleshooting" section of this chapter.

By default the publish log shows all events that occurred during publishing. By selecting a specific type of information in the Show Only dropdown as seen in Figure 16.8, you can easily view a specific kind of information.

Figure 16.8
The publish log allows you to view specific types of information by selecting an item from the Show Only dropdown.

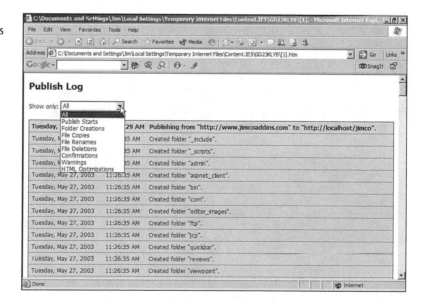

TIP

> The publish log is an HTML file that is generated on-the-fly by FrontPage and displayed in your Web browser. You can, however, save or print it from within your Web browser if you want a permanent record of the publish process.

REMOTE WEB SITE VIEW—PUBLISHING WEB SITES

After you have configured a remote Web site and set all of your publish options, you are ready to begin copying files and folders. Several options are available so that you can accomplish that:

- Publishing the site
- Copying individual files
- Copying a group of selected files
- Synchronizing individual files
- Synchronizing a group of selected files

PUBLISHING THE SITE

When you publish a Web site, FrontPage uses the options you have configured in the Remote Web Site Properties dialog to determine which files and folders are transferred. You can choose whether you want to publish from the remote Web site to the local Web site or the other way around, as seen in Figure 16.9.

Figure 16.9
The Remote Web Site view allows you to choose between transferring from the local site to the remote site or the other way around.

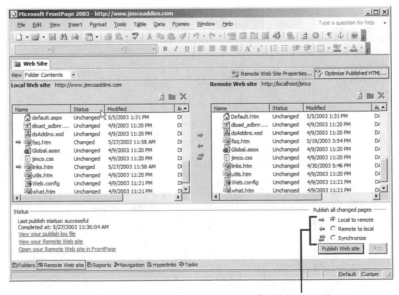

Publishing settings

If you have selected the Changed Pages Only option in the Remote Web Site Properties dialog, you also have the option to synchronize the files between the two Web servers. When the Web site is synchronized, FrontPage will ensure that both Web servers contain an identical copy of the Web site. If a file is not matched up between the two Web servers, FrontPage will copy the file from the server containing a more recent version to the server containing the out-of-date version. This is the preferred method of publishing if you have multiple authors working on the Web site.

After selecting your preferred publish method, FrontPage will display icons next to any files that will be copied to indicate what it intends to do with that file during publishing. These icons consist of a blue arrow that points in the direction that FrontPage will copy the file. For example, if FrontPage intends to copy a file from the local Web site to the remote Web site, a blue arrow will appear next to the file in the local Web site listing that points toward the remote Web site. A blue arrow pointing in both directions indicates that the file is unmatched between the local and remote sites and FrontPage intends to synchronize the file. In Figure 16.9, the icons indicate that FrontPage will copy the files faq.htm and links.htm to the remote Web site when the Web site is published.

If you have a large Web site, it might be difficult to determine which files will be published or which files are not matched on the two Web sites. By selecting an item in the View drop-down, you can filter the view in Remote Web site view, as seen in Figure 16.10.

Figure 16.10
The Remote Web site view allows you to easily filter which files are displayed.

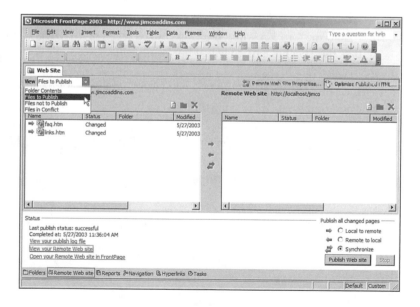

To start the publish process, select whether you want to publish local to remote, remote to local, or synchronize files, and then click the Publish Web Site button. After FrontPage successfully publishes the Web site, it will display the publish status in the lower left of the Remote Web site view (as shown in Figure 16.10). From here, you can view the publish log (if it was enabled), view the remote Web site in your Web browser, or open the remote Web site in FrontPage.

Unlike previous versions of FrontPage, FrontPage 2003 will warn you if you have unsaved pages open when you begin the publishing process as seen in Figure 16.11. If you click the Yes button, the unsaved page is saved and publishing continues. If you click No, the unsaved page is not saved and publishing continues. Cancel stops the publishing process altogether.

Figure 16.11
FrontPage will warn you if you have unsaved changes when you are publishing your Web site.

 If you publish your changes, but you don't notice any changes when browsing to your Web site, see "Published Changes Aren't Visible" in the "Troubleshooting" section of this chapter.

COPYING FILES

If you'd prefer not to publish the entire Web site, you can easily copy only those files that you choose using the Remote Web Site view. When copying files using this method, you are not actually publishing the Web site, and the publish log and other publish statistics are not modified.

To copy files between the two Web servers without publishing, perform these steps:

1. Select one or more files in either the local or the remote Web site. To select multiple files, hold the Ctrl key while you click files to select noncontiguous files. To select contiguous files, click the first file and hold Shift while selecting the last file.

2. Right-click one of the selected files and select <u>C</u>opy selected files or S<u>y</u>nchronize selected files from the context menu as seen in Figure 16.12. You can also use the copy or synchronize buttons to copy files as seen in Figure 16.13.

Figure 16.12
Copying or synchronizing multiple files is performed by right-clicking one of the files and selecting your choice from the context menu.

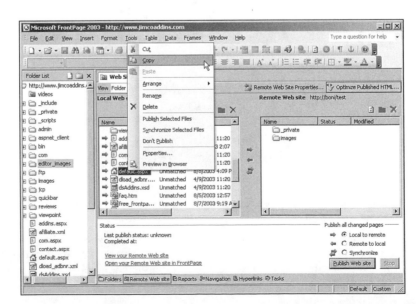

Figure 16.13
In addition to using the context menu, you can use the buttons in the Remote Web Site view to copy or synchronize files.

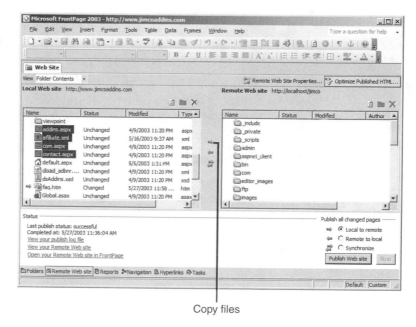

Copy files

SETTING PUBLISH STATUS

Files might exist in your Web site that you simply don't want to publish whether they've changed or not. For example, in my Web site, I don't like to publish all my add-ins every time I publish the site because they don't change often. When they do change, I just manually copy the new files. The publish status feature allows me to prevent those large files from publishing with the rest of the Web site.

The easiest method of setting publish status on a file is to simply right-click the file and select Don't Publish from the menu. The Don't Publish option is a toggle item, so selecting it will place a check next to it. Selecting it again will remove the check and reset the publish status for that file. You can also select multiple files and set the publish status on all those files in one step.

When a file's status has been set to Don't Publish, a red circle with a white x through it is displayed in FrontPage, as seen in Figure 16.14. The icon indicating publish status is not just visible in Remote Web Site view. As seen in Figure 16.15, FrontPage will indicate the publish status in all views using an appropriate icon.

TIP

To set publish status for all files in a particular folder, switch to Folder view in FrontPage and select all the files by clicking the first file and then holding the Shift key while clicking the last file. You can then right-click on any file and set the publish status for all of them.

To accomplish the same task in one step, use Jimco Selective Publish, available from http://www.jimcoaddins.com/addins.aspx.

Figure 16.14
All the files in this folder have a publish status of Don't Publish.

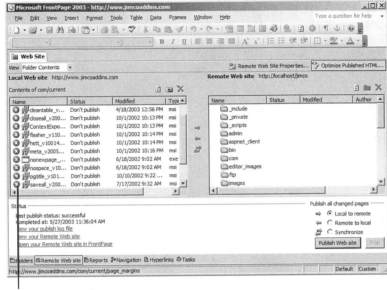

These files will not be published

Figure 16.15
Icons that represent publish status are visible in all views.

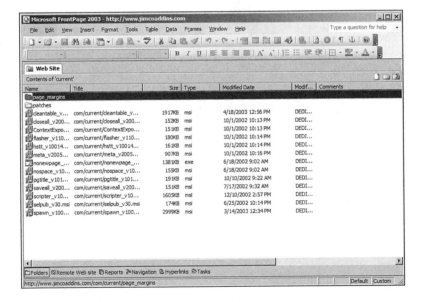

TROUBLESHOOTING

WEBDAV TRIES TO USE SERVER EXTENSIONS

When I try to publish with WebDAV, I get a message telling me that the remote Web server doesn't appear to have the FrontPage Server Extensions installed. Does WebDAV require the FrontPage Server Extensions?

No. As a matter of fact, if the FrontPage Server Extensions are installed, FrontPage won't let you publish with WebDAV. If you are getting this message, it is usually caused by a permissions problem on the remote Web server.

You'll usually see a message inside the error dialog box that will tell you the error code from the Web server. If it's a 403.# or a 401.#, it's almost certainly a permissions problem. In either case, check with the host. They should be able to correct the problem.

FTP PUBLISH ISN'T WORKING

I am publishing using FTP. FrontPage said that my Web site was published successfully, but I don't see any of my changes when I browse to my Web site.

This is most likely caused by an incorrect entry for the FTP directory when you are publishing. Check with your host and make sure that you are entering the correct directory. To avoid any confusion later, make sure to remove the files from the incorrect directory after you successfully publish your Web site.

HTML OPTIMIZATION DOESN'T CHANGE ANYTHING

I have set up some HTML optimizations, but after I copy my files to the remote Web server, I don't see any change. Is this a bug?

It's not a bug. HTML Optimizations are only applied when you publish a site. If you choose to copy a single file or a group of files, that isn't actually publishing. In order for HTML optimizations to work, you have to set publish options and click the Publish Web Site button or use the File, Publish Site menu option in FrontPage.

CHANGED FILES AREN'T PUBLISHED

I have selected to publish changed pages only, but when my Web site is published, FrontPage isn't publishing my changed files.

The most common cause of this is metadata that is out-of-date. To correct the problem, open the local Web site and select Tools, Recalculate Hyperlinks. This will refresh the metadata.

UNABLE TO VIEW PUBLISH LOG

I have successfully published, but when I try to view my publish log, I keep getting strange errors.

The Publish Log is actually an HTML file that FrontPage saves to the `Temporary Internet Files` folder on your computer before displaying it. The `Temporary Internet Files` folder has a limit on the number of files it can contain, and when that limit is reached, strange errors can occur.

Open Internet Explorer and select Tools, Internet Options and click the General tab. Click the Delete Files button and then click OK. Internet Explorer will remove all of your temporary files. It might take a while, but it should correct your problem.

PUBLISHED CHANGES AREN'T VISIBLE

I just finished publishing and it was successful. However, when I browse to `http://www.mysite.com`, *I don't see my new content. What's going on?*

This can be caused by having multiple home pages on your site. For example, say that your hosting company created your Web site for you and it had a page in it called `index.htm`, which is the home page. When you browse to `http://www.mysite.com`, it will display the `index.htm` page because it's the home page.

Now let's say that your local Web site uses `Default.htm` for the home page. When you publish, FrontPage will leave the existing `index.htm` on the remote server because there is no conflict with it and files in the local Web site. If the Web server is configured to recognize `index.htm` first as the home page, even after a successful page, you'll still get `index.htm` when you browse to your Web site.

The solution is to open the site in FrontPage and check to see which page displays the house icon indicating that it is the home page. You might need to delete or rename an incorrect home page.

FRONT AND CENTER: REMOVING UNUSED FILES

Many hosting companies will set a quota on the amount of disk space you can use on your Web site. In order to stay within that quota, you might find yourself deleting files from your Web site in an attempt to clean out the clutter. It's a great idea provided you don't make a mistake and delete a file that you need. Remember, FrontPage has no recycle bin! In order to prevent any downtime on your Web site, you can use FrontPage's synchronization features to organize and clean up your Web site.

Open your local Web site and locate and delete any files that you no longer need. Test your site after each deletion and use the FrontPage reports to ensure that you haven't broken any links. Once you have everything working after cleaning up your local site, publish your Web site to your host and select the option to synchronize the sites. FrontPage will prompt you to delete the same files on the remote Web server that you deleted on your local machine. By letting FrontPage's synchronization features handle the cleanup, you greatly reduce the risk of deleting the wrong file by mistake.

CHAPTER 17

SECURITY AND ADMINISTRATION OF A WEB SITE

In this chapter

SERVER EXTENSIONS CONFIGURATION AND ADMINISTRATION

Security is one of the most troublesome topics for many users of FrontPage, likely because a complete understanding of security requires a comprehensive understanding of not only FrontPage Server Extensions implementation, but also of Windows security. This chapter won't teach you everything about Windows security by any means, but it will teach you enough about it for you to understand how FrontPage implements security and how you can manage the security of your Web site. Administration of a Server Extensions Web site is broken down in to three separate areas; site administration, virtual server administration, and server administration.

> **NOTE**
>
> For more information on virtual servers, read *Internet Information Services Administration* from Que Publishing.

FrontPage 2003 does not ship with the FrontPage Server Extensions. However, Windows 2000, Windows XP Professional, and Windows Server 2003 all ship with the FrontPage Server Extensions. If you are running Windows 2000 or Windows XP, Internet Information Services includes the FrontPage 2000 Server Extensions. This chapter deals with the FrontPage 2002 Server Extensions, so if you want to follow along with the concepts discussed here, you will need to download and install the latest version of the Server Extensions.

You can download the FrontPage 2002 Server Extensions by visiting `http://fpse.frontpagelink.com`.

> **NOTE**
>
> Many of the settings and configurations mentioned in this chapter are configurable only by the server administrator. If you are hosting your Web site with a hosting company, you will need to contact your hosting company for changes to these settings.

→ For more information on permissions for a Windows SharePoint Services Web site, **see** "Windows SharePoint Services 2.0," **p. 943**.

To gain a better understanding of each of these areas of administration, let's discuss the configuration options available in each.

FRONTPAGE CLIENT CONFIGURATION

The majority of Web site configuration and administration is performed using the Microsoft SharePoint Administrator, but the FrontPage client does have a few places where you can make configuration changes to the Web site as well.

Two menu options are generally used to configure a FrontPage Web site from within the FrontPage client. They are the Ser_v_er menu item and the _S_ite Settings menu item, both of which are on the _T_ools menu.

 If the Server and Site Settings menu options are not available, see "Server and Site Settings Are Grayed Out" in the "Troubleshooting" section of this chapter.

THE SERVER MENU

The _A_dministration Home menu item allows you to access the Microsoft SharePoint Administrator. It launches a Web browser and loads the SharePoint Administrator in it, but only if you have sufficient privileges to do so. In earlier versions of FrontPage, there was a Security menu instead, and if you didn't have permissions to change security, the menu item would be disabled. This was a source of confusion for many users of FrontPage who were trying to configure permissions for their Web site. FrontPage 2003 has improved the situation with the Server menu.

FrontPage 2003 doesn't disable the menu item if you don't have sufficient privileges. Instead, when you select _T_ools, Ser_v_er, _A_dministration Home and you don't have a sufficient level of access to see the page, the Web server will prompt you for a username and password. If you don't enter the username and password of a user with proper credentials, you don't get in. If you select _T_ools, Ser_v_er, _P_ermissions and you don't have sufficient rights to edit permissions, FrontPage displays a dialog box informing you of that and allows you to enter the credentials of a user with sufficient rights as seen in Figure 17.1. This is a vast improvement over previous versions.

Figure 17.1
You cannot change permissions unless you have sufficient rights.

The C_h_ange Password, _B_ackup Web Site, and _R_estore Web Site items on the Server menu only apply to Windows SharePoint Services.

→ For more information on Windows SharePoint Services, **see** "Windows SharePoint Services 2.0," **p. 943**.

THE SITE SETTINGS DIALOG BOX

The Site Settings dialog box (see Figure 17.2) is a multi-tabbed dialog box that provides many settings for Web site configuration, as well as information about the Web site and Server Extensions. To access the Site Settings dialog box, select _T_ools, S_i_te Settings.

THE GENERAL TAB

The General tab shown in Figure 17.2 allows you to configure the Web site's name, but only if the Web site is a subsite. If you have opened the root Web site, the Web Name box will be disabled.

Figure 17.2
The Site Settings dialog box allows you to configure Web site settings.

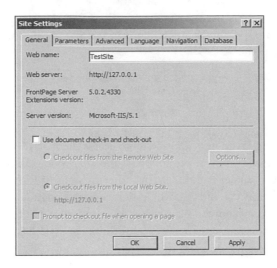

If the Web site name is changed, the URL that is used to access the Web site is also changed. For example, if you have opened `http://localhost/mySite` and you open the Site Settings dialog box, the Web Name box will read `mySite`. If you change that to `WebSite`, the URL for your Web site will change to `http://localhost/WebSite`.

Under the Web Name box is a label that displays the Web server. This is the URL of the root Web site. This label displays the URL using the same name you used to open the site. For example, if your machine name is `Jimco`, the URLs `http://localhost`, `http://jimco`, and `http://127.0.0.1` all point to the same Web site. Whichever one of these URLs you use to open a subsite on the Web server is what is displayed in the Web server label on the Site Settings dialog box. The Web server label might also display a disk location in the case of a disk-based Web site being opened in FrontPage.

The next piece of information available to you in the Site Settings dialog box is the FrontPage Server Extensions Version label. This tells you what version of the FrontPage Server Extensions the server is using. Any version that starts with a 5 indicates the 2002 version. A version that starts with a 4 indicates that the 2000 Server Extensions are installed. If the version number that is listed begins with a 6, it means that you are using a disk-based Web site.

→ For more information on disk-based Web sites, **see** "Creating a Disk-based Web Site," **p. 253**.

The Server Version label specifies the version of the Web server that is hosting the Web site. In Figure 17.2, the Web server is running on a Windows XP Professional machine because it shows Microsoft IIS 5.1. Microsoft IIS 5.0 indicates a Windows 2000 Web Server, and IIS 6.0 indicates Windows Server 2003. If the label says No Server Currently in Use, it means that you are using a disk-based Web site.

The bottom part of the General tab of the Site Settings dialog box allows you to configure FrontPage's built-in document check-in/check-out functionality.

→ For more information on the document check-in/check-out feature of FrontPage, **see** "Checking Documents In and Out," **p. 624**.

THE PARAMETERS TAB

The Parameters tab of the Site Settings dialog box provides access to Web parameters that are used in conjunction with the Substitution Web component. This is not a Web configuration setting, so we'll move on to the Advanced tab.

→ For more information on using the Substitution Web component, **see** "Using Web Components, Shared Borders, and Link Bars," **p. 167**.

THE ADVANCED TAB

The Advanced tab is shown in Figure 17.3. From here, you can configure the client-side scripting language, specify whether hidden files and folders are visible in FrontPage, and delete FrontPage's temporary files.

Figure 17.3
The Advanced tab configures advanced Web site settings.

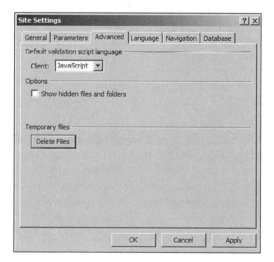

The Default Validation Script Language dropdown sets the scripting language that is used by FrontPage Server Extensions to generate client-side validation scripts. When you configure an HTML form field in FrontPage, you have the option to have FrontPage validate the information entered. FrontPage uses client-side scripting to do this, and that scripting is generated automatically by the Server Extensions when the page is saved.

If you select VBScript in the Default Validation Script Language dropdown, the Server Extensions will generate VBScript validation scripts; if you select JavaScript, the Server Extensions will generate JavaScript validation scripts; and if you select <None>, the Server Extensions will not create any client-side script to validate your form. Instead, the information that is entered is validated on the Web server and if validation fails, the user is presented with an error page.

TIP

Keep in mind that VBScript only works on Internet Explorer 3.0 and later. If you expect that people will be using a different browser, you will want to either use JavaScript or set the scripting language to <None> so that it will be taken care of on the server.

The Show Hidden Files and Folders check box allows you to configure FrontPage so that it will display hidden files and folders in FrontPage views that display files or folders. A hidden folder or file has an underscore in front of the name. By default, the only hidden item that FrontPage will display is the _private folder. If you want to see other hidden files or folders, you should check the Show Hidden Files and Folders check box and click Apply or OK. You will be prompted to recalculate the Web site as seen in Figure 17.4. Click Yes to recalculate the Web site, and FrontPage will display hidden folders and files.

Figure 17.4
When selecting to show hidden files and folders, you will need to recalculate the Web site to make them visible.

NOTE

A file that is marked as Hidden by Windows is not considered hidden by FrontPage by default. FrontPage displays all files and folders unless they have an underscore in front of the name, even if they are marked as Hidden by Windows.

The _vti folders are never visible in FrontPage. FrontPage is hard-coded not to ever show these files or folders regardless of whether you have configured FrontPage to show hidden files and folders.

The Delete Files button in the Temporary Files section deletes any temporary files that FrontPage has created for the Web site currently opened. These files might exist in the FrontPageTempDir folder located in the logged in user's Temp directory, and they might be meta-cache files (.web files) located in the C:\Documents and Settings\<User>\Application Data\Microsoft\Web Server Extensions\Cache folder.

TIP

The meta-cache files are a common source of problems in FrontPage. If these files are corrupted, you might have problems opening the Web site in FrontPage. These problems exhibit themselves by causing a lot of disk activity when trying to open a Web site, followed by a message indicating that you are either out of memory or disk space.

To correct this problem, open the C:\Documents and Settings\<User>\Application Data\Microsoft\Web Server Extensions\Cache folder and delete all .web files found there. FrontPage will re-create them when it needs them.

Many FrontPage experts recommend that you click the Delete Files button often and then manually delete all temporary files created by FrontPage to keep things cleaned up. In my experience, as long as you aren't experiencing problems, it's best just to leave these files alone. FrontPage will take care of cleaning them up when they start to use a lot of disk space.

THE LANGUAGE TAB

The next tab in the Site Settings dialog box is the Language tab shown in Figure 17.5.

Figure 17.5
The Language tab allows for the configuration of page encoding and the language used by Server Extensions for errors.

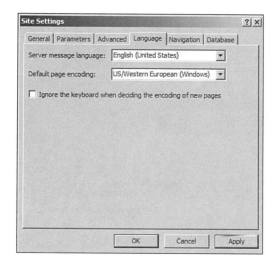

The Server Message Language dropdown configured the language that is used by the Server Extensions to display server-generated messages when form-field validation fails, when forms are submitted, and so on. The languages available to you depend on the languages that the Web server has been configured to use. In many cases, only one language is available in the dropdown.

The Default Page Encoding dropdown allows you to configure the default page encoding that FrontPage uses for the Content-Type meta tag that is inserted in to new pages. The Web browsers uses this setting to determine how the page should be displayed. Changing this setting inappropriately might cause unpredictable results when your Web pages are displayed. Setting the dropdown to <None> will cause FrontPage to leave off the Content-Type meta tag when creating new pages.

FrontPage will use your Keyboard and Regional Settings configuration from the Windows Control Panel to verify character encoding for new pages. If you'd prefer FrontPage to use your manually configured settings instead, check the Ignore the Keyboard When Deciding the Encoding of New Pages checkbox.

17

THE NAVIGATION TAB

The Navigation tab allows you to configure the labels that are seen on FrontPage Link Bars (see Figure 17.6). After making a change here, make sure that you recalculate the Web site by selecting Tools, Recalculate Hyperlinks. This will cause FrontPage to regenerate pages with your new settings.

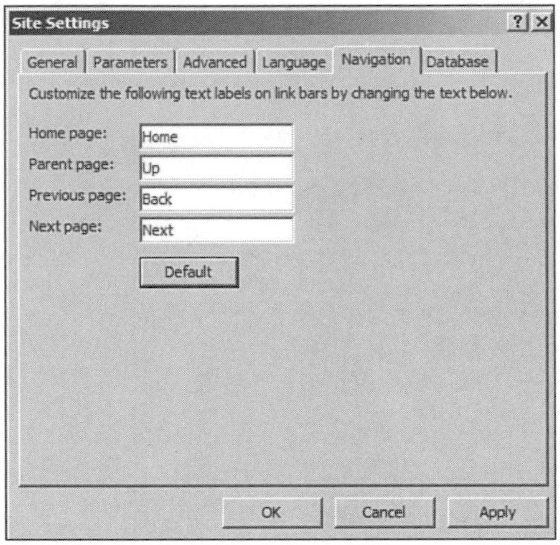

Figure 17.6
The Navigation tab allows for configuration of FrontPage Link Bars.

→ The Database tab on the Site Settings dialog box is covered in detail in "Creating a Database Connection," **p. 706**.

SITE ADMINISTRATION

Site administration is for configuration of one particular Web site. Using site administration, you can configure what users have access to your Web site and specify the type of information logged about who is visiting your Web site, what pages they are viewing, and so on.

To administer the security of a FrontPage Web site, you use the Microsoft SharePoint Administrator (see Figure 17.7) if you are using the FrontPage 2002 Server Extensions or the SharePoint Central Administration (see Figure 17.8) if you are using Windows SharePoint Services. Both are located in Administrative Tools, but you can also access them by opening the Web site in FrontPage and then selecting Tools, Server, Administration Home after opening the Web site in FrontPage.

→ For details on how to open the Web site in FrontPage, **see** "Opening and Working with Existing Web Sites," **p. 283**.

Figure 17.7
Site Administration for a FrontPage Server Extensions 2002 Web site.

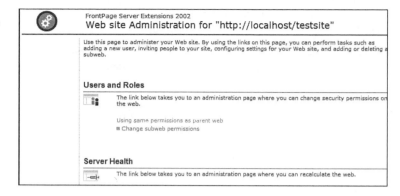

Figure 17.8
Site Settings for a Windows SharePoint Services Web site.

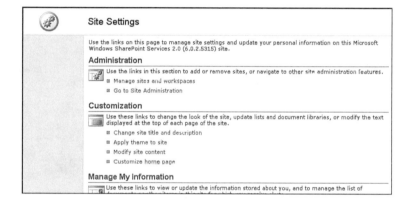

When using a FrontPage Server Extensions 2002 Web site, setting up permissions for your Web site changes the file and folder permissions on the operating system itself according to predefined roles. When using a Windows SharePoint Services site, all the content is stored in a Microsoft SQL Server database, so the usual rules don't apply. In this section, we will cover only the permissions for a FrontPage Server Extensions 2002 Web site.

→ For details on managing a Windows SharePoint Services 2.0 Web site, **see** "Windows SharePoint Services 2.0," **p. 943**.

ROLES AND RIGHTS—AN OVERVIEW

Five built-in roles are available to you on a FrontPage Server Extensions Web site. A *role* is a FrontPage group that has certain rights to a Web site. These rights can range from being able to simply browse the site to being able to administer and change permissions on the Web site. The roles that are provided by default and their default rights are as follows:

- **Browser**—This is the lowest level of access to a FrontPage Web site. A user who has been given only the Browser role can browse the Web site, but cannot post to any Web site discussions or modify the site content in any other way.

- **Contributor**—A Contributor has all the rights available to a Browser, but she can also view and post to discussions on the Web site.

- **Author**—An Author can open the Web site in FrontPage and add, edit, and delete pages, but she can't apply a theme, a shared border, or link style sheets to the Web site.

- **Advanced Author**—An Advanced Author can perform any editing task on the Web site, but she cannot set permissions on the Web site. An Advanced Author also cannot create new Web sites or subsites. This is the level of access that most hosting companies provide FrontPage users.

- **Administrator**—An Administrator has all the available rights on a Web site.

TIP

> A server administrator can configure the FrontPage Server Extensions so that they don't use roles to implement security. When roles are turned off, the Server Extensions will only allow the Browser, Author, and Administrator roles.

NOTE

> For more information on Windows users and groups and Windows administration, read *Windows 2000 User Management* from Que Publishing.

The twelve rights that can be granted to members of a particular role are as follows:

- **Author Page**—Users with this right can open the Web site in FrontPage and create, edit, or delete Web pages and folders.

- **Browse**—Users with this right can browse to any Web page in the Web site.

- **Set Source Control**—Users with this right can configure the source control database for Web sites that are under source control.

- **Theme Web**—Users with this right can apply a theme to the Web site.

- **Border Web**—Users with this right can apply a border to the Web site.

- **Link Style Sheets**—Users with this right can link style sheets to the Web site.

- **Configure Access**—Users with this right can manage permissions and roles for the Web site, but they cannot create new users.

- **Create Accounts**—Users with this right can create new users for the Web site, which are created as local Windows accounts on the Web server.

- **Manage Server Health**—Users with this right can use the Server Health tool.

- **Manage Usage Analysis**—Users with this right can manage Usage Analysis settings.

- **Manage Subweb**—Users with this right can create new subsites, rename existing subsites, and delete subsites.

- **Recalc Web**—Users with this right can run the Recalculate Hyperlinks command to recalculate the Web site.

→ For more information on the Server Health and Usage Analysis tools, see "Configuring Usage Analysis Settings" and "Managing Server Health" in this chapter, **p. 339-340**.

> **NOTE**
>
> For more information on FrontPage Server Extensions, see the SharePoint Team Services Administrator's Guide available at `http://fpserk.frontpagelink.com`.

A user can be a member of more than one role and her rights are cumulative. You can very easily change the default rights assigned to a role, as you will see later, and you can also create your own roles and change the list of rights that are available for users of your Web site. All of this will be discussed in detail as you progress through the chapter.

CREATING USERS AND ROLES

To access the Site Administration page open your root Web site in FrontPage (that is, `http://localhost`) and select Tools, Server, Administration Home.

You should now see the Site Administration page as shown previously in Figure 17.7.

→ For details on opening a Web site in FrontPage, **see** "Opening and Working with Existing Web Sites," **p. 283**.

CHANGING ANONYMOUS ACCESS

The first link in Users and Roles is the Change Anonymous Access Settings link. (If this is not your first link, make sure that you opened the root Web site and not a subsite.) Most Web sites allow for anonymous browsing, which means that you don't have to enter a username and password in order to browse the Web site. You can change whether your Web site allows anonymous access using the Change Anonymous Access Settings link.

Click the Change Anonymous Access Settings link to display the Change Anonymous Access Settings page as seen in Figure 17.9. From here, you can choose whether anonymous browsing is enabled and what role is used for anonymous browsers. In almost all cases, you will want to use the Browser role for anonymous browsing because it gives the least amount of permissions to people. If you turn off anonymous access, your site will not be accessible unless users are authenticated either by entering a valid username and password, or by having a valid user credential passed automatically from a Windows login.

> **NOTE**
>
> If you want to create a Web site where people can sign up for access and receive a password, using Web site permissions is not your best option. Instead, you can use ASP or ASP.NET to authenticate users against a database. Doing so will require skills in ASP or ASP.NET.

> **NOTE**
>
> For more information on Anonymous access and other authentication methods of Internet Information Services, read *Internet Information Services Administration* from Que Publishing.

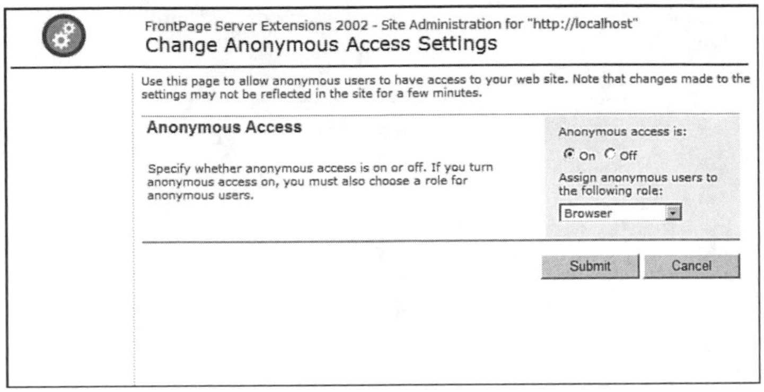

Figure 17.9
The Change Anonymous Access Settings page allows you to prevent unauthorized users from browsing your site.

ADDING AND DELETING ACCOUNTS

The next link is the Click Here to Add or Delete Accounts link, along with an informational message indicating how many accounts you've created and how many are allowed. (If this is not your second link, make sure that you opened the root Web site and not a subsite.)

By default, the FrontPage Server Extensions allow an unlimited number of user accounts, but the Web site can be configured so that the number of accounts for the site are limited to a specific number.

→ For more information on configuring user account limits, **see** "Virtual Server Administration," **p. 345**, later in this chapter.

When you click the Click Here to Add or Delete Accounts link, you are taken to the Manage Virtual Server Accounts page (see Figure 17.10), where you can see the accounts that you have created, add new accounts, and delete existing accounts. Accounts added here are Windows accounts that can then be added to roles so that they can access your Web site.

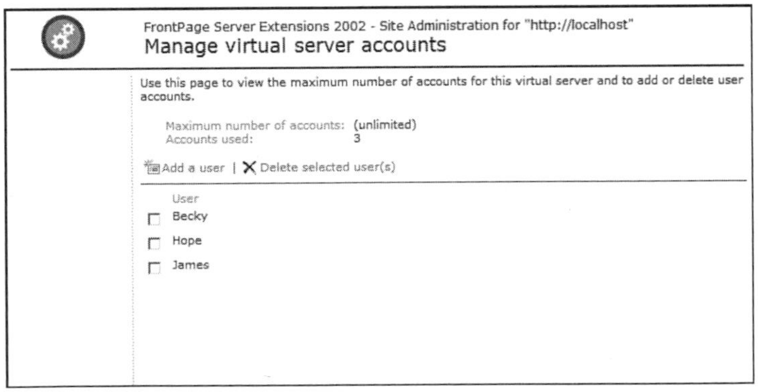

Figure 17.10
Creating new accounts for access to your site is done on the Manage Virtual Server Accounts page.

MANAGING USERS

The next link in Users and Roles is Manage Users. Using this link, you can add new users to your Web site or make existing users a member of a role. FrontPage grants access by checking the user's group membership in Windows. The FrontPage Server Extensions create Windows groups on the Web server to manage access to the Web site. Each group maps directly to a particular role. The groups for the default roles are as follows:

- `OWS_##########_admin`—Administrator
- `OWS_##########_advauthor`—Advanced Author
- `OWS_##########_author`—Author
- `OWS_##########_collab`—Contributor
- `OWS_##########_browser`—Browser

The number (#) signs in each group are replaced with a unique number for the site. The FrontPage Server Extensions create a group for each Web site with unique permissions on the Web server. However, the group is only created once a user is assigned to that role.

If all members of a particular role are removed, the group representing that role is not deleted. It is maintained so that it can be used if a user is added to the role at a later date.

NOTE

> A server administrator can configure the Server Extensions so that machine groups are not created to implement security. In those cases, the Server Extensions will set each user's permissions individually.

To assign a user to a particular role

1. Click Manage Users.
2. Click Add a User. The Add a User page is displayed as shown in Figure 17.11.

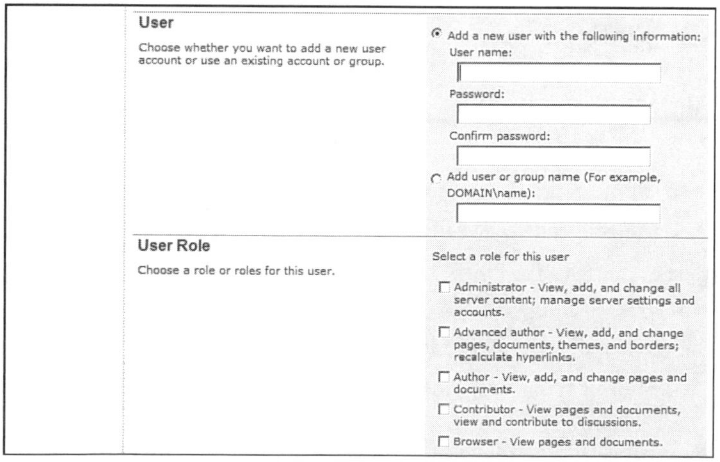

Figure 17.11
The Add a User page is where you add users for your Web site.

3. In the User Name box, enter the username to use for your new user.

4. Enter the password for the new user and enter it again to confirm it.

5. Select a role for the user. You can select multiple roles if needed.

6. Click Add User to add your new user.

Your new user should now appear in the Manage Users page as shown in Figure 17.12. In this example, the account appears as DADATOP\TestUser. DADATOP is the name of the machine or domain, and TestUser is the name of the user.

Figure 17.12
The TestUser user has been added to the Advanced Author role.

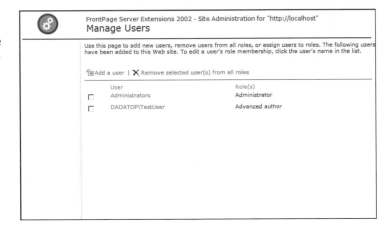

  If you are prompted for username and password after clicking Manage Users and you are not able to access the page, see "Not Authorized to Manage Users" in the "Troubleshooting" section of this chapter.

MANAGING ROLES

The Site Administration page also provides access to manage the roles in your Web site. Using the Manage Roles page, you can select which rights are available to a particular role. To add or remove rights from a particular role

1. Click the Manage Roles link to display the Edit Role page shown in Figure 17.13.

2. Click the role that you want to edit.

3. Place a check in the check box for the right you want to assign to the role and remove the check from any right that you want to remove from the role.

4. Change the description to match the new role's rights.

5. Click Submit to commit changes to the role.

FrontPage stores your role configuration inside a file called roles.ini, which is located in C:\Documents and Settings\All Users\Application Data\Microsoft\Web Server Extensions\50\W3SVC1 on the Web server. The roles.ini file is used to reapply permissions when you run the Server Health function and choose to tighten security. Therefore, if you manually alter any permissions in your FrontPage content area, the Server Extensions will change them back to what they were prior to your modifications as soon as you check server health.

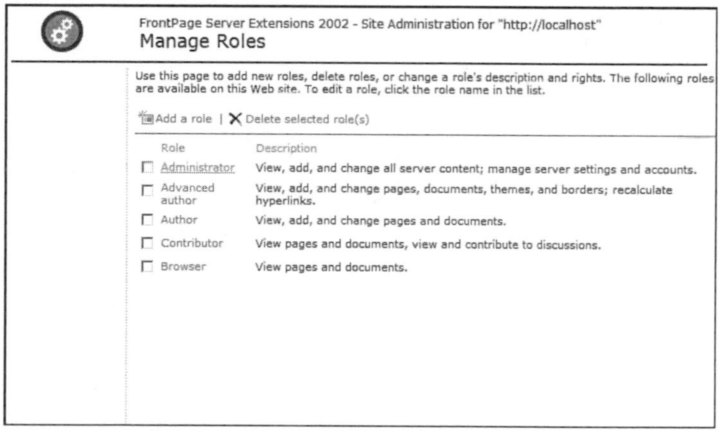

Figure 17.13
The Edit Role page provides an interface for customizing roles.

FrontPage Server Extensions 2002 - Site Administration for "http://localhost"
Manage Roles

Use this page to add new roles, delete roles, or change a role's description and rights. The following roles are available on this Web site. To edit a role, click the role name in the list.

Add a role | ✕ Delete selected role(s)

Role	Description
☐ Administrator	View, add, and change all server content; manage server settings and accounts.
☐ Advanced author	View, add, and change pages, documents, themes, and borders; recalculate hyperlinks.
☐ Author	View, add, and change pages and documents.
☐ Contributor	View pages and documents, view and contribute to discussions.
☐ Browser	View pages and documents.

Security and FrontPage Server Extensions

Windows computers control access to files and folders using file system security and permissions. Every file has permissions that determine which users have rights to that file and what level of access they have.

The permissions required to enable the FrontPage Server Extensions to operate correctly are extremely complicated. If you attempt to manage the permissions manually instead of using FrontPage, it is common to unintentionally either open security holes in the Web site or restrict access to it so that it cannot be browsed successfully.

To correct problems caused by incorrect permissions, the Server Extensions store all the permission settings inside of the `roles.ini` file. The Server Extensions can use the information in the `roles.ini` file to reapply permissions so that the Server Extensions will function correctly.

For more information on reapplying permissions using the information stored in the `roles.ini` file, see "Server Health" later in this chapter.

CAUTION

Don't ever try to manually edit the `roles.ini` file. If you do, you can prevent your Web site from working correctly.

NOTE

If you're an ASP.NET developer, don't ever allow FrontPage to tighten security on your Web content. Doing so will remove the Windows account used to run ASP.NET from the permissions and will prevent your ASP.NET files from running.

To remove one or more roles, place a check in the box next to the roles you want to delete and then click the `Delete Selected Role(s)` link.

You can also create new roles by either copying and modifying an existing role, or creating a new role from scratch. Suppose that you want to give certain people only Author access to your Web site, but you also want them to have the ability to create new sites. In that case, you can create a new role that will have all the same rights as the Author role, but will also have the right to create new sites. After you've created the role, anyone you assign to it will have the same rights as someone in the Author role, but they will have the additional right of being able to create new sites.

To copy an existing role, click the name of the role and then click the Copy Role button. You will be taken to the page>>Copy the Role <Role> page (see Figure 17.14), where a copy of the role is displayed and ready for editing. Enter a new role name and a description before creating your new role. If you want the users of the existing role to be copied to the new role, check the Copy Users from <Role> check box prior to creating the new role.

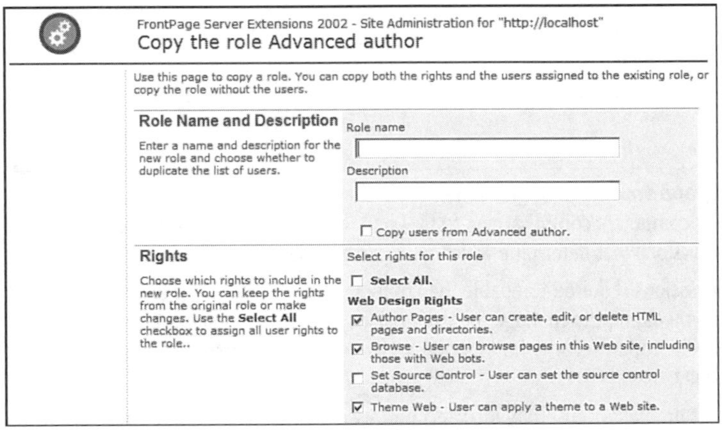

Figure 17.14
Copying roles makes creating new roles based on existing roles easy.

If you choose to create a new role from scratch, click the Add a Role link on the Manage Roles page. Enter a name and description for your new role and select the rights you want to assign to the role. If you select a right that requires another right, the required right will be selected automatically. Once you have created your new role, you can assign users to that role using the Manage Users link, as seen in Figure 17.15.

NOTE

> When you add a new role, the Server Extensions create a new group in Windows for that new role.

SENDING INVITATIONS

The final link in the Users and Roles section of Site Administration is the Send an Invitation link. Using this link, you can send a personalized invitation to anyone to whom you have given access to your site. The process is a three-step wizard.

Figure 17.15
Jack is being added to the Managers role—a new role that was just created.

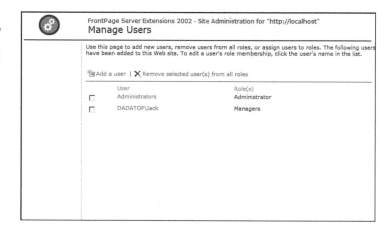

- Specify email address(es) of anyone you are inviting to your site.
- Verify the Windows account for that person. Your invitees must have accounts on the server before you invite them, so if you haven't created accounts yet, use the Manage Users link to do that before you send the invitation.
- Fill out a personal greeting and assign a role for your invitees.

The Server Extensions will send an email out to your invitees with the URL to your site, the customized greeting you entered, and a brief description of their access level.

If you get an error telling you that you must set up email before sending an invitation, see "Unable to Send Invitations" in the "Troubleshooting" section of this chapter.

CONFIGURING USAGE ANALYSIS SETTINGS

The next section in Site Administration is the Configure Usage Analysis Settings section. This section is used to configure the usage analysis for the Web site. Usage analysis provides you with details on how many hits a Web site has gotten, what browsers are being used to access it, the most popular page in the site, and so on. By checking the Process Log File Data for Full Days Only check box, you can ensure that you are getting accurate data based on full days of hit analysis.

As seen in Figure 17.16, you can configure usage analysis to run daily, weekly, or monthly. You can also configure the Server Extensions so that they delete old usage analysis data after a specific amount of time. The default is 12 months.

TIP

> Usage analysis data can end up using substantial disk space, so you will want to keep a close eye on how much space is being used by your data and make a determination as to how long you want to keep it before it's deleted.

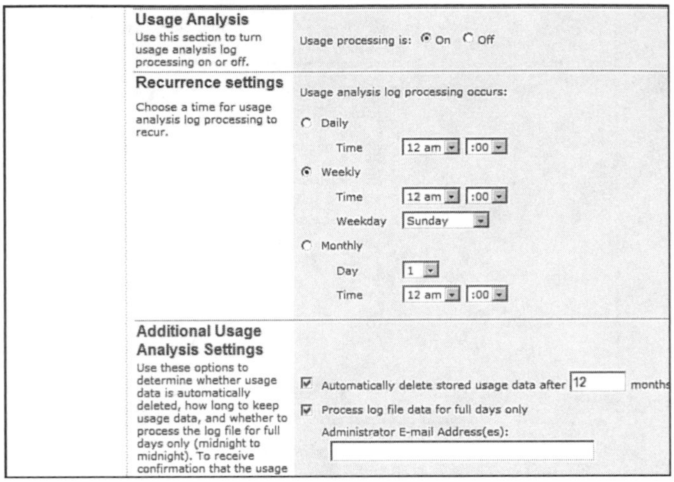

Figure 17.16
Usage Analysis data is collected at regular intervals according to the schedule you set.

The usage analysis settings also allow you to configure an email address that will receive a confirmation email as soon as usage analysis data has been successfully collected.

→ For more information on analyzing usage analysis data in FrontPage's Reports view, **see** "Reports View," **p. 70**.

MANAGING SERVER HEALTH

The Server Health section of Site Administration provides access to all the functions you need to keep your site running at full speed. The first item in this section is a label that indicates whether Server Health is on. This setting refers to the scheduling of the Check Server Health function.

> **NOTE**
>
> You don't have to schedule the Check Server Health function to run at regular intervals. However, if you have other FrontPage users editing content on your Web server, it's not a bad idea.
>
> For example, if someone were to use FTP to upload content to a Server Extensions site, forms and other Server Extensions components might be broken. By running a regular Check Server Health function, you can head off problems caused by poor authoring practices.

Click the Change Server Health Settings link to access the Change Server Health Settings page as seen in Figure 17.17. From here, you can turn Server Health on and then configure how often it runs. Unfortunately, there isn't an option to email an administrator if an uncorrectable error is encountered, but a regular check of server health is beneficial to head off such problems before they start.

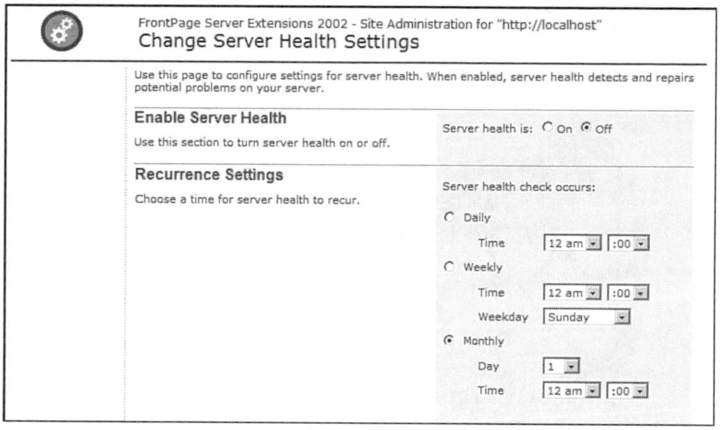

Figure 17.17
The Change Server Health Settings page helps keep your Web site running at top efficiency.

WHAT HAPPENS WHEN YOU CHECK SERVER HEALTH

If you click the Check Server Health link, you can see just what is checked and repaired when the Check Server Health function is run.

- **Reapply File Security Settings**—This option has no detect option because it really isn't applicable. When the Repair box is checked for this option, FrontPage will reapply all permissions according to the roles you have configured and the users who are members of those roles.

- **Verify Existence of Webs**—When this function is run, the Server Extensions check the services.cnf file that is located in the _vti_pvt folder of the root Web site. Inside that file is a list of all subsites that FrontPage thinks exist. The Server Extensions then check to see if the Web sites actually exist. If they do not, FrontPage removes them from the services.cnf file.

CAUTION

> You should be very careful about repairing problems found if you have content that is located on remote file systems. If the remote file system is unavailable for some reason, thereby causing FrontPage to remove the Web site from the services.cnf file, the Web site will no longer be recognized as a FrontPage Web site.

- **Check Roles Configuration**—This function checks for any problems related to roles and user accounts. It synchronizes the existing user accounts with the roles to which they are assigned and corrects any discrepancies.

- **Tighten Security**—This check ensures that only those users who are supposed to have access to your files actually have access. Web server administrators will often change permissions on files and folders within Windows instead of within FrontPage. In doing so, they may unintentionally give a user permission to a part of your Web site to which they should not have access.

When the Tighten Security function is used, if a user isn't a member of a role that should have access to a particular file or folder, she is removed from the permissions list.

CAUTION

ASP.NET developers should be very careful about running a repair on this function because it will remove the account used to run ASP.NET from your Web site permissions, thereby rendering your ASP.NET pages inoperable. Making the account that runs ASP.NET a Browser on the site will prevent this, but it can make administration more difficult for ASP.NET developers.

- **Check Anonymous Access**—This check ensures that anonymous users do not have more access than they should. The Server Extensions allow you to configure a specific role for anonymous users. This check will ensure that the role you configure is enforced and that anonymous users aren't granted additional rights.

RECALCULATING THE WEB SITE

The last item in the Server Health section is the Recalculate the Web item. This item performs the same function as the Recalculate Hyperlinks function in FrontPage. To many FrontPage users, this function is a mystery.

The Recalculate the Web function performs a whole series of checks against the Web site and corrects many possible problems. It checks the .cnf files for the Web site to make sure that there aren't any configuration problems, and it reconnects all FrontPage forms and browse-time Web components to the Server Extensions. If one or more of your FrontPage components is displaying the component name inside of square brackets (that is, [FrontPage Save Results Component]), a good first troubleshooting step is to Recalculate the Web site. That will often correct the problem.

CONFIGURING VERSION CONTROL

The Configure Version Control link takes you to the Configure Version Control page, where you can configure the source control system for your Web site. A source control system provides developers with the ability to check out files and to maintain a database of previous versions so that they can roll back to a previous version if they need to.

FrontPage has a built-in source control system that is a fairly lightweight solution and not really a good choice for a serious developer's shop. For a more robust solution, Server Extensions will also integrate with *Microsoft Visual SourceSafe (VSS)*.

If VSS is available and configured correctly, the Configure Version Control page will have the option to use an external source control system. That external system is VSS.

→ For more information on using version control with FrontPage, **see** "Checking Documents In and Out," **p. 624**.

MANAGING SUBSITES—THE SUBWEBS SECTION

The Subwebs section of Site Administration provides you with the tools necessary to create new subsites, merge subsites (convert a subsite into a folder), and delete subsites. You can also access the Site Administration page of any of your subsites by clicking on the subsite name.

TIP

> Beginning with FrontPage 2003, Microsoft refers to Web sites created under the root Web site as *subsites*. Because Microsoft is no longer releasing new versions of the Server Extensions, the terminology inside the Server Extensions dialog boxes has not changed, which can be confusing. Just remember that subwebs and subsites are the same thing.

To create a new subsite, click the Create a Subweb link to display the Create a Subweb page, as seen in Figure 17.18. Enter the name for the new subsite and select whether the new subsite should inherit the permissions from its parent or use unique permissions. If you choose the option to use unique permissions, you must also specify the username for an Administrator for the new subsite.

NOTE

> FrontPage users will find it more convenient to create new subsites inside FrontPage itself. The Subwebs Section of Site Administration is typically used by server administrators who do not have access to a copy of FrontPage.

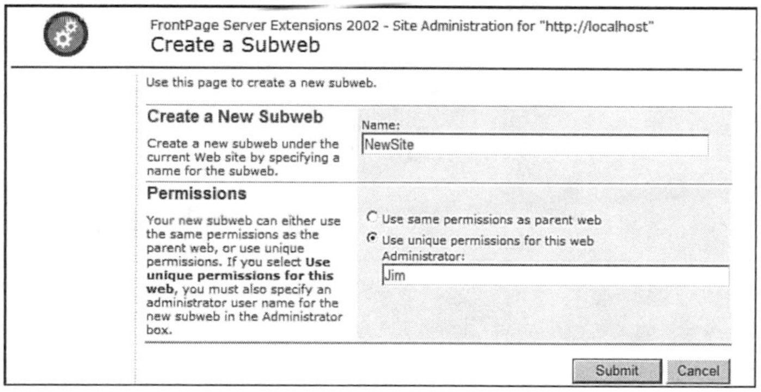

Figure 17.18
The Create a Subweb page provides the tools necessary to create new FrontPage subsites.

To convert an existing subsite into a folder, click the Merge a Subweb link to display the Merge a Subweb page as seen in Figure 17.19. Select the subsite from the Web Name dropdown and click the Merge Subweb button to convert it to a folder.

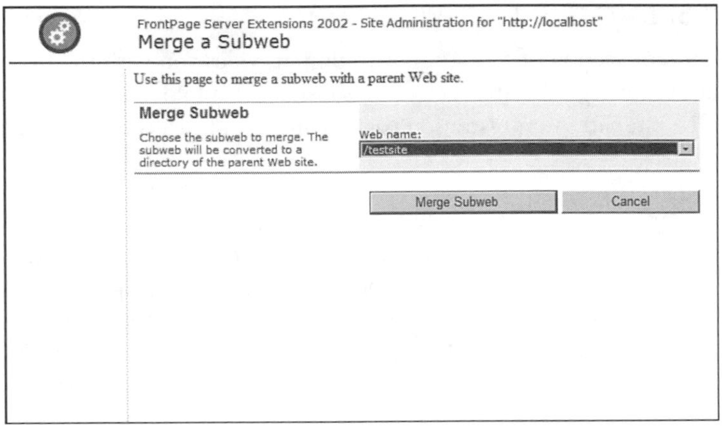

Figure 17.19
The Merge a Subweb
page converts a sub-
site to a regular folder.

To delete a subsite, click the Delete a Subweb link to display the Delete a Subweb page as shown in Figure 17.20. Select the subsite from the Web Name dropdown and then click the Delete Subweb button. The subsite and any child subsites will be permanently deleted. Remember, there is no Recycle Bin in FrontPage, so once you delete the subsite, there is no way to retrieve it.

Figure 17.20
Delete a subsite from
the Delete a Subweb
page.

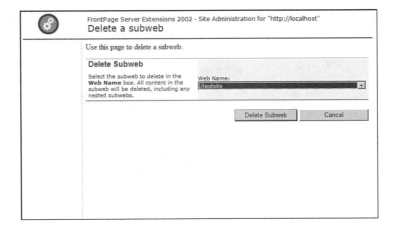

The Subwebs section also contains a list of all subsites of the current Web site. By clicking the name of the subsite, you are taken to the Site Administration page for that subsite. As shown in Figure 17.21, the Site Administration page for a subsite does not contain all the same options available to you on the root Web site's Site Administration page. Instead, you have the following tools available on a subsite's Site Administration page:

- **Change Subweb Permissions**—Allows you to configure whether the subweb inherits permissions from its parent or has its own unique permissions.
- **Recalculate the Web**—Recalculates hyperlinks on the subsite.

- **Configure Version Control**—Sets the version control options for the subsite.
- **Create a Subweb**—Creates a new subsite as a child of the current subsite.

Figure 17.21
The Site Administration page for a subsite contains fewer options than the root Web's Site Administration page.

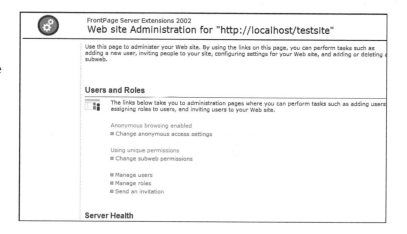

VIRTUAL SERVER ADMINISTRATION

Virtual server administration is for configuration of all of the Web sites running on a *virtual server*. A virtual server is a collection of Web sites on a Web server all sharing a common root Web site. On Windows 2000 and XP Professional, only one virtual server is allowed, and it is called the *Default Web Site*. On Windows 2000 Server and Windows Server 2003, you can create many virtual servers, each with its own configuration settings.

At the virtual server level, Server Extensions can be installed and configured, and many of the same settings configurable at the site administration level are available as well.

The Virtual Server Administration page (shown in Figure 17.22) is where you configure settings that apply to all Web sites on the virtual server.

The first link on the Virtual Server Administration is Uninstall FrontPage Server Extensions 2002. Clicking this link will take you to the page shown in Figure 17.23. You are given the option to conduct a full uninstall. If you perform a full uninstall, all metadata for the virtual server will be removed as well. *Metadata* refers to the _vti folders that contain configuration information for the FrontPage Web sites on the server. If these are removed, any FrontPage components in the Web site might not function if the Server Extensions are reinstalled at a later time.

The next link is Upgrade Virtual Server with FrontPage Server Extensions 2002 (see Figure 17.24). Clicking this link will allow you to upgrade the virtual server to the FrontPage 2002 Server Extensions in situations where an earlier version of the Server Extensions is currently installed. Enter a local user who will serve as the Administrator of the virtual server and click Submit to upgrade the virtual server.

Figure 17.22
The Virtual Server Administration page is where you configure Server Extensions settings for the virtual server.

Figure 17.23
The Uninstall FrontPage Server Extensions 2002 page allows you to uninstall the Server Extensions from the virtual server.

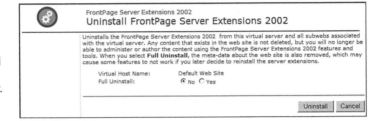

Figure 17.24
Upgrade a virtual server to FrontPage Server Extensions 2002.

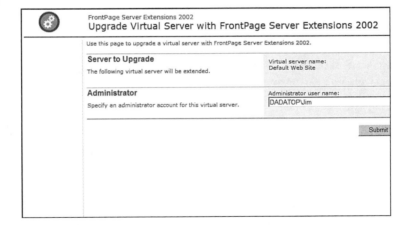

I'll discuss the Change Configuration Settings link in the next section. Let's move on to the Configure User Account Limits link. This link takes you to the User Account Limits page (see Figure 17.25) and simply allows you to restrict the number of user accounts that can be used on a virtual server. By default, the number of user accounts that are allowed is unlimited. By entering a numeric value in the text box and clicking Submit, you can restrict the number of accounts that are allowed.

TIP

> Why would you want to limit the number of user accounts for a virtual server? If there are many virtual servers configured on a Web server, the server might suffer performance problems if too many users are accessing the server. By limiting the number of users that can be created, a server administrator can more carefully control access to the server and maintain proper performance.

Figure 17.25
The User Account Limits page is where you can restrict the maximum number of user accounts for a virtual server.

CONFIGURATION SETTINGS

The Change Configuration Settings link provides an interface for configuring all the general settings for the virtual server via the Configuration Settings page shown in Figure 17.26. The Configuration Settings page is divided into several sections.

Figure 17.26
The Configuration Settings page is the place to configure virtual server settings.

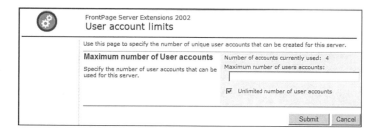

CONTROLLING AUTHORING

The Enable Authoring section allows you to disable or enable FrontPage authoring. Clear the Enable Authoring check box to turn off authoring for the server.

When authoring is disabled, FrontPage users will receive an error message if they attempt to open a Web site on the server, informing them that authoring has been disabled.

There is no way to disable authoring for specific Web sites on the server. If authoring is disabled, all Web sites will be inaccessible for authoring from FrontPage.

MAIL SETTINGS

Several features of the Server Extensions allow you to send mail. The FrontPage Save Results component sends email from a Web page. The Server Extensions can also send email to people you have invited to visit your Web site, as you saw previously in this chapter. In order for email to be sent, you must configure the Mail Settings options so that the Server Extensions will have the information necessary to send mail.

The SMTP Mail Server box configures the Simple Mail Transfer Protocol mail server that is used to send email. This is very often `mail.domain.com`, where `domain` is your hosting domain. The Server Extensions will use the SMTP mail server to relay your email. Therefore, SMTP relay must be enabled.

The From Address setting specifies the email address that appears in the From line on emails sent by the Server Extensions. Only one email address can be entered here. You cannot enter multiple addresses.

The Reply-to Address specifies the email address that an email will be addressed to if a recipient clicks the Reply button after receiving an email sent by the Server Extensions.

The Mail Encoding dropdown allows you to configure the mail encoding of the emails sent by the Server Extensions. Unless you are certain that the encoding needs to be changed, this setting should not be changed.

The Character Set dropdown configures the character set that is used to send email. As with the mail encoding settings, this setting should not be changed unless you are certain that it should be changed and are well versed in the ramifications of any change. If you are unsure about changing this setting, check with your server administrator.

PERFORMANCE TUNING

The Performance Tuning section allows you to configure a Web server for maximum performance. There are preset values for a Web server hosting fewer than 100 pages, one hosting between 100 and 1000 pages, and one hosting 1000 pages. There is also a custom setting to allow you to configure your own performance settings.

These settings are configurable at the Web site level, but only through the command line. When using the browser interface, you can only configure the settings for the entire virtual server.

> NOTE
>
> For more information on command-line administration of the Server Extensions, see the SharePoint Team Services Administrator's Guide available at `http://fpserk. frontpagelink.com`.

DOCUMENT CACHING

The In-memory Document Cache setting configures the number of documents that the Server Extensions hold in cache. When the Server Extensions are being used for authoring and when they are writing files for browse-time components, they are able to store metadata for your files in the Web server's memory in order to improve performance. By default, the Server Extensions will hold metadata for up to 4,096 files in memory. When document number 4,097 is accessed, the Server Extensions completely clear and the process starts over with one file.

The Include File Cache setting specifies the maximum number of include files (those that are included using the FrontPage Include File component) that are cached on the Web server while pages are being saved and while the Web site is being recalculated using the Recalculate Hyperlinks command. For maximum efficiency, if you have more than 16 files included with the Include File Component, you will want to change this value. It should be changed to the total number of included pages that you have in your Web site.

The Image File Cache setting specifies the number of cached images. The Server Extensions do not cache image files themselves. Instead, they cache the height and width attributes for images in your Web site when pages are saved and links are recalculated. This setting should only be changed from the default value of 16 if pages on your Web site frequently contain more than 16 images.

CONFIGURING FULL-TEXT SEARCH

The Full-text Search Index Size setting specifies the number of megabytes the Server Extensions use for the FrontPage Wide Area Information Service (FreeWAIS) search engine. The FreeWAIS search engine is commonly used by server administrators who do not enable the Microsoft Index Services option for Server Extensions.

→ For more information on the FrontPage FreeWAIS search engine, **see** "Using Web Components, Shared Borders, and Link Bars," **p. 167**.

The Max Cached Document Size setting allows you to configure the maximum size of documents that the Server Extensions will cache in memory. The default size is 256KB, and considering that anything over that would be extremely large for a Web document, that should suffice for most users.

CONFIGURING SCRIPTING LANGUAGES

One of the features of FrontPage forms is that they allow you to configure the form-field validation that runs on the client (the Web browser) to enforce restrictions on the data that can be entered in a form field. The Server Extensions generate client-side VBScript or JavaScript (based on certain settings) when the page is saved.

There are a couple of places where you can set the scripting language that the Server Extensions use. One is in the FrontPage client by selecting Tools, Site Settings and clicking the Advanced tab. The other is here on the General Settings page using the Scripting Language dropdown.

The setting on the General Settings page will override whatever is set in the FrontPage client. Therefore, if you set the Script Language dropdown to No Scripting, client-side scripting will not be generated by FrontPage even if the Web developer chooses a scripting language in the FrontPage client.

→ For more information on the Site Settings dialog, **see** "FrontPage Client Configuration," **p. 324**, in this chapter.

→ For more information on configuring form field validation, **see** "Sending Form Results to a File and Email," **p. 360**.

CONFIGURING SECURITY SETTINGS

The Security Settings section allows for configuration of three security settings for the Server Extensions.

- Log Authoring Actions
- Require SSL for Authoring and Administration
- Allow Authors to Upload Executables

All three of these settings are discussed in detail in the "Setting Installation Defaults" section of this chapter.

SERVER ADMINISTRATION

Server administration is for the configuration of all virtual servers and Web sites on the Web server. At the server administration level, you can configure settings such as how mail is sent from FrontPage forms and other global settings for all virtual servers. You can also configure the Server Extensions or remove the Server Extensions from virtual servers from server administration.

SETTING THE LIST OF AVAILABLE RIGHTS

In addition to the Site Administration page, the Server Extensions have many other options that are configurable using the Server Administration page shown in Figure 17.27.

Figure 17.27
The Server
Administration page.

To access the Server Administration page

1. Click the Start button and select Control Panel.
2. Double-click on Administrative Tools.
3. Double-click on Microsoft SharePoint Administrator.

The first link on the Server Administration page is the Set List of Available Rights link. Clicking this link will display the Set List of Available Rights page shown in Figure 17.28. By default, all rights are available. By clearing the check box next to one or more rights, you remove those rights from the list of available rights that can be assigned to new or existing roles.

Figure 17.28
By unchecking one or more boxes, you can easily make the right unavailable to new and existing roles.

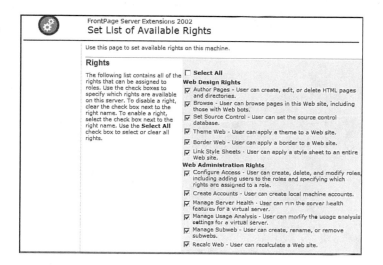

When a right is unchecked, Server Extensions will automatically uncheck any other right dependent on that right. Conversely, if a right is checked that has a dependency on an unchecked right, the unchecked right will be automatically checked.

Make sure that you fully realize the implications of removing a right before you commit the change. For example, if you remove the Author right, FrontPage developers will be unable to open the Web site in FrontPage.

SETTING INSTALLATION DEFAULTS

The Set Installation Defaults page (see Figure 17.29) allows you to configure default settings for all virtual servers. A *virtual server* is an instance of Internet Information Services configured as a root Web site. By default, Internet Information Services has one virtual server called Default Web Site.

Usage Analysis and Server Health settings set on the Set Installation Defaults page will apply to all new virtual servers created on the Web server.

→ For more information on Usage Analysis and Server Health and settings, **see** "Configuring Usage Analysis Settings," **p. 339**, and "Managing Server Health," **p. 340**.

CONFIGURING MAIL SETTINGS

In the Mail Settings section (shown in Figure 17.30), default mail settings are configured. Some features of the FrontPage Server Extensions rely on these settings being configured, so it's a good idea to set the default settings so that any new virtual servers created will be configured automatically.

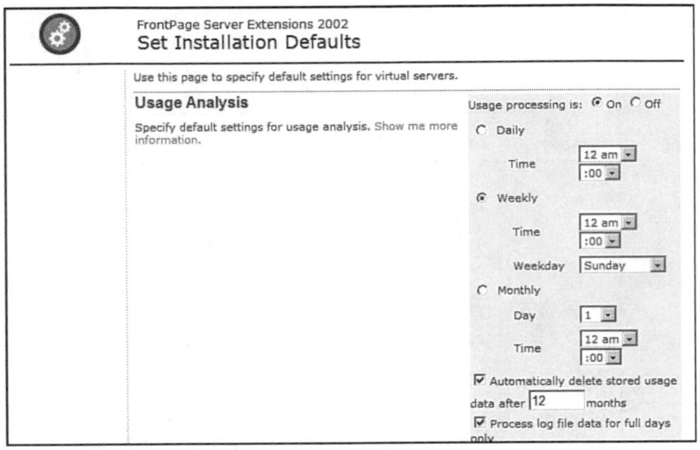

Figure 17.29
Default settings are configured on the Set Installation Defaults page.

Figure 17.30
Mail Settings configure defaults for how the Server Extensions send email.

In the SMTP Mail Server box, enter the URL of the SMTP server that handles outgoing email. The From Address box allows you to configure the email address that appears in the From field in emails sent by the Server Extensions. The Reply-to Address configures the email address that will be used when recipients of email sent by the Server Extensions reply to emails sent to them.

CONFIGURING SECURITY SETTINGS

The final section on the Set Installation Defaults page is the Security Settings section. In this section, you can configure three different security settings for the FrontPage Server Extensions—Log Authoring Actions, Require Secure Sockets Layer, or SSL, for Authoring and Administration, and Allow Authors to Upload Executables.

The Log Authoring Actions setting specifies whether the Server Extensions log authoring activity on the Web site. If this box is checked, the Server Extensions will create a log called `author.log` in the `_vti_log` folder on the Web site. Anytime someone opens the Web site in FrontPage and edits anything, the Server Extensions will add an entry to the log.

To access the `author.log` file, use Windows Explorer to browse to the `_vti_log` folder in the root folder of your Web site. Because the `author.log` file contains a record of all authoring activity, it is useful for troubleshooting when errors occur.

NOTE

For details on how to analyze the `author.log` file, see article number 278432 in the Microsoft Knowledge Base by browsing to `http://support.microsoft.com/?kbid=278432`.

The Require SSL for Authoring and Administration setting specifies whether the Server Extensions require people opening the Web site in FrontPage to connect via SSL. If this setting is checked, the Server Extensions will not allow access to the Web site via FrontPage unless that connection is using SSL.

NOTE

For more information on SSL, read *Internet Information Services Administration* from Que Publishing.

The Allow Authors to Upload Executables check box allows server administrators to control whether FrontPage authors are allowed to put executable files in folders that are marked as executable folders. If this setting is not enabled (and it is not by default), authors will be unable to add executable files to a folder marked as executable. Instead, they will receive an error message indicating that they are not allowed to upload executable files.

To make a folder executable in FrontPage, right-click on the folder and select Properties. By checking the Allow Programs to Be Run check box, you make the folder executable. Most server administrators, however, do not allow FrontPage authors to make this change. The Server Extensions have another property called `NoExecutableCgiUpload` that determines whether FrontPage users can mark folders executable. If this property has a value of 1 (which it does by default), the Allow Programs to Be Run check box will be disabled in FrontPage.

RESETTING USER PASSWORDS

The Reset User Password link allows you to reset the password for a user who has forgotten her password. When you click this link, you will be taken to the Reset User Password page as shown in Figure 17.31.

The Virtual Server dropdown contains one entry for each virtual server in Internet Information Services. By default, there is only one virtual server, and it is called Default Web Site.

NOTE

You will sometimes see the Default Web Site referred to as `/LM/W3SVC/1:`. IIS refers to it this way internally. LM stands for Local Machine, W3SVC stands for the World Wide Web Publishing SerViCe, and 1 is the instance number. If you have another virtual server on the IIS box, that new instance name would be referred to as `/LM/W3SVC/2:`, and so on.

Figure 17.31
The Reset User Password page provides the ability to reset forgotten passwords for FrontPage users.

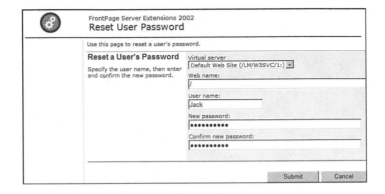

The Web Name box contains a single slash in it by default. This refers to the root Web site on the server. If you are resetting a password for a user on a subsite of the root site, you will need to add the subsite name after the slash.

After you have selected the virtual server and specified the Web site name, enter the username for the user and the new password twice. Clicking Submit changes the password for the user.

SERVER ADMINISTRATION—VIRTUAL SERVERS

The last item on the Server Administration page is the list of virtual servers. By default, only the Default Web Site is listed. Clicking the name of the virtual server will take you to the Site Administration page for that virtual server.

Along with the name of the virtual server, the Server Administration page also displays the version of the Server Extensions on that server if it has been extended with the Server Extensions. If the server has not been extended, a link will be present to allow you to configure the Server Extensions on the server.

Once a virtual server has been extended, an Administration link will be available immediately to the right of the version number. Clicking this link will take you to the Virtual Server Administration page. Working with this page is covered in the next section.

TROUBLESHOOTING

NOT AUTHORIZED TO MANAGE USERS

I am trying to manage users on my Web site, and all I can see is an error telling me that I'm not authorized to manage users.

In order to manage users on a FrontPage Server Extensions 2002 Web site, you must have the Configure Access right. The server administrator may not have given you this right. Check with your server administrator. If you are the server administrator, refer to "Creating Users and Roles" in this chapter for information on how you can change your rights.

UNABLE TO SEND INVITATIONS

I've configured some users for my site, and I'm trying to send them invitations. When I do, I get an error telling me that I must set up email first.

When you send an invitation using the Server Extensions, the Server Extensions access the SMTP mail settings that you have configured in order to send the mail. If you have not configured these settings, the Server Extensions won't know how to send mail and will display this error.

Refer to the "Configuring Mail Settings" section of this chapter for information on how to configure mail settings.

SERVER AND SITE SETTINGS ARE GRAYED OUT

I'm trying to configure site settings for my Web site, but the Server and the Site Settings menus are grayed out.

In order to configure server or site settings, you must have a Web site open. Make sure that you open a Web site before attempting to use these features.

FRONT AND CENTER: CONFIGURING SERVER EXTENSIONS USING COMMAND-LINE PROPERTIES

For those who want to configure the Server Extensions without the HTML administration pages, Microsoft offers a command-line tool that makes configuring Server Extensions fairly easy.

The Server Extensions command-line administration tool is called `owsadm.exe`, and it is located in `C:\Program Files\Common Files\Microsoft Shared\web server extensions\50\bin`. By running the tool with no parameters (just running the `.exe` file with nothing after it), you will see a partial list of the functions it can perform. For a full list, see the URL at the bottom of the help screen that displays when you run the tool, or visit `http://fpserk.frontpagelink.com`, browse to the bottom of the page, and click on Command Line Properties.

To determine the current value for a particular property, you can use the `getproperty` command. For example, if you wanted to find out if author logging is enabled (the `Logging` property), use the following command line:

```
owsadm.exe -o -p 80 getproperty -pn Logging
```

This will return the current value of the property.

TIP

> The Microsoft documentation on this command-line tool is incorrect. The documentation leaves off the dash before many of the parameters. Only commands (such as `getproperty` and `setproperty`) and property names (such as `Logging`) are entered without a dash.

Why is being able to control these settings from a command line such a great tool? Because it makes it very easy to script configurations for a Server Extensions Web site. It's quite easy to create a batch file that will set properties to your heart's content, alleviating the burden of trying to wade through administration pages trying to find the property you need.

Then there are those properties that you can't configure from the HTML administration pages. Suppose, for example, that you are trying to get Visual SourceSafe integrated with the Server Extensions and it's not working. Normally, there is no indication of what the problem might be in this situation, but if you set the Server Extensions property called `LogInitialSourceControlErrors` to 1, any errors are written into the Application log in the Windows Event Viewer. The error message is descriptive and will tell you what the problem is.

The `LogInitialSourceControlErrors` property is not available in the HTML administration pages. To set it, you need to use the `owsadm.exe` command-line tool and set the property as follows:

```
owsadm -o setproperty -pn LogInitialSourceControlErrors -pv 1
```

By creating a batch file with this line in it, you can easily give it to a server administrator and have her enable source control error logging for you without her having to know anything at all about the Server Extensions.

NOTE

Some of the Server Extensions properties might not take effect correctly or might cause problems. For example, setting the `WECCtlFlags` property used to be a way to cause the FrontPage 2000 and later Open Web dialog boxes to appear just as the FrontPage 98 Open Web dialog box—complete with the List Webs button that FrontPage 98 users were used to. Microsoft has now turned off that ability, and setting this value will generate an error or cause FrontPage to crash.

ADVANCED PAGE DESIGN CONCEPTS

CHAPTER **18**

USING FORMS

In this chapter

SENDING FORM RESULTS TO A FILE AND EMAIL

FrontPage forms have remained fairly unchanged for several versions, yet they remain one of the most widely used functions in FrontPage. The reason is simple. Any Web site worth its salt uses forms in one way or another, whether as a form of communication with the Web site owner or as a way to dig into the site to get more information. Forms are prevalent on the Internet, and FrontPage makes using them in your site straightforward and simple.

FrontPage form components can save data into a file, save data in to a database, or send email using the data entered in to a form. All these components are browse-time components, which means that they only work on Web servers running the FrontPage Server Extensions. Collectively, these components are referred to as the FrontPage Save Results component.

The most common use of FrontPage form components is to save form information in to a file or an email address. This is done using the Save Results component. As you will soon see, FrontPage offers a wide range of options for saving form results that should meet just about any need.

To insert a FrontPage Save Results component, select Insert, Form and choose any form field such as Textbox. FrontPage inserts a simple form as seen in Figure 18.1. The simplicity of this form is deceiving. There is a lot of power in this component.

Figure 18.1
A FrontPage form looks simple enough, but it is hiding some significant functionality.

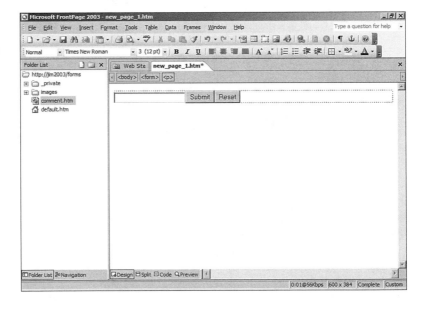

The easiest way to learn how to get the most out of this component is to use it, so let's create a Web page that will teach you how to exploit the power of the Save Results component.

CREATING A BASIC FORM

First, you need to create a new form that you can configure to save your information:

1. Create a new Web site or open an existing Web site.
2. Create a new page.
3. Select Insert, Form, Textbox to insert a single text box onto a form.
4. Press Enter twice to move the Submit and Reset buttons to the bottom of the form.
5. Press the up arrow once to move the insertion point to the line directly under the text box.
6. Select Insert, Form, Text Area to insert a multiline text box.
7. Type the text **Enter your name:** above the text box.
8. Type the text **Enter your comments:** above the text area.
9. Double-click on the text area to display the TextArea Box Properties dialog box as shown in Figure 18.2.

Figure 18.2
Configuring Text Area properties with the TextArea Box Properties dialog box.

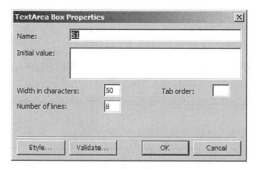

10. Change the Width in Characters to **50** and the Number of Lines to **8**.
11. Click OK.

Save the page as **comment.htm**. Your form should look like the page in Figure 18.3.

Now that you have a form, you need to configure it to save information to a file. Before you do that, you will want to change the name of your form fields. When you save the results of a form to a file, FrontPage uses the form Field Names to identify the form fields. The text box you inserted is called T1 by default, and the text area is called S1. Those aren't very descriptive names, and once you add several more form fields, you will completely lose track of them unless you give them descriptive names.

Double-click on the text box to display the Form Field Properties dialog box and change the name to **txtName**. Do the same for the text area and change the name to **txtComments**. After you've made that change, save the page again so that you won't lose your changes.

Figure 18.3
The Comment form will be used to save guest comments to a file.

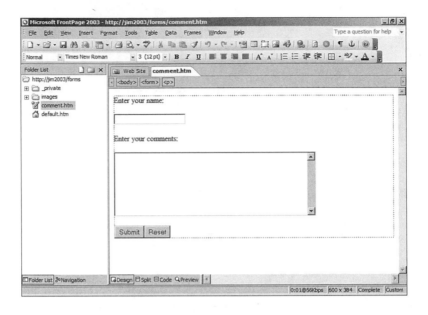

CONFIGURING FORM PROPERTIES FOR SAVING RESULTS

Now it's time to configure the form to save the results to a file. Right-click the Submit button and select Form Properties to display the Form Properties dialog box as shown in Figure 18.4.

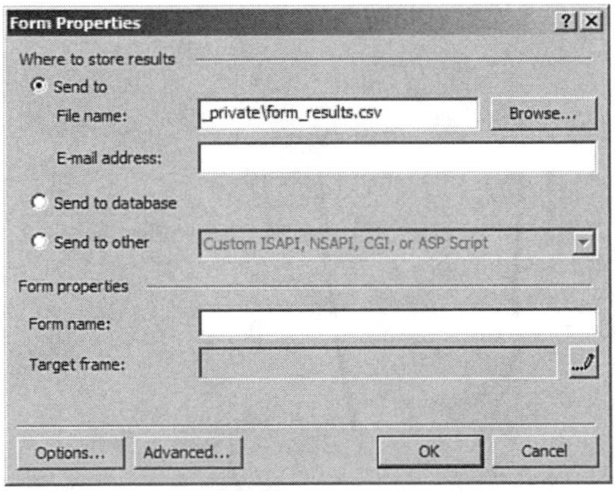

Figure 18.4
The Form Properties dialog box configures how the form is handled.

Note that the form is configured by default to save results to the _private/form_results.csv file. This file will contain the data from your form fields—with each field's data separated by a comma. This type of file is called a *comma delimited* file. The file will be written to the _private folder by the Server Extensions when a user submits your form. For now, keep the filename as it is and click the Options button to configure the rest of the form.

If only the Send to Other option is enabled in your Form Properties dialog box, *see "Form Properties Are Disabled" in the "Troubleshooting" section of this chapter.*

When you click the Options button, you are taken to the Saving Results dialog box (shown in Figure 18.5), where you can configure all the settings for the Save Results component. On the first tab, File Results, you can configure the name and format of the file to which form results are saved. If you want to save your form results into an existing file, click Browse to select the file.

Figure 18.5
The Saving Results dialog box configures the component, file results in this case.

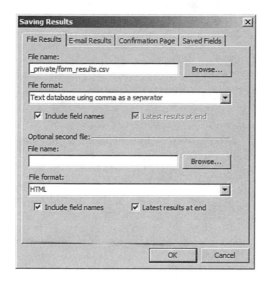

The following file formats are available:

- **XML**—Saves your results into an Extensible Markup Language (XML) file. XML files can be used in many ways, including as a data source for a FrontPage Data View.

→ For more information on using a Data View, **see** "The Data Source Catalog," **p. 736**.

- **HTML**—Saves the form results into an HTML page using the Form Insert Here FrontPage component.

→ For more information on the Form Insert Here FrontPage component, see "using Web Components, Shared Borders, and Link Bars," **p. 167**.

- **HTML definition list**—Saves the form results in HTML format using an HTML definition list.

- **HTML bulleted list**—Saves the form results in HTML format using an HTML bulleted list.

- **Formatted text within HTML**—Saves the form results in HTML format using the `<pre>` HTML tag.

- **Formatted text**—Saves the form results as text in a .txt file.

- **Text database using comma as a separator**—This is the default setting. It saves the form results in a .csv file (comma delimited file) with a comma between each value.

- **Text databases using tab as a separator**—Saves the form results in a `.txt` file with tabs separating values.

- **Text database using space as a separator**—Saves the form results in a `.txt` file with spaces separating values.

The File format dropdown provides you with the ability to save your results as XML, HTML, or text. The comma separated file, the default setting, is most often used when you anticipate that you might want to import the data in to a database at a later time. If your purpose is to collect data for a database, you might want to consider using the Send to Database component instead. Leave the File format dropdown set to a comma separated text database.

→ For more information on the Send to Database component, **see** "Sending Form Results to a Database," **p. 376**.

The Include Field Names check box stipulates whether your Field Names are included as a header row. If you don't check this box, the file will only contain the data and not the fields names. Field names are only written to the file on the first submission of the form. After that, only the data in the form is saved.

The Latest Results at End box is only available if you choose an XML or HTML format for your file. If you check this box, the results are saved from top to bottom. If this box is not checked, new results are written to the top of the file.

If you choose, you can have form results saved to a second file by entering a second filename in the Optional Second File section. This file can be a different format than the first file, but you cannot save different form fields in this file.

The E-mail Results tab (see Figure 18.6) allows you to configure an email address and format. You can only enter one address here. If you enter multiple addresses, FrontPage will not complain, but your mail will not be sent. The E-mail format dropdown contains the same options as the File format dropdown on the File Results tab.

The E-mail Message Header section of the dialog box provides you with text boxes to enter the subject line and the reply-to address for the email. You can hard-code these values, or you can check the Form Field Name check box and enter the name of a form field. For example, if you wanted the subject line of the email message to be the name of the person filling out the form on your `comment.htm` page, you would check the Form Field Name check box and type `txtName` in the Subject Line text box.

By using a form field for the Reply-to line text box, you can have the user of your form fill in her email address and use that form field for the reply-to address. By default, the mail that you receive will have a reply-to address set to whatever the server administrator of the Web server configured for the Server Extensions. By using a form field to collect the user's email address and using that as the reply-to address for your form, you can ensure that emails you reply to will be sent to the person who filled out the form and not the email address the server administrator configured.

Figure 18.6
The E-mail Results tab settings determine where emails are sent and how they are formatted.

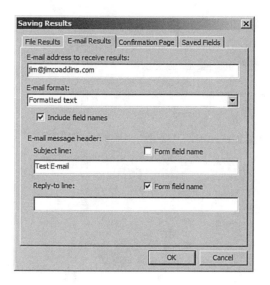

When a form is submitted, a confirmation page (see Figure 18.7) is displayed to the user of the form that recaps the information she entered and provides a link back to the form. If you'd like to present a more professional look, you can create your own confirmation page and configure your form to use it by configuring the fields on the Confirmation Page tab shown in Figure 18.8. You can also configure a validation failure page for cases in which form field validation fails and the server extensions are managing validation.

Figure 18.7
The default confirmation page doesn't look pretty, but it works.

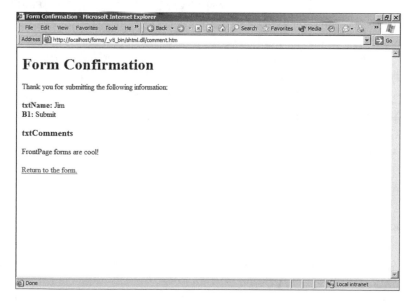

Figure 18.8
The Confirmation Page tab lets you configure your own confirmation page for a better appearance.

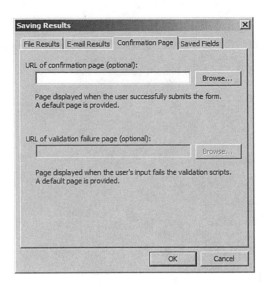

→ For more information on form field validation, **see** "Form Field Validation," **p. 370**.

NOTE

In most cases, you want form field validation to be handled by the browser and not the server so that users are presented with instant feedback if they enter incorrect information. However, in cases in which scripting is turned off in the browser, FrontPage Server Extensions will handle form field validation on the Web server.

The Saved Fields tab is used to configure which form fields are saved when a form is submitted. As you can see in Figure 18.9, the B1 field is being saved in the comment.htm file. This represents the Submit button, a field that you wouldn't normally want to save. FrontPage will always save button fields as well as data fields. If you don't want to save the button fields, remove them from the list and click OK.

You also have the option of saving the date and time that the form was submitted via the Date Format and Time Format dropdowns. By default, both of these are set to (none), which means that the date and time are not saved. By selecting a date and time format from the dropdowns, you can save this information along with your data.

If you click the Time format dropdown, you will notice that some of the time formats contain the letters TZ at the end. These formats display the time offset from UTC time, also known as Greenwich Mean Time. The time displayed is the time on the Web server, not on the user's machine.

At the bottom of the Saved Fields tab are three check boxes for saving the remote computer name, the browser type being used, and the username of the user. Unless you have password protected the Web site, the username will not be populated by the Server Extensions.

→ For more information on password protecting a Web site, **see** "Site Administration," **p. 330**.

Figure 18.9
The Saved Fields tab lists form fields that are saved as well as other information.

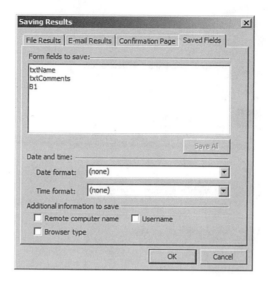

Test your form now by browsing to comment.htm in your Web browser. Fill in the form with your name and whatever comments you choose and click Submit. After submitting the form, close your Web browser and open the form_results.csv file in the _private folder in FrontPage to see your information.

 If you see a page with *FrontPage Run-time Component Page* across the top of it when submitting your form, see "Form Returns Run-Time Component Page" in the "Troubleshooting" section of this chapter.

CREATING A CUSTOM CONFIRMATION PAGE

Now let's create a confirmation page that is a bit more functional and presentable. Create a new page and save it as **confirm.htm**. Now you need to customize this page so that it will be more personal and reflect the information entered in to the form:

1. Type the text **Thank you for your submission,** at the top of the page.

2. Leave the insertion point at the end of the line and select <u>I</u>nsert, Web <u>C</u>omponent.

3. In the Component Type list, scroll down to Advanced Controls at the bottom of the list.

4. In the Choose a Control list, select Confirmation Field as shown in Figure 18.10 and click Finish. The Confirmation Field Properties dialog box appears.

5. Enter **txtName** as shown in Figure 18.11 and click OK. This is the name of the text box on your form in which your users enter their names.

6. Enter a period after [txtName] that was just inserted by the Confirmation Field component as shown in Figure 18.12.

Figure 18.10
The Confirmation Field component is used to personalize confirmation pages.

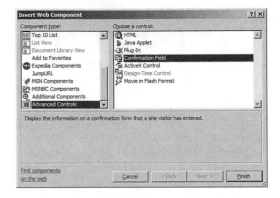

Figure 18.11
Enter the name of a form field in the Confirmation Field Properties dialog box.

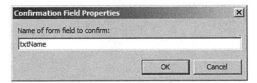

Figure 18.12
The Confirmation Field component configured to display the user's name in the confirmation page.

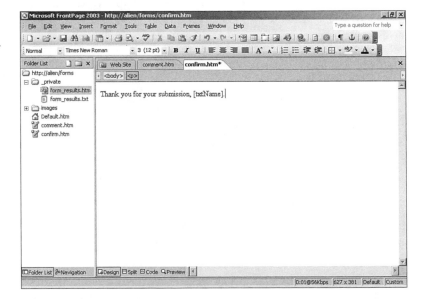

7. Format this line as an H2 style by selecting Heading 2 from the Style dropdown.

8. Press Enter to go to the next line.

9. Type the text **Your comments were:** and press Shift+Enter.

10. Insert another Confirmation Field component (see steps 2–4) and enter **txtComments** for the name of the confirmation field and click OK to insert it.

11. Click once on the [txtComments] Confirmation Field component to select it and click the I button on the toolbar to format it as italic.

12. Save the page.

Your confirm.htm page should now look like the one shown in Figure 18.13.

Figure 18.13
The finished confirmation page.

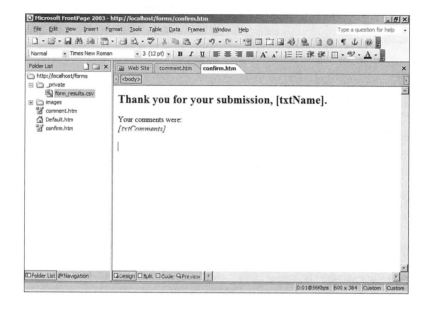

Now you will connect your form to the confirmation page that you just finished:

1. Open comment.htm.

2. Right-click the Submit button and select Form Properties.

3. Click the Options button to display the Saving Results dialog box.

4. Click the Confirmation Page tab.

5. Click the Browse button next to the URL of Confirmation Page box.

6. Browse to the confirm.htm file you just created and click OK.

7. Click OK in the Saving Results dialog box.

8. Click OK in the Form Properties dialog box.

9. Save the page.

Now preview your form in the browser and fill it out. Click Submit and you should see the confirmation page shown in Figure 18.14.

Figure 18.14
Your custom confirmation page. A much more professional look.

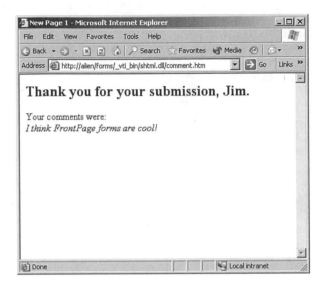

Everything is working great, but what if you user doesn't enter her name? Your confirmation form will then look pretty unprofessional. The solution to that problem is form field validation.

FORM FIELD VALIDATION

Form field validation allows you to configure constraints on the data that is entered in to a form field. It can be as simple as requiring an entry with no other constraints on the data that is entered, or as complex as requiring data in a certain format.

FrontPage can perform validation by running code on the user's Web browser or by running code on the Web server. There is a tremendous benefit to performing validation on the client. If a user enters information that does not conform to the constraints you have configured, she will be presented with a message box indicating that she needs to correct her entry (see Figure 18.15) prior to the page being posted to the Web server. If you do validation on the Web server, the user has to wait for the page to be transmitted, wait for the Web server to process the form, and then wait for the Web server to send back an error page, as shown in Figure 18.16. She then has to click a link to go back to the form and try again. Validation on the client is a much better user experience.

Figure 18.15
Client-side validation makes it easy for your users to correct their data.

Figure 18.16
Server-side validation is not nearly as user-friendly. The user had to wait for this page.

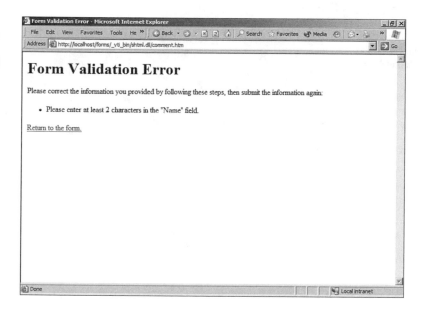

CONFIGURING FORM FIELD VALIDATION

To configure validation for your txtName form field, you will use the Text Box Properties dialog box.

1. Open comment.htm.
2. Double-click on the txtName form field to display the Text Box Properties dialog box as shown in Figure 18.17.

Figure 18.17
The Text Box Properties dialog box is used to set the properties for the form field.

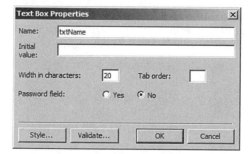

3. Click the Validate button to display the Text Box Validation dialog box as shown in Figure 18.18.
4. In the Display Name box, enter Name.

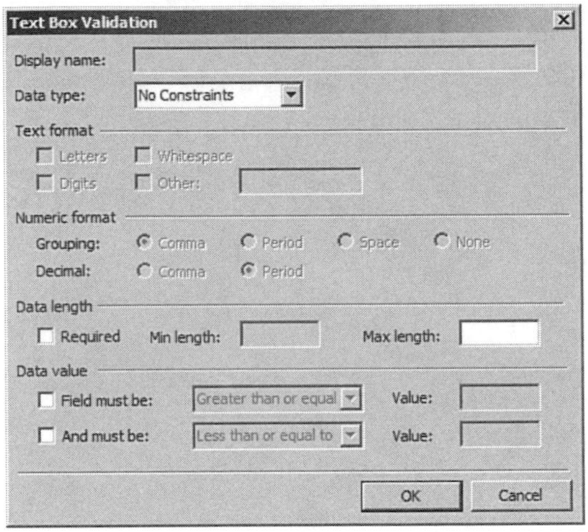

Figure 18.18
Validation is configured in the Text Box Validation dialog box.

NOTE

When you set up validation, always make sure to enter a friendly name in the Display Name box. This is the name that will be used to refer to your form field in any validation errors displayed to the user of your Web site. If you don't enter a friendly name, the user might not know which field is causing a problem.

5. In the Data Type dropdown, select Text.

6. In the Data Length section, check the Required check box.

NOTE

When you specify that a text field is required, it is a good idea to restrain the number of characters that are allowed as well. Form input is a common way for hackers to send information to a Web server in an attempt to crash it. By restricting the amount of data that can be submitted from your form, your form will be more secure.

7. In the Min Length text box, type **2**. This will prevent users from supplying only an initial instead of their names.

8. In the Max Length text box, type **30**.

9. Click OK.

10. Click OK in the Text Box Properties dialog box.

11. Save the page.

12. Select Tools, Site Settings and click the Advanced tab as shown in Figure 18.19.

13. Select JavaScript in the Client dropdown box.

14. Click OK.

Figure 18.19
The Site Settings dialog box allows you to configure what scripting language is used for validation in the browser.

Now preview your form in the browser and leave the Name field empty. Enter some text in the Comments text box and click Submit. You should be presented with a message box indicating that you need to enter your name as shown in Figure 18.20.

Figure 18.20
A validation failure telling you to enter data in txtName.

Now when you fail to enter your name, the error will be more descriptive, such as the one seen previously in Figure 18.15.

CONFIGURING VALIDATION OPTIONS

The validation options available to you differ depending on what type of form field is selected. Let's look more closely at the Text Box Validation dialog box as seen earlier in Figure 18.18.

The Data type dropdown allows you to configure the type of data you will allow in the text box. The following options are available:

- **No Constraints**—The text box can contain any type of data.
- **Text**—The text box can contain text values. Selecting this option enables the Text Format options in the Text Box Validation dialog box.

- **Integer**—The text box can contain an integer value. An integer cannot have any decimal places. It must be a whole number. Selecting this option enables the Grouping options in the Text Box Validation dialog box.

- **Number**—The text box can contain a numeric value. Selecting this option enables the Grouping and Decimal options in the Text Box Validation dialog box.

The Text format section contains several check boxes to allow you to specify what type of entry is allowed when Text is selected in the Data type dropdown:

- **Letters**—Letters are accepted as valid characters. Letters must be A-Z or a-z.

- **Digits**—Numeric values are allowed. Only the characters 0-9 qualify. If a user enters 1,095 and Digits is the only check box that is checked, validation will fail.

- **Whitespace**—Spaces are allowed.

- **Other**—When checked, a text box is made available to enter any other characters that you want to allow.

Suppose that you had a text box field for someone's telephone number and you wanted to make sure that it was in the correct format. The first thing you would want to do is provide some indication to the user for what format you expect. You would then configure validation by setting the Data type dropdown to Text and checking the Digits and Other check boxes. In the text box for Other, you would want to enter a dash character, which is the separator used in phone numbers. If you wanted to allow for area codes in parenthesis, you would enter those as well, as shown in Figure 18.21. Any other character besides a number, the dash, an opening parenthesis, or a closing parenthesis would fail validation.

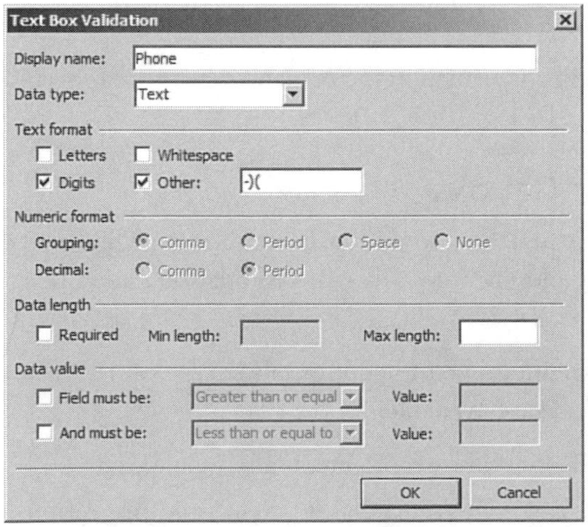

Figure 18.21
The Text Box Validation dialog box configured for validating phone number formats.

In order to avoid a phone number without an area code or one missing digits, you might also want to set a minimum and maximum field requirement. You know that a phone number formatted correctly will contain a total of 14 digits—2 for the parentheses, 2 for the dashes, and 10 for the phone number itself. The Data Length section of the Text Box Validation dialog box provides the perfect place to specify a size restriction on the data entered.

In the Data Length section, check the Required check box and type **14** in both the Min Length and the Max Length text boxes as shown in Figure 18.22. The phone number text box has now been configured to perform validation against the information entered in to it. It is also now configured as a required field. If nothing is entered in to it, validation will fail.

Figure 18.22
The Data Length section allows for restrictions on the length of the data and makes the text box a required field.

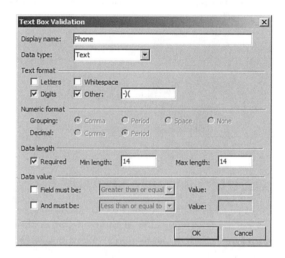

Collecting Phone Number Data

In a real-world scenario, you will probably be better off by using two separate text boxes in your form—one for the area code and one for the phone number. There are many reasons why this is a better way to collect phone number data.

The area code portion of a phone number is often used to categorize information by geographical region. For that reason, you might want to collect the area code in its own field in a database or comma delimited file so that you can use it to keep track of the demographics of your users.

Area codes also change from time to time. In many cases, when an area code changes, the phone number remains the same with the exception of the new area code. If you are using a form to collect information about a particular group of people, it will help you to keep accurate records if you separate the area code so that you can easily update area codes when they change.

Make sure that you carefully evaluate your data collection methods when you are designing your site so that you don't add additional work for yourself later on.

The final section in the Text Box Validation dialog box, the Data value section, allows you to specify a valid range for the data entered in to the text box.

You might also want to collect data on what state your site visitors are from. A dropdown box is the perfect form field for this task. When using a dropdown box for the selection of a state, you would typically include an entry such as Select a State as the first entry. You would not, however, want the form submitted until the user selected a valid state from the dropdown.

Figure 18.23 shows the Drop-Down Box Validation dialog box. Here, you can once again specify the name to display for the form field. You are also provided with a check box to specify that the field is required and another check box to disallow the first choice. The Disallow First Choice check box is convenient if your dropdown has an item such as Select a State as the first choice. Because you would obviously want someone to click the dropdown and select her state instead of leaving it set to Select a State, you would want to check the Disallow First Choice check box.

Figure 18.23
The Drop-Down Box Validation dialog box is much simpler than the Text Box Validation dialog box.

SENDING FORM RESULTS TO A DATABASE

In situations in which you want to send your form results straight to a database, the Send To Database form handler is a great option. One of the best things about this component is that you can decide what information you want to collect and design your form the way you want it, and FrontPage can automatically create a database tailor-made to your form results.

Let's reconfigure the form on comment.htm to store results in a database instead of a file:

1. Open comment.htm.
2. Right-click the Submit button and select Form Properties.
3. Select the Send To Database option (see Figure 18.4 shown previously).
4. Click Options to access the Options for Saving Results to Database dialog box as shown in Figure 18.24.

 If the Send To Database option is not available, see "Send To Database Not Available" in the "Troubleshooting" section of this chapter.

The Database Connection to Use dropdown is currently empty because there are no database connections in the current Web site. You can click the Add Connection dialog box to create a new database connection, but in this case, you want FrontPage to create a database for you so that it will contain all the necessary database fields to store results of your form. Click the Create Database button, and FrontPage will generate a new database for your form and save it to the fpdb folder in your Web site, as indicated by the message box in Figure 18.25.

Figure 18.24
The Options for Saving Results to Database dialog box.

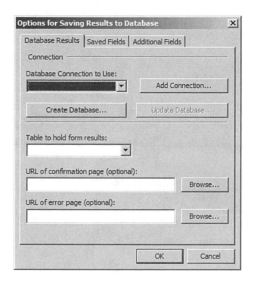

Figure 18.25
FrontPage creates a database customized for your form.

18

→ For more information on database connections in FrontPage, **see** "Creating a Database Connection," **p. 706**.

FrontPage has now populated part of the Option for Saving Results to Database dialog box for you as shown in Figure 18.26. Note that the Database Connection to Use dropdown now has comment selected. This is the name of the database connection that FrontPage created for you. The Table to Hold Form Results dropdown has also been populated with Results, the table name in the database that FrontPage created for you. If your database contained more than one table, you would need to select the correct table in the Table to Hold Form Results dropdown.

> **TIP**
>
> As with the Send to File and E-mail handler, you can configure a custom confirmation page and a custom error page. However, the confirmation page for the Send To Database handler must be an ASP page. If you would like to use confirm.htm that you created earlier, you will need to open it and resave it as an ASP page first. No other changes are necessary.

Click the Saved Fields tab. As shown in Figure 18.27, both of your form fields appear in the Form Fields to Save list and they are mapped to the database columns by the same name.

When FrontPage created your database, it created a database column for each of your form fields. It mapped the form fields to their respective database column.

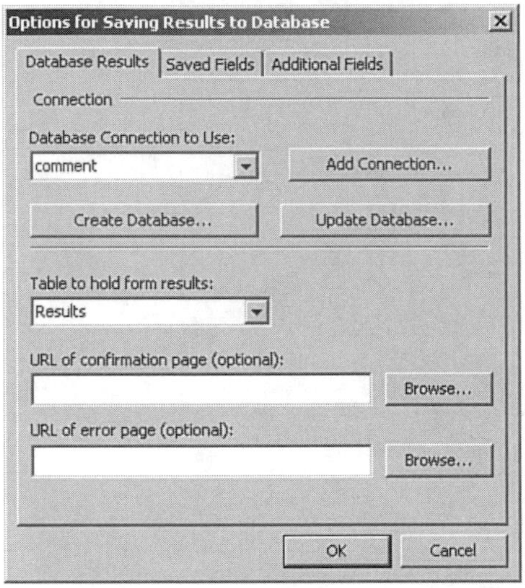

Figure 18.26
The Options for Saving Results to Database dialog is configured with the newly created database.

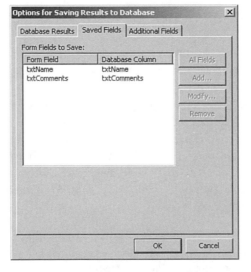

Figure 18.27
The Saved Fields tab is where you can map form fields to database columns. FrontPage mapped these for you.

Click the Additional Fields tab to configure any additional fields you would like to save. As shown in Figure 18.28, four additional fields are being saved. These are the same additional fields available to you in the Save to File or E-mail component, and these are the only additional fields available.

Figure 18.28
You have the option to include one or more of the additional fields provided by FrontPage.

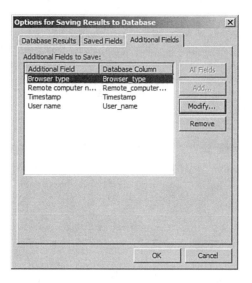

TIP

> If you cancel out of the Options for Saving Results to Database dialog box, you will have to remap all fields when you go back in to it.

Click OK in the Options for Saving Results to Database dialog box and then OK again in the Form Properties dialog box. FrontPage will inform you that you need to save this page as an ASP page, as seen in Figure 18.29. Save the page as `comment.asp`.

Figure 18.29
Send to Database pages must be saved as ASP pages.

Now preview the page in your browser, enter some information, and then click Submit. Your information is written in to the `comment.mdb` Access database in the `fpdb` folder of your Web site. If you have a copy of Microsoft Access, you can open the database and see your data. If you don't have a copy of Microsoft Access, you can create a Database Results Region to display the information in the database. A Database Results Region is a FrontPage component that can display data from a data source such as a Microsoft Access database on a Web page.

 If you submit the form without errors, but no information is written to the database, *see "Form Results Don't Appear in Database" in the "Troubleshooting" section of this chapter.*

→ For more information on using the Database Results Region, **see** "Using the Database Results Wizard," **p. 709**.

NOTE

> The Database Results Wizard pages you create with FrontPage do not require the FrontPage Server Extensions to be installed when users are browsing to them. The Send to Database form handler requires the FrontPage Server Extensions 2000 or later to be on the server, or it will not work.

ADDING NEW FIELDS

Now let's say that you have decided to also collect the email address of everyone filling out your form. FrontPage has already created a database based on what is on the form already, but that's not a problem. The Send to Database form handler has the capability to dynamically add fields to your database as your form evolves.

1. Open `comment.asp`. Make sure that you open the ASP page and not the `comment.htm` page.

2. Add a new text box form field between the `txtName` field and the `txtComments` field. For details on inserting a new form field, see "Creating a Basic Form" earlier in this chapter.

3. Name the new text box form field `txtEmail`.

4. Add any validation you would like to the new text box.

5. Right-click the Submit button and select Form Properties.

6. Click the Options button to display the Options for Saving Results to Database dialog box.

7. Click the Update Database button to update the database with your new form field.

FrontPage will add a field to the database called `txtEmail` and will display a confirmation as shown in Figure 18.30.

Figure 18.30
FrontPage can dynamically update your database when you add new form fields.

Microsoft Office FrontPage

FrontPage has successfully updated the database at "fpdb/comment.mdb" for you. When using the Database Results Wizard, use the data connection "comment".

OK

TROUBLESHOOTING

FORM PROPERTIES ARE DISABLED

I am trying to configure my form, and only the Send to Other option is available. All other options are grayed out.

If both the Send to Database and the Sent To File/E-mail options are disabled, chances are it's because you have disabled FrontPage browse-time Web components on the Authoring tab in Page Options. Select Tools, Page Options and click the Authoring tab. Make sure that there is a check in the Browse-time Web Components box.

FORM RETURNS RUNTIME COMPONENT PAGE

I have finished configuring my form and when I preview it in the browser and submit it, I get an error on a Runtime Component Page.

You must make sure that you are browsing the form on a server that has the Server Extensions installed on it. If you are sure that your server has the Server Extensions installed, recalculate hyperlinks on the Web site by selecting Tools, Recalculate Hyperlinks and try the form again.

SEND TO DATABASE NOT AVAILABLE

I am trying to configure my form and the Send to Database option is not available.

If the Send to Database option is the only option not available, it is likely because you have disabled ASP on the Authoring tab in Page Options. Select Tools, Page Options and click the Authoring tab. Make sure that there is a check in the Active Server Pages check box.

FORM RESULTS DON'T APPEAR IN DATABASE

I am submitting results to a database. I don't get an error, but there is nothing in the database.

The first thing to check is to make sure that your form fields are mapped correctly. If they are and you still aren't having success, it is possible that the problem is caused by a permissions failure when attempting to write to the database.

If you have anonymous browsing enabled on your Web site, the anonymous account on the Web server (IUSR_<machine_name> by default) doesn't have write access to the database. If you are not using anonymous access, the user who is browsing must have write access to the database.

FRONT AND CENTER: CREATING YOUR OWN FORM HANDLER

In addition to the Send to File/E-mail handler and the Send to Database handler, FrontPage also allows you to connect a form to your own custom designed form handler via the Send to Other option on the Form Properties dialog box. When you select the Send to Other option, the dropdown next to it becomes active. The dropdown contains three choices:

- **Custom ISAPI, NSAPI, CGI, or ASP Script**—Sends your form results to a custom handler.
- **Discussion Form Handler**—Sends your form to the Discussion Form Handler. FrontPage uses this handler when you create FrontPage Discussion Web sites.
- **Registration Form Handler**—Sends your form to the FrontPage Registration form handler. FrontPage uses this handler when you create Registration pages.

The first option, Custom ISAPI, NSAPI, CGI, or ASP Script, allows you to create your own form handler and point the form to it. Development of ISAPI filters, NSAPI, and CGI components is beyond the scope of this book. Instead, we will create a simple form handler using ASP.

NOTE

> For more information on ISAPI filters, read *Internet Information Services Administration* from Que Publishing.
>
> For more information on NSAPI, see Netscape Communications's NSAPI Programmer's Guide at `http://nsapi.frontpagelink.com`.
>
> For more information on common gateway interface, or CGI, read *Special Edition Using CGI*.
>
> For more information on ASP, read *Active Server Pages 3.0 From Scratch* from Que Publishing.

The form handler you will build here is not a robust solution, but is meant to show you the framework provided for creating a custom ASP form handler. You will use the `comment.htm` page that you have been using throughout this chapter.

You will need to create a new ASP page to handle your form:

1. Create a new page.
2. Save the page as **handle.asp**.
3. Type **Your name is: NAME** on the first line and press Enter.
4. Type **Your comments are: COMMENTS** on the second line.

You will configure this page so that it will display the information that was entered in the form on `comment.htm`. Start by creating the ASP code necessary to display the values from the form fields:

1. Switch to Code view.
2. Replace NAME with the following ASP code:
   ```
   <% Response.Write Request.Form("txtName") %>
   ```
3. Replace COMMENTS with the following ASP code:
   ```
   <% Response.Write Request.Form("txtComments") %>
   ```
4. Save the page.

The `handle.asp` now contains ASP code that will display the values of the form fields `txtName` and `txtComments`. It does this using the `Response.Write` statement, which writes information to the browser window, and the `Request.Form` collection, which contains one item for each form field.

Now you simply need to point `comment.htm` to the new ASP page:

1. Open `comment.htm`.

2. Right-click the Submit button and select Form Properties.

3. Choose the Send to Other option and make sure that Custom ISAPI, NSAPI, CGI, or ASP Script is selected.

4. Click the Options button to display the Options for Custom Form Handler dialog box, as seen in Figure 18.31.

Figure 18.31
The Options for Custom Form Handler dialog box lets you point your form to any handler you choose.

5. Replace `--WEBBOT-SELF--` with `handle.asp` and leave the Encoding Type set to POST.

6. Click OK in the Options for Custom Form Handler dialog box.

7. Click OK in the Form Properties dialog box.

Now save your page and browse to `comment.htm`. Enter your information and click Submit, and `handle.asp` should appear with the values you entered in the form.

18

CHAPTER **19**

USING STYLE SHEETS TO FORMAT WEB PAGES

In this chapter

UNDERSTANDING CASCADING STYLE SHEETS

Web developers have long struggled over formatting Web pages. Let's face it. HTML, although a great layout language, is not designed to be a robust formatting language. Fortunately, Web developers need not struggle with HTML for formatting page elements. *Cascading Style Sheets*, or *CSS*, is now the standard for formatting Web pages. As you will see in this chapter, CSS is well suited to the task.

CSS also solves another problem that Web developers have to contend with, and that is site redesign. Today's Internet won't tolerate a Web site that never changes. In order to keep your site fresh and desirable, you have to redesign it from time to time. If all of your formatting is implemented inside of your HTML tags, redesigning is a hassle at best. CSS solves this problem because it separates your formatting from your content. If you want to change fonts and colors, for example, you simply change your style sheet and it changes the fonts and colors in all of your pages associated with the style sheet—automatically. CSS can even be used to position your page elements right where you want them.

TIP

> If you do use CSS to position page elements, make sure that you test your page in different browsers. Internet Explorer will usually display your page as you intend it to look, but other browsers might not. This is not due to FrontPage generating code that only works right in Internet Explorer as some might say. Instead, it is because not all browsers have full support for CSS positioning.

You can apply CSS formatting to your Web site in three ways; inline styles, embedded styles, and external styles. Inline styles are configured using a `style` attribute added to an HTML tag. Embedded styles are added to the HTML document usually inside of the `<head>` section. External styles are standalone CSS files with a `.css` file extension, and they are linked to an HTML file using a `<link>` tag.

Embedded style sheets and external style sheets share the same syntax. Listing 19.1 shows a partial listing of a style sheet.

LISTING 19.1 A TYPICAL STYLE SHEET

```
a:link
{
    color: red;
    text-decoration: none;
}
a:visited
{
    color: brick;
    text-decoration: none;
}
a:hover
{
    color: red;
```

```
        text-decoration: underline overline;
}
a:active
{
    color: blue;
}
body
{
    font-family: Book Antiqua, Times New Roman, Times;
    background-color: white;
    color: black;
}
```

CSS files consist of one or more HTML elements, called *selectors* in CSS terminology, followed by CSS formatting commands enclosed in curly braces. The a selector is special in that it has several different states that can be formatted. These are referred to as *pseudo-elements* or *pseudo-selectors*. The first line of the CSS file in Listing 19.1 formats the a:link pseudo-selector, which represents an HTML <a> tag that is configured as a hyperlink. The a:link pseudo-selector represents an unvisited hyperlink that is not being clicked or hovered over, the a:visited pseudo-selector represents a hyperlink that the site visitor has already visited, the a:active pseudo-selector formats a hyperlink when the mouse button is being clicked on it, and the a:hover pseudo-selector formats a hyperlink when the mouse cursor is being hovered over it.

You can also specify multiple selectors. To use multiple selectors, separate them with commas. The following line of CSS formats both the a and the p selector:

```
a, p  { font-family: Arial; font-size: 10pt; }
```

The text inside the curly braces is the CSS text that formats the selector indicated. In Listing 19.1, the CSS text formats the color of hyperlinks at different states, the text-decoration CSS property of hyperlinks, and the formatting of the <body> tag. You will learn about how this formatting works as you read this chapter.

WORKING WITH EXTERNAL STYLE SHEETS

An external style sheet consists of a .css file containing code that defines styles for HTML elements and *CSS classes*. A CSS class is a named set of styles that can be applied to an HTML element by using the class attribute of the HTML tag.

→ For more information on CSS classes, **see** "Creating and Using CSS Classes," **p. 401**, in this chapter.

FrontPage provides the ability to create external style sheets either from preexisting templates or from scratch. External style sheets based on a template are created using the More Page Templates link in the New task pane. You click the Style Sheets tab and select a style sheet template. FrontPage will provide a brief description of the formatting that the style sheet will provide, as seen in Figure 19.1.

Figure 19.1
The Page Templates dialog box provides a brief description of each style sheet template.

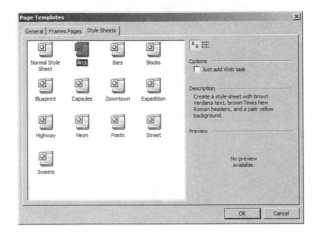

Interestingly enough, a preview is only provided for the Normal Style Sheet template that, because it is a blank style sheet, simply previews as a blank white page. However, you do get a general idea of how the style sheet will format a page from the description given.

 If you don't have a Style Sheets tab in the Page Templates dialog box, see "Style Sheets Tab Is Missing" in the "Troubleshooting" section of this chapter.

If you choose a template other than the Normal Style Sheet template, you can modify any one of the styles provided or create your own styles to add to it. If none of the provided templates suit your needs, create your own style sheet from scratch by selecting the Normal Style Sheet template.

For the most part, styles are applied to pages in the order in which they are encountered. For this reason, embedded style sheets are placed after the `<link>` tag (if present) that links to an external style sheet so that the embedded styles override the styles defined in the external style sheet. Inline styles override styles defined in an embedded or external style sheet because an inline style is applied directly to the HTML tag itself. Any style applied to a particular HTML tag also applies to any child tags of that tag. For example, if you format the `<body>` tag with a CSS style, that style will apply to the entire page unless it is overridden by another style.

TIP

> Netscape 4 has a problem with applying styles from parent tags. If you are designing a page that is going to be viewed in Netscape 4, make sure to test carefully and apply the style to all necessary selectors individually.

This process of cascading styles is how the term Cascading Style Sheets came about, but there are exceptions. Suppose, for example, you have a style in your external style sheet that formats the a selector and you don't want an embedded style sheet to override your style. You can add the ! important statement to the style in your external style sheet to give it priority over the style in the embedded style sheet. Your external style sheet style will then appear as follows:

```
a  { color: blue; text-decoration: none; ! important }
```

If a page linking to the external style sheet also has an embedded style sheet that includes a style for the a selector, the style in the external style sheet will still take precedence because of the added weight given to it by the ! important statement. However, if the embedded style sheet also uses the ! important statement when defining the style for the a selector, it will override the style in the external style sheet.

CREATING AN EXTERNAL STYLE SHEET

The best way to understand external style sheets is to create a new style sheet and use it to experiment with formatting a page. FrontPage's default Frequently Asked Questions page is the ideal page to use for this purpose because it contains many HTML elements by default. To create a new Frequently Asked Questions page

1. Select File, New and click the More Page Templates link in the New task pane.
2. Select the Frequently Asked Questions template.
3. Click OK to create the page.
4. Save the page as **CSSTest.htm**.

Now you will need a new blank style sheet that will be used to format the CSSTest.htm page. Create a new style sheet.

1. Select File, New and click the More Page Templates link in the New task pane.
2. Click the Style Sheets tab.
3. Select the Normal Style Sheet template.
4. Click OK to create the style sheet.
5. Save the style sheet as **style.css**.

The first thing you will likely notice is the Style toolbar (shown in Figure 19.2) that is floating in Design view. Using this toolbar, you can easily edit your style sheet. Click the Style button on the Style toolbar to display the Style dialog box as shown in Figure 19.3. Using the Style dialog box, you can easily start building your style sheet.

Figure 19.2
The Style toolbar floats above your page when editing style sheets in FrontPage.

19

If you don't see the Style toolbar, *see "Style Toolbar Isn't Visible" in the "Troubleshooting" section of this chapter.*

Figure 19.3
The Style dialog box makes easy work out of creating style sheets.

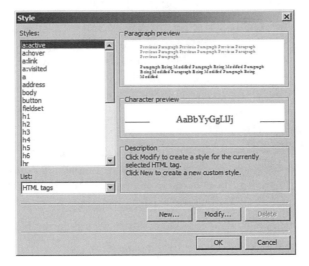

In the left side of the Style dialog box is a list of some of the HTML tags to which a style can be applied.

TIP

> You can change this list so that it contains only styles that you have defined by selecting the User-defined styles option in the List dropdown seen below the list of styles.

The Style dialog box also includes a preview of your style sheet applied to a sample paragraph and sample characters. This preview is not precise, but it's a good estimation of how the style will look on your page.

The Description box on the Style dialog box provides you with instructions on how to use the dialog box when no styles are defined for the selector that is selected in the Styles list. If a style is defined for the selector, the Description box will provide you with a rundown of the style's attributes as seen in Figure 19.4.

Three buttons on the Style dialog can be used to edit your style sheet. The New button allows you to create a new style for a selector that is not already listed in the Styles list. You can use this to create a new style for an unlisted HTML tag, or you can use it to define a new CSS class. (We'll cover CSS classes later in this chapter.) The Modify button allows you to modify styles that already appear in the Styles list, and the Delete button allows you to delete a style that was previously applied to a selector.

Figure 19.4
The Description box
provides an overview
of the selected style.

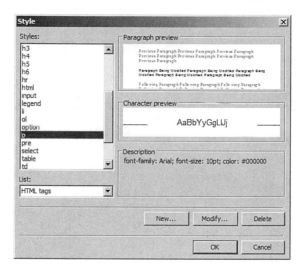

Apply a style to the hyperlinks in CSSTest.htm as follows:

1. Select the a:active pseudo-selector.

2. Click Modify to display the Modify Style dialog box as seen in Figure 19.5.

Figure 19.5
The Modify Style dia-
log box allows you to
modify the style of a
selector in one place.

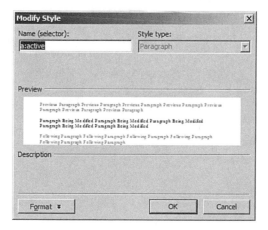

19

3. Click Format and then click Font to display the Font dialog box as shown in Figure 19.6.

4. In the Font list, scroll down to Arial and select it.

5. In the Size list, select 10pt.

6. In the Color dropdown, choose a red color.

7. Click OK twice to apply the style. Note that the Description box now indicates the style's settings and the Styles list now only contains the a:active pseudo-selector.

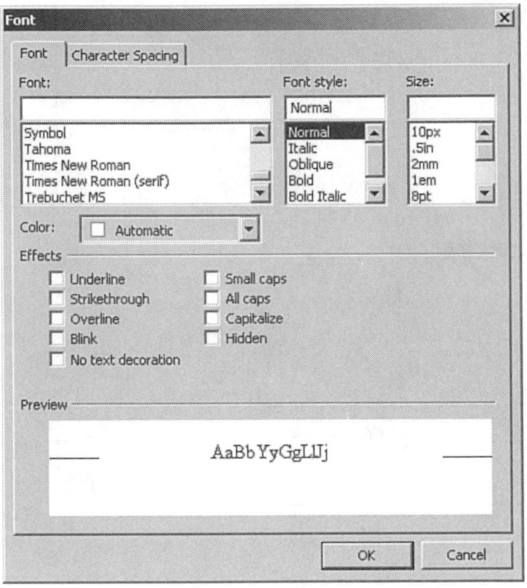

Figure 19.6
The Font dialog box
provides access to the
font style settings for
your style.

NOTE

After you modify a style for the first time, the Style dialog box displays only the user-defined styles until you select HTML Tags from the List dropdown. After you modify subsequent styles, the Styles list will continue to display all HTML tags to make editing other styles easy.

8. Select HTML Tags in the List dropdown.

9. Select the a:link pseudo-selector.

10. Click Modify to modify the style.

11. Click Format and then click Font.

12. In the Font list, scroll down to Arial and select it.

13. In the Size list, select 10pt.

14. In the Color dropdown, choose the same color that you chose for the a:active pseudo-selector.

15. Check the No Text Decoration check box.

16. Click OK twice to apply the style. The Styles list now contains an entry for the a:active pseudo-selector and the a:link pseudo-selector.

17. Select the a:visited pseudo-selector and click Modify.

18. Repeat steps 11–16, only select a color slightly lighter than the red color you chose previously.

19. Format the a:hover pseudo-selector using the same settings you used for the a:link pseudo-selector, but instead of checking the No Text Decoration check box, check the Underline check box.

20. Click OK in the Style dialog box to apply the CSS styles to the style sheet.

21. Select File, Save to save your new style sheet.

Your CSS file should now look similar to the file in Figure 19.7. Save the changes to the style sheet.

Figure 19.7
This style sheet applies styles to hyperlinks.

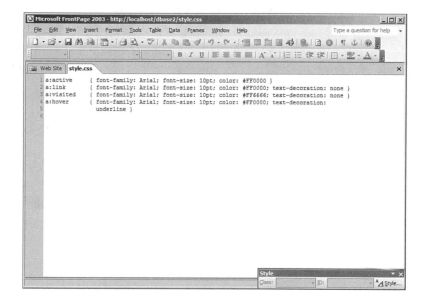

You might be wondering why you modified the a:hover pseudo-selector last instead of modifying them in the order in which they appear in the Styles list. The reason is that, as previously mentioned, styles cascade. The a:link pseudo-selector applies to all hyperlinks. Therefore, if the a:link pseudo-selector appears below the a:hover pseudo-selector, it will override the a:hover pseudo-selector.

If you review the CSS code that FrontPage generated, you will see how straightforward CSS really is. The following CSS properties were set by the changes you made in the Modify Style dialog box:

- font-family—The font-family property sets the font used to render the selector. The equivalent HTML element is the face attribute of the <font> tag.

- font-size—The font-size property sets the size of the font used to render the selector.

- color—The color property sets the color of the font. It can be expressed using hex values, RGB values, or named values. In the FrontPage-generated CSS file, it is expressed in hex values.

- text-decoration—Specifies the decoration for the text. Can be set to none, underline, overline, line-through, or blink. (blink is not supported in Internet Explorer.)

Using these four CSS properties, you have transformed your hyperlinks from the boring defaults to interactive, customized hyperlinks.

APPLYING AN EXTERNAL STYLE SHEET TO A WEB PAGE

Before you add any more styles to the style sheet, now is a good time to apply the style sheet to the CSSTest.htm page. An external style sheet is applied to a Web page by linking it to the page using a <link> tag. FrontPage provides a convenient method for linking an external style sheet to a Web page.

1. Open CSSTest.htm.

2. Select Format, Style Sheet Links to display the Link Style Sheet dialog box as shown in Figure 19.8.

Figure 19.8
The Style Sheet Links dialog box makes it easy to link your external style sheet to one or more pages.

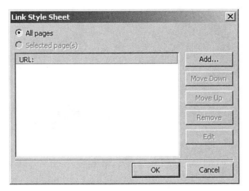

3. Click the Add button to add a new style sheet link.

4. Select style.css and click OK.

5. Make sure that the Selected Page(s) radio button is selected and click OK to apply the style sheet link.

You should see the changes to CSSTest.htm applied immediately in Design view. Switch to Preview view or preview the page in your browser and hover over the hyperlinks to see your styles in action.

ADDING MORE STYLES TO THE STYLE SHEET

When modifying the hyperlink styles, you might have noticed that an a selector appeared in the Styles list in addition to the a:link, a:hover, a:visited, and a:active pseudo-selectors. The a selector represents any HTML <a> tag. In the CSSTest.htm file, there are several HTML bookmarks so that when a user clicks on a question in the FAQ list, it will take him to the correct spot in the file. HTML bookmarks are configured with <a> tags, but they aren't hyperlinks because they don't really link to anything. Therefore, these bookmarks are not affected by the selectors that you've already formatted. To affect the bookmarks, you will need to apply a style to the a selector:

1. Open the style.css file.
2. Click the Style button on the Style toolbar.
3. Select HTML Tags in the List dropdown.
4. Select the a selector and click Modify.
5. Click Format and click Font.
6. Scroll to Arial in the Font list and select it.
7. Select 10pt in the Size list.
8. In the Color dropdown, select the same red color that you used for the a:link pseudo-selector.
9. Click OK twice to commit your change.
10. Click OK to apply the style to the style sheet.

Your style sheet should now resemble the page in Figure 19.9.

Figure 19.9
Your style sheet now has formatting for all a selectors.

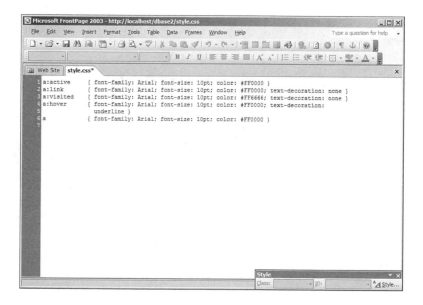

You should now have a good idea of just how powerful CSS is. If you decide to reformat hyperlinks at a later time, changing their format is as easy as changing the CSS file. Without using an external style sheet, you would have to open each page and change it individually. If you were dealing with a site with hundreds of pages in it, formatting with CSS can make an otherwise arduous task quite easy.

NOTE

The Class and the ID dropdowns on the Style toolbar are disabled when modifying selectors that are HTML tags. These dropdowns will be used later when you learn about CSS classes.

USING EMBEDDED STYLE SHEETS

An embedded style sheet uses the same format as an external style sheet. The only difference between the two is that an embedded style sheet is embedded in the HTML of the page, whereas an external style sheet exists in its own file and is linked to a page (or multiple pages).

Embedded style sheets are often used to override styles configured in an external style sheet. For example, suppose that you have configured all of your pages with a white background and black text with red hyperlinks using an external style sheet linked. You have one page in your site where you want to use all the styles configured in the external style sheet, but instead of a white background with black text, you need a black background with white text. An embedded style sheet will allow you to override the background color and font color styles from the external style sheet while keeping all the other styles.

The HTML code in Listing 19.2 uses an embedded style sheet to specify a black background and white text for the page. The rest of the page is formatted using styles specified in the `style.css` external style sheet.

LISTING 19.2 OVERRIDING STYLES WITH AN EMBEDDED STYLE SHEET

```
<html>
<head>
<title>Overridden Style</title>
<link rel="stylesheet" type="text/css" href="style.css">

<style>
<!--
body        { color: #FFFFFF; background-color: #000000 }
-->
</style>

</head>
<body>
<p>This text will appear white on a
black background.</p>
</body>
</html>
```

As shown in Listing 19.2, the embedded style is specified using a `<style>` tag. To create an embedded style sheet in FrontPage, you use the Style dialog box just as you did for the external style sheet, but you apply the styles to a Web page instead of a CSS file.

1. Open the `CSSTest.htm` file.
2. Select Format, Style to display the Style dialog box.
3. Select HTML Tags in the List dropdown.
4. Select Body in the Styles list.
5. Click Modify to open the Modify Style dialog box.
6. Select Format, Border and click the Shading tab as shown in Figure 19.10.

Figure 19.10
The Shading tab allows you to control the background shading of a selector.

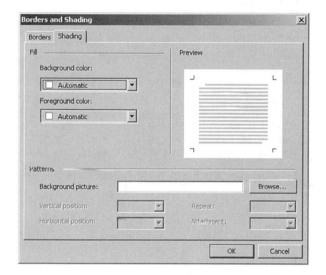

7. In the Background Color dropdown, choose a light color of your choice.
8. Click OK.
9. Select Format, Font in the Style dialog box.
10. In the Color dropdown, choose a darker color of your choice.
11. Click OK three times to commit your style changes.

FrontPage places the embedded style sheet directly under the `<link>` tag in the Web page so that the embedded styles will override the styles in the external style sheet, as shown in Figure 19.11.

Figure 19.11
This page is formatted with both an external and an embedded style sheet.

```
[Web Site] [CSSTest.htm]
[<body>] [<p>]
 1  <html>
 2
 3  <head>
 4  <meta http-equiv="Content-Type" content="text/html; charset=windows-1252">
 5  <meta http-equiv="Content-Language" content="en-us">
 6  <title>Table of Contents</title>
 7  <link rel="stylesheet" type="text/css" href="style.css">
 8  <style>
 9  <!--
10  body          { color: #FFFFFF; background-color: #000000; }
11  -->
12  </style>
13  </head>
14
15  <body>
```

USING INLINE STYLES

Inline styles are styles that are applied directly to an HTML tag and override both external style sheets and embedded style sheets. Inline styles are applied using the `<style>` tag followed by the style attributes in a semicolon delimited list.

The following code sets the style on one particular hyperlink using an inline style:

```
<p>This
<a style="text-decoration: overline underline;
        font-family: Tahoma;
        border: 1px solid #800000;"
 href="test_link.htm">link</a> is formatted with an inline style.</p>
```

The `<a>` tag has a `style` attribute that formats the hyperlink as an inline style. To format an HTML element with an inline style

1. Open `CSSTest.htm`.
2. Select one or more words in Design view.
3. Select Insert, Hyperlink.
4. Link the text to the URL of your choice.
5. Click the Style button (see Figure 19.12).

Figure 19.12
The Style button in the Insert Hyperlink dialog box inserts an inline style.

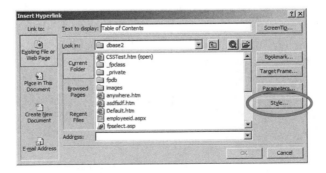

6. Select Format, Font in the Style dialog box.

7. Change the font formatting to suit you.

8. Click OK three times to commit your change.

 If you don't have a Style button in the Insert Hyperlink dialog box, *see "Style Button Is Missing" in the "Troubleshooting" section of this chapter.*

Your hyperlink is now formatted with an inline style as shown in Figure 19.13. If you review the code in Code view, you will see that FrontPage added a `style` attribute to the `<a>` tag and populated it with the correct attributes according to your selections in the Modify Style dialog box.

Formatted Hyperlink

Figure 19.13
This hyperlink is formatted with an inline style, but the page is formatted with embedded and external styles.

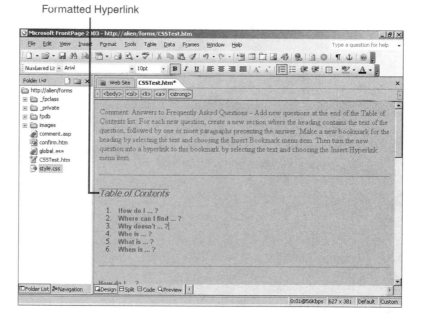

NOTE

Previous versions of FrontPage had a Style button in almost every dialog box. FrontPage 2003 places more emphasis on external style sheets and embedded styles, but the Style button is still on many dialog boxes. Anytime you use the Style button in a dialog box, FrontPage will insert an inline style.

Another way that FrontPage will insert an inline style is when editing layers or when setting absolutely positioned elements.

1. Create a new page in FrontPage.

2. Type the word **Anywhere!** onto the page.

3. Place the insertion point on the same line as the word you just typed and select F̲ormat, Po̲sition to display the Position dialog box, as shown in Figure 19.14.

Figure 19.14
The Position dialog box lets you specify an element's position on the page.

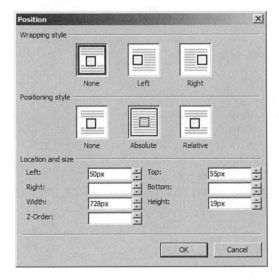

4. Click the Absolute box in the Positioning Style section.
5. Click OK.

If the Position menu item is not enabled, *see "Position Menu Is Not Enabled" in the "Troubleshooting" section of this chapter.*

You now have a layer that can be absolutely positioned by dragging the label on the layer as shown in Figure 19.15. When you drag the layer, FrontPage writes inline styles into the <div> tag, as seen in Figure 19.16.

→ For more information on creating and positioning layers, **see** "Using Layers," **p. 499**.

Figure 19.15
This layer can be dragged anywhere, and FrontPage uses inline styles to position it.

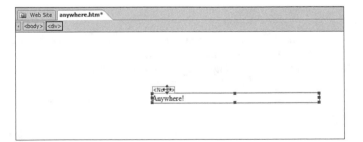

Figure 19.16
FrontPage inserts an
inline style to position
the layer.

```
<body>

<div style="position: absolute; left: 281px; top: 128px; width: 347px; height: 19px">
    Anywhere!</div>

</body>
```

Inline styles do not cascade into nested tags. This means that if you apply an inline style to a <p> tag and that tag contains an <a> tag, the <a> tag will not take on the properties of the <p> tag. If you want to format the entire paragraph with an inline style, you will have to apply the style to both the <p> and the <a> tags.

CREATING AND USING CSS CLASSES

A CSS class is a very powerful formatting tool. Some formatting tasks just cannot be easily accomplished using styles applied to HTML tags. There are also tasks that can be accomplished using styles applied to HTML tags, but are much better suited to CSS classes.

DEFINING A CSS CLASS

A CSS class is simply a collection of style elements packaged inside of a style and named with a custom name of your choice. That might not sound like much of a power tool, but it is: You will soon see why.

The following is a CSS class declaration:

```
/* Style definition for page content. */
.content      { font-family: Arial;
                font-size: 10pt;
                color: #000000;
                border: 3px solid #000000;
                padding: 2px;
                background-color: #999999;
              }
```

This CSS code defines a class called content. This new CSS class can be applied to any HTML element to format it with a gray background color, a 3 pixel black border, and black Arial text that is 10pt in size. This simple style can be used to format any page element on the page. For example, you can apply the content class to a particular table cell if you want that cell to be formatted differently than the rest of the table.

TIP

> It's a good idea to comment your style sheets when defining classes so that you will remember what they're for. To add a comment, start the comment line with /* and end it with */. Anything between those characters is a comment.

The page pictured in Figure 19.17 has a three column, three row table on it, and the center cell has been formatted with the content class.

Figure 19.17
This table doesn't have a border or background shading, but the center cell does thanks to the content class.

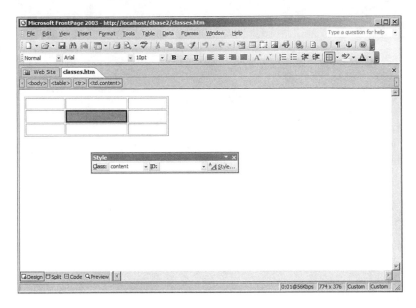

Formatting Tags Using CSS Classes

To assign the content class to the center cell, you simply add a class attribute to the HTML tag and set the value of that attribute to the name of the class. Switch to Code view and locate the tag to which you want to apply the CSS class. Click inside that HTML tag and right after the tag name, add the following:

```
class="content"
```

By adding the class attribute to the HTML tag, you are letting FrontPage know that this HTML tag should be formatted using the style defined in that CSS class.

The following HTML code assigns the content class to the table cell:

```
<td class="content">
```

TIP

FrontPage's Quick Tag Editor is an excellent tool for adding CSS classes to an HTML tag.

→ For more information on using FrontPage's Quick Tag Editor, **see** "Editing Code with the Quick Tag Editor," **p. 532**.

To reformat any HTML element to which the content class has been applied, simply edit the content class and all HTML elements using that class will change automatically.

Now take it a bit further. Suppose that you have a Web page with a banner section, header sections for your primary content sections, and content areas for your content. First, you apply the content style to all of your content areas. Then you create a CSS class called header and a CSS class called banner. You can then format the entire page by simply applying your CSS classes to the appropriate HTML elements. Your site can be easily redesigned for a fresh look by changing your CSS classes.

To create a new CSS class in FrontPage

1. Open the `style.css` stylesheet you created earlier.
2. Click the Style button on the Style toolbar.
3. Click the New button in the Style dialog box to create a new style.
4. In the Name box, enter `.content`. The period prior to the name is important.
5. Make sure that Style Type is set to Paragraph.
6. Select Format, Font in the Style dialog box and change the font format to your liking for the new style.
7. Click OK three times to commit your new style to the style sheet.

You now have a new style called `.content` listed in your style sheet. This is the style for the content CSS class. The period in front of the content style's name indicates that it is a CSS class and not an HTML tag.

To format an element on the page with your new CSS style

1. Create a new HTML page.
2. Select Format, Style Sheet Links.
3. In the Link Style Sheet dialog box, click Add.
4. Browse to `style.css` and click OK.
5. Click OK to apply the style sheet link.
6. Type the text `This is the content style.` and leave the insertion point at the end of that line.
7. Select View, Toolbars, Style to display the Style toolbar.
8. In the Class dropdown, select the content class.

As soon as you select the content class, the paragraph will be instantly formatted using the style defined in that class.

Notice that the style has been applied to your entire paragraph, as shown in Figure 19.18. This is because the content class defines a paragraph style and is applied to the parent HTML tag of the element under the current selection or insertion point. In other words, when you applied the style to the line of text you typed, the parent tag is the `<p>` tag surrounding the line, so the content class is applied to the entire paragraph.

19

Figure 19.18
The content class
applied to a Web
page.

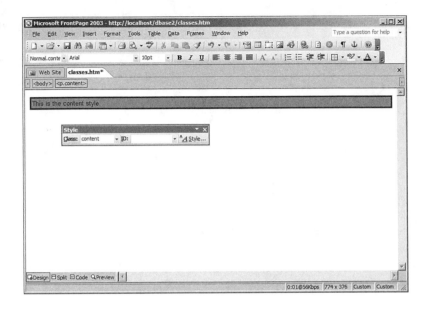

PARAGRAPH AND CHARACTER STYLES

FrontPage includes the ability for you to configure a new CSS class as either a character style or a paragraph style. The only difference between the two is that FrontPage will associate the <span> HTML tag (by naming the CSS class span.<classname>) with any CSS class defined as a character style. This doesn't seem particularly helpful to me, and I have never used a character style in FrontPage for that reason. Any style that I define in FrontPage is defined as a paragraph style.

The format that FrontPage uses to define a character style is called a *class selector*. A class selector is simply a class definition with a selector associated with it. Using this method, you can specify that the CSS class only applies to a particular selector. Because FrontPage uses span.<classname> to define a character style, the class that is defined can only be applied to the <span> HTML tag. This is not very useful because characters in your Web site are not normally contained within a <span> tag. However, there are many situations in which you can use class selectors to your advantage.

Suppose that you have many tables in your Web page. Some of these tables you want formatted using one particular style, and others you want formatted in a different style. If you create a CSS style simply for the table selector, all tables will look the same. Therefore, you will need to define some CSS classes that will format the tables the way you want them.

You could create CSS classes without associating the table selector with them, but it's very possible that the classes would contain CSS settings that apply specifically to tables. In that case, you wouldn't want to allow anyone to apply those classes to anything but tables. Using class selectors is the perfect solution. The following CSS code defines two classes for the table selector.

```
/* sidebar class for tables in borders. */
table.sidebar { font-family: Arial;
                font-size: 8pt;
                color: #FF3300;
                border: 1px solid #CC3300;
                padding-left: 4px;
                padding-right: 4px;
                padding-top: 1px;
                padding-bottom: 1px;
                background-color: #E4CBBA }

/* main class for tables in main content area. */
table.main   {  font-family: Arial;
                font-size: 10pt;
                color: #000000;
                border: 1px solid #C0C0C0;
                padding-left: 4px;
                padding-right: 4px;
                padding-top: 1px;
                padding-bottom: 1px;
                background-color: #FFF5DF }
```

When you are applying CSS styles to your Web page using the Style toolbar, the sidebar and the main class will only be available if the currently selected tag is a <table> tag. The page in Figure 19.19 shows the result of applying these classes to a Web page.

Figure 19.19
Two tables formatted with the main and the sidebar classes.

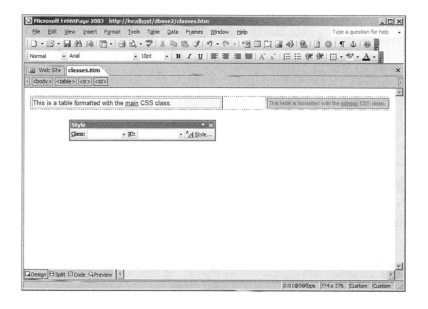

It's a little known fact that you can apply two CSS classes to one HTML element by separating each class with a space. For example, you can apply both the sidebar and main classes to one table by adding a `class` attribute to the `<table>` tag with a value of `sidebar main`, as follows:

```
<table class="sidebar main">
```

Any style element in the `main` class will now override a corresponding style element in the `sidebar` class.

TROUBLESHOOTING

STYLE SHEETS TAB IS MISSING

I am trying to create a new style sheet, but the Style Sheets tab is missing from the Page Templates dialog box.

FrontPage will remove the Style Sheets tab if you don't have CSS enabled on the Authoring tab of the Page Options dialog box. Select Tools, Page Options and click the Authoring tab. Make sure that the CSS 1.0 (formatting) check box is checked.

STYLE TOOLBAR ISN'T VISIBLE

I have created a new style sheet, but I don't see the Style toolbar.

If the Style toolbar isn't visible, you can display it by selecting View, Toolbars, Style.

STYLE BUTTON IS MISSING

I am trying to apply an inline style, but I don't have a Style button.

FrontPage will remove the Style button from all dialogs when CSS is disabled. Select Tools, Page Options and click the Authoring tab. Make sure that the CSS 1.0 (formatting) check box is checked.

POSITION MENU IS NOT ENABLED

I am trying to absolutely position something on my page, but the Position menu is grayed out.

FrontPage disables the Position menu if CSS positioning is disabled. Select Tools, Page Options and click the Authoring tab. Make sure that the CSS 2.0 (positioning) check box is checked.

FRONT AND CENTER: MORE PSEUDO-ELEMENTS

You already know that the a element has several pseudo-elements so that you can define a style for different states of a hyperlink. Most Web developers use these pseudo-elements in their style sheets, but many Web developers don't know other pseudo-elements exist that you can use to make your pages stand out.

The `first-letter` pseudo-element allows you to adjust the style for the first letter in an HTML element as long as the element is a block-level element. A *block-level element* is an element that is used to format an entire block of characters instead of specific characters within a line of text. For example, the `<table>` element is a block-level element, and so is the `<p>` element.

TIP

> FrontPage's Design view does not show the effects of block-level pseudo-elements. To see the effect, you will need to view your page in Preview view or by previewing it in a browser.

The following CSS style formats the first letter of a paragraph so that it will stand out by formatting it at twice the size of the surrounding text and in a different color. It formats the rest of the paragraph with a different font, font size, and color.

```
p:first-letter { font-family: Times New Roman;
                 font-size: 200%;
                 text-decoration: overline;
                 text-transform: capitalize;
                 color: #CC3300;
                 font-weight: bold }
p              { font-family: Arial;
                 font-size: 10pt;
                 color: #000000 }
```

Figure 19.20 shows two paragraphs on a page linked to the style sheet. Notice that the first letter of each paragraph is formatted using the `first-letter` pseudo-element.

Figure 19.20
Paragraphs formatted with the `first-letter` pseudo-element look similar to a magazine article format.

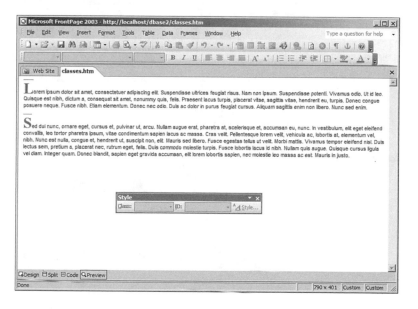

In addition to the `first-letter` pseudo-element, block-level HTML elements also have a `first-line` pseudo-element that can be used to format the first line. This is an extremely powerful pseudo-element because it can allow you to achieve results that would otherwise be impossible.

Suppose that you have a paragraph of text and you want the first line of that paragraph to appear bolded and the rest of the paragraph to appear unbolded. You could apply direct bold formatting to the characters that appear in the first line, but as soon as the browser window is resized or viewed on a monitor at a different resolution, some of the characters that were originally on the first line might move to the second line or characters the were not previously on the first line might move to the first line. Your formatting will then look sloppy and unprofessional. Using the first-line pseudo-element, you can easily apply the effect so that it works correctly at all browser window sizes, screen resolutions, and text size settings.

The following style sheet formats the first line of paragraphs as bolded and the rest of the paragraph as normal text.

```
p:first-line { font-family: Arial;
               font-size: 10pt;
               color: #000000;
               font-weight: bold }
p            { font-family: Arial;
               font-size: 10pt;
               color: #000000 }
```

Figure 19.21 shows the result of this formatting. As the browser window is resized, the bolded characters will change depending on whether they appear on the first line of the paragraphs.

Figure 19.21
These paragraphs were formatted using the first-line pseudo-element.

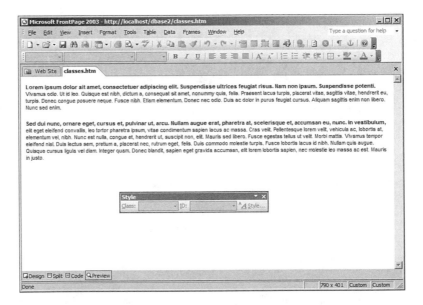

As you can see, CSS formatting is an extremely powerful tool for Web developers. You owe it to yourself to experiment with CSS and learn as much as you can about it so that you will be able to quickly and easily format your Web site with this flexible and powerful technology.

SCRIPTING, DYNAMIC HTML, AND DYNAMIC CONTENT

CHAPTER **20**

DYNAMIC WEB TEMPLATES

In this chapter

AN OVERVIEW OF DYNAMIC WEB TEMPLATES

When you're designing a Web site, it's important to maintain a consistent look and feel. FrontPage developers have often used shared borders for page elements that are shared between multiple pages, and although shared borders do allow you to share content between pages, they introduce some limitations that make your design less flexible. If you decide that some pages need a different layout or different shared content, you have to create a new subsite to contain those pages. If you have several developers working on a site, it's possible for someone else to change the content in your shared border. Shared borders also limit your design because they have to be placed on the top, left, right, or bottom of a page. You can't have shared formatting anywhere you want it.

→ For more information on shared borders, **see** "Working with Shared Borders," **p. 184s**.

Dynamic Web Templates solve all these problems and much more. Dynamic Web Templates allow you to design your Web site just the way you want it without imposing limitations on you. They also provide you with a way to design common elements and then lock parts of the Web page so that they won't be accidentally modified.

CREATING DYNAMIC WEB TEMPLATES

Dynamic Web Templates use *editable regions* to separate areas that can be edited from areas that are protected. Any content outside of an editable region is protected and cannot be edited. An editable region can be located anywhere on a page, but for the most control over the location of an editable region, you can place it in a table cell.

FrontPage will allow you to save a Dynamic Web Template before any editable regions are added to it, but FrontPage won't let you attach that template to a page until you've created at least one editable region (see Figure 20.1).

Figure 20.1
Before applying a Dynamic Web Template to a page, you must first add one or more editable regions to the Dynamic Web Template.

DESIGN A LAYOUT FOR THE DYNAMIC WEB TEMPLATE

You begin by creating the layout for your Dynamic Web Template inside of a normal Web page. Your Dynamic Web Template can be formatted using any page elements you choose. In this example, you will use a table to format the template:

1. Create a new blank page and add a table to it.
2. Give the table three columns and two rows.

3. Set the border to **0**, but leave all other settings at their default values.

4. Drag the width of the columns so that the center column is wider than the left or right column.

5. Add a graphic of your choice to the top left cell of the table as shown in Figure 20.2.

Figure 20.2
This table will be used as the basis for your Dynamic Web Template.

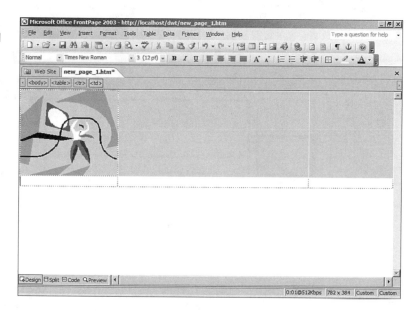

You'll use this simple table as the layout for a Dynamic Web Template you'll use as you read this chapter.

As shown in Figure 20.3, you are going to allow people editing your site to edit the left column, but you're also going to have some navigation elements there. Therefore, you'll only allow people to edit below the existing navigation buttons. You will also allow people to place main content into the center column, but you'll have some copyright text at the bottom of the column that no one will be able to modify. Finally, you'll allow developers to add content freely into the right column.

ADDING STATIC ELEMENTS

To implement this Dynamic Web Template, you will need to enter three editable regions, but first you'll need to add the content that you want to remain static and uneditable. Click inside the left column and add a few Interactive Buttons for your navigation. Press Enter after each button so that each button is on its own line, as shown in Figure 20.4.

Click inside the center column and enter some copyright information. This text will also remain locked when editing this template. Anything inserted at this point is outside of an editable region and will be locked when the Dynamic Web Template is attached to a page.

20

Figure 20.3
This page will be saved as a Dynamic Web Template and will control where content can be edited.

Navigation Buttons   Editable Region 2   Editable Region 3

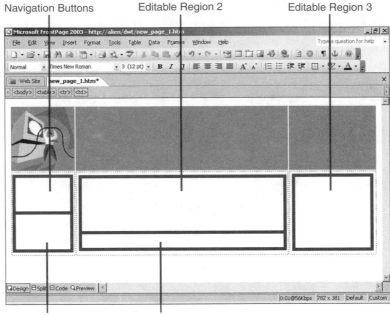

Editable Region 1   Copyright Text

Figure 20.4
These Interactive Buttons will be locked inside of an editable region.

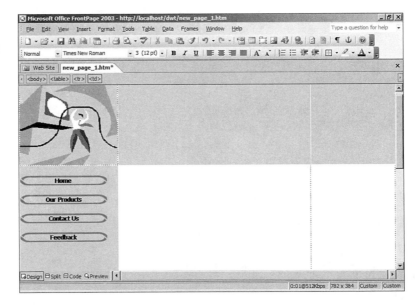

CREATING EDITABLE REGIONS

Before you create editable regions in the Dynamic Web Template, first save the template.

1. Select File, Save As to display the Save As dialog box.
2. In the Save As Type dropdown, select Dynamic Web Template.
3. Name the Dynamic Web Template **Site_Template.dwt** and click Save.
4. In the Save Embedded Files dialog box, click OK to accept the default.
5. Right-click the page and select Manage Editable Regions from the menu to display the Editable Regions dialog box as shown in Figure 20.5.

Figure 20.5
The Editable Regions dialog box allows you to insert, remove, and go to editable regions on your page.

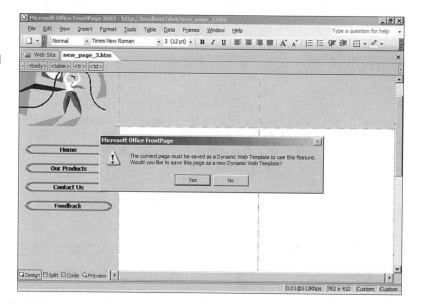

6. Enter **MainContent** in the Region name box.
7. Click Add to add this editable region to the template.
8. Click Close to close the Editable Regions dialog.
9. Place the insertion point inside the left cell below the Interactive buttons.
10. Right-click and select Manage Editable Regions from the menu.
11. Enter **LeftContent** in the Region name box.
12. Click Add to add the editable region to the template.
13. Click Close to close the Editable Regions dialog.
14. Place the insertion point inside the right cell underneath the colored top border.
15. Right-click and select Manage Editable Regions from the menu.
16. Enter **RightContent** in the Region name box.

17. Click Add to add the editable region to the template.

18. Click Close to close the Editable Regions dialog.

19. Save the page.

You now have three editable regions in the template. You might have noticed that FrontPage had already created one editable region for this page called doctitle. The doctitle editable region allows developers to change the title of pages to which this Dynamic Web Template is attached.

 If you remove the *doctitle* editable region and don't know how to get it back, or if your page doesn't have a *doctitle* editable region, *see "Developers Cannot Change the Title of Pages" in the "Troubleshooting" section of this chapter.*

The borders of the editable regions are indicated by an orange line around them. After you attach this Dynamic Web Template to a Web page, content can only be added inside these editable regions. Anything outside the editable regions will be protected.

> **TIP**
>
> You can also make a section of a paragraph an editable region. For example, you can make the year in your copyright statement an editable region so that it can be changed each year while the rest of the copyright statement stays protected.

The completed Dynamic Web Template is shown in Figure 20.6. Now that you've created a Dynamic Web Template, you are ready to attach it to a Web page.

Figure 20.6
A completed Dynamic Web Template ready to be saved and attached to a page.

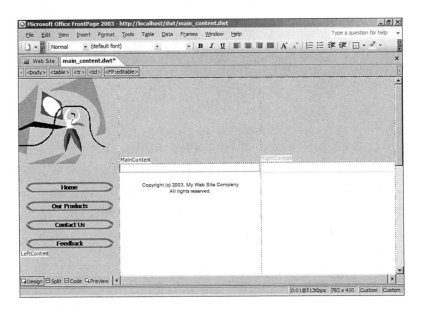

ATTACHING A DYNAMIC WEB TEMPLATE TO A PAGE

Dynamic Web Templates are attached to pages by selecting Format, Dynamic Web Template, Attach Dynamic Web Template. When you attach a Dynamic Web Template to a Web page, assuming that no other Dynamic Web Template is attached already, FrontPage will add the elements from the Dynamic Web Template to the page and display the editable regions, allowing you to begin editing the page.

To attach a Dynamic Web Template to an existing page, perform these steps:

1. Open an existing Web page.
2. Select Format, Dynamic Web Template, Attach Dynamic Web Template.
3. Select the Dynamic Web Template from the dialog and click Open.
4. If any text already exists on the page, FrontPage will prompt you to specify which editable region should contain the existing content.
5. If the editable region that FrontPage is suggesting is not correct, select the editable region in the list and click the Modify button.
6. Choose the correct editable region from the New Region dropdown, as seen in Figure 20.7, and click OK.

Figure 20.7
When attaching a Dynamic Web Template to a page with content already on it, FrontPage will allow you to map content to editable regions.

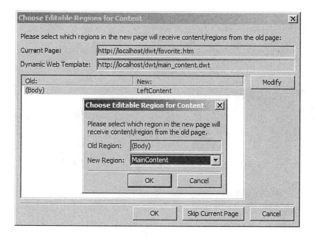

Figure 20.8 shows a page prior to attaching the Dynamic Web Template. Figure 20.9 shows the same page after attaching the Dynamic Web Template and specifying the MainContent editable region for existing content.

If you want to attach a Dynamic Web Template to multiple pages, simply select the pages in the Folder List before selecting Format, Dynamic Web Template, Attach Dynamic Web Template. You will be asked which editable region should contain any existing content in each page. After you've attached the Dynamic Web Template to your pages, you will need to save each page by either saving them individually or select File, Save All.

Figure 20.8
This page is simple and boring, but by attaching a Dynamic Web Template, it can be made very professional looking.

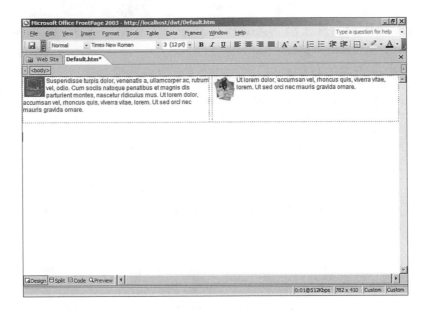

Figure 20.9
Here is our page after applying the Dynamic Web Template—quite an improvement.

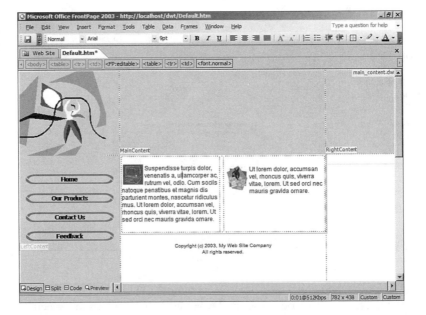

You can also automatically create new Web pages that are attached to the Dynamic Web Template. Right-click on the Dynamic Web Template in the Folder List or in Folders view and select New from Dynamic Web Template from the menu. FrontPage will create a new page and attach the Dynamic Web Template to the page in one step.

The World Wide Web is a rapidly evolving medium. If you're going to keep up, you must keep your Web site fresh and interesting. Dynamic Web Templates make it simple by allowing you to attach a new Dynamic Web Template to your pages in place of an existing one. Page content is maintained, and your site gets a face-lift with minimal effort.

Create a new Dynamic Web Template as you did before, but this time, use different graphics and a different color scheme. Because you are only using the `MainContent` editable region in this example, you can create only one editable region in your new Dynamic Web Template. Figure 20.10 shows an example of a new Dynamic Web Template with one editable region.

Figure 20.10
Implementing a new Web site design couldn't be easier than using Dynamic Web Templates.

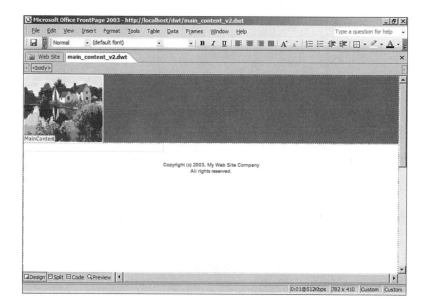

The steps to attach a new Dynamic Web Template are the same as show previously in "Attaching a Dynamic Web Template to a Page." Simply open the Web page that has the first Dynamic Web Template applied to it and select Format, Dynamic Web Template, Attach Dynamic Web Template. Choose the new template, select the editable region, and your new template is now attached to the page.

Figure 20.11 shows the result.

20

Figure 20.11
Attaching a new
Dynamic Web
Template is fast and
easy and gives your
site a facelift with min-
imal effort.

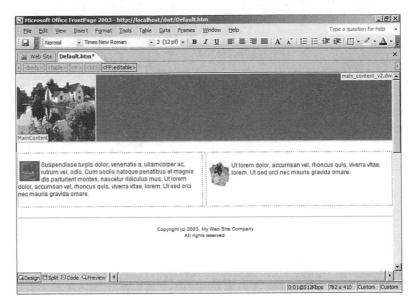

EDITING A DYNAMIC WEB TEMPLATE

In addition to completely changing your Web site using Dynamic Web Templates, you can also make small changes by editing the Dynamic Web Template itself. Any changes will automatically be applied to all pages that the Dynamic Web Template is attached to.

1. Open the original Dynamic Web Template you created earlier.
2. Change the color scheme and graphic.
3. Save the template.

FrontPage will inform you if pages are attached to the template and ask if you want to update them as shown in Figure 20.12. If you click Yes, FrontPage will immediately update pages attached to the Dynamic Web Template. If you click No, you can update attached pages later by opening them and selecting Format, Dynamic Web Template, Update Selected Page.

Figure 20.12
When modifying a
Dynamic Web
Template, FrontPage
will ask if you want to
update all pages
attached to that tem-
plate.

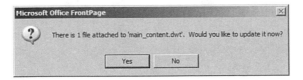

This is similar to the way that FrontPage users have worked with shared borders in the past, but it is much more powerful and intuitive. Now you can easily make global changes of graphics, color schemes, and just about anything else in one easy step.

DETACHING DYNAMIC WEB TEMPLATES

If you want to remove the formatting applied by the Dynamic Web Template, select Format, Dynamic Web Template, Detach Dynamic Web Template. All content for the page is preserved, including content provided by the Dynamic Web Template. After detaching the Dynamic Web Template, all content in the page is editable.

CHANGING CODE IN AN ATTACHED WEB PAGE

As mentioned earlier in "Creating Dynamic Web Templates," any section of an attached page that is outside an editable region is protected. However, it is still possible to access the HTML source for protected areas of the page. When you do switch to a view of the HTML code for the page, any code outside an editable region will be highlighted as shown in Figure 20.13.

Figure 20.13
Code that exists outside editable regions is highlighted in Code view.

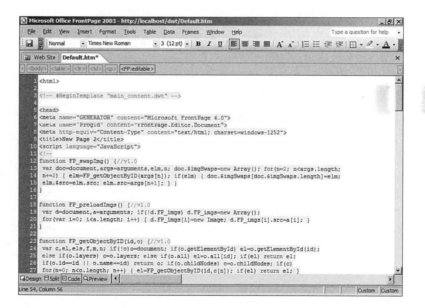

If you change any of the highlighted code, FrontPage will display the Dynamic Web Template Alert dialog (see Figure 20.14) warning you that you have made a change to a non-editable region and informing you that it will be changed back the next time the page is updated.

Figure 20.14
The Dynamic Web Template Alert dialog will warn you if you make changes outside an editable region.

You have two choices at this point:

- Always restore non-editable content while editing this page—FrontPage will always restore any changes you make to non-editable regions, and you will no longer be prompted when changing code in non-editable regions.

- Keep all changes—FrontPage will keep the change that you made, but the next time you update this page, the settings from the Dynamic Web Template will be reapplied. If you don't want this to happen, you can check the Detach from Dynamic Web Template box.

 If you are editing a page and you encounter a dialog telling you that your change cannot be applied because it is locked by a Dynamic Web Template, see "Cannot Modify an Editable Region Because It's Locked" in the "Troubleshooting" section of this chapter.

TROUBLESHOOTING

DEVELOPERS CANNOT CHANGE THE TITLE OF PAGES

I have attached a Dynamic Web Template to some pages, and now I cannot change the title of the page. What's going on?

When FrontPage saves a page as a Dynamic Web Template, it adds an editable region called doctitle that encloses the <title> tag of the Web page. This is done so that you can edit the title of the page. However, in some cases the doctitle editable region is not created. In those situations, the <title> tag is in a non-editable region and cannot be changed.

To resolve this issue, change the <title> tag in the Dynamic Web Template from this

```
<title>Page Title Here</title>
```

To this

```
<!-- #BeginEditable "doctitle" -->
<title>Page Title Here</title>
<!-- #EndEditable -->
```

This adds a new editable region called doctitle that surrounds the <title> tag and allows developers to edit the title of the page.

Make sure that you make this change in the Dynamic Web Template file and not the Web page to which the Dynamic Web Template is attached.

CANNOT MODIFY AN EDITABLE REGION BECAUSE IT'S LOCKED

I am trying to add a table to an editable region, and I'm being told that FrontPage will not accept my change because the code is locked by a Dynamic Web Template. Why is it doing that?

Certain edits are not allowed in an editable region, and inserting tables is one of them. You can change the size of text, whether the text is bold or italic, and the font, but you cannot perform any layout functions on that text (such as adding a table), and you can't apply any styles to that text.

FRONT AND CENTER

Dynamic Web Templates and editable regions can sometimes limit you more than you might like. The fact that they prevent you from adding a new table to an editable region is the perfect example. Although there are times when you want very strict control over formatting of all parts of your Web pages, there are also times when you want developers to have more freedom with design decisions than Dynamic Web Templates and editable regions allow. There is, however, a way to work around this.

If you would like to give your developers the freedom to add tables into editable regions of your Dynamic Web Template, it can be accomplished quite easily. You simply need to provide the template with a table already in the editable region.

Open the existing Dynamic Web Template that you created while working in this chapter and perform the following steps.

1. Click inside the MainContent editable region.
2. Select Table, Insert, Table and insert a table with the default settings.
3. Save the Dynamic Web Template.
4. Create a new page and attach it to the Dynamic Web Template.
5. Click inside the MainContent editable region.
6. If the table from the Dynamic Web Template is visible, select it and remove it.
7. Select Table, Insert, Table and insert a table. Change the default settings if you'd like.

Notice that FrontPage allowed you to insert the table into the editable region without complaint. You can also reformat the table any way you'd like or get rid of the table altogether. As long as a table exists in the editable region in the Dynamic Web Template file itself, you can insert and configure one in the same editable region of any page to which that Dynamic Web Template is attached.

MAKING YOUR PAGES AND SITES MORE DYNAMIC

In this chapter

DYNAMIC EFFECTS

Everyone loves to add a little flair to their FrontPage Web site, and FrontPage can assist you in the process in a number of areas.

Some of the effects we'll discuss in this chapter help lay out content in a format more attractive to the eye, whereas others do little more than add a little extra animation to the page. We'll examine both of these options in this chapter and point you to more information within this book on similar options.

We'll take a look at collapsible outlines that allow you to present list content in an interactive format, page transitions that provide Microsoft PowerPoint type transitions to your Web pages, and DHTML animation effects and FrontPage Web components that can add extra content to your FrontPage Web site.

The most effective user of such techniques knows how to make FrontPage create the exact effects he is looking for and when to use them for the best possible effect. Everyone wants to impress, but no one wants to overwhelm. We'll examine those issues as well.

USING COLLAPSIBLE OUTLINES

Collapsible outlines are a client-side JavaScript effect that lets you shrink bulleted or numbered lists to just the low level at the initial viewing of the page. Clicking the low level with your mouse will result in the subitems being shown. This is a great effect for organizing a considerable amount of information on the same page as can be seen in Figures 21.1 and 21.2.

Figure 21.1
The Web page shows only the low level bullets. Compare with Figure 21.2 and 21.3.

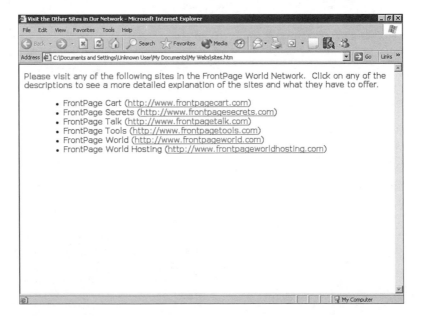

21

Figure 21.2
Compare with Figure 21.1. The first item in the list was clicked with the mouse, and the information below it is now shown.

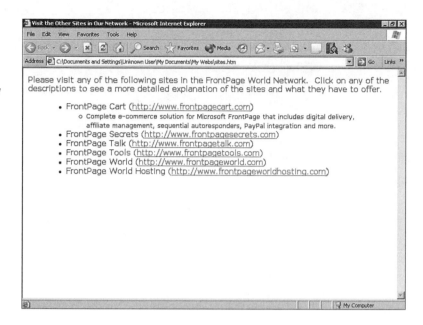

→ For more information on scripting in Web design, **see** "Client-side Scripting," **p. 475**.

NOTE

All collapsible outline content for the page is loaded to the client when the page is first viewed. Browsers that can't support JavaScript will usually show the entire outline.

TIP

There is no indication that the outline content can be expanded, such as a hyperlink. Make sure that you let the user know the option is available or he won't know it is there.

 If FrontPage has your collapsible outline options grayed out and you want to use them, *see* *"Collapsible Outline Problems" in the "Troubleshooting" section at the end of this chapter.*

BULLETED LISTS

To use this effect on a bulleted list, simply create a multi-leveled bulleted list such as the one shown in Figure 21.3.

Once the list is created, select the list content and choose List Properties from the context menu. Select any tab from the List Properties dialog box, shown in Figure 21.4. Check the Enable Collapsible Outline box and, if desired, the Initially Collapsed option.

FrontPage then writes the appropriate JavaScript code to your page, requiring no additional action on your side. If you edit list content, FrontPage will update the script accordingly.

21

Figure 21.3
This bulleted list was created with the collapsible outline shown in Figures 21.1 and 21.2.

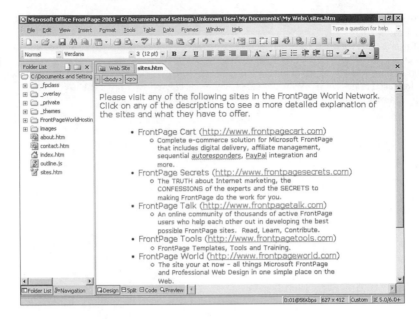

Figure 21.4
Any tab in the List Properties dialog box lets you toggle the Collapsible Outline option on and off. The Other tab is shown in this option.

TIP

Take a look at the script behind a collapsible outline—it's pretty impressive and can teach you a lot about good script design.

NUMBERED LISTS

Numbered lists work, and are created, the same way as a bulleted list. Collapsible outlines only work on these two kinds of lists and can't be utilized on a Definition, Directory, Menu, or Normal List.

→ For more information on FrontPage's list features, **see** "Developing the Basic Page: Page Properties, Text, Lists, and Hyperlinks," **p. 77**.

Collapsible Outline Use

The collapsible outline is a great tool for many kinds of data presentation options. Not only can it clean up a considerable amount of data, but it also becomes automatically "backward compatible" with other browsers so that you don't need to worry about multiple presentations of your data.

Frequently Asked Questions (FAQs), user documentation, personnel contact information, and definition lists all present well through the use of collapsible outlines.

If you have a considerable amount of data on your site that needs to be presented but can be presented in list form, consider using this technology.

USING PAGE TRANSITIONS

Page transitions are a fun little feature that help provide a more animated Microsoft PowerPoint-like transition between different pages within your Web site. As the user goes from one page to another within your site (or as he enters or exits), familiar PowerPoint transition effects (done through DHTML) such as Circle in and Horizontal Blinds can be used to bring emphasis to the jumping from one page to another. Browsers that don't support this feature (most non-Microsoft browsers don't) will simply ignore the transition effect request and will show the page as if no transition existed.

The Page Transition tool is found in the Format menu and, as shown in Figure 21.5, requires nothing more than a selection from the menu to insert the desired effect. No additional programming is required.

Figure 21.5
The Page Transitions dialog box lets you choose the event that triggers the transition, the duration of the transition, and the effect.

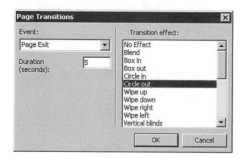

The event Page Enter (or Exit) triggers the effect for every page on the site where a transition effect is selected. If Site Enter (or Exit) is selected, the transition will only happen once for the user upon entrance (or exit) from the site. This option provides a means for using the effect without requiring a transition every time someone jumps from one page to another within the site. The Duration option lets you choose how quickly the transition renders.

NOTE

> Although page transitions are supported by most versions of Internet Explorer, they do take considerably more memory to render than the average Web page and can have the effect of slowing down slower systems surfing your Web pages. Consider this issue when using this animation effect.
>
> They are also considered by most to be as annoying as blinking (or scrolling) text and splash entry pages. Don't annoy your audience.

If your transitions are not appearing as you'd like them to, *see "Transitions Don't Work" in the "Troubleshooting" section at the end of this chapter.*

USING DHTML EFFECTS

DHTML (Dynamic HTML) is, in short, HTML tags that provide for user interaction with page content without having to request additional content from the server. Some DHTML tags also provide for animation options, again similar to Microsoft PowerPoint effects.

Both Microsoft and Netscape have different opinions on how DHTML should work and have even submitted competing proposals for the standard to the W3C. As a result, DHTML content is usually browser specific and should be used with caution. We'll also briefly discuss the hyperlink rollover effect in this section.

If you are having problems applying DTHML effects to your list items, *see "DHTML on List Items" in the "Troubleshooting" section at the end of this chapter.*

THE DHTML TOOLBAR

Insertion of DHTML effects is done through the DHTML Toolbar, seen in Figure 21.6. If the toolbar is not on your screen, it can be invoked by selecting View, Toolbars, DHTML Effects.

Figure 21.6
The DHTML toolbar provides three drop-down menus that provide for all the possible DHTML effects.

The first dropdown menu, On, indicates what will trigger the effect. This is done with a click, a mouse over, or a page load.

The second dropdown, Apply, lets you choose the desired effect. This changes based on what was chosen from the first menu.

The third dropdown offers options based on the Apply option and are different for each choice.

To insert an effect, select the item you'd like to associate with the effect. (This can be either a text block or picture.) Then choose an effect from the On field of the DHTML toolbar You then choose the three variables for the effects as described in the next section.

Items with an associated DHTML effect will be shown in Design view with a shaded box around the effect area, as seen in Figure 21.7.

Figure 21.7
Items marked with a DHTML effect are shown with a shaded box around the area. Note the shaded box around the title on this page.

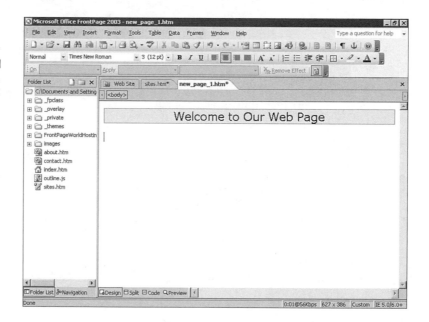

To remove a dynamic effect, simply highlight the effect with your mouse and press the Remove Effect button in the DHTML toolbar. FrontPage will both remove the effect from the page and delete the DHTML associated with it from the page code.

CLICK AND DOUBLE CLICK EFFECTS

The Click effect responds to the click of a mouse over the element selected. Once the item is clicked, your options are to have the element "fly out" of the screen or have the element switched with another picture. If you are working with text, you can apply a text formatting change.

21

NOTE

Only images can be switched with other images, and only text selections can be subject to formatting changes.

If you choose to fly out the element, the final dropdown menu will let you select where you would like the element to fly out to, as seen in Figure 21.8.

Figure 21.8
Once an item is selected to fly out, many options are made available for the element's departure.

If you choose to replace the element with another one, you will be asked to provide the path for the second element. If you choose a formatting change, the new formatting options will need to be selected.

The Double Click effect has the same options as the Click effect but requires a double-click from the user to initiate the effect.

MOUSE OVER EFFECT

The Mouse Over effect results in a change in the element when the mouse passes over that area. Once the mouse leaves that area, the original image or font formatting returns.

If the Mouse Over effect is applied to an image, the only option is to switch the image with another. You will be asked for the second image location. The Mouse Over effect can be seen in Figure 21.9.

If the Mouse Over effect is applied to text, you can either choose new formatting options or the ability to add a border around the text area. FrontPage will ask you for the specific of either option. In Figure 21.10, border options are required.

 If you are having problems applying mouse over DHTML effects to specific areas of text, *see "Mouse Over DHTML Effects on Part of a Paragraph" in the "Troubleshooting" section at the end of this chapter.*

HYPERLINK ROLLOVER EFFECT

The text rollover effect is commonly used to emphasize a URL on a Web page. It can also be used to emphasize certain areas of text by using bold font formatting.

If you would like to set all hyperlinks in a page to have a certain rollover effect, this can also be assigned in the Advanced Tab of the Page Properties dialog box, seen in Figure 21.11. You can set rollover effect specifics by pressing the Rollover style button.

Figure 21.9
The original image appears on top. The image on the bottom shows the switch effect as this is the image that will appear after the mouse touches the original image.

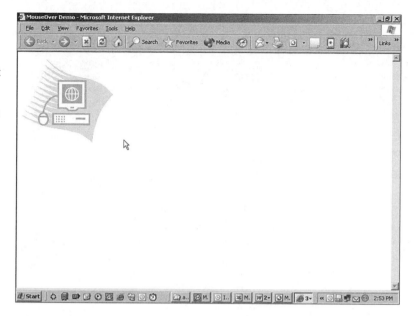

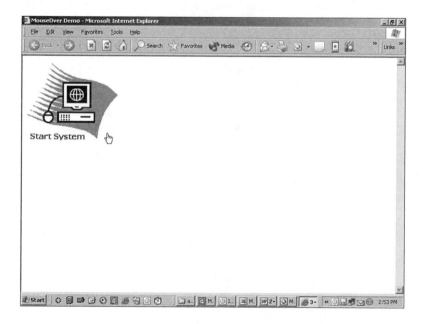

21

Figure 21.10
If a Border option is chosen from the Formatting option of a text mouse over, FrontPage will ask for border specifics from the user.

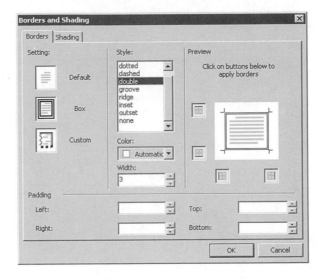

Rollover Options

FrontPage users have multiple options for creating rollovers: the page properties dialog box for simple hyperlink rollovers, FrontPage interactive buttons, CSS, and the DHTML offerings described in this chapter. They all provide great options for a rollover effect. Experiment with all of them to find the best option for you.

Do stay away from the Hover button option seen in previous versions of FrontPage. Hover buttons used way too much code (and in Java nonetheless), caused some browsers to hang, and they simply aren't as effective or stunning as any of the options previously listed.

Figure 21.11
The Advanced tab of the Page Properties dialog box lets you set hyperlink rollovers with a simple click.

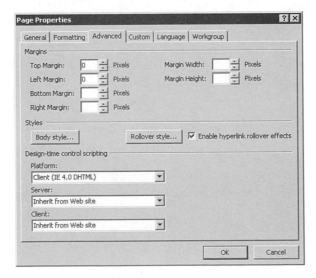

→ For more hyperlink options, **see** "Developing the Basic Page: Page Properties, Text, Lists, and Hyperlinks," **p. 77**.

PAGE LOAD EFFECT

A number of DHTML effects are used at page load. Text and image elements can be chosen to enter via animation, producing an effect similar to a Microsoft PowerPoint animation.

To select a Page Load effect, select the element you want to apply the effect to, select Page Load in the On dropdown box of the DHTML toolbar, and select the effect from the Apply dropdown list (see Figure 21.12).

Figure 21.12
Once the Page Load effect is selected, you will be able to choose from a number of animation options.

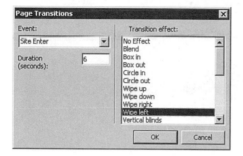

NOTE

Unlike Microsoft PowerPoint, you are unable to set the timing or order for any page loading effects.

HIT COUNTERS, TIME STAMPS, AND OTHER DYNAMIC CONTROLS

A number of items can be added to your FrontPage Web site that produce dynamic content based on user input or other system variables. Hit counters update your site every time someone visits it and time stamps automatically update site content without you having to do a thing (other than insert the time stamp). Both of these items are very easy to use and implement with FrontPage 2003. We'll show users how many others have visited your site and let them know when content on your page was last updated.

HIT COUNTERS

Hit counters can be inserted in to your FrontPage Web site quickly and easily with the Hit Counter Web component, shown in Figure 21.13. You can select your Hit Counter type from the Insert Web Component dialog box reached by selecting Web Component from the Insert menu.

→ For specific direction on using the Hit Counter tool that comes with FrontPage 2003, **see** "Using Web Components, Shared Borders, and Link Bars," **p. 167**.

 If you can't use the FrontPage hit counter on your site and need other options for their use, *see "Hit Counters Don't Work" in the "Troubleshooting" section at the end of this chapter.*

21

Figure 21.13
Pick the style of the counter (or insert a counter style of your own), and select the number on the counter.

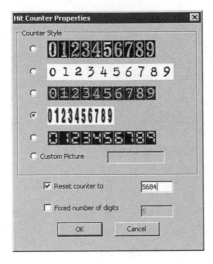

TIME STAMPS

FrontPage can automatically place the time and date a page was either updated by you or through an automatic update. You are given full control over the date and time format and don't need to add a line of code (or look up the date and time).

NOTE

Information will be taken from your Web server and will not be updated for people viewing your sites from other time zones.

To use this feature, you must be in Design view. Simply select Date and Time from the Insert menu, and FrontPage will show the Date and Time dialog box, shown in Figure 21.14.

Figure 21.14
The Date and Time dialog box lets you select what kind of updating you'd like to see on the page and how you'd like the information formatted.

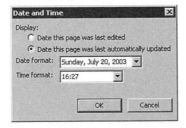

If you select the first option, FrontPage will show the date and time the page was last edited by a human editor. If you select the second option, FrontPage will also update the page if content was updated automatically, through an included file or some other server-side content update process.

21

In most cases, a date stamp is sufficient for most uses of this feature. Going down to the specific minute is a bit overboard (and confusing for people in different time zones).

Using the Date and Time dialog box, you can choose the format for the date and time to appear on your site. You can also choose to just show the date with no specific time stamp.

TIP

Be careful not to use the Time Stamp date on a page you don't intend on updating on a regular basis. Just a few short months later, it can often have the unintended effect of telling visitors that you don't care enough about your site to update it—regardless of the evergreen nature of your site content.

MARQUEE

Another dynamic effect is the Marquee, also achieved through the Web Component dialog box (accessed by selecting Web Component from the Insert menu). The Marquee effect scrolls text across your screen (like a theater *marquee*) in the direction and speed you set. FrontPage will open the Marquee Properties dialog box, shown in Figure 21.15.

Figure 21.15
The Marquee Properties dialog box lets you set every aspect of the *<marquee>* tag.

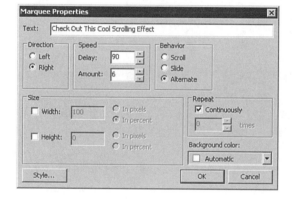

NOTE

The Marquee tag only works on Internet Explorer and is ignored on all other Web browser types. When the Marquee tag is used on a browser that doesn't support the tag, the text will be shown, but the effect will not be rendered.

After the text is entered, set the direction, speed behavior, and size accordingly. If you'd like the effect to repeat, choose how many times. You can also set background colors for the Marquee effect, if desired.

21

TIP

> If you use the Marquee effect, set it to only show once. A continuous moving effect will irritate most site visitors.

INTERACTIVE BUTTONS

The last dynamic effect we'll specifically discuss in this chapter is the Interactive Button feature, an item new to FrontPage 2003. It provides both a clean button designer with a mouse over effect that is quite impressive. It adds a certain level of effect to your site without being overwhelming and adding the Java solution seen in previous versions of FrontPage.

As seen in Figure 21.16, you can set the text and link for each button and choose from a long list of button styles and colors. In addition, you can insert any image as a button through the Image tab of the Interactive Buttons dialog box.

Figure 21.16
The Interactive Buttons dialog box gives you numerous options for setting a dynamically generated mouse over button.

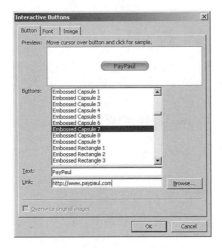

→ For a full explanation on using Interactive Buttons, **see** "Using Interactive Buttons," **p. 441**.

OTHER CONTROLS

FrontPage provides a considerable amount of additional dynamic element options through the Web components feature. This includes, but is not limited to, Flash movies, Java applets, plug-in content, and the like. A number of components also provide content from other Microsoft locations such as Microsoft Expedia (for maps) and MSNBC (for weather and news information).

→ For more information on using the additional Web components provided by FrontPage, **see** "Using Web Components, Shared Borders, and Link Bars," **p. 167**.

21

TROUBLESHOOTING

COLLAPSIBLE OUTLINE PROBLEMS

When I try to use collapsible outlines on a Definition List, FrontPage has the option grayed out. How can I make it work on this option?

Collapsible outlines only work on bulleted and numbered lists and can't be used on any other list type.

TRANSITIONS DON'T WORK

I've inserted page transitions on several pages in my site, and they aren't showing up on most browsers that I view them on.

Page transitions are a browser-specific technology that don't work on many non-Microsoft options for surfing the Web. The great thing is that the page transition information is usually ignored by these browsers. As a result, you can use page transitions without worrying about them causing problems in other browser types.

In addition, if your transitions are being done on simple white pages on fast machines, they might happen so quickly that they might not "appear" visible to the end user.

DHTML ON LIST ITEMS

I'd like to use DHTML animations on list elements, but the DHTML toolbar is grayed out when they are selected.

You can only use DHTML effects on text blocks and images.

MOUSE OVER DHTML EFFECTS ON PART OF A PARAGRAPH

I'd like to use DHTML mouse over effects on just a specific word in a paragraph, but FrontPage forces the effect on the entire paragraph.

The limitations of DHTML prevent mouseover effects for just a section of a paragraph or sentence. The effect can only be applied to an entire HTML paragraph of text (no matter how long or short it is).

HIT COUNTERS DON'T WORK

I've inserted my hit counter in to my Web page and published it at my Web site. I understand that I won't be able to view it at my disk-based Web, but it doesn't work at my Web site either. What am I doing wrong?

The hit counter system built in to FrontPage requires FrontPage Extensions and requires the content to be sent to the server via FrontPage Publish (to start the counter). If your site doesn't have FrontPage Extensions installed or you used an alternative method for publishing (such as FTP or WebDAV), the counter won't work. A number of Internet Web counters will work with all Web server types at http://bravenet.frontpagelink.com and http://dnstatistics.frontpagelink.com.

Hyperlinks in Marquees

How do I insert a hyperlink in to marquee text? Is it even possible?

You can insert a URL in marquee text either by inserting the URL directly in to the HTML through Code view or simply inserting the HTML in to the text area of the Marquee Properties dialog box.

In both tweaks, the browsers will render the HTML accordingly, but you will see the tags in the text in Design view.

Be careful inserting a hyperlink in to moving text. You don't want the effect of requiring your visitors to have to chase around one page just to get to the next one.

Front and Center: The Truly Dynamic Site

One of the things that really frustrates me about the Internet is how the same term can be used to mean many different things. The best example is how the term *ASP* can mean both **A**ctive **S**erver **P**age, a scripting technology, and **a**pplication **s**ervice **p**rovider, a paradigm for Web business.

The term *dynamic* is another one of those terms. For some, it means *on-the-fly*, as in dynamically generated content; for others it means *flashy*, as in a dynamic page transition—the kinds discussed in this chapter.

I have no problem with making a site look good. As a matter of fact, items such as a collapsible outline provide great options for presenting a lot of content in a manageable format.

CAUTION

> It is easy to go too far, too fast because FrontPage makes it so easy to do so. I've mentioned it throughout this book, but *just because you can, doesn't mean that you should.*

One perfect example of mixing an understanding of the technology with an understanding of your site and development process is the date and time stamp discussed earlier. If you update site content on a regular basis and need people to know if or when they have the latest data, this is the perfect tool for you. If, like many, you seldom update your site on a regular basis, no matter how correct the content might be, an older time stamp can result in people questioning the validity of the content. I've heard many stories of people who ask me why their Web site still brings phone calls asking when their store opens. I'd call too if a page with opening hours had a three year old time stamp.

Obviously the overuse (abuse) of any technology or flash (Flash) can distract from the purpose of your Web site. At the same time, and often in the same site, the artfully integrated combination of technology and content can provide the same level of excitement that brings us all to the Web. It is the true Web artist that understands when to do what, and no book can ever teach that lesson.

Use these dynamic elements with care and caution. When used correctly, they add to the impact and functionality of your Web site. When used incorrectly, they make you look like you have too much time on your hands.

USING INTERACTIVE BUTTONS

In this chapter

INTERACTIVE BUTTONS IN FRONTPAGE

FrontPage 97 introduced the Hover Button as a means of providing interactivity to a FrontPage Web site. The Hover Button is a Java applet that makes it easy to insert buttons onto a Web page with configurable rollover interactivity. The Hover Button, however, has its share of problems. The Hover Button relies on your Web site visitors having a Java virtual machine installed on their computer. Microsoft no longer ships a Java virtual machine with any of its operating systems, so if you're using Hover Buttons for navigation, you'll need to provide an alternative for those who won't be able to see them.

→ For more information on Hover Buttons, **see** "Using Web Components," **p. 168**.

 FrontPage 2003 replaces the Hover Button with Interactive Buttons, and it's a change that FrontPage users will find to be a good one. Because Interactive Buttons are implemented using JavaScript and DHTML, their full functionality requires only a browser that supports DHTML scripting, but even a browser that does not will fail gracefully. This means that even on an older-generation browser, links created with Interactive Buttons will still work even if the rollover effects don't.

INSERTING AND CONFIGURING AN INTERACTIVE BUTTON

There are 129 different Interactive Buttons to choose from in 31 different categories. However, because you can also configure the size of the button and the font used in the button, there are many more than 129 different combinations available to you.

To insert an Interactive Button, select Insert, Interactive Button. The Button tab of the Interactive Button dialog (shown in Figure 22.1) allows you to configure the button's appearance, the text that appears on the button, and the URL the button links to when clicked. Clicking the Browse button displays the standard Edit Hyperlink dialog. You can link an Interactive Button to a file in the Web site or to any other valid URL, including email links and links to newsgroups.

→ For more information on configuring hyperlinks in FrontPage 2003, **see** "Inserting and Formatting Hyperlinks," **p. 92**.

FrontPage uses three graphic files for each Interactive Button you insert. One graphic is used for the normal state of the button that is displayed when the mouse cursor is not hovering over or clicking on the button. Another graphic is used for the button when the mouse cursor is hovering over it. The third graphic is used for the button when it is being clicked. When you save a page after inserting an Interactive Button, you will be prompted to save these images into your Web site, as shown in Figure 22.2. FrontPage generates image file names for you.

Figure 22.1
The Button tab of the Interactive Button dialog allows you configure an Interactive Button's appearance.

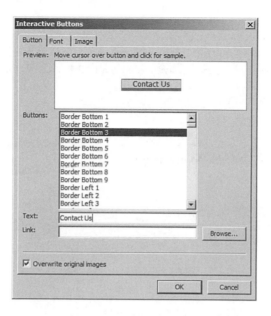

Figure 22.2
FrontPage prompts you to save the images that are used for your Interactive Button.

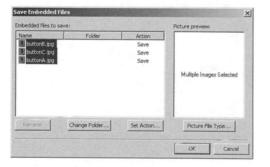

If you are editing an existing Interactive Button, FrontPage will automatically check the Overwrite Original Images check box for you. When this check box is checked, FrontPage will still prompt you to save the images for the Interactive Button, but it will default to automatically overwriting the existing images for the Interactive Button. This is recommended because the original images will no longer be used and will just take up space in your Web site. However, if you do have a need to use the original images, clear the Overwrite Original Images check box and FrontPage will generate new images for the edited Interactive Button.

TIP

> When you remove an Interactive Button, the image files are left in your Web site. To save space, make sure that you delete any image files for Interactive Buttons that you've deleted.

After selecting a button type from the Buttons list, you can preview the button and its behavior in the Preview window. The Preview window makes it very easy to pick a button that looks just the way you want it to. Any change to your button is instantly updated in the Preview window. The Preview window is available on all tabs of the Interactive Button dialog.

EDITING THE FONT AND ALIGNMENT

The Font tab (shown in Figure 22.3) is where you'll configure the font used for the button text. You can configure not only the font, but also the color of the font in three separate states.

Figure 22.3
The Font tab not only allows for changing the typeface, but also colors and alignment.

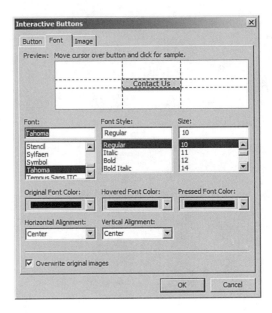

The following states are available:

- **Original**—The color of the font when the button first appears on the page and the mouse is not hovering on it
- **Hovered**—The color of the font when the mouse pointer is hovered over the button
- **Pressed**—The color of the font when the mouse is clicked on the button

Vertical and horizontal alignment can also be controlled on the Font tab. When the Font tab is selected, the Preview tab adds dashed lines to indicate text margins as a reference. As text alignment is changed, it is aligned on these dashed lines.

CONFIGURING THE BUTTON IMAGE

The Image tab (shown in Figure 22.4) gives you control over how the button itself appears. From this tab, you can adjust the size of the button using the Width and Height boxes.

Checking the Maintain Proportions check box causes any change in one dimension to be automatically sized in the other dimension. If you want to change one dimension without changing the other, uncheck the Maintain Proportions check box.

Figure 22.4
The Image tab provides all the settings necessary to control the images FrontPage creates for your buttons.

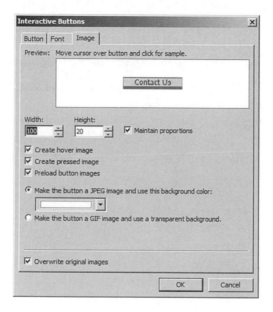

The Create Hover Image and the Create Pressed Image check boxes control whether FrontPage creates a hover image and a pressed image for the button. If a hover image is not created, the button's appearance will not change when the mouse is hovered over it. If a pressed image is not created, the button will not change appearance when pressed.

 If the graphic files for your Interactive Buttons don't appear when browsing to your Web site, *see the "Button Shows Broken Graphic Icon" in the "Troubleshooting" section of this chapter.*

The Preload Button Images check box determines whether images for the button are preloaded. Preloading images for your Interactive Buttons will provide for a much better experience for your site visitors. If you don't preload images, when the user first hovers over a button, there will be a delay while the hover image is loaded. There will be another delay when the button is clicked while the pressed image is loaded. If the Create Hover Image and the Create Pressed Image check boxes are both unchecked, the Preload Button Images check box will be unavailable because there will be no images to preload.

The Image tab also allows you to control whether FrontPage saves the images for your button as JPEG or GIF files. When the Make the Button a JPEG Image and Use This Background Color radio button is selected, FrontPage will create your images as JPEGs and will configure the background for the button in the color you specify.

NOTE

> Only if you have chosen a button type that is not rectangular will you be able to see the background color you specify.

If the Make the button a GIF Image and Use a Transparent Background radio button is selected, FrontPage will save your button's images as GIFs, and the background color of the page on which they are inserted will show through for any non-rectangular buttons.

Because JPEG images can be saved with more colors than GIF images, depending on what type of button you chose on the Button tab, you might see better image quality with a JPEG image. However, JPEG images are significantly larger than GIF images, so make your choice wisely.

→ For more information on the differences between GIF images and JPEG images, **see** "Web Graphic Formats," **p. 847**.

After an Interactive Button has been inserted, it can be edited by simply double-clicking on the button in FrontPage's Design view. The Interactive Button dialog will be displayed, and any settings can be modified.

TROUBLESHOOTING

Button Shows Broken Graphic Icon

I've moved some image files around, and now my Interactive Buttons show a broken graphic icon when I hover over or click on them. I thought FrontPage repaired links when files are moved. What happened?

FrontPage does fix hyperlinks to files and paths to images in image tags when files are moved around, but it doesn't repair links inside of scripts. Because Interactive Buttons are created using scripts, the links to the image files will be broken if you move the images used in the button.

If you want to move images for an Interactive Button, it's best to delete the original images and then double-click the Interactive Button. Remove the check from the Overwrite Original Images check box and then save the page. You will then be given the opportunity to change the path of the saved images.

FRONT AND CENTER: HOW INTERACTIVE BUTTONS WORK

Now you know how to insert and configure an Interactive Button, but you might not know exactly what an Interactive Button is and how it works. It's actually simpler than you might think.

When you insert an Interactive Button, FrontPage creates graphic files using the information you provide in the Interactive Buttons dialog. FrontPage uses the graphics located in `C:\Program Files\Microsoft Office\Templates\BUTTONS` by default. It then creates composite graphics on-the-fly to include whatever text you include on the button.

After FrontPage has created the graphic files, it generates the code to do the image swapping by using a Swap Image Behavior and a Swap Image Restore Behavior. If you select the Interactive Button and switch to the Behaviors task pane, you will see that FrontPage has automatically inserted Behaviors to add interactivity to your buttons.

For this reason, if you ever modify the Swap Image Behavior or the Swap Image Restore Behavior in any way, take note that you will also be changing the behavior of your Interactive Buttons.

If you find that the options available for an Interactive Button are not meeting your needs, you can use Behaviors in FrontPage to create your own dynamic buttons. You can either create graphics from scratch, or you can use the graphics FrontPage generated for some of your Interactive Buttons and modify them in an image editing program to suit your needs. Once you have the graphics ready for your dynamic button, you can use the Swap Image Behavior and the Swap Image Restore Behavior to add interactivity to them.

→ For more information on the Swap Image Behavior and the Swap Image Restore Behavior, **see** "The Swap Image Behavior," **p. 470**, and "The Swap Image Restore Behavior," **p. 471**.

USING BEHAVIORS

In this chapter

23

UNDERSTANDING AND WORKING WITH BEHAVIORS

Behaviors are one of the most exciting enhancements in FrontPage's history. Even after working with Behaviors for a while, you might still find yourself saying "I had no idea I could do that" as you dig deeper into the functionality of this great feature of FrontPage 2003. After reading this chapter, you will never say that again because you'll be an expert at working with Behaviors.

A *Behavior* is a FrontPage design-time component that adds script to your Web page to make it more dynamic and interactive. You can insert Behaviors that range from performing a simple task such as calling a client-side script, to complex tasks such as configuring a DHTML menu for your Web site.

NOTE

A design-time component is a component that is generated in its entirety during the design process. Unlike browse-time components, design-time components do not require the FrontPage Server Extensions, SharePoint Team Services, or SharePoint Services to function on the Web server.

USING THE BEHAVIORS TASK PANE

Behaviors are inserted from the Behaviors task pane shown in Figure 23.1. The task pane is the perfect place for Behaviors because it allows you to work with them without the interface getting in the way of your work. That's very important because Behaviors are not inserted and forgotten. After you insert a Behavior, there's plenty of tweaking you can do, and not having to dismiss a dialog box between each change makes working with Behaviors more efficient.

Figure 23.1
The Behaviors task pane makes it convenient to insert and work with Behaviors.

To access the Behaviors task pane, select Format, Behaviors from the main menu in FrontPage or press Ctrl+F1. If another task pane is already displayed, you can use the Other Task Panes dropdown at the top of the task pane to select the Behaviors task pane.

> **TIP**
>
> The Behavior task pane, like all task panes, is a dockable window. This means that you can drag it from its current position to a position convenient for you. Place your mouse in the upper-left corner of the task pane. When the mouse pointer turns to a four-way arrow, click and drag the task pane to its desired position. To redock it, drag it to the far right of the screen.

Click the Insert button and you'll see a collection of 16 Behaviors that you can insert into your page. Whether a specific Behavior is available for insertion depends on what is selected when you click the Insert button.

In some situations, it might be necessary to insert more than one Behavior for a single element. For example, when you are implementing rollover buttons, you need a Swap Image Behavior and a Swap Image Restore Behavior for the image. In cases in which you have inserted more than one Behavior on a single HTML element, depending on the type of Behavior you have selected, you can change the order of precedence using the up and down arrow buttons in the Behaviors task pane. Select a Behavior and click the up arrow to move the Behavior up in the list and the down arrow to move it down in the list. Behaviors are processed from top to bottom.

HOW BEHAVIORS WORK

Behaviors are implemented using *events* and *actions*. An event is a message that is intercepted by the Web browser when a certain action takes place. For example, when you click a hyperlink, a *onclick* event is sent to the browser. An action is what the browser does in response to the event. Behaviors allow you to add interactive scripts to your pages to take advantage of events.

> **NOTE**
>
> The events that are available in the Behavior task pane are documented on Microsoft's MSDN Web site. To access the documentation, browse to `http://msdndhtml.frontpagelink.com` and click on DHTML Reference.

The number and type of events available to you depends on what element you select before inserting the Behavior. When you insert a Behavior, FrontPage adds attributes to the closest HTML element to the left of the insertion point. (The Scripts On Tag label in the Behaviors task pane will indicate which element the Behavior is being applied to.)

23

ADDING BEHAVIORS WITHIN A PARAGRAPH

Behaviors are easily applied to hyperlinks, images, and other page elements because these elements are already associated with an HTML tag to which the Behavior can be applied. However, in cases in which you want to define a Behavior for one or more words within a paragraph, it becomes a bit more complicated. If you simply select the words and apply a Behavior, you will find that the Behavior is applied to the entire paragraph and not just the selected words.

If you want to apply a Behavior to one or more words within a paragraph, you can enclose those elements within a span tag. The easiest way to do this is to select the word or words you want to use, switch to Split view, and enclose those words in a span tag, including a unique ID. For example, if you wanted to use the words "click here" in a paragraph as the link for a Behavior, change the code from this,

```
<p>For more information, click here.</p>
```

to this,

```
<p>For more information, <span id="mylink">click here</span>.</p>
```

Switch back to Design view, and you can now click the span Quick Tag Selector to select the words "click here" prior to inserting your Behavior. Your Behavior will then be applied on to those words. Without using this method, the Behavior will affect the entire paragraph.

→ For more information on the Quick Tag Selector, **see** "Selecting Code with the Quick Tag Selector," **p. 530**.

CAUTION

> Once a Behavior has been applied to an element, there is no visual indicator that it has been applied. Because of this, it is quite easy to inadvertently apply a Behavior to an HTML element only to find that another Behavior is applied to that element's parent. In these cases, the parent's Behavior will take precedence. Hopefully, future versions of FrontPage will include some visual indication of where Behaviors are applied.

TIP

> Behaviors are implemented in FrontPage using a combination of a JScript source file and an HTML file. If you have the coding knowledge necessary, you can edit these files to enhance a Behavior to suit your specific needs. These files are located by default in the `C:\Program Files\Microsoft Office\Templates\1033\Behaviors11\ ACTIONS` folder.

FRONTPAGE BEHAVIORS

Browser compatibility is an issue with some Behaviors, mainly because of poor support for DHTML in earlier versions of Netscape. I have tested each of the Behaviors in Netscape Navigator 4.5, Netscape Navigator 6.1, Opera 7, and Internet Explorer 5.0 and later. Some

Behaviors were also tested in Netscape 7.2. I will share the results of my tests before I discuss each Behavior. However, keep in mind that there is no way to cover every possibility, so make sure that you test your pages before publishing your Web site.

THE CALL SCRIPT BEHAVIOR

Table 23.1 shows my browser compatibility findings for the Call Script Behavior.

TABLE 23.1	CALL SCRIPT BEHAVIOR BROWSER COMPATIBILITY
Browser	**Supported**
Internet Explorer 5	Yes
Internet Explorer 6	Yes
Netscape Navigator 4.5	No
Netscape Navigator 6.1	Yes
Opera 7.0	Yes

The *Call Script* Behavior runs a line of script when the event you specify is raised. You will likely want to write some script first and then call it using this Behavior, but you don't have to take that approach. If you have only one line of script to run, you can enter that line in the Call Script dialog and FrontPage will run it when the designated event occurs.

Suppose you've written a script called showInfo that you want to display when an image is clicked on your page. To do this with the Call Script Behavior, perform these steps:

1. Select the image.
2. Select Format, Behaviors.
3. Click the Insert button and select Call Script.
4. Type **showInfo();** in the Call Script dialog as shown in Figure 23.2.

Figure 23.2
The Call Script Behavior allows you to easily call a script when a specified event is triggered.

5. Click OK.

NOTE

> The event defaults to OnClick, but you can choose another event if necessary by choosing the event from the dropdown in the Behaviors task pane.

23

→ For more information on creating and using scripts in your pages, **see** "Client-Side Scripting," **p. 475**.

THE CHANGE PROPERTY BEHAVIOR

Table 23.2 shows my browser compatibility findings for the Change Property Behavior.

TABLE 23.2 CHANGE PROPERTY BEHAVIOR BROWSER COMPATIBILITY

Browser	Supported
Internet Explorer 5	Yes
Internet Explorer 6	Yes
Netscape Navigator 4.5	Yes
Netscape Navigator 6.1	Yes
Opera 7.0	Yes

The Change Property Behavior (shown in Figure 23.3) allows you to change any property on any HTML element on your page. (A *property* is a style that is applied to a particular page element.) The Change Property dialog allows you to configure some default properties such as font styles, borders, visibility, and so on, but you can also change other properties that aren't listed by clicking the Add button in the Change Property dialog.

→ For more information on using styles in a FrontPage Web site, **see** "Using Style Sheets to Format Web Pages," **p. 385**.

Figure 23.3
The Change Property Behavior is one of the most useful Behaviors for adding interactivity to your Web page.

23

NOTE

> The Change Property Behavior will successfully set properties in Netscape 4.5, but many of Netscape 4.5's properties are not the same properties that are set by FrontPage. In order for properties to work correctly with Netscape 4.5, you will likely have to use custom properties within the Change Property Behavior dialog.

Using the Change Property Behavior, it is extremely easy to add professional-quality interactivity to your Web site with minimal effort. For example, suppose that you have a series of graphics in a page, and each graphic links to a page of your site. When a user of your site hovers the mouse over each graphic, you want a text description of the link to appear on the page, and when the mouse leaves the graphic, you want the text description to disappear. In previous versions of FrontPage, this type of interactivity would have required significant hand-coding, but with the Change Property Behavior, you can easily implement this functionality without writing a single line of code.

TIP

> The following example will not work in Netscape 4.5 as given because Netscape 4.5 uses a different property for visibility. To change an element's visibility in Netscape 4.5, you have to add a custom property called `visibility`—set it to `show` to make the item visible and `hide` to make it hidden.

To create an example of interactivity using the Change Property Behavior, perform these steps:

1. Insert a table 400 pixels wide that contains three columns and three rows.

2. Add some graphics of your choice to each corner cell in the table. Feel free to use clip art if you have no graphics handy.

3. Resize the center cell so that it is 200 pixels wide and 200 pixels high. (See Figure 23.4 for the completed table.)

Figure 23.4
The completed table showing four graphics and space in the middle for layers that will contain text.

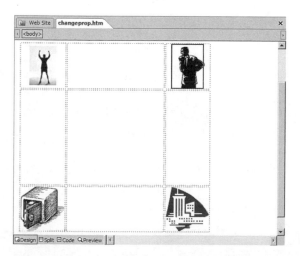

4. Insert a layer and position and size it so that it fits within the center cell. Name the layer **layer1**.

→ For more information on using Layers, **see** "Using Layers," **p. 499**.

5. Insert three more layers and position them directly on top of layer1. The easiest way to accomplish this is to copy layer1 and then paste the other layers. Name the other layers **layer2**, **layer3**, and **layer4**, respectively.

6. Select layer1 from the Layers task pane and enter some text of your choice.

7. Change the visibility of layer1 so that it is hidden by clicking the eye icon so that the eye is closed.

8. Select layer2 and enter some text of your choice.

9. Change the visibility of layer2 so that it is hidden.

10. Repeat steps 8 and 9 for the other two layers. (See Figure 23.5 for the completed Layers task pane.)

Figure 23.5
Four layers for the rollover text. They are all invisible, which is signified by the closed eye icon.

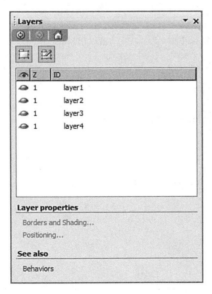

11. Select the upper-left image. From the Behaviors task pane, select Insert, Change Property.

12. In the Change Property dialog, click the Select Element radio button.

13. Choose div from the Element Type dropdown, and the choose layer1 from the Element ID dropdown.

14. Click the Visibility button and click the Visible radio button. Click OK.

15. Click the Restore on Mouseout Event check box.

16. Click OK.

17. In the Behaviors task pane, change the OnClick event to OnMouseOver.

TIP

> The Visibility property defaults to Inherit, which means that the element will be visible only if the element it is contained within is visible.

Complete steps 11–19 for the other images, and add a Change Property Behavior for layer2, layer3, and layer4 just as we did for layer1. Save the page and preview it in your browser or with the Preview tab in FrontPage. You have just created a professional-quality effect with just a few clicks of the mouse. Figure 23.6 shows the completed Change Property dialog box for one of the layers.

Figure 23.6
The completed Change Property dialog box shows the property change for layer1.

THE CHANGE PROPERTY RESTORE BEHAVIOR

Table 23.3 shows my browser compatibility findings for the Change Property Restore Behavior.

TABLE 23.3   CHANGE PROPERTY RESTORE BEHAVIOR COMPATIBILITY

Browser	Supported
Internet Explorer 5	Yes
Internet Explorer 6	Yes
Netscape Navigator 4.5	Yes
Netscape Navigator 6.1	Yes
Opera 7.0	Yes

23

The Change Property Restore Behavior is meant to be used in combination with the Change Property Behavior. It restores the most recent properties changed by the Change Property Behavior to their previous value. (When you selected the Restore on Mouseout Event check box in step 17 of "The Change Property Behavior" section seen previously, FrontPage automatically inserted a Change Property Restore Behavior to restore the property.)

No dialog exists for this Behavior. As seen in Figure 23.7, when you insert the Change Property Restore Behavior, FrontPage informs you of what it will do and then adds it to the Behaviors task pane. You can easily determine which properties are being restored by double-clicking the Change Property Behavior listed directly underneath the newly inserted Change Property Restore Behavior.

Figure 23.7
The Change Property
Restore Behavior
requires no user
input.

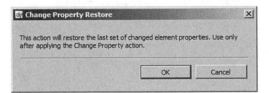

THE CHECK BROWSER BEHAVIOR

Table 23.4 shows my browser compatibility findings for the Check Browser Behavior.

TABLE 23.4 CHECK BROWSER BEHAVIOR BROWSER COMPATIBILITY	
Browser	**Supported**
Internet Explorer 5	Yes
Internet Explorer 6	Yes
Netscape Navigator 4.5	No
Netscape Navigator 6.1	Yes
Opera 7.0	No

The Check Browser Behavior (shown in Figure 23.8) allows you to easily redirect your site visitors based on which browser and which version of that browser they are using. The Check Browser Behavior can check for versions of Internet Explorer, Netscape Navigator, Opera, AOL, WebTV, AOL TV, and HotJava. However, in my testing, I found that the redirect for Opera did not work at all. I also found that the Netscape 6 redirect works, but you must set it to redirect for version 5 and later. (The reason for this is that Netscape 6 identifies itself as version 5 because it is built on Mozilla 5.0.)

The Check Browser Behavior can be added to a page itself, but it's better to attach it to a particular page element. If you attach it to a page, it is invoked from the OnLoad event of the page, and by the time that event fires, the page has already been rendered.

Figure 23.8
The Check Browser Behavior allows you to easily detect a user's browser version and redirect her appropriately.

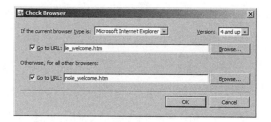

NOTE

Many Web developers fail to realize that the OnLoad event for a Web page fires after the page has completely loaded and not before the page loads. This is necessary so that any script that runs in the OnLoad event will have access to all page elements.

Unless you are detecting browsers on your site's entry page, it is best to attach the Check Browser Behavior to the OnClick event of a hyperlink that loads a new page. You can then load a particular page depending on the browser that your visitor is using, and the wrong page will never be rendered.

If you are detecting browsers on your site's entry page, create an empty page and attach a Check Browser Behavior to the OnLoad event for the page. By doing that, you can ensure that you will not load any elements that will cause errors or malformed rendering in a particular browser.

THE CHECK PLUG-IN BEHAVIOR

Table 23.5 shows my browser compatibility findings for the Check Plug-in Behavior.

TABLE 23.5   CHECK PLUG-IN BEHAVIOR BROWSER COMPATIBILITY

Browser	Supported
Internet Explorer 5	Yes
Internet Explorer 6	Yes
Netscape Navigator 4.5	No
Netscape Navigator 6.1	Yes
Opera 7.0	No

A plug-in can either be an ActiveX control running in Internet Explorer, or a plug-in running in Netscape or another browser. Using the Check Plug-in Behavior (shown in Figure 23.9), you can redirect a user based on whether she has one of the more common plug-ins. The Check Plug-in Behavior is designed to check for the existence of the Macromedia Flash, Apple QuickTime, RealNetworks RealPlayer, Macromedia Shockwave, and Microsoft Windows Media Player.

➡ For more information on using audio and video in a FrontPage Web site, **see** "Enhancing Pages with Graphics and Multimedia," **p. 113**.

Figure 23.9
The Check Plug-in Behavior makes redirecting users based on browser plug-ins quick and easy.

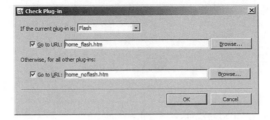

THE CONTROL PROPERTIES IN FLASH BEHAVIOR

Table 23.6 shows my browser compatibility findings for the Control Properties in Flash Behavior.

TABLE 23.6   CONTROL PROPERTIES IN FLASH BEHAVIOR BROWSER COMPATIBILITY

Browser	Supported
Internet Explorer 5	No
Internet Explorer 6	Yes
Netscape Navigator 4.5	No
Netscape Navigator 6.1	No
Opera 7.0	No

For Web developers using Flash, the Control Properties In Flash Behavior represents a major feature enhancement in FrontPage. This Behavior isn't meant to control basic Flash properties such as width and height of a Flash movie. Instead, it allows you to control the behavior of a Flash movie with script. Using the Control Properties in Flash Behavior, you can control Flash properties such as panning, zooming, and playback of the movie.

➡ FrontPage 2003 introduces the ability to intrinsically control basic Flash properties. **See** "Inserting and Configuring Flash Movies," **p. 127**, for more information.

NOTE

According to Microsoft, the Control Properties In Flash Behavior will work in Internet Explorer 5.0 or later and in Netscape Navigator 6.0 and later. However, the results of my testing indicate that only Internet Explorer 6.0 and later support control of Flash movies using the Control Properties In Flash Behavior.

Netscape 6.1 is not supported by Macromedia Flash, but even testing in Netscape 7.2 failed with the Control Properties In Flash Behavior.

To invoke the Control Properties In Flash Behavior (shown in Figure 23.10), select Insert, Control Properties In Flash from the Behaviors task pane. Select the Flash movie that you would like to control, and then select the method you would like to use.

Figure 23.10
The Control Properties In Flash Behavior is very powerful, but it only works in Internet Explorer 6.0 or later.

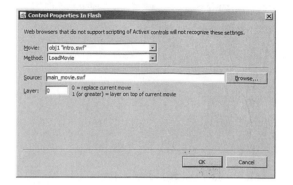

For more information on the methods listed in the Control Properties In Flash dialog, see Macromedia's DevNet Flash Development Center at
`http://www.macromedia.com/devnet/mx/flash/`.

THE GO TO URL BEHAVIOR

Table 23.7 shows my browser compatibility findings for the Go To URL Behavior.

TABLE 23.7   GO TO URL BEHAVIOR BROWSER COMPATIBILITY

Browser	Supported
Internet Explorer 5	Yes
Internet Explorer 6	Yes
Netscape Navigator 4.5	No
Netscape Navigator 6.1	Yes
Opera 7.0	Yes

The Go To URL Behavior (shown in Figure 23.11) is a simple Behavior that redirects the user to the specified URL when the event you choose occurs.

Figure 23.11
The Go To URL Behavior is a simple Behavior that does just what its name implies.

THE JUMP MENU BEHAVIOR

Table 23.8 shows my browser compatibility findings for the Jump Menu Behavior.

TABLE 23.8 JUMP MENU BEHAVIOR BROWSER COMPATIBILITY	
Browser	**Supported**
Internet Explorer 5	Yes
Internet Explorer 6	Yes
Netscape Navigator 4.5	No
Netscape Navigator 6.1	Yes
Opera 7.0	Yes

For years, FrontPage users have been asking for a way to make a menu system based off a dropdown list without having to write code. The Jump Menu Behavior answers that call.

To create a Jump Menu, select Insert, Jump Menu from the Behaviors task pane to activate the Jump Menu dialog (shown in Figure 23.12). There is no need to select anything first. FrontPage will insert a dropdown list for the Jump Menu at the insertion point's location.

Click the Add button, and enter the text that you want to appear in the dropdown list in the Choice field and the URL you want that item to link to in the Value. Click OK to add the item to the Jump Menu.

Figure 23.12
Items are added to your Jump Menu by specifying the text you want to appear and the URL you want that item to link to.

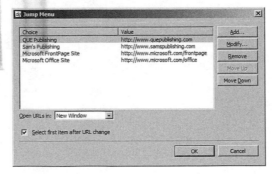

After you have added one or more items to your Jump Menu (more than one item is recommended), you can configure that item to open in either the default target for the page or in a new window.

By checking the Select First Item After URL Change box, you can force the Jump Menu to return to the first item in the list when clicking the Back button in your browser after jumping to a URL.

THE JUMP MENU GO BEHAVIOR

Table 23.9 shows my browser compatibility findings for the Jump Menu Go Behavior.

TABLE 23.9 JUMP MENU GO BEHAVIOR BROWSER COMPATIBILITY

Browser	Supported
Internet Explorer 5	Yes
Internet Explorer 6	Yes
Netscape Navigator 4.5	No
Netscape Navigator 6.1	Yes
Opera 7.0	Yes

The Jump Menu Go Behavior is designed to be used with the Jump Menu Behavior. In cases in which you don't want your Jump Menu Behavior to jump as soon as a new item is selected in the dropdown list, you can use the Jump Menu Go Behavior as a trigger for the menu.

To use the Jump Menu Go Behavior, insert a Jump Menu Behavior and then insert or select an element (such as an image that says "Go!") to use for your trigger. Select Insert, Jump Menu Go from the Behavior task pane and select the Jump Menu from the dropdown as shown in Figure 23.13.

Figure 23.13
Using the Jump Menu Go Behavior allows you to create a trigger for your Jump Menu.

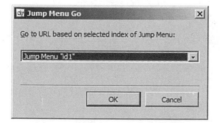

After you've done that, however, you have to stop the Jump Menu from jumping as soon as you select an item. The Jump Menu event defaults to onchange, but if you leave the event set to onchange, you won't have the opportunity to use the Jump Menu Go component because the menu will jump as soon as you select an item. To change the Jump Menu so that it doesn't jump when you select a different item, select the Jump Menu's dropdown list, and then select the Jump Menu Behavior in the Behavior task pane. Click the Delete button in the task pane to delete the onchange event from the task pane. (Don't press the Delete key on your keyboard.) This will remove the entire entry for the Jump Menu, but don't worry. After doing this, your Jump Menu Go Behavior will be the trigger for the Jump Menu.

THE OPEN BROWSER WINDOW BEHAVIOR

Table 23.10 shows my browser compatibility findings for the Open Browser Window Behavior.

TABLE 23.10 OPEN BROWSER WINDOW BEHAVIOR BROWSER COMPATIBILITY

Browser	Supported
Internet Explorer 5	Yes
Internet Explorer 6	Yes
Netscape Navigator 4.5	No
Netscape Navigator 6.1	Yes
Opera 7.0	Yes

The Open Browser Window Behavior (shown in Figure 23.14) allows you to configure a hyperlink to open in a new browser window.

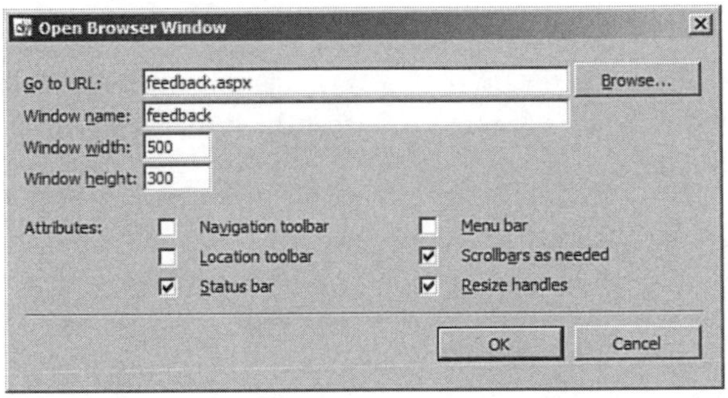

Figure 23.14
Easily create popup windows with specific configurations using the Open Browser Window Behavior.

You can control the following attributes for the new window:

- **Window Name** A unique name for the new browser window so that you can refer to it with other Behaviors or with your own scripts.
- **Window width** The width of the new window in pixels.
- **Window height** The height of the new window in pixels.
- **Navigation toolbar** The toolbar that contains the Forward button, Back button, Home button, and so on.
- **Location toolbar** The toolbar that contains the address bar.
- **Status bar** The bar at the bottom of the new window.
- **Menu bar** The menu bar at the top of the new window.
- **Scrollbars as needed** Turns scrollbars on if the content of the new window is larger than the window itself.
- **Resize handles** Allows for resizing of the new window by dragging the edges.

When adding the Open Browser Window Behavior to text, it's most useful to use a Change Property and a Change Property Restore Behavior to change the pointer to a hand when users hover over your link.

To implement this, add your Open Browser Window Behavior first. Then add a Change Property Behavior and add your own property by clicking the Add button. Use `style.cursor` for the Property Name and `hand` for the Property Value. Make sure that you also check the R̲estore on Mouseout Event box so that FrontPage will add the Change Property Restore Behavior.

 If you are having trouble with the browser window appearing behind the main window, *see "Open Browser Window Pops Up Behind Existing Window" in the "Troubleshooting" section at the end of this chapter.*

23

THE PLAY SOUND BEHAVIOR

Table 23.11 shows my browser compatibility findings for the Play Sound Behavior.

TABLE 23.11 PLAY SOUND BEHAVIOR BROWSER COMPATIBILITY	
Browser	**Supported**
Internet Explorer 5	Yes
Internet Explorer 6	Yes
Netscape Navigator 4.5	No
Netscape Navigator 6.1	No
Opera 7.0	No

The Play Sound Behavior (shown in Figure 23.15) allows you to play a sound when the selected event is triggered. The Play Sound Behavior supports wav files, midi files, RealAudio files, AIFF sound files, and AU sound files.

Figure 23.15
The Play Sound Behavior allows you to play a sound when a particular event is triggered.

THE PRELOAD IMAGES BEHAVIOR

Table 23.12 shows my browser compatibility findings for the Preload Images Behavior.

TABLE 23.12   PRELOAD IMAGES BEHAVIOR BROWSER COMPATIBILITY

Browser	Supported
Internet Explorer 5	Yes
Internet Explorer 6	Yes
Netscape Navigator 4.5	No
Netscape Navigator 6.1	No
Opera 7.0	Yes

The Preload Images Behavior (shown in Figure 23.16) allows you to preload images when a page initially loads. The most common use of preloading images is when swapping images on a mouse rollover buttons. In these situations, you want the image that displays when the user points to the button to load as soon as the page loads even though it is not initially visible. If you don't preload such images, the user experiences a delay while the image loads the first time she points to the button.

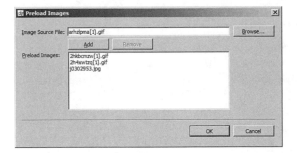

Figure 23.16
The Preload Images Behavior makes preloading images a snap.

To preload one or more images, insert the Preload Images Behavior, click the Browse button, browse to your image, and then click OK. After you have selected your image, click the Add button to add it to the Preloaded Images list. You can add as many images as you'd like to the list.

CAUTION

Be aware that preloading images doesn't make them free as far as bandwidth is concerned. You will still want to keep your image files as small as possible.

THE SET TEXT BEHAVIOR

The Set Text Behavior consists of four separate Behaviors. Because each has different compatibility results, I will list browser compatibility for each separately.

SET TEXT OF FRAME

Table 23.13 shows my browser compatibility findings for the Set Text of Frame Behavior.

Browser	Supported
TABLE 23.13 SET TEXT OF FRAME BEHAVIOR BROWSER COMPATIBILITY	
Internet Explorer 5	Yes
Internet Explorer 6	Yes
Netscape Navigator 4.5	Yes
Netscape Navigator 6.1	Yes
Opera 7.0	Yes

The Set Text of Frame Behavior sets the HTML of the frame you specify when the selected event is triggered. Suppose, for example, that you have a frames page that consists of contents on the left, main content on the right, and a small navigation frame on top of the main content frame. Using the Set Text of Frame Behavior, you can easily implement a bread crumb effect in the navigation frame as shown in Figure 23.17.

Figure 23.17
A bread crumb effect is simple with the Set Text of Frame Behavior.

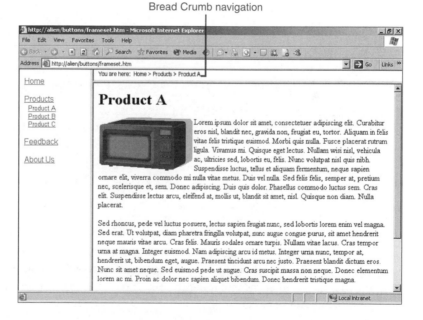

This Behavior will work with inline frames as well for those browsers supporting them. Of the browsers tested for this book, Netscape 4.5 did not work with inline frames, but the Set Text of Frame Behavior worked for framesets in all browsers.

To insert the Set Text of Frame Behavior, open a page containing a frame and select the HTML element whose event you want to trigger the Behavior. Select Insert, Set Text, Set Text of Frame from the Behavior task pane. Select the frame into which you would like to enter HTML, enter the HTML code that you would like to appear in the frame, and click OK.

If you have set the background color for the frame page or inline frame and you would like it to be preserved, make sure that you check the Preserve background color box prior to clicking OK as seen in Figure 23.18. Otherwise, the background color will revert to the default for the browser you are using.

Figure 23.18
The Set Text of Frame Behavior allows you to maintain the current background color after setting the frame's HTML.

SET TEXT OF LAYER

Table 23.14 shows my browser compatibility findings for the Set Text of Layer Behavior.

TABLE 23.14	SET TEXT OF LAYER BEHAVIOR BROWSER COMPATIBILITY
Browser	**Supported**
Internet Explorer 5	Yes
Internet Explorer 6	Yes
Netscape Navigator 4.5	No
Netscape Navigator 6.1	Yes
Opera 7.0	Yes

The Set Text of Layer Behavior allows you to specify the HTML to be rendered in the specified layer when the selected event is triggered. The bread crumb effect shown in Figure 23.17 can be implemented using the Set Text of Layer Behavior by using a layer to hold your bread crumb navigation information instead of a frame.

→ For more information on using layers in FrontPage, **see** "Using Layers," **p. 499**.

To insert a Set Text of Layer Behavior (shown in Figure 23.19), open a page containing a layer and select the HTML element whose event you want to trigger the Behavior. Select Insert, Set Text, Set Text of Layer, enter the HTML you would like to have rendered in the layer, and click OK.

Figure 23.19
The Set Text of Layer Behavior allows you to easily set the HTML used to render contents of a layer.

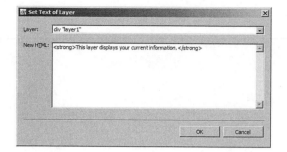

SET TEXT OF STATUS BAR

Table 23.15 shows my browser compatibility findings for the Set Text of Status Bar Behavior.

TABLE 23.15   SET TEXT OF STATUS BAR BEHAVIOR BROWSER COMPATIBILITY

Browser	Supported
Internet Explorer 5	Yes
Internet Explorer 6	Yes
Netscape Navigator 4.5	Yes
Netscape Navigator 6.1	Yes
Opera 7.0	No

The Set Text of Status Bar Behavior allows you to easily change the text that appears in the status bar at the bottom of the browser window. This can be useful to display messages of interest to visitors of your site. For example, you can use this Behavior to display a descriptive message when hyperlinks are hovered over on your Web page.

To insert the Set Text of Status Bar Behavior, select the HTML whose event you want to trigger the Behavior and then select Insert, Set Text, Set Text of Status Bar. Enter the message that you would like displayed in the status bar and then click OK, as shown in Figure 23.20.

Figure 23.20
The Set Text of Status Bar Behavior is very simple. Enter your text and click OK.

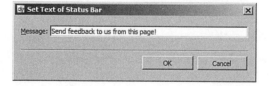

SET TEXT OF TEXT FIELD

Table 23.16 shows my browser compatibility findings for the Set Text of Text Field Behavior.

TABLE 23.16   SET TEXT OF TEXT FIELD BEHAVIOR BROWSER COMPATIBILITY

Browser	Supported
Internet Explorer 5	Yes
Internet Explorer 6	Yes
Netscape Navigator 4.5	No
Netscape Navigator 6.1	Yes
Opera 7.0	Yes

The Set Text of Text Field Behavior (shown in Figure 23.21) sets the text that appears in a TextBox or a TextArea field. This Behavior can be used when you need to set the value for a form field based on a particular event.

Figure 23.21
The Set Text of Text Field Behavior sets the text of TextBoxes and TextAreas.

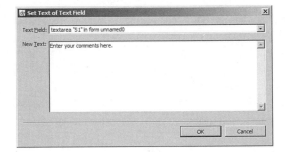

To insert the Set Text of Text Field Behavior, open a page that contains a TextBox or a TextArea field and select Insert, Set Text, Set Text of Text Field. Enter the text you would like to appear in the text field and click OK.

→ For more information about TextBox and TextArea form fields, **see** "Using Forms," **p. 359**.

THE SWAP IMAGE BEHAVIOR

Table 23.17 shows my browser compatibility findings for the Swap Image Behavior.

TABLE 23.17   SWAP IMAGE BEHAVIOR BROWSER COMPATIBILITY

Browser	Supported
Internet Explorer 5	Yes
Internet Explorer 6	Yes
Netscape Navigator 4.5	No
Netscape Navigator 6.1	Yes
Opera 7.0	Yes

The Swap Image Behavior allows you to swap one image for another when the specified event takes place. The most common use of this Behavior is to create rollover buttons. In fact, when you insert an Interactive Button, FrontPage uses the Swap Image Behavior to implement the interactivity of the button.

→ For more information on Interactive Buttons, **see** "Using Interactive Buttons," **p. 441**.

To use the Swap Image Behavior, open a page containing one or more images, select the image you would like to swap, and select Insert, Swap Image from the Behavior task pane. The Swap Images dialog (shown in Figure 23.22) contains a list of all images in the document. The image you selected is highlighted, but you can configure a swap image for as many images as you'd like before clicking OK. Just keep in mind that you are configuring one event, so if you configure a swap image for img1, img2, and img3 and you attach that to the OnMouseOver event for img1, all three images will swap when you roll over img1.

Figure 23.22
The Swap Image Behavior makes rollover button creation simple.

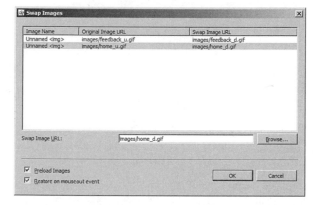

It is best to use two images the same size for your rollovers. The Swap Image Behavior will use the image dimensions of the original image for the swap image. If the proportions are different or if FrontPage is forced to resize an image, you are going to get less than optimal results.

The Swap Images dialog also provides a check box labeled Preload Images. Checking this box will automatically insert a Preload Images Behavior to preload all the swap images you have configured. Restore on Mouseout Event automatically inserts a Swap Image Restore Behavior, which we will talk about next.

THE SWAP IMAGE RESTORE BEHAVIOR

Table 23.18 shows my browser compatibility findings for the Swap Image Restore Behavior.

TABLE 23.18 SWAP IMAGE RESTORE BEHAVIOR BROWSER COMPATIBILITY	
Browser	**Supported**
Internet Explorer 5	Yes
Internet Explorer 6	Yes
Netscape Navigator 4.5	No
Netscape Navigator 6.1	Yes
Opera 7.0	Yes

The Swap Image Restore Behavior works much like the Change Property Restore Behavior. It restores the images that were swapped in the entry immediately below it in the Behaviors task pane. It is for use only after applying the Swap Image Behavior.

This Behavior is automatically inserted if the <u>R</u>estore on Mouseout Event box is checked when configuring a swap image in the Swap Images dialog.

TROUBLESHOOTING

OPEN BROWSER WINDOW POPS UP BEHIND EXISTING WINDOW

I configured a Popup Message and an Open Browser Window Behavior, and when I browse to the page I can see both, but the new browser window opens behind the main browser window. How can I fix that?

Change the order of your Behaviors by clicking the arrow buttons in the Behaviors task pane. When configuring an Open Browser Window Behavior, it should always appear at the bottom of the list because it's the last thing you want to do on that page. If you perform some other action on the page after the Open Browser Window Behavior has created a new window, the main window will resume focus and the new browser window will be moved behind it.

FRONT AND CENTER: DETECTING BROWSERS

As you've seen in this chapter, not all Behaviors work in all browsers. However, that doesn't have to keep you from using a cool Behavior that you want to use on your Web site. Using the Check Browser Behavior, you can ensure that only people who are using a compatible browser get to your page.

The recommended method for using the Check Browser Behavior is to add it to the <body> tag and fire it with the OnLoad event. By specifying a different page to be displayed for specific browsers, you can be sure that the people viewing your Web page are properly equipped to view it with all of its features intact.

The OnLoad event of the <body> tag fires after the page has completed loading. If you use the Check Browser Behavior on a page to redirect according to the browser being used, by the time the Behavior is invoked, the page has already loaded and is already visible. Your Web site visitor will see the first page load briefly and will then be redirected to the correct page as per the settings configured in the Check Browser Behavior. This results in an unprofessional look, but it can be easily avoided.

There are two methods to avoid this problem. The first method is to use a blank page and configure the Check Browser Behavior on it. The second method is to edit the code added by the Check Browser Behavior. Either of these methods will prevent users from ever seeing a page that will not display properly in their browsers.

CREATING A BLANK PAGE FOR REDIRECTING

The first method of preventing the wrong page from being displayed to your Web site visitors is to add the Check Browser Behavior to a blank page. Using this method, the page that loads initially contains no content and is only used to redirect users to the correct page based on the browsers they are using.

Using this method, you will need to create three pages; one blank page that will contain the Check Browser Behavior, one page for users who are using a browser that supports the Behavior you are using, and one for users who are using all other browsers. When you insert the Check Browser Behavior, you will need to configure a separate page for your targeted browser and another URL for all other browsers, as seen in Figure 23.23.

Figure 23.23
The Check Browser Behavior configured with one page for browsers that support your Behavior and another page for all others.

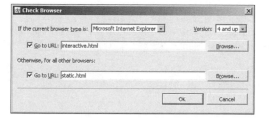

EDITING THE CHECK BROWSER CODE

The second method of preventing an unprofessional appearance when using the Check Browser Behavior involves editing the code that is inserted by the Behavior. Even though this method requires you to edit the code used by the Behavior, it involves less work than the blank page method, and it produces better results. To use this method, you first need to analyze the code that FrontPage inserts into your page when you use the Check Browser Behavior.

When you insert the Check Browser component, FrontPage inserts a JavaScript function called FP_checkBrowser that is used to determine which browser is being used to view the page. It also inserts a call to the FP_checkBrowser function in the OnLoad event of the <body> tag. The call to the FP_checkBrowser function is the code that needs to be moved.

When you insert the Check Browser Behavior, the <body> tag is rewritten to include the following function call:

```
<body onload="FP_checkBrowser('Microsoft Internet Explorer', '4+',
➥/*href*/'', /*href*/'static.htm')">
```

As mentioned earlier, because the call to the FP_checkBrowser function is in the OnLoad event of the <body> tag, the page will be displayed momentarily before being redirected. To correct that problem, you will need to move the function call so that it appears immediately after the function itself.

The following code is inserted at the beginning of the page when the Check Browser Behavior is being used:

```
//Check version
 loc=ver.search('\\+');v=parseInt(ver);if(loc>0){v=parseInt(ver);if(maj>=v)
 vm=true;}else if(maj==v)vm=true;loc=ver.search("any");if(loc>=0)vm=true;
 if(vm&&tm){ if(url1!='')location=url1;}else if(url2!='')location=url2;
}
// -->
</script>
</head>

<body onload="FP_checkBrowser('Microsoft Internet Explorer', '4+',
➥/*href*/'', /*href*/'static.htm')">
```

To alter the code so that users are redirected immediately before the page loads, remove the function call from the OnLoad event of the <body> tag and move it to the end of the <script> section of the page, as shown in the following code:

```
//Check version
 loc=ver.search('\\+');v=parseInt(ver);if(loc>0){v=parseInt(ver);if(maj>=v)
 vm=true;}else if(maj==v)vm=true;loc=ver.search("any");if(loc>=0)vm=true;
 if(vm&&tm){ if(url1!='')location=url1;}else if(url2!='')location=url2;
}

FP_checkBrowser('Microsoft Internet Explorer', '4+',
➥/*href*/'', /*href*/'static.htm')"

// -->
</script>
</head>

<body>
```

Notice that the call to the FP_checkBrowser script has been moved from the <body> tag to the end of the <script> block. Because client-side script outside of a function runs when it is encountered, this change will cause the FP_checkBrowser function to be called before the page loads. The result will be an instantaneous redirect instead of a redirect after the page loads completely.

CAUTION

> One word of warning: If you use the preceding method and edit the code that FrontPage inserts, the Check Browser Behavior will no longer be visible in the Behaviors task pane and you will not be able to remove the Behavior using the Behaviors task pane. To remove the Behavior, you will have to remove the code from Code view.

CHAPTER **24**

CLIENT-SIDE SCRIPTING

In this chapter

A HISTORY OF BROWSER SCRIPTING

Early Web sites consisted of many of the same Web page elements we use today; forms, images, hyperlinks, and static text. They also consisted of small applications called *applets* that ran inside of the Web page and were written in a new programming language called *Java*. Netscape Communications had just added Java support to its flagship product, Netscape Navigator. However, Netscape was painfully aware that many Web site developers were not Java developers, so it needed to find a way to allow non-Java developers to interact with Java applets on Web pages. It did so with the introduction of *LiveScript*, a technology that was renamed *JavaScript* by the time it made it into Netscape Navigator 2.0. The year was 1995.

Web developers were quick to embrace JavaScript, but it was not used the way Netscape intended. It was mainly being used to provide programmatic access to page content such as forms, images, and text, not to script Java applets. In fact, the most common use for JavaScript at the time is still one of its most common uses today—image swapping. Mouse rollovers were starting to appear all over the Internet.

At the same time, Microsoft released Internet Explorer 3.0, a major upgrade in its less-than-stellar Web browser. With the release of Internet Explorer 3.0, Microsoft unveiled its own flavor of JavaScript coined *JScript*. Microsoft also added its own scripting language (VBScript) and support for a new and emerging technology—Cascading Style Sheets, or CSS. The inclusion of CSS support did not buy Microsoft much, however. Microsoft's JScript implementation did not include support for image swapping, and that made it useless in the eyes of the Web developers. Developers started writing scripts that checked browser versions, and if they detected Internet Explorer, they would simply not attempt to present any of the new dynamic content that scripting provided.

NOTE

> At around this same time period, Web developers began writing scripts to check for Netscape browsers by seeing if the browser identified itself as "Mozilla," an identifier that Netscape Navigator used at the time. As browsers increased in functionality, they all began to identify themselves as "Mozilla Compatible" so that scripts would work successfully. Even today, you will see all browsers identified as Mozilla if you review server logs for your Web site.

Microsoft reacted with the release of Internet Explorer 3.02. Internet Explorer 3.02 added, among other things, support for image swapping. It also continued the divergence of scripting implementation among the major players in the Web browser world. Web developers were still not able to write a script that would easily run on any browser. Instead, they had to write a version of their scripts for each browser and use the appropriate one depending on which browser was being used to access their page. The Web developer community was aching for standards to be introduced to alleviate this problem. Sound familiar?

Netscape and Sun Microsystems, assisted by the European Computer Manufacturers Association (ECMA), standardized browser scripting with the release of ECMAScript in

1998. Ironically, Netscape was also in the process of releasing Netscape Navigator 4.0, a browser that would bring a completely proprietary document object model with it. Microsoft did the same with the release of Internet Explorer 4.0. These 4.0 series browsers introduced a robust new method of programming Web pages called *Dynamic HTML (DHTML)*, a combination of HTML, CSS, and scripting. However, they also widened the gap in compatibility between the two browsers. ECMAScript was too late to stop the momentum.

→ For more information on DHTML, **see** "The Document Object Model," **p. 480**.

The majority of client-side scripting on the Internet today is used to script DHTML effects in Web pages. While Internet Explorer still supports VBScript as a scripting language, the vast majority of Web developers use JavaScript and not VBScript because it will work in all major browsers. For that reason, this chapter sticks to a discussion of JavaScript.

FrontPage provides tools such as Behaviors and Interactive Buttons that can generate JavaScript code for you. However, if you find that you want to add more robust scripts to your page or modify the scripts FrontPage generates—or if the scripts that FrontPage generates don't perform the task you need—knowing how to write JavaScript is a vital skill to have.

The purpose of this chapter is not to teach you how to be a JavaScript programmer. Instead, it is intended to give you a taste of what client-side scripting can be used for and the basics of how it is used. If you are interested in learning how to take maximum advantage of this powerful technology, you should pick up a book specifically with that purpose in mind.

→ For a comprehensive discussion on JavaScript and how to use it to make your Web pages more interactive, read *Special Edition Using JavaScript*.

→ O'Reilly and Associates, Inc. has a Web site with great information concerning the history and evolution of JavaScript. You can access it at http:javascript.frontpagelink.com.

JAVASCRIPT BASICS

JavaScript can be difficult to learn for new programmers. There are several traits to the language that lend to this difficulty, but perhaps the most frustrating part for beginners is that JavaScript is case sensitive. Almost all JavaScript programmers have gone through the growing pains of pulling their hair out because of a lowercase letter where there should have been an uppercase one or vice versa. Debugging problems because of the wrong case can be tough. Fortunately, FrontPage provides IntelliSense for JavaScript, making it much easier to avoid many of the problems new programmers encounter.

→ For more information on using IntelliSense, **see** "Adding Tag Attributes Using IntelliSense," **p. 522**.

→ For more information on debugging JavaScript code, **see** "Front and Center: Debugging," **p. 494**.

ADDING JAVASCRIPT TO A WEB PAGE

JavaScript can be added to a Web page either right within the page's HTML code or in an external script file with a `.js` file extension. To add JavaScript to a Web page, you use the `<script>` tag. JavaScript code can consist of standalone code sections that are executed as soon as the browser encounters them and JavaScript functions that are executed only when they are explicitly called.

A *function* is a section of code that performs an action. To run the code in a function, you simply use the function name. The following code section defines a JavaScript function called `writeDateTime` in a Web page. The function is called when the page is loaded by specifying the function name in the `onload` event of the `<body>` tag.

```html
<html>
<head>
  <script language="javascript">
  <!--
    function writeDateTime() {
      document.write(Date());
      return true;
    }
  //-->
  </script>
</head>

<body onload="writeDateTime();">
</body>
</html>
```

When this Web page is opened in a Web browser, the current date and time are displayed as shown in Figure 24.1. This happens because the `onload` attribute of the `<body>` tag calls the `writeDateTime` JavaScript function. We'll discuss the details of the function later in this chapter.

Figure 24.1
The output of the `writeDateTime` () JavaScript function.

Notice that the script is surrounded by HTML comment tags `<!--` and `//-->`. These are inserted so that browsers that cannot process JavaScript will ignore the script. Modern browsers have no problems processing JavaScript code, but some older browsers do not understand JavaScript. By enclosing the script in HTML comment tags, you ensure that your page will work correctly for everyone viewing it.

Linking to an External Script File

JavaScript can also be included in an external file and linked to a Web page with the `<script>` tag. The following code calls the same JavaScript function as the previous example, but it uses an external script file:

```
<html>
<head>
  <script language="javascript" src="jscript.js">
  </script>
</head>

<body onload="writeDateTime();">
</body>
</html>
```

The `jscript.js` file contains the JavaScript function that is called in the `onload` attribute of the `<body>` tag. The code inside of `jscript.js` is as follows:

```
function writeDateTime() {
  document.write(Date());
}
```

Note that the `jscript.js` file does not contain any HTML code, including the `<script>` tag. It only contains JavaScript code.

There are benefits to including your scripts in a separate file. The primary benefit is that it is very easy to reuse the script in many files without duplicating the code in each file. This also makes it extremely easy to change the script if needed. If you include the script inside the HTML files, a change in the script has to be made in every HTML file including that script. If the script is inside a `.js` file, the script only needs to be changed in the `.js` file. All HTML files that link to that script will then run the updated script automatically.

Adding Inline JavaScript

As mentioned earlier, JavaScript can also be entered as standalone code instead of inside a function. When JavaScript is entered into a page using this method, the code is executed as soon as it is encountered. The following code produces the same output as the code you've seen previously, but it does so with a standalone code segment instead of a JavaScript function:

```
<html>
<head>
</head>
<body>
  <script language="javascript">
  <!--
    document.write(Date());
  //-->
```

```
    </script>
  </body>
</html>
```

Notice that in this example, there is no line declaring a JavaScript function. Instead, only the code inside the `writeDateTime` function is included. In the previous example, in order for the code to execute, you had to call the `writeDateTime` function from the `onload` attribute of the `<body>` tag. In this example, no function call is required because the JavaScript code is not within a function. As you can see, placing JavaScript code inside a function allows you to control when that code is run.

TIP

Because JavaScript inside a function does not run until the function is called, the Web browser will not inform you of any errors in that code until you call the function. Therefore, when you are testing pages with JavaScript functions in them, make sure that you call all of your functions during testing.

THE DOCUMENT OBJECT MODEL

Most of the interactivity in Web pages today is accomplished using DHTML. When you write DHTML code, you use scripting (typically JavaScript) to control the CSS attributes of HTML elements on a page. For example, the flyout menus that are so commonly seen on the Internet these days (see Figure 24.2) are created by causing page elements to appear when a mouse is hovered over a menu item and disappear when the mouse pointer is removed from the menu item. These types of menus are often referred to as DHTML menus because they use DHTML for their functionality.

Figure 24.2
Flyout menus, such as this one on the Jimco Add-ins Web site, are created with DHTML code.

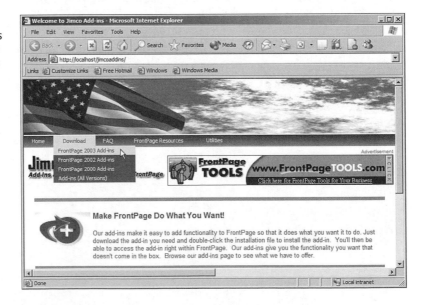

In order to script the elements on a Web page, the JavaScript code must have some way to programmatically access those elements. It does this using the *Document Object Model*, or *DOM*, for the browser. For the most part, the DOMs for the major browsers are very similar, but it doesn't necessarily mean that code that will work in one will work in the other. Even so, with a bit of work, you can write JavaScript code that is compatible with all the major browsers available today.

NOTE

> The *World Wide Web Consortium (W3C)* does have a standard for the DOM, but most Web browsers do not strictly conform to it. Instead, most browsers implement their own DOM that includes specific functionality only for that browser.

At the top of the DOM hierarchy is the window object. Underneath the window object, you will find an extensive list of objects—far too many to cover in a single chapter of this book. However, you will learn about some of the commonly used objects in the DOM.

NOTE

> For complete coverage of the Internet Explorer DOM, visit `http://iedom.frontpagelink.com`. For complete coverage of the Netscape DOM, visit `http://nsdom.frontpagelink.com`.

THE window OBJECT

The window object refers to the browser window itself and is used to manipulate the browser window and its elements. For example, if you want to change what is displayed in the status bar (the lower portion of the browser window), you use the status property of the window object.

The following code example changes the status bar message:

```html
<html>
<head>
   <script language="javascript">
   <!--
      function changeStatus(msg) {
         window.status = msg;
         return true;
      }
   //-->
   </script>
</head>
<body onload="changeStatus('Welcome!');">
</body>
</html>
```

When this page is opened in the Web browser, the status bar text will say Welcome!. Note that when the changeStatus function is called, the text Welcome! is passed to it in parenthesis. When the function runs, the text that is passed to it is assigned to the msg variable, which is then displayed in the status bar.

Using this method of passing a value to a function makes it convenient to reuse the function for other purposes. For example, if you need to display a different message in the status bar of the browser at a different point in the page, you simply call the `changeStatus` function again and pass the text that you want to display to it. This function can be made even more robust by saving it an external `.js` file and simply linking that file to each page that needs to use the `changeStatus` function.

> **TIP**
>
> I offer an add-in on my Web site called Scripter that makes it easy to link a `.js` file to multiple files in one easy step. You can download it from `http://www.jimcoaddins.com`.

THE document OBJECT

One of the objects under the `window` object in the DOM hierarchy is the `document` object. The `document` object is one of the most frequently used objects by JavaScript programmers because it provides access to all the elements on the Web page.

In Internet Explorer, the `all` collection of the `document` object contains a reference to every element on the Web page and is often used by Internet Explorer developers to reference a particular item. For example, consider this `<div>` tag:

```
<div id="border">Web page border goes here.</div>
```

If you wanted to get a reference to this `<div>` tag, you would simply use the following line of code:

```
document.all("border")
```

By appending the ID of the `<div>` to the `all` collection, this line of code returns a reference to the `<div>` with that ID.

That works great in Internet Explorer, but it won't work in Netscape because Netscape doesn't support the `all` collection of the `document` object. Therefore, a better method to get a reference to the `<div>` tag is to use the `getElementById` method of the `document` object. The following code will get a reference to the `<div>` tag, and it will work in both Netscape and Internet Explorer:

```
document.getElementById('border')
```

This code will return a `div` element that references the `<div>` tag called `border`. Once you have that reference, you can then programmatically interact with the `<div>` tag, as you will see later.

> **NOTE**
>
> Many JavaScript developers use the `document.all` collection to determine if a user is using Netscape or Internet Explorer. If `document.all` doesn't return anything, you know that the browser must be Netscape.

There are many other objects in the browser's DOM. By reading through the documentation provided by Microsoft and by Netscape Communications, it should be easy for you to take advantage of what the DOM has to offer. The best way for you to start down that road is to write a little code, so let's write a few sample scripts that implement some real-world scenarios.

WRITING SIMPLE SCRIPTS

Now that you have a general idea of how to write JavaScript code, you are ready to look at a few examples of how you can use JavaScript in your Web pages. In this section, you will learn how to hide and show page elements using JavaScript, how to access elements on a page and read and change their attributes, and how to check information entered into a form before it's submitted. These three tasks are the most common tasks taken on by JavaScript developers.

I have tested the scripts used in this section in Internet Explorer 6 and Netscape 7.1, but they are simple scripts that should work in earlier versions as well. As always, before you implement any scripting solution, you should thoroughly test it in all Web browsers you think your Web site visitors might be using.

24

NOTE

> The finished pages and files for all these scripts are located in the CH24 folder on the CD accompanying this book.

SHOWING AND HIDING PAGE ELEMENTS

One of the most common techniques in browser scripting is changing page content based on certain conditions, such as when the mouse pointer passes over a particular graphic. This type of effect is extremely easy to implement with FrontPage Behaviors, but you might find that you want to edit the code that FrontPage generates. You might also find that a FrontPage Behavior doesn't do exactly what you need and decide to implement your own script. In these cases, understanding how this type of effect is achieved with JavaScript is invaluable.

In this example, you will create a Web page with a list of links on the left side. When you pass over a link, text on the Web page will change to indicate the nature of the link you are pointing to. All of this will be accomplished using DHTML that is programmed using JavaScript.

1. Create a new Web site or open an existing Web site.
2. Create an empty Web page.
3. Insert a table with 1 row and 2 columns, no border, and a width of 100%.
4. Right-click on the left column and select Cell Properties.
5. Check the Specify Width check box.

6. Select the In Pixels option and enter **150** for the width.

7. Click OK.

8. Save your page.

The left column will contain links to parts of the Web site. When you hover over each link, text describing that link will appear in the right column of the table. To implement this, you will need to insert a `div` to hold the text description for each link. When you hover over a link, you will display the `div` for that link and hide all the other `div`s.

Enter the following items in the left column and press the Enter key after each item:

- **Home Page**
- **Our Products**
- **About Us**
- **Contact Us**

In a real-world Web site, you would link each of these to their respective pages in the Web site; but for now, simply link each one to the page you are currently editing so that you will have a hyperlink to work with.

Now you will need to create some `<div>` tags to hold the text for each link. To do this, you will use the Layers feature in FrontPage:

1. Select Insert, Layer.

2. Size and position the layer so that it appears in the right column of your table.

3. Right-click the layer and select Copy.

4. Right-click the layer again and select Paste.

5. Right-click the layer and select Paste three more times so that there are four total layers—one right on top of the other.

6. Select View, Task Pane to show the task pane.

7. Right-click the first layer and select Modify ID.

8. Change the first layer's ID to **Home**.

9. Change the second layer's ID to **Products**.

10. Change the third layer's ID to **About**.

11. Change the fourth layer's ID to **Contact**.

12. Right-click the Home layer and select Set Visibility: Hidden.

13. Repeat step 12 for the remaining layers.

16. Save the page.

Your page should now look like the one shown in Figure 24.3.

Figure 24.3
The Web page is now ready for you to add some code.

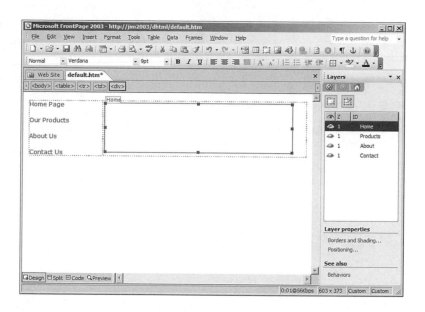

TIP

FrontPage uses absolute positioning for layers. All the layers you inserted are stacked on top of each other. Therefore, any text added to each div will appear in the same place on the page because they each sit on their own layer at the same position on the page.

→ For more information on using Layers, **see** "Using Layers," **p. 499**.

When you make the layers hidden using the task pane, FrontPage simply adds a CSS property to the <div> tags to make them hidden. That property is the visibility property. For example, the following <div> tag is hidden:

```
<div id="Products" style="visibility: hidden;">I am hidden.</div>
```

When the Web page containing this <div> tag is loaded, the div will be invisible.

TIP

In situations in which a div is not absolutely positioned, hiding it using the visibility property makes it invisible, but the browser still reserves space for the div. The result is an empty area where the div is on the page. To prevent this, use the display property for a div that is not absolutely positioned. When the display property is set to none, the div will not be displayed and the browser will close up the space where the div used to be.

Enter some text for each layer that describes the content for that link. To do this, first click the layer in the Layers task pane and then click inside the layer. Enter any text you choose for each layer.

When someone visits your Web site, you want the text for the Home layer to be visible right away. If the site visitor then hovers over one of your other links, you want the layer for that link to be displayed. To do that, you will need to enter some code.

Switch to Code view and add the following JavaScript code before the closing `</head>` tag:

```
<script language="javascript">
  <!--
  function hideAllDivs() {
    document.getElementById('Home').style.visibility = 'hidden';
    document.getElementById('Products').style.visibility = 'hidden';
    document.getElementById('About').style.visibility = 'hidden';
    document.getElementById('Contact').style.visibility = 'hidden';
  }

  function changeVisibility(layer) {
    document.getElementById(layer).style.visibility = 'visible';
    return true;
  }
//-->
</script>
```

→ For more information on entering code in Code view, **see** "Working in Code View and Split View," **p. 519**.

Two JavaScript functions exist in this code. The first one is the `hideAllDivs` function. This function sets the `visibility` property of each `div` to `hidden`. Remember that when you set the layer to be invisible, FrontPage set an inline style by adding a `style` attribute to the `<div>` tag. The value of that `style` attribute is `visibility: hidden`. To programmatically set an inline style on an element, you use the `style` attribute of the element. In the `hideAllDivs` function, you are setting an inline style for each `div`, and that inline style sets the `visibility` property to `hidden`.

The second function is the `changeVisibility` function. This function makes whatever layer name is passed to it visible by setting the `visibility` property to `visible`. For example, if you wanted to make the Products layer visible, you would call the `changeVisibility` function using the following code:

```
changeVisibility('Products');
```

When the `changeVisibility` function is called with this line of code, the `layer` variable in the function is assigned the value `Products`, and the `getElementById` function then returns a reference to the Products layer on the page. The `style` attribute is then used to set the `visibility` property to `visible`.

Now you will need to add some code that will call these functions at the appropriate times to finish out the page. First, you will want to make sure that the Home layer is visible when the page is first loaded. To do that, you will call the `changeVisibility` function for the Home layer when the page loads.

Make sure that you're still in Code view and edit the `<body>` tag of your page so that it resembles the following code:

```
<body onload="changeVisibility('Home');">
```

The `onload` event of the `<body>` tag is triggered automatically as soon as the page has finished loading. When an event is triggered, that event is said to have *fired*. By adding a call to the `changeVisibility` function in the `onload` event of the `<body>` tag, you cause the Home layer to become visible when the `onload` event is fired.

The final step is to edit the hyperlinks you created so that they cause the correct layers to appear and disappear as the mouse moves over them. To add this functionality, you will use two different events—the `onmouseover` event and the `onmouseout` event. The `onmouseover` event is fired when the mouse moves over the element, and the `onmouseout` event is fired when the mouse moves off the element.

Locate the `<a>` tag for the Products link and edit it so that it resembles the following code:

```
<a href="default.htm"
onmouseover="hideAllDivs();changeVisibility('Products');"
onmouseout="hideAllDivs();changeVisibility('Home');">
```

The `onmouseover` event first calls the `hideAllDivs` function. This causes any visible `div` to be hidden in preparation for displaying the Products layer. It then calls the `changeVisibility` function and passes `Products` to it. This causes the Products layer to become visible. Note that a semicolon appears between the two function calls.

When the mouse is moved off the Products link, the `onmouseout` event is fired. This event again calls the `hideAllDivs` function, which hides the Products layer. It then calls the `changeVisibility` function to make the Home layer visible again because we're on the home page.

To finish out the page, edit the About and Contact hyperlinks just as you did with the Products hyperlink. Make sure that you pass the correct layer name to the `changeVisibility` function in the `onmouseover` event. After you've finished editing your hyperlinks, save the page and preview it in your browser to see your layers swapped out as you hover over the hyperlinks.

 If the *divs* don't change when you mouse over them, see "Divs Don't Change on Rollover" in the "Troubleshooting" section of this chapter.

ACCESSING AND CHANGING ATTRIBUTES

JavaScript code is often used to access attributes of HTML tags. Using JavaScript, you can read the value of a particular attribute and also change the value of an attribute. Web pages that use image swapping use this technique to change the image file that is displayed when the mouse hovers over an image. In this section, you will write some JavaScript code that will swap an image when your mouse hovers over it.

The HTML `<img>` tag has an attribute called `src` that specifies the image file to be displayed. By using JavaScript to change the `src` attribute of an image tag, you can easily create the effect of swapping the image with another image. To do this, you will need to perform two primary tasks—preload the images and write the code to swap the images.

Before you get started, you will need a couple of images to work with. You can use the parrot_gray.jpg and the parrot_color.jpg images in the CH24/Swap folder on the CD accompanying this book, or you can use your own images. Just make sure that the images are the same size so that the rollover effect will work correctly. Save whatever images you decide to use into the images folder of your Web site.

PRELOADING IMAGES

Your first step is to add a JavaScript to preload the images that will be swapped. You want to preload the images because if you don't, when your Web site visitors hover over your original image, they will have to wait for the browser to download the second image before the images are swapped. This delay can take several seconds on a dial-up Internet connection, and that delay makes your effect seem unprofessional.

Preloading images with JavaScript is an easy task. Open a new page and enter the following JavaScript code before the closing </head> tag:

```
<script language="javascript">
  <!--
  grayImg = new Image();
  grayImg.src = "images/parrot_gray.jpg";
  colorImg = new Image();
  colorImg.src = "images/parrot_color.jpg;
  //-->
</script>
```

This code defines two variables called grayImg and colorImg. It then sets these variables equal to a new Image object. An Image object is an object that represents an HTML <img> tag. You then set the src attribute of the new Image object to the image file that you want to display for that object. After this code runs, you will have two Image objects—one for the parrot_gray.jpg image (the initial image) and one for the parrot_color.jpg image.

Note that this code does not exist within a function call. That's because you want this code to run when the page loads. You could place this code within a JavaScript function and call it in the onload event of the <body> tag, but doing that would cause the script to run immediately *after* the page loads. If your Web site visitor were to mouse over the image as soon as the page finishes loading, you wouldn't get the benefit of the image preloading.

> **TIP**
>
> You can use the Preload Images Behavior to preload the images if you want. However, because I feel that understanding what goes on when you use that Behavior is important, I have included the code necessary to preload images.

WRITING A FUNCTION TO SWAP IMAGES

The next step is to write a function that will swap the images. Because this is a function that you might want to reuse in other Web pages, it makes sense to write it so that it isn't specific to the images you are using in this example. Instead, the function should be written as a generic function that can swap images based on the information passed to it.

Edit your script to include the swapImage function as follows:

```
<script language="javascript">
  <!--
  grayImg = new Image();
  grayImg.src = "images/parrot_gray.jpg";
  colorImg = new Image();
  colorImg.src = "images/parrot_color.jpg;

  function swapImage(imgID, imgObj) {
    if (document.images) {
      document.images[imgID].src = imgObj.src;
    }
  }
  //-->
</script>
```

The swapImage function takes two parameters—imgID and imgObj. The imgID variable will contain the id attribute of the image that's being swapped. This allows you to refer to the correct page element. The imgObj variable is the object name for the image that you want to display in place of the original image. When the function runs, the src attribute of the original image is changed to the src attribute for the swapped image. Since the images have been preloaded, the result of this function is that the image instantly changes.

ADDING THE IMAGES

Now the JavaScript code is in place. All that's left is to insert the original image into a new Web page and then add some JavaScript function calls to the <img> tag. Insert the parrot_gray.jpg image onto your page. Using the Quick Tag Editor, edit the <img> tag so that it appears as follows:

```
<img border="0" id="parrot" src="images/parrot_gray.jpg"
width="92" height="122" onmouseover="swapImage('parrot', colorImg);"
onmouseout="swapImage('parrot', grayImg);">
```

→ For more information on the Quick Tag Editor, **see** "Editing Code with the Quick Tag Editor," **p. 532**.

The <img> tag now contains code for the onmouseover event that calls the swapImage function and passes 'parrot' and colorImg to it. This tells the JavaScript function that you are changing the image for the tag with an id attribute of parrot. It also tells the JavaScript function that you want to change the src attribute of the tag so that it's equal to the src attribute of the colorImg object. The src attribute of the colorImg object is set when the images are preloaded, so when the mouse hovers over the grayscale picture of the parrot, it changes automatically to a color picture right before your eyes. The onmouseout event calls the swapImage function again to change the images back again. Using this exact same procedure, you are now equipped to write your own JavaScript rollover buttons.

 If there is a delay when the images swap, see "Images Don't Swap Instantly" in the "Troubleshooting" section of this chapter.

FORM FIELD VALIDATION

Another common use of JavaScript in Web pages is validation of form fields. In this section, you will write JavaScript that will validate an HTML form and make sure that data was entered in each form field. It will also check to ensure that only numeric characters are entered in a particular field and that no more than three digits are entered.

CREATING THE FORM TO VALIDATE

First, you will need to create an HTML form that will be validated by your script:

1. Create a new page in your Web site.
2. Select Insert, Form, Textbox to insert a form and a textbox control.
3. Insert another textbox control on the form under the first text box.
4. Type the text **Enter your name:** above the first text box.
5. Type the text **Enter your age:** above the second text box.
6. Double-click the first text box and change the name to **txtName**.
7. Double-click the second text box and change the name to **txtAge**.
8. Save the page.

Your page should now resemble the page in Figure 24.4.

Figure 24.4
The finished HTML form that will be validated with JavaScript.

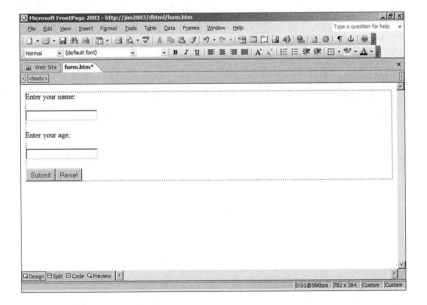

→ For more information on working with Forms, **see** "Using Forms," **p. 359**.

ADDING THE JAVASCRIPT VALIDATION FUNCTION

Now you will need to enter some JavaScript code to validate the form. Here's the JavaScript function to validate both of the form fields.

```
<script language="javascript">
  function validateForm(theForm) {
    var txtName;
    var txtAge;
    var nums = '0123456789';

    txtName = theForm.elements[0];
    txtAge = theForm.elements[1];
    if ((txtName.value == '') || (txtAge.value == '')) {
      alert('Please specify both your name and your age.');
      return false;
    }
    for (var i = 0; i < txtAge.value.length; i++) {
      if (nums.indexOf(txtAge.value.charAt(i)) == -1) {
        alert('You can only specify numeric data for age.');
        return false;
      } else if (txtAge.value.length > 3) {
        alert('You cannot possibly be that old.');
        return false;
      }
    }
    return true;
  }
</script>
```

This script is the most complicated yet, but it's not quite as complex as it looks at first glance. The first three links set up three variables—one for the txtName form field, one for the txtAge form fields, and one for the numeric characters you will validate the txtAge field against.

Next, you set the txtName and the txtAge variables equal to their respective form fields. To get a reference to each form field, you use the variable called theForm. This variable will hold a reference to whatever has been passed into the validateForm function. As you will see later, a reference to the form itself is passed to this function. The elements collection contains one object for each form field in the form. The first form field is called elements[0], the second elements[1], and so on. The first element in your form is the txtName form field, so the txtName variable is assigned to theForm.elements[0]. The txtAge variable is then assigned to theForm.elements[1], the txtAge form field.

VALIDATING THE FORM FIELDS

Now that you have a reference to both the txtName and the txtAge form fields, you check to ensure that both of them contain data. You do this by checking to see if their value property is an empty string with the following line of code:

```
if ((txtName.value == '') || (txtAge.value == ''))
```

The value property returns the data entered into the from field. If the value property returns an empty string, you know that the user hasn't entered any data and you display an appropriate message using the `alert` method. (Notice that to check whether one value is equal to another value in JavaScript, you use double equal signs.) The double pipe symbol (¦¦) is the logical OR operator in JavaScript. Therefore, if either `txtAge` or `txtName` contain no data, validation will fail.

The next validation to perform is checking whether the `txtAge` form field contains any non-numeric values. To do this, you use a string variable (`nums`) that contains all the valid numerical values. You then check each character in the `txtAge` form field against that string variable. Here is the code segment that performs that check:

```
for (var i = 0; i < txtAge.value.length; i++) {
  if (nums.indexOf(txtAge.value.charAt(i)) == -1) {
```

The first line sets up a *for loop*. A `for` loop runs through a particular code segment repeatedly as long as a particular condition is met. When you define a `for` loop, you specify three items that control how the loop is executed—a variable that will be used to indicate how many times the loop has run, a condition that must be met in order for the loop to continue running, and an incrementer for the loop counter that adds 1 to its present value each time the loop runs.

In the loop example, the variable that will indicate how many times the loop has run is called `i`, and it is initialized to 0 at the beginning of the loop. The condition is then specified so that as long as `i` is less than the length of whatever is entered into the `txtAge` form field, the code segment will continue to be executed. Finally, `i` is incremented with the `i++` statement which adds 1 to its present value.

NOTE

The ++ symbol mean to increment the value to the left of it by 1. This syntax is used in many languages other than JavaScript, including C and C++. In fact, C++ got its name from the fact that its developers believed it to be one better than C.

When this code runs, the loop runs once for every character in the `txtAge` form field. Each time it runs, it checks a single character in the `txtAge` form field (using the `charAt` function) to see if it contains any value other than one of the numbers in the `nums` variable. It does this using the `indexOf` function. The `indexOf` function returns the position of one string within another string. If the string is not found, a value of -1 is returned. Each character in the `txtAge` form field should be found somewhere within the `nums` string variable. If it is not, you know it is not a numeric value and you display the appropriate message.

The final check is to determine if the length of the text entered into the `txtAge` form field exceeds three digits. If it does, you display a message letting the user know that he has lied about his age. If any of the previous validations fail, you return a value of `false` from the `validateForm` function because validation has failed. After a value is returned from a function, processing of that function stops. Therefore, the last line in the function returns a value of `true` because you know if you've gotten that far, validation has succeeded.

ADDING THE CALL TO THE JAVASCRIPT FUNCTION

Now you need to add one final bit of code to make this all work. You need to add a call to the `validateForm` function. You do that in the `onsubmit` event of the form. Using the Quick Tag Editor, edit the `<form>` tag as follows:

```
<form method="POST" action="--WEBBOT-SELF--"
onsubmit="return validateForm(this);">
```

The `onsubmit` event fires when the form is submitted. In this event, you call the `validateForm` function and pass a reference to the form using the `this` keyword. The `this` keyword will always contain a reference to the particular element containing it. It is a convenient way to pass a reference to an element to a function. Because you have used `return` when calling the function, the `return` statement inside the `validateForm` function will return either `true` or `false`. If the value is `false`, the form will not be submitted. If the value is `true`, the form will submit as usual.

Save the page now and preview it in your browser. Submit the form without entering any data and see the result. Then enter your name in both fields and note that you are told that the `txtAge` form field can only contain numeric data. Then enter an age of `1000` and try to submit the form.

This is a simple validation script. In a real-world environment, you would want your validation script to be much more robust than this. However, this script gives you a solid foundation on the methods used when validating forms.

TROUBLESHOOTING

Divs DON'T CHANGE ON ROLLOVER

When I roll the mouse over my links, the text doesn't change.

The most common cause of this is a typographical error in your code. Look in the status bar of the browser and make sure that an error doesn't appear in your script. If it does, carefully review the code you entered to make sure that you haven't made a mistake.

This can also be caused by having scripting turned off in your browser. To check that in Internet Explorer, select Tools, Internet Options and click the Security tab. Select the appropriate zone (select Internet if using a URL with dots in it and Intranet if using a URL without dots) and click the Custom button. Make sure that the Enabled option is selected for Active Scripting. To check that in Netscape, select Edit, Preferences, and then double-click the Advanced category. Select the Scripts & Plugins category and make sure that the Navigator check box is checked.

IMAGES DON'T SWAP INSTANTLY

I've entered in all the code including the preloading code, but my rollover image doesn't swap instantly. Instead, there is a delay while the second image loads.

Internet Explorer can be configured so that it checks the Web server each time a file is requested to see if a newer version is on the server. This check can cause a delay in the display of rollover images.

To correct this, select Tools, Internet Options. Make sure that the General tab is selected and click the Settings button. In the Check for Newer Versions of Stored Pages section, choose the Automatically option and click OK.

FRONT AND CENTER: DEBUGGING

So far, the assumption has been that all the JavaScript you're entering will run without problems. As long as you enter it correctly, it will, but that's because I've already debugged it for you! In the real world, code almost never runs successfully on the first try. Sometimes you get lucky and your code runs without debugging, but almost all code requires some level of debugging in order to get the desired results.

There are two types of problems you can encounter with code—syntax errors and logic errors. Syntax errors are often the easiest errors to resolve. For example, the following line of code will generate an error:

```
document.Write('Welcome!');
```

Remember, JavaScript is case sensitive. The write method does not start with a capital W, so when this line executes, it will generate an error.

Logic errors are much harder to track down. A logic error occurs when code is written so that it will run without syntax errors, but the code produces undesired results. Logic errors are hard to track down because when an error occurs, it will often point you to a part of code that is nowhere near where the actual error is located. Suppose, for example, you have a function that returns a specific numeric value and that function contains a logic error. You have code in a completely different area that relies on the number returned from the function. When the code runs and an error occurs, the error message might point to the section of code that is using the number returned from the function, not the function itself.

There are many approaches to debugging JavaScript code. Some people use the JavaScript alert method to display messages at certain places in code. For example, if a function returns a specific numeric value, you can place an alert method at the end of the function call and display the value the function returns as shown in the following code example:

```
function debugTest() {
  var i;
  i = document.getElementById('txtYears').value;
  alert(i);
  return i;
}
```

When this function runs, an alert dialog box will display indicating the value of i. This method of debugging can help in some situations, but it is far more useful to use a debugger so that you can execute code in a controlled way and examine values as you progress through it. FrontPage offers just such a debugger in the Microsoft Script Editor.

To use the Microsoft Script Editor, open a Web page in FrontPage that contains client-side script and then select Tools, Macro, Microsoft Script Editor. If the Microsoft Script Editor menu option is not enabled, you will need to install HTML Source Editing, an option in your FrontPage installation (see Figure 24.5). If HTML Source Editing is already installed, you might still have to install the Script Editor, but FrontPage will prompt you to do so when you click the menu item.

Figure 24.5
The HTML Source Editing component of FrontPage must be installed to use the Script Editor.

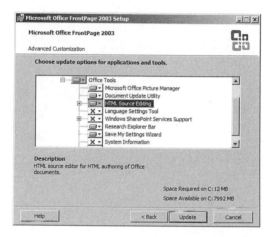

Once the Script Editor is installed, you will still need to install Web Debugging in order to use the debugging feature. To install it, select Debug, Install Web Debugging from within the Microsoft Script Editor. Once Web Debugging has been installed, you are ready to start debugging.

1. Switch to FrontPage and open the Web page with the form validation script in it that you created during this chapter. If you are using the files from the CD, the filename is form.htm.

2. Select Tools, Macro, Microsoft Script Editor to open the page in the Script Editor.

3. Set a breakpoint at the beginning of the validateForm function by right-clicking on the line and selecting Insert Breakpoint. A *breakpoint* is a place in code where the debugger will automatically stop, allowing you to control when subsequent code is executed.

4. Select Debug, Start to launch your Web browser and load the page.

5. Click the form's Submit button to run the validateForm function.

When you submit the form, the debugger will break on the validateForm function as shown in Figure 24.6. Note that the debugger does not stop at the very first line. Certain lines are not valid breakpoints because they do not execute any code. If you set a breakpoint on an invalid line, the Script Editor will break on the first valid line after your breakpoint.

The arrow indicates the line currently being executed

Figure 24.6
The debugger has stopped and is waiting for you to execute the next line of code.

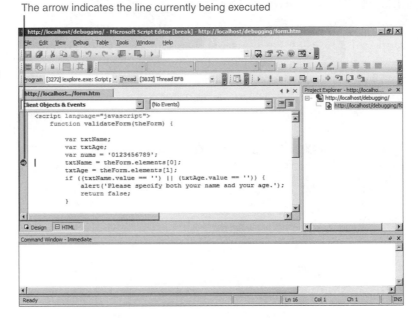

The three primary methods of continuing execution of your code are as follows:

- **Step Into**—By pressing F11, you can step into the next line of code. Each press of F11 causes the debugger to go to the next line.

- **Step Over**—By pressing F10, the debugger steps over code. Step Over works in much the same way as Step Into, but if the current line of code is a function call, Step Over will cause the debugger to execute the entire function in one step, whereas Step Into will cause the debugger to stop on each line of the function.

- **Step Out**—By pressing Shift+F11, the debugger will step out of the current function and stop again at the line where the function returns.

While the debugger is sitting on a breakpoint, it is very easy to examine the current state of your script. The Locals Window is the most convenient way to analyze the variables in your script. In Figure 24.7, you can easily see the variables that were declared in the validateForm function. Note that theForm, txtAge, and txtName all have a plus sign next to them. By clicking the plus sign, you can analyze all the properties of each of those variables. For example, by clicking the plus sign next to txtName, you would be able to look up the value property to see what text was entered into that text box.

Figure 24.7
The Locals Window provides details on all variables in one place.

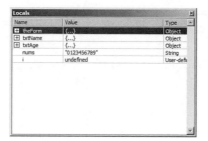

The Help file for the Script Editor contains details on all the tools available to you to make debugging your scripts easy. By utilizing the powerful debugging tools that the Script Debugger offers, you can spend more time writing new scripts and less time fixing problems in existing scripts.

24

USING LAYERS

In this chapter

INTRODUCTION TO LAYERS

In the early days of Web sites, Web developers were content with having a Web page with columns of text for their hyperlinks. Web pages were boring and drab, but they served their purpose. As the Internet became more popular, Web sites became more interactive and dynamic. Instead of plain text and graphics, it is much more common now to see dynamic graphically-oriented Web pages with content that changes in real-time as you interact with the page.

A Web developer can use many techniques to create a Web page in which certain areas of the Web page change as the user interacts with it. Many Web developers use <DIV> tags to implement this kind of funationality because by using the style attribute of the <DIV> tag, you can easily control the <DIV> tag's position, size, and many other attributes.

FrontPage 2003 uses <DIV> tags to implement *layers*. A layer is a <DIV> tag that is *absolutely positioned* so that you have fine control over its position on the page. When an item on a Web page is absolutely positioned, it means that the tag used to render that item contains attributes that specify exactly where that item is to appear on the Web page. The position is specified using three attributes:

- left—The distance between the left side of the Web page and the left side of the item.
- top—The distance between the top of the Web page and the top of the item.
- z-index—The position of the item in relation to other absolutely positioned items if you were to stack the items one on top of the other. A higher z-index indicates the item is higher in the stack.

The z-index is what defines a <DIV> as an actual layer. Because the z-index allows you to stack <DIV> tags in layers on a page, absolutely positioned <DIV> tags are known as layers.

CAUTION

If you change the properties of a layer and turn off the absolute positioning for the layer or if you edit the page in Code view and remove the style attribute, the <DIV> is no longer considered a layer and FrontPage will no longer provide you with the tools to edit it as a layer.

You encounter layers almost every time you go to a Web site. For example, when you see a menu system that pops up a submenu for items you point to, chances are that functionality is implemented with layers. Previous versions of FrontPage would allow you to add this kind of functionality to a Web page, but in order to do so, you had to hand-code it inside of Code view. FrontPage 2003 introduces the Layers task pane, which provides you with an intuitive interface with which to add and configure layers on your Web page without hand-coding.

NOTE

> Layers can be used for much more than just menu systems. You can use layers to control any element on your page including graphics, blocks of text, and even other layers.

Over the course of this chapter, you will create a Web page with a dynamic menu system and other dynamic content using layers, Behaviors, and Interactive Buttons. Previous versions of FrontPage would have required that you do all of this by writing code. But by using FrontPage 2003, you will create it all without even looking at a single line of code!

NOTE

> If you'd prefer to use a completed copy of the Web page described in this chapter, see the file `layers.htm` in the `Ch25` folder on the CD-ROM that accompanies this book for the completed example.

→ For more information on using Behaviors in FrontPage, **see** "Using Behaviors," **p. 449**.

→ For more information on using Interactive Buttons, **see** "Using Interactive Buttons," **p. 441**.

INSERTING AND CONFIGURING LAYERS

Layers are inserted and formatted in FrontPage using the Layers task pane. There are other ways to insert a layer, but the Layers task pane is the most efficient way because it is also used to format and arrange layers. To insert a layer in to your Web page, simply select Format, Layers to display the Layers task pane seen in Figure 25.1. From the Layers task pane, you can click the Insert Layer button or the Draw Layer button to insert a new layer into the page. In addition to using the Layers task pane, you can also select Insert, Layer to insert a new layer.

 If the controls inside of the Layers task pane are grayed out and unavailable, see "Layers Task Pane Is Disabled" in the "Troubleshooting" section of this chapter.

In addition to the Insert Layer and Draw Layer buttons, the Layers task pane is made up of three columns. The leftmost column, the Layer Visibility column, allows you to control whether a particular layer is visible and to see at a glance which layers are visible and which ones are not. The second column, the Layer Z-Index column, provides for a quick reference to the z-index for each layer. The rightmost column, the Layer ID column, displays the ID for each layer.

TIP

> Choose the ID for each layer carefully and try to choose an ID that describes the layer's purpose. You will use the ID of the layer to refer to the layer in Behavior dialogs and if you are writing client-side code. By naming your layers with descriptive names such as mainContent and navButtons, you will be less likely to confuse them later.

Figure 25.1
The Layers task pane is where you insert and configure your layers.

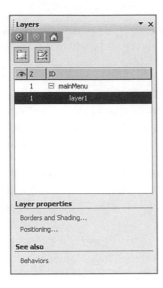

ADDING CONTENT TO A LAYER

Let's begin creating the Web page you'll use throughout this chapter to learn about layers in FrontPage.

1. Create a new blank page.

2. Select Format, Layers to display the Layers task pane.

3. Click the Draw Layer button and draw a layer the same width as your page and half the height of the page by clicking in the upper left corner of the page and dragging the mouse to draw the layer.

4. Click inside the layer to place the insertion point in it.

5. Select Insert, Interactive Button to insert an Interactive Button.

6. Choose the Border Bottom 1 button.

7. Enter **Home** for the text of the button and click OK.

8. Continue this process by repeating steps 6 and 7 to create button for **Products**, **Support**, and **Contact Us**. Your page should look like the one shown in Figure 25.2.

9. Double-click the layer to display the Layers task pane if it's not already displayed.

10. Right-click layer1 and select Modify ID to rename the layer.

11. Change the layer name to **mainMenu**.

12. Right-click on the mainMenu layer and select Modify Z-Index.

13. Change the Z-index for the mainMenu layer to **3**.

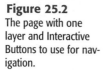

Figure 25.2
The page with one layer and Interactive Buttons to use for navigation.

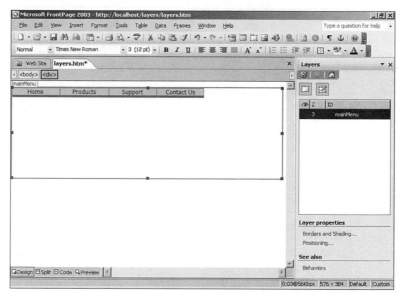

RESIZING A LAYER

The layer you have just inserted needs to be resized so that it is the same size as the four Interactive Buttons inside it. Change the width and height of the layer to match the height of the size of the Interactive Buttons. To do that, follow these steps:

1. Move the mouse over the blue border on the layer until the mouse pointer changes to a four-way arrow.

2. Single-click on the border to activate the sizing handles. The sizing handles appear as small blue squares at each corner and in the middle of each side of the layer.

3. Move the mouse pointer over a sizing handle until the mouse pointer changes to a two-way arrow.

4. Click and hold the left mouse button while you drag the sizing handle to change the width or height of the layer.

Resize the mainMenu layer until it matches the width and height of the Interactive Buttons. You should now have a new layer containing four Interactive Buttons, as shown in Figure 25.3. The buttons represent the top-level menu. You will create submenus that will display when a user hovers over the Products or Support menu buttons.

CREATING AND WORKING WITH CHILD LAYERS

You now need to create a layer to hold each submenu. You will then control the visibility of the layer based on the position of the mouse. To do that, you'll use Behaviors and the Layers task pane.

25

Figure 25.3
These Interactive Buttons will be the top-level menu for your dynamic menu built using layers.

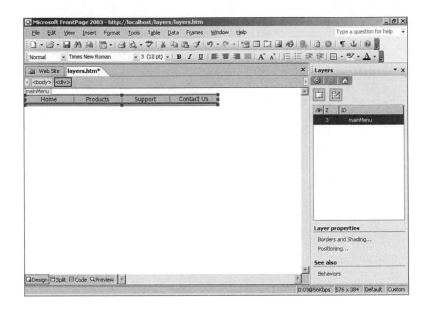

One of the great things about layers is that because they are absolutely positioned, you can design them anywhere on the page and then simply drag and drop them where you want them to appear when your page is complete. In the case of your menu, you will be creating three separate layers. As you'll soon see, being able to design these layers and then place them in their final positions makes the development of menus much more convenient.

The mainMenu layer is the parent layer for all the other layers in the menu system. By making the mainMenu layer the parent layer, all the layers that make up your menu will be attached to the mainMenu layer. If you move the mainMenu layer, it will move the entire menu system and keep all of your layers in place.

You now need to create the first child layer for the mainMenu layer. To do that, follow these steps:

1. Select Format, Layers to display the Layers task pane if it's not already visible.

2. Select the mainMenu layer so that the new layer will be inserted as a child layer.

3. Click the Insert Layer button to insert a new layer.

4. Because the new layer is inserted directly on top of the existing layer, select the layer and drag it below the mainMenu layer as shown in Figure 25.4.

5. Insert an Interactive Button in to the layer by selecting Insert, Interactive Button.

6. Choose the Border Left 1 button.

7. Enter **Software** for the text of the button and click OK.

8. Press Shift+Enter to insert a line break.

9. Insert another Border Left 1 Interactive Button immediately below the first button.

10. Enter **Hardware** for the text of the button and click OK.

Figure 25.4
The new layer is posi-
tioned right under the
mainMenu layer.

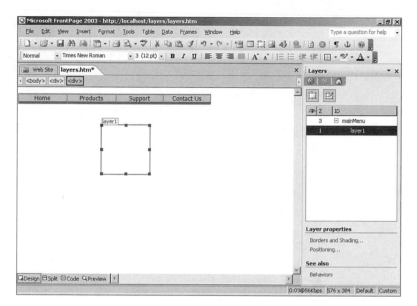

The mainMenu layer now has a child layer called layer1, and that layer contains two
Interactive Buttons. Resize the layer so that its height and width matches the height and
width of the Interactive Buttons.

You should now rename the layer and give it a more descriptive ID. Right-click the layer1
layer in the Layers task pane and select Modify ID. Type **ProdSubmenu** for the layer ID. Your
page should now resemble the page in Figure 25.5. Note that the ProdSubmenu layer
appears slightly indented below the mainMenu layer in the Layers task pane, and there is
minus sign next to the mainMenu layer. This indicates that the ProdSubmenu layer is a
child layer.

The layer is still not in its final position. When you've finished this page, the ProdSubmenu
layer will appear just below the Products menu button. However, it's easiest to design your
layers first and then move them into their correct positions later. Because the ProdSubmenu
layer is a child layer to the mainMenu layer, it will always move with the mainMenu layer.
Therefore, when you place it into its final position, you'll never have to worry about it losing its position relative to the mainMenu layer.

NOTE

When you insert a child layer, FrontPage simply inserts the <DIV> tag for the layer
nested within the parent <DIV> tag.

25

Figure 25.5
The ProdSubmenu layer is a child layer of the mainMenu layer.

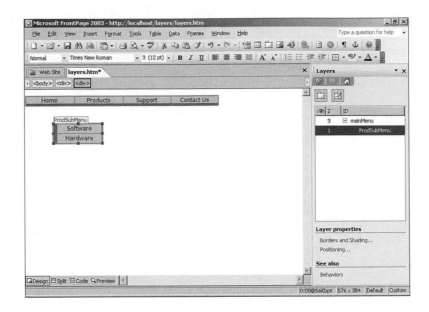

The final popup menu you need to create is the Support menu. Copy the ProdSubmenu layer and paste it as a new layer. Rename the new layer **SupportSubmenu**. This layer also needs to be a child of the mainMenu layer. To make it a child layer, click the SupportSubmenu layer in the Layers task pane and drag and drop it on top of the mainMenu layer in the Layers task pane. They layer is now a child layer at the same level as the ProdSubmenu layer.

You now need to change the Interactive Buttons in the new SupportSubmenu layer. Double-click the first button and change its text to **FAQ**. Double-click the second button and change its text to **Ask Us**. You now have all the layers complete for your interactive menu, and your page should look like the one seen in Figure 25.6.

NOTE

When using Interactive Buttons in a real application, you would also configure the button to link to another page. In the example you're building in this chapter, you don't configure a hyperlink because you're only designing one page to illustrate the use of layers.

Figure 25.6
The layers have all been inserted for your dynamic menu.

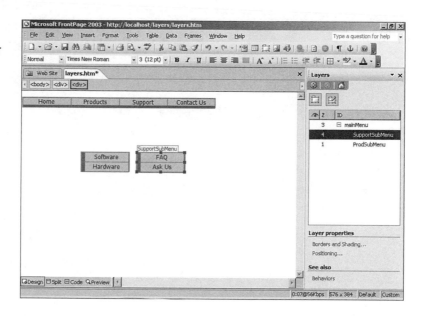

POSITIONING LAYERS

As mentioned previously, none of the layers on your page are in their final position. However, because layers are often stacked on top of each other, they are difficult to edit when they are placed in their final positions prior to finishing their content. That's why you added all the items to your layers while they were all separated. Now it's time to position the layers into their final positions.

The dynamic menu you are building will display a submenu of products when you hover over the Products button and a submenu of support options when you hover over the Support button. You'll want to position the ProdSubmenu layer so that it appears underneath the Products button and slightly overlaps the bottom of the button. You will also want to position the SupportSubmenu layer so that it appears underneath the Support button.

Drag the ProdSubmenu layer so that it appears underneath the Products button and the SupportSubmenu layer so that it appears underneath the Support button, as shown in Figure 25.7. Make sure that the ProdSubmenu layer and the SupportSubmenu layer do not overlap. After you have positioned the ProdSubmenu and the SupportSubmenu layers, select the mainMenu layer and drag it to the position where you want your menu to appear on the page. Notice that as you drag the mainMenu layer, the positions of the ProdSubmenu and the SupportSubmenu layers do not change in their relation to the mainMenu layer. That's the benefit of making those layers child layers to the mainMenu layer.

25

Figure 25.7
The completed user interface for your dynamic menu.

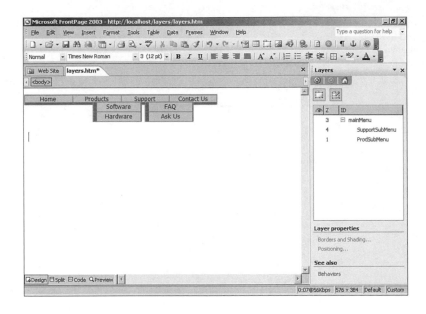

TIP

> If you have multiple layers on top of one another, it can become difficult to select the layers in Design view. By clicking the layer in the Layers task pane, you can easily control which layers you are selecting.

SETTING LAYER PROPERTIES WITH BEHAVIORS

Now you're ready to add interactivity to your menu. When the page first loads, the only layer that you want to be visible is the mainMenu layer. When a user hovers over the Products button, the ProdSubmenu layer will display. When a user hovers over the Support button, the SupportSubmenu layer will appear.

In addition to configuring these layers to appear at the correct time, you will also need to configure when each layer should disappear. You wouldn't want your menus to appear and stay visible forever. When the user has moved the mouse out of the menu, you want the menu to disappear.

The perfect way to implement all of this is using Behaviors. By using the Change Property and Change Property Restore Behaviors, you can easily configure your layers to appear and disappear just when you need them to.

→ For more information on using Behaviors, **see** "Using Behaviors," **p. 449**.

SETTING THE VISIBILITY OF LAYERS

When the page loads, the only layer that you want people to see is the mainMenu layer. All the other layers should be invisible. The Layers task pane provides for an easy method of controlling the visibility of layers using the Layer Visibility column.

The Layer Visibility column is empty by default, but by clicking next to a specific layer, an eyeball icon will appear, as shown in Figure 25.8. The open eye icon means that the layer is visible. There are three visibility states for each layer in the Layers task pane:

- Default—Indicated by the absence of an eye icon.
- Visible—Indicated by an open eye icon.
- Invisible—Indicated by a closed eye icon.

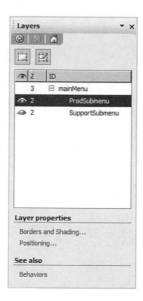

Figure 25.8
The Layer Visibility column provides for full control over layer visibility.

Click the eye icon on the ProdSubmenu layer so that it appears closed. The Products submenu will now appear hidden when the page is first browsed. Click the Layer Visibility column next to the SupportSubmenu menu twice so that the SupportSubmenu layer is invisible as well. Now save your page and browse it. You will see that the only layer that is visible is the mainMenu layer, as seen in Figure 25.9.

TIP

Even if a layer is set to be hidden, it is visible if it is selected in the Layers task pane.

ADDING LAYER INTERACTIVITY

Now you need to add some interactivity. Remember that the ProdSubmenu layer needs to be made visible when a user hovers over the Products button. To add that interactivity, you will use the Change Property Behavior to change the Visibility property for the ProdSubmenu layer.

→ For more information on the Change Property Behavior, **see** "The Change Property Behavior," on **p. 454**, and Change Property Restore Behavior," **p. 457**.

Figure 25.9
The main menu appears, but all other layers are hidden.

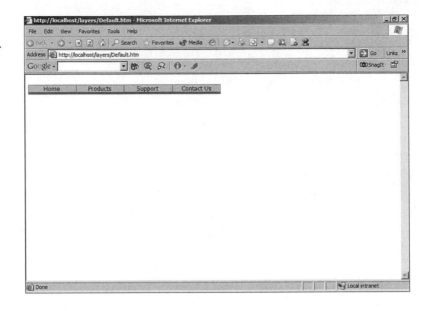

CONFIGURING THE PRODUCTS SUBMENU

Click the Other Task Panes dropdown in the Layers task pane and select Behavior or select Format, Behaviors to display the Behaviors task pane. To add the interactivity for the Products submenu, follow these steps:

1. Select the Products button.
2. In the Behaviors task pane, click the Insert button.

> **NOTE**
> Behaviors will already be listed for each of your Interactive Buttons. These are the Behaviors that FrontPage added automatically to make your Interactive Buttons work.

3. Select Change Property from the Behaviors menu.
4. Select the Select Element radio button.
5. Select div from the Element Type dropdown.
6. Select ProdSubmenu from the Element ID dropdown.
7. Click the Visibility button.
8. Select the Visible radio button and click OK.
9. Make sure that the Restore on Mouseout Event check box is unchecked.
10. Click OK to add the Behavior.
11. Locate the Behavior in the Behaviors task pane and change the Events from onclick to onmouseover. The Behavior will change position in the Behaviors task pane when the event is changed.

Now if you browse the page, the ProdSubmenu layer will appear when you hover over the Products menu. However, there is a problem. The Products submenu will never disappear unless you reload the page. You want the Products submenu to disappear if the user moves the mouse off the menu.

 If the submenu does not appear when you hover over the Products button, **see** *"Behaviors Don't Work" in the "Troubleshooting" section of this chapter.*

Switch to the Layers task pane and select the ProdSubmenu layer to make it visible so that you can apply the Behaviors to it. Without deselecting the ProdSubmenu layer, switch to the Behaviors task pane.

To configure the ProdSubmenu layer so that it disappears at the correct time, follow these steps.

1. Select Insert, Change Property to display the Change Property dialog.
2. Leave the Current Element option selected.
3. Click the Visibility button and select the Hidden option.
4. Click OK.
5. Make sure that the Restore on Mouseout Event box is unchecked.
6. Click OK.
7. In the Behaviors task pane, change the Events column from onclick to onmouseout.

Now the Products button is configured to show the submenu when you hover over it, and the ProductSubmenu layer is configured to hide itself when you move the mouse outside the menu.

Save and test your page to see how it's working out so far. Hover over the Products button, and you'll notice that the ProductSubmenu layer appears. Move the mouse over the ProductSubmenu layer, and you'll notice a problem. When you hover over the buttons on the ProductSubmenu layer, the entire menu disappears! This is obviously not what you expect to happen. To correct this, you need to add a Behavior to each button on the ProductSubmenu layer.

Switch back to FrontPage, activate the Layers task pane, and select the ProdSubmenu layer to make it visible again. Switch to the Behaviors task pane and configure the Behaviors for each button as follows:

1. Select the Software Interactive Button.
2. In the Behaviors task pane, select Insert, Change Property.

NOTE

Several Behaviors will already be listed for the Software button. These are the Behaviors that FrontPage added automatically to implement the functionality of your Interactive Button.

25

3. Select the Select Element option.

4. Select div in the Element Type dropdown.

5. Select ProdSubmenu from the Element ID dropdown.

6. Click the Visibility button.

7. Select the Visible option.

8. Click OK.

9. Make sure that the Restore on Mouseout Event check box is unchecked.

10. Click OK.

11. Change the onclick event to onmouseover.

Perform the same steps for the Hardware Interactive Button. After configuring the Hardware button, save and preview your page in the browser. Hover over the Products button to display the Products submenu, and then hover over the Software and the Hardware buttons. Move the mouse below the Products submenu and notice that the menu disappears as expected.

One problem still remains. If you hover over the Products button and then move the mouse off the Products button to any other button or off the menu itself without hovering over the submenu, the ProdSubmenu layer will remain visible. You actually want the ProdSubmenu layer to disappear if a user hovers over one of the other mainMenu layer buttons, or if the user moves the mouse off the menu altogether. To correct that, follow these steps:

1. Switch back to FrontPage.

2. Select the Home button.

3. Switch to the Behaviors task pane.

4. Select Insert, Change Property.

5. Select the Select Element option.

6. Select div from the Element Type dropdown.

7. Select ProdSubmenu from the Element ID dropdown.

8. Click the Visibility button.

9. Select the Hidden option.

10. Click OK.

11. Make sure that the Restore on Mouseout Event check box is unchecked.

12. Click OK.

13. Change the onclick event to onmouseover.

Make the same Behavior configuration change for the Support button. After you've done that, create a new Behavior for the mainMenu layer that will hide the ProdSubmenu layer as follows:

1. Select the mainMenu layer.
2. From the Behaviors task pane, select Insert, Change Property.
3. Select the Select Element option.
4. Select div from the Element Type dropdown.
5. Select ProdSubMenu from the Element ID dropdown.
6. Click the Visibility button.
7. Select the Hidden option.
8. Click OK.
9. Make sure that the Restore on Mouseout Event check box is unchecked.
10. Click OK.
11. Change the event from onclick to onmouseout.

Save your page and browse it to preview the menu. The Products submenu should now work perfectly and should display and hide itself in response to the correct events.

Configuring the Support Submenu

The next step is to configure the Support submenu. The steps are the same as the steps you completed for the Products submenu.

1. Create a Behavior for the Support button to display the SupportSubmenu layer in the onmouseover event.
2. Create a Behavior for the FAQ and Ask Us buttons to display the SupportSubmenu layer in the onmouseover event.
3. Create a Behavior for the SupportSubmenu layer that hides the SupportSubmenu layer in the onmouseout event.
4. Create a Behavior for the Products and Contact Us buttons that hides the SupportSubmenu layer in the onmouseover event.
5. Create a Behavior for the mainMenu layer that hides the SupportSubmenu layer in the onmouseout event.

Save the page again and preview it. Your dynamic menu should be fully functional at this point.

TROUBLESHOOTING

Layers Task Pane Is Disabled

I can pull up the Layers task pane, but I can't select anything on it because everything's disabled.

Layers rely on absolute positioning, a feature of the Cascading Style Sheets (CSS) 2.0 specification. If your authoring settings in FrontPage are configured so that CSS 2.0 is not enabled, you will not be able to access any of the settings on the Layers task pane.

To enable CSS 2.0 features in FrontPage, select Tools, Page Options and click the Authoring tab. Make sure that the CSS 1.0 (formatting) and CSS 2.0 (positioning) check boxes are checked.

BEHAVIORS DON'T WORK

I configured the Behaviors for my menu, but they don't do anything.

When you insert a Behavior, the event defaults to onclick. If you are expecting the Behavior to work when you hover the mouse on a page element, but you forget to change the onclick event to onmouseover, the Behavior will not work.

Make sure that you always change the event if necessary.

FRONT AND CENTER: BUILDING NESTED MENU SYSTEMS

The dynamic page you created in this chapter demonstrated the power behind layers in FrontPage when combined with other features. However, the menu system you built is not as powerful as it could be. Most menu systems are nested instead of being single layer. The Layers task pane and Behaviors feature of FrontPage will allow you to create a nested menu feature with little additional effort.

1. Create a new layer and change the ID to **Nested**.
2. Add two Interactive Buttons to the new layer. Use **Nested 1** for the text on one button and **Nested 2** for the text on the other.
3. Resize the layer so that it is the same size as the two Interactive Buttons.
4. Position the new layer next to the Software button, as shown in Figure 25.10.

Figure 25.10
Adding a nested sub-menu is easy with Layers and Behaviors.

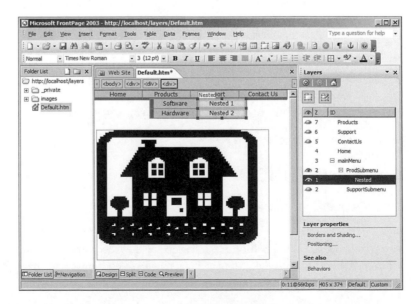

Now you need to add some new Behaviors to control the nested submenu. First, add a new Behavior to the Software button that displays the Nested layer in the onmouseover event.

1. Display the ProdSubmenu layer and select the Software button.
2. Switch to the Behaviors task pane and select Insert, Change Property.
3. Select the Select Element option.
4. Select div in the Element Type dropdown.
5. Select Nested in the Element ID dropdown.
6. Click the Visibility button.
7. Select the Visible option and click OK.
8. Change the event from onclick to onmouseover.

The new nested submenu will now appear when you hover over the Software button. If you'll remember how the other submenus were configured, you know already that we need a few more Behaviors for this to work right. We need

- A Behavior on each of the buttons in the Nested layer that changes the Visibility property of the Nested layer to Visible when you hover over them.
- A Behavior on the Nested layer that hides the Nested layer when the mouse moves off it.
- A Behavior on the Nested layer that hides the ProdSubmenu layer when the mouse moves off the Nested layer.
- A Behavior on the ProdSubmenu layer that hides the Nested layer when the mouse moves off the ProdSubmenu layer.
- A Behavior on each of the buttons in the Nested layer that changes the Visibility property of the ProdSubMenu layer to Visible when you hover over them.

To add these Behaviors, follow these steps:

1. Switch to the Layers task pane and display the ProdSubmenu layer and the Nested layer.
2. Switch to the Behaviors task pane.
3. Select the first button in the Nested layer.
4. In the Behaviors task pane, select Insert, Change Property.
5. Select the Select Element option.
6. Select div in the Element Type dropdown.
7. Select Nested in the Element ID dropdown.
8. Click the Visibility button.
9. Select the Visible option and click OK.
10. Click OK.
11. Change the event from onclick to onmouseover.

25

12. Complete steps 4–11 for the second button in the Nested layer.

13. Select the Nested layer.

14. From the Behaviors task pane, select Insert, Change Property.

15. Select the Current Element option.

16. Click the Visibility button.

17. Select the Hidden option and click OK.

18. Click OK.

19. Change the event from `onclick` to `onmouseout`.

20. From the Behaviors task pane, select Insert, Change Property.

21. Select the Select Element option.

22. Select div from the Element Type dropdown.

23. Select ProdSubmenu from the Element ID dropdown.

24. Click the Visibility button.

25. Select the Hidden option and click OK.

26. Click OK.

27. Change the `onclick` event to `onmouseout`.

28. Select the ProdSubmenu layer.

29. From the Behaviors task pane, select Insert, Change Property.

30. Select the Select Element option.

31. Select div from the Element Type dropdown.

32. Select Nested from the Element ID dropdown.

33. Click the Visibility button.

34. Select the Hidden option and click OK.

35. Click OK.

36. Change the `onclick` event to `onmouseout`.

Add a Behavior to each Interactive Button in the Nested layer. Connect the Behavior to the `onmouseover` event, and set the visibility of the Products layer to `Visible` in that event. As a final step, add another Behavior for each button in the Nested layer for the `onmouseover` event. In the event, change the visibility property of the ProdSubMenu layer to `Visible`.

Now switch back to the Layers task pane and make the ProdSubmenu and the Nested layer invisible. Save the page and browse to it to see your completed nested dynamic menu in action.

Using the lessons you've learned in this chapter, you can easily create a very complex menu system and Web page using Layers and Behaviors without knowing anything about writing client-side script. Even if you know how to write script to accomplish these tasks, you might find yourself preferring the Layers task pane and the Behaviors task pane because of the sheer amount of time that they will save you.

WORKING WITH CODE

WORKING IN CODE VIEW AND SPLIT VIEW

In this chapter

EDITING HTML AND SCRIPT

FrontPage certainly excels at being a WYSIWYG design tool, but there are times when editing code directly is your best option. FrontPage 2003 is the first FrontPage release that directly caters to professional developers in this area, and it does so in a very big way. From IntelliSense to full-page color-coding, FrontPage 2003 is a full-featured code editor.

> **TIP**
>
> FrontPage 2003 allows you to enter code bookmarks so that you can easily mark specific lines of code in your page.
>
> To insert a code bookmark, make sure that line numbers are enabled, place the insertion point anywhere on the line where you want the bookmark, and press Ctrl+F2. You can then easily locate the line later because FrontPage puts a colored block in the margin.
>
> Bookmarks are not saved with the page, so after closing the page, the bookmark will be gone.

→ For more information on setting line numbers, **see** "Code Formatting Options", **p. 524**.

The familiar HTML view has been replaced in FrontPage 2003 by two different views; Split view and Code view.

- **Split view**—A split between Code view at the top and Design view at the bottom.
- **Code view**—The page's code appears in the full window. This view is the same as HTML view in previous versions.

Split view (see Figure 26.1) is a feature that FrontPage developers have wanted for a long time. In previous versions of FrontPage, it was often difficult to synchronize Design view and HTML view, making it hard to tweak HTML code for complex pages. Split view was designed to address this problem.

By selecting an element on the page in one part of the view, it is automatically selected in the other, making it simple to edit code for complex page elements such as tables. You can select page elements using the QuickTag Selector or by clicking on the item itself. In the Code view pane, clicking on the opening tag for an element will select that entire element in the Design view pane.

→ For more information on using the QuickTag Selector, **see** "Selecting Code with the QuickTag Selector," **p. 530**.

> **TIP**
>
> To adjust the splitter between Design view and Code view, move the mouse pointer over the splitter between the two panes until the pointer changes to an up and down arrow and then drag the splitter to the desired position.

Figure 26.1
Split view allows you to easily synchronize Design view and Code view.

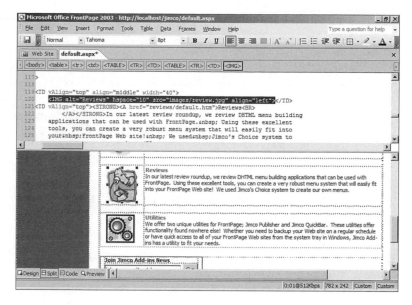

USING THE INTELLISENSE FEATURE

Entering and editing code has been made much more user-friendly with the introduction of IntelliSense. To see IntelliSense in action, perform these steps:

1. Create a new blank page.
2. Switch to Code view by clicking the Code tab.
3. Place the insertion point after the opening <body> tag and press Enter.
4. Press < to begin a new HTML tag.
5. IntelliSense displays a list of all applicable HTML tags for the current location, as seen in Figure 26.2.

26

Figure 26.2
IntelliSense provides quick access to applicable code entries.

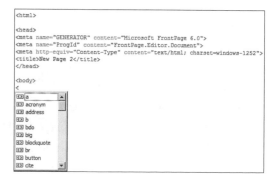

6. Select the `table` tag by either scrolling down to `table`, by pressing T, or by clicking on `table`.

7. Insert the `table` tag by pressing Space.

> **TIP**
>
> You can enter the currently selected item in IntelliSense by pressing Tab, Space, or Enter. Space has the advantage of inserting a space after the selected item, which is convenient if you need to insert another attribute prior to closing the tag. For the purpose of the examples in this chapter, Space will be used.

8. IntelliSense displays a list of all attributes of the `table` tag.

9. Select the `border` attribute by scrolling to `border`, by pressing B+O, or by clicking on `border`.

10. Insert the `border` attribute by pressing Space.

11. Type `="0">` after the border attribute to set the border to 0.

Note that after you typed the > character, FrontPage automatically inserted a closing `</table>` tag for you. You can now enter as many table rows and cells you would like by inserting `<tr>` and `<td>` tags, respectively. IntelliSense allows you to quickly insert these tags.

→ For more information on inserting and using tables in FrontPage, **see** "Using Tables," **p. 189**.

ADDING TAG ATTRIBUTES USING INTELLISENSE

You probably noticed that each time you inserted a new HTML tag, IntelliSense displayed a list of attributes for that HTML tag. You might not have noticed that IntelliSense will also provide you with applicable values for many of these attributes. Tables provide an excellent example of this because many attributes are available for `table` tags, `tr` tags, and `td` tags. Perform the following steps to add tag attributes:

1. Insert a table with default settings on to a new page.

2. Place the insertion point immediately after the r in a `<tr>` tag.

3. Press Space.

4. IntelliSense displays a list of all attributes of the `tr` tag.

5. Select the `align` attribute by clicking on `align` or by pressing A.

6. Insert the `align` attribute by pressing Space.

7. Type `="` to indicate that you are entering a value for the `align` attribute.

8. IntelliSense displays a list of all applicable values for the `align` attribute.

9. Select `center` by pressing C.

10. Insert the `center` value by pressing Space.

11. Type `"` to close the attribute value.

Using this method, you can very easily enter code to your Web page without having to remember all the attributes and values.

SETTING INTELLISENSE OPTIONS

IntelliSense options are controlled by selecting Tools, Page Options, and clicking the IntelliSense tab. Auto Popup options specify when IntelliSense's popup list is displayed, and Auto Insert options control what is automatically inserted when entering code.

The following Auto Popup options are available:

- **HTML statement completion**—Enables IntelliSense for HTML tags and HTML attributes.

- **Scripting statement completion**—Enables IntelliSense for client-side scripts.

- **Script parameter information**—Enables IntelliSense for client-side script parameters such as parameters passed to functions, and so on.

The following Auto Insert options are available:

- **Close tag**—If checked, automatically enters a close tag for applicable tags when the start tag is entered. A close tag is applicable if a close tag is valid for the HTML tag entered and if you have not configured the tag to omit a close tag in the Code Formatting tab.

- **HTML attribute value quotes**—If checked, HTML attributes selected from IntelliSense are automatically enclosed in quotes.

- **XSL attribute value quotes**—If checked, XSL attributes selected from IntelliSense are automatically enclosed in quotes.

COLOR CODING HTML AND SCRIPTING CODE

Color coding has been much improved in FrontPage 2003. You can now control all elements of your HTML and scripting code. You can control colors displayed in Design view as well as Code view.

→ For more information on color coding for elements in Design view as opposed to Code view, **see** "FrontPage's Views," **p. 61**.

To customize colors used in Code view, select Tools, Page Options, and click the Color Coding tab (see Figure 26.3). The color entries on the left side of the dialog apply to Code view. The entries on the right apply to elements within Design view.

26

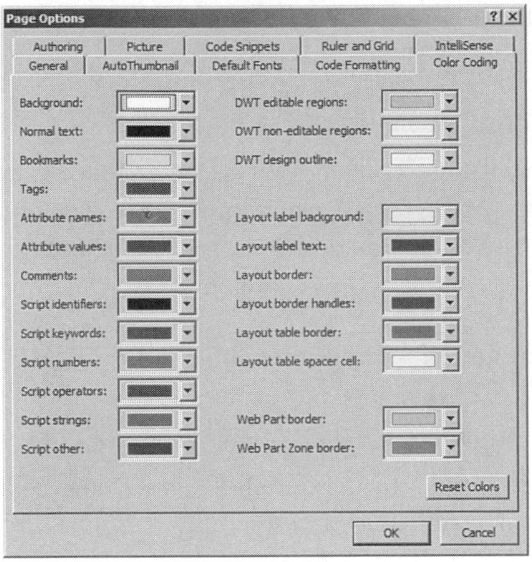

Figure 26.3
The Color Coding tab
of the Page Options
dialog provides com-
plete control over
color coding of code
and design elements.

You can adjust the color of the following items:

■ **Background**—The background color of the page in Code view. This setting does not
affect the background of the page in Design view or when viewing in a browser.

■ **Normal text**—Text that is not part of an HTML tag or script.

■ **Bookmarks**—The color of code bookmarks.

■ **Tags**—HTML tags.

■ **Attribute names**—Attributes of HTML tags.

■ **Attribute values**—Values of HTML tag attributes.

■ **Comments**—HTML and client-side script comments.

■ **Script identifiers**—Variable names and function names in client-side script.

■ **Script keywords**—Keywords in client-side script.

■ **Script numbers**—Numeric values in client-side script.

■ **Script operators**—Operators in client-side script (that is, =, +, &, and so on).

■ **Script strings**—Strings (text values) in client-side script.

■ **Script other**—Script not recognized by FrontPage. ASP and ASP.NET scripts fall into
this category.

Clicking the Reset Colors button will reset all colors to their default values.

CODE FORMATTING OPTIONS

The Code Formatting tab of the Page Options dialog (shown in Figure 26.4) gives you
extensive control over how code is formatted in Code view.

Figure 26.4
Control over how code is formatted is specified in the Code Formatting tab of the Page Options dialog.

 If you make a change to formatting and it doesn't take effect, see "Formatting Changes Don't Take Effect" in the "Troubleshooting" section of this chapter.

The Code Formatting tab allows you to configure the following settings:

- **Tag names are lowercase**—If checked, HTML tags are added in lowercase. Also causes HTML tags appearing in IntelliSense to appear in lowercase.

- **Attribute names are lowercase**—If checked, tag attributes are added in lowercase. Also causes attributes appearing in IntelliSense to appear in lowercase.

- **Allow line breaks within tags**—If checked, line breaks are added inside HTML tags once the tag length reaches the number of characters specified in the Right margin box.

- **Tab size**—The number of spaces represented by a press of the Tab key. The size of a single space depends on the font selected on the Default Fonts tab.

- **Indent # tabs/spaces**—The number of characters inserted when code is indented. The dropdown determines whether the characters inserted are spaces or tabs.

- **Right margin**—The number of characters before a line break is inserted. If Allow line breaks within tags is not checked, FrontPage will not insert a line break within a tag even if the right margin has been reached.

- **Insert tabs as spaces**—If checked, will insert spaces instead of tabs when indenting code. The number of spaces inserted per tab is indicated by the value entered in the Tab size box.

- **Tags**—Allows for configuration of specific HTML tags. By selecting a specific tag from the list, you can modify settings specific to that tag.

- **Base on current page**—Clicking this button will set code formatting options based on the page currently active.
- **Reset**—Resets all code formatting options to their defaults.

> **NOTE**
>
> Changes made in the Code Formatting tab apply only to the appearance of code in FrontPage's Code view. They do not affect the appearance of the page when viewed in a browser.

 If you notice lines breaking before reaching the specified right margin setting, see "Lines Breaking Too Soon" in the "Troubleshooting" section at the end of this chapter.

By selecting a specific HTML tag in the Tag list, you can configure the following settings, which apply only to that tag:

- **Line breaks before start**—The number of line breaks inserted before the start tag.
- **Line breaks before end**—The number of line breaks inserted before the end tag.
- **Line breaks after start**—The number of line breaks inserted after the start tag.
- **Line breaks after end**—The number of line breaks inserted after the end tag.
- **Omit start tag**—If checked, the start tag for the selected tag is omitted.
- **Omit end tag**—If checked, the end tag for the selected tag is omitted.
- **Indent contents**—If checked, tags that are enclosed within the selected tag are indented.

The Omit Start Tag, Omit End Tag, and Indent Contents check boxes are enabled and disabled based on the tag that is currently selected. For example, because the `<form>` tag requires both start and end tags, the Omit Start Tag and the Omit End Tag check boxes are disabled. Likewise, when tags that cannot contain child tags are selected (such as the `<br>` tag), the Indent Contents check box is disabled.

> **TIP**
>
> Many ASP developers have a need to create pages that have no `<html>` or `<body>` tags. By selecting each one of these tags and checking the Omit Start Tag and the Omit End Tag check boxes, FrontPage will allow you to create pages without `<html>` and `<body>` tags.

FrontPage 2003 also provides options for code display on the General tab of the Page Options dialog, as shown in Figure 26.5.

Figure 26.5
The General tab provides basic display options for the Code view.

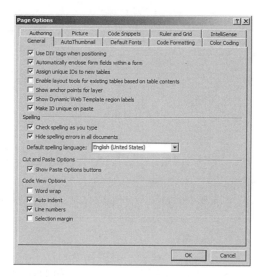

The following Code view options are available:

- **Word wrap**—Forces lines to wrap at the right edge of the document window.

- **Auto indent**—Automatically indents lines of code as necessary to line them up with previous lines.

- **Line numbers**—Displays lines numbers in the left side of the document window. Note that enabling line numbers will automatically also show the Selection margin even if the Selection Margin box is not checked.

- **Selection margin**—Displays a shaded left margin for quick selection of lines of code. Clicking inside this margin on a particular line selects that line of code. Dragging the mouse down multiple lines selects multiple lines of code.

TROUBLESHOOTING

FORMATTING CHANGES DON'T TAKE EFFECT

I have changed some of the formatting options, but these changes aren't affecting my code. Why not?

Changes made on the Code Formatting tab of the Page Options dialog only apply in two cases; code that has not been changed in any way since FrontPage generated it and new code that is generated after the change is applied. Any existing code is unchanged by formatting changes.

LINES BREAKING TOO SOON

I have set the right margin to 80 characters, but my lines are breaking before reaching 80 characters. Why?

Make sure that you don't have Word Wrap enabled on the General tab of the Page Options dialog. If Word Wrap is enabled, lines will wrap at the right edge of the document window regardless of whether they have reached the right margin set on the Code Formatting tab.

FRONT AND CENTER: SAVING CUSTOMIZED HTML TAGS

A common troubleshooting step when FrontPage won't launch is to delete the HKEY_CURRENT_USER\Software\Microsoft\FrontPage Registry key. FrontPage re-creates that key when launched, and if there is corruption in that key, removing it will often resolve launching problems.

Keep in mind, however, that FrontPage stores important information in this key, and one of those things is all of your code formatting settings for individual HTML tags. These are stored in the following Registry location:

HKEY_CURRENT_USER\Software\Microsoft\FrontPage\Editor\HTML\<tag>

If you have customized the properties for HTML tags and you are going to remove the FrontPage Registry key in an attempt to troubleshoot a startup problem, you might want to first export the key containing your HTML tag customizations. You can then merge this information back in to FrontPage after FrontPage re-creates the FrontPage Registry key.

To export your HTML tag code settings, perform these steps:

1. Open Registry Editor by selecting Start, Run, entering **Regedit**, and clicking OK.
2. Click the plus sign next to HKEY_CURRENT_USER.
3. Click the plus sign next to Software.
4. Click the plus sign next to Microsoft.
5. Click the plus sign next to FrontPage.
6. Click the plus sign next to Editor.
7. Right-click on the HTML key and select Export.
8. In the Filename box, enter **FPTagsBackup**.
9. Click Save.

This will save a file called FPTagsBackup.reg on your Desktop. Anytime that you need to reapply your HTML tag code formatting settings, simply double-click this file and click Yes when asked to confirm that you want to merge the file into your Registry.

CHAPTER 27

EDITING CODE WITH QUICK TAG TOOLS

In this chapter

OVERVIEW OF THE QUICK TAG TOOLS

The Quick Tag Tools provide you with a powerful method for analyzing and editing code in your FrontPage Web site. The Quick Tag Tools are a combination of two features: the *Quick Tag Selector* and the *Quick Tag Editor*. The Quick Tag Selector can be used to select code in Code view or Split view, or it can be used to easily select items in Design view. The Quick Tag Editor provides a robust set of options for editing HTML tags in your code.

→ For more information on working in Code view or Split view, **see** "Working in Code View and Split View," **p. 519**.

→ For more information on working in Design view, **see** "Working with Page Related Views," **p. 64**.

SELECTING CODE WITH THE QUICK TAG SELECTOR

The Quick Tag Selector (shown in Figure 27.1) is a toolbar that appears at the top of the document window in Design view, Split view, and Code view. Each tag in the Quick Tag Selector toolbar is represented by a *tag selector*, a button that allows you to easily select the tag and perform editing actions on it.

The Quick Tag Selector toolbar

Figure 27.1
The Quick Tag Selector makes selecting specific HTML tags fast and easy.

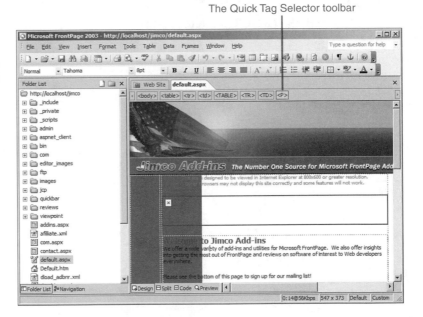

 If you do not see the Quick Tag Selector toolbar, *see "Quick Tag Selectors Don't Appear" in the "Troubleshooting" section at the end of this chapter.*

As you navigate through your Web page, the tag selectors change to reflect the location of the insertion point. Tag selectors are available for the tag at the insertion point's current location as well as all of that tag's parent tags. In other words, if the insertion point is inside a <FONT> tag that appears inside a table cell, you will have a tag selector for the <FONT> tag, <TD> tag, <TR> tag, <TABLE> tag, and—assuming that the table is not nested—the <BODY> tag as shown in Figure 27.2.

Figure 27.2
Tag selectors appear for tags based on your current location in the document.

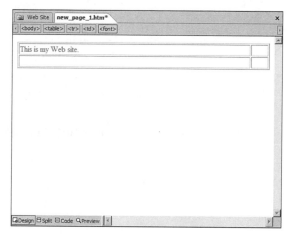

As you hover over tag selectors in Design view, FrontPage will draw a box around the page element represented by the tag selector you are hovering over. This makes it very easy to determine exactly which tag represents a specific element. After you have identified the correct tag selector for the element you want to select, click on the tag selector to select that element, as shown in Figure 27.3.

Figure 27.3
Selecting page elements in Design view is made simple with tag selectors.

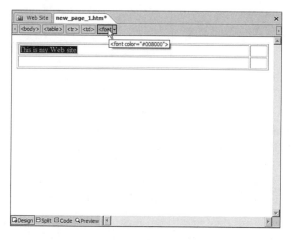

The tag selector for the currently selected tag will be highlighted in blue and will have a dark blue border. If the number of tag selectors exceeds the number that can be displayed in one row of the Quick Tag Selector, you can use the Scroll Left and Scroll Right buttons on the left and right side of the Quick Tag Selector to display additional tag selectors.

> **TIP**
>
> If you hover over a tag selector, a ScreenTip will display the entire HTML tag and all of its attributes.

By right-clicking the tag selector or by hovering over the tag selector and clicking the arrow button, you can access the options menu for the tag as seen in Figure 27.4. Selecting <u>S</u>elect Tag from this menu is the same as clicking the tag selector. Selecting Select Tag <u>C</u>ontents from the options menu allows you to select only the contents of the tag and not the tag itself. This is a useful way to select, for example, all the contents of a table cell without selecting the table cell itself.

The other items on the options menu are options for the Quick Tag Editor, which is discussed in the next section.

Figure 27.4
The options menu allows you greater control over what is selected.

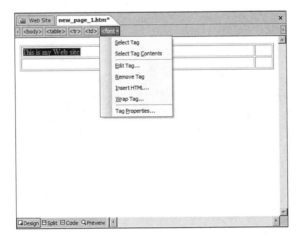

EDITING CODE WITH THE QUICK TAG EDITOR

The Quick Tag Editor is where the true power of the Quick Tag Tools exists. Using the Quick Tag Editor, you can easily examine an HTML tag, change the HTML tag, or completely replace the HTML tag. FrontPage provides color-coding and IntelliSense for code editing within the Quick Tag Editor making it a full-featured tool for editing specific areas of code.

→ For more information on using IntelliSense, **see** "Using the IntelliSense Feature," **p. 521**.

To best get an idea of how all the Quick Tag Editor tools operate, let's create a simple page you can use to experiment with this powerful toolset:

1. Open a Web site or create a new Web site.
2. Create an empty Web page.
3. Insert a table with the default settings.

4. Place the insertion point inside the upper-left cell and insert another table using default settings inside that cell.

5. Click inside the upper-left cell of the table created in step 4.

6. Enter `Using the Quick Tag Editor is easy!` in to the table cell, as shown in Figure 27.5.

Figure 27.5
This page is used throughout the chapter to experiment with the Quick Tag Tools.

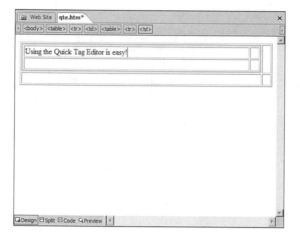

7. Select the text and change the font color to red.

8. Save the page.

You will use this page throughout this chapter to experiment with the Quick Tag Editor.

To access the Quick Tag Editor, either click the arrow button on a tag selector or right-click the tag selector to access the Options menu seen in Figure 27.4. The following Quick Tag Editor options are available to you:

- **Edit Tag**—Displays the Quick Tag Editor dialog, which allows you to make changes to the HTML code for the tag.

- **Remove Tag**—Removes the selected HTML tag, but not the contents wrapped by the HTML tag.

- **Insert HTML**—Displays the Quick Tag Editor dialog, which allows you to insert HTML.

- **Wrap Tag**—Wraps the current tag with the HTML tag entered.

- **Tag Properties**—Displays the Properties dialog for the selected tag if applicable. If the selected tag does not have a Properties dialog, a Modify Style dialog for the selected tag is displayed.

27

THE EDIT TAG OPTION

The Edit Tag option displays the Quick Tag Editor dialog with the selected HTML tag ready for editing, as shown in Figure 27.6. The code displayed in this dialog is fully color-coded, and FrontPage provides full IntelliSense support.

Figure 27.6
The Edit Tag option allows for fast editing of your HTML tags.

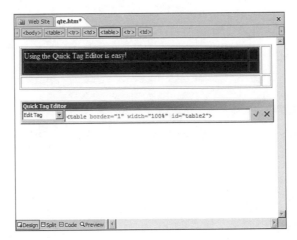

Open the Web page you created and click anywhere inside the text you entered in to the table cell. Notice that a tag selector appears for the <FONT> tag, and if you hover over that tag, a dark border appears around the text you entered. This feature of the Quick Tag Selector makes it simple to select exactly the tag you need when using the Quick Tag Tools.

Suppose you have defined a CSS class called `tableText` that will be used to format any table text in your Web pages. You want to apply the style defined in that class to the text in the table cell. Although you can certainly use Split view to locate the <FONT> tag in code and then edit it there, the Quick Tag Editor makes quick work of the task.

To edit the <FONT> tag so that your CSS class applies to it, follow these steps:

1. Right-click the tag selector for the <FONT> tag or click the arrow button on the tag selector.
2. Select <u>E</u>dit Tag from the Options menu.
3. Place the insertion point just to the left of the closing tag delimiter for the <FONT> tag.
4. Press Space to display IntelliSense for the <FONT> tag, as shown in Figure 27.7.
5. Double-click Class from the IntelliSense popup to insert the `class` attribute.
6. Add the following text after the `class` attribute:
   `="tableText"`
7. Click the green check button or press Enter to commit your code change.

➔ For more information on using CSS classes, **see** "Creating and Using CSS Classes," **p. 401**.

Figure 27.7
When you press Space, IntelliSense appears, making adding the class attribute effortless.

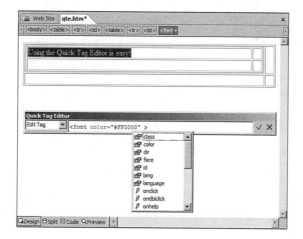

FrontPage will perform syntax checking on the HTML that you enter in to the Quick Tag Editor. If you enter invalid HTML and attempt to commit it to the page, FrontPage will display an error message (see Figure 27.8) and will not allow you to add the HTML to the page.

Figure 27.8
The Quick Tag Editor will not allow you to enter invalid HTML.

After adding the class attribute to the `<FONT>` tag, notice that the tag selector for that element changes to `<font.tableText>` to indicate the CSS class for the element, as shown in Figure 27.9. If you commonly format your Web pages using CSS classes, the tag selectors make it even more painless to quickly locate tags.

Figure 27.9
Tag selectors also indicate the CSS class where appropriate.

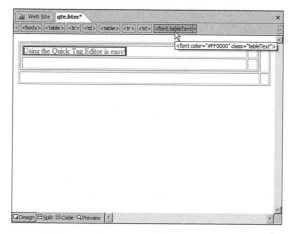

27

THE REMOVE TAG OPTION

The Remove Tag option allows you to quickly remove a tag wrapping other HTML elements. This option is only available when the current tag selector represents an HTML tag that is an optional container for other HTML elements. In other words, you can remove a <FONT> tag around some text or a <P> tag around an element because they are optional tags. However, you cannot remove a <TR> tag from a table row because the <TR> tag is not optional.

To use the Remove Tag option, follow these steps:

1. Click inside the text to display the <font.tableText> tag selector.
2. Right-click the <font.tableText> tag selector or click the down arrow to display the Options menu.
3. Select Remove Tag from the Options menu.

When you remove the tag, the <FONT> tag is removed (see Figure 27.10), but the text contained within the <FONT> tag is retained. Because the tag you removed was responsible for formatting the text, the formatting that you previously applied to the text is removed as well.

Figure 27.10
After removing the
<font.
tableText> tag,
the text remains.

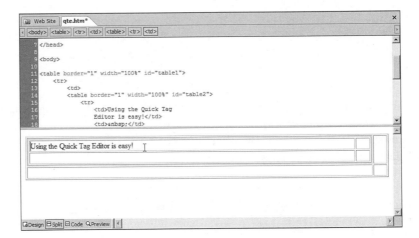

TIP

To easily tell which part of a page is affected by a tag, hover over the tag selector and FrontPage will draw a dark border around the area.

If you display the Options menu for the <TABLE> tag, you'll notice that the <u>R</u>emove Tag menu option is disabled. Once again, the Remove Tag menu option will always be disabled when removing the selected tag will result in invalid HTML on the page. In the case of the <TABLE> tag, removing it would leave <TD> and <TR> tags without a corresponding <TABLE> tag, which would not be valid HTML.

27

THE INSERT HTML OPTION

The Insert HTML option allows you to insert HTML in to your document. The behavior of the Insert HTML option is sometimes hard to predict because it will insert the code in different places depending on whether you have text selected. When you insert HTML using the Insert HTML option, the HTML is inserted at the location of the insertion point if no page elements are selected. If any part of the page is selected, the HTML that you enter is inserted immediately to the left of the tag closest to the selection.

In order to truly understand how the Insert HTML option works in different situations, it's best to try out an example.

1. Create a new page in FrontPage.
2. Place the insertion point on the page and press Enter.
3. Enter the text **Inserting HTML is easy.** and press Enter.
4. Click the Split button to switch to Split view so that you can easily see the text both in Design view and in Code view.
5. Click to place the insertion point right before the "e" in the word "easy."
6. Right-click the <P> tag selector or click the arrow button to display the Options menu.
7. Select Insert HTML from the Options menu.
8. Enter the following code in to the Quick Tag Editor, as shown in Figure 27.11.
   ```
   <font color="red">super</font> 
   ```
9. Click the check mark button or press Enter to commit the new HTML code.

Figure 27.11
Enter the code shown here in to the Quick Tag Editor to add HTML to your page.

Note that the word "super" now appears before the word "easy" and "super" appears in red. If you look in Code view, you'll see that the HTML you entered was inserted exactly at the insertion point's position, as shown in Figure 27.12.

TIP

The Quick Tag Editor dialog contains a dropdown box that allows you to quickly switch between Quick Tag Tools. Simply click the dropdown and choose Edit Tag, Wrap Tag, or Insert HTML.

27

Figure 27.12
The code you entered is inserted right where you placed the insertion point.

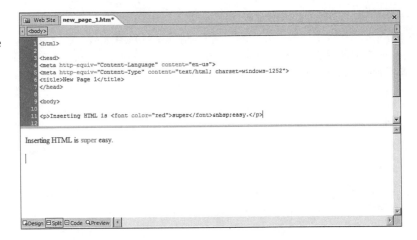

As you can see by this example, inserting HTML with the Insert HTML option is straightforward when you haven't selected anything before inserting the HTML. However, if you have selected a page element prior to inserting the HTML, figuring out where your HTML will go when you enter it takes a bit more work.

1. Select the word "super" that you inserted previously.
2. Right-click the <FONT> tag selector or click the arrow button to display the Options menu.
3. Select Insert HTML.
4. Type **strong** between the "<" and ">" characters in the Quick Tag Editor.
5. Click the green check mark button or press Enter to commit the code change.

> **NOTE**
>
> When entering code, the Insert HTML option will add an opening and closing <strong> tag to the page. FrontPage will always check the code you enter for validity. If you enter an opening tag but not a closing tag, FrontPage will automatically add the closing tag if it is required.

You might have thought that adding the <strong> tag with the Quick Tag Editor would surround the word "super" with <strong> tags, but instead, an empty set of <strong> tags appears just to the left of the <font> tag, as seen in Figure 27.13. Anytime you insert HTML with an active selection, the HTML you enter is inserted immediately to the left of the tag represented by the tag selector you choose. In other words, the Insert HTML option will never affect a selection. If you want to enter HTML that will format your selection, use the Edit HTML option or the Wrap Tag option instead.

Figure 27.13
The Insert HTML option will always insert the HTML to the left of your selection.

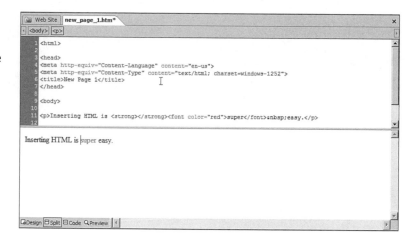

THE WRAP TAG OPTION

The Wrap Tag option will wrap an HTML tag with the tag you enter. The tag that is wrapped is determined by the tag selector you choose.

1. Select the word "super" that you inserted previously.
2. Right-click the <FONT> tag selector or click the arrow button to display the Options menu.
3. Select Wrap Tag from the Options menu.
4. Enter **\<strong\>** in the Quick Tag Editor dialog.
5. Click the check mark button or press Enter to commit the code.

The Wrap Tag option wraps the <FONT> tag with the HTML tag you enter in the Quick Tag Editor dialog. Once again, FrontPage will check the HTML you enter for validity. If the HTML you enter is not valid, FrontPage will warn you and will remove it.

You can wrap an HTML tag with more than one HTML tag by entering a series of HTML tags in the Quick Tag Editor. For example, in step 4, if you had entered **\<strong\>\<i\>** in the Quick Tag Editor dialog, the word "super" would have appeared as bold and italic text, as seen in Figure 27.14.

THE TAG PROPERTIES OPTION

The Tag Properties option will display a Properties dialog that is applicable to the type of HTML tag you have selected. For example, if you were to choose the Tag Properties option from a tag selector for the <STRONG> tag you entered, FrontPage will display the Font Properties dialog because the <STRONG> tag is a tag that formats fonts. If there is no Properties dialog for the tag that you have chosen, the Modify Style dialog is displayed as shown in Figure 27.15.

27

Figure 27.14
Using the Wrap Tag option, it is easy to surround an existing HTML tag with another tag.

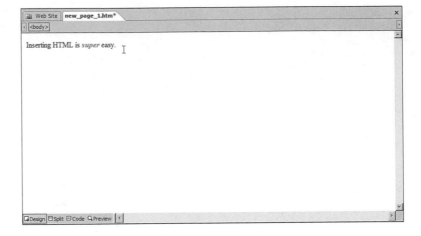

Figure 27.15
The Modify Style dialog appears if there is no applicable Properties dialog for the HTML tag you choose.

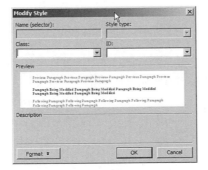

When changes are made in a Properties dialog, FrontPage will generate code automatically to affect those changes. In some cases, this might cause undesirable effects. To remove the <STRONG> tag from the text you've already entered, follow these steps:

1. Click anywhere on the word "super" that you inserted previously.
2. Right-click the <STRONG> tag selector or click the arrow button to display the Options menu.
3. Select Tag Properties.
4. In the Font Properties dialog, clear the check in the Strong check box.
5. Click OK.

When you remove the <STRONG> tag using this method, FrontPage also removes the <I> tag that you inserted. To correct that, follow these steps:

1. Right-click the <FONT> tag selector or click the arrow button to display the Options menu.

2. Select Tag _P_roperties.

3. In the Font Properties dialog, select Italic in the Font Style list, as seen in Figure 27.16.

Figure 27.16
The Font Properties dialog box is displayed using the Tag Properties option.

4. Click OK to commit your change.

If you now look at the code that FrontPage generated, you'll see that FrontPage didn't just add the `<I>` tag back. It also added a `<SPAN>` tag to format the text. This might not be what you expect to happen, so when editing code with Properties dialogs, it is sometimes useful to remain in Split view so that you can always see what code FrontPage has generated to represent the selections you made in the Properties dialog.

TROUBLESHOOTING

QUICK TAG SELECTORS DON'T APPEAR

I'm clicking around in Code view, but the Quick Tag Selector toolbar doesn't appear.

In certain situations when FrontPage has reformatted code in Code view, the Quick Tag Selector toolbar will not be visible. To display the Quick Tag Selector toolbar, switch to Design view and click the page.

FRONT AND CENTER: WHY USE QUICK TAG TOOLS?

Now that you know how to use the Quick Tag Tools, why would you want to use them as opposed to just editing your code in Code view? There are many answers to that question, but one of the most useful reasons to use the Quick Tag Tools is that you can edit your HTML code in a non-destructive manner.

If you edit your code in Code view, any changes you make are applied to your page in real-time. Usually this isn't a big deal, but if you make a mistake in your code editing inside of a complex page (such as a page with nested tables), it is easy to get the page into a state that is hard to get out of. FrontPage's undo feature will help in some cases, but it's not always a lifesaver if you aren't sure exactly what you did.

With the Quick Tag Tools, you can carefully edit HTML tags in the Quick Tag Editor dialog. If you make a mistake while editing a tag, you can stop and safely click the Cancel button and your change isn't applied to the page. If you're editing a complex style tag or other complex tag structures, the Quick Tag Tools are often the best method of tag editing.

CHAPTER 28

USING CODE SNIPPETS

In this chapter

THE CODE SNIPPETS TOOL

If you work a lot in Code view, you know that there are groups of code that you insert on a considerable basis. As you've already seen in Chapter 26, IntelliSense will help considerably on a word-by-word basis, but another tool will help you insert information in to your sites blocks at a time. If you are considering learning code to expand your design skills, an understanding of the Code Snippet tool will help you maximize your efforts.

→ For a detailed look on using IntelliSense during the coding process, **see** "Working in Code View and Split View," **p. 519**.

New to FrontPage 2003 is the Code Snippets tool that provides a simple means for quickly adding snippets of code in to your site without having to enter or paste the code directly in to your site. Although FrontPage 2003 comes with a small batch of Code Snippets installed, the true power in the product comes from developing your own and using them as needed. In this chapter, we'll examine how Code Snippets work, how to add them to your system, and how to use them to help you speed up your design process.

> **NOTE**
>
> Code Snippets only work in Code or Split view. You can't use them in Design view.

WORKING WITH CODE SNIPPETS

A code snippet is a short batch of code (HTML or script) or text that you can define and reuse many times with an easy keyboard shortcut. FrontPage has several predefined code snippets, but it also offers you the ability to build and edit your own.

To make the use of code snippets even easier, you can associate a keyword to the code snippet, letting you select and enter the snippet even quicker.

> **NOTE**
>
> Code Snippets are stored on the system they were entered or modified on. A code snippet library can't be transferred to another site or system.

USING CODE SNIPPETS

To use the Code Snippet tool, you must be in either Code view or the coding area of Design view. To open the Code Snippet box, press Ctrl+Enter. As shown in Figure 28.1, the Code Snippets box will open, allowing you to scroll through and pick the snippet of your choice. You can scroll through the choices with the arrow keys or your mouse. You can also enter the first letters of your keyword, and the list will jump to the desired location. Press Enter (or double-click) to select a snippet.

28

Figure 28.1
With the Code Snippet interface used in Code view, you can scroll through your choices and select with the Enter key.

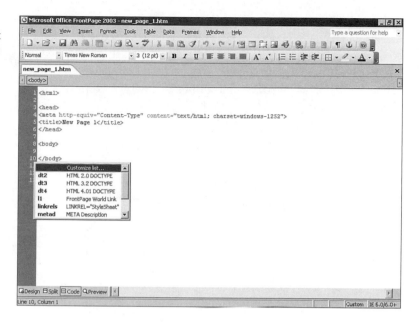

ADDING, MODIFYING, AND DELETING CODE SNIPPETS

The first option in the Code Snippet interface (seen in Figure 28.1) is the Customize List option. Selecting this option will open the Code Snippets tab in the Page Options dialog box, as seen in Figure 28.2. You can also access the Page Options dialog box by selecting Tools, Page Options.

Figure 28.2
Code snippets can be added to, modified, or removed from your system.

The Add and Modify buttons offer the same interface as shown in Figure 28.3. The three options allow you to enter a keyword for the snippet, a description of the snippet, and the snippet content. There is no limit to the size of the snippet.

Figure 28.3
There is no limit to the size of the snippet that you can create.

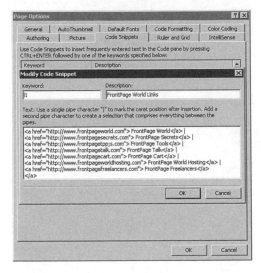

NOTE

Any code entered by hand into a code snippet is not validated by FrontPage. Double check that your code is good before you make it a snippet.

To delete a snippet from the list, click the Remove button.

NOTE

When you click the Remove button on the Page Options dialog box, there is no verification of your choice and there is no way to undo the delete.

 If you are having problems finding your code snippets, *see "Where Did My Snippets Go" in the "Troubleshooting" section at the end of this chapter.*

TIP

Make use of the free SnipView add-in that comes with the CD with this book. It manages your snippets for you and lets you back them up and move them around from computer to computer as needed. This product is exclusive to this book and can't be purchased online at any price.

28

USING CODE SNIPPETS TO SPEED UP DESIGN

The simple ability to quickly add code content to your site with the click of a button is obvious, but the following tips will help you make the most of the code snippets interface.

- **Keyword, keyword, keywords.** Now that you have optimized your coding process through the use of Code Snippets, don't waste time scrolling through your snippets to choose. A few letters of your keyword will quickly jump to the snippet of your choice and cut another half second off the process.

- **Let FrontPage do the hard work.** Code Snippets can expedite the development process if you have elements in your site that are entered over and over again. Use the Code Snippet tool to take the repetition out of your work.

- **Put some thought into your keyword scheme.** After just a little use of the Code Snippets tool, you will find that your snippets library is considerable in size. If you don't plan ahead of time and design a manageable keyword scheme, you will find yourself scrolling through your choices and taking considerable time to do so.

- **Don't limit your library.** If you use a batch of code more than just a few times, consider adding them to your library. A common link or menu item takes as much time to enter as does anything else. You aren't limited to the amount of items you can keep in your library, so don't limit yourself.

- **Think before you code.** Taking a short time to build a code snippet library before you start your project will speed up the design process considerably. Often once involved in the design process, a coder will seldom take the short time needed to add a snippet to the snippet library. Take the time needed before the project begins to create a good snippet library.

TROUBLESHOOTING

WHERE DID MY SNIPPETS GO?

I started to work on my site from another computer and wasn't able to use the Code Snippets I designed for the site. I connected to the site directly. What did I do wrong?

Code Snippets are stored on the computer they were entered on. If you are using another system, it won't have them installed. You will need to enter the snippets on any system where you intend to use them.

FRONT AND CENTER: NEVER UNDERESTIMATE THE POWER OF A SNIPPET

Take a look at the HTML or script of any page in your site. Notice how often the same batches of text and tags are repeated over and over? Even simple things such as the same text link can be found several times on a page or site, and for most developers, each instance is entered by hand.

Some smart coders use cut and paste for this kind of process, but that shortcut still requires going back and forth between your code to find the item. When used properly, Code Snippets can speed up any design project considerably.

If you are taking on a Web project of any size, you could easily identify a number of elements that will be used over and over again on your site. From items as basic as internal hyperlinks to issues a bit more complex such as client-side form field validation scripts, if an element is going to be used throughout a site, its addition as a Code Snippet should be considered.

In addition, if you design using CSS, the ability to place your styles as Code Snippets can quickly expedite your design process.

There are limits to the Code Snippet tool.

You can't save, export, or share your snippets. In some ways, this is good because it encourages each developer to create her own library, but it certainly discourages the combined efforts that could come from a team working together on a shared library.

In addition, because there is no external storage or archive system, your library will die if your system does. As a result, make sure that your system is backed up on a regular basis should something go wrong.

This is why we created the SnipView product mentioned previously in this chapter and located on the CD that comes with this book.

Not only do you have the upper hand with FrontPage 2003 and Code Snippets, but you just made it better by buying this book.

28

CHAPTER 29

OPTIMIZING FRONTPAGE'S HTML

In this chapter

FRONTPAGE AND HTML

FrontPage HTML. These two words, when used together, have caused more pain and strife for Microsoft and the average FrontPage user than either would care to admit. To be nice, in many ways FrontPage creates its own "flavor" of HTML that, finally, can be controlled with the tools provided by FrontPage 2003.

To understand how FrontPage can now optimize HTML, FrontPage's approach to HTML needs to be understood first. After that, the tools FrontPage 2003 offers to optimize FrontPage HTML can be examined and better understood. We'll do both in this chapter.

With FrontPage 2003, you can reformat existing HTML to a cleaner, more compliant format: An optimize HTML dialog box is now part of your toolset, and FrontPage can also optimize HTML during the publishing process so that the world will never know what program you used to create your Web page.

We'll start with a real-world example. Figures 29.1 and 29.2 show the HTML of a page created in a previous version of FrontPage before and after the page was considerably optimized by FrontPage 2003 through the publishing process.

In this chapter, we will show you how to get the best possible HTML with FrontPage 2003.

Figure 29.1
The last 28 lines of a 423 line "older" FrontPage HTML page loaded into FrontPage 2003.

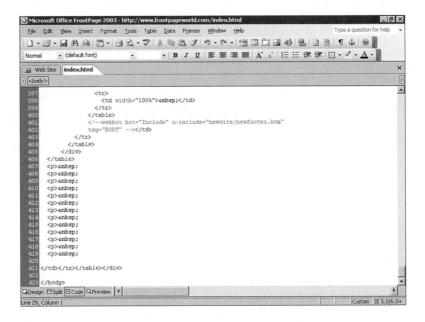

Figure 29.2
The page of HTML from Figure 29.1 after it has been published and optimized by FrontPage 2003. Note that the same page is now only 58 lines long.

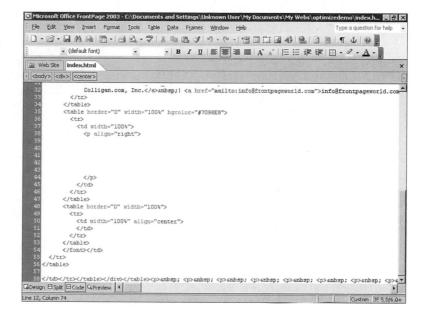

WHAT'S WRONG WITH FRONTPAGE'S HTML?

At a quick look, the HTML created by FrontPage seems harmless enough. Any user can quickly enter the Coding view and edit the HTML at will. It looks a lot like the HTML found all around the Net, doesn't it?

In short, FrontPage has three issues surrounding its use of HTML:

- The HTML produced by FrontPage isn't always that good. It has gotten better with each revision of FrontPage and now, Microsoft claims that the code produced by FrontPage 2003 is so clean that it is virtually interchangeable with products like Dreamweaver MX. We've seen nothing in the development of this chapter that would lead us to believe otherwise.

- A great number of legacy issues surround the way FrontPage produces HTML. From multiple tags for the same font to legacy and meta data added with the hover buttons, the "old" FrontPage HTML was much "fatter" than it needed to be.

- Because FrontPage writes HTML on-the-fly based on conditions in the site, it must include a considerable amount of metadata in the HTML.

For the first issue, take heart—FrontPage produces considerably better HTML than it ever has before. The other two issues are explored a bit deeper in the sections that follow. FrontPage 2003 offers help for all three of these issues and provides additional tools to further massage and clean up the style of HTML it produces.

 If you are having problems eliminating the FrontPage specific HTML, see "Make the FrontPage Specific HTML Go Away" in the "Troubleshooting" section at the end of this chapter.

LEGACY MARKUP ISSUES

Themes, navigation bars, include files, Web components, and the list goes on: All the tools that add to the HTML from FrontPage need FrontPage to write the HTML. Unlike simple design and markup HTML, FrontPage can't let you edit code associated with these elements because they require specific coding that changes as does the file and Web site.

For example, the addition of a new page to a site with a navigation bar across every header requires the addition of navigational metadata across every single page in the Web.

In order to use the tools described previously, the HTML produced by FrontPage must also contain whatever additional information is needed for these tools to provide the functionality they were implemented for. This information is commonly referred to as *metadata*.

In short, because a FrontPage Web site holds more than just traditional HTML markup, it makes sense that it will often contain more than just the HTML.

WHAT YOU SEE ISN'T WHAT IT CODES

If you use a FrontPage-specific tool (such as included content) in your FrontPage Web site, the HTML for that tool, as seen in the Coding view, is not the same HTML as is presented when you view your site.

There is no way around this because the core HTML needs to store FrontPage data (such as interactive button content, link bar locations, and so on) so that they can be quickly edited with the click of a button in the Design view. No option exists within FrontPage to turn off this feature because doing so would negate the product's power. If you use a FrontPage tool in the design process, you will need to let FrontPage write the appropriate HTML code as needed.

This is really only an issue if you are going to take HTML content directly from your FrontPage Web content on your desktop and move it to a Web server, circumventing the publishing features available with the product. If you need to do this, we recommend publishing the site from one area of your hard drive to another, allowing FrontPage to produce the optimized HTML that you adapt as needed.

 If you are having problems with FrontPage specific HTML and using Site Build It's HTML upload feature, see "Using FrontPage with Site Build It" in the "Troubleshooting" section at the end of this chapter.

→ For a detailed look at the publishing process, **see** "Publishing a FrontPage Web Site," **p. 299**.

USING THE OPTIMIZE HTML DIALOG BOX

All is not lost. An Optimize HTML dialog box, as seen in Figure 29.3, can be implemented on any page in your site and used to quickly clean up the HTML. Anything not specifically controlled by FrontPage-related features can be modified with this powerful tool. The tool can be called at any time (and as many times as needed) in the design process.

Figure 29.3
The Optimize HTML dialog box gives you considerable strength in optimizing your FrontPage HTML.

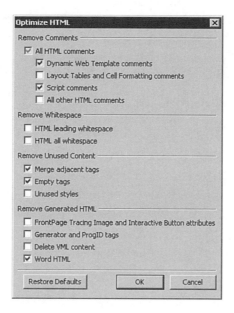

> **NOTE**
>
> Once you have set a page to optimize HTML a certain way, all code produced from that point on will follow the rules you set.

OPTIMIZE HTML DIALOG BOX PROPERTIES

Each option in the Optimizing HTML dialog box will optimize certain elements of your HTML.

The first series of elements deals with *HTML comments*. Dynamic Web Templates, layout tables, cell formatting, scripting, and general HTML can contain a considerable amount of comments. These comments are only for the developer's reference and contain no information to help render the HTML. Selecting any of these items will simply erase the comment HTML from the Web page.

The second series deals with HTML whitespace. If you look at the HTML in a Web page, the HTML is usually lined up nicely, allowing a user to easily find the area or information he is looking for. If you would like, you can eliminate leading whitespace (spacing and tab whitespace) or all of your HTML whitespace, resulting in a Web site that is simply a single line of code. Whitespace is only an aesthetic element with the single purpose of making HTML code easier to read by developers. Figures 29.4 and 29.5 show how powerful this tool is.

> **TIP**
>
> Certain scripting elements do not allow the elimination of all whitespace. If this is the case, FrontPage will leave the script as it needs to appear.

Figure 29.4
HTML in FrontPage 2003 before the white-space is removed.

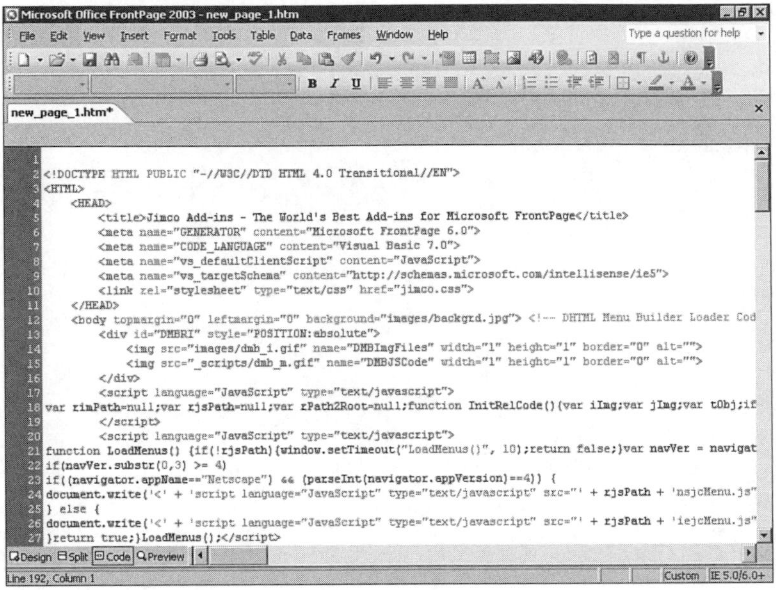

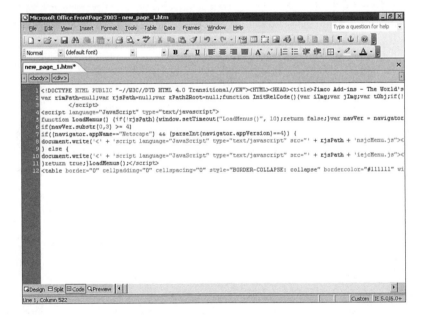

Figure 29.5
The same HTML in FrontPage 2003 after all whitespace is removed.

Older versions of FrontPage (and sloppy developers) can often produce a considerable amount of unused HTML information. This includes similar adjacent tags, empty tags, and unused styles. Toggling these options from the Remove Unused Content area will help you rid your pages of these elements.

The last area of this tool removes HTML specifically generated by FrontPage. These include image tracing, interactive button, generator and progid tags, VML content, and World HTML. You can have FrontPage eliminate these tags with the click of a button.

NOTE

> The Remove Generated HTML does not remove *all* FrontPage specific HTML such as Theme and navigational elements. Using this tool will not eliminate all traces of FrontPage-specific HTML from your Web site.

WARNINGS AND CONSIDERATIONS

TIP

> If you are going to do considerable modification of your site HTML, backing up your content is always a good idea.

It might seem beneficial for all users to optimize every HTML element on every page in their Web site. However, there are reasons why this isn't the case.

In addition to the reasons listed previously, you might find that you want to optimize your HTML when your site is published. This gives you the benefit of simple layout, meta information, and extensive commenting combined with the thinnest possible code at your site's final destination. We discuss HTML optimization at publish time later in this chapter.

HTML comments have the dual purpose of reminding you what you were thinking in the development process and enabling other users tasked with working on your project an insight into your development process. Eliminating your comments could result in a few bits of HTML eliminated but a few hours of design work when you (or another) try to "figure out" your coding.

Eliminating whitespace requires the same considerations. It might seem like a great idea at the time, but can result in a coding nightmare when trying to come back and make sense of a large Web page made of a single line of HTML.

The removal of unused content has little affect at any point in the design process. You can optimize for unused content at any time without having to worry that the loss of such data would affect your site in any way.

TIP

> If you remove generated HTML that kills elements that you need to edit, you can regenerate the elements from within FrontPage. Just run the specific tool within FrontPage that creates the elements and fill in the needed data.

USING OPTIMIZE HTML ON OLDER WEB PAGES

Previous versions of FrontPage produced code that was considerably less than optimized. This was shown previously in Figure 29.1. Opening a site designed in previous versions of FrontPage and optimizing a page at a time can quickly result in sites with cleaner code that often run faster.

Don't ever "assume" that code cleaned with FrontPage's Optimize HTML tool will perform exactly as the original code. Double-check that your optimized efforts produce the effect you are looking for before you save the file as final. HTML can be a tricky little beast, and the assumption of anything without verification is never a good idea.

OPTIMIZING HTML AT PUBLISH TIME

As mentioned earlier, you can let FrontPage optimize HTML at publish time and place the optimized code at the published destination. This is beneficial because it enables optimization of an entire site's code as opposed to a page at a time. It also provides the benefits of HTML optimization at the Web site without taking away the strength of a heavily commented site with considerable amounts of metadata. The options for published optimization are slightly different from the Optimize HTML dialog box discussed previously, but provide similar results.

REMOTE WEB SITE PROPERTIES DIALOG BOX

→ For a detailed look at the publishing process, **see** "Publishing a FrontPage Web Site," **p. 299**.

When you publish a site with FrontPage 2003, you can choose to optimize your HTML during the process. This results in a final site with optimized HTML produced from a site with bulkier code.

> **NOTE**
>
> This process results in you having two different sites—one with the original FrontPage HTML and one optimized for viewing on the Web. The first site will always be able to produce the second site, but the reverse is not true.
>
> Many people treat their published site as a backup of the content they developed before publishing. If considerable HTML is eliminated during the publishing process and the original source is lost, re-creating the site from the optimize HTML might be nearly impossible. If you take this approach, consider alternative backup options.

To optimize the code during the publishing process, you need to select settings in the Optimize HTML tab of the Remote Web Site Properties dialog box, seen in Figure 29.6. This tool provides an option list similar to the Optimize HTML dialog box, but takes items that are applicable to the publishing process into consideration.

Figure 29.6
The Optimize HTML tab of the Remote Web Site Properties dialog box lets you set which elements of HTML you want optimized at publish time.

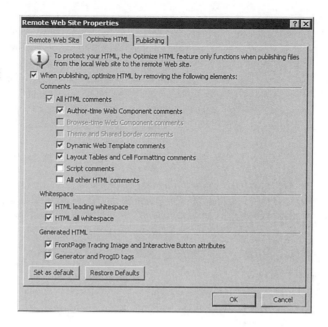

As seen in Figure 29.6, the tool to remove comments has more options than provided in the Optimize HTML dialog box. The ability to also eliminate author and browse time Web component and Theme and Shared Border comments has been added to the list.

In some cases, the elimination of these comments will have no effect on the final site. If they do, FrontPage will grey out the options, preventing you from using them.

The removal of whitespace options are the same as with the Optimize HTML dialog box.

The removal of generated HTML items is reduced to Tracing Image, Interactive Button, Generator, and ProgID tags. If you want to eliminate Word HTML or VML content from your site, you will need to do that before the publishing process.

REFORMATTING HTML

In addition to the way FrontPage produces HTML, many are frustrated with FrontPage's handling and formatting of HTML. Although it is not specifically an optimization issue in the truest sense of the word, you can set FrontPage to follow specific code formatting rules and reformat any existing HTML to those rules.

By formatting, we mean the spacing, tabbing, and tag elements FrontPage places in the HTML. The HTML is, in fact, a text file and is not subject to font sizes, and so on.

TIP

> Some users seem to obsess over their HTML formatting, whereas others don't care as long as it works. If you find yourself in the second category, don't worry: HTML formatting is 99% a matter of designer preference.
>
> Obviously, if you are working with a team or intend on handing your site off to another programmer (or team) later, the HTML formatting issues should be discussed and determined as part of the initial design process.

CODE FORMATTING

Selecting Page Options from the Tools menu will open the Page Options dialog box. The Code Formatting tab, seen in Figure 29.7 lets you set, specifically, how you would like FrontPage to format the HTML it produces.

Figure 29.7
You can tell FrontPage exactly how you would like it to code HTML through the Code Formatting tab of the Page Options dialog box.

NOTE

> Code Formatting is set on a page-by-page option and is not standardized across your entire site.

The tool divides HTML formatting into two areas: Formatting and Tags.

Formatting options can be set as follows:

- **Tag names are lowercase**—Some users prefer uppercase, whereas others prefer tags be in uppercase. You can set that issue here.

NOTE

A lot of the industry is moving toward lowercase tags by default. This both encourages standardization and helps in issues of markup through XHTML and the like. It is a good idea to use lowercase in most cases.

- **Attribute names are lowercase**—Similar to the previous option, you can toggle this option on or off based on preference.

- **Allow line breaks within tags**—Some like to see all tag content contained within a single line, whereas others like to see a tag opened and closed on a separate line for easier distinction. You can set that option here.

- **Tab size**—Lets you set the exact spacing for a tab.

- **Indent**—You can set how far an indent is spaced in either tabs or characters.

- **Right margin**—Some developers don't like scrolling left/right and want a specific right margin set for their code. You can do that here.

- **Insert tabs as spaces**—If you would like to see all tabs set as spaces, check this option.

The second Tags area lets you set how FrontPage handles each specific tag. A modification of the `<script>` tag is shown in Figure 29.8. To set tag handling, select a tag from the Tags list and set the variables as desired.

Figure 29.8
The Code Formatting for the `<script>` tag is now set to have a dual line break before and after the tag. Contents are also sent to indent to make for easier reading.

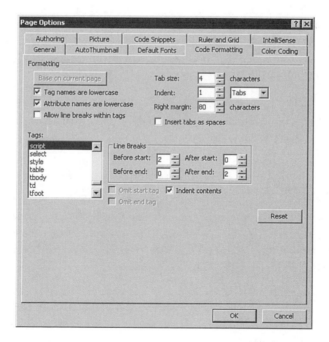

29

The first option is to set line breaks before and after the start and before and after the end of each tag. If you want to set apart a certain tag with clear whitespace, you can set this accordingly.

If you want to omit the start or end tag for any selection, you can toggle that choice. In addition, you can choose whether contents within a tag are indented.

NOTE

If HTML standards don't allow the omission of start or ending tags, the option will be grayed out. In XHTML, all tags **must** have a start and an end.

TIP

If you are one of the many who dislike the way FrontPage formats the paragraph tag with the unnecessary open tag, you can turn that off with this option.

If you find that you've made a mess of your HTML formatting rules, the Reset button at the bottom corner will bring things back to the default settings.

FORMATTING CODE BASED ON AN EXISTING PAGE

If you have brought an externally coded page in to FrontPage (or coded a page from hand using the Code view) and want FrontPage to mimic the formatting options set by the page, you can tell FrontPage to base formatting on the existing formatting in that page. To do so, click the Base on Current Page button at the top of the Code Formatting tab. FrontPage will then set the site-wide and tag-specific formatting to the standards found within the page you are working on.

NOTE

This option sets formatting based on HTML currently in that page and doesn't call formatting from any other page.

BROWSER COMPATIBILITY CHECK

A good Web developer is concerned with ensuring that his site is compatible on the browser choice of his audience base. Although it is the role of the developer to understand what browser platform will be used, FrontPage provides a tool for helping to ensure browser compatibility during the Web design process.

The Browser Compatibility tool will let you check your HTML for compatibility with different browser types and technologies. FrontPage has a limited number of specific browser and version types listed but allows for a custom option if you are checking against a browser not found within the interface.

RUNNING THE TOOLS

To run the Browser Compatibility tool, select Browser Compatibility from the Tools menu. As seen in Figure 29.9, you can set the tool to check compatibility of anything from a single page to all pages within a Web site.

Figure 29.9
The Browser Compatibility tool will let you check any number of pages for compatibility with a target browser.

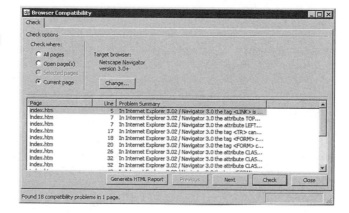

The use the tool, choose which pages you want FrontPage to examine and set the target browser through the Page Options dialog box—set by clicking the Change button within the tool's interface. The Page Options dialog box is shown in Figure 29.10.

Figure 29.10
The Page Options dialog box lets you check against specific FrontPage and SharePoint Technologies, browser types, and browser versions.

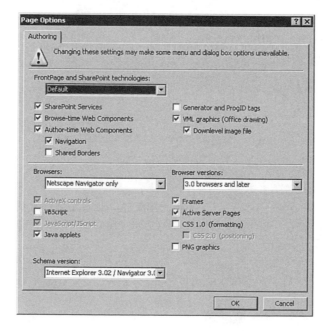

The dialog box allows for the toggling of any technology that you would like to check against, known as Authoring Options. The four dropdown menus in the dialog box will toggle the correct items on and off when selected. In Figure 29.10, I selected a complete FrontPage and SharePoint technologies check for Internet Explorer and Netscape Navigator versions 4.0 and higher.

NOTE

Surprisingly, the introduction of new browser versions has not always carried complete assumption of all technologies previously supported. When the versions of the browsers 7.0 and later are introduced (at the time of writing, Netscape was already at version 7.0), you can't assume that FrontPage's take on "later" versions will be complete. As always, double check your sites with the browsers you expect to be able to view your sites on.

TIP

Although the Browser Compatibility tool in FrontPage 2003 only lists and provides data for Microsoft Internet Explorer and Netscape 6.0 and earlier, you can easily check support for other browser types by toggling choices on and off with the Custom option.

Any page with all the advanced authoring options turned off would be compatible with almost any browser. You can decide if you want to take that extreme.

When using the Browser Compatibility tool, most users will find that they will want to check against specific requirements and not the defaults offered by the dropdown menus.

After the elements you want to compare your page or pages against are chosen, a click of the Check button will return the report. Figure 29.11 shows how the results are presented.

Figure 29.11
You can sort results in the Browser Compatibility check by page, line, or problem summary. Note that when a specific issue is selected, the corresponding issue is shown in Split view.

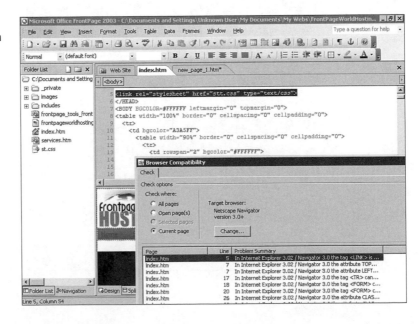

If you find that your HTML compatibility report doesn't accurately reflect reality, *see "The Report Is Wrong" in the "Troubleshooting" section at the end of this chapter.*

GENERATING AN HTML REPORT

Another option with the Browser Compatibility tool is the ability to generate an HTML report of the findings. After a check has been performed, clicking the Generate HTML Report button will produce the report as a separate HTML page. Figure 29.12 shows an example.

Figure 29.12
The Browser Compatibility Report Template generated through the Browser Compatibility Tools can be edited within FrontPage.

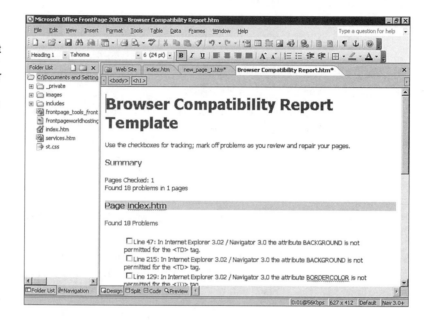

The report can be edited, printed, or emailed as desired.

TROUBLESHOOTING

MAKE THE FRONTPAGE SPECIFIC HTML GO AWAY

I want to use FrontPage to strip every single piece of FrontPage-specific HTML from my site.

It is simply impossible to eliminate all FrontPage-specific HTML in your site if you use FrontPage Themes, Web components, included files, or navigational elements in your Web site. If you use these tools, FrontPage will create FrontPage-specific HTML that can't be edited from within FrontPage.

If you must completely eliminate all FrontPage-specific elements, you can publish an optimized site and then edit the optimized site content in another editor to eliminate these tags.

USING FRONTPAGE WITH SITE BUILD IT

I want to use FrontPage 2003 to develop my Site Build It site (http://sitebuildit.frontpagelink.com). How can I create a site with FrontPage 2003 that I can use with Site Build It?

Site Build It can't support any FrontPage specific technologies. To develop a site for Site Build It, simply refrain from using the FrontPage-proprietary tools. This includes any of the Web components, Themes, navigational elements, or included file content.

Web sites such as FrontPage Tools (`http://frontpagetools.frontpagelink.com`) sell Site Build It specific FrontPage Templates.

THE REPORT IS WRONG

I ran a browser compatibility report, and it said that a certain feature won't work in the browser I was testing. I checked the feature in the browser, and it worked. Is the browser compatibiliy checker not working correctly?

The Browser Compatibility tool checks against specific stated compatibility standards. Sometimes a browser might not support a specific tag or issue, but the end result might be the same.

At the end, the final test is really in the browser you are checking against.

FRONT AND CENTER: MUCH ADO ABOUT ANYTHING?

Some "serious" Web developers will tell you that they won't touch FrontPage because of the way it "handles" HTML. No matter what you tell them about this most recent release, they will avoid FrontPage 2003 like the plague. Although some hesitance is understandable, the changes made in this release require a serious examination for anyone with this prejudice.

Another important question should be asked—"Why is there so much noise about the HTML produced by FrontPage?"

Before I discuss this issue, I want to make it perfectly clear that historically, the HTML produced by previous versions of FrontPage was bloated and filled with unnecessary data.

The fact is simple: FrontPage 2003 now produces HTML code as clean as any other WYSIWYG Web development product (yes, that includes Dreamweaver and GoLive). If FrontPage-specific technologies are utilized, metadata is necessary but provided for in the thinnest possible manner.

In addition, the HTML optimization tools described in this chapter can help you produce HTML code that will make even the most avid fan of HTML compliance happy.

But this is not, and never will be, the end of the issue. Clean HTML code is certainly a good goal for every Web designer, but other issues are equally as important.

However, some character types obsess about HTML compliance. They spend hours digging through line after line of code to make sure that the content meets every single specification known to man.

Although compliance is a very important issue and producing code that "works" should be the goal of anyone who creates a Web site, there is such a thing as going to far.

Do what you can to make sure that your site is accessible, as compliant as possible, loads as quickly as possible, and doesn't contain information or content that will slow down your customers. They've taken the time to visit your site—the least you can do is give them the information they are looking for as quickly as possible.

If you are looking for a solid resource on HTML that can assist you further in this matter, I certainly recommend Molly Holzschlag's *Special Edition Using HTML/XHTML* book. There is nothing else like it out there.

In terms of obsessing about the process, leave that to the people with too much time on their hands.

29

WORKING WITH VBA AND FRONTPAGE

In this chapter

30

INTRODUCTION TO PROGRAMMING WITH VISUAL BASIC FOR APPLICATIONS

Visual Basic for Applications (VBA) is easily one of the most powerful features of FrontPage. It is also one of the least utilized. Unlike most other Office applications, FrontPage does not provide a macro recorder. If you want a macro for FrontPage, you have to write it yourself, and many users of FrontPage are uneasy about delving into this area. In fact, writing macros is much easier than most people think, and once you start writing code, you'll find that there's almost no limit to what you can accomplish.

The purpose of this chapter is not to teach you the syntax of VBA code or to teach you all the facets of programming macros in FrontPage. Instead, the intent is to give you enough information to get your feet wet. It's important to realize that the best method for learning how to write any kind of code is to jump right in and start coding. Hopefully, this chapter will provide you with the foundation to do just that.

Macros are developed with the *Visual Basic Editor*. To start the Visual Basic Editor, select Tools, Macro, Visual Basic Editor, or use the keyboard shortcut Alt+F11.

NOTE

> Even though Microsoft calls the macro editor the Visual Basic Editor, it is not the same as Microsoft Visual Basic. When you are writing macro code in FrontPage or any other Office product, you are writing VBA code.
>
> VBA is a subset of Visual Basic and does not have all the same capabilities. One of the limitations of VBA is that the code must run within a host application. You cannot write a standalone application with VBA as you can with Visual Basic.

When you first launch the Visual Basic Editor, you will see two windows on the left side of the screen as shown in Figure 30.1—the Project Explorer and the Properties window. The Project Explorer displays a tree view of all files that are part of your macro project. The Properties window provides access to the properties of items within your project. Let's briefly discuss the files that make up a macro project.

UNDERSTANDING MODULES, CLASS MODULES, AND USERFORMS

Three types of files are available to you in a macro project; modules, class modules, and UserForms. Modules and class modules contain only code, whereas UserForms contain both code and user-interface elements. A macro project must have at least one module. It can also contain one or more class modules and UserForms, but is not required to have either.

MODULE

A *module* is a file that contains VBA code. It is common practice for VBA programmers to create many modules when programming complex macros. For example, you might have one module that contains code to perform certain editing functions in your Web pages and another module that performs specialized tasks such as sending email if a failure occurs. The choice is yours, but organization is critical if you want to keep track of your code.

Figure 30.1
The Visual Basic Editor provides all the tools necessary to write macros for FrontPage.

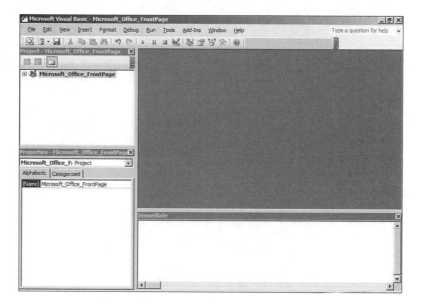

30

When you start the Visual Basic Editor, one module is automatically created for you. To create new modules, right-click inside the Project Explorer and select Insert, Module from the menu.

> **NOTE**
>
> The time to get organized is *before* you write your first line of code. When approaching a macro project, try to break your project into logical sections, and then clearly define the requirements for each section.

CLASS MODULE

A *class module* is a special kind of module that defines a class. A *class* is an object that has definable characteristics and performs certain tasks. Characteristics of a class are called *properties*, and the code that enables the class to perform a certain task is called a *method*. FrontPage has many of its own classes that you can use, but you can also create your own classes with their own properties and methods. Any classes you create are defined in class modules.

To insert a new class module into a macro project, right-click in the Project Explorer and select Insert, Class Module. The use of class modules is outside the scope of this book.

30

NOTE

For more information on defining classes within a class module you can check out *Special Edition Using Visual Basic 6.0*. Although it discusses Visual Basic and not VBA, the concepts of classes and class modules does not differ between VBA and Visual Basic.

USERFORM

A *UserForm* provides a user interface for your macro. Many macros do not include a UserForm, but if you require more than basic interaction with the users of your macro, a UserForm might be required.

To add a new UserForm to your macro project, right-click in the Project Explorer and select Insert, UserForm as seen in Figure 30.2. We will be designing a UserForm for the sample macro we'll write later in this chapter.

Figure 30.2
A UserForm allows users to interact with your macro.

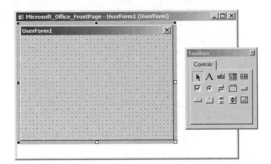

ACCESSING WEB SITES WITH VBA

Now that you have a general understanding of the pieces that make up a VBA macro, let's take a look at how we can use a macro to automate FrontPage.

When you write macros, you access parts of the application you're developing against using a predefined set of classes, properties, and methods called an *object model*. FrontPage actually has three different object models that you can use; the *Application* object model, the *Web* object model, and the *Page* object model. As you might have guessed, you access the FrontPage application using the Application object model, you access Web sites with the Web object model, and you access Web pages and their content using the Page object model.

THE APPLICATION OBJECT MODEL

The top-level object in the Application object model is the *Application* object. The Application object represents the current instance of the FrontPage application itself.

Suppose that we want to display the version of FrontPage that we are running. We can do that using the following code:

```
MsgBox Application.Version
```

This code displays the Version property of the Application object in a message box.

THE WEB OBJECT MODEL

At the core of the Web object model is the *WebEx* object. A WebEx object represents a FrontPage Web site. You can get a reference to a WebEx object as follows:

```
1  Dim oWeb As WebEx
2  Set oWeb = Webs.Open("http://localhost", , fpOpenInWindow)
```

Line numbers are included for reference only and are not part of the code. In the first line we declare a variable called oWeb and indicate that it will contain a WebEx object. We then open the Web site located at http://localhost and set the oWeb object equal to that Web site. After this code executes, oWeb will contain a reference to the root Web on the local machine and we can begin accessing the properties of that site and calling its methods.

For example, suppose that we want to publish the root Web of the local machine to http://www.mysite.com. We can do that using the code in Listing 30.1.

LISTING 30.1   PUBLISHING TO ROOT WEB

```
1  Dim oWeb As WebEx
2  Set oWeb = Webs.Open("http://localhost", , fpOpenInWindow)
3  oWeb.Publish "http://www.mysite.com", fpPublishAddToExistingWeb
```

As you can see, writing code to automate functionality in FrontPage is easy once you get the hang of it.

Figure 30.3
The Object Browser provides quick and easy access to all the objects in your project. Help is easily accessible by selecting an object and pressing F1.

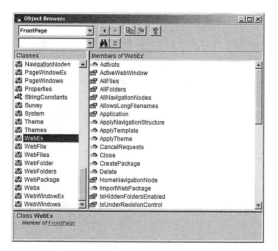

The Object Browser
The *Object Browser* is an excellent tool for viewing all the objects, properties, and methods of FrontPage's object models. You can open the Object Browser by selecting View, Object Browser (or press F2).

As seen in Figure 30.3, the Object Browser provides a comprehensive list of all the objects, properties, and methods in your macro project. When a class is selected in the Classes frame on the left, the Members pane on the right displays all the properties and methods of that class. By right-clicking on any class, property, or method and choosing Help from the menu, you have quick access to the documentation for that object. You can also select the object and press F1 to get help.

The Object Browser is fully searchable. Suppose that you want to find the documentation on the *Open* method of a FrontPage WebEx object. Simply enter `"open"` in the search box and click the Search button—the button that looks like a pair of binoculars. Using this method, you will often not only find the specific item you need, but you will also likely see other objects of interest that will help you to increase your knowledge of the FrontPage object models.

Experiment with the Object Browser for a while. Find an interesting object in the FrontPage object model and try to write a macro that uses that object. You'll find that taking this approach will dramatically increase your knowledge, and you'll learn skills that you can draw on for many years to come.

THE PAGE OBJECT MODEL

Now that we've got a WebEx object, we can easily access that Web site's files by using the *WebFile* object. If, for example, we wanted to open the page called `default.htm` in the root folder of the Web site, we would do it by adding the code in Listing 30.2 to the code we entered in Listing 30.1.

LISTING 30.2 OPENING PAGE FROM ROOT

```
1  Dim oFile As WebFile
2  Set oFile = oWeb.RootFolder.Files("default.htm")
3  oFile.Open
```

WRITING A MACRO

Now that you know about the Visual Basic Editor and the FrontPage object models, it's time to put that knowledge to work and write a macro.

NOTE

The files for the macro you will write are on the CD-ROM in the CH30 folder. Instead of entering the code and creating the UserForm, you can install the files from the CD and then drag and drop the files for the macro to the Project Explorer window.

One of the many exciting new features to FrontPage 2003 is the ability to specify HTML code optimizations that are applied when you publish a FrontPage Web site. Everything from FrontPage webbot comment tags to FrontPage's GENERATOR and ProgID meta tags can be automatically cleaned up from your pages when you publish a FrontPage Web site. Naturally, the FrontPage object model provides us with programmatic access to this functionality, so we'll use that functionality to write a useful macro.

You will want your macro to allow for the entry of a server name. It will then access that Web server and will provide a list of all the FrontPage Web sites on that server. When one of those Web sites is selected, it will show what HTML optimizations are applied for that Web site, and it will allow you to easily change those settings with the click of the mouse.

Let's have a look at the requirements for your macro. You'll need

- A UserForm that will be used to interact with your macro
- A method to retrieve the list of FrontPage Web sites from a given server
- A method to determine the current HTML optimization settings for a given Web site
- A method to set the HTML optimizations for a given Web site as specified by your macro.

CREATING THE USERFORM

The first thing to do is create a UserForm. You'll need to provide a way for users to enter the name of a Web server, a button for the user to click to get a list of FrontPage Web sites on that server, a method of displaying the list of Web sites to the user, and some check boxes that will display the current HTML optimization settings. The UserForm will also allow the user of your macro to change the HTML optimization settings and to specify new settings.

Start the Visual Basic Editor if it's not already running and insert a new UserForm by right-clicking inside the Project Explorer and selecting Insert, UserForm. A new UserForm is inserted into your project, and the *Toolbox* window appears. The Toolbox contains all the tools you will need to create the user interface for your macro.

NOTE

> You're not limited to the tools that are in the Toolbox by default. By right-clicking on the Toolbox and selecting Additional Controls from the menu, you can add other controls that are installed on your system.

After adding the UserForm, the Properties window will contain a listing of the properties for the UserForm. All objects in a macro have certain properties that control their behavior, and each of these properties has a value associated with it that describes that property. In the case of our UserForm, one of the properties is the Name property; the value for that property is currently set to UserForm1. We can change the Name property, but other properties are read-only and can only be read.

A discussion of all the UserForm properties is outside the scope of this book, but by selecting a property and pressing F1, you can review the context-sensitive help on that property.

At the top of the list of properties is the Name property. This property defines the name used to refer to the selected object in your macro code. Select the Name property and change it from UserForm1 to **frmMain**. After changing the name of the UserForm, change the Caption property to **HTML Optimizer**, the Height property to **277**, and the Width property to **375**.

30

Next you'll need to add some controls to the UserForm. Add a Label control from the Toolbox to the UserForm by clicking the Label control button (the button marked with the letter A) and then drawing the Label on the UserForm. After drawing the Label on the UserForm, change the Left property to 12, the Top property to 18, the Height property to 12, the Width property to 210, and the Caption property to Enter the server name:.

Add the controls in Table 30.1 and set their properties as indicated. If you aren't sure which Toolbox button represents which control, hover over the button with your mouse and the name of the control will display in a ToolTip. If you'd prefer, you can install the files from the CD accompanying this book and import the frmMain.frm file from the CH36 folder.

TABLE 30.1   CONTROLS FOR THE USERFORM

Control	Control/Property	Value
TextBox	TextBox	
	Name	txtServerName
	Height	18
	Left	12
	Top	30
	Width	216
CommandButton	CommandButton	
	Name	cmdGetSites
	Caption	Get Site List
	Default	True
	Enabled	False
	Height	18
	Left	235
	TakeFocusOnClick	False
	Top	30
	Width	100
Label	Label	
	Name	lblSelectSite
	Caption	Select site:
	Enabled	False
	Height	12
	Left	12
	Top	66
	Width	210

Control	Control/Property	Value
ComboBox	ComboBox	
	Name	cboSites
	Enabled	False
	Height	18
	Left	12
	Style	2- fmStyleDropDownList
	Top	80
	Width	215
CheckBox	CheckBox	
	Name	chkAuthorComponents
	Caption	Author-time component comments
	Enabled	False
	Height	15
	Left	12
	Top	125
	Width	180
CheckBox	CheckBox	
	Name	chkBrowseComponents
	Caption	Browse-time component comments
	Enabled	False
	Height	15
	Left	12
	Top	141.75
	Width	180
CheckBox	CheckBox	
	Name	chkDynamicTemplates
	Caption	Dynamic Web Template comments
	Enabled	False
	Height	15
	Left	12
	Top	158.45
	Width	180

30

continues

30

TABLE 30.1   CONTINUED

Control	Control/Property	Value
CheckBox	CheckBox	
	Name	chkGenerator
	Caption	GENERATOR and ProgIdProgID Meta tags
	Enabled	False
	Height	15
	Left	12
	Top	175.2
	Width	180
CheckBox	CheckBox	
	Name	chkWhitespace
	Caption	HTML whitespaces
	Enabled	False
	Height	15
	Left	12
	Top	192
	Width	180
CheckBox	CheckBox	
	Name	chkHTMLComments
	Caption	HTML comments
	Enabled	False
	Height	15
	Left	186
	Top	125
	Width	180
CheckBox	CheckBox	
	Name	chkLeadingWhitespace
	Caption	Leading whitespaces
	Enabled	False
	Height	15
	Left	186

Control	Control/Property	Value
	Top	141.75
	Width	180
CheckBox	CheckBox	
	Name	chkScriptComments
	Caption	Script comments
	Enabled	False
	Height	15
	Left	186
	Top	158.45
	Width	180
CheckBox	CheckBox	
	Name	chkThemeComments
	Caption	Theme comments
	Enabled	False
	Height	15
	Left	186
	Top	175.2
	Width	180
CommandButton	CommandButton	
	Name	cmdClose
	Caption	Close
	Height	20
	Left	228
	Top	222
	Width	60
CommandButton	CommandButton	
	Name	cmdOK
	Caption	OK
	Height	20
	Left	294
	Top	222
	Width	60

Figure 30.4 shows the completed version of the UserForm.

30

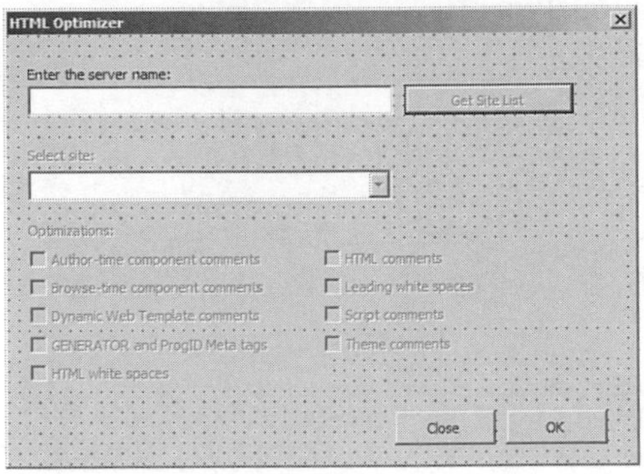

Figure 30.4
The completed UserForm provides all the controls necessary for users to control the operation of your macro.

30

IMPLEMENTING THE FUNCTIONALITY

Now that the UserForm is complete, it is time to write the main sub procedure for the macro. This sub procedure is what you will run to start executing the macro. If Module1 is not visible in the Project Explorer, click the plus sign next to Microsoft_Office_FrontPage, click the plus sign next to the Modules folder, and then double-click Module1 to open the code window. You'll enter the main sub procedure in the Module1 code window because it must be available in the Macro dialog in FrontPage. Only public sub procedures are available in the Macro dialog, and you can only enter a public sub procedure in a module.

Code for a macro can be written inside a sub procedure or a function. A sub procedure and function are defined as follows:

- **Sub procedure** A block of code that performs a certain task but returns no value
- **Function** A block of code that performs a certain task and returns a value

Click inside the Module1 code window and enter the code seen in Listing 30.3.

LISTING 30.3   PROCEDURE TO EXECUTE MACRO

```
1  Public Sub StartHTMLOptimizer()
2      frmMain.Show
3  End Sub
```

The code in Listing 30.3 declares a public procedure that shows the macro's UserForm. If you now switch from the Visual Basic Editor to FrontPage and select Tools, Macro, Macros, you will see the StartHTMLOptimizer macro listed as seen in Figure 30.5. If you run that macro, it will display your UserForm.

Everything looks great so far, but if you click around on the UserForm, you will find that it doesn't do much. In fact, it doesn't do anything at all! You need to write some code to add functionality to the UserForm, and the Visual Basic Editor makes this very easy to do.

 If you run the UserForm but you cannot seem to click anything on it, see "UserForm Seems Hung" in the "Troubleshooting" section at the end of this chapter.

Figure 30.5
Your macro will now allow you to display the UserForm, but until the code that provides the functionality is added, none of the controls do anything.

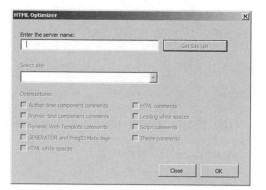

Switch back to the Visual Basic Editor and double-click the Get Site List button. When you do this, the code window for the UserForm opens, and the cursor is placed inside the cmdGetSites_Click procedure. When you are running the macro and you click the Get Site List button, a Click event is fired for that button. This event automatically runs the code in the cmdGetSites_Click procedure. Therefore, any code written in this procedure will run whenever the button is clicked.

Place the cursor inside the Click event for cmdGetSites and enter the code in Listing 30.4.

LISTING 30.4   CODE FOR Click EVENT

```
1     ' Variable to hold return value of GetWebSites.
2     Dim bGotWebSites As Boolean
3
4     ' In case we're searching on a new site, reset the form.
5     ResetForm
6
7     ' Call the GetSubwebs procedure and pass the server name to it.
8     bGotWebSites = GetWebSites(txtServerName.Text)
9
10    If bGotWebSites Then
11
12        ' A variable to hold a control.
13        Dim c As Control
14
15        ' Iterate through all of the controls on the form and enable each one.
16        For Each c In Me.Controls
17            c.Enabled = True
18        Next
19
20        ' Select the first item in cboSites.
21        cboSites.ListIndex = 0
22
23    End If
24
25  End Sub
```

When the Get Site List button is clicked, FrontPage takes the server name that was entered and gets a list of all the FrontPage Web sites on that server. Let's have a look at the code we just entered to implement this.

TIP

> You'll notice that many of the lines of code in our macro start with a single quote. These lines are comments that serve as inline documentation on what the code is doing. It is good practice to always comment your code, and as you write more complex macros, it becomes a necessity. Without comments, you almost certainly won't remember what you were thinking when you revisit code later.

Line 2 in Listing 30.4 declares a Boolean variable that will hold the return value of a call to a function that gets the FrontPage Web sites on the server we enter. A *Boolean* variable is a variable that has a value of either True or False. Our function will return True if successful and False if something goes wrong. (You will write that function later.)

Line 5 makes a call to a sub procedure called ResetForm. This sub procedure (which you will also write later) will be responsible for resetting the UserForm. It will return the UserForm to its initial state and prepare it for displaying information for a new server.

Line 8 sets the value of the Boolean variable to the value returned by the GetSubWebs function. It also passes the text entered into the txtServerName control to that function. When you call a function or sub procedure, you can pass values to it by appending them to the function's or sub procedure's name. The function or sub procedure has to be written to expect these values to be passed to it, and we'll have a look at how that's done in Listing 30.6. In this case, the server name is passed to the GetSubwebs function.

TIP

> The code in Listing 30.4 illustrates an important point in programming. By separating the implementation of the button into separate sub procedures and functions, it is very easy to keep track of code and to change implementation later. If all the code existed within the Click event itself, the code would quickly become unmanageable, and any change in implementation would increase the risk of introducing bugs.

Line 10 checks the value returned by the call to GetWebSites. If this value is True (meaning that we successfully contacted the Web server and got a list of the FrontPage Web sites on it), the code between the If statement on line 10 and the End If statement on line 23 is executed. If the value of bGotWebSites is False (meaning that something prevented you from successfully getting the list of FrontPage Web sites from the Web server), the code between lines 10 and 23 is not executed.

Line 13 declares a variable of type Control. You will use this variable to cycle through all the controls on your UserForm in lines 16–18. This is a common technique that will become familiar to you after working with code for a while. The Controls collection of a

UserForm represents all the controls on that UserForm. Any time you want to cycle through all the items in a collection programmatically, declare a variable of the same type as the objects in the collection (a variable of type Control in this case), and then use a For...Each statement to cycle through the collection. This is referred to as "iterating through the collection."

Remember that when the UserForm was created, the Enabled property of many of the controls was set to False. We did that because those particular controls are not applicable unless a list of FrontPage Web sites has already been obtained from the server. Since we now have a list of Web sites from the server, we are ready to enable all the controls so that the user of the macro can interact with those controls. Lines 16–18 accomplish this by iterating through each control on the UserForm and setting the Enabled property to True.

After the Get Site List button is clicked, we want the ComboBox to display the settings for the root Web site of the server, which will be the first item in the ComboBox. To do that, we set the ListIndex to 0 in line 21.

Now enter the code for the ResetForm procedure. Place the cursor at the end of the code window for frmMain and enter the code in Listing 30.5.

LISTING 30.5 CODE FOR THE ResetForm PROCEDURE

```
1   Private Sub ResetForm()
2
3       ' Clear entries in cboSites.
4       cboSites.Clear
5
6       ' Variable to hold a reference to a control.
7       Dim c As Control
8
9       ' Iterate through all controls and disable all CheckBoxes.
10      For Each c In Me.Controls
11          If TypeName(c) = "CheckBox" Then c.Enabled = False
12      Next
13
14      ' Disable labels and the ComboBox.
15      lblSelectSite.Enabled = False
16      lblOptimizations.Enabled = False
17      cboSites.Enabled = False
18
19   End Sub
```

The code in Listing 30.5 resets the UserForm to its original state. Line 4 begins the process by clearing all items in the ComboBox. After that is done, lines 7–12 iterate through the controls on the form in the same manner used in Listing 30.4. The difference here is that instead of setting the Enabled property to True, we are setting the Enabled property to False just as it was when the UserForm was first displayed.

Take a look at line 11. We're using the TypeName function and passing the current control to it. The TypeName function returns a string that indicates the type of the control passed to it. In this particular case, we only want to set the Enabled property to False if the control is a

CheckBox, so we use the TypeName function to check the control's type before we set the Enabled property. If the control is a CheckBox, the TypeName function will return "CheckBox" and we'll disable the control.

After we've disabled all the CheckBox controls, the procedure is ended by disabling the two label controls and the ComboBox control.

To complete the functionality of the Get Site List button, you need to enter the code for the GetWebSites function. Position the cursor at the end of the code window for frmMain again and enter the code in Listing 30.6.

LISTING 30.6 CODE FOR THE GetWebSites FUNCTION

```
1   Private Function GetWebSites(serverName As String) As Boolean
2
3       ' Variables for this sub procedure
4       Dim oWeb As WebEx
5       Dim oFolder As WebFolder
6
7       ' Display an hourglass on our UserForm while we work.
8       Me.MousePointer = fmMousePointerHourGlass
9
10      ' Set up error handling so that we can inform the user of any problems.
11      On Error GoTo ErrorHandler
12
13      ' Get a reference to the root Web site of the server.
14      Set oWeb = Webs.Open("http://" & serverName, , , fpOpenNoWindow)
15
16      ' Recalculate hyperlinks on the root Web site.
17      oWeb.RecalcHyperlinks
18
19      ' Loop through all folders in oWeb.
20      For Each oFolder In oWeb.AllFolders
21          ' If the current oFolder is a Web, add it to cboSites on
            ➥our UserForm.
22          If oFolder.IsWeb Then
23              cboSites.AddItem oFolder.URL
24          End If
25      Next
26
27      ' Destroy our WebEx object.
28      Set oWeb = Nothing
29
30      ' Return the mouse pointer to the default.
31      Me.MousePointer = fmMousePointerDefault
32
33      ' Return True.
34      GetWebSites = True
35
36      ' Exit the sub procedure to avoid running ErrorHandler code when
        ➥no error occurs.
37      Exit Function
38
39  ' Error Handling code.
40  ErrorHandler:
```

```
41
42      ' If we've reached this point, an error occurred.
        ➥Display the error to the user.
43      MsgBox Err.Number & ": " & Err.Description, vbExclamation + vbOKOnly,
        ➥"HTML OPTIMIZER"
44
45      ' Restore the mouse pointer.
46      Me.MousePointer = fmMousePointerDefault
47
48      ' Return False.
49      GetWebSites = False
50
51  End Function
```

30

In line 9 of Listing 30.4, we called the GetWebSites function and passed the server name to it. As I said then, the function must be written to expect this value to be passed to it. By examining what's inside the parenthesis in line 1 of Listing 30.6, we can see that the GetWebSites function expects a string value (which means a text value) to be passed to it, and it assigns that value to a variable called serverName.

Line 4 declares a variable that will hold a reference to the root Web on the server, and line 5 introduces a new object in the FrontPage Web object model, the WebFolder object. A WebFolder represents a folder in a FrontPage Web site, and one of its properties is IsWeb, which returns True if the folder is a FrontPage Web site and False if it is not. This property is the perfect way for us to get a list of all the FrontPage Web sites on the Web server.

Line 8 sets the mouse pointer to an hourglass so that the user will know that we're processing some information while we parse the Web site. Using the Me keyword here simply refers to the UserForm itself. The Me keyword is not required here, but it makes the code more readable.

Line 11 sets up error handling just in case something goes wrong. When you are accessing an external resource (such as opening a Web site), there's always a chance that something can go wrong. If you don't account for that possibility, your macro might crash with an ugly error message. For that reason, it's always a good idea to implement some error handling if you anticipate that unwanted results are possible.

In VBA, you implement error handling by using the On Error GoTo <line_label> statement, where <line_label> is a label defined inside the same method. The ErrorHandler line label in this case appears on line 37; line 11 specifies that if an error occurs, code execution will skip to line 39 and a message containing the error will be displayed to the user. We will then return a value of False indicating that something went wrong.

Line 14 sets the oWeb variable to a valid WebEx object by opening the root Web on the server that was passed to the function. To do that, we call the Open method of the Webs collection.

Line 17 recalculates hyperlinks on the Web site. We do this so that any new Web sites added to the server since the current session of FrontPage was started will be recognized. Without doing this, we cannot guarantee that new Web sites have been added to

FrontPage's configuration files. Recalculating hyperlinks forces FrontPage to update its configuration files for the Web server and guarantees that we will have fresh information to work with.

Beginning at line 19 we iterate through all the folders in the Web. If the folder is a Web site (which we determine via the IsWeb property as discussed earlier), we add its URL to the cboSites ComboBox on line 23.

After we've run through all the folders, we destroy our WebEx object on line 28, reset the mouse pointer to the default pointer, and return a value of True. Finally, on line 37 we explicitly exit the function so that our error handling code won't run when no errors are encountered.

> **NOTE**
>
> Whenever you explicitly create an object (such as the WebEx object oWeb we created previously), you should destroy that object by setting it equal to Nothing when you have finished using it. When you do this, all resources and memory used by that object are freed.

Now that you've gotten a list of Web sites on the server, you need to write some code to read the current HTML optimization values. You want to do that whenever a new site is chosen from the cboSites ComboBox. Therefore, you'll write that code in the Change event of the ComboBox.

Double-click the cboSites ComboBox and enter the code in Listing 30.7 into the Change event.

LISTING 30.7   THE cboSites_Change EVENT

```
1   ' Check to see if there are any entries in the ComboBox.
2   If cboSites.ListCount > 0 Then
3
4       ' A variable to hold a reference to a WebEx object.
5       Dim oWeb As WebEx
6
7       ' Set up error handling.
8       On Error GoTo ErrorHandler
9
10      ' Open the Web.
11      Set oWeb = Webs.Open(cboSites.SelText, , , fpOpenNoWindow)
12
13      ' Reset error handling.
14      On Error GoTo 0
15
16      ' Run through each CheckBox and check the flag to see if we
        ➥should check it.
17      With Me
18          .chkAuthorComponents.Value = (oWeb.OptimizeHTMLPublishFlags
            ➥And fpHtmlOptAuthorComponents)
```

```
19        .chkBrowseComponents.Value = (oWeb.OptimizeHTMLPublishFlags And
          ➥fpHtmlOptBrowseComponents)
20        .chkDynamicTemplates.Value = (oWeb.OptimizeHTMLPublishFlags And
          ➥fpHtmlOptDwtCmnts)
21        .chkGenerator.Value = (oWeb.OptimizeHTMLPublishFlags And
          ➥fpHtmlOptGenerator)
22        .chkWhitespace.Value = (oWeb.OptimizeHTMLPublishFlags And
          ➥fpHtmlOptHTMLAllWhitespace)
23        .chkHTMLComments.Value = (oWeb.OptimizeHTMLPublishFlags And
          ➥fpHtmlOptHTMLCmnts)
24        .chkLeadingWhitespace.Value = (oWeb.OptimizeHTMLPublishFlags And
          ➥fpHtmlOptHTMLLeadWhitespace)
25        .chkScriptComments.Value = (oWeb.OptimizeHTMLPublishFlags And
          ➥fpHtmlOptScriptCmnts)
26        .chkThemeComments.Value = (oWeb.OptimizeHTMLPublishFlags And
          ➥fpHtmlOptThemes)
27      End With
28
29      ' Destroy the Web object.
30      Set oWeb = Nothing
31
32   End If
33
34   Exit Sub
35
36   ErrorHandler:
37
38      MsgBox "An error occured while trying to open the Web site " &
          ➥cboSites.SelText & "." & _
39          vbCrLf & vbCrLf & Err.Description, vbCritical + vbOKOnly,
            ➥"HTML OPTIMIZER"
```

In line 2, we check to see if there are any items in the ComboBox. This might seem like a strange thing to do because you would think that if the selection in the ComboBox has changed (which is, after all, what causes this code to run because it is in the Change event), there would obviously be an item in the ComboBox. In fact, the Change event does run once when there are no items in the ComboBox. When you run the ResetForm sub procedure in Listing 30.5, the Change event is fired when the ComboBox is cleared in line 4. We don't want the code that opens the Web site and applies optimization settings to run in this case, so we enclose the code within an If...End If block and only run it if the ListCount property is greater than 0.

The code up to line 14 should be familiar to you by now, but line 14 probably isn't. You will notice that line 8 sets up error handling just as we've done in some of our other code. However, in this case, we are resetting that error handling in line 14. Our error handling code is designed to handle an error occurring when we open the Web site in line 11. After we've successfully accomplished that, we reset the error handling in line 14.

Lines 17–28 also introduce a new concept. In these lines, we are determining the current HTML optimization settings for the Web site by checking the OptimizeHTMLPublishFlags property of the Web site. This property contains a value that is of type fpOptimizeHTMLFlags, which is a special type of value called a *flag*. Flags are commonly used when writing programs because they are binary values and the computer can efficiently manipulate them. Fortunately, VBA provides an efficient means of manipulating them as well.

In lines 18–26, we use the And operator to check the current HTML optimization settings. The return value of `OptmizeHTMLPublishFlags And <flag>` will return True if the flag denoted by `<flag>` is set and False if it is not.

The rest of the code in Listing 30.7 uses concepts we have already covered and should already be familiar to you.

The functionality of the macro is almost complete. You've written the code necessary to get a list of FrontPage Web sites on the server specified by our user, as well as the code necessary to determine what the current HTML optimizations are for the selected Web site. When the current HTML optimizations are displayed to the user, your macro allows them to change those settings and then apply them to the Web site. That's the code that you will write next.

Double-click the OK button on the UserForm and enter the code in Listing 30.8 into the Click event.

LISTING 30.8   Click EVENT CODE

```
1   ' Variable to hold return value of OptimizeSite
2   Dim bOptimized As Boolean
3
4   ' Call OptimizeSite and pass the selected URL.
5   bOptimized = OptimizeSite(cboSites.SelText)
6
7   ' If optimization was successful, display appropriate message.
8   If bOptimized Then _
9       MsgBox "Optimizations applied successfully.", vbInformation + 
            ➥vbOKOnly, "HTML OPTIMIZER"
```

This code is very similar to the code in Listing 30.4. We are setting the Boolean value bOptimized to the value returned by the OptimizeSite function in line 5. Enter the code for the OptimizeSite function now.

Place your cursor at the end of the code window for the UserForm and enter the code in Listing 30.9.

LISTING 30.9   THE OptimizeSite FUNCTION

```
1   Private Function OptimizeSite(sURL As String) As Boolean
2
3       ' Set up error handling.
4       On Error GoTo ErrorHandler
5
6       ' A variable for a WebEx object.
7       Dim oWeb As WebEx
8
```

```
 9        ' Get a reference to the Web site URL we passed in.
10        Set oWeb = Webs.Open(sURL, , , fpOpenNoWindow)
11
12        ' Determine the OptimizeHTMLPublishFlags for the site.
13        With oWeb
14
15            ' Reset flags.
16            .OptimizeHTMLPublishFlags = fpHtmlOptEmpty
17
18            If Me.chkAuthorComponents.Value = True Then _
19                .OptimizeHTMLPublishFlags = .OptimizeHTMLPublishFlags + _
                   ➡fpHtmlOptAuthorComponents
20
21            If Me.chkBrowseComponents.Value = True Then _
22                .OptimizeHTMLPublishFlags = .OptimizeHTMLPublishFlags + _
                   ➡fpHtmlOptBrowseComponents
23
24            If Me.chkDynamicTemplates.Value = True Then _
25                .OptimizeHTMLPublishFlags = .OptimizeHTMLPublishFlags + _
                   ➡fpHtmlOptDwtCmnts
26
27            If Me.chkGenerator.Value = True Then _
28                .OptimizeHTMLPublishFlags = .OptimizeHTMLPublishFlags + _
                   ➡fpHtmlOptGenerator
29
30            If Me.chkWhitespace.Value = True Then _
31                .OptimizeHTMLPublishFlags = .OptimizeHTMLPublishFlags + _
                   ➡fpHtmlOptHTMLAllWhitespace
32
33            If Me.chkHTMLComments.Value = True Then _
34                .OptimizeHTMLPublishFlags = .OptimizeHTMLPublishFlags + _
                   ➡fpHtmlOptHTMLCmnts
35
36            If Me.chkLeadingWhitespace.Value = True Then _
37                .OptimizeHTMLPublishFlags = .OptimizeHTMLPublishFlags + _
                   ➡fpHtmlOptHTMLLeadWhitespace
38
39            If Me.chkScriptComments.Value = True Then _
40                .OptimizeHTMLPublishFlags = .OptimizeHTMLPublishFlags + _
                   ➡fpHtmlOptScriptCmnts
41
42            If Me.chkThemeComments.Value = True Then _
43                .OptimizeHTMLPublishFlags = .OptimizeHTMLPublishFlags + _
                   ➡fpHtmlOptThemes
44
45            If Not (.OptimizeHTMLPublishFlags And fpHtmlOptEmpty) Then _
46                .OptimizeHTMLPublishFlags = .OptimizeHTMLPublishFlags + _
                   ➡fpHtmlOptOn
47
48        End With
49
50        ' Destroy the oWeb object.
51        Set oWeb = Nothing
52
53        ' Return True
```

30

continues

30

LISTING 30.9   CONTINUED

```
54      OptimizeSite = True
55
56      ' Exit the function
57      Exit Function
58
59  ErrorHandler:
60
61      ' Display the error.
62      MsgBox "An error occured while processing optimization." & vbCrLf &
        ➥vbCrLf & Err.Description, _
63          vbCritical + vbOKOnly, "HTML OPTIMIZER"
64
65      ' Return False
66      OptimizeSite = False
67
68  End Function
```

The `OptimizeSite` function is our longest code listing yet, but there's not as much here as you might think at first glance. The code up to line 16 follows the same concepts we covered in Listing 30.7.

Line 16 sets the `OptimizeHTMLPublishFlags` property of the Web site to `fpHtmlOptEmpty`. This clears all the existing HTML optimization settings in preparation for applying the new settings our user has specified. Lines 18–43 check each CheckBox's `Value` property, and if it is checked, the corresponding `OptimizeHTMLPublishFlags` bit is set.

Line 45 performs a check to see if the `OptimizeHTMLPublishFlags` property is still set to `fpHtmlOptEmpty`. If it is, the user of your macro hasn't checked any of the CheckBoxes and we need not apply any HTML optimizations. However, if the user has checked one or more of the CheckBoxes, we add the `fpHtmlOptOn` flag to the current `OptimizeHTMLPublishFlags`. This has the effect of turning on HTML optimization so that your user's settings will be applied the next time the Web site is published.

The rest of Listing 30.9 consists of concepts covered in Listing 30.6.

FINISHING THE CODE

The main functionality of your macro is complete now. However, there are some finishing touches that you need to add.

First you'll add the code for the `Close` button. Double-click the `Close` button and add the following code to the `Click` event.

```
' Unload the form without making any changes...
Unload Me
```

This is pretty simple code that does exactly what it appears to do. It unloads the UserForm from memory, which causes it to close and our macro to end. That's all we need for the Close button.

Finally, we don't want the users of your macro to be able to click the Get Site List button if they haven't entered a server name. In order to add that functionality, we'll add some code to the Change event of the txtServerName TextBox control.

Double-click the txtServerName TextBox control and enter the following code in the Change event.

```
' If no server name is entered, disable the Get Site List button.
If txtServerName.Text = "" Then
    cmdGetSites.Enabled = False
Else
    cmdGetSites.Enabled = True
End If
```

The code in the Change event of txtServerName will run whenever the text in the TextBox changes. Each time the user of our macro presses a keyboard key while the cursor is in the txtServerName TextBox, we check to see if any text is in it. If there is, we enable the Get Site List button. If there isn't text in the TextBox, we disable the Get Site List button.

> **TIP**
>
> For the most part, we rely on FrontPage itself to handle any incorrect entries in the txtServerName TextBox. However, the macro can be made more robust by adding your own logic to check for invalid entries. Challenge yourself by adding some code to check for invalid entries.

RUNNING THE MACRO

That's it! We are now ready to run the macro. Close the Visual Basic Editor (and make sure to save your changes when prompted) and then select Tools, Macro, Macros in FrontPage. Select the StartHTMLOptimizer macro and click Run.

Once the UserForm displays, enter the name of a Web server and click the Get Site List button. Your macro gets a list of the FrontPage Web sites on the server and populates the ComboBox with them.

Once the site list has populated, select a Web site from the ComboBox and examine the current HTML optimization settings. Change some of the settings and click the OK button to apply them. Figure 30.6 shows the macro with optimization settings applied. Figure 30.7 shows the Remote Web Site Properties dialog in FrontPage. Note that the changes applied with your macro are reflected in the Remote Web Site Properties dialog.

 If you've specified that browse-time comments be removed, yet they still remain in your pages after publishing, see "Browse-time Comments Still Exist" in the "Troubleshooting" section at the end of this chapter.

→ For more information on the Remote Web Site Properties dialog, **see** "Security and Administration of a Web Site," **p. 323**.

Figure 30.6
The completed macro. Note that we have configured the current site to remove the Author-time comments, the GENERA-TOR and ProgID meta tags, and HTML comments.

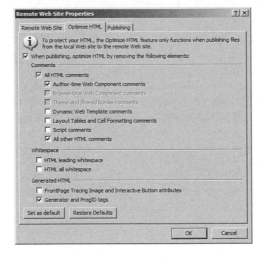

Figure 30.7
The Remote Web Site Properties dialog shows that the changes we made to the Web site with our macro did take effect.

The next time this Web site is published, it will be published using the HTML optimizations set with your macro.

 If the Remote Web Site Properties dialog does not reflect the settings you specified when you ran your macro, see "New Settings Don't Take" in the "Troubleshooting" section at the end of this chapter.

WHEN SOMETHING GOES WRONG—DEBUGGING

One of the tried and true rules of programming is that something will always go wrong. When it does, knowing how to debug a macro is the key to finding the problem and getting it fixed.

Breakpoints are a vital aid in the debugging process. The Visual Basic Editor will automatically stop execution when a breakpoint in code is hit. You can then use the Debug toolbar (accessible from View, Toolbars, Debug) to step through your code. When hovering your mouse pointer over objects and variables in your code, a ScreenTip will display with the current value of that object or variable.

To set a breakpoint at a line of code, right-click the line of code and select Toggle, Breakpoint from the menu. You can also click in the left border of the code editor at a specific line to set a breakpoint on that line, or click anywhere on the line of code and press F9. You can create as many breakpoints as you would like. You can remove all of your breakpoints in one step by selecting Debug, Clear All Breakpoints.

The *Locals Window* is available by selecting View, Locals Window. It displays all objects available to you and their properties and values in a tree view structure. As you step through your code when debugging, the Locals Window allows you to see what properties of an object are changing and what their values are. When I am debugging code, I use the Locals Window more than any other debugging tool because it shows me everything in one convenient location.

The *Immediate Window* is available by selecting View, Immediate Window. It allows you to enter commands and view or change the value of variables and properties while your code is paused at a breakpoint.

The *Watch Window* is available by selecting View, Watch Window. It allows you to watch a particular variable while code executes or to set a conditional breakpoint so that the Visual Basic Editor breaks when a particular condition is met or when the value of an expression you specify changes. To add a new Watch in the Watch Window, right-click anywhere within the Watch Window and select Add Watch.

For detailed information on debugging and the Locals, Immediate, and Watch windows, see the Visual Basic Help available by selecting Help, Microsoft Visual Basic Help within the Visual Basic Editor.

TROUBLESHOOTING

USERFORM SEEMS HUNG

When I run the macro, I can see the UserForm, but when I click anywhere on it, nothing happens and my computer just dings at me. What's wrong?

Make sure that you haven't disabled the UserForm. When we added controls to the form, we set the Enabled property of many of them to False. If you accidentally set the Enabled property of the UserForm itself to False during that process, you won't be able to interact with the UserForm at all.

BROWSE-TIME COMMENTS STILL EXIST

I checked the box so that FrontPage would remove the browse-time Web component comments, but after publishing my Web site, they're still there! Is the macro broken?

The macro's not broken. Browse-time Web components rely on the comments to run. Therefore, if you are publishing to a Web site that is running the FrontPage Server Extensions or any version of SharePoint Team Services, FrontPage will always leave these comments in. If FrontPage did remove them, it would break your FrontPage Web components!

NEW SETTINGS DON'T TAKE

I selected the optimization options the way I wanted them, but when I checked the Remote Web Site Properties dialog box in FrontPage, the options I selected don't seem to have taken effect.

Make sure that the Web site you are configuring is not currently open in FrontPage. FrontPage caches the information for the currently opened Web site, so even though you've changed the settings, FrontPage still sees the old settings.

If you really want to see the latest settings, select Tools, Recalculate Hyperlinks in FrontPage and then check the Remote Web Site Properties dialog again and the settings you applied will be visible.

FRONT AND CENTER: USING EVENTS AND VBA

It is often useful to write code that will run when the FrontPage application performs some type of action, such as opening a Web site. The Application object model provides several events that allow you to do this.

Suppose that you wanted to write a macro displaying a message when a Web site is opened that tells you the type of Web server that the Web site is running on and what version of the FrontPage Server Extensions the server is running. To implement this, you will need to do the following:

- Create a new class module.
- Declare a public variable to hold a reference to the FrontPage application.
- Write code that will determine the version of the Web server and the FrontPage Server Extensions when a Web site is opened.
- Intercept the FrontPage Application object event.

CREATE A NEW CLASS MODULE

In order to write code that runs when FrontPage opens a Web site, we must create a class module. A class module is just like a module except that a class module defines a class. (See the section "Class Module" earlier in this chapter for more information.) Insert a new class module into your macro project by right-clicking inside of the Project Explorer and selecting Insert, Class Module. Change the Name property of the class module to ServerInfo.

The Name property of a class module is very significant. You use the code in a class module by creating a new object from that class. (This new object is known as an *instance* of the class.) When you do that, the type of the instance is the name of the class module. In other words, when you create a new instance of the object defined in your new class module, that new instance is a ServerInfo object.

DECLARING THE FRONTPAGE APPLICATION VARIABLE

Now that you have a new class module, you need to declare a variable that will represent the FrontPage Application object. You'll need to do this using the WithEvents keyword. The WithEvents keyword exposes the events to you so that you can write code that will run when those events occur.

Double-click the ServerInfo class and enter the following code in the code window:

```
Public WithEvents fpApp As FrontPage.Application
```

The Public keyword allows you to access the fpApp variable from anywhere in your macro. After you have declared this variable, you need to add code that will set that variable equal to the current instance of FrontPage. You want that code to run as soon as your ServerInfo object is created. Class_Initialize is the event that gets triggered when a new instance of your class is created, so that's where we'll enter that code.

At the top of the ServerInfo code window, you will see two dropdowns; the Object dropdown on the left and the Procedure dropdown on the right. Select ServerInfo in the Object dropdown, and then select Initialize in the Procedure dropdown. This creates an empty code block for the Class_Initialize event. Click inside that event and enter the following code:

```
Set fpApp = Application
```

Now your fpApp variable contains a reference to the current instance of FrontPage.

WRITING CODE TO DISPLAY SERVER INFO

Now you need to write code that runs when a Web site is opened that displays the type of Web server and the version of the FrontPage Server Extensions. The event that will contain this code is the OnWebOpen event of the fpApp object you created.

Select fpApp from the Object dropdown and select OnWebOpen from the right dropdown. This inserts a block of code for the OnWebOpen event. Click inside that code and enter the following code:

```
Dim sWebServer As String
Dim sExtensionsVersion As String

sWebServer = pWeb.Properties("vti_httpdversion")
sExtensionsVersion = pWeb.Properties("vti_extenderversion")

MsgBox "Web server:" & vbTab & sWebServer & vbTab & vbCrLf & _
    "FPSE Version:" & vbTab & sExtensionsVersion, _
    vbInformation + vbOKOnly, "Server Information"
```

This code introduces a new property of the WebEx object; the Properties property. The Properties property contains a collection of properties that describe the Web site. In this particular case, we are concerned with the vti_httpdversion item, which returns the version of the Web server, and the vti_extenderversion, which returns the version of the FrontPage Server Extensions. (For a complete list of properties and their values, go to http://webproperties.frontpagelink.com.)

30

INTERCEPT THE FRONTPAGE APPLICATION EVENT

The last step in writing your macro is to add the code that will intercept the OnWebOpen event. You'll need to add this code to Module1 as a Public sub procedure just as you did with the StartHTMLOptimizer macro.

Double-click Module1 to open the code window and enter the following code at the top of the code window before any other code:

```
Public cServerInfo As ServerInfo
```

This is a public declaration, so it must be outside of any sub procedures or functions. By making it public, you are making it available to your entire macro for the life of your macro.

Now you need to create a new instance of the ServerInfo class and assign the value of the cServerInfo variable to that instance. Place the insertion point at the bottom of the code window and enter the following code:

```
Public Sub InterceptFPEvent()
    Set cServerInfo = New ServerInfo
End Sub
```

This code will be the name of the macro that we will run from the Macro dialog in FrontPage. It creates a new instance of the ServerInfo class, which will run the Class_Initialize event of the ServerInfo class and intercept the FrontPage application events.

To test your macro, switch back to FrontPage and select Tools, Macros, Macro. Select the InterceptFPEvent macro and click Run to run it. It will seem as though nothing happens, but you have actually instantiated a new instance of your ServerInfo class, and it is now waiting for you to open a Web site. Open a Web site in FrontPage, and you should see a dialog much like the one in Figure 30.8.

Figure 30.8
The Server Information dialog indicating server version and FrontPage Server Extensions version.

Web Collaboration

CHAPTER 31

MANAGING TEAM DEVELOPMENT PROJECTS

In this chapter

THE TEAM DEVELOPMENT PROCESS

Web design and development is no longer a solo activity. Simply too many skills and talents are required to put together an effective and powerful Web site. More times than not, you need a team to help you accomplish the task of developing a successful Web site. The good news is that FrontPage 2003 can help in the process of working with a design team.

On the most basic level, design-related tools such as the dynamic Web templates allow you to develop templates that can't be "broken" by the careless information worker or FrontPage Themes. Another is CSS, which makes sure that a Web maintains a similar look and feel no matter how many people are working on it.

→ For more information on the use and design of Dynamic Web Templates in the design process, **see** "Dynamic Web Templates," **p. 411**.

→ For more information using style sheets to manage a site look and feel, **see** "Using Style Sheets to Format Web Pages," **p. 385**.

Tools are also built in to FrontPage that assist with the management side of working with a group of developers. We'll examine those issues in this chapter and section of the book.

In this chapter, we'll examine developing a team to manage the project and then look at the technology decisions that need to be made before the project can begin.

In the Chapter 32, "Collaboration with FrontPage 2003," we'll look at the collaboration process and the tools FrontPage 2003 provides to make it easier to manage and entire team. In Chapter 33, "Managing Workflow and Tasks in the Design Process," we'll look at management of workflow and tasks from the FrontPage interface.

DEVELOPING THE TEAM

Putting together the right team is key to any collaborative effort. The right team is made up of willing participants with the right talents that enable them to get the job done.

More than anything else, developing the team requires a solid understanding of the project at hand. Participants should be chosen in light of their abilities in relation to the project requirements. All too often, a Web site has been designed with far too many artists or programmers, without the necessary qualified writers and content editors. Choose your team based on what is needed, not based on a preconceived notion of how many people should be on the team.

FrontPage 2003 provides a series of tools and capabilities that make the development of a team-based site easier than it has ever been before. A solid understanding and proper implementation of these tools can make the process as painless as possible.

In this chapter, we'll look at the technological and personal aspects that must integrate into any team-based Web development project. We'll look at the people who should make up any team and look at the technology that provides the means to manage them and their project.

CHOOSING PARTICIPANTS

Bringing a lot of people into a Web-based project might seem like a good idea. Many managers decide that everyone can be a part of the project when the only thing required is access to the Web site (or even corporate network).

This reasoning is never a good idea. In the same way that too many cooks spoil a soup, an oversized team can work a project into the ground. The meetings and planning sessions that exponentially multiply with the size of a group seldom do more than get in the way.

Like any other project, a collaborative Web-based effort needs to have a clear beginning and end. Effective leadership is required to move the project from concept to completion. Including everyone in the process will most likely keep both from occurring.

At the same time, beware of thinking that you need fewer people than you do. There is a common misunderstanding in Web design that *just because you can*, *you should*. Sometimes subtlety and brevity work better than any fancy graphic or layout ever can.

31

TIP

> No matter how wonderful the tool, an understanding of what to do with the tool is always more important than having the tool. Be careful with participants who think that because they have a graphic program, they suddenly are artists; be careful also of those who believe they can suddenly program now that they have FrontPage Wizards at their disposal.

As mentioned in the previous chapter, FrontPage 2003's reporting features provide a number of valuable options for tracking the movement and progress of the teams. Use these reports on a regular basis to understand and react to what your participants are doing. They compose a very powerful toolbox for understanding your project's status in its entirety.

TALENTS TO SEEK OUT

Seven talents are required for a successful collaborative Web-based project:

- Ability to create content
- Effective layout skills
- Graphics capabilities
- Programming capabilities
- Knowledge of the data that's to be presented (and how to present it)
- Understanding of the project flow
- Management skills

A single person obviously can provide more than one talent. It also goes without saying that some talents are important enough to require multiple participants. The best collaborative team blends these talents.

TIP

> The ability to work with a team is an obvious but often disregarded requirement for any-one participating in a collaborative online effort. Don't assume that just because some-one spends his time in front of a computer, he lacks people skills. Nothing slows a team project more than someone who doesn't work well with others.

CONTENT

The ability to create clear and concise content is one of the most overlooked talents in a collaborative project. All too often, people assume that anyone who has a keyboard in front of him can create good content for the site. This is simply not the case. Understanding what to present does not come naturally to everyone. Team members will sometimes use a Web site as a dumping ground for every piece of information available. Key elements will at other times be missing because it is assumed that "everyone knows that." Nothing frustrates a user faster than a Web site lacking the information he is looking for.

Get someone who has an understanding of content presentation. English majors, copywriters, and communication specialists are always a good place to start. Many times, it is the same people who write your marketing or training material who should be brought into that part of the project.

The type of content required for intranet projects can be very different from traditional copy sources. This content often contains phrasing and slang understood by the company but that is Greek to the outside world. This is understandable, but it needs to be carefully monitored; the documents one day might be ported to a traditional Internet or extranet, which might be viewed by individuals unfamiliar with the corporate lingo. The audience for any project must be clearly understood before the first line of copy is written.

"Content is king" remains a popular Internet catch phrase. Without good content, the rest of the site isn't worth much at all, so be sure your people in charge of content understand that.

LAYOUT

A firm understanding of Web design layout requirements is mandatory whenever a site is being created. This is especially important in a collaborative effort; as you divide the project into manageable pieces, it will become even more important to trust that the other participants are completing their ends of the project. Someone who writes good copy or codes database searches well should not be expected to understand how his work will look on various platforms. As can be seen in Figure 31.1, lousy layout can have the effect of overshadowing fabulous content.

To put things simply, someone with skills for layout simply has an "eye" for it (usually trained by a lot of experience). He must understand the maximum amount of words that should be onscreen at any one time and has the ability to place them together in a way that is pleasing to the eye. He knows how to create a look and feel that flows through the entire site. It is obviously best if he has worked on a Web site before. Figure 31.2 shows how good layout can help direct the user in whatever direction you want him to go.

Figure 31.1
Although the content might be great, an unattractive layout prevents the reader from ever getting to that content.

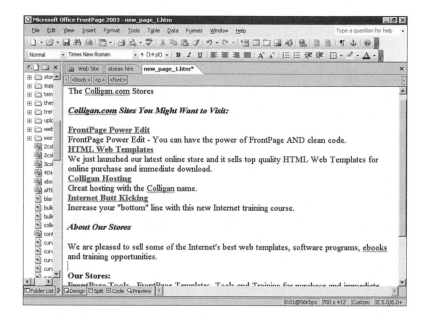

Figure 31.2
Good layout directs the eye to the content and leads the reader along. Compare this to Figure 31.1.

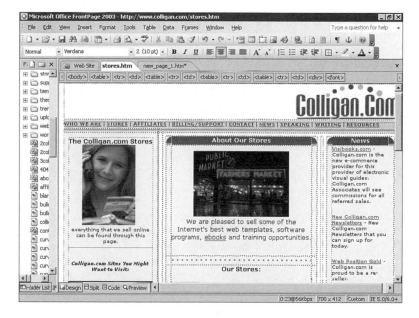

Often, the person with the layout talent should be one of the first involved in the development process. FrontPage 2003's template capabilities can help prevent some layout mistakes made by the uninformed or the overly zealous, but those capabilities should never take the place of team talent on a large project.

GRAPHIC SKILLS

Graphic skills require more than the ability to use the graphics programs available to the group. An eye for aesthetics and an understanding of the requirements and limitations of a screen-based presentation are required for anyone who is put in charge of the graphics and images for the site.

It might seem that everything is different on the Internet, but this is seldom the case. Many of the same skills taught to and understood by traditional graphic designers can be used in a Web environment. The effect of certain colors on mood or the impact gained from a certain font can help make a powerful Web project.

Go for the "eye" first if you must decide whom to assign to layout. Someone in charge of layout or content can always manipulate the users' work so that it can be presented online. The graphics chapters in this book can help walk you through that process.

→ Help on the art of using graphics with Web design can be found in Part X, "Creating and Adapting Graphics for the Web," **p. 823**.

PROGRAMMING CAPABILITIES

In the life of a Web-based project, programming skills are sometimes required. They might not be required in the beginning, but the chances of programming becoming necessary at some point are too strong to ignore.

In addition, the reality is that many Web project requirements can be better performed via a program rather than traditional HTML. If you understand the options, you can make the best decision. In short, FrontPage is not always the right tool for Web design—it is simply my favorite.

Someone should be available from the project's beginning who can help you determine whether (and when) programming will ever be needed. Even if you think you don't need a programmer immediately, you should have one available for both project consulting and possible later use. No one knows better than a programmer when a programmer is needed.

> **TIP**
>
> Programming must be approached carefully in Web-based projects. In traditional programming, the developer can control considerably more than he can on the Web, and this reality is sometimes lost. Make sure that your programmer understands that he has *no* control over system, OS, browser type, screen size, and also can't be assured that the top plug-ins are installed or that they are even allowed on the desktop of the user.

Scripting is the first type of programming you will see in a Web project. In this approach, the programmer writes scripts (on either the server or client side) that interact directly with the data or the user. Typical examples of this programming type include reactions to mouseovers and direct responses to entered data. Scripting typically is accomplished in DHTML, JavaScript, or VBScript. JavaScript and VBScript should never be confused with their executable-based Visual Basic or Java counterparts.

Behaviors, new to FrontPage 2003, provide limited client-side scripting options to your site with just a few clicks of the button. In some cases, you won't need to code a thing, but having someone who understands scripting will let you further define the behaviors. In Figure 31.3, the Jump Menu behavior dialog box is shown. Entering the desired choices and value will produce a scripted jump menu, seen in Figure 31.4.

Figure 31.3
The Jump Menu dialog box lets you set variables without scripting.

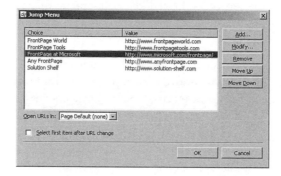

Figure 31.4
The Jump Menu behavior is an example of client-side scripting.

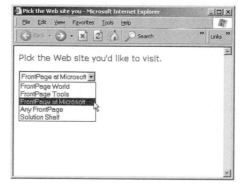

You also can optionally use *server-side scripts* (scripts that are stored and executed on the server). Such scripts result in HTML being written based on user input or other external data sources. This typically is used when the user is searching information in a database and HTML code has to be written on-the-fly to respond to the search. Active Server Pages (ASP) is one of the most popular implementations of server-side scripting.

Because it doesn't require program execution, scripting is one of the most popular practices for Web-based programs. If your programming requirements can be accomplished via scripting, you should use it.

The second type of programming is more traditional. It results in individual programs that run in conjunction with the Web browser or server. These can be found in the form of traditional .exe executables, Java programs, and COM controls.

When looking for a programmer, bring someone to the team who can program in Visual Basic and VBScript for Microsoft-specific projects or C++, Java, and Perl for more universal applications. Be sure that you hire someone who understands both programming approaches and understands when to use each. If you don't know enough about programming to make a good decision, bring on board someone who does.

You also should use programmers who use additional software tools. Although programmers will have to code something by hand at some point, the assistance given by such tools almost always speeds the development process. Beware of programmers who say that they don't need additional development tools: They sometimes separate themselves from the tools because they fear being replaced.

The third programming skill that shouldn't be overlooked is the ability to develop FrontPage macros with VBA. Many times a certain project or team will need the same basic function over and over again and quick macro developed by someone proficient in VBA could save untold hours.

→ For more information on some basic client-side coding options and FrontPage 2003 behaviors, **see** "Using Behaviors," **p. 449**.

→ For more on coding on the client-side, **see** "Client-side Scripting," **p. 475**.

→ For directions on programming FrontPage to provide specific functionality based on your specific needs, **see** "Working with VBA and FrontPage," **p. 567**.

DATA MANAGEMENT

Web sites often contain tremendous amounts of data. Whether it is in the form of a database or hundreds of pages of copy, the amount can sometimes be overwhelming. Making sense of all the data is an important skill set for successful Web design. Sometimes site data management requires more than effective layout skills and an understanding of flow.

Someone on the team needs to understand and be able to manipulate the amount of data presented at the site. The requirements are minimal if the amount is relatively small. Having a person skilled in data management is always a good idea, however, if the amount of data is as large as is typical to intranet and extranet applications.

TIP

> Sometimes the requirements of a Web site seem capable of being met through traditional HTML. If the amount of data contained on the site is expected to grow on a regular basis, you should examine whether the site could best be designed and implemented via a database-driven interface. Obviously, FrontPage is not the only tool used in such an approach.

INFORMATIONAL FLOW

Understanding (and controlling) how the information flows from one page of the site to the next is mandatory for an effective site design. This concept is discussed in greater detail in the first two chapters of this part and should be reviewed if necessary.

Either an individual or a tightly knit team should be responsible for how the project's information flows. The larger the number of people working on the project, the better the chance that the content will be haphazardly thrown together. This must be prevented.

Someone often meets this talent need with previous site design and Web building experience. Chances are good that he will have made mistakes in the past and can bring his current knowledge to the project. The larger the site he has worked with in the past, the more experience he has with issues of informational flow.

The type of person required is someone who understands the site as an entity as well as understands how everything relates to everything else. These are certainly "big picture" people who see things in terms of the site instead of the Web page.

MANAGEMENT SKILLS

Someone must manage the project. Introducing a new leader to the perils of command when working on a collaborative Web project is never a good idea. The person in charge of the project should have some past management experience and should enjoy working with people; he will work with others more often than anything else. All the clichés in this case are true: You will want a people person with good communication skills.

Someone with previous online or computer-based management experience is especially desirable. Someone with the experience of communicating with a team via email (or other forms of electronic communication) will have an advantage. Anyone who has used a computer system to track his progress is in the right location as well.

DIVISION OF LABOR

Dividing the work among your team members is always easier said than done. Expecting everyone to complete his work in such a way that no one else in the group is adversely affected is nothing short of wishful thinking. Because the relationships between various elements in every Web are so interconnected, great care must be taken in dividing the tasks between the team members.

The best way to approach the division of labor problem is to divide the project into smaller tasks, as many as you can. If at all possible, design the project so that everything comes together as late in the process as possible. Follow each of the teams as they complete their tasks and ensure that they follow some kind of schedule.

It is often wise to have content developed independently of the rest of the site. Upon completion, the content can be added to the final product without requiring constant revisions.

Putting placeholders in a Web project is no problem. Filling pages with dummy text or a database with multiple copies of the same entry is fine in the initial stages. Placing "graphic goes here" placeholders on the pages is also completely acceptable—until your site goes live, of course.

DECIDING ON THE PLATFORM

Deciding which platform the final product will be created in and reside on is not an easy task. You should consider several things: an understanding of the desired Web type, the server type, the best possible physical location of the server, the type(s) of browsers expected to be used by the project audience, and any additional tools that might be part of the development process.

Platform decisions vary greatly based on the type of project being developed. Whereas Microsoft Personal Web Server is a fine platform for an intranet of a company of fewer than 100 employees, an extranet designed for a worldwide client base certainly requires something a bit more robust. The tools used in the Web and design process also help dictate the project's final shape.

WEB SITE TYPE

Too often, Web projects begin with the purchase of the server or hosting service without any consideration for what you expect the Web site to do. When starting a project, first consider the Web site type you intend on developing and then make a decisions on the server (hardware and software) you'll need to serve that content.

The Web site type is the first decision that needs to be made because from there, you'll need to decide what kind of server you'll be placing your Web site on (examined in the next section). *Web site type* is defined as the technical means by which the information is presented. This dictates the requirements for the development and deployment platform.

If your site will use only HTML, your options are unlimited and you are free to use any Web server available. If you expect to use additional features—such as dynamic content, database integration, streaming media serving, or other server-side applications—new decisions need to be made.

TIP

> Don't be surprised that the complexity of your site grows over a short amount of time. Many sites that start out as a few short pages about a subject become multimedia presentations in a short amount of time. Consider what might happen in the future when considering Web type.

SERVER TYPE

Once you understand the type of Web project you are going to be developing, the next question you will ask about the server type is whether FrontPage extensions will be required. If so, be sure that the final placement of the project is on a server with the extensions installed.

Obviously, installation of the server extensions makes the development and update process easier. Server extensions also enable people to log on to the site and make changes from their own machines. It is still one of the most powerful aspects of the program and should not be underestimated. The power provided by Office server extensions is also very attractive in light of the collaborative process.

31

NOTE

> Although FrontPage extensions are available for most professional Web servers today, it is important to note that Office server extensions must be run on Microsoft's Internet Information Server, which runs only on a Microsoft 2000 or 2003 Server.

But server extensions are only one part of the story. If you want to run other server-side applications, such as database integration, make sure that the server supports the tools you are looking for. If you want to use Microsoft applications on the server side, you probably need to run your site on Microsoft Internet Information Server on a Windows 2000 or 2003 Server.

Different server-side applications—such as electronic commerce, databases, and media streaming—work best on different server platforms. Spend some time researching your options (they change all the time) so that you can make the right decision.

 If you are having a hard time setting the security settings in FrontPage to allow multiple users, *see "Can't Set Security Settings with FrontPage 2003" in the "Troubleshooting" section at the end of this chapter.*

Another option to consider for server type is SharePoint Team Services 2.0. This server system, built in to Windows Server 2003, not only provides Windows Server and .NET functionality, but also provides a number of tools that integrate directly with FrontPage 2003.

→ For more information on FrontPage and SharePoint Team Services, **see** "Windows SharePoint Services 2.0," **p. 943**.

TIP

> It is no secret that computer costs decrease on a regular basis. A platform priced in one month could be considerably less in 60–90 days. If you are going to host the site internally or will buy your server (and software), consider developing the project on a simple server and having it published to a robust platform upon completion.

It is important to point out that not all Web servers provide the same degree of reliability. When investigating Web servers, be sure that you have either a reliable server or a response plan for when things go wrong. On the Internet, it is never a question of if your server will go down; it is a question of *when it will go down and what you plan to do about it.*

SERVER LOCATION

The server's physical location isn't as obvious a decision as you might think. Even though many companies locate their servers at their geographical locations, this might not be a good idea.

If the project is an intranet and serves people in only one physical location, the server's typical location is the local network. There is often little need to place the information outside.

If the project is a traditional Internet Web site, you should place the server where as many potential customers as possible can easily reach it by making the fewest hops. If your company is located far away from some of the Internet *Network Access Points* (*NAPs*), you should place the server in a location that takes fewer hops to a NAP. Whereas it might seem strange to locate your Web server hundreds (even thousands) of miles away, the speed at which your customers can connect to your server is well worth the effort.

An extranet is also best served in a location where it is as few network jumps as possible away from the most customers.

In all circumstances, including the corporate intranet, you should examine possibilities for outsourcing the server to an Internet service provider or Web hosting firm. Their connectivity most often rivals what any company can bring, or afford, and the pressures of keeping hundreds of sites running can result in an uptime guarantee that the average IT staff simply can't provide.

→ For more information about Web hosting, **see** "Publishing a FrontPage Web Site," **p. 299**.

In addition, some security issues obviously are associated with placing your server in a location anywhere other than your own property. Spend some time considering these issues as well.

Browser Type

The audience browser question is an important one. Browser type dictates which technology can be used at the site, and the addition of every type and version increasesof the project.

TIP

> Remember that when viewing a Web site, browser version is not the only variable that dictates the way the Web is viewed. The viewer's screen size and resolution also can dictate certain elements. Don't assume that any site will be viewed in the same screen dimensions in which it was designed. FrontPage Page Preview lets you view your site on a number of screen resolutions. Make constant use of this option.

Many times, an intranet can be developed for a single browser version. A corporate decision or mandate can require that anyone wanting to view the site must do so on a certain browser type and version. If this is the case, development in terms of browser type is an easier task.

Making the Browser Choice

The choice of browser is by far the most personal (and in many cases, politically charged) of software decisions. Feelings about Microsoft (pro and con) sometimes cause individuals to insist on a certain browser type at their desktops. Performance issues also often dictate browser choice. Different browser types simply work better on different systems. It is also important to point out that just because a corporate decision has been made about a browser type doesn't mean that it always will be followed. Telling people a site is "best viewed" in a certain browser type is not enough.

Extranet results are also subject to specific browser versions, but they introduce probabilities that the site might be viewed on another platform. Users might not think that using a specific browser is as necessary as the developers think it is and approach the site accordingly. A traveling sales force might be forced to use handheld devices or someone else's platform during their travels. In addition, it might not be a good idea politically to dictate which browser any customers or resellers use if your extranet is being positioned as a service.

TIP

> If you are developing an extranet for a single browser version, consider making copies of that browser available to everyone who will use the Web site. Choices that you can offer include a simple download option on the site's home page and the distribution of CDs to all participants.

A traditional Web site opens the possibilities of dozens of browser versions and types viewing your site. Interestingly enough, some surfers are running version 1 or 2 of their programs and simply refuse to upgrade. In addition to that reality, remember that nontraditional Web devices—such as Windows PocketPC machines, Palm Pilots, and television set top devices (such as Microsoft WebTV and the Sega Web Browser)—are surfing the Internet as well. Also remember that some browser versions are available on multiple platforms, including the PC, Macintosh, Linux, and more.

FrontPage 2003 does offer some help in this area.

The Page Options dialog box's Authoring tab lets you choose a number of variables for a specific page (see Figure 31.3). These variables can affect the browser in use. You can choose to include or exclude specific features and browser versions. The browser versions are limited to Internet Explorer, Netscape Navigator, and Microsoft WebTV and should not be mistaken as a list of all possible options.

Figure 31.5
The Authoring tab lets you define exactly which commands that page will support.

TIP

> If you are not going to use the Compatibility option on a site-wide basis, consider designing a series of template pages with the desired options for the site and designing all pages in the site from that initial template.

TIP

> If, for some reason, browser version is an absolute requirement for your Web site, consider coding your site home page such that it permits only that specific browser version. You can do this easily with FrontPage Behaviors, discussed in Chapter 23, "Using Behaviors."

ADDITIONAL DEVELOPMENT TOOLS

FrontPage 2003 is obviously not the only development tool available for Web site design. Not only must you consider previous versions of FrontPage, but you also must consider other products such as Microsoft Visual InterDev and non-Microsoft products, such as Macromedia Dreamweaver, NetObjects Fusion, Adobe GoLive, and others.

You can't always assume that everyone in the group will use FrontPage 2003. Some users might have previous versions of the program, and others might be using the Macintosh implementation of the program. You must understand the implications of this and react accordingly.

What FrontPage does, it does well. What it doesn't do well requires the use of additional software.

USING OTHER FRONTPAGE VERSIONS

Because FrontPage allows collaboration in the FrontPage Web site, other versions can be used in the development process. They might not be capable of using the latest technologies provided by the new program, but they will always be capable of accessing and editing site content.

NOTE

> The Macintosh version of FrontPage (1.0, Macintosh Edition) is based on the FrontPage 97 era of the product and contains a number of issues that would make it difficult to integrate effectively in a team environment.

MICROSOFT VISUAL INTERDEV AND MICROSOFT VISUAL STUDIO .NET

Microsoft Visual Internet development tool from Microsoft and is part of Visual Studio .NET. The program enables a higher degree of programming than is provided by traditional HTML. Typical uses for InterDev include database integration and Active Server Page (ASP) and .NET development. It is a powerful tool that adds a degree of programming capability FrontPage is simply incapable of delivering.

FrontPage 2003 does provide a tiny amount of database support. Oftentimes, you will want to use an additional tool if you intend to do any significant work with databases in your site.

InterDev's purposeful integration with the FrontPage environment makes it the ideal tool for such integration.

TIP

> FrontPage 2003 is designed to be as simple to use as possible. The program purposely looks and acts like other programs in the Microsoft Office suite. Microsoft Visual InterDev is meant to be a powerful application development tool that requires an understanding of programming and database integration. Don't feel that you can pick the program off the shelf and learn it much the same way that you can learn FrontPage.

More information about Microsoft Visual InterDev can be found online at http://visualinterdev.frontpagelink.com, and in *Special Edition Using Visual InterDev*, 0-7897-1549-x.

In addition to Visual InterDev, Microsoft also has an entire line of development products that fall under its Visual Studio .NET line. The programs include Visual Basic, Visual C++, Visual FoxPro (a database development program), and Visual J++ (a Java development program). Similar to InterDev, these products require a high degree of programming proficiency, but all are excellent tools designed to work within the FrontPage development environment.

More information about Visual Studio can be found online at http://visualstudio.frontpagelink.com and in *Special Edition Using Microsoft Visual Studio*, 0-7897-1260-1.

OTHER WEB DEVELOPMENT PROGRAMS

If in the past you used a third-party Web development program to edit content for a FrontPage Web site, you might have noticed that FrontPage would often rewrite certain elements of the code and sometimes undo edits. This was a frustrating problem and generated more complaints than any other issue. Microsoft fixed that problem with FrontPage 2000.

Microsoft claims that FrontPage 2003 supports 100% HTML preservation and promises not to edit any HTML placed within the site. As a result, you can use additional HTML editing programs (or any other additional Internet development applications) within the FrontPage environment. This can be done either by editing the files externally and importing them into the Web site or by opening the files directly on the server and editing them with the specific application.

CAUTION

> Although you can use other development programs during the development process, you always should take great care when doing so. As with most computer projects, regularly backing things up is a good idea. This is especially smart if you work with third-party applications.
>
> And, don't think that FrontPage is the only program that could alter Web site HTML when multiple design products are used.

31

SERVERS AND THE DEVELOPMENT PROCESS

Traditionally, team-based development is done in a two-phase process. The site is first built and approved on a production server in which the entire team has access. Once completed or ready for viewing by the entire world, the content from the production server is published to a launch server. Production and launch servers are called many different things in the industry. What is important is this two-tiered approach.

Whereas everyone in the team has access to the development server, traditionally only a few have access to the launch server. This helps prevent all sorts of potential problems. The benefits of this two-tiered approach are obvious: It prevents the audience from viewing content not yet ready for its consumption, and it provides an experimental platform for the development team to preview its ideas and concepts before letting the world see them.

Use this two-tiered approach if possible. The benefits are plentiful, and the potential problems from not implementing such an approach are obvious.

TIP

> Another benefit to the two-tiered approach is the fact the two servers act as an additional backup system. If one server goes down completely, the other one can be used to bring it back to a certain level of functionality.

PRODUCTION SERVER

The production server does not have to be a costly endeavor. The number of people accessing the site usually would be small and could almost always be handled on an individual user's machine. The exception to this rule is a highly complex Web site on the server side that would require a production server capable of testing the implementation.

LAUNCH SERVER

Choosing the launch server for your final product is one of the most important decisions you can make. Who has access to the launch server is another important issue that must be decided.

It is good practice to store the launch server in a location other than where the production server is. This is in case any problems occur with the physical location of either.

TROUBLESHOOTING

CAN'T SET SECURITY SETTINGS WITH FRONTPAGE 2003

I'm trying to set security settings in my site, which has FrontPage Server Extensions installed, and am unable to do so.

FrontPage Server Extensions aren't perfect all the time. Sometimes they simply "don't take" and need to be reinstalled. If you are having problems with your security settings, try reinstalling your extensions or having them reinstalled for you.

If that doesn't work, it is also possible that you have not been given the right permissions on the server side to make the security settings you desire. If this is the case, you will need these set for you by whoever has the permission to do so.

One other possible solution is that you are trying to set the security options on your local version of the server. Make sure that you open up the remote server if you want to edit the settings there through FrontPage.

FRONT AND CENTER: WORKING WELL IN A TEAM ENVIRONMENT

A team-based Web site is one of the more exciting opportunities for the *true* designer. Whereas the old paradigm of a single Webmaster required that he learn all aspects of the development process (including Web security and database programming), a true team environment can allow people to perform the duties they are the most skilled at.

The biggest challenge for a designer in a team environment is often in convincing others in the team to follow your design—not develop their own. Because the design process (as opposed to the skill) is so easy with FrontPage 2003, many will fancy themselves developers, regardless of their talents. Effective project management obviously also requires an appreciation (and understanding) of the role of the design in the development process.

This is why the role of the project manager is so important. This individual is tasked with ensuring that everyone on the team complete the tasks assigned to them while letting others do what they do well. On any project in which the design process seems to get out of control, a good manager can help bring everything back into focus.

The question every project manager should ask is how many people are actually needed for a team project. Too few will prevent the project from getting completed, but too many will slow down the project to the point of a snail's crawl. Choosing which (and how many) people will be working on your project is as important as the technology you might choose to implement.

CHAPTER 32

COLLABORATION WITH FRONTPAGE 2003

In this chapter

DEVELOPING A COLLABORATIVE AUTHORING ENVIRONMENT

Developing a collaborative authoring environment is a delicate blend of the technology and workflow process. FrontPage 2003 provides the technology; developing the workflow process is the project manager's job.

In the previous chapter, we examined the "art" of managing a team development project. In this chapter, we examine the tools for doing the same. We'll first explain the role of the project manager, show you how to check documents in and out, assign documents to a specific user, publish (all or part of) the site as needed, and assess where the project stands at any given time. In the next chapter, we'll get more specific about managing workflow and tasks as we examine the specifics of the collaborative authoring environment.

FrontPage 2003 can help with the collaborative development process by providing a means to track each team member's tasks simply and quickly. Without a proper understanding and communication of the project at hand, a team can waste countless hours trying to achieve a goal that isn't possible because it doesn't exist or wasn't communicated well.

THE ROLE OF THE MANAGER

An effective collaborative development environment will never be accomplished without a single individual in charge of the process with whom the "buck stops." The project needs one person whose job is to watch the entire project from above and ensure that the task at hand is being met—a *manager*. Although it is the nature of Web designers to want to work in an atmosphere of teamwork, someone still needs to be in charge. Choosing the right manager is at least as important as choosing the technology with which you will implement the project.

Once the technology decisions have been made, the more important issues of working with the people who will be helping you develop your Web project need to be examined. More than anything else, your team will need a manager who understands both the technology and the people he will be working with.

The Manager position has been called by other names that include, but are not limited to, Webmaster, Web mistress, Web architect, Web facilitator, project lead, program lead, and boss. What's important in collaborative design is that a single individual has a final say in the development process. The proper name for that individual is unimportant. For the rest of this text, we will refer to the position as "the manager."

The job of the manager is a difficult and complex one. The first role is responsibility for the growth of the site. Equally important is the role of assessing the site during the development process to bring the project back on course should it sway. This requires a firm understanding of the development process, the tools provided by FrontPage 2003, and how those tools interact with FrontPage 2003. We'll cover that issue in this chapter and the next.

Typically, the duties of the manager are best performed by a single individual. Even though a large project can have many people in a leadership position, a single leader who heads the project still best suits a collaborative effort.

CHOOSING THE RIGHT TECHNOLOGY

Technology use and implementation is a key part of the successful collaborative development environment. For example, a development team no longer needs to communicate task requirements by random email or spend a great deal of time tracking anything that the computer could track better. FrontPage 2003 provides a set of tools that help make a collaborative environment much easier and effective while letting the computer track the elements as required.

FrontPage Server extensions let teams access the site from wherever they are (each with different logins and passwords), letting your team be located anywhere that has an Internet connection. Although they are no longer "required" for the publishing process, they still offer a number of benefits to the team development process. We'll examine them in this section.

Tasks tracking is the most powerful feature provided by FrontPage when working with a team. Making use of this tool from the very beginning of your project will help the collaborative process considerably.

Previously in FrontPage 2000, the only option for task management was a limited tasks file, seldom used by anyone and with no direct impact on the Web site. In FrontPage 2002, the tasks tracking capabilities were greatly increased in scope, and a number of new collaborative features that directly benefit the collaboration process were added. These features were upgraded slightly for the latest version and remain a powerful tool in any collaborative authoring environment.

FRONTPAGE SERVER EXTENSIONS

The FrontPage *Server Extensions* are a series of programs and executables that work in collaboration with FrontPage and a Web server to provide a lot of its server-side capabilities (often found in the FrontPage components). FrontPage Server Extensions have been part of the program since the beginning, and although no longer emphasized by Microsoft, they provide a number of tools that assist in the collaborative design process.

Unlike typical Microsoft programs that require the Windows platform to run, versions of the FrontPage extensions for most of the Web server programs are available today.

To check which version of the FrontPage extensions your Web server has, select Tools, Site Settings and select the General tab.

→ For more information about the roles of FrontPage Server Extensions and Web servers, **see** "Publishing a FrontPage Web Site," **p. 299**.

32

Most of the features described in this chapter require FrontPage Server Extensions. Despite Microsoft's decision to no longer emphasize their use, they are well worth the effort when working on a collaborative authoring environment.

WORKING WITHOUT SERVER EXTENSIONS

Much to the frustration of many previous FrontPage users, FrontPage Server Extensions were once required for Web development. This is no longer the case. If desired, a Web site could be placed on a shared directory and edited by anyone with access to the directory or at a Web site accessible by the entire team via FTP.

Without Server Extensions, other Web development products such as Dreamweaver and GoLive could be used to help develop your site. The manager will have to decide if the benefits of other products outweigh the features offered through FrontPage Server Extensions.

Although this is possible, it is not a recommended development platform—especially when working with the collaborative features provided by the program and explained here.

TASKS TRACKING

From the Tasks view (see Figure 32.1), FrontPage 2003 assigns and tracks tasks during the development process. Users assigned to the tasks can go directly to their jobs and complete them as required by double-clicking the task. FrontPage opens the document immediately, and when a document is closed, FrontPage asks the user to assign a status to the task such as whether the task is completed or in process.

Figure 32.1
The Tasks view in FrontPage 2003 shows the status for each task, to whom it is assigned, its priority, with which document it is associated, the last date it was modified, and any comments.

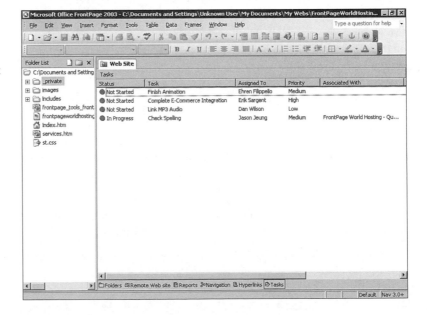

The tasks tracking feature provides two services: It allows an overview of the entire project status as necessary and provides a jumping-off point for team members. The project manager can easily see what remains to be done from a simple view, and team members can quickly get to work without bothering the manager with a typical "What should I do now?"

Clicking any of the field buttons in the Tasks view sorts the list by the field. This is useful for assessing priority, status, modification dates (to see which task has been around the longest), or the amount of tasks assigned to an individual.

ESTABLISHING A WORKFLOW

A Web site is an entirely different entity from a traditional document (or any other traditionally linear work). Multiple items within a single document are linked at various locations, and the final product might be the result of many people, including (but not limited to) a graphic designer, copy editor, page layout director, and programmer. Because a change in any of the elements can have an immediate effect on the complete document, establishing a set of rules and project etiquette is necessary.

Blending the provided technology with a firm understanding of the project is the key to successful collaborative efforts. It might seem that because FrontPage 2003 provides such powerful collaboration tools, developing workflow would be easy as well. This is not the case. The workflow for any project might be many times more complicated than the development of the project itself.

Establishing workflow is a three-step process consisting of developing a site goal, designing the project flow, and assigning duties to the team in charge of the project. After these three things are complete, workflow has been established and the site development process is both well under way and on a path to success.

A number of computer programs are available on the market today that can help with the design and establishment of a project workflow. If you are looking for one, make sure that the program assumes multiple participants in the project, not a single user. Microsoft Project 2002 is one such powerful tool and can help in the workflow process. More information about Microsoft Project can be found online at `http://project.frontpagelink.com`.

DETERMINING THE SITE GOAL

All too often, technology gets in the way of the task at hand. The desire to jump right into a project, embracing the forgiving nature of Web design, is a powerful draw. It might seem obvious, but a very clear site goal should be developed and communicated to all team members before the site's first page is designed.

An effective Web site goal takes into account the user and platform base, aesthetic requirements, team assignments and responsibilities, and a growth and maintenance schedule. The Web site your team is building might be viewed on various platforms (different browser versions on different operating systems) and on various devices (handheld devices, WebTV-type machines, computers, and cell phones). This new presentation paradigm requires a level of attention that simple print projects have never required. The user and platform base is very important when working with a team. A technology restriction must be put into place if the site is to be viewed by users without the latest technology. Everyone must understand what to do with technology that might not be supported or understood by the user base. Questions to ask about the use of such technology include

- Should it be utilized at all?
- Should there be alternative pages for users without the technology?
- Should the site provide information for users on how to download and install the latest technology?
- Do you want to provide technical support to users who try to use the technology but are unable to do so on their own?
- Do potential viewing platforms, such as handheld devices or television set top browsers, have an effect on the technology that will be used?

→ For more on making sure that your FrontPage Web site can be accessed on as many browser types as possible, **see** "FrontPage's Accessibility Features," **p. 235**.

Aesthetic requirements are especially important when working with a team because all members must understand, and be able to reproduce, a specific look and feel for the entire site. Questions to be asked include the following:

- Will this be done with the use of FrontPage themes? CSS? Will Dynamic Web templates be used?
- Does your team understand how to design sites so that the sites can be effectively managed and updated by using any of these FrontPage technologies?
- Will you use Web page templates?
- Will you require that everyone use them?
- Who will design them?
- What will the color scheme for the site be?
- Where will the graphic library come from?
- Do your graphic designers understand the graphic and color palette issues specific to Web design?

Team assignments and responsibilities must be carefully understood and communicated from the very beginning. Everyone needs to know what is expected of him in the site development (and maintenance) process:

- Who is in charge of proofreading and editing?
- What sections of the site should be legally approved before publication?
- Who has the authority to change look and feel, colors, or themes?
- Who is responsible for providing links to newly added pages?

- What will be done to ensure that your site is accessible?
- What steps will be taken to ensure that these decisions are followed?

What happens after the site is up is always very important. A Web site is usually a constantly changing entity that requires an upkeep schedule. The Tasks view mentioned earlier works only when team members go to FrontPage to view their tasks. Everyone on the team needs to understand what is expected of him in terms of site maintenance and upkeep and should also know what type of update schedule he is required to follow.

DESIGNING WORKFLOW

After the site goal questions have been answered, the workflow design must be created. *Workflow* is best described as the specified order in which projects are completed, reported, and verified. In what order are the elements of site design going to come into play, and who is going to be responsible for what? If one element takes too long to complete (or is completed early), how does that affect the project? How much has to be done before the first page is designed, and how much effect on the site does any one page or user have?

The elements of workflow include content development, structure development, establishment of site look and feel, publication, alpha testing, beta testing, and maintenance. Although not all sites will contain all the elements listed, the workflow elements that will be used need to be put into place.

The workflow design should be simple enough to fit on a single page that can be distributed and communicated to the entire team so that they know what is expected.

32

TIP

> Consider adding a special section to your site, which is accessible only by the team, that clearly states the site goal and workflow requirements. Ask your team to refer to this section on a regular basis so that they are reminded of the project requirements. You also can update the area as things change, and your team can automatically be updated when such changes occur via the use of subscriptions.

Content development is one of the more important issues in Web design. A popular catch phrase in the world of Web design is "content is king." If the project you are working on has a team of writers attached to it, the source for your content is clear. If (as is often the case) your team does not contain professional writers, the source of your content won't always be so. Don't automatically assume that everyone on your team has the skills required to write for the Web.

After the content is completed (or at least started), the content presentation and linkage structures must be determined. Documents that are hard to find and documents offering too many choices can create unnecessary confusion at the site. If utilized, the Navigation view is a powerful tool for determining structure development.

The site's look and feel is extremely important because it dictates how content is to be imported into the Web site. If the site will use themes, templates, or CSS, it is especially important that the team uses similar style tags so that all pages look the same. If style tags aren't used and the site theme is changed, the result could be awkward. If templates are used, the templates' sources, the templates' numbers, and the final templates' approval need to be determined as well.

→ For a further discussion of the use of FrontPage themes in Web design, **see** "Using Themes," **p. 133**.

Issues of site publication include

- How often is the site going to be published?
- Who has the authority to publish the site?
- Should any elements of the site be prevented from being published?

A publishing schedule and rule set must be established in the workflow design.

Alpha testing is the process of bringing in external users to examine the site's basic flow before it is completed. A shell must be put into place before alpha testing can take place, but site usability can be examined after this has been done. If the initial alpha testing team determines that the initial flow or feel of the alpha site is ineffective, a restructuring plan can be put into place without requiring a remake of the entire site.

Beta testing is the process of bringing users to the final site before it is open to the public (or specified audience) to catch bugs and problems that are seen much more easily by someone who has not spent hours on the project. The results of the beta test can range dramatically from simple bug fixes and content edit to large overhauls of issues missed during the design process.

Maintenance is key and sometimes more complicated than the rest of the issues mentioned earlier because it determines the life of the site after it has been published to the initial audience. Understanding and communicating who is in charge of each level of maintenance ensures that the site is updated as required.

ASSIGNMENT OF DUTIES THROUGH THE TASKS FEATURE

After the purpose of the site has been determined and the workflow process has been established, the next step for the manager is to assign duties to the team.

Select Edit, Tasks while in Tasks view to assign a generic task to a Web. Enter the task name, who it is assigned to, the priority for the task, and a short description. To associate a task to a specific document, have the document selected in Folder view before you create the new task.

THE DEVELOPMENT ENVIRONMENT

Collaborative development is typically done on what is called a *development server*. The development server holds the collaborative project until it is ready to be published to a live server for the intended audience to see and interact with.

Traditionally, the development server is built on the same hardware and software platform on which the final project will be launched, which provides a means of testing all aspects of the final project. This practice is encouraged because it not only gives the developers a chance to work on the same system they expect the audience to work on, but it also helps identify unforeseen problems with the chosen platform. Development servers also have been used to provide backup systems when the deployment server goes down.

Budgets and other issues sometimes prevent a separate development server. It is possible, although not recommended, to develop the site on a disk-based Web or in a section of the site rendered unavailable to anyone but the development team.

TIP

> Don't let the term *development server* scare you away. If you are developing a basic site, your development server can be something as simple as a shared folder on your network.
>
> Development servers aren't about the technology; they are about making sure that you have things right before you publish your work to the entire world.

32

PUBLISHING ISSUES

To prevent the wrong information from being placed online, FrontPage 2003 offers the capability of marking a page or document to prevent it from being published during the normal publication process. All documents are marked for publishing by default, but you can quickly change the status of anything on the site.

This is powerful because it keeps the development Web from becoming an all-or-nothing situation. You can publish your development server on a regular basis without fear of half-completed documents or other such problems that can come from the use of multiple participants in the Web design process.

To exclude a specific file from being published with the rest of the Web, select the Exclude option from the Properties dialog box's Workgroup tab, shown in Figure 32.2; do so by right-clicking the document and selecting Properties from the menu.

Use the Publishing Exclude option when a document needs review or an edit before it should be published. This is an important issue when holding content for legal, content, or code review. Upon completion of the review, the reviewer can deselect the option. Make a note to the person in charge of the document to be sure to deselect the option when the task is completed.

Figure 32.2
You can exclude a file from being published to the Web until you are sure that the file is ready to be published.

> **TIP**
>
> Getting a team to remember to deselect the Publishing Exclude option might be difficult. This could result in a complete site that isn't allowed to be published. Before publishing the site, run the Publish Status report (described later) to determine whether any pages require additional work.

CHECKING DOCUMENTS IN AND OUT

Another FrontPage 2003 feature key to the collaborative authoring environment is the capability to check documents in and out from a Web site. During the time that a document is checked out, the individual who checked it out is the only person allowed to edit it. This option can be used to both prevent users from making multiple edits to a single file and editing a file they shouldn't (see Figure 32.3). This option was not available in earlier versions of FrontPage and was the source of a number of problems. The implications of such a tool quickly become obvious the first time one user overwrites the changes made by another.

Figure 32.3
FrontPage makes it clear when the document is not yours to check out. It also lets you know whom you must contact to get the document.

This option originally was available only on Web sites hosted on a Windows servers running an additional program called Microsoft Visual SourceSafe. Now the feature comes built in to the program.

TIP

> Be sure to stress to your team the importance of checking a document back in after it has been edited. Finding that someone who has gone home for the day, weekend, or year has checked out the document and not checked it back in is very frustrating.

 If you need to edit a document under someone else's control, *see "Can't Edit a Document Currently Checked Out" in the "Troubleshooting" section at the end of this chapter.*

CONFIGURING CHECK IN/OUT SETTINGS FROM WITHIN FRONTPAGE

To turn on the check in/out feature (it works in all Webs, including disk-based ones), simply click the Use Document check-in and check-out option in the General tab of the Site Settings dialog box. This can be reached by selecting Tools, Site Settings. The option can be turned on and off as needed.

After the feature has been turned on, every document opened by a user will result in the user being asked whether he wants to check out the document just requested. If he says no, he is given a read-only version of the document that can be saved under a different filename. If the user wants to check out a document without opening it, he can right-click the document in the folder list and select Check Out from the menu. This option is useful for preventing unauthorized edits to important pages.

 If site documents are being edited despite the fact that they are locked, *see "Problems with Check In and Check Out" in the "Troubleshooting" section at the end of this chapter.*

CAUTION

> This feature will only work by users editing site content with FrontPage. If anyone else tries to access and edit the content with another program (even Notepad), they will not be allowed to do so.
>
> Make sure that your team realizes the limitations of this tool if you are using any other development products with them.

DOCUMENT CHECK IN/OUT WITH VISUAL SOURCESAFE

Although FrontPage 2003 enables checking documents in and out, it does not contain all the functionality of Microsoft Visual SourceSafe. Visual SourceSafe also provides extensive version control capabilities that can be very powerful during a collaborative effort.

Version control is a tool that keeps copies of previous document and program versions. It makes returning to a specific date and time's version possible. Mistakes made aren't often realized until later in the project, and the capability to go back and undo a mistake at its point of origin is powerful.

Visual SourceSafe also provides more features to the documentation check-out process: cross-project tracking and separate access level control. The degree of power offered to the administrator is considerably more than is given with FrontPage 2003.

32

Visual SourceSafe runs only on Microsoft Internet Information Server on Windows servers. At this time, no plans exist to port it to any other server platform.

Although the cost of Visual SourceSafe might make it appear a bit out of reach, that cost is often recovered in simple man hours when one problem is promptly fixed because of a revision history.

More information about Microsoft Visual SourceSafe can be found online at `http://visualsourcesafe.frontpagelink.com`.

ASSIGNING DOCUMENTS

FrontPage 2003 gives you the ability to mark documents with a specific user assignment or review status. Although the markings have no direct affect on the file, the marking can be used to help the project team better understand the site's needs and requirements. By viewing either the Review Status or Assigned To report, participants in the development process have an additional view of the project status.

To assign a specific file to a specific user, open the properties dialog box for that page and click the Workgroup tab (seen in Figure 32.4). Select or type in the name of the person you want to assign the document to in the Assigned To dropdown box. You also can assign review status to any document using the same procedure in the Review Status dropdown.

Figure 32.4
The Workgroup tab shows who the document has been assigned to and what Review Status has been assigned to the document.

Remember that assignment of documents to users or the assignment of Review Status is little more than a label that has no control over who has authority to edit or delete the document. Assignment status should be used for reference purposes only.

ASSIGNMENT

The first duty of the Manager is that of assignment. This includes the assignment of documents to specific categories, documents to specific individuals, specific tasks to groups, and specific tasks to individuals.

FrontPage 2003 has the capability to assign variables to specific documents and users. This helps the collaborative environment by providing a clear online presentation of who is responsible for what and what is expected from each person in the project. Variable assignment is new to FrontPage and helps the Manager distribute the project requirements as needed in an effective and manageable format.

Assignment is accomplished through the Properties dialog box for each document. To reach the Properties dialog box, either right-click the document in FrontPage and select Properties or select File, Properties in an already open document.

Figure 32.5 shows the information made available in the Workgroup tab.

Figure 32.5
The Workgroup tab of the Properties dialog box lets you assign categories, users, review status, and publishing status to any document in your Web.

CATEGORIES

A document can be assigned to one or more categories. By assigning documents to categories, the Manager can assess and modify the workload distribution, and the Developer can quickly determine which documents have been placed under his responsibility.

Category variables can be added, edited, or deleted at any time. A site-wide Master Category List is reached by selecting Categories in the document Properties dialog box. In the Master Category List dialog box, categories can be added and deleted as necessary. No limit exists to the number of categories that can be assigned to a Web site. Feel free to get as specific as you like. See Figure 32.6 for a look at a simple Master Category List.

The ability to assign categories to a specific document helps distribute the workload of the total project. It also helps make maintenance of the site a bit more approachable. Instead of being an unwieldy mass of hundreds (or thousands) of documents, a Web can be divided into manageable categories with an individual or a group assigned to each. The site reports (discussed later in this chapter) help assess how documents are assigned and the effectiveness of such a distribution.

Figure 32.6
The Master Category List lets you assign category possibilities for the entire Web site.

ASSIGNING DOCUMENTS TO USERS

As well as being assigned to categories, a document also can be assigned to a single individual. As with category assignment, this is done in the Workgroup tab of the document Properties dialog box. Unlike category assignment, however, assigning a document to more than one individual is not possible. Document assignment is a powerful tool because it provides a working environment and site profile where a Developer can go directly to the site, see which documents are assigned to him, and work on the documents as necessary. It also helps the Manager see the load balance for the site.

Through this approach to assignment, no need exists for constant, direct interaction between the Manager and Developer. Often, members of a project team are in different physical locations and communication is scarce at best. A pattern of document assignment enables a clear workflow process without a need for constant meetings and other distracting nuisances.

A Manager can choose to assign documents on a category or user level or, for a higher level of specificity, assign documents to both levels with users being viewed as a subcategory. For example, a Manager might assign document A to Mary in Marketing and document B to Mark, also in Marketing. Documents can share categorization but have different Developers assigned to them.

Similar to the Master Category List, a Usernames Master List is also available. This is reached by clicking Names in the document Properties dialog box. See Figure 32.7 for a sample Usernames Master List.

NOTE

The Usernames Master List is independent of the Users list assigned to the site reached through Tools, Server, Permissions. Assignment of a name to the Usernames Master List does not automatically grant that name access to the site.

Figure 32.7
The Usernames Master List lets you assign username assignment possibilities for the entire Web site.

 If you need to edit site permissions but can't get into the interface, see "Can't Change Web Site Permissions" in the "Troubleshooting" section at the end of this chapter.

REVIEW STATUS

The third element on the Workgroup tab in the document Properties dialog box is Review Status. Review Status is an optional indicator for documents that require review before publication. Possible statuses include, but are obviously not limited to, Legal, Marketing, and Sales. Review Status also could include technical requirements, such as code review or proper use of color palettes (see Figure 32.8).

Figure 32.8
The Review Status Master List lets you review status possibilities for the entire Web site.

Like the previously mentioned master lists, a Review Status Master List is available. This is reached by clicking Statuses in the Page Properties dialog box.

DOCUMENT SUMMARY

The Summary tab is available only in the document Properties dialog box—reached by right-clicking the document in the Folder List and selecting Properties. You can place text in the Comments box that can be viewed (and edited) by anyone with access to the FrontPage Web. Figure 32.9 shows the Summary tab.

> **NOTE**
>
> Text placed in the Page Summary tab is not placed in the HTML—unlike the Comments Component, which places the comment text directly into the HTML (although not viewable through the browser). Be careful to put sensitive information about a page in the Page Summary tab, where it can be seen only by members of the collaborative team.

Figure 32.9
You can make comments about a specific document in the Summary tab of the document Properties dialog box.

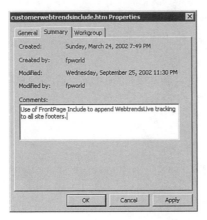

The Comments box for each document is a great place to present information about the document that you don't want made available in the HTML of the final document. Typical information found in the Comments box includes, but is not limited to, workflow commands, document purpose statements, editing requirements, and documentation-specific requests.

ASSIGNING TASKS

The assignment abilities of the Manager are not limited to categories, users, and review status. A Manager also can assign tasks to a Web that either are assigned to a specific document or are independent in nature. By providing tasks as a common reference point, developers can quickly determine which jobs are expected of them by examining and reacting to the Tasks view. See Figure 32.10 for an example of the Tasks view.

The Manager can assign a task at any time by selecting Tasks from the Edit menu while in Task view. The New Task dialog box lets the Manager enter the task name, who it is assigned to, the priority of the task, and a description for it. The rest of the variables are completed automatically by FrontPage.

Figure 32.10
The Tasks view shows all necessary information about a task.

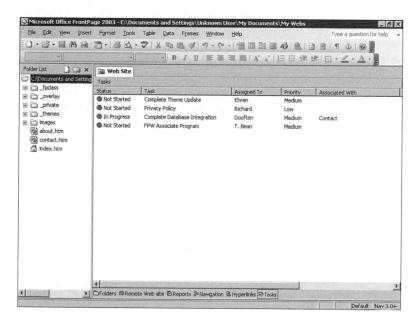

32

TIP

> During the site development and maintenance process, you will find that a number of tasks can be accomplished by anyone in the group. Consider creating an Assigned To variable of "Anyone" or "Volunteer" so that you can place the tasks in the Tasks view with an open call to anyone who will take it on.

PROJECT ASSESSMENT

The second job of the Manager is assessment of the project. One person needs to understand how the overall project is doing so that workflow can be adjusted accordingly. With a team of developers who are each focused on a specific page, file, or program, it is extremely important to have someone who concentrates on the overall project. Without such focus, a Web can quickly degrade into little more than a collection of individual documents.

FrontPage 2003 provides the tools to make an assessment of a document and the review process. The program also provides a number of reports that can help the Manager understand how various aspects of the project are doing and how they all relate to each other.

THE REPORTS

FrontPage 2003 provides great site-wide reports that can be used to assess the status of the site. Each report provides a different picture of the project's overall health. These reports were enhanced in FrontPage 2003, providing even more assessment capability than before, and are accessible through the Reports view.

The first report, Site Summary, acts as an overview or inventory of all the reports and lists the total number of files, pictures, unlinked files, linked files, slow pages, older files, recently added files, hyperlinks, unverified hyperlinks, broken hyperlinks, external hyperlinks, internal hyperlinks, component errors, uncompleted tasks, unused themes, stylesheet links, and dynamic Web templates. The Site Summary report appears automatically when the Reports view is accessed. Double-clicking any of the lines of the report takes you directly to the specific reports, described in the following. An example of the report can be seen in Figure 32.11.

Figure 32.11
The Site Summary reports gives a great overview of the site and contents.

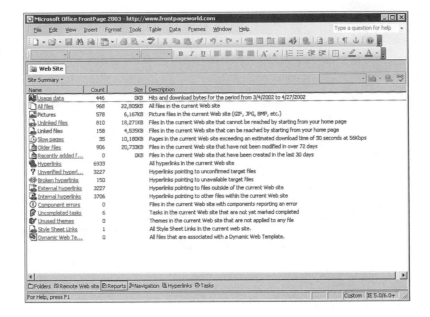

TIP

In all reports with elements that can be defined variably (how long does a slow page take anyway), the definitions of each report can be changed when viewing the report by clicking the appropriate variable in the Reports toolbar. Although the default variables for each report often provide a valuable view of the site, consider manipulating the variables for a more specific reading of your site. The default values for some of the reports can be changed in the Reports View tab of the Options dialog box—reached by selecting Tools, Options.

All Files shows all the files in the Web site in one long list. As is true with all the reports, selecting any of the column headers in the report enables you to sort by that variable.

Use this report to assess just how big your site has become. A quick glance through all the files at once can give you a powerful overview of the project and can quickly point you in the direction of immediate site needs and requirements.

Pictures obviously states the amount of pictures in your Web site. A constantly updated Web site with a lot of pictures can quickly become a cemetery for them. If your list of pictures seems a bit much, select the report and consider eliminating the ones that aren't currently serving a purpose.

Unlinked Files are files without a link to or from the file. They tend to signify either a forgotten or an incorrect link or a document that should have been deleted from the site. The Manager should take time to verify the purpose of any unlinked file and act as necessary.

TIP

> Instead of deleting files from a site, consider creating a Deleted folder in which all documents marked for deletion could be placed. This will allow you to quickly bring back a file if you realize later that you really didn't mean to delete it.

Linked Files reports on files in the Web site that can be linked from the home page. This is always an interesting report when examining site flow.

The Slow Pages report can help the Manager identify potential problem files that should either be reduced in size or be split in to two or more files.

Remember that the default for the Slow Pages report is meant to rate the site in relation to a typical modem connection. If your project is an intranet with typical LAN connectivity, this is hardly an issue.

The Older Files report shows you the oldest files in the site. A Manager might choose to remove older files as a result of the report or use the information to identify which documents need updating or archiving.

Recently Added Files shows you which elements have recently been added to the site. This is an especially powerful option for the Manager who wants to ensure that nothing has been added to the project that shouldn't be there.

If you aren't sure of the purpose or validity of a document, open or view it to get a better idea of what it is. The Modified By column lets you know who placed the item into the Web in the first place should you need to take action.

Hyperlinks reports the total amount of hyperlinks within the Web site. This can be used as an interesting metric of the size and health of your site.

Unverified Hyperlinks is a list of hyperlinks pointing to unverified files (internal or external). This report is used to determine whether you have any broken hyperlinks. Selecting the report provides you with the chance to verify the hyperlinks (if you are connected to the Internet, of course).

Broken Hyperlinks cause user frustration and inhibit site success. They often are the result of a simple typographical error but are hard to trace because the link path doesn't appear in the WYSIWYG FrontPage interface. The Broken Hyperlinks report quickly lists all broken hyperlinks and provides a quick repair option through the Edit Hyperlink dialog box—reached by double-clicking the specific broken link.

32

Where External Hyperlinks report lists links outside your site; Internal Hyperlinks shows links inside your site. These also are a good metric of the size and scope of your site.

The Component Errors report lists problems with any FrontPage components in the site. This report prevents the Manager from having to double-check every component in the site to ensure that they work. Just because a component has been placed in a Web does not mean that it will automatically work. Most components call for additional files and variables that, if not listed, will result in the component not working.

Uncompleted Tasks is a great way to get a quick overview of what needs to be done at your site. It provides a quick reminder of what still needs to be done, whereas the regular Tasks screen lists all tasks (including those completed and those already in progress).

If you use them, the Unused Themes report can be very valuable. Themes installed at your site that aren't used simply take up disk space and slow everything else down. Ideally, the number of unused themes should be 0 as they represent only wasted disk space.

Style Sheet Links (new to FrontPage 2003) shows you all links to stylesheets (internal or external) and lets you quickly sort by the link. Use this report to make sure that all CSS links within your site are valid.

Dynamic Web Templates shows you all files in your site associated with any Dynamic Web Templates installed on your site. Use this report to make sure that no Dynamic Web Template content has been accidentally deleted.

Five other (non-site traffic) reports are available by selecting the dropdown list in the Reports toolbar and selecting the Workflow option. These reports are also useful when assessing the state of your Web site.

The Review Status report lists every file in the site, providing a column for Review Status, if any. The Reviewed By column is marked with the person who assigned the review. Use this report to determine which files still need to be reviewed before project completion.

The Assigned To report, similar to the Review Status report, lists every file in the Web, with a column for whom the document was assigned to and who assigned it.

Use this report to determine the distribution of work in the project. Sometimes a Manager might not realize that he has placed a large amount of work on a single individual, and the report can help identify such trends.

Categories lists all files in the Web, with a column provided for category assignment. You can use the report to ensure that the correct pages were assigned to the correct categories and review the category distribution.

 If you find the default category features assigned by FrontPage to be a bit limiting in scope, see "Categories Don't 'Work' for Me" in the "Troubleshooting" section at the end of this chapter.

Publish lists all files, their review statuses (if any), and their publish statuses. Documents that were excluded from publication are marked as Don't Publish in the report.

It's always a good idea to review the Publish report right before you think a project is completed. A file might still need to be reviewed (or has already been reviewed and needs to be marked accordingly).

The Checkout Status reports on which documents are currently checked in and out of your Web site.

THE ROLE OF THE DEVELOPER

As the world of Web design moves from simple text and graphics to interactive multimedia, not only does the need for a team-based approach to Web design become obvious, but it also becomes necessary. Very few people can provide all the skills necessary to produce an effective Web site. Those who think that they can tend to have a higher opinion of themselves than they probably should.

The Developer in a collaborative project could be a Mac user accessing the site with Dreamweaver, a programmer accessing the site with a version of Microsoft Visual InterDev, or a technical writer who only feels safe using Microsoft Word. Sure, the Developer might have the same system you do (it sure makes communication and training easier), but it's not always so. Sometimes the Developer might be using a third-party development tool instead. Yes, the development process can get that complicated.

 If you find that working with multiple site development products tend to wreck havoc on elements of your site, *see "Other Products Mess Things Up" in the "Troubleshooting" section at the end of this chapter.*

The Developer can use the same tools provided to the Manager to make his daily job a little more productive. As you will see here, the Tasks view and reporting features are as useful to the Developer as they are to the Manager.

TIP

> Although Microsoft Visual InterDev and previous versions of FrontPage (including the Macintosh version) can access a FrontPage Web, they will not be capable of making full use of all the features provided by this release of the program. Be aware of exactly which options are available to team members who aren't using FrontPage 2003.

THE TASKS VIEW

The most powerful tool for the Developer is the Tasks view. It lets the Developer quickly check the site for a list of any tasks that might be assigned to him and react accordingly. Instead of task meetings or waiting for an email note with the work for the day, a Developer can go directly to the Web to see what is required/expected of him in the project.

Assigned tasks also can be generic in nature, not necessarily assigned to a particular individual. The smaller the team, the more likely a Developer will wear multiple hats. This is provided for in the program.

32

When the Developer double-clicks the task, the Task Details dialog box opens, giving all the specifics for the task. From there, the Developer can click Start Task to open the document so the work can be performed. When the Developer closes the document, FrontPage automatically asks whether he wants the task to be marked as completed. If the user says yes, the Tasks view will list it as such. If the user says no, the Tasks view will list the task as In Progress. See Figure 32.12 for an example of the Task Details dialog box.

Figure 32.12
The Task Details dialog box shows the Developer exactly what is expected of him in the collaborative process.

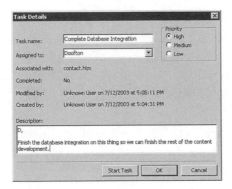

REPORTING

The Developer also can use a number of the reports in the Reports view to determine which tasks are expected from him.

If the Developer is in charge of elements of the site specific to a report, he can select the report from the list to determine site requirements and individual action. For example, a developer in charge of making sure that the site loads quickly can select the Slow Pages report to determine which pages require action.

Developers should understand which of the reports apply to their specific tasks and should be trained in how to view the reports and react appropriately. Any Manager can quickly show their Developers how to select the report from the list and guide them in the appropriate action items.

TIP

> Site reports are a new concept in Web design. Experienced developers might not immediately recognize their purpose in the development process or the extra power these reports provide. It is the job of the Manager to communicate the benefits of site reporting to everyone involved in the project.

DEVELOPERS NOT USING FRONTPAGE

You might be faced with developers on the team who aren't using FrontPage. Although this provides an additional level of complexity, it is not an impossible problem to solve.

The key to developers working in a FrontPage Web without FrontPage is the program's commitment to 100% HTML preservation. In other words, if a document is edited by a third-party program, FrontPage will not re-edit the HTML to make it work inside the system. A developer could edit a page inside a Web with any program (including Notepad) and expect it to remain as edited.

If development work in a FrontPage Web is going to be done without FrontPage as the proprietary editor, you should use the Recalculate Hyperlinks option on a regular basis by selecting the option from the Tools menu. Recalculating hyperlinks makes FrontPage aware of all the files in the Web so that it can act and report accordingly.

TIP

> You do not want to recalculate hyperlinks when any part of the site is being edited by any of the developers because it might not provide a complete view of the site.

TROUBLESHOOTING

CAN'T EDIT A DOCUMENT CURRENTLY CHECKED OUT

Another user has a document checked out that you must edit immediately. You don't have time to track the user down.

If you must make edits to a page currently checked out by another user, consider making a copy of the page and then editing the copy instead. To make a copy, select the file, right-click it, and select copy. Paste the copied page wherever you prefer. Edit the copy of the page. Once completed, notify the user who has the page checked out where your changes can be found.

Of course, this means that two copies of the file will be floating around at some point and someone will have to come in and compare the two and create a best of breed file. FrontPage can't do this for you; you'll need a "human" to take on this task.

CAN'T CHANGE WEB SITE PERMISSIONS

You need to change the permissions in your site and are unable to do so through the FrontPage interface.

If you are unable to set the permissions of your Web site through the FrontPage interface, the Web administrator has not given you Administrator access. Ask the Web administrator to give you such access. If you are in a virtual hosting situation, you might have to pay extra for such access.

→ For more on server security setting, **see** "Security and Administration of a Web Site," **p. 323**.

CATEGORIES DON'T "WORK" FOR ME

The workgroup categories assigned to your site are not sufficient enough to effectively manage your site.

More categories can be assigned to your site through the Workgroup tag of the Properties dialog box. This is done by selecting the Categories option and entering additional categories into the Master Category List.

OTHER PRODUCTS MESS THINGS UP

Members of your team want to use other Web development tools, but they want to use the collaborative tools offered by FrontPage 2003.

Using the collaboration features provided by FrontPage requires that people actually use FrontPage in the design process. No safeguards exist to ensure that this important rule is followed outside the program. Care should be taken to make sure that the development team understands this issue. If users must use other development tools, they can enter the HTML produced by these tools into their FrontPages through either the HTML tab or the Insert HTML option.

PROBLEMS WITH CHECK IN AND CHECK OUT

Documents in your Web site are somehow being edited, despite the fact that they are checked out.

A document opened in any program other than FrontPage won't be affected by the Check In and Out features. For example, nothing prevents authors from editing or deleting a file from within the Windows Explorer (if it can be accessed through Windows Explorer, common in a development environment). If you have users who plan on editing files within the Web site using programs other than FrontPage, the feature becomes pointless and a more robust change control system is required.

FRONT AND CENTER: COLLABORATION VERSUS COMMUNICATION

Collaborative authoring adds many people to a procedure that was at one time completed by only one. Having a team decide on (or even develop) design elements might be an invitation to disaster and should be approached carefully. Just because you have the tools to collaborate doesn't mean that you have the tools to communicate.

Everyone on your team needs to know what is expected from them and what you expect the final site to look like. Whiteboarding a site and providing initial planning screenshots to an approval team is an effective way to handle the design process. Making sure that everyone understands exactly what the site is going to look like and requiring that everyone follow the directions is a mandatory step.

The best way to get around the problems associated with group design is to divide the team in such a way that the actual design process is limited to as few participants as possible. Make a decision about who is in charge of the design and aesthetic aspects of the project, and trust him to bring the project to completion.

Consider using your FrontPage Web site to store the results of your whiteboarding sessions. This way, everyone on the team will be able to reference back to them. Obviously, set the permissions so that the normal public isn't able to access that information.

CHAPTER 33

MANAGING WORKFLOW AND TASKS IN THE DESIGN PROCESS

In this chapter

ASSESSING YOUR SITE

In the first chapter of this section, we examined the issues surrounding management of a team development project and how FrontPage can play a role. In the previous chapter, we took a high-level overview of the tools and technologies that a Web project manager would want to use when taking on such a project. Both FrontPage-specific tools and other platforms were examined. In this chapter, we'll take a look at the specifics of the tools that come with FrontPage 2003 and how to make them an integral part of the site management process. We'll also explain how to truly "read" the different reports to understand the health and status of your site and how to respond to problems that will inevitably come up in the Web development process.

From file assignment to reporting, many of the tools and features in FrontPage 2003 help the user better understand the status of the project she is working on. This focus on site assessment assists greatly in the collaboration process.

As sites grow larger and larger, it is extremely important to have an accurate understanding of the entire project. When building a bridge, construction quality means little if the foundation is sinking. In site design, the quality of the graphics means little if the site has ineffective flow or the task load on any one member of the team prevents that member from performing her assigned job. Proper use of the tools provided by FrontPage 2003 gives the user an understanding of the project, which enables her to make proactive decisions in terms of continued site development.

UNDERSTANDING SITE FLOW

The Internet contains millions (if not billions) of pages of great content. The problem has always been finding an effective way to direct people to that content. Greater than the problem of bandwidth, technology, or crashing operating systems is the problem of site flow. Very few sites provide a clear path to the content they work so hard to present.

How many pages does someone need to click to get to the information she is looking for? In much the same way that people get disgusted when they have to push 10 numbers before they can speak to a real human in a phone tree, clicking through 10 pages to get to the content they are looking for is equally as discouraging.

Site flow is defined as the means by which a user goes from one page to another. Are the possible paths well defined? Do they make sense? Is there more than one option for getting to the information the user is seeking? After the user has gone down one path, does she need to return to the beginning to go down another one?

Effective site flow comes from an effective navigation scheme and manageable and navigational depth level.

NAVIGATION

One option in assessing site navigation is the Hyperlinks view (shown in Figure 33.1). This view enables you to see each file and how it relates to each other file in terms of links from and to the document.

Figure 33.1
The Hyperlinks view lets you examine your site in terms of links to and from each document.

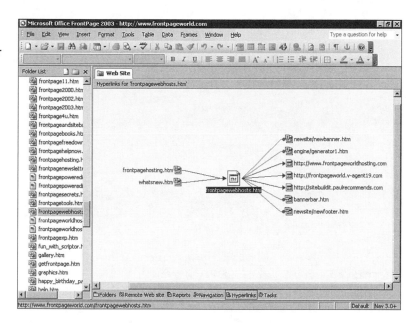

Hyperlinks view lists ach document and folder in the Web on the left side of the screen. To assess how any document relates to the rest of the Web, select the document from the Folder List. The view shows the document in the middle of the screen with documents that link to the item on the left and items the document links to on the right. Selecting the plus symbol on any of the documents in the screen results in the same presentation for that document. You can follow this view as many times as you'd like, placing as many hyperlinks on the screen as desired. This is shown in Figure 33.2.

It is important to examine the possible paths to each document in the site when assessing the navigation options on your site. If a document has only one path to it, the chances of a user finding that document are greatly diminished. The power of hyperlinked text is in the fact that is nonlinear, allowing the user to approach the text however he wants to.

TIP

> You should have at least two paths to every document in your site. People aren't guaranteed to follow any specific direction, so providing multiple roads helps increase chances that a user will find what she is looking for.
>
> Do name your pages in such a way that people know which road they are on. If you have numerous pages with the same title (or similar titles), even if they are working their way through your site, they just might not know how far they've gone.

Figure 33.2
Hyperlinks view lets you examine the link relationships to multiple documents on the same screen if desired.

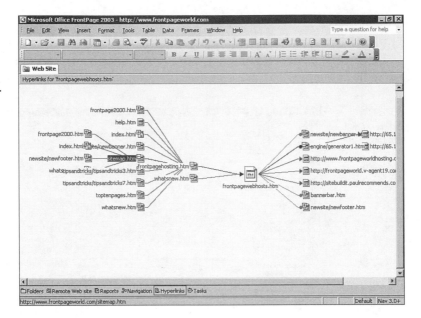

If a document has only one possible path, track back through the path and see whether any other path options can be offered. For example, a document could also be listed in a general page of important site documents or in a New Links section that points users directly to documents recently added to the site.

T I P

Another popular site navigation tool is a site map, which provides a map or an overview of the entire site for the first-time visitor. You either can create one by hand or use the Table of Contents Web component to make one for you.

Navigation also can be assessed through a simple examination of the Web site. Take a look at your site through a browser and consider how the first-time user might approach navigation. You can also bring in an outsider to view the site for the first time. Ask her what she thinks of the site and documents links.

T I P

Shared borders and the Include component are tools that can be used effectively in promoting a simpler site navigational scheme.

→ For more on the navigational tools that come with FrontPage 2003, **see** "FrontPage's Navigation Tools and Elements," **p. 147**.

Depth

The depth of your site is also very important. If it takes too many clicks for a user to get to a certain document, the chances are good that she either won't take the time to do so or will get extremely frustrated in the process. Most users come to a Web site looking for a specific item, and if that item is too hard to find, they often leave quickly and disappointed.

If your site was developed using the Navigation view, shown in Figure 33.3, you already have a great overview of the site depth; use the view to see just how deep the site goes. You can't examine a site in Navigation view unless it was created with that tool.

→ For more information regarding development with FrontPage's navigation tools, **see** "FrontPage's Navigation Tools and Elements," **p. 147**.

Figure 33.3
Navigation view quickly lets you see how many documents are required to get to any particular item on your site.

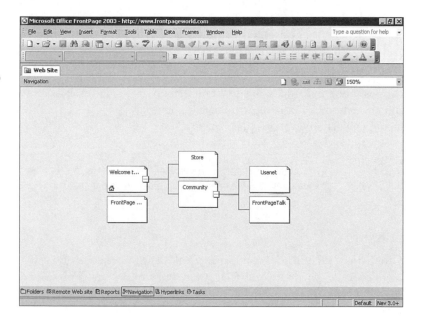

If you didn't build your site in Navigation view, you must assess the site depth on your own. You can use the Hyperlinks view mentioned previously to some success, but effective assessment requires an understanding of the site that, at this point, can be reached only by clicking your way through the site.

TIP

One good way to manage site depth is to put each level in a new folder on the site. You will quickly be able to determine how deep a site is if you follow this design process from the beginning.

There is no need for a site to become too deep. FrontPage's capability to rewrite paths on the file makes site reorganization a simple and worthwhile task. All you need to do is move a file from one folder to another, and FrontPage will make sure that all the HTML in the site is updated accordingly. If the site has become too deep, it is time to reorganize the site navigation.

TASK LOAD

A domino effect of inefficiency can take place if too much responsibility lies on the shoulders of a single individual or team. If team members are waiting on someone else to complete her part of the project, you can have a cyber traffic jam in your design process.

Examining the task load on any one individual or one area of influence is as vital as examining site health or any of the other subjects discussed in this chapter. If too much is waiting on one person or one area, other groups won't be able to do their part. Managing the task load is the "human" part of managing a collaborative project. The Task view can only alert the manager of the symptoms.

Cross training individuals in your team is always a good idea. Not only does it provide a certain protection from the repetition factor, but it also provides an additional workforce should one group's workload become too heavy.

TIP

A quick look at a site's Task view on a regular basis can help the manager quickly assess if too much of the project has been placed on one particular person.

OTHER ISSUES

33

Other issues exist that a good manager will want to keep eye on during the Web development process. The first is verifying accessibility of the site. The second is checking for speedy download times and identifying potential problems through the FrontPage site reporting features.

Throughout the development of a project, it would be a good idea to check the Web site's accessibility and make sure that no one in your team is developing content that can't be accessed by those wanting to view it. Run the accessibility checker on a regular basis to both identify problems as well as stop unhealthy development trends early in the development process.

→ For more on the FrontPage 2003 Accessibility checker and other issues related to making your site accessible, **see** "FrontPage's Accessibility Features," **p. 235**.

The second issue a good site manager will want to check on a regular basis is the general health of the site. FrontPage 2003 comes with a series of site reports, discussed in the next section of this chapter, that can help you assess how your site is doing and make necessary changes to keep your site as healthy as possible.

USING SITE REPORTING

The 16 site reports provided with FrontPage 2003 provide an incredible overview of the site workflow and task status. Understanding how to use and respond to each of the reports is key to managing the site development and maintenance process.

Sites reports are accessed through the Reports view.

TIP

> Remember that the variables assigned to each of these reports are defaults and might not necessarily represent a realistic view of your site. Make sure that you adapt the variables in each of the reports to your requirements.

SITE SUMMARY REPORT

The Site Summary report provides a basic snapshot of the site, which can be used to make a number of important decisions and assessments. It lists the basic elements of all the reports listed below, allowing you to quickly determine your next step.

Use this report as a jumping-off point for your site maintenance duties; refer to it on a regular basis because it provides a view of your *entire* site—not just a single aspect of it. You can click any of the items to jump to the corresponding report.

ALL FILES REPORT

The All Files report, shown in Figure 33.4, provides a way to quickly view and sort through a list of every document in the entire site. You can sort by any aspect in the report by clicking it. For example, you can click the Type column header to sort all the files by type, enabling you to quickly identify all non-HTML files. You also can use the feature to sort by Name or Title if you aren't sure exactly which file you are looking for.

Use this view to assess a number of things, including how many types of a specific file are in the site, an overview of the site's history in the modified date field, and a list of people who have been modifying documents in the site. You can also use the report to tell just how many files exist, where they are located, and who is modifying them.

You must have a good understanding of just how big your site is. Depending on the site's purpose, it might be a good idea to institute a practice of archiving or deleting files after they have met their purposes. A site can sometimes become simply too big to handle.

UNLINKED FILES REPORT

An *unlinked* file is an interesting problem. It identifies either a file no longer needed or a file that can't be reached because it is missing an important link to it. The first problem requires either deletion or archiving, whereas the second problem requires further investigation and action. All files should have at least one link; otherwise, they will not be capable of being found.

33

Figure 33.4
The All Files report can be quite long. It gives a powerful, exhaustive overview of everything contained in the site.

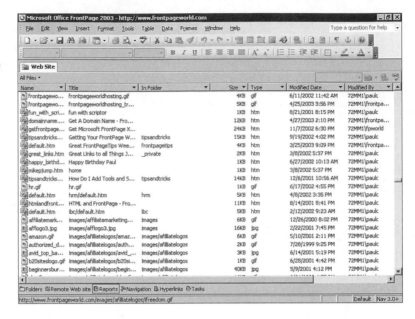

TIP

> If you know that there should have been a link to an unlinked file, chances are good that the link to the file was misspelled. If this is the case, you can use the Broken Hyperlinks report to determine potential sources for the link.

An unlisted file that shouldn't have been deleted obviously requires some sort of link to it. If it is unclear from where the document should be linked, create a task that requires the correct team member to find and implement the link.

SLOW PAGES REPORT

A common problem in Web development is the developer or team who forgets that the average user will be connecting to the site over a modem (often at speeds less than optimal), instead of over the high-speed network on which the site was developed. A lot of FrontPage developers don't even have a network to deal with; most have likely developed their sites on the Web server that came with the program.

Because some developers might have the tendency to forget the reality of the world for which they are designing, the Slow Pages report is a powerful tool; it enables a quick view of all potential download speed problems in the entire site without requiring a look at each individual page.

The Slow Pages report provides a look at pages that might have speed problems when being downloaded by modem. You can choose which speed you consider a slow download to have and examine your site from that perspective.

How slow is a slow page? How long should you expect your audience to wait for a page to be viewed? These are some of the great questions of Web design that can't be answered here. You must determine who your audience is, what they are looking for, and how long they are willing to wait for it. If you want a hint at what works best, look at the world's most popular Web sites (Yahoo!, MSN, Amazon, and Excite) with a stopwatch and see what they do.

TIP

You always should design your pages to load as quickly as possible, despite the rapid proliferation of broadband. Although you might be designing your site for a high-speed network, such as an intranet, the chances are good that users will want to access the site from a traditional dial-up line (either through the Internet or via a direct-dial connection into the network).

Telecommuters and remote staff are becoming more and more common in today's workspace. You should do what you can to be ready for them. It is always easier to design with them in mind than it is to later modify a site for their use.

You can do three things with slow loading pages: split them into pieces, decrease graphic sizes in the document, or leave the document as is.

Splitting a document into pieces is by far one of the easiest ways to solve the slow page problem. You can complete the entire process in a few seconds with FrontPage's cut-and-paste capabilities. Be sure that you identify and hyperlink the files accordingly.

TIP

If you split a document into pieces, you should take note of what might happen if a person enters the site from one of the middle pages. Spider-based search engines make a note of a site's every page and might, for example, send one of your users to page 4 of 7. In a multiple-page document, hyperlinked notations (such as page 4 of 7) are a great navigation tool and help prevent potential confusion.

33

Decreasing graphic size on a page is another means of decreasing page download time. A simple tweak to a color palette or a change in file type can result in a significant decrease in image file size. Another option is to shrink the physical size of the image, which always results in a smaller file size (as shown in Figure 33.5).

Sometimes you just need to leave the file as it is. Some pages need every item to remain just the way it was designed. Although this is rare, it is still an option that must be considered. If the document is valuable enough and people know the wait is coming, it can be worth the slow load time.

Figure 33.5
Decreasing the size of
an image on a page
and cropping for focus
can quickly decrease
its download time.

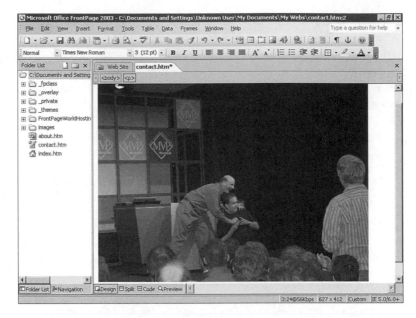

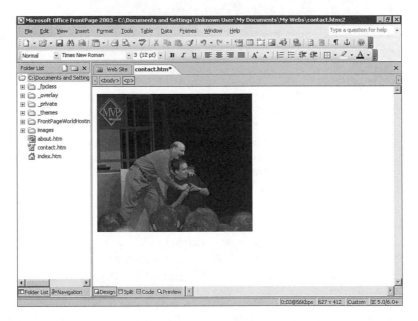

33

TIP

If you have a page on your site that takes a long time to download, it is always a good
idea to make a note of that fact on all hyperlinks to that document.

OLDER FILES REPORT

The Older Files report does just what its name implies: lists the oldest files in your site. The report is useless if your site performs the role of archive and you need to keep a copy of everything. If, however, you want to maintain a site of specific size or need help weeding out older documents and files, this report is for you.

Many designers commonly keep a copy of everything the site has ever presented online. Although this can have a certain nostalgic appeal, it can create a site that is simply too large to manage. A site quickly can become tens of thousands of pages and at the same time become a large management headache. Use this report to identify older files and determine a plan for them.

TIP

> If you need to keep an online copy of every file ever posted to your Web site, consider storing documents of a certain age in an archive file. It makes them more easily identifiable.

RECENTLY ADDED FILES REPORT

The Recently Added Files report gives you the chance to see what was recently added to the site. Double-clicking any item in the report opens the document for your inspection or approval. You can sort by any of the fields in the report by clicking the field header.

On a more serious note, a hacker might have placed an item into the Web site that shouldn't be there. A regular peek at the Recently Added Files report can help you identify such suspicious files.

TIP

> Don't assume that HTML files can't contain viruses or other forms of malicious code. They can call viruses from an outside source; scripts in the file can contain malicious code as well. If a suspicious file has been added to your Web site and you are not sure what it does, consider bringing in a scripting or programming expert to examine the file to ensure it is acceptable.

33

HYPERLINKS REPORT

The Hyperlink report lists every hyperlink in your site. Although some might find the report overwhelming, it does serve the powerful purpose of being able to give you a very quick idea of how big your site actually is.

Web sites can get out of control. They can, simply, get too big to be of use to anyone. In addition, if you have too many links pointing outside of your site, you are spending a great amount of time directing people away from your business.

Use the report to get a good feeling for your site. Are there plenty of hyperlinks to the pages that matter? Are there too many links outside of your site? Are there just too many links and not enough content for a site of that size?

UNVERIFIED HYPERLINKS REPORT

Unverified hyperlinks are links outside the site, which FrontPage can't verify are "good" or not. Even a link to something as steadfast as http://www.microsoft.com comes up as unverified in this report—(initially) so don't worry.

When you first open the report and there are some unverified links in your site, FrontPage asks if you would like it to verify the hyperlinks for you. Let it do so.

This is a powerful report because it gives you the chance to double-check that the hyperlinks in your site are going to the right places and actually exist. Once you've collected a number of external hyperlinks, you can quickly have FrontPage double check that you didn't misspell a URL or direct people toward a dead site.

Nothing is more frustrating than links that go nowhere. Be sure that your site's links take the users where they are supposed to.

NOTE

> FrontPage will only verify that a hyperlink goes to a live site and not that it is the right page in the site or even the correct URL.

BROKEN HYPERLINKS REPORT

Broken hyperlinks are always a problem in a site of any size. A broken hyperlink can be a frustrating experience to anyone who is looking for specific information and can result in the perception that the site is sloppy.

Webmasters sometimes receive an email note that says little more than "Your link to that page is down." In the past, they had no choice other than to check each hyperlink individually. In the past, third-party programs (some costing more than the retail price of FrontPage 2003) helped track down such hyperlinks. This feature is now included with FrontPage 2003 (see Figure 33.6).

A broken hyperlink's source is usually either a typographical error or a file or an external Web site that has been deleted. You can use the broken hyperlink path in conjunction with the All Files report to make a solid guess at what the hyperlink might be.

TIP

> It takes a great deal of time (especially when using a modem), but be sure that you run the Broken Hyperlinks report when you are connected to the Internet. If generated while online, the report also tells you which links are down outside your Web site.

Figure 33.6
The Broken Hyperlinks report provides a quick listing of all such links (internal and external) in your site.

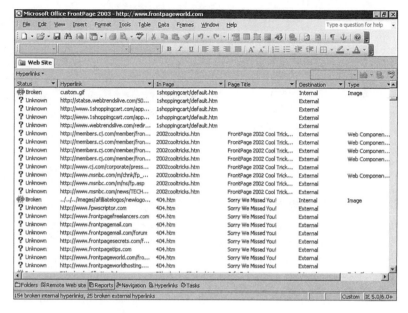

EXTERNAL AND INTERNAL HYPERLINKS REPORTS

These two reports help give you an idea of the internal and external links within your site.

If your goal is to keep people at your site, but you find that you have many more external than internal links, you might want to reexamine the links. If you find that your site has a disproportionately large number of external links—that might be a good indication that your site doesn't have a lot of information, internally, to point to.

COMPONENT ERRORS REPORT

FrontPage components provide the site design process a high level of power and interactivity. They enable you to provide interactive elements to your site that are traditionally assigned to complicated (and expensive) programming or programmers.

FrontPage components require a number of elements that aren't as obvious as other files in a Web site. The chances for problems are many, and care should be taken to prevent them. Problems could be as simple as a missing file or could result from something as complicated as the server permissions not being properly set.

The Component Errors report is a valuable timesaver because it identifies problems in site components without requiring that you test every element individually. You should run the Component Errors report on a regular basis to identify any potential problems early.

If you find a component error on a page in your site and aren't certain what is required to fix it, consider eliminating the component from the page altogether and then reinserting it.

➔ For more on the FrontPage Web components, **see** "Using Web Components, Shared Borders, and Link Bars," **p. 167**.

33

UNCOMPLETED TASKS REPORT

This important report gives you an instant look at what still needs to be done on the Web site.

It is hard to look at a site and have a good idea of what is missing. As Web sites get bigger and bigger, their holes become less obvious to the eye (with the exception of course, of the user's eyes). Frequent examinations of the Uncompleted Tasks report equips you with an instant overview of what remains to be done.

 If you find that there are simply too many tasks in the system to deal with effectively, *see "Tasks Out of Control" in the "Troubleshooting" section at the end of this chapter.*

UNUSED THEMES REPORT

If your site uses FrontPage themes and changes them frequently, the possibility for unused themes to remain in your site is always there. Other than the fact that they take up space, they also can be a distraction to the developers because the developers might not understand which theme they should be designing under.

If your site has unused themes, eliminate them. You can always, obviously, put them back in later if you find you need them again.

STYLE SHEET LINKS REPORT

All style sheet links in a Web site are shown with this report. This includes internal and external links and can be used to quickly assess the status of your style sheets.

Like everything else on the Internet, style sheets get edited and updated on a regular basis. This report might show you that certain style sheets are no longer called or, more importantly, certain sheets are being called and they aren't available.

Because so many are involved in the site design and maintenance process, you will want to check this on a regular basis to make sure that no one has undone the work of another.

DYNAMIC WEB TEMPLATES REPORT

The use of Dynamic Web Templates in the design of a Web site built collaboratively is obvious. Sites can be developed in such a way that some developers have to do little more than update a few sentences here and there.

As with style sheets, if Dynamic Web Template content is erased by anyone on your team, the content will not work as desired or planned. Consult this report on a regular basis to ensure that no necessary Dynamic Web Template content has been removed from your site.

RESPONDING TO REPORTED PROBLEMS

After the site has been assessed and the reports have been run, you need to know how to respond to the gathered information. Although the natural instinct is to immediately issue a new set of tasks and assignments, this might not be the best first step.

Responding to site status requires identifying site problems and then implementing the proper corresponding solution. Establishing a means to further prevent such problems is a good idea as well.

WHY PROBLEMS OCCUR

Problems in project workflow come from either ineffective assignments or an unequal workload. In short, problems arise when your team members are unable to accomplish the tasks at hand in the amount of time given them. It is the manager's job to keep track of the project workload as well as ensure that the assignments are effective.

You usually can identify a problem via a quick assessment of the tasks list or from the Assigned To or Publish Status report. An individual or a group often rises to the top as having much more to do than anyone else. This unequal distribution results in others waiting for elements from the slowest team and, because of a domino effect, being unable to accomplish their tasks as a result.

A group or an individual who can't keep pace with the rest of the team needs discipline, training, or additional help. Discipline is an individual matter, but FrontPage can assist with training or help.

> **TIP**
>
> Be sure that your entire team understands the tools made available to them. Take a few minutes to point out to everyone on the team the tools that will have the biggest impact on their project and make sure that they know how to use them.

SOLUTIONS

Solutions to workflow and task assignment problems are found either in better training or by task reassignment. Solutions can also be reached by creating wizards and templates that guide a team member through a process not previously understood or handled well.

Sometimes team members are hard workers with the potential to complete their requirements and are simply unaware of how to use FrontPage's tools. Web design requires a special way of thinking and understanding that is sometimes forgotten in the world of the WYSIWYG interface.

Training can take many forms. Possibilities include direct training by the manager, letting users work their way through this book (or others), and sending team members to third-party training.

Sometimes the manager must walk the team member through the fundamentals of design with FrontPage—especially in terms of the project being worked on. Even though there are some aspects of FrontPage a team will never use, there are an equal number of tools that, although not obvious, will greatly assist in the development process. Don't assume that the team knows and understands what has been made available to it. A few examples of using the tools often provide the team members with all the required information and enable

33

them to make great production advances that they wouldn't have made with just a simple understanding of the program. The tutorial that comes with FrontPage, although basic, walks the user through the fundamentals of the program as well and might be a great place to start.

Task reassignments, shown in Figure 33.7, can be based on a logical shifting of responsibilities to one group or another. Another option is to create "virtual" users and groups, and that can be claimed by anyone who has the time to accomplish the task. For example, assigning a document to *Anyone* or to a group called *Extra* is a viable option that gives team members with time on their hands additional direction toward project completion. Because it is assigned to *Anyone*, anyone in the team can complete the task. This practice, used in conjunction with the ability to check documents in and out, provides a smooth workflow.

Figure 33.7
Assigning tasks to virtual users can be a subtle means of offering the task to anyone with the time to complete the project.

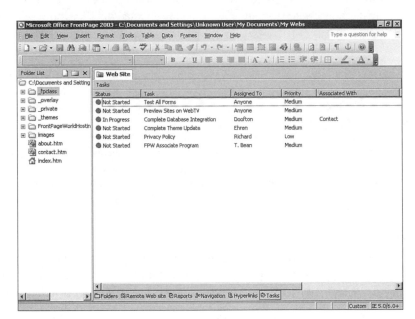

Use of this tactic requires a team capable of completing each other's work. Whereas it is fine to let anyone transfer a preexisting memo to a Web site, it is not a good idea to let a temp undertake the legal review tasks on his first day.

Web templates (dynamic and otherwise) are another possible solution to problems that can arise during the collaborative process. The team might not have the skills or time to create pages and sections from scratch. Not everyone has the eye for layout that another team member might have.

If desired, you can make page templates in FrontPage as you would any other page and simply save the file as a FrontPage template (as shown in Figure 33.8). Be sure that you select the Save Template in Current Web check box (in the Save As Template dialog box). This ensures that the template is saved to the entire Web site and not to your local machine.

Figure 33.8
Selecting the Save Template in Current Web check box saves the template to the entire Web site so that it can be used by everyone on the team.

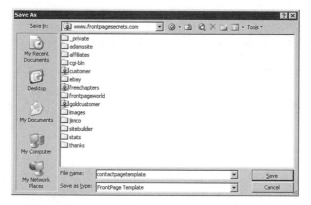

In template design, remember to use the Insert Comment option; this further directs users regarding what is expected of them on the page. Comments are viewable only in FrontPage and are not seen when the page is viewed through a Web browser.

> **TIP**
>
> When assigning a task that requires a template, be sure to note that fact specifically on the task assignment. There is no way to force anyone to use a template, so good training is the best way to ensure that one is used.

PREVENTION

Good preventative measures for protecting against potential problems are a necessity in the collaborative process. Use of the assessment tools described earlier in this chapter is most effective if they are used to spot trends and problems the manager can help protect against in the future.

Problems and corresponding preventative measures vary greatly from project to project. However, it is important to stress that FrontPage 2003's assessment tools can be used in combination with the rest of the program to provide a number of powerful preventative measures.

Some preventative measures are quite clear. An overzealous team member who tends to edit or create more than she should can quickly be identified and dealt with accordingly. Likewise, older files can be archived, and broken hyperlinks can be fixed. A quick note to the team about a current problem and its probable cause is often all that is needed to prevent it from happening again.

In issues of greater importance—bottlenecking, for instance—prevention comes from identifying problems before they become too big and acting accordingly. Reassigning tasks to another individual or group as necessary is the typical response.

TIP

> Sometimes users view the task list once and don't return until they complete what they originally were assigned. It is not always the practice of everyone to view the task list on a regular basis. If you tend to edit a user's task list (especially in terms of task reassignment) on a regular basis, you might want to notify the user via an additional means of communication.

New Task Load

When assigning a new task load, be sure that the recipient(s) understands the tasks and why they were reassigned. Help the team understand that they are working for the sake of the project and everything is assigned accordingly based on that need. You don't want to foster low team morale by not giving team members a reason to work hard. You don't want to encourage slow workers to continue to be so by taking their tasks away from them. Everyone should be encouraged to work their hardest, and a new task load should be implemented in a way that does so.

Because of the way Web sites are so closely interwoven and the types of action required by developers, balancing the requirements of new task loads with the personal implications of assigning them is difficult. Good management requires effective communication skills as much as it does effective design talents.

Often, the best method is to assign a few tasks at a time so that users are gently guided to the task ahead of them; it helps avoid their being too overwhelmed with the scope of the project. This obviously requires that the manager have an excellent understanding of the site needs and requirements.

TIP

> If you choose to assign tasks a few at a time, be sure to foster a practice within your teams of looking to the tasks list on a regular basis for the latest updates. You also should put future tasks on the list without specific user/group assignments so that the team can become aware of what is coming ahead on the project.

Publishing

Excluding a file from publishing with the rest of the Web site is another possible solution to workflow and task problems. If separating some of the problem issues from the rest of the general site is possible, publishing a good chunk of the site while waiting for the problem areas to be fixed is also possible.

If possible (if, that is, it doesn't affect the site flow too much), tag the problem files (to prevent them from being published) as shown in Figure 33.9 and continue to publish the completed areas of the site on a regular basis.

Figure 33.9
Selecting the Exclude
This File When
Publishing the Rest of
the Web option in the
Workgroup tab keeps
you from publishing a
page that isn't ready.

Choosing not to publish certain areas of a Web site is always a risky undertaking. It requires that you break the site into different sections. In much the same way as separating part of a spider web, taking away part of a Web site without deeply affecting the remainder of the project is difficult.

 If you find that files you marked as not to be published are ending up at the final site, *see "Files Published Anyway" in the "Troubleshooting" section at the end of this chapter.*

TIP

> You should be careful when marking files not to be published. Be sure that no hyperlinks to the file exist that are otherwise published. This results in broken hyperlinks.

DAMAGE CONTROL

Mistakes will be made. The more people are involved in the development process, the more mistakes will be made. As mentioned earlier, it is never a question of *if* you will have problems; it is a question of what you will do when you have problems.

Effective damage control comes from a gentle balance of preventing mistakes, undoing mistakes, backing up the project on a regular basis, and, if possible, using some form of version control.

PREVENTING MISTAKES

You can help prevent mistakes in a collaborative environment in many ways. These ways can be summed up as making effective use of the tools provided and working with intelligent people during the process.

The most common mistake made in collaborative Web design is a user editing or deleting a file he shouldn't have. This stems from a variety of problems, which include an improper understanding of what files and tasks are assigned to him and making simple mistakes. The remedy is preventing the user from being able to edit or delete the wrong file in the first place. This can be controlled somewhat through the use of the FrontPage document check in and check out process. Figure 33.10 shows the warning that FrontPage shows when someone attempts to modify a locked file.

→ For more information on the document check in and check out process, **see** "Collaboration with FrontPage 2003," **p. 615**.

Figure 33.10
A document that has been checked out quickly prevents an unauthorized user from modifying or deleting the file.

Another way to help prevent mistakes is to assign every document in the Web site to a specific user. Then you must ensure that users pay attention to the assignments and react accordingly.

You can also use the FrontPage 2003 security options. By making certain directories available to certain groups or users, unauthorized access is not permitted and mistakes are less likely to be made.

NOTE

> The security options are maintained through FrontPage 2003, but require FrontPage Server Extensions on the server side to maintain. If you are working on a Web server without FrontPage Extensions, you will need to maintain the security and access issues through whatever means are required by your server.

Nothing prevents you from creating as many directories on your site as you want. Consider placing each user's work in his own folder so that he deals only with (and has the potential to damage) a small area of the Web site. Set the security permissions for each folder so that only the people responsible for the content are able to change/edit/create it.

BACKING UP THE WEB

Backing up anything on a regular basis is always a good idea. Disk drives are prone to failure, and the constant accessing of files typical to a Web server puts a lot of strain on any drive.

Back up both your production and launch servers on a regular basis. Removable media that can be stored somewhere else. CD-ROM or tape drives, for example, provide ideal archiving capabilities.

TIP

> Consider maintaining an archive of backups for your Web site. If you make your backups on the same media, you will have only the most recent backup to return to. Many times, a mistake made on a site isn't realized until a significant amount of time has passed. Without a series of different backups, you will be unable to get a backup as close to the mistake as possible.

INTEGRATING WITH SOURCESAFE

Microsoft Visual SourceSafe is one way to provide version control and change management for your site. *Version control* is the practice of making an actual copy of every change made to a project; that enables any problems noticed in the future to be fixed. SourceSafe automates the entire process on any server on which it is running.

If you perform collaborative work in Visual SourceSafe, all changes made at any time to the site are recorded in an exhaustive database. If a mistake is realized anywhere in the process, the exact change can be tracked and the correct modifications made.

More information about Visual SourceSafe can be found online at
`http://sourcesafe.frontpagelink.com`.

WORKING WITH SHARP PEOPLE

The ease with which anyone can approach Web design is often confused with the idea that anyone should be allowed to do it. The skill set required to make a Web page is small.

It is also sometimes difficult for people to begin working together as a virtual team. Put those people in a room together, and they can accomplish almost any task. Place that same group in front of computers, and they are unable to perform because they're part of a group they can't see. Virtual teaming is hard for some people.

Collaborative teams are special groups of people. They must understand the need to be self-starters, realize their positions in a larger picture, and know how to work in a team environment in which they might never see the face of anyone with whom they are working.

Hiring a good team to produce your product is as important as any technology or platform decision you will ever make. People who are unable to take on the challenge often make mistakes that can have a disastrous effect on the entire group.

TROUBLESHOOTING A TEAM-BASED WEB SITE

How do you troubleshoot a site that you haven't developed?

Troubleshooting on a team-based site is much more difficult than on one you developed yourself. Not only are there mistakes that might have been made, but also you might not be aware of them because you weren't part of their creation. Fixing a problem you didn't create, or know nothing about, is difficult.

In short, before you can effectively troubleshoot a team-based site, you first must view the thing before you can identify the problems to fix. This means every single page, like it or not. The role of the manager is to know the entire site so that troubleshooting it is possible.

If you are unable to view every page in the site, a few tools can help you with some of the biggest potential problems.

Viewing the site-wide reports discussed in the last chapter can provide a great snapshot of potential problems. This suite of reports points in the direction of many of the biggest problems with a site. If you are unable to review a site completely, at least run all the reports to identify the biggest problems.

TROUBLESHOOTING

TASKS OUT OF CONTROL

With the history of my tasks and all existing tasks, my tasks view is out of control and simply too much to handle.

Right-click anywhere in the Tasks view screen and deselect Show History. This will remove historical links from your Tasks view and allow you to focus on what still needs to be done.

FILES PUBLISHED ANYWAY

I've set certain files as not to be published, but I'm finding them on the final site anyway.

If you assign a file as not to be published, the only program that will pay attention to the setting is FrontPage. If someone in your team is using a third-party product to FTP the site to the final destination, it will not adhere to the FrontPage Web site settings.

FRONT AND CENTER: BEING AN EFFECTIVE PROJECT MANAGER

If you previously found yourself in a position of Web designer and have now found yourself in a position of managing a team of developers, two courses of action can be taken. Your first choice is to humbly take on your new position and pat yourself on the back for advancing in the world. If, on the other hand, you need to continue being the designer that you were in the midst of your new role as manager, there is a way to do both.

No rule prevents a manager from designing the templates to be used by the team. There is also nothing preventing the same manager from designing a site theme or even Web shells and bringing the team in to "fill in the blanks." Not everyone has an eye for design, and designing the basic building blocks for the project that your team must take on can be a good idea.

It is important to point out that some designers feel that they need to do everything on a project, despite team size. This often can cause all sorts of problems and is something you want to be careful not to do. If you have been given a team of people to work with, be sure that you make use of this valuable resource. You will find that your team is more valuable to the project than FrontPage will ever be.

PART **VIII**

ACCESSING DATA WITH FRONTPAGE 2003

CHAPTER **34**

TYPES OF DATA USED WITH FRONTPAGE: AN OVERVIEW

In this chapter

UNDERSTANDING DATABASE TECHNOLOGIES

A database is a collection of related data and consists of types of data, called *fields*, and the data itself, frequently referred to as *records*. You will also often see people refer to a database field as a *column* and the data itself as a *row*. That's because most databases can display data in a *table*, which is a collection of columns, one for each database field, and rows, one for each record.

An example might be a database table called Addresses. In that table, you might have a column called `LastName`, a column called `FirstName`, a column called `Address1`, and so on. You would then have one row for each person in your Addresses table.

ACCESSING DATABASES WITH FRONTPAGE

Technologies for accessing databases over the Internet have been available for a long time. Database integration with FrontPage debuted with FrontPage 97 and a technology known as IDC/HTX. Since that time, data access has come a long way, and FrontPage 2003 provides data access using both *Active Server Pages (ASP)* and the latest technology in data access, *ASP.NET*.

ACTIVE SERVER PAGES (ASP)

ASP pages consist of HTML code and server-side script written in either VBScript or JScript. When an ASP page is requested, the Web server processes the script in the file and dynamically generates HTML code that is then sent back to the browser. ASP pages can be used to access data in a data source or to display other dynamic information such as the user currently logged in to the Web site.

> **NOTE**
>
> VBScript is a subset of Microsoft Visual Basic and is most commonly used to write ASP pages. JScript is Microsoft's flavor of JavaScript.

ASP.NET

ASP.NET is very different from ASP in most respects. ASP.NET is not a scripting language. Instead, ASP.NET applications are written using full-fledged programming languages. ASP.NET developers can choose to use Visual Basic .NET, Microsoft's newest version of Visual Basic, or C# (pronounced C-sharp), Microsoft's newest programming language.

ASP.NET applications run on the .NET Framework. The .NET Framework provides developers with a powerful base on which to develop applications. ASP.NET applications are *object-oriented* applications, which means that developers create sections of specialized code called *objects* that provide the functionality for the application. This approach is commonly considered the most productive way to write applications because each type of functionality in the application is isolated to the code that defines the object. If a problem is encountered or if code has to be rewritten, the developer only has to address the code that defines the object.

ASP.NET also provides developers with a more secure development environment because the code used to write the application does not have to be deployed to the Web server. With classic ASP, the programming code is inline within the HTML document. With ASP.NET, the programming code can be compiled into a single file and then the Web server can use that file to run the application. Not only does this keep your code more secure, but also the separation of the user-interface HTML code from the programming code allows you to let designers worry about the user-interface while programmers add the code necessary to make it all work.

For those FrontPage developers who are not inclined to write any code, ASP.NET also brings radical improvements. Because FrontPage 2003 now has support for ASP.NET, users of FrontPage can take advantage of the enhanced user-interface elements that ASP.NET provides (see Figure 34.1). Instead of displaying database results in a table, FrontPage users now have access to an ASP.NET control called the *DataGrid*. The DataGrid gives FrontPage users access to many options to control the appearance of their data. As an added benefit, FrontPage developers can open their FrontPage Web sites in Microsoft Visual Studio .NET and make changes there as well. For more information on developing with Visual Studio .NET, check out *Special Edition Using Visual Basic .NET*.

 If you browse to an ASP.NET page on Internet Information Services 6 and receive a 404 error, *see "ASP.NET Generates 404 Error in IIS 6" in the "Troubleshooting" section of this chapter.*

Figure 34.1
The ASP.NET DataGrid provides you with more control over appearance than classic ASP.

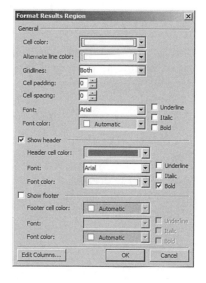

→ For more information on ASP and ASP.NET and the requirements for each, **see** "Data Access Technologies," **p. 679**.

→ For more information on accessing data with ASP and ASP.NET, **see** "FrontPage and Databases," **p. 705**.

TYPES OF DATA FRONTPAGE CAN ACCESS

FrontPage can access data from the following databases:

- Microsoft Access—A database stored in a single file with a `.mdb` file extension.
- Microsoft SQL Server—A professional level database server that is very robust and designed to operate under heavy loads
- Oracle—A non-Microsoft database technology that is comparable to Microsoft SQL Server
- Other *Open Database Connectivity (ODBC)*–compliant data sources

FrontPage's database features are designed explicitly to connect to Microsoft Access, Microsoft SQL Server, or Oracle using Microsoft's ODBC driver for Oracle. However, if you want to connect to another ODBC-compliant data source, FrontPage will allow you to manually specify a connection string for that data source. A *connection string* contains information about a data source, such as what type of data source it is, how the connection to it should be established, what settings to use for the connection, and any authorization information required for the connection.

TIP

The documentation for your specific data type should contain example connection strings. As long as the connection string is ODBC-compliant (and the documentation should specify this), it should work with FrontPage.

CHOOSING A DATABASE TYPE

When choosing the type of database to use, several factors need to be considered. Perhaps the most important is how many users you expect to access your data simultaneously. Many Web developers will tend to dissuade you from using Microsoft Access as a data access platform because it does not provide a robust solution for high volume Web sites. However, for many personal sites, a Microsoft Access database is a perfectly viable option and offers some advantages.

NOTE

If your Web site is hosted on SharePoint Services, the only database type available to you is SQL Server. If you want to use a Microsoft Access database as your data source, you must not run Windows SharePoint Services on your Web site.

Being able to back up your database simply by copying one file is very attractive to those who are not experts in the area of database management. Microsoft Access also requires significantly less technical expertise to administer than SQL Server or Oracle. Many Web developers may also not have access to a SQL Server or Oracle database. Even if they do have access to it on the production Web server, many Web developers are not running SQL

Server or Oracle on their local machines to use for testing while developing the application. In these cases, Microsoft Access might be an attractive alternative.

In cases in which you expect high volume or anticipate that you might have more than 10 or so users simultaneously accessing data on your Web site, you might want to consider moving to a more robust solution, such as Microsoft SQL Server. In addition to being a more robust database engine and management system, SQL Server also provides numerous other benefits. With a small amount of study, a developer can learn how to use data from other data sources to populate a SQL Server database and to transform that data in any way necessary. SQL Server also provides development tools and comprehensive documentation that can aid a developer in building a Web application.

NOTE

For more information on using SQL Server in your applications, read *Microsoft SQL Server 2000 Programming By Example* from Que Publishing.

Many hosting companies now provide access to a SQL Server database for very little money. Most of the time, this means that they are running not only your database, but many other databases as well on the same SQL Server. In these cases, performance might suffer, but you likely won't notice too much of a slowdown. Most of the time, performance is very acceptable.

TIP

Many development languages that Microsoft ships come with a version of SQL Server, usually *Microsoft Desktop Engine*, or *MSDE*. MSDE is a scaled-down version of SQL Server designed for developers.

XML DATA SOURCES

NEW *Extensible Markup Language (XML)* is a relatively new technology that came on the scene in 1998. XML has experienced much more attention recently because of the introduction of XML Web Services with Microsoft's .NET Framework. FrontPage 2003 is the first version of FrontPage that provides the capability to use XML data natively in the user interface. However, in order to do so, your site must be hosted on a server running Windows SharePoint Services.

→ For more information on Windows SharePoint Services, **see** "Windows SharePoint Services 2.0," **p. 943**.

Listing 34.1 shows a simple example of an XML file.

34

LISTING 34.1   AN EXAMPLE XML FILE

```
<?xml version ="1.0"?>
<AddressBook>
    <Contact ID=1>
        <firstName="Jack" />
        <lastName="Smith" />
        <address="252 Any Street" />
        <city="Ft Worth" />
        <state="TX" />
    </Contact>
    <Contact ID=2>
        <firstName="Joe" />
        <lastName="Johnson" />
        <address="432 Some Street" />
        <city="Portland" />
        <state="OR" />
</AddressBook>
```

Unlike a technology such as HTML that describes how data should be displayed, XML simply categorizes data and provides a description of the data. Developers can then use the XML in many different ways—whether in a Web page or a Windows application. As you will see when we discuss XML Web Services in Chapter 38, "FrontPage and Web Parts," XML is a great solution for accessing raw data.

As seen in Listing 34.1, an XML file is somewhat like a database. It contains a series of name/value pairs that describe data. This makes it ideal for use as a data source in FrontPage. FrontPage connects to XML files within the current Web site. If the XML file you attempt to use does not reside in the current Web site, FrontPage will prompt you to import it.

FrontPage 2003 has the capability to not only use XML files for data sources, but, as you will see later, it can also use XML Web Services as data sources. These new capabilities provide an exciting new era in FrontPage data access.

USING WEB PARTS

Web Parts are new to FrontPage and are a dramatically enhanced method of providing interactivity to your Web site. Many of the data sources you've already seen are composed of Web Parts—SharePoint Lists, SharePoint Libraries, XML files, and XML Web services are all Web Parts.

Although Web Parts can be inserted into a SharePoint site using the SharePoint Web interface, inserting them in FrontPage offers additional functionality. You can configure Web Parts in FrontPage so that they share information and feed off each other. For example, you can configure a Web Part that returns a list of cities and ZIP Codes from an XML file. You can then configure the site so that when a ZIP Code is clicked, a Web service automatically pulls weather information for the ZIP Code. That kind of power has never before been available to FrontPage developers.

→ For more information about inserting and configuring communication between Web Parts, **see** "Connecting Web Parts," **p. 754**.

Server Extensions and SharePoint

FrontPage users are accustomed to using the Database Results Wizard and the Database Interface Wizard to connect to databases. Those tools are still available, but only if your Web site is not hosted on a Windows SharePoint Services site. If you are using SharePoint Services, the only database that you can use for a data source is SQL Server. SharePoint Services does add considerable functionality to your Web site, but if you require a connection to a database type other than SQL Server, you will want to make sure that you don't use SharePoint on your site.

If you are using the Database Results Wizard or the Database Interface Wizard to connect to a database, you do not need FrontPage Server Extensions on the server when the pages are browsed. You must have Server Extensions on the Web server if you want to be able to open the Web site in FrontPage and reconfigure the database access, but when the pages are browsed, the Server Extensions are not used in any way.

SHAREPOINT LISTS

Windows SharePoint Services stores content for Web sites in a SQL Server database. Among the types of data that a Windows SharePoint Services Web site can store is the *SharePoint List*.

A SharePoint List can consist of many different types of data. Users of your SharePoint site who have sufficient access rights to the application can add information to your SharePoint List directly from the Web site. You can then access the data in that list using the FrontPage 2003 data access toolset. This is an extremely powerful ability.

An example of a SharePoint List might be a list of contacts shared by the team at your office, as shown in Figure 34.2. By configuring this as a SharePoint List, members of the team can update their information directly from the team Web site. Using the data tools in FrontPage, you can then create a Web page that accesses that list in real-time without having to manually connect to the database where the data is stored. Such features can save developers many hours of development time.

Another advantage of the SharePoint List is that Windows SharePoint Services allows you to develop a user interface for SharePoint List management by simply selecting options on a Web page, as seen in Figure 34.3. This makes it quite easy to change the fields contained in a list and to modify the list's settings as the need arises. After such modifications, you can quickly modify your FrontPage data-connected pages to connect to any new fields that are configured in the list.

Using these tools, it becomes very easy to adapt your Web page to changes quickly and efficiently and with minimal downtime.

34

Figure 34.2
A SharePoint List displays dynamic content that can easily be updated via the SharePoint Web site.

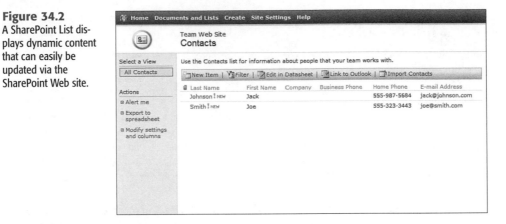

Figure 34.3
Reconfiguring a SharePoint List is simply a matter of choosing which fields you want from a Web page.

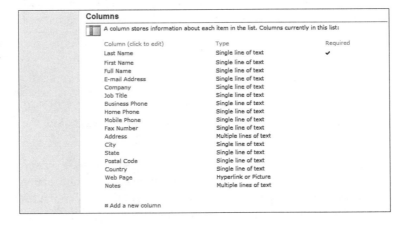

SHAREPOINT LIBRARIES

A SharePoint Library is a collection of documents as well as information describing those documents, such as the document's author, the name of the document, where the document is located on the network, and so on. SharePoint Libraries are very convenient in situations in which you want to keep a central repository of documents.

Users of your SharePoint Services Web site can upload documents to the SharePoint Library. Depending on their level of access, users can connect to the site and edit the document or make other changes to the document library. You can also give users access to create their own SharePoint Libraries so that your documents can be organized according to the criteria you define.

As seen in Figure 34.4, Windows SharePoint Services provides users the ability to see a version history of documents in a library, discuss a document using a SharePoint Discussions feature that allows users to add non-destructive notes to documents, and set up alerts that will email them when a document is changed.

Figure 34.4
Users have many options when it comes to SharePoint Document Libraries.

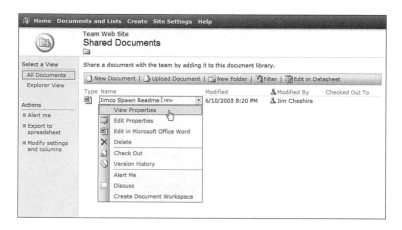

FrontPage 2003 can connect to a SharePoint Library and can display information about documents in it, such as the user who created the document, when it was last modified, when it was created, how large it is, and so on. You can configure any one of these fields to display in numerous ways, including displaying the field as a link directly into the SharePoint site so that the item can be edited in ready-made SharePoint forms.

In situations in which you would like to incorporate data from a SharePoint Library into a Web page containing no other SharePoint information, FrontPage 2003 provides you with all the tools necessary and also gives you the ability to connect that page directly to the editing facilities provided by SharePoint for even greater power.

Understanding Server-side Scripts

Server-side scripts consist of code that runs on a Web server and returns data. In the case of the Server-side Script data source in FrontPage, the data returned is XML data. The URL for the server-side script is entered, and any necessary parameters are entered as well. You can then insert a view of the data returned by the script.

In many cases, you will use an XML Web service for obtaining XML data, but there are often cases in which a developer might write a Web page that returns XML data instead of a Web service. For example, suppose a colleague writes an ASP.NET page that takes a manager's name in your company as a parameter and returns an XML document containing all that manager's employees. By connecting to that data in FrontPage using the Server-side Scripts data source, you can easily insert a view of that data inside your Web page.

XML Web Services

With the release of the Microsoft .NET Framework, XML Web services appeared on the Internet scene. XML Web services are perhaps one of the most misunderstood technologies available to Web developers today. Because XML Web services return their data in XML format, many developers are unsure of how to use them and what advantages they offer over more traditional methods of data generation.

In fact, Web services fill a very important need in the world of Web development. They provide a means for developers to feed data to applications running on multiple platforms and being delivered on multiple devices with a minimal amount of effort. Because the data returned by a Web service is in XML format, the Web service itself doesn't have to be concerned with what kind of application consumes that data.

The Web service architecture is quite complex, but using a Web service is not. A Web service typically has one or more methods that can be called and that will return data based on information passed to them. A *method* is simply a piece of programming code designed to perform a certain task. In the context of Web services, a Web method is used to take data that you pass it, process that data, and return additional data in the form of an XML response.

A good example of the use of a Web service is a stock quote service. Suppose that you wanted to provide your Web site with real-time stock quotes for any stock symbol your site visitor requests. A Web service is the perfect solution. The Web service can take the stock symbol, access information stores of stock value data, determine the value of the stock, and then return the value of the stock in XML format. Because the value is returned in XML format, it can easily be used in a Web page, a Windows application, a cell phone application, or any other device that can consume a Web service. The developer of the Web service doesn't have to be concerned with how the content will be displayed. That's the sheer beauty of Web services.

Many Web services are available for public use and can be used in your Web applications. For a searchable list, visit `http://uddi.microsoft.com/search`. Click on the tModels tab and enter a search string such as stock. A list of XML Web services is returned, as shown in Figure 34.5.

Figure 34.5
Microsoft's UDDI Web site provides access to Web services you can use in your applications.

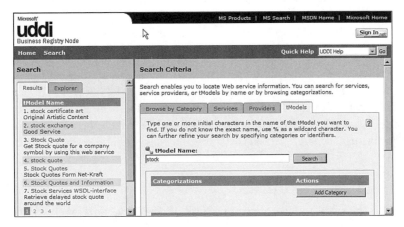

Select one of the Web services listed in the results window and then click the Overview tab to see the URL for the overview document. An overview document is written in XML and displays all the information required for the Web service to work. It consists of a link to a .asmx file with ?WSDL at the end of the link. If you browse to the link without the ?WSDL, you can run the Web service from within your Web browser. In Figure 34.6, you can see the .asmx page for a Web service's method called GetQuote. By entering a stock symbol in the text box and clicking Invoke, you can run the Web service. Figure 34.7 shows the results of the GetQuote method when the stock symbol MSFT is passed to it. The page shown here is an example of a test page provided by all Web services. In a real-world environment, you would call the Web service programmatically and not from a Web page.

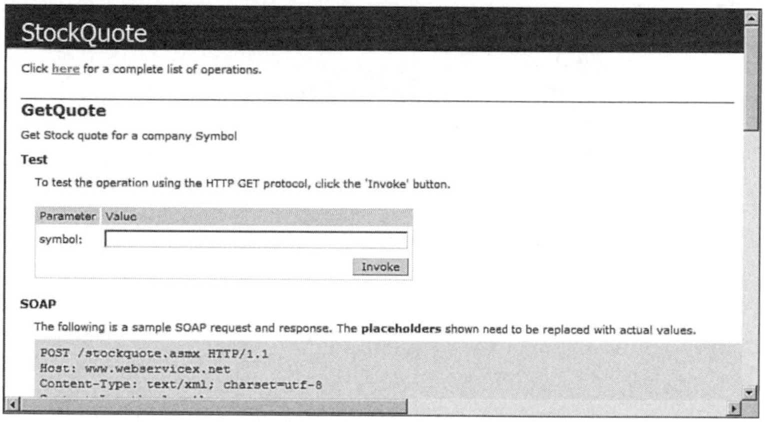

Figure 34.6
This page allows you to test the GetQuote method of the StockQuote Web service.

Figure 34.7
By entering MSFT into the StockQuote Web service, XML data is returned detailing the stock performance of Microsoft.

To add a reference to the GetQuote Web Service, follow these steps:

1. Select Data, Insert Data View to display the Data Source Catalog.

2. Click the Add to Catalog link under the XML Web Services section of the Data Source Catalog as shown in Figure 34.8.

Figure 34.8
Add a new data source to the Data Source Catalog using the Add to Catalog link.

3. In the Service Description Location text box, enter
   `http://www.webservicex.net/stockquote.asmx?WSDL`.

4. Click Connect Now to access the Web Service and populate the Data Source Properties dialog box as shown in Figure 34.9.

Figure 34.9
The Data Source Properties dialog box provides all the information necessary to use the Web Service.

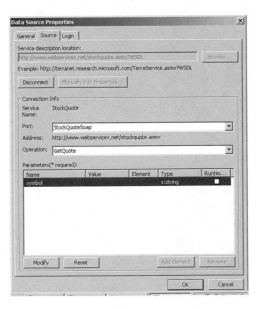

5. Click the Modify button to display the Parameter dialog box as shown in Figure 34.10.

Figure 34.10
The Parameter dialog box allows you to send a parameter to the Web Service.

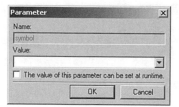

6. Enter **MSFT** in the Value text box and click OK.

7. Click OK to add the new data source to the Data Source Catalog.

When a Data view is inserted using a Web Service, the data returned is in XML format. In order to format the data for display on a Web page, you will need to write some XSL to format the data. *XSL* is a formatting language that is used to format XML data. A discussion of XSL is outside of the scope of this book, but for a comprehensive explanation of XSL and how to use it to format data, read *Special Edition Using XSLT* from Que Publishing.

TROUBLESHOOTING

ASP.NET GENERATES 404 ERROR IN IIS 6

 I am trying to browse to an ASP.NET page on an IIS 6 server, and I know it exists. However, when I browse to it, I receive a 404 error saying that file is not found.

IIS 6 prohibits ASP.NET pages by default. To allow ASP.NET pages to run, follow these steps:

1. On the Web server, double-click on Internet Information Services (IIS) Manager in Administrative Tools.

2. Click the plus sign if necessary to expand the node for the computer name of the Web server.

3. Click once on the Web Service Extensions folder.

4. Click once on ASP.NET in the right-hand pane and click the Allow button as shown in Figure 34.11.

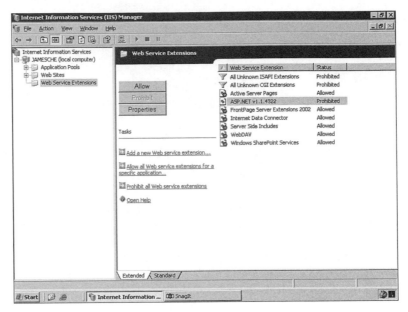

FRONT AND CENTER: REAL-WORLD USES FOR DATABASES

Many FrontPage users think that databases are only used for e-commerce sites or other sites that store large amounts of data. In fact, databases are useful on any site where the information being displayed might change from time to time. Databases are also useful for discussion Web sites.

When I started Jimco Add-ins, I used a static HTML page to display all of my add-ins. The maintenance of that page quickly became a nightmare. Whenever I redesigned my Web site, I had to reenter all the content for that page. I often wasn't able to copy and paste the data from the old page because the layout of the new page was different. The solution was to make the page a dynamic database-driven page using ASP and eventually ASP.NET. I was then able to easily update the site and reformat the page without reentering any of the information. I was also able to build a Web page that allows me to add, edit, and delete add-ins from a Web browser so that I can update my add-ins page from any computer with Internet access.

Chances are that your Web site also contains information that gets updated or changed frequently. If it does, you should carefully evaluate whether you should use ASP or ASP.NET to present that information. By doing so, you can allow users of your site to specify the information they want to see and use a database query to pull just that information. You will also be able to easily redesign your site and plug the information into a new page layout with minimal effort.

There are some considerations you should keep in mind. Developing an ASP or ASP.NET Web site takes considerably longer than developing a static HTML Web site. You will also need to make sure that your host supports ASP or ASP.NET, and some hosts might want to charge you an extra fee for that support. Making the move to ASP or ASP.NET requires extra development time and a steeper learning curve, but in the long run the payoff is likely going to be worth the extra effort.

34

CHAPTER **35**

DATA ACCESS TECHNOLOGIES

In this chapter

UNDERSTANDING ACTIVE SERVER PAGES (ASP)

Active Server Pages (ASP) is a technology that was introduced in 1997 by Microsoft, and it revolutionized dynamic content for the Internet. Prior to ASP, there were other technologies that existed for dynamic Web content, but ASP was the first technology that was widely accessible to most Web developers. Writing ASP pages doesn't require complex knowledge of confusing concepts. Instead, Web developers can leverage existing knowledge to add dynamic and interactive content.

When Microsoft first released ASP, it was available as an add-on to *Internet Information Server (IIS) 3.0*, the free Web server that Microsoft made available for use on Windows NT Server. ASP also worked with *Peer Web Services*, a Web server for Windows NT Workstation, and for *Personal Web Server*, the Web server that shipped with FrontPage 98. Starting with IIS version 4, ASP is a part of the Web server and nothing else needs to be installed for ASP support.

ASP applications run on a Web server, but the user interface for the application runs in a Web browser on the user's machine. There is actually no connection between the Web server and the user's browser. Once the Web server generates the page and sends it to the browser, the work is done and the Web server no longer has any knowledge of the user. This is obviously not conducive to an interactive and dynamic Web application. Therefore, the ASP *object model* gives ASP developers the ability to store information about a particular user's browser session. (An object model provides a method by which a developer can programmatically access a particular technology.)

→ For more information on object models and how they're used, **see** "Introduction to Programming with Visual Basic for Applications," **p. 568**.

THE ASP OBJECT MODEL

The ASP object model provides several objects that can be used, among other things, to store and retrieve information between browser requests.

- **Application object**—An object that is shared between all users of a Web application. Allows an ASP developer to get information about and manipulate an ASP application.

- **ObjectContext object**—Allows ASP developers to write ASP code that uses *transactions*. Transactions allow an ASP developer to take specific actions depending on whether the ASP page executed successfully in its entirety.

- **Request object**—Gives the ASP developer programmatic access to the user's request for the page being displayed. Provides access to things such as form fields in a form.

- **Response object**—Gives the ASP developer programmatic access to the Web server's response to a user's request.

- **Server object**—Provides for programmatic access to the Web server on which the ASP application is executing.

- **Session object**—An object that is unique to each application session a user has open. Allows an ASP developer to programmatically access a user's session and store and retrieve information about it.

→ For more information on the ASP object model, read *Active Server Pages 3.0 By Example* from Que Publishing.

ANATOMY OF AN ASP PAGE

ASP pages consist of both HTML code and *server-side script* and have a .asp file extension. The server-side script is written using either VBScript or JavaScript, or JScript as Microsoft calls it. Server-side script is separated from the HTML code by using either ASP delimiters (<% and %>) or <SCRIPT> tags with a runat attribute that specifies the script is to run on the Web server.

The following code will display the current date and time of day as reported by the Web server:

```
<HTML>
<BODY>
    <% Response.Write Now() %>
</BODY>
</HTML>
```

Any code between the <% and %> delimiters is ASP code, and the Web server processes that code prior to sending the Web page to the Web browser. In the preceding example, the Web server will replace <% =Now() %> with the current date and time, as shown in Figure 35.1. The user browsing to this page will not see the ASP code. She will only see the result of that code running on the Web server.

 If you browse to an ASP page and you are asked to download the file instead of the file being displayed in the browser, *see "ASP Page Generates Download Prompt" in the "Troubleshooting" section of this chapter.*

The following code produces the same output, but uses <SCRIPT> tags instead of the ASP delimiters.

```
<HTML>
<BODY>
    <SCRIPT language="VBScript" runat="server">
        Response.Write Now()
    </SCRIPT>
</BODY>
</HTML>
```

35

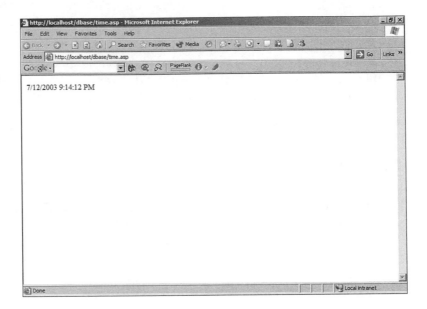

Most ASP developers will use <SCRIPT> tags for writing functions that perform a series of computations and will use the ASP delimiters <% and %> for inline ASP code. If you use both to produce output on the page, you might be surprised at the output. Consider the following ASP page:

```
<HTML>
<BODY>
    <SCRIPT language="VBScript" runat="server">
        Response.Write Now()
    </SCRIPT>
    <% = "The current date and time is " %>
</BODY>
</HTML>
```

The result of this page is shown in Figure 35.2. Note that the result of the code inside the ASP delimiters is displayed prior to the ASP code inside the <SCRIPT> tags even though the latter appears first in the page. Code that appears inside <SCRIPT> tags will always execute after inline script.

Using ASP, it's easy to make a page very dynamic. For example, you can use ASP to access a database of users and customize a page's appearance depending on who is accessing the page. In Listing 35.1, a user's role is used to determine how the page is laid out.

Figure 35.2
ASP code inside ASP delimiters will always run before code inside <SCRIPT> tags.

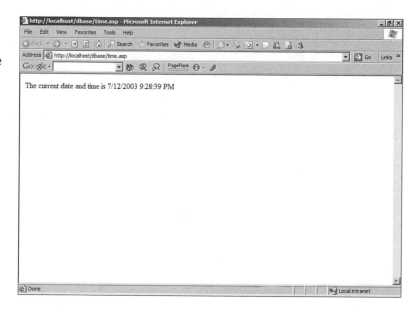

The current date and time is 7/12/2003 9:28:39 PM

LISTING 35.1   USING ASP TO CUSTOMIZE PAGE CONTENT

```
<HTML>
<!--#include file="dbconnect.inc"-->
<BODY>
  <%
    userRole = rs("Role")
  %>
  <TABLE>
    <TR>
      <TD>
      <% If userRole = "employee" Then %>
          From this page, you can:<BR>
          <UL>
            <LI>Check your vacation balance.</LI>
            <LI>Review your current goals.</LI>
            <LI>Review your personal statistics.</LI>
          </UL>
      <% ElseIf userRole = "manager" Then %>
          Manager's Toolset<BR>
          <UL>
            <LI>Edit your employee's information.</LI>
            <LI>Get team metrics.</LI>
            <LI>Review employees.</LI>
          </UL>
      <% End If %>
      </TD>
    </TR>
  </TABLE>
</BODY>
</HTML>
```

35

In this example, the code to connect to the database and retrieve the value for userRole is stored in an external file called dbconnect.inc. The second line specifies that the file dbconnect.inc should be included in this page. The dbconnect.inc file is not listed here, but in this example, that page would contain ASP code that connects to a database and pulls out the role of the current user.

Once we know the role of the current user and have stored it in userRole, ASP code is used to determine the layout of the page based on that role. If userRole is equal to employee, the page displays a list of tasks that an employee can accomplish using the Web page. If userRole is equal to manager, the page will display tools for a manager to use.

As you can see, inline server-side code makes it easy to make an interactive Web application, but it does have drawbacks. Listing 35.1 is simple and uncluttered, but in a real-world environment, ASP pages can become very large. ASP code inline with HTML code can get confusing for a developer to deal with. This is one of many reasons that Microsoft created a new version of ASP from the ground up.

USING ASP.NET

In 2002, Microsoft released the *.NET Framework*, and a new way to write applications was born. The .NET Framework provides a common framework that developers can use to create Windows applications, Web applications, and *XML Web services*. In order to run ASP.NET on a Web server, the Web server must be IIS version 5 or greater, and it must have the .NET Framework installed on it. This means that you must have Windows 2000 or greater.

NOTE

> Windows XP Home Edition cannot run ASP or ASP.NET pages because it does not support the installation of a Web server. If you want to test the ASP or ASP.NET pages you develop on Windows XP, you must use Windows XP Professional Edition. You can develop ASP or ASP.NET pages on Windows XP Home Edition, but before they can be browsed, they must be published to a Web server that supports the technology you're using.

THE COMMON LANGUAGE RUNTIME

An application written using the .NET Framework runs under *Common Language Runtime*. When a developer writes software using the .NET Framework, she compiles her program into *intermediate code* known as *Microsoft Intermediate Language* or *MSIL*, which is code that only the Common Language Runtime understands. When someone runs that software, the MSIL code is compiled again into executable code that the operating system can run in a process known as *Just In Time compilation*, or *JIT*.

→ For more information on the Microsoft .NET Framework including XML Web Services, the Common Language Runtime, MSIL, and JIT compilation, read *Think Microsoft.NET* from Que Publishing.

Microsoft released a version of the Common Language Runtime in combination with the .NET Framework release and the release of Visual Studio .NET. The current Common Language Runtime runs on Windows machines, but work is underway by independent software developers to develop a version of the Common Language Runtime that will run on Unix or Linux machines as well. Because of the way Microsoft designed the .NET Framework, once a version of the Common Language Runtime is developed for another operating system, developers will simply have to compile their code on the new operating system and then they will be able to run applications originally written to run on Windows. If everything works as it should, no code will have to be rewritten. There are exceptions to this, such as those situations in which an application was written to take advantage of Windows-specific functionality.

How ASP.NET Applications Are Developed

ASP.NET is the latest version of Microsoft server-side Web application development technology, and it runs on the .NET Framework. An ASP.NET application is not made up of inline script in a Web page. Instead, ASP.NET is a full-featured development technology, and ASP.NET applications are written following the same principles used when building a Windows application. Instead of VBScript or JScript, ASP.NET developers use VB.NET or C# to develop their applications.

ASP.NET offers many advantages over the legacy ASP application model. A few of the more prominent advantages are

- Familiar programming approach for developers who aren't used to writing Web applications
- Full-featured development environment as opposed to a simple scripting language
- ASP.NET server-controls that provide robust built-in functionality
- Complete separation of user-interface and server-side code if desired
- Extremely powerful and flexible control for caching of data

NOTE

> Microsoft provides two applications that were specifically designed for developing ASP.NET applications—Visual Studio .NET and Web Matrix. Visual Studio .NET is a professional-level suite of tools for developers, whereas Web Matrix is a free ASP.NET development tool that is similar to a very basic and stripped down version of Visual Studio .NET. FrontPage 2003 supports ASP.NET and can generate ASP.NET code in addition to performing rudimentary editing of existing ASP.NET content, but it is not the best choice for designing ASP.NET sites from scratch.

→ For more information on Visual Studio .NET, read *Sams Teach Yourself Visual Studio .NET 2003* from Sams Publishing.

→ For more information on Web Matrix, **see** "Front and Center: Developing ASP.NET with Web Matrix" at the end of this chapter.

→ For more information on using FrontPage to develop ASP.NET pages, **see** "FrontPage and Databases," **p. 705**.

35

USING ASP.NET SERVER CONTROLS

ASP.NET ships with many server controls that make adding functionality to a Web page very easy. Because these controls are server controls, they run on the Web server and the Web server generates the HTML necessary for the control to be rendered on the Web page. It also means that you can programmatically access these controls in your ASP.NET code.

Listing 35.2 shows a page with an ASP.NET Label server control.

LISTING 35.2   A SIMPLE ASP.NET PAGE

```
<%@ Page Language="vb" Codebehind="sample.aspx.vb" Inherits="jcaApp.sample"%>
<HTML>
<BODY>
<asp:Label id="lblTime" runat="server">Current Time</asp:Label>
</BODY>
</HTML>
```

The only part of this page that resembles ASP code is the first line. That line is called the *page directive*, and it tells ASP.NET what language to use for the page (either vb for VB.NET or c# for C#), what file contains the server-side code (the code that provides most of the page's functionality) if necessary, and what *class* the page is inherited from. Classes and inheritance are important concepts in ASP.NET. A class is a component of code that stores certain information about itself (called *properties*) and knows how to perform certain tasks (called *methods*). In the page in Listing 35.2, the class is called jcaApp.sample, and it is defined in the file sample.aspx.vb.

The sample.aspx.vb file is called the *code behind* file. This is the means by which ASP.NET allows you to separate the user-interface from the server-side implementation. The code behind file contains all the ASP.NET code for your Web page. To access one of the controls on the Web page from the code behind file, you use the control's id attribute.

Listing 35.3 shows The code behind file for the page in Listing 35.2.

LISTING 35.3   THE CODE BEHIND FILE

```
Public Class sample
    Inherits System.Web.UI.Page
    Protected WithEvents lblTime As System.Web.UI.WebControls.Label

    Private Sub Page_Load(ByVal sender As System.Object, _
      ByVal e As System.EventArgs) Handles MyBase.Load
        lblTime.Text = Now.ToLongTimeString
    End Sub
End Class
```

The first and last lines of Listing 35.3 show that the code is defining a class called sample. The next line indicates that the sample class inherits the System.Web.UI.Page class. This is a class that is included with ASP.NET, and it contains many properties and methods that are specific to Web pages. (The Page_Load event that is listed is an example of a method that is included in the `System.Web.UI.Page` class.) Next is the line that creates the server-side Label control in the code behind page. Note that the name of this control in Listing 35.3 is `lblTime` just as it is in Listing 35.2. Finally, the `Page_Load` event indicates what code is to run when the page is loaded by the Web server. In this case, we are setting the `Text` property of the `lblTime` Label to the current time.

The server controls included with ASP.NET are contained in a special folder installed by the .NET Framework called the *Global Assembly Cache*, or *GAC*. ASP.NET will automatically see these controls without you having to specify any additional configuration settings because it's designed to always look in the GAC for controls and other classes. If you have some controls in other folders on your hard drive that you would like FrontPage to include in your ASP.NET pages, select <u>T</u>ools, <u>O</u>ptions and click the ASP.NET tab to access the dialog box shown in Figure 35.3. From this dialog box, you can choose a folder for additional ASP.NET controls for all Web pages or for Web pages in the current Web site.

Figure 35.3
The ASP.NET tab on the Options dialog box in FrontPage gives you the ability to specify folders for additional ASP.NET controls.

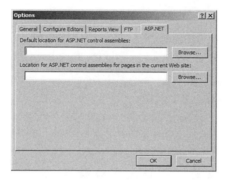

→ For complete coverage of programming ASP.NET pages with VB.NET, check out *ASP.NET By Example* from Que Publishing.

COMPILING ASP.NET APPLICATIONS

Before you can run this ASP.NET page on a Web server, it has to be compiled. This is the process of creating a DLL file that contains all the programming code for the page. That DLL file and the Web page containing the HTML code are then copied to the Web server, and the page is ready to run.

NOTE

The fact that you can compile your ASP.NET code in to a DLL file is another huge advantage over traditional ASP applications. By compiling your code in to a DLL file, you can keep it secure from other people. The code behind file that contains the server-side code for your Web page is not required to be present on the Web server when the page is being browsed.

You can also write your ASP.NET code inline with the HTML page. If you choose that route, the application does not have to be compiled prior to browsing. Instead, it is automatically compiled the first time it is browsed.

35

When the page is run, the current time on the Web server is printed to the browser window.

TROUBLESHOOTING

ASP PAGE GENERATES DOWNLOAD PROMPT

I've created an ASP page, but when I browse to it, I get a prompt to download the file instead of seeing the page in my browser.

ASP pages must be served from a Web server that supports ASP. If you are browsing an ASP page on a server that does not have support for ASP, you will be prompted to download the file instead of seeing the page in your browser.

If you are unsure whether your Web server supports ASP, check with your hosting company.

FRONT AND CENTER: DEVELOPING ASP.NET WITH WEB MATRIX

So you want to try your hand at developing some ASP.NET pages, but you don't have a lot of money to invest in Visual Studio .NET? Microsoft has made it easy for you to get started without spending a dime. ASP.NET Web Matrix is a free ASP.NET development tool that makes developing ASP.NET pages much easier than writing them all by hand. It's not nearly as robust as Visual Studio .NET, but it is a great way to get started with ASP.NET.

You can get Web Matrix free from http://webmatrix.frontpagelink.com. Once installed, the Help menu provides quick links to documentation on Web Matrix and Microsoft's .NET Framework.

Web Matrix doesn't have many of the features that make Visual Studio .NET or FrontPage easier to use. For example, Web Matrix doesn't provide any IntelliSense support for ASP.NET code. It also doesn't provide a user interface for easy configuration of many of the properties of ASP.NET controls. However, it is quite a bit easier to develop with Web Matrix than it is with Notepad or another text editor.

CHAPTER 36

FRONTPAGE'S DATA TOOLSET

In this chapter

INTRODUCTION TO THE DATABASE RESULTS WIZARD AND DATABASE INTERFACE WIZARD

FrontPage first introduced data access technologies with FrontPage 97's IDC/HTX database connectors. The technology was cryptic, and FrontPage's feature-set wasn't very robust. Developers struggled with adding the interactivity and dynamic content they wanted to their site. The result wasn't very pretty. Not many developers embraced data access with FrontPage, and those new to FrontPage and Web design didn't even bother to explore the features at all. Then Microsoft introduced Active Server Pages (ASP), and everything changed. Suddenly, data access was well within the reach of all Web developers. Sites started appearing all over the Internet that used ASP to connect to databases and provide site visitors with great dynamic content. The Internet had certainly changed, but FrontPage users were left in the dust. FrontPage 97 just didn't have the toolset to develop ASP pages very easily.

FrontPage 98 changed everything. Microsoft introduced the Database Region Wizard, and finally FrontPage users had ASP firmly in their grasp. Plenty of FrontPage users were developing Web sites that displayed data fed from a Microsoft Access or Microsoft SQL Server database. With the release of FrontPage 2000, the Database Region Wizard got a new name, the Database Results Wizard. It also got a few new features, but not many. Still, it was a good tool that enabled most FrontPage developers to design a data-driven Web site without knowing any code. It wasn't long, however, before FrontPage users had pushed the Database Results Region to its limit and were feeling the limitations of it bearing down on them. They were crying out for a suitable method for adding new records to their databases and for editing existing records. Enter the Database Interface Wizard.

FrontPage 2002 introduced the Database Interface Wizard, and for the first time, FrontPage developers had a full ASP toolset at their fingertips. Not only could they easily design Web pages to display data from their database, but they could also create a full-featured database editing system complete with password protection.

THE DATABASE RESULTS WIZARD

The Database Results Wizard, shown in Figure 36.1, is a five step wizard that makes it easy to insert a Database Results Region. A *Database Results Region* is a section of a Web page that displays dynamic data generated from a database. Very few users of the Database Results Wizard fully realize the potential of this tool.

The Database Results Wizard has grown over the years. Beginning with FrontPage 2003, both ASP and ASP.NET, Microsoft's latest data-driven Web application development technology, are now supported. Using the Database Results Wizard, you can connect to many different data sources:

- Microsoft Access database
- Delimited text files
- Microsoft Excel worksheet

- Microsoft dBase files
- Microsoft Paradox database
- Microsoft Visual FoxPro
- System data source (DSN) on the Web server
- Microsoft SQL Server
- Oracle (using Microsoft's ODBC provider)
- Other data sources using a `.dsn` file, `.udl` file, or a custom connection string

Figure 36.1
The Database Results Wizard provides an easy interface for adding database interactivity to your Web site.

→ For more information on ASP and ASP.NET, see "Data Access Technologies," **p. 679**.

USING THE DATABASE RESULTS WIZARD

The features of the Database Results Wizard go far beyond simply displaying database results such as those shown in Figure 36.2. Using the Database Results Wizard, FrontPage users can create complex pages that allow for searching databases and displaying appropriate records as well.

When you insert a Database Results Region, FrontPage adds several files to your Web site. First, it adds the `global.asa` file, a file used by most ASP applications. The `global.asa` file stores information for use by the Database Results Wizard and also contains some functions that provide more functionality to the Database Results Wizard. FrontPage also adds several files to the `_fpclass` folder. The files that it adds differ depending on whether you use ASP or ASP.NET.

→ For information on how to insert a configure a Database Results Region, see "Using the Database Results Wizard," **p. 709**.

If you are using ASP, FrontPage adds the following files to the `_fpclass` folder:

- **fpdblib.inc**—This file contains numerous functions used by Database Results Wizard pages in order to provide for data access.
- **fpdbrgn1.inc**—This file contains ASP code used to format database results.
- **fpdbrgn2.inc**—This file contains ASP code that implements paging in Database Results Wizard pages.

Figure 36.2
This page was generated with the Database Results Wizard.

ProductName	SupplierID	CategoryID	QuantityPerUnit	UnitPrice	UnitsInStock	UnitsOnOrder	ReorderLevel
Chai	1	1	10 boxes x 20 bags	18	39	0	10
Chang	1	1	24 - 12 oz bottles	19	17	40	25
Aniseed Syrup	1	2	12 - 550 ml bottles	10	13	70	25
Chef Anton's Cajun Seasoning	2	2	48 - 6 oz jars	22	53	0	0
Chef Anton's Gumbo Mix	2	2	36 boxes	21.35	0	0	0
Grandma's Boysenberry Spread	3	2	12 - 8 oz jars	25	120	0	25
Uncle Bob's Organic Dried Pears	3	7	12 - 1 lb pkgs.	30	15	0	10
Northwoods Cranberry Sauce	3	2	12 - 12 oz jars	40	6	0	0
Mishi Kobe Niku	4	6	18 - 500 g pkgs.	97	29	0	0
Ikura	4	8	12 - 200 ml jars	31	31	0	0
Queso Cabrales	5	4	1 kg pkg.	21	22	30	30
Queso Manchego							

If you are using ASP.NET, FrontPage adds the following files to the _fpclass folder:

- **fpdbnet.cs**—A file written in C#, Microsoft's newest programming language, that contains common database functionality for ASP.NET pages.

- **dbregion.ascx**—This file is an ASP.NET user control, a control that can be reused easily in multiple pages. It implements the DataGrid that contains database results in ASP.NET pages generated by the Database Results Wizard.

- **dbquery.ascx**—This is another ASP.NET user control that is used to implement database queries in search forms inserted by the Database Results Wizard.

- **fputil.cs**—This is a C# file that contains ASP.NET code to format the database results.

In addition to these files, FrontPage also adds a file called web.config to your root folder when you create an ASP.NET page with the Database Results Wizard. This file contains configuration information for the ASP.NET application.

→ For more information on ASP and ASP.NET, see "Data Access Technologies," **p. 679**.

If you are unable to see the _fpclass folder in FrontPage, see "The _fpclass Folder Is Not Visible in FrontPage" in the "Troubleshooting" section of this chapter.

If you can see the _fpclass folder, but you don't see the files you expect in it, see "Files Aren't in _fpclass Folder" in the "Troubleshooting" section of this chapter.

TROUBLESHOOTING DATABASE RESULTS APPLICATIONS

The global.asa file is responsible for storing information on database connections used by the Database Results Wizard. Therefore, the global.asa file must exist in the *application root* of the Web application. The application root is configured in Internet Information Services (IIS), and it indicates the top-level folder for the Web application. When you browse any ASP page, the Web server looks in the application root folder for a `global.asa` file. If it finds one, it runs certain code in that file to set up the Web application.

If the root folder of your Web site is not configured in IIS as an application root, you can get very strange results or error messages from your Database Results Wizard pages. To check for these types of problems, Microsoft provides a special ASP file called `fpselect.asp` that you can run. It will do automated diagnostics on your Web site to ensure that everything is configured as it should be. It will also allow you to run a test query against any of the database connections in your Web site.

Figure 36.3 shows the `fpselect.asp` file displaying a successful test against a Web site. Figure 36.4 shows a failure caused by the root folder of the Web site not being set as an application root. When your Database Results Wizard files don't run successfully, the `fpselect.asp` file can make troubleshooting much easier and will often tell you exactly what the problem is.

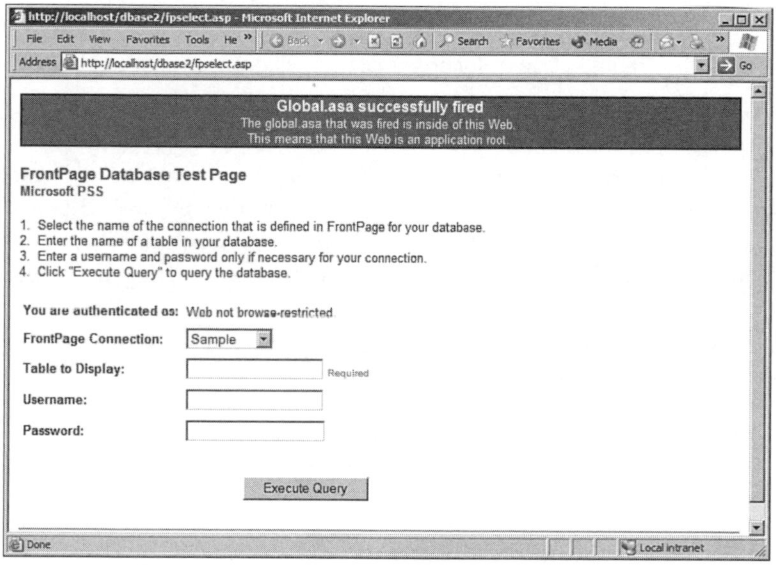

Figure 36.3
The `fpselect.asp` utility makes troubleshooting database pages easy. In this case, everything's fine.

NOTE

You can obtain the `fpselect.asp` file from Microsoft Product Support Services Knowledge Base article 294960 or from `http://fpselect.frontpagelink.com`.

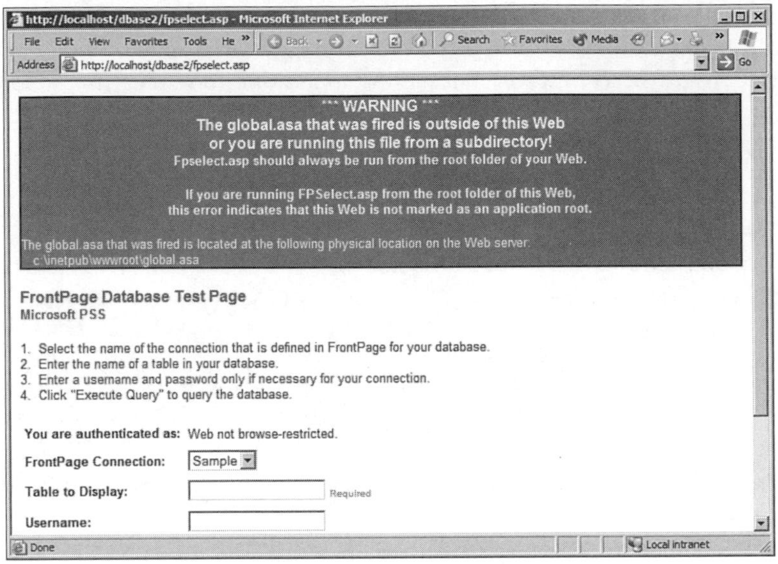

Figure 36.4
The `fpselect.asp` utility has found a problem and told us what we need to know to fix it.

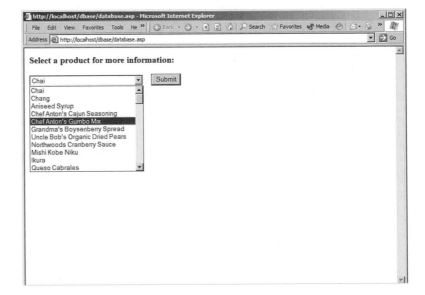

CREATING A DRILL DOWN SEARCH WITH THE DATABASE RESULTS WIZARD

As discussed previously, the Database Results Wizard can do much more than simply display database results. Figure 36.5 shows a page with a dropdown list that was populated from the Products table in the FrontPage sample database called `fpnwind.mdb`. When a product is selected and the button is clicked, another Database Results Region page is displayed with the details on the selected product as shown in Figure 36.6. All of this was done with the Database Results Wizard and without even looking at a single line of code!

Figure 36.5
This search page was created with the Database Results Wizard.

Figure 36.6
The details page displays details on the product selected, and it all happens without writing any code.

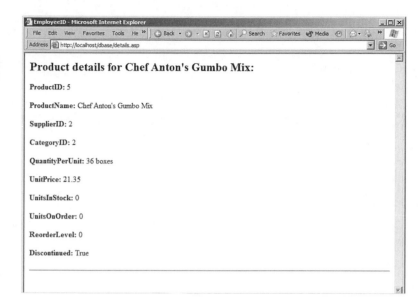

Product details for Chef Anton's Gumbo Mix:

ProductID: 5

ProductName: Chef Anton's Gumbo Mix

SupplierID: 2

CategoryID: 2

QuantityPerUnit: 36 boxes

UnitPrice: 21.35

UnitsInStock: 0

UnitsOnOrder: 0

ReorderLevel: 0

Discontinued: True

→ For more information on using the Database Results Wizard, see "Using the Database Results Wizard," **p. 709**.

THE DATABASE INTERFACE WIZARD

FrontPage 2002 introduced a new database tool to the FrontPage arsenal; the Database Interface Wizard. The Database Interface Wizard is a Web site wizard that can either be created as a new Web site or added to an existing Web site. You can insert multiple sets of Database Interface Wizard pages into a single Web site in situations where you have multiple database connections in a single Web site.

The Database Interface Wizard (shown in Figure 36.7) can connect to the same types of databases as the Database Results Wizard, but in addition to displaying the contents of the database, the Database Interface Wizard also provides the ability to edit database records, add new records, and delete existing records.

Figure 36.7
The Database Interface Wizard.

36

The page shown in Figure 36.8 is the Database Editor created by the Database Interface Wizard. All the code necessary to run the Database Editor was generated automatically by the Database Interface Wizard. The Database Interface Wizard also allows you to password protect the Database Editor so that only those people with the password can edit, add, or delete records.

Figure 36.8
The Database Editor, created by the Database Interface Wizard, allows for editing of database records.

AN OVERVIEW OF THE DATA SOURCE CATALOG AND WEB PARTS

In addition to the Database Results Wizard and the Database Interface Wizard, when coupled with Windows SharePoint Services, FrontPage 2003 adds a new set of features for adding dynamic data-driven content to your Web site. These new features use the power of Windows Server 2003 and ASP.NET to provide access to data.

THE DATA SOURCE CATALOG

The Data Source Catalog is a new task pane that provides access to many different data sources. In addition to the Access and SQL Server data sources you are already familiar with, you can also use the Data Source Catalog to access new data sources provided by Windows SharePoint Services and XML data sources.

The Data Source Catalog relies on the Web server running Windows SharePoint Services, and Windows SharePoint Services requires Windows Server 2003. If you are hosting your Web site on Windows 2000 or earlier, you won't have access to these features. Instead, FrontPage will present you with a dialog box informing you that you need Windows SharePoint Services, as seen in Figure 36.9. After you've seen all that these features can do, you will be switching your site to a Windows Server 2003 and Windows SharePoint Services host in no time.

Figure 36.9
The features on the Data menu in FrontPage rely on Windows SharePoint Services.

To access the Data Source Catalog, select <u>D</u>ata, Insert Data <u>V</u>iew to display the Data Source Catalog as shown in Figure 36.10.

Figure 36.10
Data is quickly displayed in the Data View Details task pane.

AN OVERVIEW OF THE DATA SOURCE CATALOG

The Data Source Catalog provides access to all the data sources that can be accessed using Windows SharePoint Services. Many of the data sources available in the Data Source Catalog are features of Windows SharePoint Services such as SharePoint Lists, but you can also use the Data Source Catalog to access generic data sources such as XML files and XML Web Services.

→ For more information on data sources available in the Data Source Catalog, see "Inserting Web Parts Using the Data Source Catalog," **p. 736**.

TIP

The Data Source Catalog and other Windows SharePoint Services data access features are also available by selecting Insert, Database. However, the Data menu provides quicker access to these features.

NOTE

Depending on the kind of Web site you have open, one or more of these data sources might initially be unavailable. FrontPage will provide a link to allow you to create a new data source if one does not already exist.

In addition to Windows SharePoint Services and Windows Server 2003, the Data Source Catalog also relies on ASP.NET being properly configured on the Web server. ASP.NET automatically installs with Windows Server 2003, but in order for ASP.NET pages to run, they have to be explicitly enabled using the Internet Information Services console. To enable ASP.NET on Windows Server 2003, follow these steps:

1. Click Start, Control Panel.
2. Double-click on the Administrative Tools icon in Control Panel.
3. Double-click on Internet Information Services in Administrative Tools.
4. Click the plus sign to expand the computer name node if it isn't already expanded.
5. Click once on the Web Service Extensions folder.
6. In the right-hand pane, select ASP.NET and click the Allow button.

After following these steps, ASP.NET will be enabled on the Web server.

After you have added a data source to the Data Source Catalog, you can preview the data returned by that data source by clicking the data source name and selecting Show Data from the menu. The data from the data source is displayed in the Data View Details task pane. When you have verified that this is indeed the data you want to display on your page, click the Insert Data View link to insert a view of that data onto the page, as shown in Figure 36.11. After the data has been inserted into a page, it is called a *Web Part*.

A Web Part is extremely customizable, and there are many ways to access the dialogs used to customize them. The easiest way is to select the Web Part and click the Data View Options button, as seen in Figure 36.12. The Data View Options menu provides access to all the formatting and configuration properties for the Web Part.

This doesn't even begin to scratch the surface on what you can do with Web Parts. For example, Web Parts are able to communicate with each other. This makes it very easy to build an interactive page or series of pages where data is passed from one Web Part to another. You could have a Web Part that displays information on your suppliers from a local database. When you click a supplier in the list, it communicates that supplier's address to another Web Part that contacts an XML Web service and displays a map of the supplier's location. All this can easily be configured right within the FrontPage interface without a single line of code!

Figure 36.11
The Insert Data View link in the Data View Details task pane inserts a new Data View using the data currently displayed.

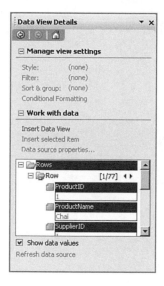

Figure 36.12
The Data View Options button is an easy way to access configuration settings for a Web Part.

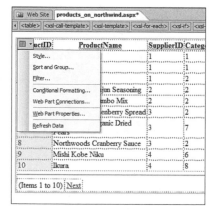

After you've inserted a Web Part, you can configure the style of the Web Part using the View Styles dialog box shown in Figure 36.13. There are 15 different styles to choose from. The Options tab, seen in Figure 36.14, allows you to add additional features to the Web Part such as headers and footers; forms to allow users to configure filtering, sorting, and grouping; and how many records are displayed at once.

The Sort and Group dialog box (see Figure 36.15) allows you to configure how your data is sorted and lets you easily group results into expandable sections. The page shown in Figure 36.16 is grouped by supplier with one supplier's records expanded and the rest collapsed. This kind of grouping is easy with the Sort and Group dialog box.

Figure 36.13
The View Styles dialog box makes changing the format of a Web Part a quick job.

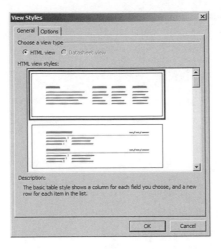

Figure 36.14
The Options tab provides many options to customize your Web Part.

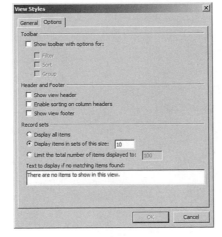

Figure 36.15
The Sort and Group dialog box allows you to sort your data and group it into expandable/collapsible sections.

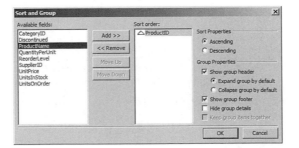

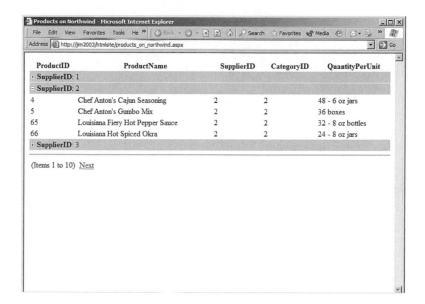

The Filter dialog box, seen in Figure 36.17, filters your data based on filtering clauses that you enter. In Figure 36.18, the Web Part is configured to show only those items with a unit price of less than 20 dollars. As soon as that filtering is configured and committed, FrontPage refreshes the data displayed in Design view to reflect the results of the filtering. This makes it very easy to ensure that you're getting the data you want without even having to preview the page in a browser.

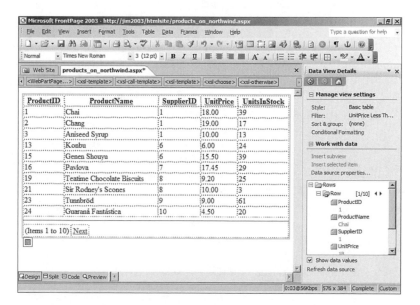

The Conditional Formatting task pane (see Figure 36.18) provides very powerful formatting abilities based on whatever criteria you specify. For example, suppose that you wanted to format any dollar amount with a unit price of over 20 dollars in red. The Conditional Formatting task pane makes it very easy to do, and once formatting is applied, you can review it and the rule attached to it at a glance. Modifying the style is as simple as clicking it in the Conditional Formatting task pane and selecting Modify from the menu.

Figure 36.18
The Conditional Formatting task pane is another powerful formatting tool for Web Parts.

The Web Part Properties dialog box is a five-section dialog box that gives you the ability to quickly and easily format additional Web Part options. In the first section (see Figure 36.19), *XSL*, or *Extensible Stylesheet Language*, is used to format the results. XSL is a formatting language for XML data, and the information returned by a Web Part is returned in XML format. Therefore, an XSL stylesheet is used to format the results.

NOTE

> FrontPage provides default XSL to format the results. If you are well versed in writing XSL code, click the ellipses button to display the XSL editor where you can edit the existing XSL or write your own.

The Web Part Properties dialog box also allows you to easily format the appearance and behavior of your Web Part, as seen in Figure 36.20. The frame settings are only valid for Web Parts that exist inside of a *Web Part Zone*, a configurable section of a page that is designed to hold a Web Part.

Figure 36.19
Formatting of a Web Part is accomplished using XSL.

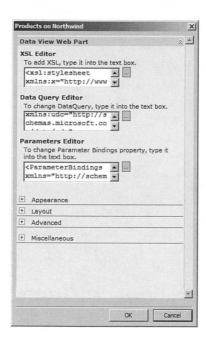

Figure 36.20
Formatting the appearance and behavior of a Web Part using the Web Part Properties dialog box.

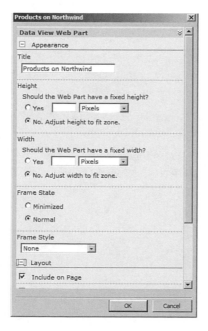

→ For more information on Web Part Zones, **see** "Configuring a Data View and Web Parts," **p. 743**.

TROUBLESHOOTING

THE _fpclass FOLDER IS NOT VISIBLE IN FRONTPAGE

I've inserted a Database Results page, but I am unable to see the _fpclass folder in my Web site.

The _fpclass folder is a hidden folder that is only visible if you have configured the Web site to show hidden files and folders. Select Tools, Site Settings and click the Advanced tab. Place a check in the Show Hidden Files and Folders check box and click OK. When asked to refresh the Web site, click Yes. You should now be able to see the _fpclass folder.

FILES AREN'T IN THE _fpclass FOLDER

I have inserted some database results, and I can see the _fpclass folder, but there are no files in it.

FrontPage doesn't add any files into the _fpclass folder until your pages are saved. Save your page, and the files needed for your database results will be added automatically.

FRONT AND CENTER: DATA SOURCES THROUGH A FIREWALL

Many FrontPage developers sit behind a firewall and have to use a proxy server to access the Internet. That can pose a problem if you are trying to connect to a data source on the other side of the firewall.

Fortunately, ASP.NET provides a way to get through the proxy via the web.config file, an XML configuration file that configures the way that ASP.NET pages are run on the site. To enter in proxy server configuration for your site, you can edit the web.config file.

1. Open the web.config file in the C:\Program Files\Common Files\Microsoft Shared\web server extensions\60\CONFIG folder. Notepad is a sufficient XML editor.

2. At the bottom of the file after the </system.web> tag and before the </configuration> tag, add the following code, replacing http://proxy:80 with the address of your proxy server:

```
<system.net>
    <defaultProxy>
        <proxy
        proxyaddress="http://proxy:80"
        bypassonlocal="true"
        />
    </defaultProxy>
</system.net>
```

Save the web.config file, and you will now be able to access data sources outside of the firewall.

TIP

> When the web.config file is saved, ASP.NET will automatically use the new settings. No other action is required.

CHAPTER 37

FRONTPAGE AND DATABASES

In this chapter

CREATING A DATABASE CONNECTION

FrontPage has offered database connectivity since FrontPage 97. It started as the simple ability to pull information from a database and list it on a page in an HTML table, but as FrontPage has matured, so have the database features it offers. Using the database features available in FrontPage 2003, you can easily store information about the people visiting your site, present an online catalog in an e-commerce store, and so on. Dynamically building content for your Web site using information in a database is a quick and easy way to make your site retain its appeal and freshness.

The database capabilities of FrontPage require a database connection. A *database connection* consists of information that is necessary to make a connection to your database. The information included in a database connection varies depending on what type of database you are connecting to. For example, if you are connecting to a SQL Server database, the database connection will specify the database server name, the name of the database to connect to, and a username and password if necessary. For a Microsoft Access database, the connection string will contain the path to the Access database, as well as other information as needed.

To add a new database connection, select Tools, Site Settings and click the Database tab. Click the Add button to access the New Database Connection dialog box, as shown in Figure 37.1. After creating the database connection and clicking OK, you can verify it by clicking the Verify button.

TIP

> FrontPage will display a check mark next to the connection name if it successfully verifies. However, a check mark doesn't necessarily mean that the database connection will work successfully when you run the page. In order to ensure that the connection is a good one, test the page that uses the connection by browsing to it in your Web browser.

Figure 37.1
The New Database Connection dialog box allows you to manage database connections to various data sources.

NOTE

> The New Database Connection dialog box can also be accessed from the Database Results Wizard or Database Interface Wizard by selecting the option to create a new database connection.

The four options for a new database connection are as follows:

- **File or Folder in Current Web Site**—Connect to a data source using a file in the current Web site.

- **System Data Source on Web Server**—Connect to a data source using a System DSN on the Web server.

- **Network Connection to Database Server**—Connect to a Microsoft SQL Server database or an Oracle database using Microsoft's ODBC provider for Oracle.

- **Custom Definition**—Connect to another data source using a `.dsn` file, a `.udl` file, or a custom connection string.

USING A FILE OR FOLDER IN THE CURRENT WEB SITE

To use a file in the current Web site, first import the file in to your Web site. After you've imported the file, select the File or Folder in Current Web Site radio button in the New Database Connection dialog box and then click Browse to display the Database Files In Current Web Site dialog box, as shown in Figure 37.2. Select the file to use and then click OK to add a connection to that file.

Figure 37.2
The Database Files in Current Web Site dialog box allows you to select a file as a data source.

USING A SYSTEM DSN

To use a System DSN on the Web server, select the System Data Source on Web server radio button and click Browse. Choose the System DSN from the list displayed as shown in Figure 37.3 and click OK. If a System DSN is not displayed for your data source, you can create one using the Data Sources (ODBC) applet in the Control Panel or by contacting your hosting company or server administrator.

Figure 37.3
Use the System Data Sources On Web Server dialog box to select a System DSN.

For information on creating a System DSN in Windows XP Professional Edition or Windows Server 2003, see article number 305599 in the Microsoft Knowledge Base (`http://support.microsoft.com?id=305599`).

For more information on creating a System DSN in Windows 2000, see article number 300596 in the Microsoft Knowledge Base (`http://support.microsoft.com?id=300596`).

USING A NETWORK CONNECTION TO A DATABASE SERVER

To connect to a SQL Server or Oracle database server, select the Network Connection to Database Server radio button. Click the Browse button to display the Network Database Connection dialog box, as shown in Figure 37.4. Select SQL Server to connect to a SQL Server instance or Microsoft ODBC for Oracle to connect to an Oracle server. If you select SQL Server, enter the name of the SQL Server and the name of the database to use for the data source and click OK. If you select Microsoft ODBC for Oracle, enter only the name of the Oracle server and click OK. If you need to use a username and password to connect to your database server, you will need to click the Advanced button in the New Database Connection dialog box and enter that information in order to successfully use the database.

Figure 37.4
Setting up a connection to SQL Server or Oracle is easy with the Network Database Connection dialog box.

A SQL Server connection might successfully verify when you click Verify, but might not necessarily work when you browse the page. It all depends on what type of authentication is being used on the SQL Server and the configuration of the Web browser and the Web server. In most cases on the Internet, SQL Server requires a username and password. In an Intranet environment, many Web developers rely on Windows to authenticate users to SQL Server. In these cases, a username and password might not be required.

> **NOTE**
>
> For more information on connecting to SQL Server databases, read *Microsoft SQL Server 2000 Programming By Example* from Que Publishing.
>
> For more information on connecting to Oracle databases, get *Oracle 9i Development By Example* from Que Publishing.
>
> For detailed information on security and SQL Server, check out *SQL Server System Administration* from Que Publishing.

USING A CUSTOM DEFINITION

If none of the selections on the New Database Connection dialog box are appropriate for your particular data source, you can use a custom definition to connect to your data source using the Custom definition option. Using this option, you can point FrontPage to a `.dsn` file or a `.udl` file. Both files contain connection information to allow you to easily connect to many different data sources.

> **TIP**
>
> To easily create a `.udl` file to connect to your data source, create a new text document with Notepad and then change the file extension from `.txt` to `.udl`. Double-click the new `.udl` file and the Data Link Properties dialog box will appear, allowing you to easily configure a new `.udl` file.
>
> Click OK after configuring your settings, and they will be saved in your `.udl` file and ready for use in FrontPage.

> **NOTE**
>
> For more information on `.dsn` and `.udl` files, read *Sams Teach Yourself ADO 2.5 in 21 Days* from Sams Publishing.

USING THE DATABASE RESULTS WIZARD

The FrontPage Database Results Wizard has been around since FrontPage 98 and has largely remained unchanged since FrontPage 2000. FrontPage 2003 adds the ability to generate ASP.NET pages with the Database Results Wizard, as well as ASP pages.

The Database Results Wizard can be used to display data from many different data sources:

- Microsoft Access database
- Delimited text files
- Microsoft Excel worksheet
- Microsoft dBase files
- Microsoft Paradox database
- Microsoft Visual FoxPro
- System data source (DSN) on the Web server
- Microsoft SQL Server
- Oracle (using Microsoft's ODBC provider)
- Other data sources using a .dsn file, .udl file, or a custom connection string

NEW The first step in inserting database results with the Database Results Wizard is to select either ASP or ASP.NET for your Web page. Before you make this choice, make sure that your Web host supports the technology you plan to use.

TIP

> The Database Results Wizard dialog box indicates that FrontPage detects whether your Web server is best suited to using ASP or ASP.NET. In fact, FrontPage makes no attempt to detect which technology to choose. The choice is purely your own.

→ For more information on the requirements of ASP, **see** "Understanding Active Server Pages," **p. 680**.

→ For more information on the requirements for ASP.NET, **see** "Using ASP.NET," **p. 684**.

Whether you choose ASP or ASP.NET, there is almost no difference in the steps taken to insert database results with the Database Results Wizard. ASP pages allow you to select from a wider array of options for presenting your data, but ASP.NET allows greater control over the appearance of your data. When deciding between ASP and ASP.NET, it is best to first carefully evaluate the purpose of the data and how you want to display it.

If you simply want your data displayed in a grid, ASP.NET might be your best option because it allows you to easily configure the appearance of data displayed in a grid. If you need to display your data in list format or in a dropdown box, ASP is the option you should choose. We'll look at the differences between using ASP and using ASP.NET after we've finished configuring and inserting some database results.

CONFIGURING THE DATABASE RESULTS WIZARD

You're probably eager to see the Database Results Wizard in action at this point, so let's insert some database results and see some of this powerful tool's functionality. You will need to either create a new Web site on a server capable of running ASP pages, or publish your Web site to an ASP-enabled Web server before testing the ASP pages.

STARTING THE DATABASE RESULTS WIZARD

Create a new one-page Web site and create a new document. Select Insert, Database, Results to display the Database Results Wizard as shown in Figure 37.5. Choose ASP as your technology and choose the option to use a sample database connection. Click Next: FrontPage will create a new folder in your Web site called fpdb, and a Microsoft Access database called fpnwind.mdb will be created in it. Click Next to go to step 2 of the Database Results Wizard.

Figure 37.5
The first step in the Database Results Wizard allows you to choose whether to use ASP or ASP.NET.

NOTE

> You will also notice that FrontPage has created a file global.asa in the root folder of your Web site. This is a special file used in ASP applications. FrontPage uses the global.asa file for storage of database connection information as well as for special functions that the database features rely on. For more information on the use of the global.asa file, check out *Active Server Pages 3.0 By Example* by Que Publishing.

CHOOSING A RECORD SOURCE

In step 2, you select a record source for your database results. FrontPage provides two options for you, as shown in Figure 37.6. The first option is the Record Source dropdown, which contains an entry for each table in the sample database that FrontPage created for you. The dropdown will also contain any queries that have been saved in Microsoft Access, but the fpnwind.mdb file doesn't contain any queries.

The second available option is to use a custom SQL statement. Using a custom SQL statement, you can easily customize the data that is returned by the Database Results Wizard, but it requires a knowledge of SQL syntax. Select Employees from the Record Source dropdown and click Next to move to step 3.

Figure 37.6
Choosing a record source in step 2 of the Database Results Wizard.

CONFIGURING YOUR DATA

Even though the dialog box in step 3 appears to be very simple at first glance(see Figure 37.7), much of the advanced functionality of the Database Results Wizard is configured here. In the top half of the dialog box, you can configure which fields are displayed in your database results. By default, all the fields in the table or query you select are displayed. If you'd like to remove some of those fields or change the display order of those fields, you can do so by clicking the Edit List button.

Figure 37.7
Step 3 of the Database Results Wizard provides access to advanced features.

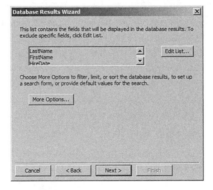

> **NOTE**
>
> Even though you might change the fields that display in your database results via the Edit List button, FrontPage will still generate ASP code that returns all the fields from the database. Whether you display all those fields is your choice.

Displaying all the fields in the Employees table is going to be a little unwieldy, so click the Edit List button and select all the fields in the Displayed Fields list except for EmployeeID, LastName, FirstName, Title, and HireDate. After you've selected the fields, click the Remove button to remove them from the list.

Move the HireDate field so that it will be displayed in the second column of your database results by selecting the field and then clicking the Move Up button three times so that it appears under the EmployeeID field, as seen in Figure 37.8.

Figure 37.8
The Displayed Fields dialog box configured so that only specific fields are displayed.

TIP

> You can easily select multiple fields in the Displayed Fields list by holding the Ctrl key while clicking noncontiguous fields or clicking the first field then clicking the last field while holding the Shift key to select contiguous fields.

Clicking the More Options button displays the More Options dialog box (see Figure 37.9), where you can configure many of the advanced features of the Database Results Wizard.

- **Criteria button**—Allows you to filter your database results based on whatever criteria you choose. As you will see later in this chapter, you can filter based on a fixed value or a value entered in a form field on a Web page.

- **Ordering button**—Allows you to change the order of the items in your database results.

- **Defaults button**—Allows you to set default values for any form fields that are used to filter results. If a user does not enter a value for a field, FrontPage will use the default value entered here.

- **Limit Number of Records Returned**—Allows you to control how many records are returned by your database results. This enables you to prevent long-running queries that might take longer than desired.

- **Message to Display if No Records Are Returned**—Indicates what message should be displayed to the user if the Database Results Wizard returns no results.

To order the list of results by LastName and then by FirstName, click the More Options button and then click the Ordering button. Select the LastName field in the Available Fields list and then click the Add button to add the LastName field to the Sort Order list. Click the Add button again to add the FirstName field to the Sort Order list. The Ordering dialog box should now appear as shown in Figure 37.10. When the Database Results

Wizard displays the results, they will be ordered by the LastName field and then the FirstName field in ascending order.

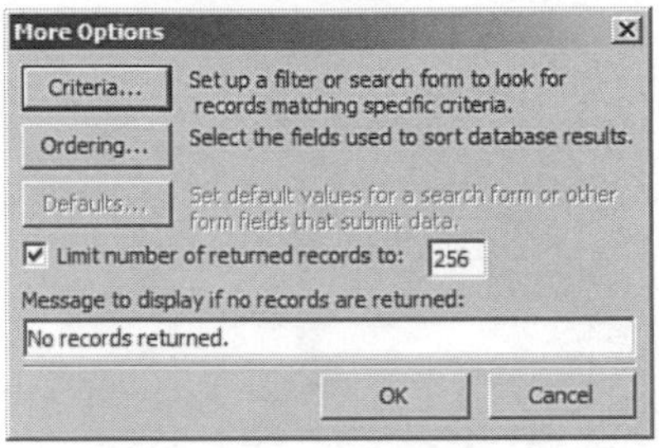

Figure 37.9
The More Options dialog box provides access to some of the advanced features of the Database Results Wizard.

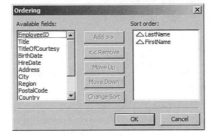

Figure 37.10
The Ordering dialog box makes it easy to sort your results.

Click OK to dismiss the Ordering dialog box and then click OK again to dismiss the More Options dialog box. Click the Next button to move to step 4 of the Database Results Wizard, where you will choose the formatting options for your database results.

FORMATTING YOUR DATA

When using ASP to display your database results, you have three options for formatting your results. The first option is to use a table with one record per row. When you choose this option, you are given three check boxes to configure the appearance of the table.

- **Use Table Border**—When checked, the table will have a border around each cell.
- **Expand Table to Width of Page**—When checked, the table will expand to 100% of the page's width. If left unchecked, the table will expand as necessary to account for the data contained in it.
- **Include Header Row with Column Labels**—Displays a header row at the top of the table containing the name of the field contained in each column.

In addition to the option of displaying the results in a table, you can also choose to display the results in list format. You have the option to display labels for all field values and to include a horizontal separator bar between each record. The List Options dropdown provides for a high level of customization of the list.

- **Paragraphs**—Displays the database results as a single paragraph for each field using <p> tags. This has the effect of making the list double-spaced.

- **Line breaks**—Displays the results in list format with a <br> tag separating each field. This has the effect of making the list single-spaced.

- **Bullet list**—Displays the results in list format as a bulleted list with each field represented by a bulleted item.

- **Numbered list**—Displays the results in list format as a numbered list with each field representing a numbered item. Numbering restarts for each record returned.

- **Definition list**—Displays the results in list format as a definition list using <dt> and <dd> tags.

- **Table**—Displays the results in table format with each record in its own table.

- **Formatted**—Displays the results as preformatted text using the <pre> tag.

- **Text fields**—Displays the results in text input fields in a <form> tag, one <form> tag per record. This option is best used when your results return one record and you want to perform a search based on that record.

- **Scrolling text fields**—Displays results in scrolling text fields using <textarea> tags. As with the Text Fields option, this is best used when performing a search based on a single returned record.

Your last formatting option is to display the results in a dropdown list. This option displays your results in a dropdown inside of a <form> tag so that a user of your page can select a value from your results and then submit the form. When you select this formatting option, you are presented with two dropdowns, as shown in Figure 37.11. The first dropdown specifies the database field used to populate the text that users of your Web page will see in the dropdown. The second dropdown specifies the database field that is submitted when the form is submitted.

Figure 37.11
The dropdown list option requires you to select the value to display and the value to submit.

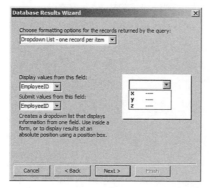

Select the Table option in the formatting dropdown, and then click Next to go to step 5.

37

CHOOSING DISPLAY OPTIONS

In step 5, you have the option of displaying all records that are returned or splitting the records into groups (see Figure 37.12). Splitting records into groups is a good idea if your database results page returns a large number of records. Returning a large number of records can take a long time to load. If you split the records into groups, the number of records that you specify in step 5 will be returned and the user can then click a button to select the next group of records. The Add Search Form check box is disabled at this point because you haven't chosen any form fields in previous options. You will use that option later.

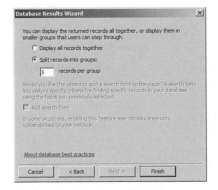

Figure 37.12
Step 5 of the Database Results Wizard allows you to break large results up in to groups.

Click Finish to insert your database results. Your page in FrontPage should be similar to Figure 37.13. Save your page as **database.asp** and preview it in your browser. You should see a list of five employees and buttons to allow you to go to the next page to see the remaining employees, as shown in Figure 37.14. All this information is being dynamically pulled from the Microsoft Access database in the fpdb folder of your Web site.

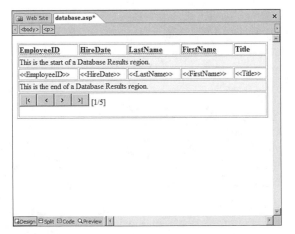

Figure 37.13
The inserted database results ready to be previewed in your browser.

Figure 37.14
The information on this page is dynamically populated from your database.

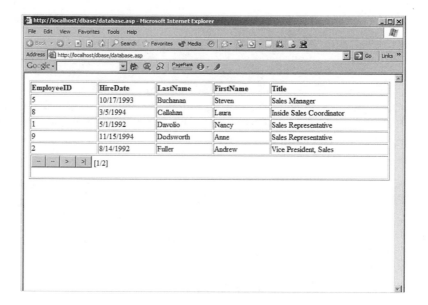

USING ASP.NET TO DISPLAY DATA

The page you created in the previous section uses ASP to display the data from your database. You can also choose to use ASP.NET to display your results instead of using ASP. Doing so gives you easier control over the appearance of your data, but it limits you to one formatting option—the ASP.NET DataGrid. The DataGrid is a very powerful control, but to get the maximum benefit from it, you either need to have a solid understanding of how to hand-code the DataGrid in HTML view, or you need to use a tool such as Visual Studio .NET that has a user interface for editing the properties of the DataGrid. Displaying your database results using ASP.NET still has some unique benefits.

CAUTION

If you attempt to switch an ASP database results page to ASP.NET or vice versa, FrontPage will warn you that the page may not display correctly or may not display at all. Heed that warning. A page switched from ASP to ASP.NET or ASP.NET to ASP will almost always not display. To be safe, always create a new page before inserting new database results.

To create a new page using ASP.NET to display database results, follow these steps:

1. Close your browser and switch back to FrontPage.
2. Create a new page and select Insert, Database, Results.
3. In the first step, select ASP.NET and then click Next.
4. Select Employees as the record source and click Next.

5. Click the Edit List button and select the Notes field in the Displayed Fields list. Click Remove to remove the Notes field from your results and click OK.

6. Click Next to move to step 4.

In step 4, you will notice that the three formatting options available to you for ASP pages have been replaced by one formatting option, the DataGrid. The DataGrid is rendered by ASP.NET using a `<table>`, so it's very similar to the Table formatting option when configuring an ASP page. However, when using an ASP.NET DataGrid, you have much more control over the appearance of the table.

As shown in Figure 37.15, three options are available to you when using an ASP.NET DataGrid:

Figure 37.15
When using ASP.NET, the only formatting option available is the DataGrid, but it's highly customizable.

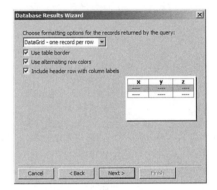

■ **Use Table Border**—As with the ASP table, selecting this option places a border around each cell of the DataGrid. This is configurable after the DataGrid has been inserted, as you will see later.

■ **Use Alternating Row Colors**—Selecting this option causes every other row in the DataGrid to be highlighted with a different color. The color used can be changed easily after the DataGrid has been inserted.

■ **Include Header Row with Column Headers**—Selecting this option makes the first row in the DataGrid into a header row. This is also configurable after the DataGrid has been inserted.

For now, leave all three options selected, click Next, and then click Finish to insert the DataGrid. Your page should now resemble the page shown in Figure 37.16. Save your page as **employeeid.aspx** (the default name FrontPage will give it) and preview it in your browser to see the result as shown in Figure 37.17. The page is almost identical to the ASP page except that alternating rows of the table are in a different color.

Figure 37.16
This page uses the ASP.NET DataGrid to display database results.

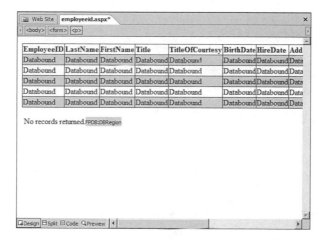

Figure 37.17
This ASP.NET page shows the DataGrid with alternating row colors.

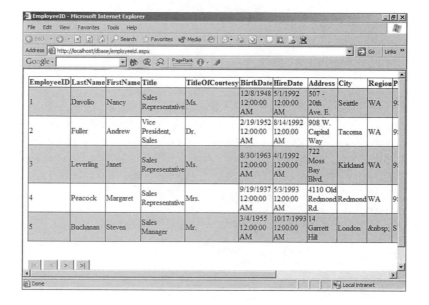

TIP

> Remember that you must have the Microsoft .NET Framework installed for ASP.NET pages to display correctly, and you must be using Internet Information Services (IIS) 5.0 or later on Windows 2000 or later.

 If the ASP.NET page shows up but the DataGrid doesn't display, *see "DataGrid in ASP.NET Page Doesn't Show" in the "Troubleshooting" section of this chapter.*

One of the major benefits of using the DataGrid (and really the only benefit if you don't know how to hand-code ASP.NET) is that you can very easily configure the appearance of the DataGrid right within the FrontPage interface. Right-click on the DataGrid in

FrontPage and select Format Results Region from the menu to display the Format Results Region dialog box as shown in Figure 37.18.

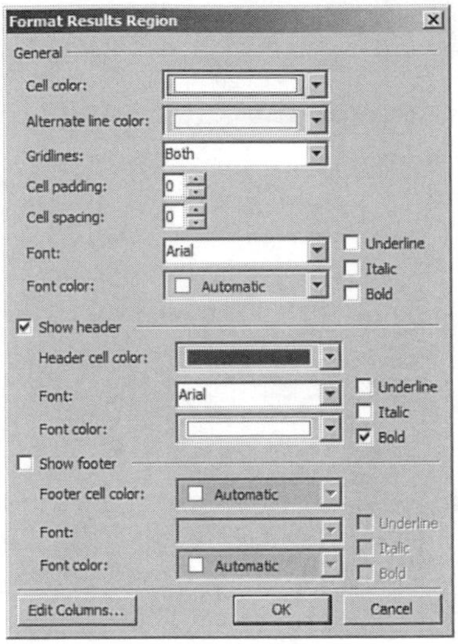

Figure 37.18
The Format Results Region dialog box makes formatting the DataGrid in an ASP.NET page simple.

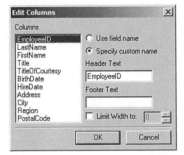

Using the Format Results Region dialog box, you can change the color scheme of the DataGrid, change the formatting of the border, and set the formatting for a header and a footer. By clicking the Edit Columns button, you can configure the header and the footer text for each column, as shown in Figure 37.19. Figure 37.20 shows the database results after the results region has been formatted with custom colors and fonts using the Format Results Region dialog box.

Figure 37.19
The Edit Columns dialog box allows you to customize the text displayed in the header and footer columns.

TIP

After making formatting changes using the Format Results Region dialog box, the DataGrid displays differently in Design view in FrontPage. Instead of seeing the DataGrid, you will only see a single line that says ASP.NET Control: DataGrid. This is normal, and the page will display correctly in the browser.

Figure 37.20
The database results are much more visually pleasing with a few formatting changes.

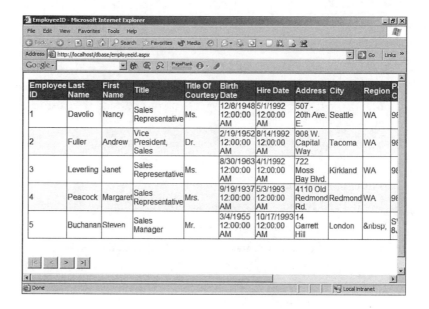

DRILLING INTO DATA WITH THE DATABASE RESULTS WIZARD

It's impressive that you can insert a dynamic data-driven Web page with no coding at all, but these pages are not very useful by themselves. There really isn't any interaction going on with the user. For example, suppose that you wanted to be able to get detailed information on an employee when you click her name in the list? This kind of interaction would be pretty difficult to code by hand, but with the Database Results Wizard, it's easy.

CREATING A DRILL-DOWN PAGE

Close your browser, switch back to FrontPage, and open the database.asp page. Double-click on one of the yellow bars surrounding your database results to display the Database Results Wizard. In order to provide for a data drill-down page, you will reconfigure this page so that the employee's last name is a hyperlink to another page. When that link is clicked, it will display details on the employee whose name was clicked.

1. Click Next twice to move to step 3 of the Database Results Wizard.
2. Click Edit List and remove the EmployeeID field.
3. Select the HireDate field and click Move Down to move it just above the Title field.
4. Click OK.
5. Click Next twice and Finish to regenerate the Database Results Region.
6. FrontPage will ask if you want to regenerate the Database Results Region. When it does, click Yes.

CREATING THE DETAILS PAGE

Now you will need to create a new ASP page to display the details on the employee whose name is clicked.

1. Create a new page and select Insert, Database, Results.
2. Make sure that ASP is selected and that you are using the existing Sample connection and click Next.
3. Select Employees as the record source and click Next.
4. Click the More Options button and click Criteria.
5. In the Criteria dialog box, click Add.
6. In the Field Name dropdown, make sure that EmployeeID is selected.
7. In the Comparison dropdown, make sure that Equals is selected.
8. In the Value dropdown, make sure that EmployeeID is selected.
9. Make sure that the Use This Search Form Field check box is checked. This tells FrontPage that EmployeeID in the Value dropdown is a value that will be passed from a search form and not an explicit value.
10. Click OK three times to return to the Database Results Wizard and click Next.
11. Choose the List—One Field per Item formatting option and click Next.
12. Uncheck the Add Search Form check box. If this is checked, FrontPage will add a form at the top of your database results so that users can enter an employee ID to search on. In this example, you are passing the employee ID from another page, so you don't want a search form.
13. Click Finish to insert the database results.

> **TIP**
>
> When using a form field to search on as you are doing here, it is a good idea to enter default values in the More Options dialog box. However, in this case, no one will be browsing directly to the details.asp page, so no default values were entered.

Save this page as **details.asp**. This page is now configured to display details on whatever employee ID is passed to it. You now need to configure the database.asp page so that it passes the employee ID to details.asp.

CONNECTING THE PAGES

Switch back to the database.asp page. In your database results, right-click on <<LastName>> and select Database Column Value Properties from the menu to display the Database Column Value dialog box. Place a check mark in the Display as Hyperlink checkbox and click the Hyperlink Parameters button to display the Hyperlink Parameters dialog box.

The Hyperlink Parameters dialog box is used to configure the URL that the database column links to. It also enables you to configure query string values. A *query string* value is a name/value pair that is passed in a hyperlink. In this case, you want to pass the employee ID for the employee whose last name you click. You will pass that employee ID in the hyperlink URL as a query string.

Click the Add button to display the Add Parameter dialog box. In the Name dropdown, choose EmployeeID. FrontPage will automatically populate the Value dropdown with the ASP code necessary to pass the employee ID for the employee you click, as shown in Figure 37.21. Click OK to insert the parameter and then click OK again to dismiss the Hyperlink Parameters dialog box. The Column to Display dropdown now contains a hyperlink to details.asp, and the query string value is added to it as shown in Figure 37.22.

Figure 37.21
The ASP code necessary to populate the employee ID is entered automatically.

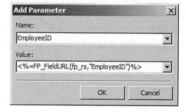

Figure 37.22
The Database Column Value dialog box now contains a URL for the details.asp page and the employee ID query string.

Click OK in the Database Column Value dialog box. Note that the LastName column is now configured as a hyperlink. However, it is now configured to display the EmployeeID field and not the LastName field. Because you want to make the employee's last name a hyperlink to the details page, double-click on <<EmployeeID>> and select LastName in the Column to Display dropdown. Click OK to commit that change. If you now hover over the <<LastName>> column value, you will notice that the status bar in FrontPage displays the hyperlink to the details.asp page.

TIP

> The fact that FrontPage changed the column to display the EmployeeID field is a quirk of the Database Results Wizard. If you configure a database column as a hyperlink, you can still reconfigure the column to display the desired database column value by double-clicking the column value and changing the column that it displays. Your hyperlink settings will be maintained.

Save the `database.asp` page and preview it in your browser. Each employee's last name should be a hyperlink, and when it is clicked, you will be taken to `details.asp` and the complete details on that employee should be displayed.

NOTE

> Microsoft FrontPage MVP (Most Valuable Professional) Kathleen Anderson has an excellent Web page with great resources and some of her own tips and tutorials on the Database Results Wizard at `http://dbrw.frontpagelink.com`. This is a highly recommended resource for getting the most out of the Database Results Wizard in FrontPage.

→ The FrontPage Database Results Wizard, like any wizard, is limited in what it can do. To really get full database functionality, consider learning how to code your own ASP. For resources on learning ASP, **see** "ASP and .NET Resources," **p. 916**.

WORKING WITH THE DATABASE INTERFACE WIZARD

In the previous section, you learned how to display existing records in a database using FrontPage. FrontPage also offers the ability to edit, add, and delete records from a database using the Database Interface Wizard. The Database Interface Wizard will add all the pages necessary for you to display records from your data source, edit those records, add new records, and delete existing records. It will even provide a password protected editing interface so that only those users you choose can edit your data source.

The Database Interface Wizard is a Web site wizard. Therefore, you can either create a new Web site with the Database Interface Wizard or you can add the Database Interface Wizard to an existing Web site. It is usually most convenient to add it to an existing Web site because you will then have the option to use an existing database connection. Let's add a Database Interface Wizard to your existing Web site and create some pages that will allow you to edit your database.

CREATING A SITE WITH THE DATABASE INTERFACE WIZARD

To insert the Database Interface Wizard, follow these steps:

1. Select File, New and click the More Web Site Templates link in the New task pane.
2. Select the Database Interface Wizard template.

3. Check the Add to Current Web Site check box.

4. Click OK to display the Database Interface Wizard, as shown in Figure 37.23.

Figure 37.23
The Database Interface Wizard makes it easy to create pages to edit your database.

CHOOSING ASP OR ASP.NET

As with the Database Results Wizard, you can choose between ASP and ASP.NET. Choose ASP and select the Use an Existing Database Connection option. Make sure that the Sample database connection is selected and click Next to proceed to step 2 of the wizard.

 If the Use an Existing Database Connection option is disabled, *see "Use an Existing Database Connection Is Disabled" in the "Troubleshooting" section of this chapter.*

CONFIGURING THE RECORD SOURCE

In step 2, select Employees from the dropdown so that the Database Interface Wizard will connect to the Employees table just as you did with the Database Results Wizard. FrontPage chooses a location for your Database Interface Wizard files using the `<connection_name>_interface/<record_source>` naming convention. You can change this if you want, but for now, leave it as the default and click Next.

> **TIP**
>
> The Database Interface Wizard places all of its files in the folder specified in step 2. If you decide to remove the Database Interface Wizard from your Web site, simply delete that folder and it's gone.

FORMATTING YOUR DATA

Step 3 of the Database Interface Wizard is where you choose the order of the columns in your record source and how they are configured. The EmployeeID field has an asterisk next to it to indicate that it is the *primary key*, a field in the database that must be unique for every record. If you leave it configured as is, when a user enters a new employee, she will have to enter an employee ID for that person. It would be preferable if the number could be generated automatically so that the user of your page doesn't have to worry about entering a number that already exists. To set that up, do the following:

37

1. Select the EmployeeID field and click Modify.

2. In the Column type dropdown, select Autonumber.

3. Click OK.

The EmployeeID field now shows a column type of Autonumber and the form field type is empty, as shown in Figure 37.24. This will cause the Microsoft Access database to automatically assign the next available employee ID to newly entered employees. Because the form field type is empty, the EmployeeID field will not display to users of your site, which is exactly the way it should be. Click Next to move to step 4.

Figure 37.24
The EmployeeID field has been modified so that it is an autonumbered field.

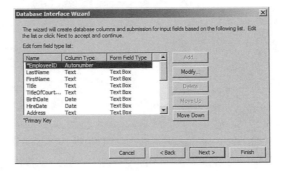

CHOOSING THE PAGES FOR YOUR SITE

In step 4 of the Database Interface Wizard, you choose what pages you want the Database Interface Wizard to generate for you, as shown in Figure 37.25.

- **Results Page**—The page that displays the contents of your database

- **Submission Form**—The form that allows for the creation of new records for your database

- **Database Editor**—A series of Web pages that allow for complete administration of your database from your Web browser

Figure 37.25
The Database Interface Wizard allows you to choose which pages to include.

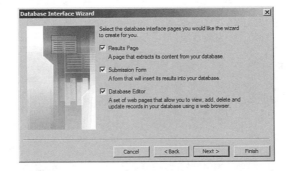

Select all three check boxes and click Next to move to step 5.

SPECIFYING A USERNAME AND PASSWORD

In step 5, you can specify a username and password that will be required to access your database editor. If you password protect your editor, the only page that people can view without the correct username and password is the results page, `results_page.asp`. Any editing, deletion, or addition of records requires the correct username and password. Enter the username and password of your choice and then click Next and Finish to insert your Database Interface Wizard pages.

→ To see how to use the Database Interface Wizard's password protection on any page you prefer, **see** "Front and Center: Password Protecting Pages of Your Choice," **p. 732**.

CONTENT ADDED BY THE DATABASE INTERFACE WIZARD

After the Database Interface Wizard has finished adding pages to your site, you will have a new folder named whatever you specified in step 2 of the wizard. Inside that folder, you will have folders and files that will differ, depending on which pages you chose to have inserted, as shown in Figure 37.26.

Figure 37.26
The Database Interface Wizard inserts many pages in to your site, depending on the options chosen in step 4.

> **CAUTION**
>
> Even though the Database Interface Wizard uses Database Results regions, don't ever edit the pages with the Database Results Wizard. If you do, it will break the functionality of the Database Interface Wizard pages.

Assuming that you checked all three check boxes in step 4 of the Database Interface Wizard, the following pages will be added to your site:

37

- **results_page.asp**—Displays all the records in your database, much like the Database Results Wizard page that you created earlier. This is the only page that is not protected by a password if you chose to have your editor password protected in step 5 of the wizard.

- **confirm.asp**—A confirmation page that is displayed after a new record is added to the database.

- **database_editor.asp**—A frames page that displays the database editor.

- **delete.asp**—Appears in the bottom frame of database_editor.asp when you are deleting records from the database.

- **detail.asp**—Displays in the bottom frame of database_editor.asp when a record is selected from the top frame by clicking an employee ID.

- **edit.asp**—Appears in the bottom frame of database_editor.asp and allows for editing of records.

- **list.asp**—Appear in the top frame of database_editor.asp.

- **login.asa**—This page is included in each ASP page of the database editor when they are protected with a password. It contains the username and password that you configured for the database editor.

- **login.asp**—The login page for the database editor if it is protected with a password. If a user requests a page in the editor without logging in, she is automatically redirected to this page.

- **Login_Validate.asp**—Contains ASP code that validates the username and password entered in the login page. If the login entered is correct, the user is taken to either the database_editor.asp page or the page she originally requested.

- **new.asp**—Appears in the bottom frame of database_editor.asp when a new record is being added.

- **submission_form.asp**—A standalone (nonframed) version of new.asp that appears whenever the Submission Form link is clicked from database_editor.asp.

- **update.asp**—Contains the ASP code necessary to update a record that is being edited.

The entry point for a Database Interface Wizard site is usually results_page.asp. From there, a user can access all the other pages in the editor.

> **TIP**
>
> The Database Interface Wizard can also create a new database in your Web site. In step 1 of the Database Interface Wizard, select the Create a New Microsoft Access Database Within your Web Site radio button to have a new database created for you in the fpdb folder of your Web site.

USING THE DATABASE INTERFACE PAGES

Now you can check out your database editor in action. Browse to the results_page.asp that the Database Interface Wizard created, and you should see a page similar to the one shown in Figure 37.27. In the upper-right corner of this page are links to the Submission Form and the Database Editor. The Submission Form allows you to add new records to the database. You can also add new records from the Database Editor in addition to editing and deleting existing records.

Figure 37.27
The Results Page generated by the Database Interface Wizard contains links that will allow you to edit your database.

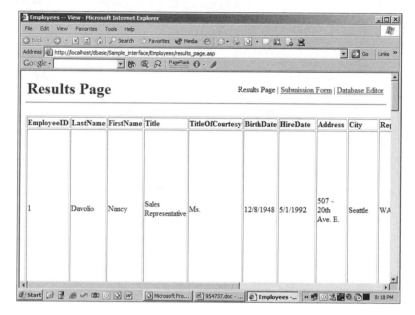

Click the Database Editor link. You should be prompted to log in as shown in Figure 37.28. Enter your username and password and click Login to log in to the Database Editor. When the Database Editor appears (see Figure 37.29), you can add a new record by clicking the Add New Record button, delete one or more records by selecting them and clicking the Delete Selected Records button, or edit a record by selecting that record and then clicking the Edit button at the bottom of the page.

Click the Add New Record button. Fill in information for yourself and click the OK button to add yourself to the database. After you have been added, click the next page button (the > button) at the bottom of the top frame to go to the next page. Your record will appear last in the list (see Figure 37.30) because the list is ordered by the EmployeeID field, and since you are the last employee entered in the database, you have the highest employee number.

Click your employee number to display details on yourself. The bottom frame will refresh with the details on your record. At the bottom of the details page are Edit button and Delete buttons. From here, you can edit or delete your record. You can also remove one or more records by checking the box next to the record in the top frame and clicking the Delete Selected Records button.

Figure 37.28
The login page protects access to the Database Editor.

Figure 37.29
The Database Editor provides all the functions necessary to maintain the records in your database.

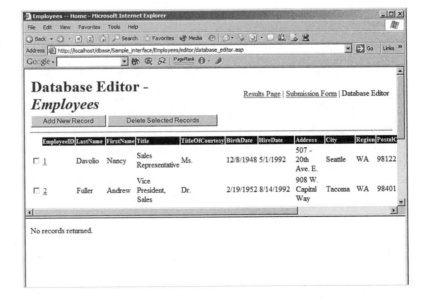

As you can see, building a full-featured database editing system is very easy with the Database Interface Wizard, and you can do it all without writing a single line of code.

Figure 37.30
A new record has been added with the information entered.

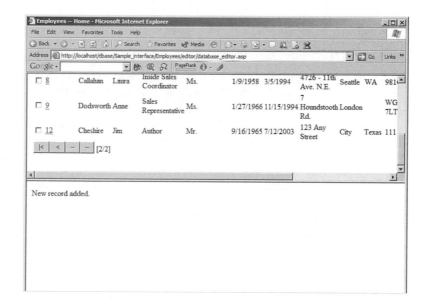

TROUBLESHOOTING

DATAGRID IN ASP.NET PAGE DOESN'T SHOW

I chose ASP.NET for my database pages. The page shows up, but the DataGrid doesn't display.

First, make sure that your Web server supports ASP.NET and that the .NET Framework is installed. If you check out for both of those, it is likely that ASP.NET has not been correctly registered on IIS.

Go to a command prompt, switch to the `C:\<Windows_Folder>\Microsoft.NET\Framework\<Framework_Version>` folder, and run the following command:

```
aspnet_regiis -i
```

After the command has finished installing ASP.NET onto IIS, try your page again, and the DataGrid should display.

USE AN EXISTING DATABASE CONNECTION IS DISABLED

I am trying to insert a Database Interface Wizard, but the option to use an existing database connection is not available.

The option to use an existing database connection is only available if you are adding the Database Interface Wizard to an existing Web site. Make sure that you have checked the Add to Current Web Site check box before starting the Database Interface Wizard and that you have a database connection created in the existing Web site.

37

FRONT AND CENTER: PASSWORD PROTECTING PAGES OF YOUR CHOICE

One of the most common questions from FrontPage users is "how can I password protect one or more pages in my Web site?" It just so happens that the Database Interface Wizard adds the ASP code necessary to handle all this for you as long as you don't mind having a single username and password for all of your users. Only ASP pages can be protected using this method because the protection relies on the ASP code generated by the Database Interface Wizard.

Open the edit.asp page that the Database Interface Wizard generated and switch to Code view. Select the code at the top of the page all the way down to, but not including, the <html> tag. Create a new page and save it in the same folder as the edit.asp. Save the page as protected.asp. Switch to Code view and paste the code that you copied from edit.asp into the page at the top of the page before the <html> tag. Edit the line of code that performs the Response.Redirect and change edit.asp to protected.asp. The code before the <html> tag should now be as follows:

```
<!-- #include File='login.asa'-->
<%
    If Session(SiteID) <> true Then
        Response.Redirect("Login.asp?requester=protected.asp")
    End If
%>
```

Note that the only change made was to the requester query string value. Now change to Design view and type **This page is password protected.** in to the page. Save the page and preview it in a new browser window. When the page is first requested, you will be prompted to log in. Only after you enter the correct username and password will you be served the protected.asp page.

How does this work? FrontPage stores a long string called SiteID in the login.asa file. This string is a *GUID*, a string of 32 hexadecimal digits guaranteed to be unique. FrontPage uses the SiteID value to name a specific value associated with your ASP session to the dbase Web site. By using a GUID, FrontPage can be certain that there are no other ASP Session values by that same name.

FrontPage also stores the username and password that you configure for the Database Editor in the login.asa file. It does this so that it can verify them when you enter them on the login page. The first line you pasted into protected.asp tells ASP to stick the contents of login.asa into the protected.asp page. By doing that, you now have access to the correct username and password that are stored in login.asa and you also have access to the unique value for SiteID.

FrontPage then inserts some ASP code to verify if the ASP Session variable for SiteID is equal to true. It will only be equal to true if you have previously logged in successfully. If you haven't logged in successfully, the value represented by the SiteID GUID will not be equal to true and you will be redirected to the Login.asp page.

When you are redirected to the Login.asp page, FrontPage includes a query string parameter called requester that contains the name of the page you originally requested. FrontPage uses this to send you back to that page after you successfully log in. The page responsible for checking the credentials you enter on the Login.asp page is the Login_Validate.asp page. If the username and password you entered are correct, it redirects you to the page passed in the requester query string. If the credentials you entered are not correct, you are notified of that and are not allowed to continue.

So what if you want to password protect some pages, but you don't want to include all the Database Interface Wizard pages in your Web site? The only pages you need to implement password protection are Login.asp, Login_Validate.asp, and login.asa. After you've run the Database Interface Wizard to generate those pages, you can delete all the other pages.

There is one more important consideration when modifying the structure of the Web site. It's important to make sure that the paths in your ASP code are relative to the current page. For example, suppose you want the protected.asp page that you've been working on in this chapter to be located in the root of the dbase Web site. You can't just move the page to the root folder and expect FrontPage to update the links because the links are in ASP code and FrontPage doesn't update links in ASP code. Instead, you have to change the links yourself.

Move the protected.asp page to the root of the dbase Web site and browse to it again. You will get an error message. To correct that error, you have to edit the code so that it appears as follows.

```
<!-- #include File='Sample_interface/Employees/editor/login.asa'-->
<%
If Session(SiteID) <> true Then
  Response.Redirect("Sample_interface/Employees/editor/Login.asp?
  ➥requester=/dbase/protected.asp")
End If
%>
```

Now that all the paths are correct, the page will work as expected.

CHAPTER 38

FrontPage and Web Parts

THE DATA SOURCE CATALOG

A significant new feature-set has been added to FrontPage, and it represents the most exciting new addition to FrontPage since the Database Region Wizard added in to FrontPage 98. That new feature-set is called *Web Parts*. Web Parts are XML-driven data access components that are extremely powerful. Using Web Parts, you can configure complex data queries. You can have multiple Web Parts on one page, and you can configure them to talk to each other so that they share data. You can access just about any data you can conceive using Web Parts, and you can do it all without a single line of code!

Web Parts rely on Windows SharePoint Services, and Windows SharePoint Services rely on Windows Server 2003. If you are hosting your Web site on a Windows 2000 Server, you won't be able to use Web Parts. However, Windows Server 2003 hosting plans are popping up all over the Internet, and Windows SharePoint Services support is appearing as well. Once you see the awesome power of these features in FrontPage, you will be beating down the door at your hosting company asking for Windows SharePoint Services. Web Parts really are that cool.

→ For more information on Windows SharePoint Services, **see** "Windows SharePoint Services 2.0," **p. 943**.

INSERTING WEB PARTS USING THE DATA SOURCE CATALOG

You can access Web Parts from many different places in FrontPage, but the most comprehensive area is the Data Source Catalog. The Data Source Catalog (shown in Figure 38.1) is a FrontPage task pane that acts as a repository of data sources that you have added to the site. By default, there are no data sources in the Data Source Catalog, but adding them is very easy.

Figure 38.1
The Data Source Catalog is a very powerful task pane.

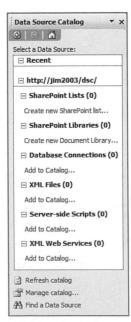

NOTE

> You must have access to Windows SharePoint Services in order to walk through the steps outlined in this chapter. If you don't have access to Windows SharePoint Services, don't let that stop you from reading through this chapter and exploring all the capabilities that Web Parts have to offer.

To access the Data Source Catalog, select <u>D</u>ata, Insert Data <u>V</u>iew. A *Data View* is the most commonly used Web Part because it allows you to dynamically populate a Web page using content from any one of six different data sources. The data sources available to you are

- **SharePoint Lists**—Contain any Windows SharePoint Services Lists. A SharePoint List can contain any type of information and is usually a part of a Windows SharePoint Services Web site.

- **SharePoint Libraries**—Contain any Windows SharePoint Services Libraries. A SharePoint Library is a collection of documents or pictures and is often a part of a Windows SharePoint Services Web site.

- **Database Connections**—Contain any database connections that you have configured. You can connect to a Microsoft SQL Server or an Oracle database server using the user interface provided by FrontPage. You can also access any other OLE DB compliant data source by specifying a custom connection string.

- **XML Files**—Contains any XML files that you have configured. The XML file must exist in the current Web site. If it does not, FrontPage will prompt you to import it when you create the data connection.

- **Server-side Scripts**—Contains any server-side script data sources. These are usually ASP.NET or ASP pages to which you pass parameters to get data. The data should be returned in XML format so that the Web Part can properly consume it.

- **XML Web Services**—Contains any XML Web Services that you have created a reference to. An XML Web Service is a URL that takes parameters from you and returns data based upon those parameters in XML format. As you'll see in this chapter, XML Web Services are a very powerful part of the Data Source Catalog.

 If the Insert Data View option is disabled on the Data menu, see "Cannot Insert Data View" in the "Troubleshooting" section of this chapter.

At the top of the Data Source Catalog is a link to recently used data sources. If you select a recently used data source and it is no longer available, FrontPage will inform you of that fact and allow you to remove it from the list. Directly underneath the recently used data sources list is the top-level item for the current Web site. The top-level item displays as the URL of the current Web site. You can easily add data sources from other URLs by using the Manage Catalog link at the bottom of the Data Source Catalog, as shown in Figure 38.2.

TIP

> Everything on the Data menu in FrontPage relies on Windows SharePoint Services. If you don't have Windows SharePoint Services on your Web site and you try to use these features, FrontPage will politely remind you that you need Windows SharePoint Services.

Figure 38.2
The Manage Catalog dialog box allows you to quickly add new data sources to the Data Source Catalog.

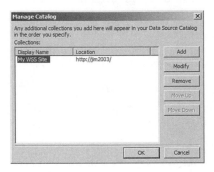

ACCESSING DATA SOURCES FROM OTHER WEB SITES

When you install Windows SharePoint Services, the root Web site of your Web server is configured as a Windows SharePoint Services Web site. By default, a Windows SharePoint Services Web site contains six SharePoint Lists and one SharePoint Library. If you want to access those Lists or the Library in a different Web site, all you have to do is add the Windows SharePoint Services Web site to the Data Source Catalog. You do that as follows:

1. Click the Manage Catalog link at the bottom of the Data Source Catalog task pane to display the Manage Catalog dialog box (shown previously in Figure 38.2).

2. Click the Add button.

3. In the Display Name text box, enter a name of your choice to use for your new data source collection. This name will be displayed in the Data Source Catalog and also in the header for your Data View.

4. In the Location text box, browse to the URL for the Web site that contains the data sources that you want to use. For example, if you want to connect to the data sources for the root Web site that was configured as a Windows SharePoint Services Web site, enter **http://localhost**.

5. Click OK.

As shown in Figure 38.2, the new data source collection appears in the Manage Catalog dialog box. Click OK to add the new collection to the Data Source Catalog, as shown in Figure 38.3.

Figure 38.3
The Data Source Catalog now contains new data sources from the newly added collection.

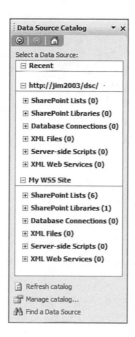

INSERTING A DATA VIEW

When the Data Source Catalog is displayed initially, there are no data sources available. To add data sources to the Data Source Catalog, click one of the Add to Catalog links under a data source name. For example, to create a connection to a Microsoft SQL Server database

1. Expand the Database Connections data source if it is not already expanded.
2. Click the Add to Catalog link to display the Data Source Properties dialog box as shown in Figure 38.4.

Figure 38.4
The Data Source Properties dialog box is the interface to create new data source connections.

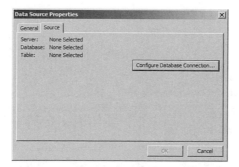

3. Click the Configure Database Connection button to display the Configure Database Connection dialog box as shown in Figure 38.5.

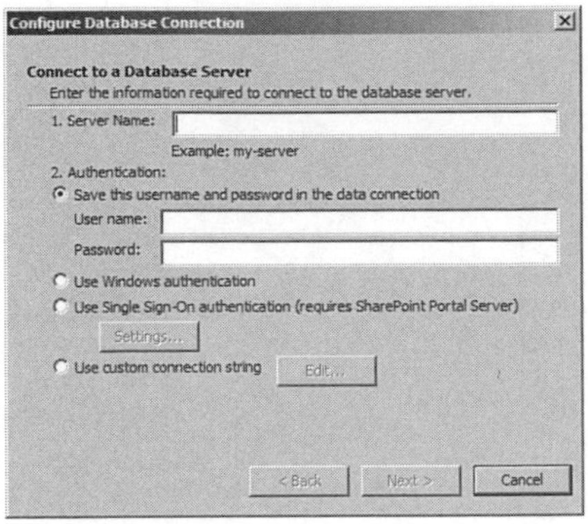

Figure 38.5
The Configure Database Connection dialog box allows you to connect to any OLE DB compliant data source.

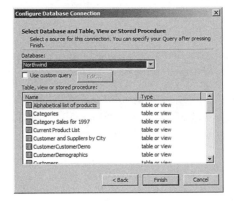

38

4. In the Server Name text box, enter the name of your database server.

5. In the Authentication section, select the desired authentication method to use to connect to your database and enter a username and password if necessary.

6. Click Next to go to the next step as seen in Figure 38.6. If the database connection information you provided is not correct, FrontPage will display an error and you will have to correct the connection information before you can proceed.

Figure 38.6
After entering server information, select the table, view, or stored procedure from the list or create a custom query.

7. In the Database dropdown, select the database to use for your connection from the list of databases available on the data source you have connected to.

8. Select a table, a view, or a stored procedure. If you'd prefer, you can check the Use custom query check box and click Edit to create a custom query. FrontPage will display a text box where you can type in your query.

9. Click Finish. The Data Source Properties dialog box now contains configuration information for your data source, as shown in Figure 38.7.

10. Click OK to add the connection to the Data Source Catalog.

Figure 38.7
The Data Source Properties dialog box is now populated with information on your data source.

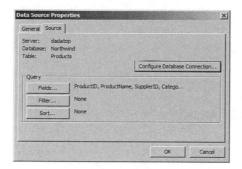

The Data Source Catalog now contains a new entry for your data source. By clicking the data source, you can access the data source menu as seen in Figure 38.8.

Figure 38.8
The data source menu provides access to a lot of functionality.

If you are trying to connect to Microsoft SQL Server running on a computer other than the Web server and you receive an error when trying to connect, see *"Cannot Connect to SQL Server"* in the *"Troubleshooting"* section of this chapter.

Instead of jumping right in and inserting your data right away, you might want to review it first and make sure that it shows you what you want. To do that, click the down arrow next to the data source and select <u>S</u>how Data. When you do, you will be taken to the Data View Details task pane, as shown in Figure 38.9. From here, you can review the data your data source connects to, and after you confirm that this is the data you want, you can click the Insert Data View link to insert a Data View of that data onto your Web page.

Figure 38.9
The Data View Details task pane provides a view of your data and much more.

Using the data source menu, you can also choose to save the data source by selecting Save As or email it to someone by selecting Mail Recipient (as Attachment). Both of these options will generate an XML file that contains all the information for the data source. To add the saved data source to FrontPage later, simply copy the XML file into the _fpdatasources/fpdatasources folder in the Web site (which is created when you add a data source to the Data Source Catalog) and recalculate links on the Web site by selecting Tools, Recalculate Hyperlinks.

To insert a new Data View into your Web page, select Insert Data View from the Data View Details task pane or select Insert Data View from the data source menu in the Data Source Catalog. When you do, two things happen. The first is that FrontPage inserts a Data View into your Web page that displays the data as shown in Figure 38.10. The second is that the Data Source Properties link activates in the Data View Details task pane. (If you selected the Insert Data View option from the data source menu in the Data Source Catalog, FrontPage will automatically activate the Data View Details task pane.)

Figure 38.10
A new Data View is inserted into your Web page. This Data View is displaying live data.

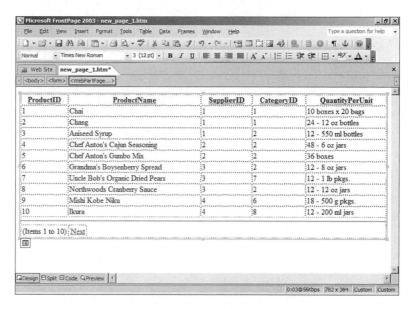

CONFIGURING A DATA VIEW AND WEB PARTS

A Data View can be configured quickly and easily using the Data View Options button to display the Data View Options menu as shown in Figure 38.11. The Data View Options button is made available by clicking inside of the Data View, and because it's a floating button, it can appear in many different places depending on where you clicked.

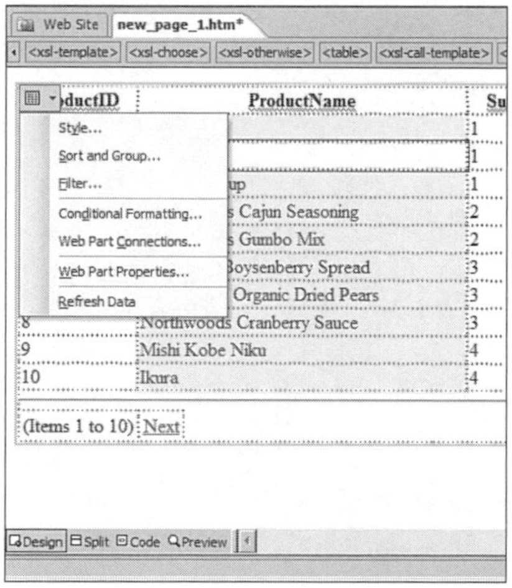

Figure 38.11
The Data View Options menu is a quick way to format a Data View.

THE STYLES OPTION

The first option on the Data View Options menu is Style. This allows you to apply broad formatting style changes to the data. As shown in Figure 38.12, the General tab provides many different styles from which to choose. When selecting a style in the HTML View Styles list, the Description will update to reflect a brief description of the style.

Figure 38.12
The General tab of the View Styles dialog box provides many templates to choose from.

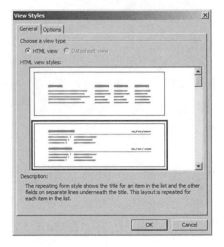

The Options tab, shown in Figure 38.13, provides access to some of the functionality settings of the Data View. Changes to settings here affect the Data View when it is being displayed in a Web browser.

Figure 38.13
The Options tab sets the behavior and appearance of your Data View when it is being browsed in a Web browser.

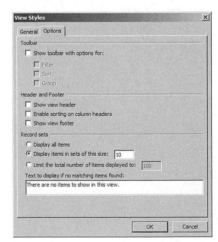

You can configure toolbars for the Data View by checking the Show Toolbar with Options For check box and selecting one of the following options:

- **Filter**—Displays a Filter link that allows people browsing your Data View to filter the data based on the criteria they choose.

- **Sort**—Adds a dropdown list of all the fields in your data source. The Data View will be sorted by the field chosen from the dropdown by the user browsing your Data View.

- **Group**—Displays a dropdown list of all the fields in your data source. By selecting a field name in the dropdown, users browsing your Data View can group the Data View by that field in expanding and collapsing sets of data.

The Header and Footer section allows you to choose to display a header and/or footer. Depending on the style you have chosen on the General tab, you can also choose to allow viewers of your Web page to sort the Data View. If sorting is enabled by clicking the Enable Sorting on Column Headers check box, users of your Web site can sort the data by clicking on a column header.

The Record Sets section configures whether the Data View displays all records at once or displays paging links. You can also configure the message that is displayed if you or the user of your Data View configure it so that it doesn't return data.

Figure 38.14 shows a view in the browser of a Data View that is configured with the Filter, Sort, and Group toolbar options. Note that the user has chosen to group by SupplierID and the Data View is showing the data with supplier 1 expanded and the rest collapsed. Also notice that there is a small downward-pointing arrow to the right of the Group By dropdown. This indicates that the Data View is grouped in ascending order. By clicking this arrow, you can reorder the Data View in descending order.

Figure 38.14
A Data View viewed in the Web browser with some advanced features.

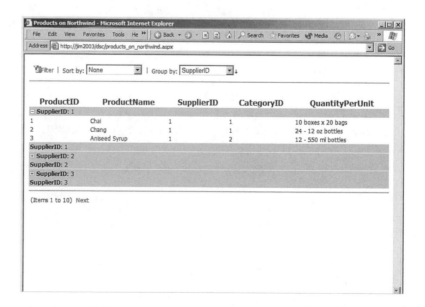

THE SORT AND GROUP OPTION

The second option on the Data View Options menu is the Sort and Group option. Selecting this option displays the Sort and Group dialog box shown in Figure 38.15. The Sort and Group dialog box allows you to configure the Data View by sorting the data and grouping it in design-time so that when it initially appears on the Web page, it will appear already sorted and grouped. The effect is the same as the effect seen in Figure 38.14, but is applied at design-time instead of when a user is browsing the Data View.

Figure 38.15
The Sort and Group dialog box configures the way data is displayed.

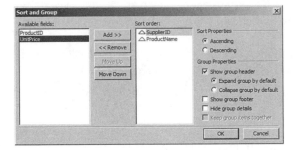

NOTE

By selecting a field name in the Available Fields list in the Sort and Group dialog box and clicking the Add button, you can configure the Data View to be sorted by that field. The Sort Properties radio buttons allow you to configure the sort as ascending or descending.

In the Group Properties section, you can configure grouping for the Data View. The grouping settings that you configure apply to the field that is currently selected in the Sort Order list. This enables you to create complex groupings. The page shown in Figure 38.16 is sorted by SupplierID and then by ProductName. Grouping is enabled for both with SupplierID set to be expanded by default and ProductName set to be collapsed by default.

THE FILTER OPTION

The next option on the Data View Options menu is Filter. This option allows you to filter the Data View by one or more criteria as shown in Figure 38.17. Click the first row to add a filter clause. Once you have configured your filter clauses, click OK to update the Data View with your settings.

Figure 38.16
Creating complex groupings is easy with the Sort and Group dialog box.

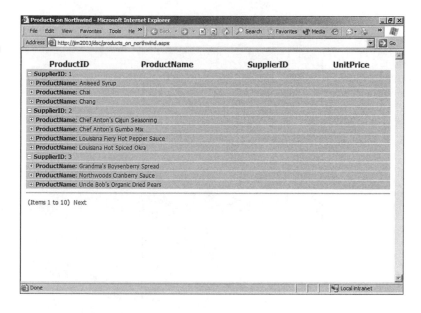

Figure 38.17
The Filter Criteria dialog box filters a Data View based on one or more criteria.

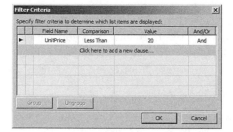

THE CONDITIONAL FORMATTING OPTION

The next item on the Data View Options menu is Conditional Formatting. Selecting this item takes you to the Conditional Formatting task pane, as shown in Figure 38.18.

Figure 38.18
The Conditional Formatting task pane allows you to format values in a Data View based on certain conditions.

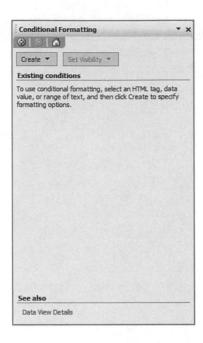

Suppose that you want to display your list of products, and you want any product with a unit price of greater than twenty dollars to be displayed with a black background and white text. Using the Conditional Formatting option, such formatting is simple.

1. Select one of the rows in your Data View.
2. In the Conditional Formatting task pane, click Create and select Apply Formatting from the menu. This displays the Condition Criteria dialog box.
3. Click the first row to add a new clause as shown in Figure 38.19.

Figure 38.19
The Condition Criteria dialog box contains clauses to apply formatting based on specified conditions.

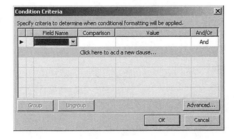

4. In the Field Name dropdown, select UnitPrice.
5. In the Comparison dropdown, select Greater Than.
6. In the Value dropdown, enter the value **20** as shown in Figure 38.20.
7. Click OK to apply the condition criteria. The Modify Style dialog box appears as shown in Figure 38.21.

Figure 38.20
A new clause configured for all prices greater than 20.

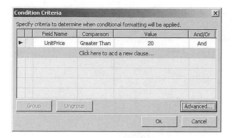

Figure 38.21
The Modify Style dialog box provides access to all the formatting options you'll need.

8. Click the Format button in the Modify Style dialog box and select Border from the menu.

9. In the Borders and Shading dialog box, click the Shading tab.

10. In the Background Color dropdown, select black, as shown in Figure 38.22.

Figure 38.22
The Borders and Shading dialog box showing the new background color for the conditional formatting.

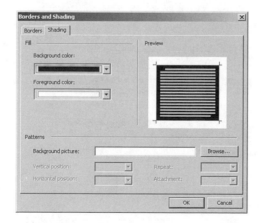

11. Click OK to return to the Modify Style dialog box.

12. Click Format and select Font from the menu.

13. In the Color dropdown, select white, as shown in Figure 38.23.

Figure 38.23
The Font dialog box with the new color selected for the conditional formatting.

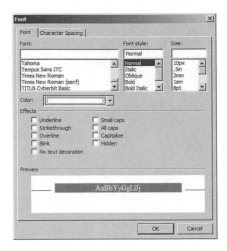

14. Click OK to return to the Modify Styles dialog box.

15. Click OK to apply the conditional formatting.

As shown in Figure 38.24, the Conditional Formatting task pane now shows the condition you just applied, and the Data View has been formatted according to the condition.

Figure 38.24
The Conditional Formatting task pane and the Data View have been updated.

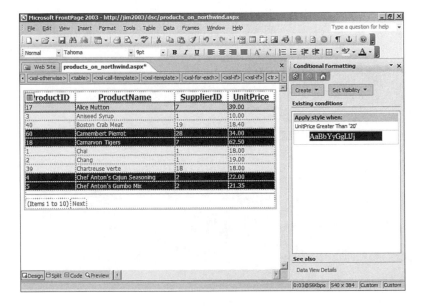

WEB PART OPTIONS

The next option on the Data View Options menu is Web Part Connections. This option is used to connect Web Parts together.

→ For more information on connecting Web Parts, **see** "Connecting Web Parts," **p. 754**.

The next option on the Data View Options menu is Web Part Properties. The options available to you in the Web Part Properties dialog box are dependant on the type of Web Part being edited. However, all Web Part Properties dialog boxes will allow you to display and edit the *XSL* and the *XSLT* code that make up the Web Part.

XSL and XSLT
XSL and XSLT are languages that allow you to take XML data from one data source and transform and format it for use in another data source. It isn't necessary to understand these technologies in order to work with Web Parts because FrontPage will write all the XSL and XSLT code for you as you work in the user interface. As of this writing, FrontPage is the only tool available that can generate standards-compliant XSL and XSLT code from a WYSIWYG interface. For more information on XSL and XSLT, read *Special Edition Using XSLT* by Que Publishing.

38

Many of the properties of a Web Part apply only to Web Parts that are a part of a *Web Part Page*—a collection of page templates that are included with FrontPage. Web Part Pages already have containers for Web Parts arranged on them. These containers are called Web Part Zones, and they allow you to easily change the design of a page that contains Web Parts. You can insert your own Web Part Zone onto a Web page as well, but Web Part Pages contain other design elements that make editing Web Parts more powerful.

To create a new Web Part Page

1. Select File, New and click the More Page Templates link in the New task pane.
2. Click the Web Part Pages tab.
3. Select the Header, Left Column, Body template and click OK.
4. Save the page as **WebPart.aspx**.

You should now have a new page that resembles the page in Figure 38.25.

Preview the WebPart.aspx page in your browser. You will notice that the page is empty except for a few graphics and a link that says Modify Shared Page, as seen in Figure 38.26. That link is your window into the power of Web Part Zones and the reason why you want to use a Web Part Page for Web Part Zones instead of inserting them on a normal Web page.

Figure 38.25
A new Web Part Page complete with several Web Part Zones.

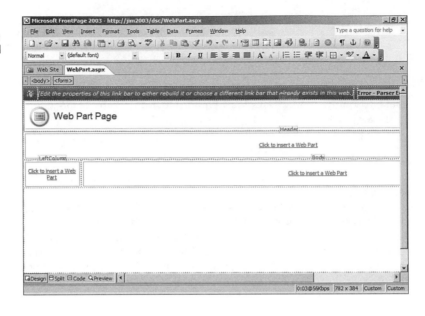

Figure 38.26
The empty Web Part Page. The power lies in the Modify Shared Page link.

Modify Shared Page link

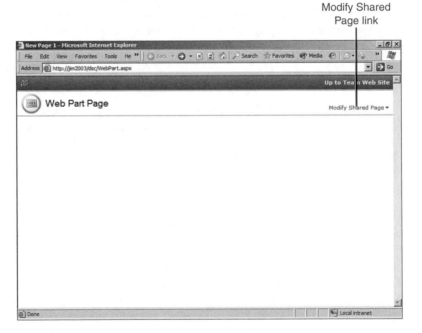

Click the Modify Shared Page link to display the Modify Shared Page menu as seen in Figure 38.27.

Figure 38.27
The Modify Shared Page menu allows you to edit the page and its Web Parts.

The options available to you are as follows:

- **Add Web Parts**—Hovering over this menu produces a submenu that allows you to Browse, Search, or Import Web Parts. Clicking one of these displays the Add Web Parts pane in the browser as shown in Figure 38.28. You can drag Web Parts from this pane to the main window to add the Web Part to the page.

- **Design This Page**—If the page already contains Web Parts, choosing this option allows you to change the layout of the page and move Web Parts around.

- **Modify Shared Web Parts**—When you hover over this menu item, you will see a list of all Web Parts that exist within a Web Part Zone. Selecting one of the Web Parts allows you to modify that Web Part. Any Web Part that is not inside of a Web Part Zone is not a shared Web Part that can be edited.

- **Shared View**—Activates the view of the page that is shared among all visitors to the site.

- **Personal View**—Activates a view of the page that is customized per user. Only applicable if the site is not browsed using anonymous access.

Figure 38.28
Adding Web Parts to a Web page is done right within your browser window.

→ For a full walkthrough of Web Parts and editing Web Part Pages, **see** "Windows SharePoint Services 2.0," **p. 943**.

CONNECTING WEB PARTS

Web Parts can be extended even further by configuring a connection between them. Using Web Part connections, you can easily pass data between Web Parts and have the Web Parts use the data to decide what data to display.

To provide you with a simple example, suppose that you are displaying a list of your products from a SQL Server database. You want to be able to click the product name in one Web Part and have that product name passed to another Web Part that will then display the supplier information for that product. Configuring this type of interaction is simple using Web Part connections.

You will need two data sources to complete the task:

1. Select Data, Insert Data View.
2. Click the Add to Catalog link in the Database Connections section of the Data Source Catalog as shown in Figure 38.29.

Figure 38.29
The Add to Catalog link allows you to easily add a new connection to the Data Source Catalog.

3. Click Configure Database Connection.
4. Configure a connection to a SQL Server database and click Next.
5. Select Northwind in the Database dropdown.
6. Select the Products table.
7. Click Finish.

8. Click the Fields button.

9. Remove all fields except for ProductName, UnitsInStock, and UnitsOnOrder as seen in Figure 38.30.

Figure 38.30
Select only the
ProductName,
UnitsInStock,
and
UnitsOnOrder
fields for the data
source.

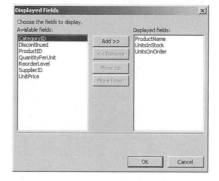

10. Click OK.

11. Click OK again to add the data source.

12. Click the Products on Northwind connection to display the context menu.

13. Select Copy and Modify from the menu as shown in Figure 38.31.

Figure 38.31
The Copy and Modify
menu option makes it
easy to create a new
data connection based
off of an existing con-
nection.

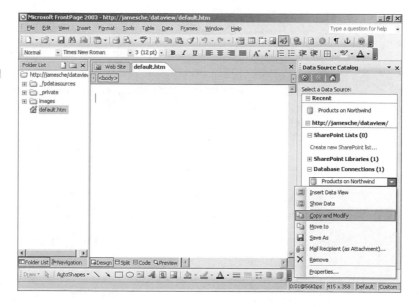

14. Click the Fields button.

15. Remove the UnitsInStock and UnitsOnOrder fields.

16. Add UnitPrice and SupplierID and shown in Figure 38.32.

Figure 38.32
Only
ProductName,
UnitPrice, and
SupplierID are
used for the second
data connection.

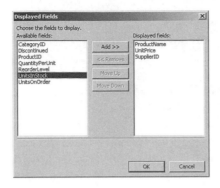

38

17. Click OK.

18. Click the General tab.

19. Enter **Supplier Details** in the Name text box.

20. Click OK to add your data source.

Now that your data sources are ready, click the Products on Northwind data source and select Insert Data View from the menu. Place the insertion point below the Data View and insert another Data View for the Supplier Details data source. Your page should now resemble the page in Figure 38.33.

Figure 38.33
Two Web Parts ready
to talk to each other.

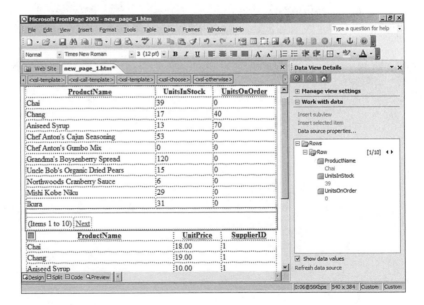

In order to configure the Supplier Details Data View so that it shows the information only for the product name that was clicked in the first Data View, you will need to filter it using the Filter Criteria dialog box.

1. Click the Data View Options button for the Supplier Details Data View and select Filter from the menu.

2. Click the first row in the Filter Criteria dialog box to create a new filter clause.

3. In the Field Name dropdown, select ProductName.

4. Leave the Comparison dropdown set to Equals.

5. In the Value dropdown, select [InputParameter].

Your Filter Criteria dialog box should now resemble the dialog box shown in Figure 38.34. The [InputParameter] setting simply specifies that you are going to pass a parameter to this Web Part from somewhere else. In this case, we will pass the parameter from the other Web Part. Click OK to commit the criteria. The Supplier Details Data View should be filtered so that it currently shows no records.

Figure 38.34
The Filter Criteria dialog box configured to accept an input parameter as a filter.

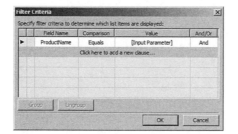

The next step in the process is to set up the Web Part connections so that the first Web Part on the page feeds data to the second Web Part. We will do that by configuring the Web Part connection on the Supplier Details.

1. Click the Web Part Options button for the Supplier Details Web Part and select Web Part Connections from the menu. You should now see the Web Part Connections Wizard shown in Figure 38.35.

2. In the Choose the Action on the Source Web Part to Use for This Connection dropdown, select Modify View Using Parameters From. This action is used to modify the Data View using parameters from another Web Part.

3. Click Next to proceed to step 2 of the wizard, shown in Figure 38.36.

4. Your only option here is Connect to a Web Part on This Page. That is what you want to do, so click Next.

Figure 38.35
The Web Part Connections Wizard walks you through setting up a Web Part connection.

Figure 38.36
Step 2 of the Web Part Connections Wizard specifies the location of the Web Part to connect to.

38

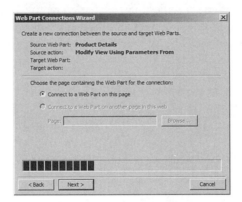

5. In step 3 of the wizard, shown in Figure 38.37, you will accept the default values. Because your page only contains one other Web Part, there are no other options available. However, if other Web Parts were on the page, you would have a choice of which Web Part to connect to.

Figure 38.37
Step 3 of the Web Part Connection Wizard indicates the specific Web Part to use and how to use it.

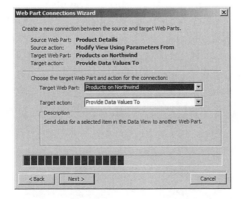

6. Click Next to proceed to step 4 of the wizard.

7. Here you can see that there are two parameters. The first is [InputParameter], and that is the parameter we are using. In the Columns in Products on Northwind column, click <none> and select ProductName in the dropdown, as shown in Figure 38.38.

Figure 38.38
Step 4 of the Web Part Connection Wizard is where you configure what data you are sending between Web Parts.

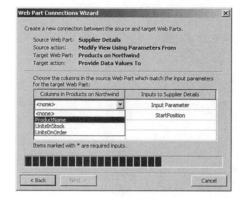

8. Leave the StartPosition parameter as <none> because you will not be using it and click Next.

9. In step 5 of the wizard, you can choose which field in the Data View you want to use for a hyperlink. This hyperlink will kick off the communication between the two Web Parts. In this scenario, you want to use the ProductName field, so select it.

10. The Indicate Current Selection Using check box allows you to configure a field that will indicate the item being displayed in the details Web Part. FrontPage will indicate the selected field by bolding it. Check the check box, check the ProductName field in the Modify Key Columns dialog box as shown in Figure 38.39, and click OK.

Figure 38.39
Step 5 of the Web Part Connection Wizard allows you to choose a hyperlink field on the Web Part.

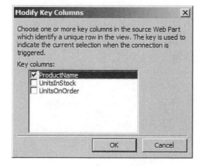

11. Click Next to proceed to the final step of the wizard.

12. In step 6 of the wizard, shown in Figure 38.40, the Set Up Conditional Formatting on Consumer Web Part check box will cause the Conditional Formatting task pane to appear when you click Finish. In this case, you will not be setting up conditional formatting, so leave it unchecked and click Finish to complete the connection.

After you have inserted the connection, save your Web page.

Figure 38.40
Step 6, the final step of the Web Part Connection Wizard.

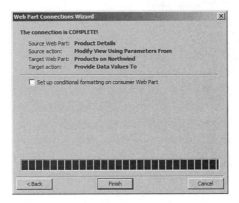

The Web page is now ready to be browsed. Preview the page in your browser and click on any product name to display supplier details on that product, as shown in Figure 38.41. When you click the product name, the Web Part displaying the links communicates that product name to the Supplier Details Web Part, and it filters the Data View based on the product you selected.

Figure 38.41
Two Web Parts—one built by using data passed to it from the other.

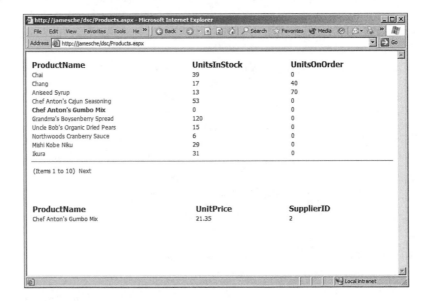

TROUBLESHOOTING

CANNOT INSERT DATA VIEW

I'm trying to insert a Data View, but the Insert Data View menu option is not enabled.

The Data View relies on Windows SharePoint Services being enabled in the Page Options dialog box. Select Tools, Page Options and click the Authoring tab. Make sure that the SharePoint Services check box is checked.

Even though the Insert Data View menu option is enabled, you will still not be able to insert a Data View if you are not connected to a server running Windows SharePoint Services. The Insert Data View menu option will also fail if you try to use it on a disk-based Web site.

CANNOT CONNECT TO SQL SERVER

I have opened a Web site in FrontPage on a remote Web server and am trying to connect to another server running SQL Server, but it is failing.

When you are creating a connection to SQL Server, there are two methods you can use to authenticate—Windows Integrated and SQL Server authentication. When using Windows Integrated, Windows will try to automatically authenticate you to SQL Server. When using SQL Server authentication, you must specify a username and password when configuring the connection.

If you choose Windows Integrated as your authentication method, in most cases the SQL Server must be running on the same computer as the Web server. This is because Windows Integrated authentication to SQL Server is designed to fail when your credentials are being *delegated*.

What that means is that you are logged in to your workstation computer and when you open the Web site on a remote Web server, your user credentials are used to authenticate to the Web server. When the Web server then attempts to authenticate to SQL Server, it automatically passes your credentials to SQL Server to try and authenticate you. This is called *delegation of credentials*, and it will always fail. The solution is to either use SQL Server authentication or run SQL Server on the Web server.

For performance reasons, it is best not to run SQL Server on the same computer that is running the Web server if you expect a lot of traffic on your Web site. Therefore, SQL Server authentication might be a better option, depending on your needs. The downfall to SQL Server authentication is that the username and password are saved in the connection string as clear text.

You will need to weigh the pros and cons of both methods and decide which is best in your environment.

Front and Center: Formatting with XPath

You already know that Data Views are created using XSL and XSLT. What you might not know is that the data returned by a Data View can be formatted using another technology known as *XML Path Language*, or *XPath*.

XPath is a standards-based language designed to allow a developer to easily refer to specific elements in an XML file. However, XPath also allows the developer to use expressions and functions to act upon XML elements.

FrontPage uses XPath to format specific data in a Data View. As a user of FrontPage, you don't have to know anything at all about XPath. FrontPage will generate the necessary XPath code for you based on options you choose in the user interface.

Suppose that you want to format the UnitPrice field as currency. You can do so as follows:

1. Open a Web page on which you have a Data View displaying the UnitPrice field.
2. Click once on one of the values in the UnitPrice field. The value will be bordered by a yellow border when it is selected.
3. Right-click on the value and select Format Item as, Currency from the menu to display the Format Number dialog box as shown in Figure 38.42.

Figure 38.42
The Format Number dialog box is a WYSI-WYG editor for XPath.

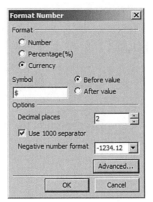

4. Change the options as desired or click OK to accept the defaults.

The UnitPrice field is now formatted as a currency value, and FrontPage is applying that formatting using XPath.

The Format Item as menu item will contain different options based on what type of field you have selected. For example, if you have selected a field that consists of text, the options on the Format Item as menu are Text, Boolean, Hyperlink, and Picture.

Using XPath, FrontPage makes it easy to format your Data View just the way you want it.

INTEGRATING FRONTPAGE 2003 WITH OFFICE 2003

WORKING WITH MICROSOFT WORD

WORD AND FRONTPAGE 2003

It seems as if Microsoft Word has been around forever. It is hard to believe that Word 2003 represents the 11th version of this workhorse for the information worker.

As the popularity of the Internet grew, different camps at Microsoft tried to do different things with Word. Some of them made a lot of sense, and some of them were just plain weird. (Remember Word as Web browser?)

With Word 2003, Microsoft has produced a solid word processing product that meets the needs of anyone developing content for the page—*printed or Web*. They seemed to finally have let each product do what it does best. In Word's case, the product excels (pun not intended) in the creation of content. When used in combination with FrontPage 2003, you can utilize the tools offered by Word to leverage the capabilities provided by FrontPage.

You will find that Microsoft Word can be a powerful tool and prove to be a strong ally in the Web development process.

On the very basic level, content from Word can easily be transferred to a Web page with the traditional cut and paste features we all know so well. FrontPage 2003 increases this integration by providing new means to edit Word content directly in FrontPage. And Word's capability to publish content directly to the Web makes it a viable companion in the content development process. We'll examine all those issues and approaches in this chapter and, as always, examine the human issues of working with these two products in our "Front and Center" section at the end.

COPYING WORD CONTENT INTO FRONTPAGE

Content from Microsoft Word can be easily cut from Word and pasted in to FrontPage. If any of the file formats used in the content aren't "Web friendly" (such as a WMF image file), FrontPage will translate the content as needed when the file is saved to a Web site. In addition, FrontPage makes it easy to import Word content into a Web site.

CUTTING AND PASTING CONTENT

Content can be cut from Word and pasted elsewhere the same way it is in any other Windows program. In FrontPage 2003, a paste options box, seen in Figure 39.1, will let you either keep the source formatting of the original content or reformat the text to match the formatting of the area in which the content is pasted.

NOTE

> Although the different Office System products have a similar look and feel, the paste options dialog box offers different options for each product.

Figure 39.1
When content is cut and pasted from a Word document (as well as most other programs), FrontPage provides a paste options box with numerous ways to format the copied text.

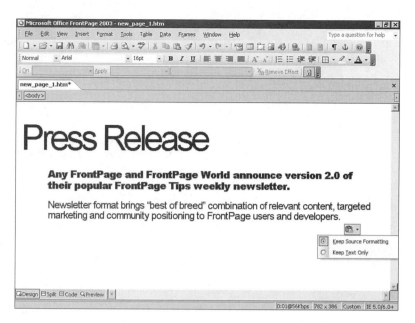

It is important to point out that if you don't select the option to reformat your text, FrontPage will save a considerable amount of additional Word specific HTML with your content. An example of this can be seen in Figure 39.2.

Figure 39.2
A simple paragraph cut and paste from Word 2003 contains a considerable amount of metadata in the HTML.

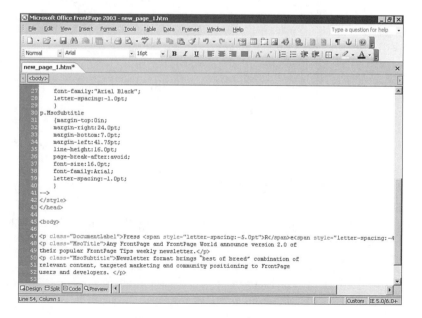

39

In most cases, you won't want or need this additional data. You should either use the reformat to match text option when pasting the content or use FrontPage's HTML optimization tools to eliminate the extra content.

→ For more information on FrontPage's HTML optimization capabilities, **see** "Optimizing FrontPage's HTML," **p. 549**.

TIP

> Sometimes content from a Word document contains multiple formatting elements such as tables and font sizes that look terrible when pasted on a Web page. Simply select the option from the paste options box to reformat text to match and then begin the process of reformatting the text as needed from within FrontPage. You will find many times that this approach is considerably faster.

Importing Web Content

Sometimes users simply want to offer Word documents on a Web server for users to access when and as needed. This is typical in many Intranet projects and is easily done with FrontPage. When a Web site is opened, a Word document can be imported by selecting the File, Import option, seen in Figure 39.3. You can also drag and drop the page from your desktop into your FrontPage Web site.

39

Figure 39.3
The import file option lets you import any folder, file, or file type, into your FrontPage Web site.

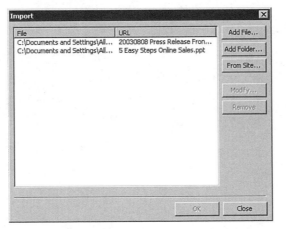

Once a Word document is part of your FrontPage Web site, you can link to it as you would any other file type.

NOTE

> If you import a Word document into a Web site and a person views the site with Word installed on his system, Internet Explorer will open the document as a Word file.

THE MICROSOFT WORD WEB LAYOUT VIEW

Word content is, by default, fitted for the printed page. Most of the views in Microsoft Word present content aligned to this paradigm. The one exception is the *Web Layout* view, which lets you view Word content closer to how it would be viewed if it were to be later converted to HTML (or if Word is in fact directly editing HTML content).

TIP

> To get an idea of how formatting in Word for the printed page is different, take a regular Word document and view it in Web Layout view—notice the differences? Right margins are based on the window size, and images aren't formatted as specifically as they were in Word.

By creating and editing content in Web Layout view, the developer can get a better idea of the constraints of HTML and how the content will look in a Web page.

NOTE

> Web Layout view in Word helps provide a better view of how content will look in a browser, but it is still Microsoft Word, not a Web browser. Make sure to check all content in a browser so that you get the desired effect.

 If you are having problems reconciling your Word document with the Web version, *see "Web Page Looks Nothing Like Word Document in Web View" in the "Troubleshooting" section at the end of this chapter.*

WORD CONTENT AS HTML

If you look at the New Document task pane for Word 2003, shown in Figure 39.4, you will note that from the very beginning Word asks which file format you intend to create in. Although you can easily switch from one file format to another (through the Save As option in the File menu), you still need a place to start. We examine the different document creation options in Word in this section.

Word 2003 also provides the means to save Word content as HTML that can be easily integrated in to a FrontPage Web site. By saving content as HTML, it can be viewed on any browser and doesn't require a copy of Microsoft Word to view. Word content is saved as HTML through the Save As option in the File menu.

NOTE

> Word files are different from HTML files because they maintain all elements of the file (images, multimedia, and the like) within the single Word file rather than linking to files outside the document.

Figure 39.4
The Word 2003 New Document task pane offers the ability for you to create XML, Web, and Email documents from Word (in addition to the traditional blank Word document).

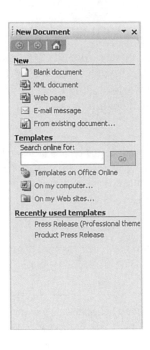

39

As seen in Figure 39.5, Word 2003 offers three options for saving a Word file as HTML: Single File Web Page, Web Page, and Web Page, Filtered. These options are also described in this section.

Figure 39.5
Word 2003 lets you save a Word document in three different Web page options.

WORD DOCUMENT FILE TYPES

As seen in Figure 39.5, Word lets you create a file as a Web page or as an XML file from the very beginning of the design process. If Word is going to be used to create Web content, there is really no reason to create the document in Word and then step through the process of saving the Word document later as HTML. You can instead just create the content in FrontPage.

If you do create your content initially in Word, the Web Layout view can be used to get a better feel for how the page will be viewed in the browser window and expedite the Web content design process.

→ For more basic information on how FrontPage works with XML documents, **see** "Types of Data Used with FrontPage: An Overview," **p. 663**.

SAVE AS A SINGLE FILE WEB PAGE

When Word is saved as a Single File Web Page, the entire document is saved into a single file browser format supported by Internet Explorer 4.0 and later. The file format is saved in the .MHT format, taken from the official term for this file type, *MIME encapsulated aggregate HTML document (MHTML)*.

> **TIP**
>
> If you attempt to open a Word file saved as a .MHT file from FrontPage, by default FrontPage will open Word to edit the file (if Word is installed on that system).
>
> You can change this in the Configure Editors tab of the Options dialog box.

 If you are having problems viewing your single file version in Netscape, see *"Single File Web Page Option Doesn't Work on the Latest Netscape"* in the "Troubleshooting" section at the end of this chapter.

SAVE AS A WEB PAGE

When the file is saved as a Web Page, Word will save the entire document as a series of files within the specified directory. This file format contains a considerable amount of Word-specific metadata that can be used to re-create the original Word file if the content is ever re-imported back into Word.

> **NOTE**
>
> Supporting files for the document are saved in a `filename_files` directory that is hidden by default.
>
> You can toggle hidden folders on/off through the Advanced tab of the Site Settings dialog box.

WEB PAGE, FILTERED

When the file is saved as a Web Page, Filtered, Word will save the entire document as a series of files within the specified directory. The Web Page, Filtered format removes the Word-specific metadata seen in the regular Web Page version.

The warning message displayed by FrontPage, illustrated in Figure 39.6, shows that the text will be permanently changed and cannot be returned to the original Word file.

Figure 39.6
Word files saved as a
Web Page, Filtered
can't be converted
back.

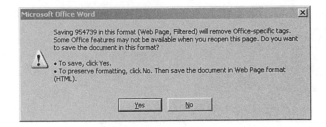

NOTE

Supporting files for the Web Page, Filtered document are saved in a `filename_files` directory that is *not* hidden by default.

WORKING WITH WORD DOCUMENTS IN FRONTPAGE

Content cut and pasted from a Word document into a FrontPage HTML file is edited as any other page in your FrontPage Web site would be. If you want to edit content in FrontPage that was developed and saved in Word, you will need to tell FrontPage to react accordingly. We examine both processes in this section.

EDITING WORD CONTENT IN FRONTPAGE

By default, in a FrontPage Web site, content created in a certain application will be edited by that product (if the product is installed on the machine). As a result, clicking content created by Word within FrontPage will open the content in Word unless otherwise specified.

To edit Word created HTML content from within FrontPage, right-click the file in the Folder List and choose FrontPage (Open as HTML) from the Open With option, as seen in Figure 39.7.

If you need to edit content created by Word, consider editing the original source files and then re-saving the content as HTML. The other option is to open and edit the files from within Word through FrontPage so that edits are saved directly to the site with the proper Word content. Using FrontPage to edit content created in Word should only be done as a final resort.

When you use Word to edit your content, you have all the tools provided by Word and won't always know when these were used in the design process. It is always a good idea to go back to the original source program when editing content.

Other Versions of Word

Word 2002 and 2000 both have options directly in the product for saving content as HTML. They are not detailed as the features provided in Word 2003, but they provide a solid option for HTML translation.

You can also load a Word file saved in a previous version of Word and save it as HTML in Word 2003 to take full advantage of the new features.

Figure 39.7
Right-clicking a file in
FrontPage lets you
choose the applica-
tion you want to edit
the content with.

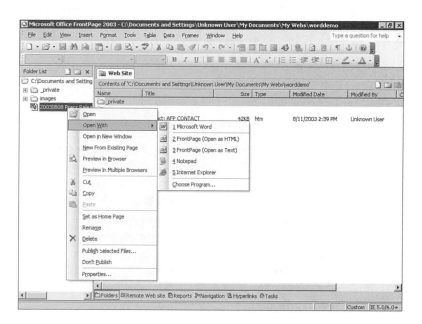

TROUBLESHOOTING

SINGLE FILE WEB PAGE OPTION DOESN'T WORK ON THE LATEST NETSCAPE VERSION

*I published my presentation as a Single File Web Page. I know that it isn't supported on earlier ver-
sions of Netscape, but it also can't be viewed on the most recent release. How can I make this format
work?*

The Single File Web Page option is only supported by Internet Explorer version 4.0 and
higher. In addition, the format is only supported by Microsoft technologies and is not an
industry standard. It contains Microsoft-specific metadata that will only be supported by
those browser types.

WEB PAGE LOOKS NOTHING LIKE WORD DOCUMENT IN WEB VIEW

I saved a Word file as a Web page, and the document isn't in the font I saved it as when I view it.

If the browser you view the Word as HTML file on has a preset font or the system you are
viewing the content on doesn't have the selected font installed, you will not be able to view
the file in your chosen font. This is one of the limits of HTML, not one of the problems of
combining these two applications. There is no way to force the user to view a page in a specific font.

FRONT AND CENTER: A FEW WORDS ON WORD

When you talk to some people about creating content for the Web or helping you out with
your Web site, they get a glazed look on their face and you know, no matter how hard you

try, that these people just don't "get it." Funny thing is, tell these same people that you need a Microsoft Word document and you have a willing helper.

In the end, the Web is about content. If you run the numbers, many more people are going to create content with Word than will ever create content on all the Web development products anywhere.

Use this fact to your advantage in any of the following ways:

- **Let others create in whatever program they want to create.** The hardest part is the content creation, and if you have people willing to create content, let them. Have them send you the content in whatever file format they want, and all you have to do is simply cut and paste the content into your FrontPage Web site.

- **Let others create HTML content in Word.** If you can get others to create HTML content in Word, they've done even more of the work than in the first option. If they want to create your Web content for you, let them. Sure, you will have to reformat the content to meet your site look and feel, but they've already done the hard work. Even though the HTML created by Word isn't as optimized as you might like, you can always use Word's html optimization features to clean it up.

→ For more on optimizing HTML in FrontPage, **see** "Optimizing FrontPage's HTML," **p. 549**.

In addition to these two options, another approach to Web development should be considered. **Forget content creation—it is often already available.** I've been to offices and consulted on too many projects too many times with people who feel that they have to create content from scratch for the Web. Often, content has already been created, and, more time than not, it has been created in Word. Take these already existing files and either cut and paste them in to your Web or use Word to product the HTML files.

Finally, the issue of Word files saved as HTML needs to be examined.

When Word content is pasted directly in to a Web page, FrontPage will also keep a significant amount of Word metadata in the HTML. Unless the Save as Type option of Web Page, Filtered is selected when a document is saved for the Web site, the content will be saved with the additional Word-related metadata. Best practices state that you remove this additional data through the HTML optimization tools that come with FrontPage.

Two other issues should be mentioned in the discussion of Word and Web development with FrontPage 2003:

- Don't forget how Dynamic Web Templates radically change the Web design process. When .DWTs are used, you can simply grab text from any source, apply the DWT, and...bam! You have the formatting for the rest of your site. With that kind of ease of use and formatting power, it would be silly to have anyone do any of the work in Word.

- Simply have people design the content in whatever program they want and email it to you. Heck, have them email the content. Paste the content into a Web page, apply the Dynamic Web Template, and everything else is done for you. It couldn't be easier.

→ For more detailed information on the design of Dynamic Web Templates, **see** "Creating Editable Regions," **p. 415**.

Finally, you need to remember to use each tool for what it is worth. I'm not a big fan of people who try to squeeze too much functionality out of a product that was never meant for the task. How many flyers have you seen developed in PowerPoint or how many tables have you seen made in Excel because the user didn't know that Word had a table option?

If you need to use Word, great. If you are just creating simple content, remember that FrontPage has a good chunk of the functionality and interface that Word does and can meet the needs of most users.

Here's one more thing: Word content tends to be long because it is typically designed for the printed page. When you write for the Web, you need to be short and to the point. If your Word content is long and drawn out and doesn't "translate" well for the Web, make sure to edit as needed.

But Word is there for you to use when and as needed.

39

WORKING WITH MICROSOFT EXCEL AND FRONTPAGE

In this chapter

METHODS FOR INSERTING EXCEL DATA INTO FRONTPAGE

Microsoft Excel is one of Microsoft's flagship products. Excel is a spreadsheet application that allows for the complex (or simple) analyzation of numbers. Excel is often used by accountants and others who have a need to scrutinize numerical data, but its use is not limited to them. Homeowners might use Excel for entering their budgets and tracking other financial information.

FrontPage can access data in an Excel spreadsheet in three ways:

- Database Results Wizard
- Office Web Components
- Windows SharePoint Services DataView

In this chapter, we will review using the Database Results Wizard and Office Web Components to access Excel data. You will use the Excel spreadsheet Expenses.xls located in the CH40 folder on the CD accompanying this book. However, you can use a different spreadsheet if you choose.

→ For more information on accessing data with Windows SharePoint Services DataViews, **see** "Inserting a Data View," **p. 739**.

PREPARING AN EXCEL SPREADSHEET FOR FRONTPAGE

Before you can insert Excel data into your Web site, you have to prepare your Excel spreadsheet. FrontPage uses database connections to access external data. When you create a database connection, you specify the data source that contains the data (such as a Microsoft Access database file or a Microsoft SQL Server) and a record source, usually the name of a table in the data source.

→ For more information on database connections in FrontPage, **see** "Creating a Database Connection," **p. 706**.

An Excel spreadsheet doesn't have tables in it. Therefore, there is nothing in the file that you can point to as a record source. Before you can use your Excel spreadsheet in FrontPage, you must create a named range in Excel. A *named range* is simply a section of a spreadsheet to which a name is applied. Once you've defined a named range in your spreadsheet, FrontPage will see the named range as a record source and will allow you to access the data in the named range.

To create a named range in your Excel spreadsheet, follow these steps:

1. Copy the Expenses.xls file from the CH40 folder on the CD accompanying this book to the location of your choice on your hard drive.

2. Open the Expenses.xls file in Excel.

3. Select all the cells containing data except for the bottom row and column H, as shown in Figure 40.1.

Figure 40.1
Select all the data you want to include in your named range.

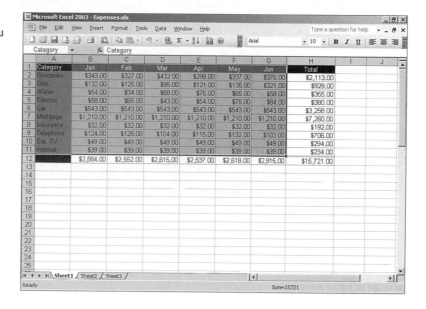

4. Select Insert, Name, Define.

5. Excel will suggest Category as the name. Change this to **Expenses** as shown in Figure 40.2.

Figure 40.2
Change Excel's suggested name to Expenses to add a new named range.

6. Click Add to add the new name.

7. Click OK to return to the spreadsheet.

8. Save the spreadsheet.

If you receive an error telling you that the file is read-only, see "Spreadsheet Is Read-Only" in the "Troubleshooting" section of this chapter.

You now have a named range that FrontPage can use as the record source when you are inserting data from this spreadsheet into your Web pages. The named range contains all the data in the spreadsheet except for the bottom row. The bottom row is not included because it's a total row. It shows a total for all the data rows, but it's not really data itself. However, if you choose to include it, you can.

INSERTING EXCEL DATA WITH THE DATABASE RESULTS WIZARD

Most FrontPage users use ASP to display data from a Microsoft Access database or from a SQL Server database, but you can also use ASP to display data from an Excel spreadsheet.

→ For more information on using the Database Results Wizard, **see** "Using the Database Results Wizard," **p. 710**.

IMPORTING THE EXCEL SPREADSHEET

The first step in creating an ASP page to display Excel data is to import the Excel spreadsheet into your Web site so that you can connect to it with a database connection. To do that, follow these steps:

1. Open a Web site or create a new Web site. The Web site must be on a server that supports ASP.
2. Select File, Import.
3. Click the Add File button.
4. Browse to the Excel file, select it, and click Open.
5. Click OK to import the file.

→ For more information on the requirements for ASP pages, **see** "Understanding Active Server Pages (ASP)," **p. 680**.

CREATING THE DATABASE CONNECTION

Once the Excel spreadsheet has been imported, you need to create a new database connection that points to the Excel file. The database connection allows you to connect to the Excel file with the Database Results Wizard.

1. Select Tools, Site Settings.
2. Click the Database tab.
3. Click the Add button.
4. In the Name text box, enter **Expenses**.
5. Select the File or Folder in Current Web Site option.
6. Click Browse.
7. In the Files of Type dropdown, select Microsoft Excel Driver (*.xls).

8. Browse to the folder containing the Expenses.xls file as shown in Figure 40.3, select it, and then click OK.

9. Click OK in the New Database Connection dialog box to close the dialog.

Figure 40.3
Select the Expenses.xls file to create a database connection to it.

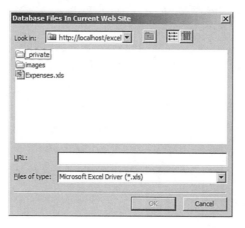

 If the Site Settings option is not enabled, see "Site Settings Is Disabled" in the "Troubleshooting" section of this chapter.

The Site Settings dialog box now shows a new database connection. Notice that the Status column shows a question mark. You can go ahead and click OK at this point, or you can select the connection and click Verify just to make sure that FrontPage can access the file successfully. Once you've verified the connection, FrontPage will display a check mark in the Status column as shown in Figure 40.4. The check mark indicates that FrontPage sees the Excel file; however, it does not indicate that FrontPage can access data inside of it. After you've verified the connection, click OK to add the connection to your Web site.

Figure 40.4
The database connection to the Excel file has been verified.

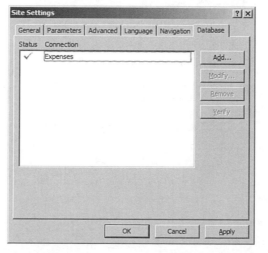

40

FrontPage has now added two items to your Web site. It has added an fpdb folder (which is empty) and a global.asa file. The fpdb folder is a restricted folder so that anything put into it cannot be accessed by people browsing to your Web site. Because you wouldn't want people to download your Excel spreadsheet file, you might want to move it into the fpdb folder by dragging and dropping it on the fpdb folder. FrontPage will automatically update the database connection for you.

The global.asa file contains special ASP code that defines your database connection. It also contains other ASP code that FrontPage will use when you create your ASP page connecting to your Excel file.

→ For more information on the global.asa file and its use in ASP pages, read *Active Server Pages 3.0 from Scratch* from Que Publishing.

INSERTING THE DATABASE RESULTS

Now it's time to create a new ASP page and connect to the data inside of the Excel spreadsheet.

1. Create a new Web page.

2. Select Insert, Database, Results.

3. In the first step of the Database Results Wizard, select the ASP option.

4. Select the Use an Existing Database Connection option and select Expenses in the dropdown as shown in Figure 40.5.

Figure 40.5
The first step of the Database Results Wizard. You will use the existing database connection you created earlier.

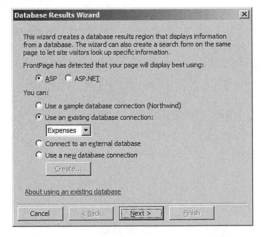

5. Click Next.

6. Select the Record Source option as shown in Figure 40.6. The only option in the dropdown is Expenses because that is the only named range in the Excel spreadsheet.

Figure 40.6
You will use the Expenses record source. This record source refers to the named range in your Excel spreadsheet.

7. Click Next.

8. Leave all fields as they are and click Next.

9. Select the Table—One Record per Row option and leave all check boxes checked as shown in Figure 40.7.

Figure 40.7
Choose the option to display the results in a table. This more closely resembles the original format in Excel.

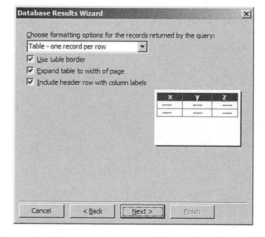

10. Click Next.

11. Select the Split Records into Groups option and type **5** in the Records per Group text box as shown in Figure 40.8.

12. Click Finish to insert the database results.

Your page should now look like the one in Figure 40.9. Save the page as **expenses.asp**.

→ For more information on all the options in the Database Results Wizard, **see** "Using the Database Results Wizard," **p. 709**.

Figure 40.8
It isn't necessary to split into groups for your small spreadsheet, but you might be adding more data later.

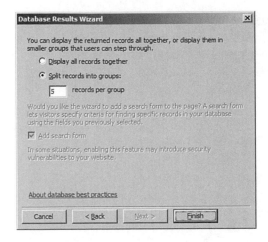

Figure 40.9
The completed page in FrontPage. Notice that FrontPage pulled out the columns from your Excel spreadsheet.

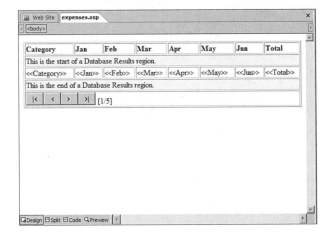

 If the Results option is not available on the Database menu, *see "Cannot Insert Database Results" in the "Troubleshooting" section of this chapter.*

Now that you've saved the page, preview it in your browser. When you do, the Web server will connect to your Excel spreadsheet, pull the data from it, and display the data in the browser as shown in Figure 40.10. If you open the original Excel spreadsheet and change the data, the Web page will automatically show the updated data.

TIP

> If you're going to edit the Excel spreadsheet that your Web page is connected to, you should make a copy and edit the copy. After you've finished editing, copy the updated file into your Web site and overwrite the existing copy.

Figure 40.10
This Web page was generated dynamically from the data in the `Expenses.xls` spreadsheet.

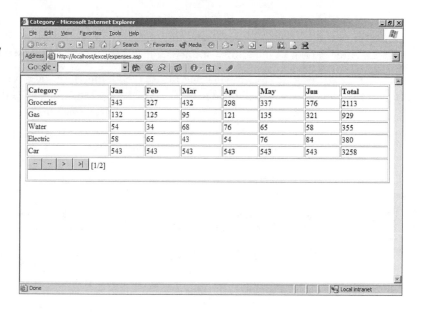

INSERTING EXCEL DATA WITH THE OFFICE WEB COMPONENTS

FrontPage can also connect to Excel spreadsheets using the Office Web Components. The Office Web Components are ActiveX controls that run inside a Web page and look just like their Office counterparts. For example, the Office Spreadsheet Web Component (shown in Figure 40.11) looks and acts just like an Excel spreadsheet.

Figure 40.11
The Office Spreadsheet Web Component is essentially Excel inside a Web page.

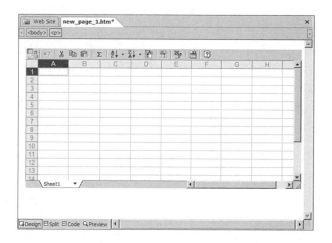

40

Because Office Web Components are ActiveX controls, they are also editable inside the FrontPage interface. In fact, once you've inserted an Office Spreadsheet Web Component, you can enter data in to it and format the data inside it just as you can in Excel.

In order for your site visitors to view an Office Web Component, they must be using Internet Explorer 5.01 with Service Pack 2 or newer, and they must have the Office Web Components installed. Users of Netscape Navigator will not be able to see Office Web Components. Instead, they will see a message informing them of what needs to be installed in order to view the components as shown in Figure 40.12.

Figure 40.12
The Office Web Components are installed on this machine, but they will not work because Netscape does not support them.

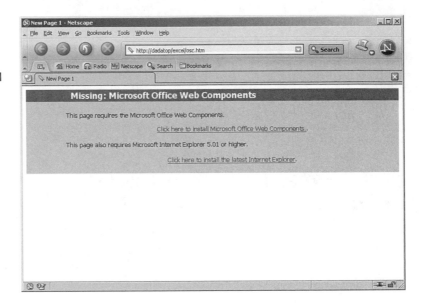

The Office Web Components are automatically installed during a default install of Office 2003. If you haven't installed them, you can run the installation for Office 2003 and select them from the Office Shared Features section of the install, as shown in Figure 40.13.

For users who do not have Office 2003 installed, the Office Web Components can be installed separately using files included in the Office 2003 Resource Kit.

NOTE

For more information on the Office Resource Kit, visit the Microsoft Office Web site at http://www.microsoft.com/office.

An Office Spreadsheet Web Component is composed of a workbook and one or more worksheets. A *worksheet* is the visible area of the Office Spreadsheet Web Component and is made up of cells arranged in columns and rows. A *workbook* is a collection of one or more worksheets. When the Office Spreadsheet Web Component is first inserted, it contains three worksheets called Sheet1, Sheet2, and Sheet3. Sheet1 is active and visible when you first insert the Office Spreadsheet Web Component. You can activate other worksheets by clicking the Sheet1 tab in the lower left corner of the Office Spreadsheet Web Component as shown in Figure 40.14.

Figure 40.13
The Office Web Components are part of the Office Shared Features section of Office 2003.

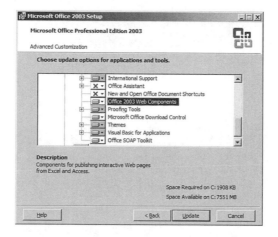

Figure 40.14
The sheet tab in the Office Spreadsheet Web Component provides access to the sheets in the spreadsheet.

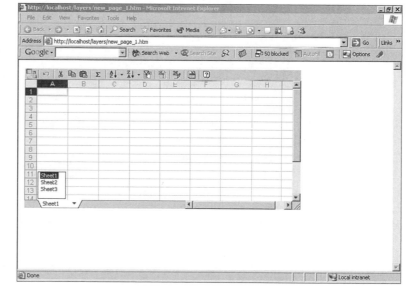

INSERTING THE OFFICE SPREADSHEET WEB COMPONENT

The Office Spreadsheet Web Component is listed in FrontPage as a Web Component and is inserted from the Insert Web Component dialog box.

1. Create a new empty page.
2. Select Insert, Web Component.

3. Select Spreadsheets and charts in the Component Type list.

4. Select Office Spreadsheet from the Choose a Control list as shown in Figure 40.15.

5. Click Finish.

Figure 40.15
The Office
Spreadsheet Web
Component is located
in the Insert Web
Component
dialog box.

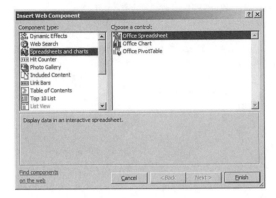

 If the Spreadsheets and Charts option is not available, see "Cannot Insert Office Spreadsheet Web Component" in the "Troubleshooting" section of this chapter.

CONFIGURING THE OFFICE SPREADSHEET WEB COMPONENT

As previously mentioned, the Office Spreadsheet Web Component acts just like an instance of Excel inside your Web page. You can enter information into it, and you can perform calculations on that information just as you can in Excel. In addition to that, you have complex control over how that information is displayed to users and what they can do with it.

There are two ways to access the properties of the Office Spreadsheet Web Component. One way is to right-click inside the component and select Commands and Options, and the other way is to right-click an edge of the component and select ActiveX Control Properties from the menu. The ActiveX Control Properties menu provides all the options available on the Commands and Options menu in addition to some others, but is not available when the component is rendered in the browser. The Commands and Options menu is available when in FrontPage and when the Web page is rendered in the browser, but not all the design-time options are available at browse-time.

The following tabs are available in the Commands and Options menu when viewing the page in the browser:

- **Format**—Formats the cell font, color, alignment, and so on.
- **Formula**—Defines formulas and named ranges.
- **Sheet**—Provides search functionality and formatting for the selected worksheet.
- **Workbook**—Provides the interface for creating, deleting, and arranging worksheets and for formatting worksheets.

In addition to the preceding tabs, the following tabs are available in the Command and Options menu only when accessed within FrontPage at design-time:

- **Import**—Allows you to import data from an external source.
- **Protection**—Configure which options are available during browse-time.
- **Advanced**—Configures the advanced options such as width and height of columns and what type of programmatic access the component provides.
- **Data Source**—Configures the data source for the component when accessing external data.

You can also access properties for the component by clicking once on the Office Spreadsheet Web Component; then right-click one of its edges and select Active**X** Control Properties from the menu to display the ActiveX Control Properties dialog (seen in Figure 40.16).

Figure 40.16
The Format tab provides all the tools to format the appearance of cells.

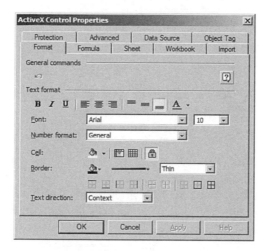

The ActiveX Control Properties dialog box contains the tabs discussed in the following sections.

FORMAT TAB

The Format tab formats the currently selected cells. You can configure the font, the numeric format, the appearance of the cells, and the direction of text. The Format tab also contains an undo button (the reverse arrow in the top-left of the tab) so that you can undo any previous changes to the Office Spreadsheet Web Component.

The Format tab is available both at design-time and browse-time.

FORMULA TAB

The Formula tab (shown in Figure 40.17) displays the formula for the currently selected cell, allows you to enter a new value for the cell, and lists the named ranges in the current worksheet. It also allows you to create new named ranges and delete existing named ranges.

The Formula tab is available both at design-time and browse-time.

Figure 40.17
The Formula tab lets you work with formulas and named ranges in your Office Spreadsheet Web Component.

SHEET TAB

The Sheet tab (see Figure 40.18) provides search functionality for the active worksheet and allows you to control what features are available in the worksheet. There is also a button to allow you to freeze panes in the sheet so that certain cells remain stationary while the sheet is scrolled.

The Sheet tab is available both at design-time and browse-time.

Figure 40.18
The Sheet tab enables you to format the look of the active sheet and lets you search for information in the sheet.

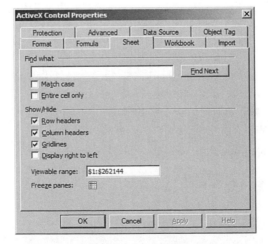

WORKBOOK TAB

The Workbook tab (see Figure 40.19) controls the calculation options and appearance of all worksheets in the workbook. It is also where you can manage the worksheets in the workbook. You can insert new worksheets, delete existing worksheets, reorder worksheets, and hide worksheets from the Workbook tab.

The Workbook tab is available both at design-time and browse-time.

Figure 40.19
The Workbook tab controls the appearance of the workbook and manages worksheets.

IMPORT TAB

The Import tab (shown in Figure 40.20) allows you to import data from an HTML file, a comma-separated values file, or an XML file. By checking the Refresh Data from URL at Run Time check box, you can configure the Office Spreadsheet Web Component to automatically update with the latest data each time the Web page is browsed.

The Import tab is only available at design-time.

Figure 40.20
The Import tab is one way to connect the Office Spreadsheet Web Component to external data.

40

PROTECTION TAB

The Protection tab (seen in Figure 40.21) configures the options that are available in the Office Spreadsheet Web Component when it is being viewed in a Web browser. By default, users of your Office Spreadsheet Web Component can access the Command and Options dialog box and can insert, remove, and rename worksheets. If you want to allow for additional functionality, check the necessary boxes in the Protection tab.

The Protection tab is only available at design-time.

Figure 40.21
The Protection tab controls what users of your Office Spreadsheet Web Component can and cannot configure in the browser.

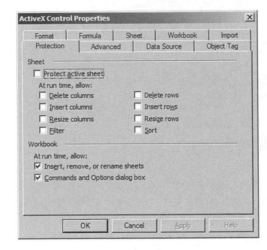

ADVANCED TAB

The Advanced tab (shown in Figure 40.22) is where you can configure the size of columns and rows, the maximum size of the spreadsheet, and other advanced settings.

The Advanced tab is only available at design-time.

Figure 40.22
The Advanced tab configures the advanced features of the Office Spreadsheet Web Component.

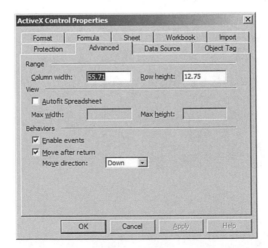

40

DATA SOURCE TAB

The Data Source tab (see Figure 40.23) allows you to configure data connections to other data sources, such as SQL Server databases and other ODBC data sources.

The Data Source tab is only available at design-time.

Figure 40.23
The Data Source tab configures advanced data connectivity for the Office Spreadsheet Web Component.

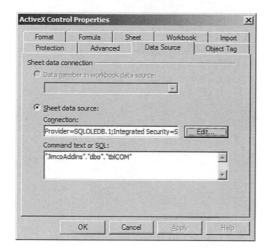

OBJECT TAG TAB

The Object Tag tab (shown in Figure 40.24) configures the HTML <object> tag for the Office Spreadsheet Web Component. You can configure the CSS styles for the Office Spreadsheet Web Component, the layout, and the HTML used for browsers that do not support the Office Spreadsheet Web Component. You can also configure a code source URL for those who need to download and install the control.

The Object Tag tab is available for all ActiveX controls and is not specific to the Office Spreadsheet Web Component. It is the only tab that is available in the ActiveX Control Properties dialog box and not available in the Command and Options dialog box of the Office Spreadsheet Web Component.

40

Figure 40.24
The Object Tag tab configures generic ActiveX control settings.

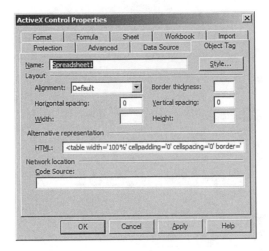

TROUBLESHOOTING

SPREADSHEET IS READ-ONLY

I am trying to save the Expenses.xls file, but I get an error telling me that it's read-only.

Make sure that you copied the file from the CD to your hard drive. You will also likely have to turn off the read-only attribute for the file because it was copied from a CD. Right-click the file and select Properties from the menu. Uncheck the Read-only check box and click OK.

SITE SETTINGS IS DISABLED

I am trying to create a new database connection, but the Site Settings option is disabled.

The Site Settings menu option is only available if you have a Web site open. Make sure that you have opened a Web site and not just a Web page.

To open a Web site, select File, Open Site and enter the URL of the Web site. Click the Open button to open the Web site.

CANNOT INSERT DATABASE RESULTS

I am trying to insert Database Results, but the Results menu option is not enabled.

The Database Results feature in FrontPage relies on Active Server Pages, or ASP. If Active Server Pages are not enabled in your Authoring options, the Results menu item will be disabled.

Select Tools, Page Options and click the Authoring tab. Make sure that the Active Server Pages check box is checked and click OK.

CANNOT INSERT OFFICE SPREADSHEET WEB COMPONENT

I'm trying to insert an Office Spreadsheet Web Component, but the Spreadsheets and Charts option is turned off and I can't select it.

If the Spreadsheets and Charts option is not available, it is because the Office Web Components are not installed. Run the FrontPage 2003 setup in Add/Remove Programs and click the plus sign next to the Office Shared Features section. Make sure that Office Web Components is set to Run from My Computer.

FRONT AND CENTER: MORE WAYS TO LOOK AT DATA

The Office Spreadsheet Web Component is just one of three Office Web Components that provides access to Excel data. There is also an Office Chart component and an Office PivotTable component—both of which provide the same amount of interactivity as the Office Spreadsheet Web Component.

The Office Chart component (shown in Figure 40.25) makes it easy to provide users of your Web site with interactive charts populated with data from an external data source or another Office Web Component on the same Web page. Figure 40.26 shows the same Office Chart component running inside a Web page. Notice that the toolbar provides much of the same functionality in the browser that you have when using a chart in Excel or other Office products.

Figure 40.25
The Office Chart component creates dynamic charts for display on your Web site.

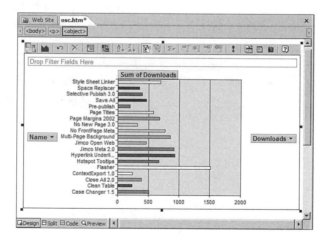

The Office PivotTable component is the most powerful Office Web Component of the three, and along with that power comes a considerable amount of complexity. Users of Excel spend a great deal of time learning how to use a PivotTable, and most users never fully grasp the power and function of this feature.

Figure 40.26
The Office Chart component running inside a Web browser. Notice the toolbar providing advanced options right within the browser.

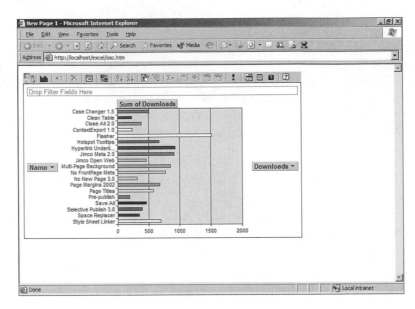

A PivotTable presents data so that it can be manipulated and massaged to show you exactly what you need. It essentially allows you to build a spreadsheet on-the-fly based on what fields you choose to display from a particular data source. You can configure how the data is grouped and how much of it is displayed. Until you use a PivotTable, the concept of it is hard to understand.

Figure 40.27 shows what an Office PivotTable component looks like when it's first inserted. Note the link that says Click here to connect to data. When you click that link, the Commands and Options dialog box is displayed and the Data Source tab is selected as shown in Figure 40.28. Once you configure a data source, the Office PivotTable component changes to look like the one shown in Figure 40.29.

Figure 40.27
The Office PivotTable component without any data connections configured.

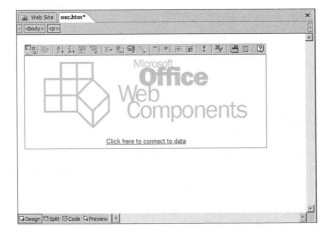

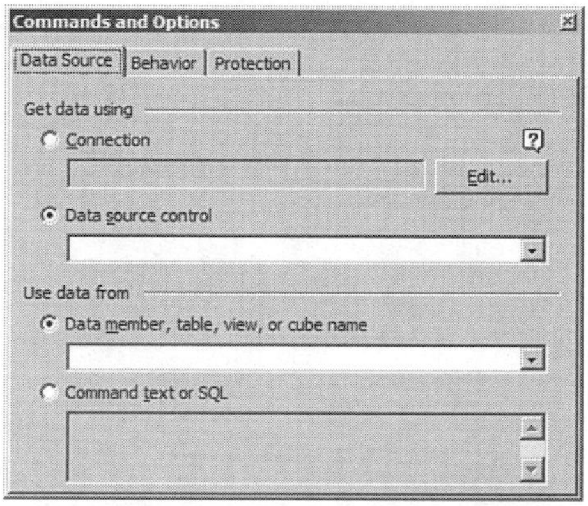

Figure 40.28
The Commands and Options dialog box provides the interface to connect the Office PivotTable component to data.

Figure 40.29
This Office PivotTable component is connected to a data source and is ready to be populated with data.

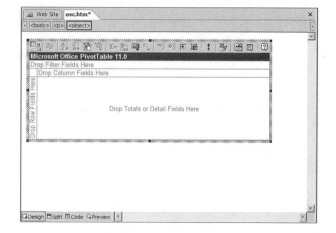

To populate the Office PivotTable component with data, right-click on it and select Field List from the menu to display the PivotTable Field List dialog box shown in Figure 40.31. Figure 40.32 shows a PivotTable component configured to show sales data for a particular period. By dragging and dropping fields from the Field List, changing the data that is displayed and how it is being displayed is very easy.

Figure 40.30
The PivotTable Field List allows you to choose what data is displayed in your PivotTable component.

Figure 40.31
This PivotTable shows a complex view of sales data. Getting this kind of view would be nearly impossible without a PivotTable.

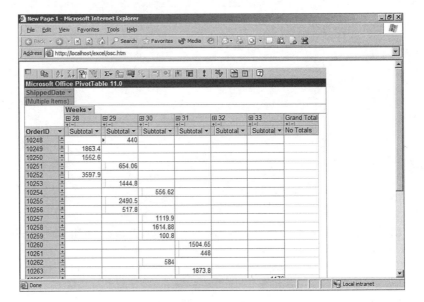

WORKING WITH MICROSOFT POWERPOINT 2003

In this chapter

Microsoft PowerPoint is one of the more popular products in the Microsoft Office System. The wizards and templates provided by this presentation product have helped put together millions of slideshows since the product was released. Most users will agree that it is one of the simplest products to use in the Office System and helps produce some of the most impressive results in the shortest amount of time.

In some ways, the jump for a PowerPoint presentation from the desktop (or laptop) to the Web makes a lot of sense. The ability to share your presentations with the world is obviously attractive to anyone who considers it, as the PowerPoint user's audience moves from the boardroom to the world.

The integration of Microsoft PowerPoint and FrontPage needs to be examined on two levels. The first level should examine the simple issue of inserting PowerPoint content directly into your FrontPage Web. The second level covers the creation of PowerPoint content for the Web and how to integrate it with FrontPage. Finally, we'll examine the use of PowerPoint content in a Web site in our Front and Center section at the end of this chapter.

INSERTING POWERPOINT CONTENT INTO YOUR WEB SITE

Elements from a PowerPoint presentation can be easily cut and pasted from PowerPoint into FrontPage. If any of the file formats used in the presentation aren't "Web friendly," (such as a .WMF clip or file or something similar) FrontPage will translate the content as needed. In addition, there are options for translating PowerPoint files to a number of other file formats that can be more readily called from a Web site. We'll examine those options in this section.

INSERTING SIMPLE POWERPOINT ELEMENTS

Any element from a PowerPoint presentation can be cut from the presentation and pasted into FrontPage.

Basic text is cut and pasted from PowerPoint the same way it is in most other Windows programs. A paste options box will let you reformat the text to match the formatting of your page.

Text blocks are added to a FrontPage Web page as layout table content. FrontPage offers a paste options button with three options for handling the text content. This can be seen in Figure 41.1.

41

Figure 41.1
A text block from a PowerPoint presentation is pasted to FrontPage as layout table content. Note the Paste Options box and the three options.

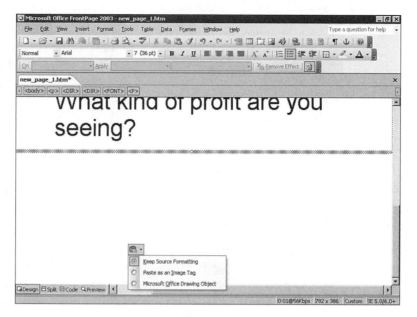

The first option, Keep Source Formatting, keeps the content pasted as a layout table and makes no additional changes. The second option, Paste as an Image Tag, converts the text to an image. The third option, Microsoft Office Drawing Object, converts the text to a Microsoft Office Drawing object that can be more easily edited and transferred between other Microsoft programs if needed.

→ For more information on FrontPage's handling of tables and the new layout table technology, **see** "Using Tables," **p. 189**.

NOTE

> If you keep source formatting, VML image files are included in the content. These images can only be viewed on the most recent browsers.

When an image is copied from a PowerPoint presentation, FrontPage treats the image as it would any other: When the page file is saved back to the Web site, FrontPage will offer the chance to change the name of the file and file type, if necessary.

TIP

> Most PowerPoint images aren't usually in a Web friendly format. Make sure that any graphic content transferred is saved as either a GIF or JPEG file.

41

NOTE

> Most content copied from a PowerPoint presentation will contain a considerable amount of metadata important to PowerPoint but not that important to your Web page. Consider cleaning some of the data from your page either by hand or using the HTML optimization tools provided with FrontPage.

→ For information on cleaning up FrontPage html from content of this type, **see** "Optimizing FrontPage's HTML," **p. 549**.

INSERTING ENTIRE PRESENTATIONS

The PowerPoint file format is proprietary to PowerPoint. Historically, Microsoft has provided a PowerPoint player product with previous versions that let people view PowerPoint content who didn't have the main program.

Most people don't realize that Internet Explorer versions 4.0 and higher have contained a PowerPoint player inside the program. These versions of IE can easily read and play a PowerPoint presentation, which can easily be added to a FrontPage Web. Simply add the PowerPoint file to your site and link to it as you would any other file in your site. Figure 41.2 shows a PowerPoint presentation being viewed in Internet Explorer. IE will read either .PPT (the native PowerPoint file format) or .PPS (the PowerPoint Slideshow Format that allows only viewing of the slideshow without the ability to edit it) files.

Figure 41.2
A PowerPoint file can easily be added to a Web site and viewed with Internet Explorer. There is no need to edit the file in any way.

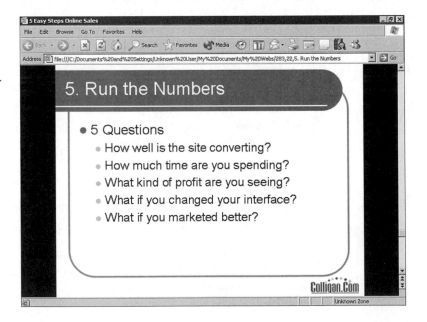

Obviously the entire world doesn't use Internet Explorer so this approach can't be an entire solution. But for the large majority of people to use IE, there is no simpler way to let them view PowerPoint content.

TIP

> If you save raw PowerPoint files to the Web for your readers to view, save the file as a .PPS instead of a .PPT. The same content is there, but it prevents readers from being able to download your entire presentation and make edits accordingly.

CREATING WEB CONTENT FROM POWERPOINT SLIDES

You are not limited to copying content from PowerPoint or forcing users to view PowerPoint files through Internet Explorer. You can use PowerPoint 2003 to create individual graphics of each of your slides or create Web HTML content that contains both the slide content as well as a simple navigation scheme.

CREATING GRAPHICS FROM POWERPOINT SLIDES

As seen in Figure 41.3, PowerPoint 2003 provides a means to save a presentation in a number of graphic formats. The images are saved as *Slide1*, *Slide2*, and so on. No text or notes content associated with the slideshow is saved in this method.

Figure 41.3
A PowerPoint file can be saved as a number of different graphic files formats.

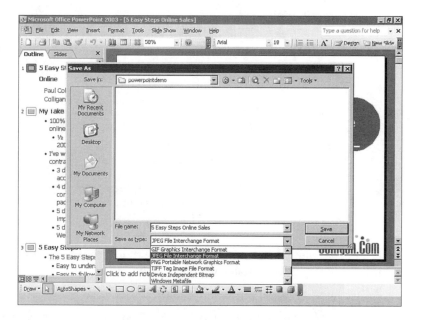

You can have PowerPoint save the slides directly to a FrontPage Web site and develop Web content to call each slide as needed or let PowerPoint develop the navigation for you, as described in the next section.

41

TIP

If you save your presentation as graphic slides to be used in a Web site, make sure to use a Web friendly format such as JPEG or GIF. PowerPoint offers the other file format options because this tool is used for other things than producing Web content.

Creating Web Pages from PowerPoint Slides

As seen in Figure 41.4, PowerPoint offers the ability to save a presentation as a Web Page or a Single File Web Page. When the presentation is saved as a Web page, PowerPoint will save the entire presentation as a series of files within a chosen directory. When a file is saved as a Single File Web Page, the entire presentation is save into a single file browser format that is only supported by Internet Explorer 4.0 and later.

Figure 41.4
PowerPoint lets you save a presentation as a Web Page or a Single File Web Page.

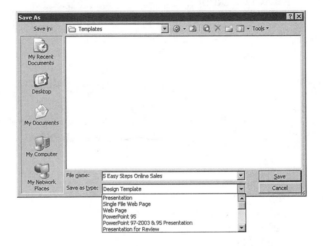

 If you can't view your Single File Web Page version of your presentation in Netscape, *see "Single File Web Page Option Doesn't Work on the Latest Netscape Version" in the "Troubleshooting" section at the end of this chapter.*

Once a PowerPoint presentation is saved as a Web page, the content can be imported into FrontPage and quickly integrated into your Web site.

41

TIP

It isn't necessary to make the "import" process any more complicated than it needs to be. Have PowerPoint save directly to the Web site or simply drag the content into your FrontPage Web in one simple step. The Import option in the File menu is another way to bring content (or entire files of content) into your FrontPage Web site.

SAVING POWERPOINT PRESENTATIONS FOR USE ON THE WEB

When you save a PowerPoint presentation as a Web page, you will need to configure the specific publishing options that match the need of your Web site.

When a PowerPoint presentation is saved as a Web page in PowerPoint 2003, a browser-specific framed interface is created that presents the PowerPoint content. In Figure 41.5, this content is shown in Internet Explorer 6.0.

Figure 41.5
PowerPoint files saved as Web pages produce an impressive framed interface for showing presentation content.

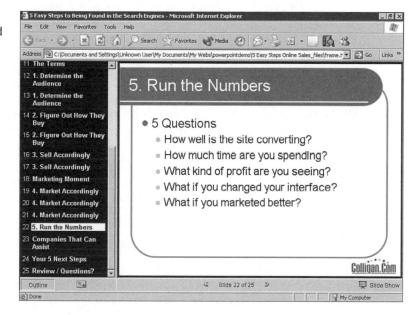

PUBLISH AS WEB PAGE DIALOG BOX

The Publish button in the Save As dialog box for PowerPoint, (shown previously in Figure 41.4), opens the Publish as Web Page dialog box, shown in Figure 41.6.

The variables of the Publish What area are obvious. Select the slide numbers you want presented and choose if you'd like speaker notes to be published as well.

TIP

> PowerPoint slide decks often contain speaker notes made up of content that makes sense only to the presenter. If you are going to publish your speaker notes with your presentation, make sure that your notes make as much "sense" as your slide content does.

41

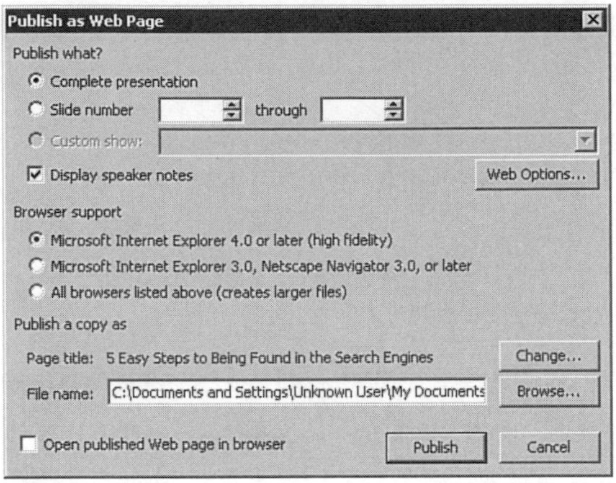

Figure 41.6
The Publish as Web Page dialog box gives you specific control over how you would like your PowerPoint content to be saved.

The Browser Support area lets you choose the desired level of older browser support you'd like the HTML to publish to. You can choose either support for the more recent browsers (which presents the content in a format that sizes with the screen), support for older browsers (which presents the content as HTML with static sized graphic slide files), or both. If the final option is chosen, additional HTML is generated that checks for browser type and directs the browser to the appropriate content. The dual version option takes up considerably more space because it ends up saving two different versions of the PowerPoint presentation for access by the different browser types.

The Publish a Copy as area lets you set the destination for the final HTML content.

TIP

> If possible, save the content directly to your FrontPage Web site and save yourself the extra steps of important the content into your site.

EDITING POWERPOINT WEB CONTENT IN FRONTPAGE

By default, content created in a certain application will be edited by that product (if the product is installed on the machine). As a result, clicking content created by PowerPoint within FrontPage will open the content in PowerPoint unless otherwise specified.

To edit PowerPoint created HTML content from within FrontPage, right-click the content and choose FrontPage (Open as HTML) from the Open With option, as seen in Figure 41.7.

If you need to edit content created by PowerPoint, consider editing the original source files in PowerPoint and then resaving the content as HTML. The other option is to open and edit the files from within PowerPoint through FrontPage so that edits are saved directly to the site. Using FrontPage to edit content created in PowerPoint should be done only as a final resort. If you had PowerPoint create only graphic files of the slides, there will be no way to edit the text content within these slides.

Figure 41.7
Right-clicking a file in FrontPage lets you choose the application you want to edit the content with.

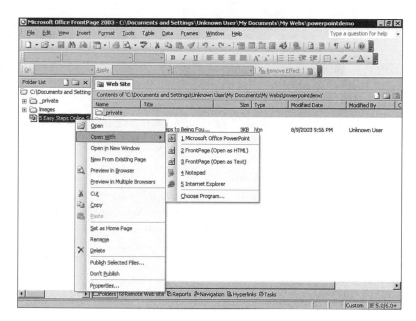

 If you edited PowerPoint content in FrontPage and are having problems accessing it, *see* *"PowerPoint Content Is Damaged"* in the *"Troubleshooting"* section at the end of this chapter.

TIP

> If you edit your slide content in FrontPage, make sure to edit both copies of the created HTML if multiple copies were made in the save as process described earlier.

CALLING POWERPOINT CONTENT FROM FRONTPAGE

Once your PowerPoint presentation is in your Web site, you can link to the PowerPoint content through the FrontPage hyperlink button. The Insert Hyperlink box will show all content in your site, including PowerPoint content. This is seen in Figure 41.8.

Figure 41.8
The Insert Hyperlink dialog box identifies all possible links in your site, include PowerPoint content.

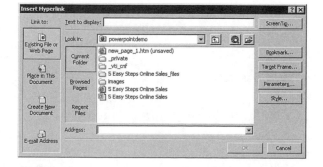

41

Do You Need FrontPage at All?

In reality, no. You don't need FrontPage at all to create Web content from PowerPoint files. Obviously, the creation of links from your Web site to your presentation content requires an HTML editor. FrontPage provides for this need, but the two products work well independently of each other.

FrontPage is, however, the ideal product for bringing multiple slideshows together and integrating them into the larger Web site structure and format.

Other Versions of PowerPoint

The fact that Internet Explorer provides a simple PowerPoint viewer is relevant to all previous versions of PowerPoint. However, because they aren't supported by all browsers, other options for porting PowerPoint content are still needed.

The option to save slide content as graphics files is only supported by PowerPoint 2003.

PowerPoint 2002 and 2000 both have options directly in the product for saving slide content as HTML. They are not detailed as the features provided in PowerPoint 2003 but provide a solid option for HTML translation.

PowerPoint 2003 can read .PPT files created in previous versions of PowerPoint. You can then save these files as Web content using any of the options described previously.

Troubleshooting

Single File Web Page Option Doesn't Work on the Latest Netscape Version

I published my presentation as a Single File Web Page. I know it isn't supported on earlier versions of Netscape, but it also can't be viewed on the most recent release. How can I make this format work?

The Single File Web Page option is only supported by Internet Explorer version 4.0 and higher. It contains Microsoft-specific metadata that will only be supported by those browser types.

Your only options for Netscape compatible PowerPoint content is either by saving the presentation as a Netscape compatible file (don't save as single file) or having PowerPoint save the screens as graphic files and calling the content from a Web page developed for this purpose. You can also cut and paste content from a PowerPoint presentation and save it directly into your Web pages as desired.

PowerPoint Content Is Damaged

I made a simple edit to some HTML content created by PowerPoint. The PowerPoint slides now don't present as required through the HTML interface. How can I fix this?

HTML content created by PowerPoint contains a significant amount of XML data that enables PowerPoint to further edit the content if needed. If this content was deleted or altered, the results could be less than desirable. Your best bet is to resave the PowerPoint file as HTML and redo the edits, being careful to not touch the additional XML metadata.

FRONT AND CENTER: DOES POWERPOINT "TRANSLATE"?

At first impression, it might seem like a great idea to place PowerPoint content in your Web site. With the tools provided by PowerPoint 2003, you can quickly produce impressive Web content from your PowerPoint presentations, considerably increase the size of your site, and establish how content is presented.

Be careful when placing PowerPoint content at a Web site.

When used as a reference for people who already have seen the presentation, it is a great reference tool similar in impact to printed slides handed out to the audience. It is the effective presenter who gives her audience the ability to return to content presented when and as needed.

The "problem" with placing such content on the Web can come from the user who is attempting to re-create a presentation on the Web and provides a means for participants to get around the initial presentation by reading the presentation slides and notes. Nothing Web-based can re-create the impact of a presentation by a human.

As mentioned throughout this book, *just because you can, doesn't mean you should*. If you are going to place PowerPoint content online, make sure that the information needed to process the content is there.

41

WORKING WITH MICROSOFT PUBLISHER

In this chapter

CREATING WEB SITES WITH PUBLISHER

Microsoft Publisher is designed for creating print publications, but as the Internet has become more popular, more people are using Publisher to create Web sites. Designing Web sites is not simple, even with FrontPage. FrontPage users have to understand how to use tables and other complex layout tools, and they must have a rudimentary understanding of the limitations imposed by HTML. If you're a Publisher expert, learning all the ins and outs of Web development just might not be worth it.

Microsoft realizes that many people are very comfortable with the easy page layout tools of Publisher and want to put content on the Web without learning the complexities of Web development. For those people, Publisher provides the ability to save a publication in HTML format. That ability, however, does not come without a price. As you will see in this chapter, HTML files generated by Publisher can carry a significant amount of code, and they might not always display the way you expect them to.

Publisher's Web site templates (shown in Figure 42.1) are quite simple compared to FrontPage's templates. Depending on which template you choose, Publisher will create one or more pages in your publication. As shown in Figure 42.2, Publisher provides an easy way to navigate between pages using the Page Sorter. By right-clicking a page in the Page Sorter, you can add a new page based off of that page or any other page template. Figure 42.2 also shows the Web Tools toolbar, where all the Web-specific tools are located.

Figure 42.1
Publisher's Web templates are not as complex as FrontPage's.

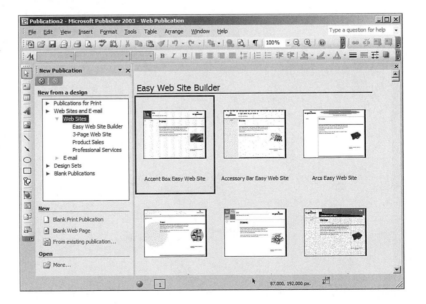

Figure 42.2
The Page Sorter makes navigating between Web pages in Publisher an easy task.

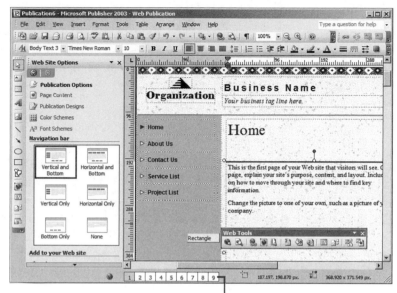

Tho Page Sorter

Now that you know that Publisher can help you create a Web site, you might be wondering whether you should use it to create your Web site. The answer to that question depends entirely on what your needs are. If you are designing a Web site from scratch, using Publisher is probably not your best option. You'd be better off starting out with FrontPage and sticking with FrontPage because it is designed for Web site design. However, if you simply want to make a desktop publishing project available on the Internet, Publisher can do a fairly good job at making that happen.

MOVING PUBLISHER CONTENT INTO FRONTPAGE

There are three different techniques you can use to move Publisher content into FrontPage:

- Copy and Paste
- Save As a Web Page or Graphic
- Publish to the Web

Each one of these has benefits and disadvantages, and each of them is going to carry some consequences that you will need to be aware of. You should also be aware that when you move Publisher content to FrontPage, it might not look exactly the same. A Publisher document rarely looks as good after saving in HTML format as it does in Publisher.

42

COPY AND PASTE

The copy and paste method provides you with the highest level of control over how Publisher content appears in FrontPage. When you paste content from Publisher, FrontPage will display the Paste Options button as shown in Figure 42.3. The Paste Options button provides you with different options for pasting the content depending on the type of content you are pasting.

- **Keep Source Formatting**—FrontPage will use CSS and *Vector Markup Language (VML)* to attempt to lay out the page the same way it was presented in Publisher. This method produces pretty good results, but the output is not supported in browsers that do not support VML. Content pasted using this option is absolutely positioned.

- **Paste as an Image Tag**—FrontPage will convert the pasted content into a graphic file. Text can no longer be edited, and the size of the file might be fairly large. However, this method does guarantee that the page will appear exactly as it did in Publisher.

- **Microsoft Office Drawing Object**—FrontPage will convert the pasted content into an Office Drawing Object. This option is very similar to the Keep Source Formatting option, but content pasted using this option has no positioning properties set.

- **Keep Text Only**—If you are pasting text without any graphic or drawing elements, you can choose the Keep Text Only option to paste the text into FrontPage without any of the formatting from Publisher.

- **Use Destination Styles**—If the current FrontPage document has existing styles, you can choose to apply those styles to pasted content by selecting this option. Content pasted using this option is absolutely positioned.

→ For more information on CSS, **see** "Using Style Sheets to Format Web Pages," **p. 385**.

Paste Options

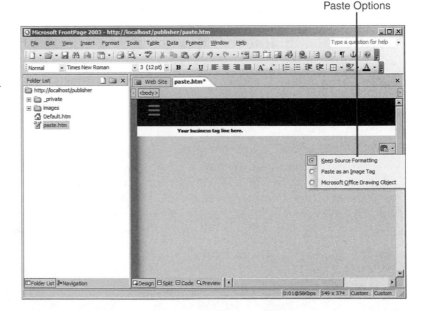

Figure 42.3
The Paste Options menu controls how FrontPage deals with pasted Publisher content.

All the paste options other than Paste as an Image Tag and Keep Text Only will use VML to draw any shapes on the page. VML is a language that uses code to define shapes generally called "vectors." Because vector shapes are created using numerical data, they can be resized as needed without losing quality. Figure 42.4 shows a Publisher file. Figure 42.5 shows the Publisher content in a Split view in FrontPage after pasting using the Keep Source Formatting option. Notice the large amount of code necessary to retain the formatting of the original content.

Figure 42.4
A simple Publisher document.

Figure 42.5
The same Publisher content in FrontPage. Notice the large amount of code necessary to create the same content in FrontPage.

42

Only Internet Explorer 5 or newer and Netscape 6 and newer support VML. FrontPage includes code so that if the page is viewed in a browser that doesn't support VML, it will display the content as images instead. However, as you will see later, this doesn't always translate into a Web page that displays the way it should.

When you use the Paste as an Image Tag option, FrontPage will convert all content pasted into the page as a single graphic. When you save the page, you will be prompted to save the new image as shown in Figure 42.6. Notice that FrontPage defaults to saving the image in GIF format. If you would like to change the format, click the Picture File Type button and select the desired format.

Figure 42.6
FrontPage defaults to saving pasted Publisher image tags as GIF files. This might not be the best choice.

→ For more information on graphic file formats, **see** "Web Graphic Formats," **p. 847**.

Not all of FrontPage's paste options will present your content in the same way. When pasting as a Microsoft Office Drawing Object, content is not absolutely positioned. This can cause individual objects from Publisher to be pasted into unintended positions. Figure 42.7 shows the Publisher content from Figure 42.4 pasted as a Microsoft Office Drawing Object into FrontPage. Note that the text is no longer inside the oval. Instead, it has shifted above the oval because the content is no longer absolutely positioned. If you want to reposition the objects so that they appear as they did in Publisher, select Format, Position in FrontPage and select Absolute in the Positioning Styles section of the Position dialog box.

TIP

> Not all browsers will handle absolutely positioned elements equally. Netscape 4.*x* versions and older are not likely to render absolutely positioned objects as you intend. Make sure that you test your pages in all browsers.

SAVE AS A WEB PAGE OR GRAPHIC

42

In addition to copying and pasting one or more objects from your Publisher document, you can also save the entire publication as an HTML file by selecting File, Save As and choosing Web Page from the Save As Type dropdown.

Figure 42.7
Content pasted as a Microsoft Office Drawing Object can be shifted into unwanted positions on the page.

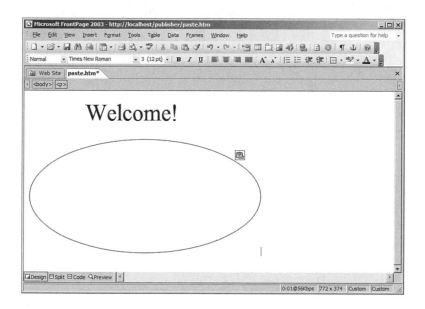

Choosing this option carries a bit more baggage than you might like because Publisher will add code that is necessary to open the document in Publisher again. Microsoft refers to this technology as *round-tripping*. Even though the Publisher file is saved in HTML format, code added to the file enables it to convert back to a Publisher document when it is reopened in Publisher.

Figure 42.8 shows a partial view of the code generated when the Publisher file from Figure 42.4 is saved as a Web page. Much more code that is not visible is required to implement round-tripping.

Figure 42.8
Publisher adds a lot of code to your file when you save as a Web page. This code is added so that Publisher can reopen the file later.

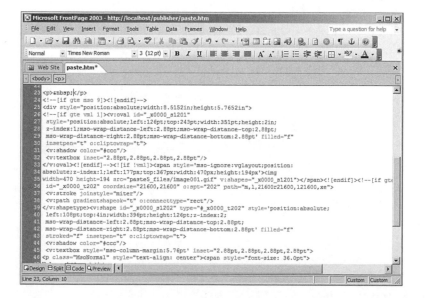

42

TIP

> If you try to open an HTML page in FrontPage that was saved in Publisher, it will open in Publisher. If you would prefer that Office files not be opened in the application that created them, open FrontPage and select Tools, Options and click the Configure Editors tab. Remove the check from the Open Web Pages in the Office Application that Created Them check box.

PUBLISHING TO THE WEB

Publisher can also save your Publisher file in HTML format as *filtered HTML* using the Publish to the Web option. Filtered HTML is HTML without all the extra code that enables round-tripping. Saving your file in filtered HTML can make the file substantially smaller.

You might also find the Publish to the Web option more convenient if your Publisher file consists of multiple pages. When you use the Publish to the Web option, Publisher will save all the files and related files in one step.

To save a Publisher file using the Publish to the Web option, select File, Publish to the Web in Publisher. In the Publish to the Web dialog box (shown in Figure 42.9), select the location for your files and click Save. When the files are saved, Publisher will save your publication as an HTML file. It will also save any supporting files in a folder named `<document_name>_files`. If your publication consists of more than one page, the home page will be saved to the path you specify and all other pages will be saved to the `<document_name>_files` folder.

Figure 42.9
The Publish to the Web dialog box makes saving publications as HTML files easy.

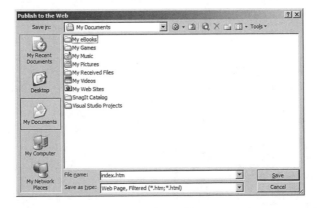

When you save your publication, Publisher will inform you that it is being saved as filtered HTML for faster downloads, as shown in Figure 42.10. After a publication is saved as filtered HTML, it cannot be opened again as a Publisher file.

42

Figure 42.10
When publishing to the Web, Publisher saves the file as filtered HTML.

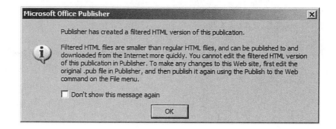

You can choose to save your publication to a disk location and then import the files into your FrontPage Web site, or you can save it directly into your FrontPage Web site using a Web Folder in My Network Places as long as the Web server is running the FrontPage Server Extensions. A *Web Folder* is a special folder that points to a FrontPage Web site. Using Web Folders, you can save your publication directly to your FrontPage Web site using the HTTP address. When you save a file using a Web Folder, the file is saved using the FrontPage Server Extensions. Therefore, if you save your Publisher document using a Web Folder, no other action is necessary in order for FrontPage to recognize the new files in your Web site.

 If you receive a "The folder is inaccessible" error when trying to save your publication to a Web Folder, *see "Unable to Save to Web Folder" in the "Troubleshooting" section of this chapter.*

When you save your publication using a Web Folder, Publisher saves the <document_name>_files folder as a thicket folder. A *thicket* folder is a folder saved into an HTTP location by an Office application. Inside the thicket folder is an _vti_cnf folder containing a file called .fp_folder_info. This file identifies the folder as a thicket folder.

 If you are unable to see the _vti_cnf folder, *see "_vti_cnf Folder Not Visible" in the "Troubleshooting" section of this chapter.*

FrontPage is specifically designed to hide thicket folders. Even if you configure the Web site to show hidden files and folders, the thicket folder will still be invisible. If you want to see the thicket folder in FrontPage, you will need to delete the .fp_folder_info file in the _vti_cnf folder as shown in Figure 42.11.

Figure 42.11
The .fp_folder_info file identifies this folder as a thicket folder and one that is not visible in FrontPage.

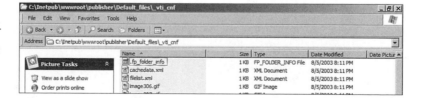

There is one other special consideration for publications saved out of Publisher (or any other Office application for that matter) as HTML files. The <document_name>_files folder is connected to the HTML file associated with it. If you delete the <document_name>_files folder, Windows will automatically delete the associated HTML file as well because of a new feature called *Connected Files*, which was introduced beginning with Windows 2000.

If you attempt to rename a connected folder, you will see a warning message (shown in Figure 42.12) informing you that if you rename the folder, you will break the connection. As long as you are aware of what's going on and you are comfortable breaking the connection, you will be fine. If you want to restore the connection later on, simply rename the folder back to what it was originally.

Figure 42.12
Windows will warn you if you try to rename a connected folder.

> **TIP**
>
> Publisher does have an option to not save supporting files in a separate folder. See the Publisher Help files for more information.

TROUBLESHOOTING

UNABLE TO SAVE TO WEB FOLDER

I am trying to save my files to a Web Folder, and I am getting an error message saying that the folder is inaccessible.

This message indicates that you might have broken Web Folders. Web Folders are complicated components of Windows, and they can be damaged quite easily. When that happens, repairing them is not easy. However, Microsoft has written a Knowledge Base article that can assist you in repairing them.

To access the article, browse to http://support.microsoft.com and search for article number 287402.

vti_cnf FOLDER NOT VISIBLE

I am trying to delete the .fp_folder_info file from a thicket folder, but I cannot see the _vti_cnf folder.

The _vti_cnf folder is a hidden folder. If you cannot see it, in Windows Explorer, select Tools, Folder Options and click the View tab. Select the Show Hidden Files and Folders options and click OK.

FRONT AND CENTER: SHOULD YOU USE PUBLISHER?

The general consensus in the Web development community is that Publisher is a great solution for desktop publishing, but a mediocre solution at best for Web development. While the features surrounding Web development in Publisher have been dramatically improved in Publisher 2003, it still does not excel as a Web development tool.

One problem you might encounter when using Publisher to generate your HTML pages is an inconsistent appearance in different browsers. Figure 42.13 shows a simple Web page in Publisher. Figure 42.14 shows the same page in Internet Explorer after it was saved as a Web page in Publisher. Figure 42.15 shows the same page in Netscape. It doesn't take a sophisticated eye to see that the Web page is useless when viewed in Netscape. These are the kinds of problems you might encounter if you use Publisher as a Web design tool.

Figure 42.13
A simple Web page in Publisher.

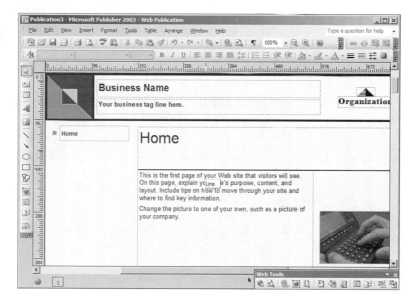

42

Figure 42.14
The same page in
Internet Explorer after
being saved as a Web
page in Publisher.

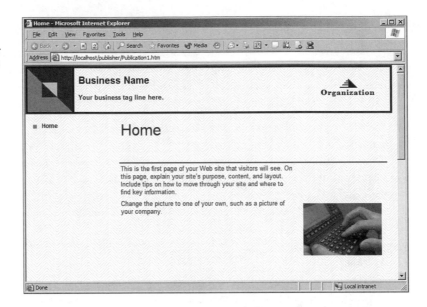

Figure 42.15
The same page
viewed in Netscape
Navigator. Notice that
the content has been
moved around and
the page is no longer
useful.

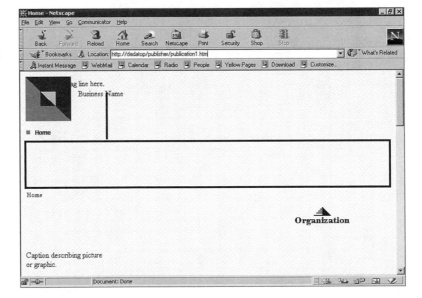

42

CREATING AND ADAPTING GRAPHICS FOR THE WEB

CHAPTER **43**

COLOR CONCEPTS AND WEB DESIGN

In this chapter

COLOR THEORY

43

If you have a window nearby, look out. In the natural world, you have a wide range of colors. There's everything from the bright green of a new leaf to the shocking orange of an Arizona sunset. Between these bold extremes, nature shows her subtle hand in the soft blue sky, a slate gray rock, and the light tan patches on a cat's fur.

It should be of no surprise to you that the computer environment is more limited than nature. When you take a closer look at the Web environment, these limitations become even more stringent. Yet, an understanding of the colors that exist and how they work gives you an edge when it comes to using color in a way that leaves a lasting impression and works across all available browsers and platforms.

This part will help those of you who do not have a strong background in design look at a variety of color elements that impact design, including color types, properties, relationships, and special effects. For those of you with an artistic background, revisiting these elements will help you put them into the perspective of the Web.

You will find that FrontPage's approach to handling color is solid and offers color amateurs the ability to produce impressive results while giving the more professional developer options for creating the exact color schemes they are looking for.

SUBTRACTIVE COLOR

Colors in the natural world are made up of pigments. *Pigment* is a substance that reacts to light. You might have heard it said that without light, there is no color. This is true, and without pigment, there is no variation in color.

Subtractive color is the theoretical premise on which color in the natural world is based. It's called *subtractive* because it absorbs light before transmitting or reflecting the results that your eyes perceive as color.

Subtractive color theory exists to help both industrialists and artists understand and try to re-create nature's own design. With this premise as a guide, pigments are re-created chemically in paints, dyes, and inks.

Remember the color wheel? A *color wheel* is a circular representation of subtractive color, with different colors making up pie slices within the wheel. The color wheel begins with what are known as the *primary* colors: red, blue, and yellow.

Each of these colors can be mixed together to come up with an entire spectrum of colors.

Digital information, however, is dealt with quite differently. Computers and computer hardware are limited in their capability to deliver color to a screen. You can't compete with Mother Nature! Those who attempt to compete with Mother Nature, especially in the Web environment, end up looking silly because they don't understand the limitations of color on the Web.

Because it's impossible for a computer to absorb light, it must generate light. Therefore, the type of color you see on your computers is backed by a theory referred to as additive synthesis.

ADDITIVE SYNTHESIS

In *additive synthesis*, color is created by the addition of colors. Computers use three colors to do this: red, blue, and green. It's almost as if three individual paint guns are being fired at your screen, combining color and light to create variations.

Red, green, and blue color is referred to simply as *RGB*. As you work with digital color, this will be the technical foundation for the decisions you make. However, it's the subtractive world from which you gain your inspiration. It's important to keep this distinction in mind.

Why can the natural world make all colors from red, blue, and yellow, but computers cannot? It goes back to the difference between the capability to absorb versus the capability to transmit light, and how light then interacts with what is absorbed or transmitted. If you mix red and green paint, you'd get brown. But guess what happens when a computer mixes those same colors? The resulting color is yellow.

COMPUTER DELIVERY OF COLOR

Computers rely on three primary pieces of hardware to deliver color information to you:

- The computer
- The graphics card
- The monitor

It stands to reason, then, that the quality of color you see on your computer depends on the quality and capability of these components. If any one of these components is incompatible or unequal in its properties, the end result will not be as true and refined as possible.

NOTE

> Unlike the print medium, where you can control how your final work is presented, the variables provided in the previous list dictate that you will never be able to get the exact result you are looking for.

Furthermore, computer platforms and operating systems have differing capabilities when it comes to color. The color capabilities on older systems usually are substandard when compared to the newer operating systems. Windows XP and 2000, Macintosh, and various Linux systems all have very good color control, but they use different methods to represent color. This can spell trouble if you view graphical images on different systems.

You must learn to work with (and understand) the color limitations and standards that exist. Knowing your own machine, and the capabilities of your viewing audience, will help you do just that.

Add to this the fact that any graphical interface, such as a browser, will affect the management of color, and you've got an important issue in color technology: In Web design, it is the browser that limits color significantly.

This is the bane of the Web designer's existence when it comes to color, but it's not insurmountable. FrontPage provides a number of color controls that will help you manage color effectively.

If you come from a graphics background or have worked with Photoshop or other professional graphics programs, you're probably familiar with other color management methods. One of the most familiar is CMYK (Cyan, Magenta, Yellow, Black). *CMYK* is a method used for print output. Other management systems include grayscale (which contains black, white, and gradations of gray) and indexed color (a limited palette of specific colors defined by the designer). In Web design, indexed color is extremely important.

→ For more information on issues of index color, **see** "Web Graphic Formats," **p. 847**.

COLOR DEPTH

If you pay any attention to the difference in video cards, the measurements of 8-bit, 16-bit, and 24-bit color should sound familiar. These values refer to the number of bits of computer memory required to represent the various levels of color depth.

These values mentioned aren't the only possible color depths, only the most popular. The simplest level is 2-bit color. This requires only two memory places—one for the color white and another for the color black.

For every additional bit of memory, the number of possible colors increases. 3-bit color has 8 unique colors, and 4-bit color has 16. The next major color depth worth mentioning is 8-bit color. 8-bit color can display 256 colors. This is what Photoshop refers to as *indexed color*, and the GIF format still uses this color depth.

16-bit and 24-bit color include colors your eyes cannot even detect, with 65,536 and 16,777,216 colors, respectively. Somewhere among these colors are the hues of that Arizona sunset and the patches of a cat's fur. 24-bit color is often called *photographic-quality color*. The JPEG format uses 24-bit color.

Web designers use all these color depths, and FrontPage deals with each of these separately.

NOTE

If you've shopped around for scanners while looking for video cards, you've no doubt seen ads mentioning 30- and 36-bit color depths. These are 24-bit color scanners with an additional 6 or 12 bits added to measure the opacity of an image. These extra bits are called the *alpha channel* and define how much of the underlying image shows through—used for *transparent* images.

WORKING WITH ELEMENTS OF COLOR

As mentioned earlier, no color exists without light. Although light is necessary, color is not. In fact, many people cannot perceive color, or they perceive color improperly, such as in the common condition known as color blindness. However, for those with normal color perception, color is a significant aspect of their emotional and artistic lives. In fact, it's so much a part of them that they might not necessarily even know what motivates them to pick out certain colors for their wardrobes—yet they do it.

Artists and designers have been trained to understand and use the elements of color as a method of communication. Web designers, like artists and traditional designers, also need to possess a full understanding of what color can do, what it means, and how to harness its power and use it to create sites with maximum communicative potential.

CATEGORIES OF COLOR

Color is defined by how colors are combined. Even though the method of combination is going to differ when you compare the subtractive, natural world to the digital, additive one, the end results are the same in terms of your perception of color.

Subtractive color categories are defined as follows:

- **Primaries**—All subtractive colors are the results of some combination of three colors: red, yellow, and blue. These colors are referred to as primary because they are the first colors to technically exist. Without them, no other color is possible.

- **Secondaries**—The next step is to mix pairs of the primaries together. If you mix equal parts of red and yellow paint, you come up with orange. Blue and yellow create green, and violet is created by mixing red with blue. Orange, green, and violet are therefore the secondary colors found on the color wheel.

- **Intermediates**—When two or more primaries, or secondaries, are mixed together in unequal parts, the results are referred to as intermediate colors. These colors are gradations that lie between the primary and secondary colors, such as light blue and pink.

NOTE

> Colors that are next to each other on the color wheel, such as blue and violet, have a distinct relationship and are considered to be *similar*. Opposing colors, such as orange and blue, are *complementary*. Red and green, which are three colors removed from each other on the wheel, are *contrasting* colors.

In the digital world, additive color is used. The additive color categories are different from their subtractive counterparts as follows:

- **Primaries**—All additive colors are the results of some combination of red, green, and blue (RGB).

- **Secondaries**—The secondary colors for an additive system are also different from the subtractive system. Mixing red and green produces yellow. Combining green and blue

43

43

makes cyan, which is similar to light blue. When red and blue are mixed, the result is magenta. For additive color, yellow, cyan, and magenta are the secondary colors.

- **Intermediates**—This includes everything else.

Figure 43.1 shows FrontPage's version of the color wheel. The wheel is separated into discreet colors that can be easily selected, but you can see how the primary colors blend into the secondary colors. Each corner of the hexagon has a primary or secondary color.

Figure 43.1
FrontPage's Color Selector is a modified color wheel.

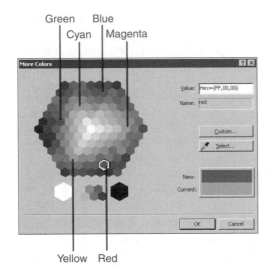

Green Blue
Cyan Magenta

Yellow Red

Along with these categories, you can achieve additional categories by adding white or black. When you add white to a given color, you achieve *tint*, which lightens the color saturation. Black added to a color darkens it. This is referred to as *shade*.

PROPERTIES OF COLOR

Bordeaux. Banana. Spice. Where do these colors fit into the spectrum? What determines the difference between cobalt and peacock, even if they are both blue? Do these issues even matter on the Web?

The way in which differentiation of this nature is made is by defining the *properties* of color. Color properties are determined by the type and amount of color as well as how much light is used in that color, as follows:

- **Hue**—This term is used to differentiate one color from another. For example, red is different from green, and purple is different from brown. Whether a color is primary, secondary, intermediate, or tertiary (third level) isn't important with regard to hue; that they are different in terms of actual color is.

- **Value**—Chocolate brown is darker than tan, and sky blue is lighter than navy. A color's value is defined by the amount of light or dark in that color.

- **Saturation**—Also referred to as intensity, you can think of saturation as being the brightness of a color. Peacock blue is very bright, whereas navy is rather dull. Similarly, those popular neon lime greens reminiscent of the 1960s are much more intense than a forest green.

- **Warmth**—Hues found in the yellow-to-red range are considered to be warm. They emit a sense of heat.

- **Coolness**—Cool colors are those ranging from green to blue. Think of ice blue or the cool sense of a forest a deep green can inspire.

If you look at these definitions, you can see that a given hue can contain a value and saturation. When you think of all the variations that are potentially held within each of these properties, you can begin to see that color is much more than meets the eye.

Of course, you might notice that black and white are missing from this list. Black can be described as absence of light, and white as being light. A more technical way to think about black and white is to refer to the properties of hue and saturation. The fact? Neither black nor white possess hue *or* saturation.

NOTE

> Why then do "shades" of gray exist? The reason is found in value. The amount of light or dark in white or black determines the resulting value of gray.

COLOR RELATIONSHIPS

Colors are emotional, and they have emotional relationships with one another. In a compatible relationship, harmony reigns. In a discordant relationship, clashing occurs. These color-based emotional relationships can be part of your Web designs if you understand how they work in the great scheme of things.

In design, relationships are very important because both harmonious as well as discordant color schemes can be effective, depending on the circumstances.

If I'm trying to convey a peaceful environment, I'm going to want to use harmonious colors. An example of this would be creating a palette from soft, subtle pastels. The end result is going to be calm and even feminine.

However, if I want to wake people up and jangle them up a bit, I might try a discordant relationship. Bright yellow and red with black creates discord, but the visual impact is intense. Depending on the audience and the communication issues at hand, the discordant relationship might be a more appropriate choice than the harmonious one.

43

COLOR SIGNIFICANCE

To those of you who are familiar with it, the *Wired* look is memorable. Using neon and discordant colors, the magazine—as well as the HotWired Web site (`http://hotwired.frontpagelink.com/`)—communicates energy. If you've never been to the site, take a look—you will be quite impressed.

Ever notice how all-night restaurants are usually very brightly lit? This is thought to help keep people awake.

The more you look for examples of the significance of color, the more you will find. Colors are even associated with specific professions, ages, and sexes: white and green for doctors and nurses, darker or more neutral colors for older people, pink for girls, and blue for boys.

None of this is accidental. In fact, it's very specific. Color has very strong impact on the human psyche. This has been shown to be true in countless studies.

However, the intriguing issue is that color alone doesn't create this impact. Culture has a profound influence in how you perceive color, too.

Recently, a trend occurred in some Western countries to marry in black: the bride and her bridesmaids as well as the men used black material in their formal bridal wear. This upset a lot of people because Westerners tend to associate black with death and mourning.

But in some cultures, the color Westerners normally associate with purity and brides (white) is the color of death. In East India, for example, white is the color of the death shroud and mourning costumes.

It's important for you, a Web designer working in a global medium, to have some sense of what colors signify. Although it's not possible to give you a rundown of cultural color significance in one chapter, giving some general meanings of color is. Be advised that if you're doing work for a client from a different culture, asking about color perception in that individual's culture will be well worth your while. This can help you avoid uncomfortable, time-consuming situations. It is a World Wide Web, after all.

Here's a bit about color significance in the Western world. Remember, these are generalizations, and other interpretations do exist.

Color	Significance
Black	Death, darkness, elegance, sophistication
White	Purity, cleanliness, refinement
Red	Passion, intense energy, anger
Green	Healing, nature, earth
Blue	Dignity, power, stability
Yellow	Happiness, vibrancy, youth
Purple	Royalty, riches, sumptuousness

43

Now that you are familiar with the types and meanings of color and have a good foundation in color theory, it's time to apply these ideas to the Web.

WEB COLOR TECHNOLOGY

You've already become familiar with color management methods for the computer screen. The one emphasized as a starting point for Web-based color is RGB (or red, green, blue) color management.

To effectively work with color on the Web, however, you have to take RGB a step further and convert it into a system of values HTML will recognize. This system is known as *hexadecimal*.

Hexadecimal, referred to simply as "hex," is the base-16 number system. Base-16 is an *alphanumeric* system, consisting of both numbers and letters in combinations that translate into a color. Hexadecimal uses the numbers 0–9 and the letters A–F. All hexadecimal color values should contain a total of six characters for HTML to understand it. The first pair in the series of six equals the amount of red in the color; the second pair equals the amount of green; and the third pair equals the amount of blue.

TIP

> If at any time you get a single character in hex conversion, such as a single 0 or letter D, simply enter a 0 before the hex character so that the resulting binary information will be accurate.

Remember your computer science classes way back when? A single byte is made up of 8 bits of information. Every two characters within a hex value makes up one byte, or 8 bits. This means that each hex value contains 24 bits of color information.

It's no accident that RGB color is also known as *24-bit color*.

How do you find the hex value of RGB colors? You're in luck. FrontPage automatically does the conversion and shows you these values when you select a color.

Imagine Web design without all these tools and having to do these things by hand. Now you know why your authors are such fans of FrontPage.

USING HEX COLOR VALUES

If you examine HTML code, you will find places where colors are specified in hex values. These are easy to identify because they begin with the # sign followed by six characters.

Although FrontPage uses the standard Windows color selector dialog box, an additional dialog box shows a range of colors useful on the Web. This is the More Colors dialog box, and it also shows the hex values for all the colors (refer to Figure 43.1).

You can use these hex values to replace the hex values in the HTML code to change colors manually. To find the hex value for a color, follow these steps:

1. Find one of the many color selection dropdown lists through FrontPage, such as the ones in the Page Properties dialog box on the Background tab. You can access this directly by selecting the Format, Background menu.

2. Clicking the Background dropdown list opens a small popup menu showing the Standard Colors, Document Colors, and a link to the More Colors dialog box. Figure 43.2 shows these options. Click the More Colors option.

Figure 43.2
Choose a color or click More Colors in the Background drop-down list in the Page Properties dialog box.

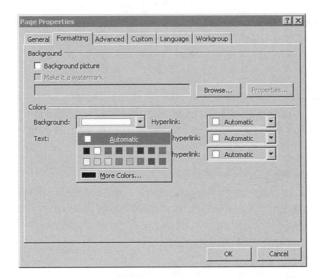

3. The More Colors dialog box presents a hexagonal array of colors (see Figure 43.3). Select a new color by clicking it.

Figure 43.3
The More Colors dialog box shows the hex value for each color.

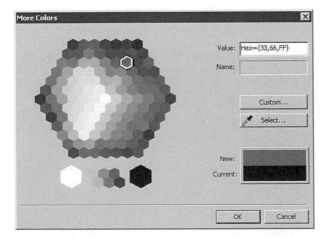

4. The hex value for this color is shown in the Value field at the upper right. Remember to drop the commas when using the hex value in code.

NOTE

> A select few colors have familiar names associated with them. When a color in the More Colors dialog box shows a value in the Name field, that color can be specified within HTML code by that name. These names include blue, cyan, lime, fuchsia, yellow, red, maroon, white, silver, gray, and black.

BROWSER-BASED COLORS

If your pages were all text and your users never had to download any graphics, your pages would load very quickly. Would you sacrifice speed for visual attraction?

The answer: probably. But it doesn't mean that you can't use color to create a rich base for the graphics you will use. What this does is offer the opportunity to have faster loading pages because you're using fewer graphics to achieve visual appeal.

Smoke and mirrors? Hardly! But if you understand how to tap into the colors native to your browser, you will have stable, attractive splashes of color before a graphic is ever downloaded.

To make this happen, you must understand the *Web safe palette*. This is a palette of 216 colors that are reserved by browsers on the Macintosh and Windows platforms for immediate access. Instead of having to download information from a remote server, the browser parses the hexadecimal color codes from the page right away.

Does this sound great? The FrontPage creators are one step ahead of you. The colors in the hexagonal array within the More Colors dialog box just happen to be these 216 colors.

THE SAFE PALETTE

A safe palette is the palette made up of 216 colors that remain as stable from one browser to another, between platforms, and at various monitor color capacities and resolutions as possible.

TIP

> In some cases, the term "safe palette" can be a bit of an overstatement. If you've ever looked at an old monitor days away from death or surfed the Internet on a black and white Palm pilot, you know that these graphics are anything but as the developer originally intended. Remember that not everyone is surfing with the monitor power that you have.

You should use the safe palette in most instances because it ensures cross-browser, cross-platform stability. If you use colors outside the safe palette, you can run into serious problems.

43

Picture this: You choose a soft, pale blue color for your background and a very dark blue for your text. Enough contrast exists to be readable, and you're happy with the look of your hard design work done on an upper-end machine capable of full 24-bit color.

You put your page up on the Internet, and along comes a friend to check out your work. He gets to the page and sees that you've chosen a bright peacock blue for your background and a very similar color for your text. He can't read the content on your page, and he's confused.

How did this happen? Well, you didn't use safe color. Your friend came along with a more limited set of hardware and software, and his color management system chose to *dither* the colors. This means that his computer grabbed the first blues available because it couldn't identify your unsafe color.

To avoid this, you must choose from the safe palette. It might seem that 216 colors is a very limited number, and it's true. My only words of solace are to encourage you to be creative. Enough colors are available within the safe palette to create beautiful designs—it's done every day on the Web.

NOTE

If most color systems can display at least 256 colors, how did the safe palette end up with only 216? It's a complicated story that involves older versions of Windows having reserved colors for the operating system that were different from the reserved colors on the Macintosh. Browsers then went on to use just the available colors to avoid the problem, and the end result was a limited palette. The good news is that the 216 color palette is very stable and addresses many problems that occur across platforms—something over which Web designers can breathe a sigh of relief.

To work effectively with the safe palette, you must draw from all the information covered in this chapter. Beginning with what you know of color, you can think about the look-and-feel and emotion you want to express on your site.

Let's say that you want to create a warm and welcoming personal presence that expresses your personal energy. Begin by selecting colors that are warm as well as vibrant: orange, red, and yellow. Then find an appropriate combination of hues: You want the site to be harmonious, not discordant. The harmony of colors will help express the welcoming and personal presence, offering comfort while still conveying energy.

Turn to your understanding of RGB and hexadecimal values. Add to that the fact that you know you want to choose your colors from a safe palette, and you've narrowed down your choices to a very specific set of colors.

What you can do at this point is create what is called an *individual* palette, which is a selection of five to seven colors you choose from the safe palette.

FrontPage offers an easy way to keep track of the colors you've selected. In the dropdown menu on any color selector is a section of Document Colors; these are the unique colors you've chosen for this document. By examining these colors and checking the harmony between them, you should be able to tell which colors need to be changed.

So where do you go from here? By using the hexadecimal values in combination with HTML and Cascading Style Sheets, you can employ your colors to create a design. Be creative, combining your colors for backgrounds, links, text, and table cells.

NOTE

> As computer display technologies get better and better, the rising majority of users have video displays that are simply capable of handling a much wider range of colors. As these numbers continue to rise, the importance of the Web safe palette decreases.
>
> As a result of these significant changes in technology, it is important to point out that a lot of professional Web designers are now ignoring the Web safe palette.

→ For more information CSS and Web design, **see** "Using Style Sheets to Format Web Pages," **p. 385**.

SPECIAL CONCERNS

There are two issues to bring to your attention regarding color. The first is contrast and readability; the second is the use of unsafe colors.

CONTRAST AND READABILITY

Contrast is a necessary element when designing with color. Simply defined, *contrast* is two colors that are different enough from one another to provide an obvious separation to the eye. Contrast is necessary to produce readable sites.

Many of you have undoubtedly visited sites where the background and body text have been very difficult to read. In most cases, the problem is because of poor contrast. A black on a light red isn't going to have enough contrast to be readable, as you can *try* to see in Figure 43.4. However, black on white is going to be very readable (see Figure 43.5).

TIP

> Accessibility experts have found that for visually impaired individuals, severe contrasts (such as black and white) are the best for readability in low vision circumstances. If you know that your audience is made up of a lot of older individuals or visually impaired persons, it's wise to plan ahead and ensure that your contrast colors are as solid as possible: black on white for body text is a surefire way to go.

Another approach is to *reverse* this concept, placing light colors on dark colors. This is known as *reverse type*, and, if the contrast is good enough, it can be quite effective. Bottom line? Be sure that your content is readable on your background to ensure that people are able to get to the information you're delivering.

Figure 43.4
Not enough contrast creates readability problems.

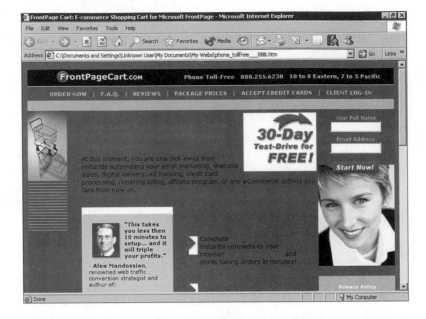

Figure 43.5
Black on white is high contrast, so it's easy to read.

Usually, body text should be darker than the background—dark enough so that significant contrast is created, enabling maximum readability.

UNSAFE COLOR

Using unsafe color is risky, and it's not recommended. However, sometimes unsafe color can be used. Here's a helpful set of guidelines:

- When you know your audience. And I *mean* know them! One situation in which you might know them well would be a corporate intranet.
- If you're less certain about your audience, but still interested in using unsafe color, test the colors for dithering at lower resolutions.

To test colors, drop your monitor down to 256 colors when viewing your page. If the color appears differently from what you originally determined, you probably should revert to a safe color. You will also want to be very thorough, testing your pages on a variety of browsers, platforms, and computer systems.

COLORS IN FRONTPAGE 2003

FrontPage doesn't have a single control for managing color, but rather, several entry points to the color controls. Whether it's text color, a background, or a complete color theme, the controls always seem to be there when you need them.

SELECTING COLORS

If you look at the Web, you see a lot of color. It seems to fill every corner of every page, and it isn't just found in graphics. Most of the color selection tools are part of the various format dialog boxes. Table 43.1 contains a list of which elements can be colored and where the color selector is found.

TABLE 43.1	COLOR SELECTOR LOCATIONS IN FRONTPAGE
Element	**Location**
Text	Font dialog box or Formatting toolbar
Borders and Shading	Borders and Shading dialog box
Normal Hyperlinks	Page Properties dialog box, Formatting tab
Active Hyperlinks	Page Properties dialog box, Formatting tab
Visited Hyperlinks	Page Properties dialog box, Formatting tab
Page Text	Page Properties dialog box, Formatting tab
Page Background	Page Properties dialog box, Formatting tab
Table Background	Table Properties dialog box
Table Borders	Table Properties dialog box

continues

43

TABLE 43.1 CONTINUED	
Element	**Location**
Cell Background	Cell Properties dialog box
Cell Borders	Cell Properties dialog box
Horizontal Lines	Horizontal Line Properties dialog box

All the color selection dropdown menus are initially set to Automatic. This setting enables FrontPage to manage the color by using themes or predefined style sheets. Selecting a color overrides this automatic setting, but the first option in the color popup menu will allow you to re-enable the automatic setting.

STANDARD AND DOCUMENT COLORS

The next section in the color popup menu contains the Standard Colors. These 16 colors are standard across a broad range of operating systems and browsers. They also make choosing and applying a basic color to an element quick.

Any new colors selected and applied to your current Web page are added to the Document Color section. This provides a quick look at the range of colors your page is using. This is a good reference for piecing together a pleasing color scheme. If the Document Color section shows a mess of disharmonious colors, you should rethink your color selections.

BROWSER-SAFE COLOR PALETTE

The More Colors option opens a dialog box with the browser-safe colors presented in a pleasant hexagon shape. You can safely select any of these colors and rest assured that the same peacock blue you designed your site with will show up the same no matter the system or browser.

NOTE Obviously this isn't the case for browsers that don't show color.

If the safe colors still don't have what you need, you can select a color by using the Eye Dropper tool or selecting a custom color.

USING THE EYE DROPPER

Have you ever painted a room? Choosing the perfect color can be the trickiest part of the process. To find the matching color requires several trips to the paint store. Each time you return with several small strips of colors. When you finally find the right one, you are usually holding it in your hot little hand. If you lose the color strip, it's back to the drawing board to start the process over again.

43

Sometimes this happens when designing a site. If you have an image that holds the exact tones you need, you might struggle to match the same tones from a palette. The Eye Dropper tool, found in the More Colors dialog box, lets you grab any color you can see, including colors in other applications. After you click the Select button to enable the Eye Dropper tool, the tool stays active until you click again. You can make the tool disappear by pressing the Esc key on the keyboard.

Suppose that you want to grab a color for your page background; this is how it works:

1. Open the Page Properties dialog box's Formatting tab by selecting Format, Background.

2. Click the Background dropdown list for the background color.

3. Select More Colors.

4. Select the Eye Dropper tool by clicking the Select button shown in Figure 43.6. The cursor will change to an eye dropper tool.

5. Click the color you want to select. This color becomes the new color.**Figure 43.6**

Selecting existing colors with the Eye Dropper tool.

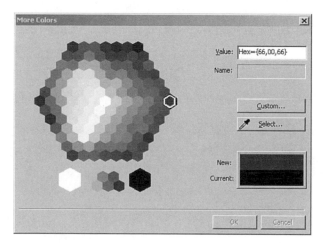

> **TIP**
>
> The power of the Eye dropper tool can not be overstated. You can use it to pull colors from any graphic on any program on your desktop—pull color from a Web page, desktop image or anything else you can imagine.
>
> Because the eye dropper can only capture color that can be seen on the screen, you will need to resize FrontPage to take up less than the entire screen if you want to pull from another program.

 If you are having a hard time choosing the "right" color for a Web page with all the technologies we've detailed, see "Choosing Proper Colors" in the "Troubleshooting" section at the end of this chapter.

43

CUSTOM COLORS

The Custom button takes you to the final option for colors. This opens the Color dialog box, which is the default Windows color selector (see Figure 43.7). By using the controls on the right, any color within the 16.7 million colors in the 24-bit spectrum are possible. This should be more than enough colors for even the most demanding designer.

Figure 43.7
The default Windows color picker is used for custom colors.

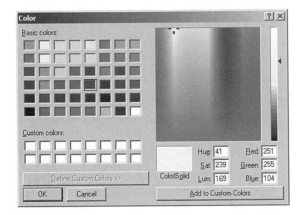

Any custom colors selected become instantly available in the color popup menu thereafter.

THEME COLORS

A surefire way to make your colors match is to use themes. Chapter 7, "Using Themes," covers the details about themes, but theme colors are unique enough to be mentioned here.

→ For more information on FrontPage and themes, **see** "Using Themes," **p. 133**.

The Themes task pane has a toggle button for turning vivid colors on or off, but the really interesting color options show up when you click the Create New Theme link. This makes three buttons appear, as shown in Figure 43.8. One of these buttons is Colors.

Clicking the Colors button opens the Customize Theme dialog box for colors. Three tabs are available in this dialog box: Color Schemes, Color Wheel, and Custom. The Color Schemes tab (see Figure 43.9) shows the color schemes for each of the loaded themes. You can choose any of these schemes for your current theme by clicking it. The Preview of New Theme pane shows the current theme with the new color scheme.

If none of the current color schemes fit the bill, click the Color Wheel tab. This opens a color wheel where you can select a new custom color scheme. The five colors that make up the color scheme are interrelated, so when a new default text color is selected in the color wheel, complementary colors are automatically updated. Figure 43.10 shows the color wheel at work.

Figure 43.8
Themes can be modified in three ways.

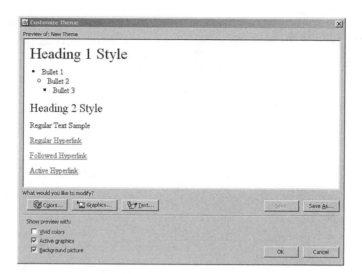

Figure 43.9
Choosing a theme's color scheme.

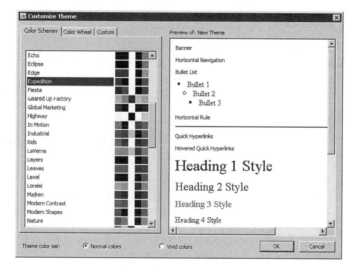

The Custom tab enables you to handpick the colors for a variety of Web page elements, including hyperlinks, background, and all heading levels.

After you've applied a theme, the theme colors will show up in the color popup menu for easy selection.

Figure 43.10
Selecting a custom
color scheme by
using the color wheel.

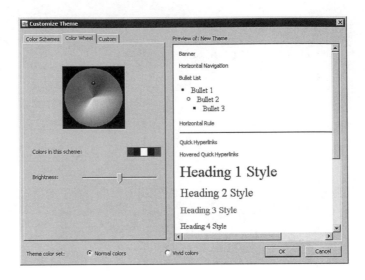

CREATING A COLOR-SAVVY TEMPLATE

Creating a template with positive, correlating colors can be tricky. It is also one of the most important aspects of Web design. The colors you choose will define the mood of the site to your visitors. If incorrectly defined, the site can alienate visitors.

The first step is to understand the theme and mood you want to convey. This example uses a site for a water park. The imagery I want to portray will include water, waves, oceans, beaches, and sun. I hope to present a cool, calm, and relaxing mood. Given these definitions, my colors will be light blues and tans.

Next, consider the graphic formats you intend to use. I plan to use mainly GIF images, so my colors should be selected from the 216 browser-safe colors in the More Colors dialog box. Visit the dialog box and look at the possible colors; then think of the places in your pages where you will need these colors.

To create a template of site colors, follow these steps:

1. Open a new Web page by selecting File, New. Choose the appropriate page type from the New task pane.

2. The first colors to select can be found in the Page Properties dialog box. Open this dialog box by right-clicking your new page and selecting Page Properties from the popup menu; then click the Formatting tab.

3. Select a color for the background by clicking the arrow to the right of the Background dropdown list. Then, select the More Colors option and select light blue (#CCFFFF), and click OK.

4. Repeat step 3 for selecting a text color. Make sure that the text color has a good contrast to the background color (#000066).

5. With the Page Properties dialog box still open, select Hyperlink (#0000FF), Visited Hyperlink (#0000CC), and Active Hyperlink (#000099) colors.

6. With the Page Properties colors defined, add some text to the page to check the results.

7. Next, add a table with the Table, Insert, Table menu and open the Table Properties dialog box. Set the Background color to be the same as the page background, and select some colors for the border (#FFCC99), light border (#FFFFCC), and dark border (#FFCC66).

8. Add a Horizontal Line by selecting Insert, Horizontal Line; open its properties dialog box. Select its color to be the same as the dark border color on the table (#FFFFCC).

9. Finally, save the page as a template by selecting File, Save As. Select FrontPage Template in the Save As Type dropdown list. In the Save As Template dialog box, include the colors used in the Description box.

Once you've created a color savvy template through this method, you can use the template throughout your Web site and even forward the template for use by others on your team.

You can also use the same approach to develop one of the new Dynamic Web Templates.

→ For more about the use and design of Dynamic Web Templates, **see** "Dynamic Web Templates," **p. 411**.

TROUBLESHOOTING

CHOOSING PROPER COLORS

I'm having trouble choosing colors. Can you give me some tips?

Colors are everywhere. Take a look at the purpose of the site. What type of images do you expect on the site? If it's a company site, start with the colors in the company logo. Look for brochures, signs, or business cards that have colors. If you don't have some basic colors to start from, select some colors from magazines or ads that look good together and use them.

Remember that with the Eye dropper tool described earlier, you can lift colors from anything you can get on your desktop.

MAINTAINING A COLOR SCHEME

I'm working on some pages for events taking place around the holidays. How do I use the holiday colors and not mess up my color scheme?

If you have a color scheme established, don't be afraid to deviate on one or two pages. The holiday colors provide a great chance to add some variety to your pages. Try using small splashes of the holiday colors, or you can abandon your basic scheme for hot pink during Valentine's Day. Visitors will be understanding because they know it's only temporary, and they'll know you have a festive attitude.

FRONT AND CENTER: COLOR AND THE REAL WORLD

43

I'm quite fond of this chapter because it gives you a bunch of great theory and information related to color and Web design. It is good stuff that needs to be taken into consideration. If this is all new to you, go ahead and read the chapter again—good stuff in here.

But, let's shake things up a bit:

I'd like to offer a number of additional ideas related to color and Web design that you should also consider. They come more from the "real world" than they do the "artsy world" that produced the first part of this chapter.

Take a look at the top five sites on the Internet and see what they have in common—yup, simple graphics (maybe 16 colors at the most), a white background, and an easy to read font. Yes, there is a time and a place to be artsy, but there is also a time to get the information to your users quickly and easily. Sometimes Web design is art. Sometimes, it isn't.

Nothing turns off a Web site visitor more than a site that wastes a visitor's time. Do you need millions of colors on a page? Do you really need those background images, multiple images, or huge photos? Is it necessary to have fancy graphics that take forever to load, or would a more simple approach work better? Don't waste your time giving your audience more than they are looking for.

More and more people simply aren't surfing the Internet in color—let alone with a color safe palette. Remember that I often surf the Net on a black and white HipTop phone and that a significant number of people need Web pages read to them—either by a human or a machine. Not everyone sees the colors you are working so hard to perfect—make sure that you have something for them as well.

WEB GRAPHIC FORMATS

In this chapter

UNDERSTANDING GRAPHIC FORMATS

If you are going to place graphics and images on the Internet, you need to understand the different graphics formats and how each of them are used. This is, honestly, an issue independent of FrontPage but belongs in a book such as this in order to provide a complete overview of the Web design process.

The Web and most browsers support three pixel-based formats—GIF, JPEG, and PNG. Subtle differences exist between each of these formats, and understanding these differences can have a big impact on the final look of the graphic.

For example, the GIF format supports only 256 colors, so if you use this format to represent a scanned photo of a forest scene, the image will look like a cartoon because all the colors will be changed to one of the 256 colors the format supports. This can be tragic to the images on your Web pages. A better choice for scanned photographs is the JPEG format, which supports 16.7 million colors.

In addition to color ranges, the formats differ in how they are compressed. To reduce the file size of graphic images to download more quickly over the Web, these Web-based formats compress the image information using compression algorithms.

In this chapter, we'll examine the popular Internet graphic and vector formats and how they work from within FrontPage. We'll also briefly discuss graphic optimization and the conversion between final formats. At the end of the chapter is a section about standards and how they should affect your design process.

GRAPHIC INTERCHANGE FORMAT

The Graphic Interchange Format (GIF) is a file format that uses a *lossless* type of compression, which means that none of the image quality is lost during the compression process. The GIF image compression algorithm works by scanning the image row by row to find sections of color that are the same and storing them as a block instead of as individual pixels.

This compression algorithm works because the GIF format is limited to a total of 256 colors. With only 256 unique colors, the chance of having similar colors appear next to one another is fairly high. Suppose that you have an image of a flag. The information read for this image could be something such as pixel number 1, blue; pixel number 2, blue; pixel number 3, blue; and so on. The long stretch of redundant colors could be more efficiently represented with this: The next 31 pixels are blue. This method of compression is built in to the GIF format.

You can increase the compression ratio even more by limiting the number of colors to less than 256. For instance, images containing only black and white pixels can be compressed to a very small file size.

NOTE

> A bit of confusion exists over the pronunciation of GIF. Many people say it with a hard "g" because logically, if the *G* stands for *graphic*, it would follow that *GIF* (as in GIFt) would be the proper pronunciation.
>
> However, many people, including myself, pronounce the G like a J, or JIF as in JIFFY.

GIFs have been the longest supported graphic file type on the Web, and they are extremely useful for a number of graphic file applications.

WHEN TO USE GIF FILES

Several types of graphics can be saved using the GIF format, including

- **Line-drawn images**—Any graphic that uses few lines, such as a cartoon, is a good choice for the GIF format.

- **Logos**—Company logos created with a drawing package typically use a minimum number of colors.

- **Images with few, flat colors**—With only a few colors and no light sources or gradations in that color, there's not going to be a lot of competition for those 256 colors in the compression method.

Figure 44.1 shows the single color graphic for FrontPage World, which is an excellent choice for the GIF format. Figure 44.2 shows the image bar for FrontPage Talk, with a couple of basic colors, with no light sources or gradations; it also makes the image perfect for the GIF format.

Figure 44.1
The single color FrontPage World logo is the perfect choice for the GIF format.

FRONTPAGE W🌐RLD

Figure 44.2
The FrontPage Talk header graphic is also a good choice for the GIF format.

JOINT PHOTOGRAPHIC EXPERTS GROUP (JPEG)

Frustrated with the limitations of GIF images, a group of photographic experts went to work on compression methods that would allow high-quality compression while retaining millions of colors. The results are what is known today as Joint Photographic Experts Group (JPEG or JPG).

44

The compression algorithm used with the JPEG format is by nature more complicated than the GIF format. JPEGs use a *lossy* compression method, which means that some image quality is sacrificed during the compression process. The algorithm focuses on removing data that is considered unimportant, instead of first mapping out areas of information that should be saved.

The JPEG method does this by dividing the image data into rectangular sections before applying the algorithm. On one hand, this method gives you a lot of control in terms of how much information you're going to toss away; at high compression ratios, however, you can end up with a blocky, blurry result.

These blocky sections are known as *artifacts*. Artifacts occur when you've overcompressed an image. You will look at this a bit later when you step through the optimization process. Working with JPEGs, just as with GIFs, requires a bit of skill and a fine hand to achieve the best results.

The JPEG format enables you to set the amount of compression that is applied. The greater the compression setting, the smaller the file size, but the poorer the image quality.

WHEN TO USE JPEGs

Because the JPEG format was specifically designed to manage files with a lot of color, certain types of images best lend themselves to JPEG compression. The following list is a helpful guide to use when determining whether JPEG is the best format for your image:

- A lot of colors, such as with color photographs (see Figure 44.3)
- Graphics using gradient fills
- Graphics using light sources

Figure 44.3
Pictures, particularly when in full color, contain a lot of gradation and will normally be processed via the JPEG format.

PORTABLE NETWORK GRAPHICS

Another file format supported by most newer Web browsers is the Portable Network Graphics format, PNG for short. This format is newer than the other formats, but it is widely supported by all the latest graphic tools. It is felt that PNG offers even better compression than a GIF while allowing for 16.7 million colors.

Using a lossless compression method, the PNG format offers the color range of JPEG images without the image destroying lossy compression. Another major difference between the PNG and JPEG formats is that PNG images, like GIF images, can be interlaced, making it a very attractive option for the future. Interlacing causes the image to appear line by line as it is downloaded. This gives users an idea of how the image looks as the it downloads.

44

> **NOTE**
> ┌───┐
> │ Older browser versions don't support PNG.   │
> └───┘

FrontPage—as well as many graphic imaging programs, such as Photoshop—includes PNG support for file development and optimization. For more information on the PNG format, visit the World Wide Web Consortium's specification for PNG at http://pngspec. frontpagelink.com.

WHEN TO USE PNGs

The PNG format is best when you find yourself in middle ground, in need of a lot of colors, and still desiring lossless compression. Interlacing images with a lot of colors is another reason to use PNG. This isn't an option with standard JPEG images.

 If you are still having a hard time deciding if you should use the PNG format, see "Use of the PNG Format" in the "Troubleshooting" section at the end of this chapter.

Keep in mind that users who view Web pages with older browsers might not be able to see your PNG images. This format is better used on an intranet with a homogenous browser base. It can be used for the following:

- Line-drawn images with more than 256 colors
- Interlaced graphics with a lot of colors
- GIF images in need of better compression rates

USING VECTOR FORMATS

In addition to the standard bitmap formats, several new vector formats are available, such as Flash and SVG. The Flash format, developed by Macromedia, requires a plug-in to work. Why would anyone want to use a graphics format that requires a plug-in? Vector graphics are represented by mathematical formulas and numbers. This makes their file sizes much smaller when compared to bitmap images.

Animations are another area in which vector formats are a huge advantage. GIF animations require the space of several images shown one after another, but vector animations need to know only how the mathematically defined lines, curves, and colors change over time. This yields a dramatic size savings and can really open your Web presentations to some elaborate full-screen effects.

NOTE

You can import vector images, such as WMF, into FrontPage, but these get converted to a Web friendly graphic format when the Web page is saved.

Make sure that you do the same if you create Word Art with FrontPage or use the FrontPage drawing tools.

MACROMEDIA FLASH

The most popular vector format currently is Macromedia's Flash. The latest version offers advanced features such as music, sound effects, and interactivity. FrontPage supports the Flash format directly. After a Flash file is added to a Web page, several properties can be set. Figure 44.4 shows the Flash Properties dialog box. To access this dialog box, right-click the Flash object and select properties.

→ For more information on inserting Flash files into your FrontPage Web site, **see** "Enhancing Pages with Graphics and Multimedia," **p. 113**.

Figure 44.4
FrontPage lets you change the properties of a Flash file.

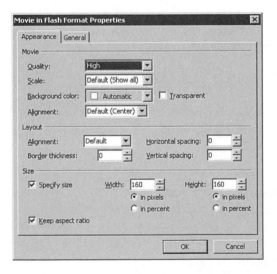

SVG

SVG stands for *Scalable Vector Graphics*. The SVG format is a vector-based format sponsored by the World Wide Web Consortium with broad industry support. SVG is based on XML, which enables the image definitions to be included as text within an HTML document. You also can control the image elements using a scripting language, such as JavaScript.

Because SVG graphics are based on XML, FrontPage can accept SVG images, but the internal FrontPage browser cannot interpret or preview the graphics. Selecting the HTML tab at the bottom of the FrontPage window will let you view the SVG code.

CAUTION

> Currently, only browsers with an SVG Viewing plug-in installed can view SVG files. One such plug-in can be found at the Adobe Web site: `http://svg.frontpagelink.com`. As a result, use this format with caution.

GRAPHIC OPTIMIZATION

Optimizing graphics is the technique by which a Web graphic designer reduces a graphic's file size for acceptable download times while maintaining a high-quality image.

Optimization is all about reducing an image's file size. The file size can be reduced by getting rid of graphical information—preferably, the unnecessary information, such as extra whitespace that surrounds an image. One way to reduce file sizes is to reduce image size; with fewer pixels, less information exists and the file is smaller.

Before optimizing any image, you must determine which file format is appropriate for the image. This will impact your optimization strategy. To recap: The general rule of thumb is to use the GIF file format for line art and images with mostly areas of flat color. JPEGs are more appropriate for full-color, gradient images; PNG is useful if you have an image with more than 256 colors and you're certain that the people accessing the image are using a browser that supports PNG graphics.

CAUTION

> Interestingly, the guidelines discussed within this chapter for these formats are not always accurate for every possible situation. Often, determining which format that will help you achieve the smallest file size while retaining the most important information takes a little experimentation and a good dose of *trial and error*.
>
> Use these guidelines as guidelines only and double test all of your graphic file options.

OPTIMIZING A GIF IMAGE

Several additional ways to optimize GIF images are available. One of these is to throw away colors that aren't being used. A GIF image holds the information for 256 colors, but if an image uses only 56 colors, the extra 200 colors are unnecessary information that can be deleted. You will need a software package such as ImageReady, the image optimization tool that comes with Photoshop, to eliminate the extra colors.

Another optimization method for GIF images is to replace large sections of multiple colors (such as dithered areas) with a single color; the resulting image saved using the GIF format will be much smaller.

OPTIMIZING A JPEG IMAGE

JPEG optimization is easier to control. The capability to optimize an image is one of the key benefits of the JPEG format. Because the JPEG format is a lossy format, it automatically throws away image information based on the user-specified settings. It first throws away the information that no one will miss; but eventually, if you squeeze hard enough, it will discard some noticeable information.

You can use FrontPage to control the level of JPEG compression using the Picture File Type dialog box. This dialog box becomes available when you save a Web page containing graphics. The section "Additional Graphic Techniques," later in this chapter, shows how to use this dialog box. Here's a list of helpful optimization guidelines for the JPEG format:

- Images appropriate to optimization as JPEG files should have many colors, light sources, or color gradients.
- Your initial file should be saved using the maximum quality JPEG setting with no compression.
- The file to be optimized should be appropriately sized for Web use.

NOTE

> Quality settings of 75 and 50 are often similar in visual quality but not always similar in terms of weight. Most of your JPEGs will be saved at a setting of 50, with some at 75, and—if you truly are looking to keep image integrity—very few will be saved at 25 or lower. A setting of 100 is a good setting should you have a reason to want full color with absolutely no degradation.

The more you practice optimization techniques, the more skilled you will become at knowing which type of file format to use, how much or how little to optimize a graphic, and when your specific circumstances allow you leeway for variation in file weight.

ADDITIONAL GRAPHIC TECHNIQUES

Several graphic techniques involving the GIF and JPEG file formats are critical to your Web graphic production work. They include progressive rendering, transparency, and animation. FrontPage can be used for progressive rendering and transparency, but you will need an additional tool to create animations such as Ulead's Gif Animator (http://gifanimator.frontpagelink.com).

PROGRESSIVE RENDERING

This feature keeps a site visitor's visual attention while graphics are downloading from a server to a Web page. The concept is that the individual will see portions of the graphic until all of its binary data is loaded into the browser.

It's an effective method. If you prefer to have your images "pop" into a page, the downloading process appears to be smoother when progressive rendering is in place. You should learn progressive rendering techniques and make your own decisions based on personal and professional preferences.

Progressive rendering can be achieved in both the GIF and JPEG formats.

INTERLACED GIFs

Interlacing is the term used for GIFs that progressively render.

Most popular Web graphic applications support interlacing. When you save a Web page in FrontPage that contains GIF images, the Save Embedded Files dialog box, shown in Figure 44.5, appears. This dialog box enables you to rename the graphic file, change the image folder, set actions, or set various picture options.

Figure 44.5
The Save Embedded Files dialog box lets you rename any images in a Web page.

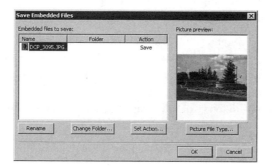

Clicking the Picture File Type button opens the Picture File Type dialog box (see Figure 44.6). This dialog box lets you specify the image format as JPEG, GIF, or PNG. It also lets you specify GIF images as interlaced if desired.

An interlaced GIF will first appear fuzzy and then slowly clarify as the GIF data downloads to the Web browser.

NOTE

> If you view these images in the Preview window or in a browser on your local machine, you might not see the interlacing effect. Even large images will take almost no time to load from your local hard drive, so the interlacing effect isn't noticeable. To see the effect, load the image from a Web server over a slow Internet connection.

Figure 44.6
The Picture File Type dialog box lets you set several image format options.

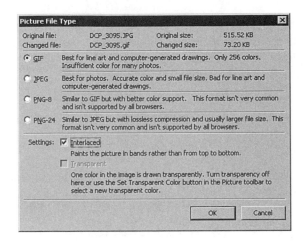

PROGRESSIVE JPEGs

It's important to note that you cannot interlace a JPEG. However, a technology has been developed to enable JPEGs to progressively render. This is the *progressive* JPEG format. FrontPage, as well as many contemporary Web imaging programs, enables you to create JPEGs that render progressively.

As mentioned earlier in the chapter, the JPEG algorithm works by reducing rectangular sections of color data within an image. If you conceptually reverse this process and imagine data flowing in to the rectangular blocks, you will be visualizing the way a progressive JPEG renders. An integrated series of blocks creates the image and first appears with little graphic data. With each new delivery of information from the server, the JPEG blocks receive more data until the download is complete.

Whereas interlaced GIFs first appear fuzzy and then get clearer, progressive JPEGs first appear blocky and blurry.

> **NOTE**
>
> When serving progressive JPEGs at high speeds, the blurry effect is reduced or eliminated, improving the visual experience.

A JPEG image can be made into a progressive JPEG using FrontPage's Picture File Type dialog box. In this dialog box, you can specify the number of progressive passes. These passes are divided by the total time to load the image. If you have a fairly small JPEG image that takes five seconds to load with a setting of five passes, each pass will take roughly one second. This will create a rippling effect as the graphic comes into view.

TIP

Standard GIFs and JPEGs scroll into place rather than render progressively. Some people prefer this look. Still, most usability studies and anecdotal information suggest that progressive rendering helps keep individuals on a page. Therefore, in many cases it's usually wise to progressively render your graphics.

TRANSPARENCY

Transparency can be described as an effect that places your graphic on a clear piece of tape. This means you can place that tape on a background and the background will show through the tape.

This is particularly effective when you're creating graphics that sit on a background—especially graphics that aren't a standard rectangular shape.

The technique takes a little bit of time, patience, and an excellent hand and eye to learn.

Again, FrontPage can create transparent images, but your favorite Web graphics program is likely to have a helpful method by which to make an image transparent.

NOTE

Only GIFs can be transparent. JPEG technology does not include a transparency option.

Assume that you want to place a text header image over a background texture. The text selection is ornate, with a lot of circular shapes. Follow these steps to create a transparency:

1. Open a new page in Normal view.
2. Add a background image by selecting Format, Background. This opens the Page Properties dialog box with the Formatting tab selected.
3. Check the Background Picture box, and then use the Browse button to locate the background image.
4. Click OK to accept the background image. The view should tile the background image.
5. Load the header image by selecting Insert, Picture, From File. If the file doesn't include transparency information, it will look similar to Figure 44.7.
6. Click the image to access the Picture toolbar; click the Set Transparent Color tool.
7. The cursor will change to look like an eraser. Click the color in the image that you want to make transparent.
8. The color you clicked becomes transparent (see Figure 44.8).

TIP

Creating transparent GIF images can leave ragged edges around your image. To reduce the visibility of this edge, try to match the background color in the image to the background color on the Web page. This is something you'll want to do in the program you are designing your graphics in.

Figure 44.7
Adding a non-transparent image to a page with a color.

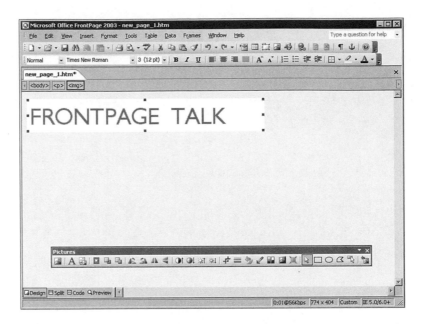

Figure 44.8
A transparent GIF appears seamless over background color.

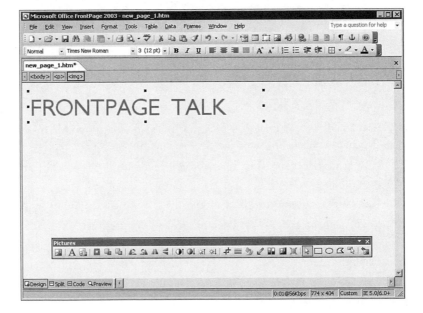

GIF ANIMATION

Another inherent feature of the GIF format is GIF animation. This very handy effect is actually an exploitation of GIF technology. This chapter briefly mentions animation because the GIF animation is directly tied to the file format that parents it.

GIF animations are essentially several GIF images stitched together into one file. You can create an animation effect by crafting your images carefully. FrontPage cannot be used to create GIF animations, but it can place any such animations on a page.

FrontPage won't show the animation in Design view (it will only show you the first frame of the animation) but will show you the animation if you view the file in Preview view.

Special Concerns

Several considerations regarding graphic file formats should be discussed before moving on to other aspects of Web page creation. These include using low-resolution (lo-res) images, splitting large images into several smaller ones, and working with optimization tools.

44

Using Lo-Res Images

As an alternative to progressive rendering, consider the lo-res approach. FrontPage supports, in the Picture File Type dialog box, a lo-res alternative to any image. This lo-res alternative loads before the actual image loads. If you can create a compressed or black-and-white version of the actual image, visitors will have something akin to the image to look at while the actual image is downloaded.

FrontPage can help create a lo-res alternative. With the image selected, click the Black and White tool in the Picture toolbar. This creates a black-and-white version of the image. Save this version with a name that is unique, and include this name in the Lo-Res Alternatives field of the Picture Properties dialog box.

Slicing Images

Another trick for managing large images that are slow to download is to *slice* it, cut the large image into several smaller ones. As the page loads, these pieces will download and become visible before the entire image does.

This technique gives visitors a quick look at portions of the image without the blurry blotches that are common with progressively rendered images.

When using this technique, you should place the cut-up images within a table so that they won't wrap if the browser window is reduced. Be sure to set the borders, cell padding, and cell spacing properties to 0 in the Table Properties dialog box.

 If you are having a hard time putting the pieces of a sliced image back together, *see "Putting the Slices Back Together?" in the "Troubleshooting" section at the end of this chapter.*

Optimization Tools

The optimization tools in FrontPage are limited, so you might need to rely on additional tools to complete your optimizations. For example, Adobe's graphical tools have adopted a common interface for optimizing graphics for the Web. Whether you're using Photoshop,

Illustrator, or InDesign, the Save for Web dialog box will let you visually check the various optimization options.

Several good tools to assist you with image optimization are as follows:

- **ImageReady**—This tool is part of PhotoShop and is available from `http://photoshop.frontpagelink.com/`. It has quickly become the industry standard for image optimization tools.

- **Debabelizer Pro**—This is available from `http:// debabelizer.frontpagelink.com/`. It's the professional-level graphic production tool. It manages the optimization process and includes a batch processing utility that lets you optimize many graphics at once. This is a particularly good choice for Web graphic designers, but it's an expensive program.

- **Ulead Systems SmartSaver Pro**—This is available from `http://ulead.frontpagelink.com/`. For the Windows platform only, this helpful utility enables you to import and then compare graphic optimization types and weights before saving.

- **GIF Optimizer**—This is available from `http:// gifoptimizer.frontpagelink.com/`. You can optimize your GIFs online using this tool, free of charge.

CONVERTING BETWEEN FORMATS

FrontPage makes working between different graphic formats easy. Although you would expect FrontPage to support only the GIF, JPEG, and PNG formats, FrontPage actually can place images in any of the following formats:

- Internet formats (GIF, JPEG, PNG)
- Windows bitmap (BMP)
- Tagged image format (TIF)
- Windows metafile (WMF)
- Sun raster format (RAS)
- Encapsulated PostScript (EPS)
- Zsoft Paintbrush (PCX)
- Kodak PhotoCD (PCD)
- Targa (TGA)

Although FrontPage can import any of these graphic formats, FrontPage automatically converts the image to GIF, JPEG, or PNG when the page is saved. The format depends on the setting in the Picture Properties dialog box. When the page is saved, you are given a chance to rename the image in the Save Embedded Files dialog box before it is saved along with the HTML file for this page. Follow these steps to convert between formats:

1. Open FrontPage in Page View mode by selecting View, Page.
2. Add an image to the page by selecting Insert, Picture, From File.

3. Click the Files of Type drop-down list in the Picture dialog box to see the formats FrontPage can import (see Figure 44.9). Select the file to import.

Figure 44.9
FrontPage supports many industry-standard graphic formats.

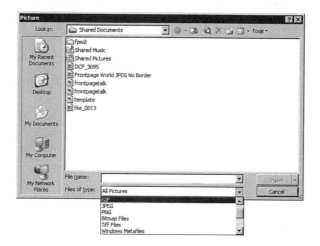

4. Right-click the image and select Picture Properties from the popup menu.
5. Switch to the General tab in the Picture Properties dialog box. Click the Picture File Type button. Select the file type you want to use; then click OK. Figure 44.10 shows a GIF image being changed to a JPEG image.

Figure 44.10
Converting between the JPEG and GIF formats.

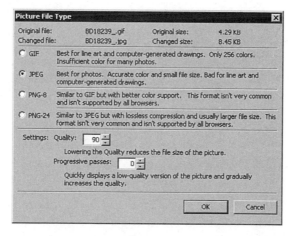

6. Save the page by selecting File, Save. The Save Embedded Files dialog box lets you rename or save the image to a different folder.

TROUBLESHOOTING

USE OF THE PNG FORMAT

PNG and GIF are comparable. I have a graphic tool that can output to PNG; should I use it instead of GIF?

Although the PNG format has better properties, many people on the Web are still using older browsers that cannot display PNG images. If you are worried about this group of surfers, stick with GIF images. If the advantages of using PNG are of more concern than visitors with older browsers, use PNG.

PUTTING THE SLICES BACK TOGETHER?

I sliced an image to cut down on size. How do I get the pieces to fit back together?

The fastest and easiest way to put together a sliced image is by using FrontPage 2003's new Tracing Image tool as a guide. Take the original figure, set it as the tracing image, and then place the image slices around it.

→ For more on FrontPage's new tracing image feature, **see** "Using FrontPage's Image Tracing Feature," **p. 879**.

FRONT AND CENTER: SETTING STANDARDS

It has been said that the Internet loves standards—*that's why there are so many of them on the Internet.*

Everyone wants to set the standards because whoever sets the standards, becomes, *well*, the standard. Makes sense, right? You didn't think Microsoft, Netscape, IBM, or Sun were doing this for posterity, did you?

I continue to read articles about "the next standard" in *x*, where the new standard is often honestly better (smaller, faster, easier, *insert adjective here*) than the standard but because the standard is…well…*the standard*, the new standard simply will never become the standard.

Am I confusing you? Good.

When does a new standard become *the standard*? When enough people say it is. How many is enough? That's the question of the ages.

I love Flash; I do. It is a great product and a lot of fun, and it is certainly the standard for online animation and multimedia. Macromedia continues to release press releases of considerable market penetration.

However, not everyone who comes to your Web site is going to be able to view your Flash animations. Not everyone who comes to your Web site is going to be able to view your PNG graphics.

Heck, not everyone who is going to visit your Web site is going to be able to view your GIFs (optimized or not).

A good Web master keeps on top of these issues.

We presented the major Web graphic formats in this chapter as they apply in October 2003. Although we presented them as standards, new standards might come and old standards might go. You are going to need to keep up-to-date on these issues and, eventually, make the final decisions on what standards you are going to use at your site.

And if everyone can't view your standard files, how standard are they?

The W3C keeps an updated page on the latest in graphics formats at `http://graphicsnews.frontpagelink.com`.

44

CREATING PROFESSIONAL WEB GRAPHICS

In this chapter

PUTTING IMAGES ON YOUR PAGES

At times in the Web design process, clip art provided by FrontPage and Microsoft (or anywhere else for that matter) simply isn't enough and you will need to actually create your own graphics and content for your Web site.

→ For more on the surprisingly considerable clip art collection provided to you, the FrontPage user, **see** "Enhancing Pages with Graphics and Multimedia," **p. 113**.

In this chapter, we look at the different options for graphics on your Web pages and look at ways to both edit existing items to better meet your needs or create new graphics and images from scratch. In the "Front and Center" section at the end of the chapter, we'll examine the use (and abuse) of graphics by the "non-artists" of the world and offer a few options for the "creatively challenged."

A Web site typically uses graphics to design, identify, and navigate.

Some of the images you will use throughout your site include the following:

- **Background images**—These are images that load into the background of the page. Sometimes referred to as wallpaper, background images set the tone of a page.
- **Headers**—Headers give an individual page its identity. They can also include the site's logo.
- **Navigation buttons**—One click of a navigation button, and you're on your way to another page within a site.
- **Bars and rules**—Used to separate text or elements on a page, graphic bars and rules can customize a site's look.
- **Spot art**—This is the term used to describe clip art or photography that will accentuate the textual content on a page.

FrontPage has some unique dialog boxes to create some of these types of images, but you will want to use a graphics tool, such as Photoshop, to create others.

→ For content specifically related to the development of graphics with third-party graphic programs, **see** "FrontPage and Graphic Tools," **p. 887**.

Within these types of images are a variety of techniques to employ to ensure professional quality.

OBTAINING IMAGES FOR YOUR SITE

How do you get images? Essentially, three ways exist:

- Scanning and manipulating photographic and printed materials
- Working with clip and stock art and photography
- Designing your own graphics from scratch or considerably editing other content to meet your needs

Sometimes you will employ all three methods to create a single image. It all depends on the look and feel you've planned for your site.

One thing to remember in the development of graphics for your Web site: *If you begin with poor images, whether from scan or stock, you will end up with poor images.*

To avoid that, you will learn some basic scanning tricks and then take a look at how to choose quality clip art, stock art, and photos.

NOTE

> If you prefer to design your own graphics, an entire section of this chapter walks you step by step through Web graphic creation. See, "Creating Your Own Web Graphics," later in this chapter.

SCANNING IN FRONTPAGE

Scanning is, in and of itself, an art. The good news is that for the Web, you don't need high-resolution scans. This translates into less money spent on hardware, as well as a shorter learning curve for those individuals wanting to get right to the business at hand.

For hardware, a flatbed color scanner or a digital camera is highly recommended. You can buy very inexpensive scanners that will work well for the Web. The guideline is in resolution—because your final image will be 72dpi (dots per inch), you need a scanner capable of scanning only at this resolution. Just be sure that it supports millions of colors and will work with your computer and imaging software.

Here are some guidelines to follow as you prepare to scan your work:

- Be sure that photos are crisp, clean, and free of dust.
- Drawings and prints should be free of smudges and speckles.
- The scanner screen itself should be clean and free of dust. Follow your manufacturer's guidelines when cleaning your scanner.

On the software side, FrontPage is all you need. The Insert, Picture menu has an option called From Scanner or Camera. Selecting this option opens the Insert Picture from Scanner or Camera dialog box (see Figure 45.1). This dialog box supports multiple scanning devices. You can select the scanning device to use in the dropdown list. It also lets you specify the resolution as Web Quality or Print Quality. Clicking the Insert button invokes the scanner's control. The actual software that does the scan depends on the scanner or camera type. If you want to add your scan to the Clip Organizer, select that option in the check box.

After your item is scanned, you should crop it. *Cropping* an image removes any unwanted areas. At this point, you're probably working larger than any recommended Web graphic—both in terms of dpi and dimension. For now, your crop is a preliminary one to remove any whitespace or extra information that you don't want (see Figure 45.2).

Figure 45.1
The Insert Picture from Scanner or Camera dialog box will let you scan or upload a photo directly into FrontPage.

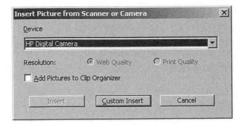

NOTE

> DPI stands for *Dots Per Inch* and represents how many pixels are stored per inch of your image. The higher the DPI, the bigger the image file. Whereas low-end printers print at 300 to 600 DPI, high-end professional printers go as high as 1200 DPI. On a computer monitor, you only need a DPI of 72. As a result, anything over 72 DPI will be lost on your computer screen.
>
> Dimension is the length and width of your file. On a Web page, images only need to be an inch or two long because with DPI, reduction of the image size can greatly reduce the file size (and download time required).

Figure 45.2
Cropping the scan.

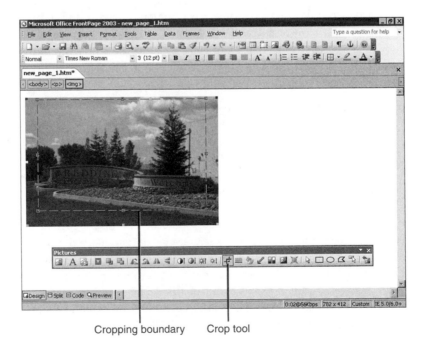

Cropping boundary   Crop tool

TIP

> On occasion, you will find that certain items need a higher resolution scan to truly catch the feel of the image. If this is the case, scan the item at the needed DPI and then resize it to the 72dpi resolution.

The Crop tool can be found on the Picture toolbar. Click it once to enable the cropping boundaries. Move the boundaries by dragging the edges or corners. After you are comfortable with the crop marks, click the Crop tool again to complete the action.

Now you should look for any problems with the scan. Is everything smooth and crisp, or are there smudges and speckles? If the scan isn't acceptable, go back and do it right. It can be time-consuming, but it's well worth it.

If you're happy with the scanned results, set your dpi to 72. If you scanned in at a higher resolution (check your scanning hardware and software for adjusting this), you will see an automatic reduction in the image's dimension.

If you're at 72dpi, you're ready to make any adjustments to the scan. Make alterations to the color; blur or sharpen; and generally sweep, dust, and clean the image to your taste. FrontPage has a number of tools to help modify your scanned images, including Brightness and Contrast.

→ For more information on working with FrontPage's image tools, **see** "Enhancing Pages with Graphics and Multimedia," **p. 113**.

When you're satisfied with the size and quality of your image, save the file as a master image. If you decide to later resize the image or add an edge effect such as a drop shadow or bevel, work with a copy of the master image and retain the master image should you need to start over. It is best to save photographs in the JPEG format to maintain the entire range of colors.

If you're looking to create a page that is accessible across all platforms and browsers (no matter how old), you're working at 640×480 screen resolution. This includes pixels for your scrollbar and other screen real estate. No graphic should exceed 512 pixels in this case, with the exception of backgrounds, which will be explained in just a bit. As for height, some occasions exist in which you will be designing longer graphics; but typically, you want to stick to sizes that fit within the screen.

NOTE

The 640x480 screen resolution rule is pretty extreme. Most designers are working in 800x600, and many are designing for screens bigger than that. You will have to decide which resolution you will design against.

In some instances, you will want to design for higher resolutions in instances in which you are sure of the user. One example is a corporate intranet in which hardware and software specifications are highly controlled.

You're now ready to make additions or changes to your scanned image or to put it aside for later use.

THE MICROSOFT CLIP ORGANIZER

The Office 2003 System ships with a common Microsoft Clip Organizer product that lets you organize your clip art pieces and easily access them from any program in the suite. If you are going to do any amount of work with clip art, this tool, seen in Figure 45.3, is easy to use and highly recommended.

Figure 45.3
The Microsoft Clip Organizer lets you keep all of your clip art pieces in one simple place.

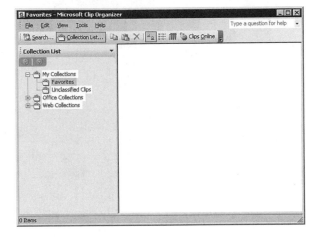

→ For more information on the Microsoft Clip Organizer and how to use it, **see** "Enhancing Pages with Graphics and Multimedia," **p. 113**.

THE PHOTO GALLERY WEB COMPONENT

FrontPage 2003 ships with a Photo Gallery Web component, which enables you to quickly organize photos within pages of thumbnails that are created and annotated automatically by the Web component. If you are going to use a large number of photographs at your site, this tool is recommended.

→ For more information on the Photo Gallery Tool and how to use it, **see** "Enhancing Pages with Graphics and Multimedia," **p. 113**.

SELECTING STOCK IMAGES

Sometimes the right effect can come from a stock image resource. You can obtain stock images from Web sites that sell them or by purchasing them on a CD.

TIP

> Make sure that you have the legal right to use the image or photograph at your site. Most stock image sources have specific requirements to what you can and can't do with their content.

The following are some guidelines for choosing stock images:

■ **Photographic images should be crisp and clear, not blurry.**

■ **Line drawings should have no marks or speckles on them.**

- **You should be able to choose from the file type**—Typically, a JPEG file is acceptable, particularly if it has been saved to maximum capacity. Avoid optimized GIFs, unless you're going to use that file as is or make very minimal changes to it.

- **Read the licensing agreements *very carefully***—You want to be absolutely certain that you have the legal right to use the image.

NOTE

> Photodisc (`http://photodisc.frontpagelink.com/`) gives you a number of stock image options in which you are allowed to choose the kind of file you want to purchase—options are available for file type as well as resolution.
>
> Another great option is ArtToday (`http://arttoday.frontpagelink.com`), which provides links to numerous low cost options for everything from photos to clip art.

Free art sites are variable. You can find great stuff, but you also need to use the guidelines stated earlier to make good decisions when selecting from free clip art and photos.

TIP

> Just because someone claims that you are free to use a graphic from his site (a common claim at free graphics sites), it doesn't mean that you are. If he has no right to give you such permission, you can be penalized for taking it.

CREATING YOUR OWN WEB GRAPHICS

In this chapter, I'll step you through a variety of tasks and demonstrate and describe features, problems, and helpful hints that will help you create your own Web graphics for your specific needs.

 If you are having a hard time figuring out the specific term for the specific type of image you are looking for, *see "Categorizing Images" in the "Troubleshooting" section at the end of this chapter.*

WORKING WITH BACKGROUND IMAGES

Three kinds of background images exist:

- **Wallpaper patterns**—These are small squares that tilè in to create a smooth, seamless texture that looks like well installed wallpaper (no burps, seams, or bungles).

- **Margin tiles**—Also referred to as *strips* because they are wide and short, margin tiles can be functional or decorative in nature.

- **Watermark style**—This is one large background graphic, usually square, that adds an image, logographic material, or color to the background of a page.

One important issue to remember is that *all backgrounds are tiles.* They might not look like tiles, but they will always act like tiles whenever the resolution of a screen changes.

Wallpaper patterns, which are squares, will tile into the browser one by one until the available space is filled.

Margin tiles fill the browser in the same way—except it might seem as though they don't because of their sizes and shapes.

Finally, watermark tiles, which are very large squares, tile in the same way that wallpaper and margin tiles do. Therefore, you have to be careful when creating watermarks.

 If you are having a hard time making your backgrounds visible on an older system, *see "Making Backgrounds Visible" in the "Troubleshooting" section at the end of this chapter.*

WATERMARKS

Watermarks are especially difficult to create because of the tiling issue. The idea with watermarks is to keep them simple, with very few colors, because this is the only way you can make larger graphics look good.

To develop your own watermark, create a very large tile, 1024×1200 pixels. At that size, no matter the resolution, the effect will generally be the same.

Use as few colors as possible. By limiting colors and saving the image using the GIF format, the large, consistent areas of color are efficiently compressed. Save the file as a GIF with no dithering.

To see the results, create a new page in FrontPage and load the watermark graphic as the background image (see Figure 45.4). One of the options in the Formatting tab of the Page Properties dialog box in FrontPage is a Make it a Watermark check box. This check box causes the background graphic to remain stationary as the page is scrolled. This is supported only in browsers that support this feature.

NOTE

You can get the same effect by setting the large watermark image as a background graphic. It won't tile if it's large enough, and serves the same purpose, without the potential browser problems.

HEADER GRAPHICS

Headers are used to identify a site and a page within a site. One type of header is the *splash header*. This typically fills a larger piece of real estate on the opening page only. It identifies the site with the company logo or brand and sets the visual tone for the rest of the site.

A *page header* is smaller but still boldly visible along the top and left, middle, or right edge of an internal page.

TIP

A great product that does nothing other than create impressive header graphics can be found online at `http://headergenerator.frontpagelink.com`.

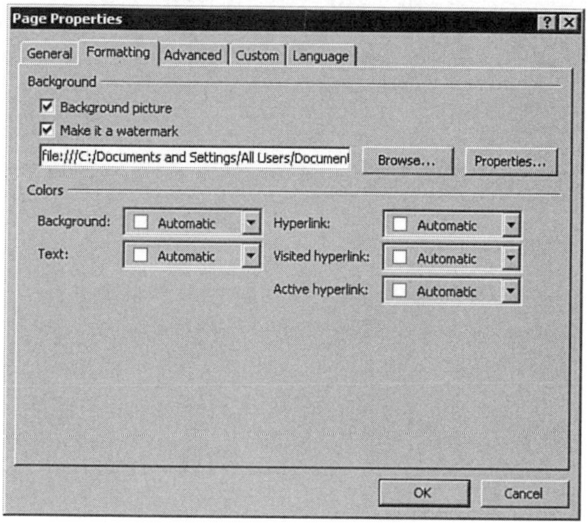

Figure 45.4
A watermark-style
background is set in
FrontPage.

BUILDING A SPLASH PAGE

Creating a splash page is easy to accomplish with any graphic development tool and FrontPage:

1. Create the new graphic file.
2. Enter the desired dimensions in pixels of the splash screen image.
3. Add the graphic in the center of the workspace.
4. Use a text tool to add text on top of the graphic.
5. When the graphic is complete, save it as a JPEG image (because the image contains many unique colors).

To create the splash page using the splash image you just made, use FrontPage's Insert, Picture, From File command. The resulting splash page will look similar to Figure 45.5.

From the original splash header, creating internal page headers is just a matter of resizing the original. In FrontPage, just grab one of the corners and drag it to the desired size. To resize the actual graphics file, click the Resample button on the Picture toolbar. This page header can then be used on additional pages as needed or loaded into the Navigation bar.

TIP

> A large percentage of Internet users consider a splash page to be little more than an annoyance. They were interesting years back but now do little more than frustrate your audience.

Figure 45.5
The splash graphic in place.

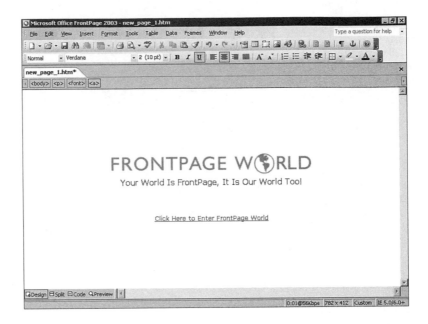

BUTTONS IN FRONTPAGE

Navigational buttons can be made up of text, images, or a combination of both.

In this section, you learn how FrontPage can be used to make a simple beveled button.

For this exercise, start with a simple graphic image that you want to make into a beveled button. Then, do the following:

1. In FrontPage, load the button graphic by selecting Insert, Picture, From File.
2. Select the graphic and click the Bevel button on the Picture toolbar.

The beveled button was added to the page. The result is shown in Figure 45.6.

> **TIP**
>
> The Interactive Button tool, new to FrontPage 2003, also produces impressive buttons with just a few clicks of the mouse.

→ For more information creating Interactive Buttons with FrontPage, **see** "Using Interactive Buttons," **p. 441**.

BARS AND RULES

At times, you might like an effective, decorative bar or rule to demarcate sections of a Web page. You can either create your own bars to match the look and feel of your site or use FrontPage to modify horizontal rules accordingly.

Figure 45.6
A simple beveled button created in FrontPage.

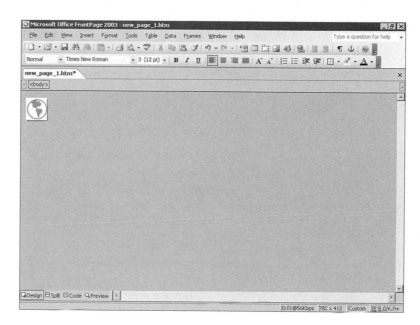

If you're going to create your own bar, I'd recommend the following:

- **Don't stretch the bar from margin to margin**—Instead, make a bar that is either centered with some whitespace to either side or aligned to the right or left. Cutting the margins separates space dramatically and could cause disruption in cohesiveness of both the design and the content.

- **Use a treatment**—This can be something such as a drop shadow, curved or angled lines, something that's hand drawn, or broken lines (anything to give the rule a fresh look).

FrontPage can create a variety of horizontal rules for you, or you can make your own and import them as a normal graphic. Figure 45.7 shows a number of horizontal rules options.

STANDARD HORIZONTAL RULES

To use FrontPage's horizontal rules (or *lines* as FrontPage calls them), select Insert, Horizontal Line. Within the Horizontal Line Properties dialog box, you can specify width, height, alignment, and color. You can also toggle shading on or off (see Figure 45.8).

SPOT ART

Spot art serves to enhance and accentuate text. It can be clip art or photographs.

Figure 45.7
Several attractive horizontal rule options.

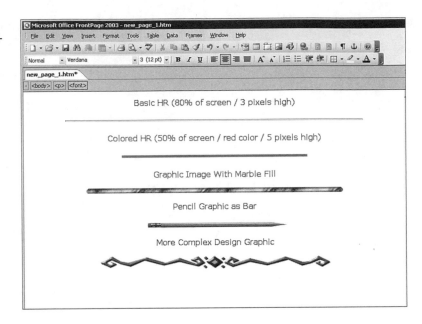

Figure 45.8
Setting the horizontal line properties.

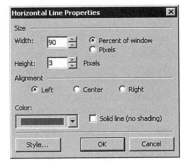

To make spot art stand out from the norm, it's fun to add edges, shadows, or bevels for effect. However, you do have to be careful with the use of effects because of the additional weight they can add to a page.

Hand-drawn art, cartoons, and clip art can add variety and personality to your sites as well.

Whichever you choose, you should be consistent and creative—not conflicting and clichéd—throughout a site. It always surprises me to find that people have created slick graphics only to mix them with a piece of overused, worn out clip art.

Another concern is dimension. Spot art is akin to italic or bold on a page—it's about emphasis, not dominance. You want your spot art to blend well into the overall scheme of your design. Pay close attention not only to the dimension in relation to the screen size, but also from one photo to another.

Backgrounds, headers, rules, and spot art—you're wrapped up and ready to go!

TROUBLESHOOTING

CATEGORIZING IMAGES

I've seen images used on the Web that don't fall into any of the categories mentioned here. How would you categorize them?

Web page design is a creative process. There are no hard, fast rules on using images. The categories in this chapter represent some of the more common uses, but it isn't a complete list. Don't be afraid of trying different ideas of your own.

MAKING BACKGROUNDS VISIBLE

If I use a background image, how can I ensure that visitors to the page will be able to read the text?

If you use a background image with a lot of details and colors, you could be in danger of making the text on your page illegible. One good method to try is to use the Wash Out tool on the Picture toolbar in FrontPage. This reduces the brightness of the image and makes the text easier to read.

FRONT AND CENTER: MODERATION

It is so much fun for many people to create a Web site full of fun graphics, cool backgrounds, great pictures, and cute clip art. With a product such as FrontPage 2003, all these effects can be done with a few clicks of the mouse and are almost always guaranteed to make someone say "Wow!"

That's the good news.

Now for the bad news:

You don't always need to. As a matter of fact, you seldom need to. Admit it, what do you do when you visit a site with ugly backgrounds and more graphics than needed?

I'd bet a good steak dinner that if you removed 80% of the graphics from the Web, no one would notice, the Web would work a lot faster, and a lot more business would be done.

Take a look at your Web site. Why are those graphics there? Here are some questions you should really ask yourself.

Do I need this background image? What does it really do for my site?

That clip art—why is it there? Does it need to be there? What would happen if I took it away?

That slideshow—does anybody care? Could I reduce the pictures by 50% and have the same effect?

Do I need so many horizontal rules to break up my text? Is a paragraph break enough?

Why did I put that Splash Screen there? If I finally get people to my site, do I really want a page that says "Welcome to my site, click here to visit my site?"

Moderation. Moderation. Moderation.

Another simple question should be asked, *"Am I the one best qualified to create the graphics for my site?"* Many people who aren't graphics designers or artists by any means somehow feel qualified to produce images for a Web site because the tools are so simple to use.

The tools might be simple, but you still want someone who knows what he is doing on the other end. Yes, hammers are very impressive, but I'm still going to let someone else build my house for me.

If you aren't qualified to build your own graphics, what can you do? Sometimes, someone on your team can help. Ask around; you might be surprised with what you find.

There are several other options for you: You might need to purchase the talents of an artist to help you design the graphics you need. You might want to purchase a clip art or stock photography CD to assist you in your needs. Or, you could consider buying a third-party Web theme or Web template to help push you in the right direction.

45

USING FRONTPAGE'S IMAGE TRACING FEATURE

In this chapter

IMAGE TRACING

It is hard to design a Web site from scratch. Sitting at a desk with little more than FrontPage to create how your site will look is both overwhelming and, in some ways, impractical. Sometimes you need a little push to start the process.

For others, the process of design is simply beyond their reach. This type requires a standard from which to start the design process.

New to FrontPage 2003 is the ability to place an image in the background of the Design view so you can "trace" your site around the image. This gives you the ability to create a Web site layout from a single image.

> **NOTE**
>
> Image tracing is only a tool used from within FrontPage. Any images used in this feature will not be seen by anyone viewing your site content.

By tracing a site from an image, a designer can quickly lay out a site with a graphical representation of how it should look. Developing a site design from an existing graphic through this method also allows you to divide the design elements in to a layout that is considerably faster to render and load.

WORKING WITH THE IMAGE TRACING TOOL

Use of the tool is a simple as telling FrontPage which image you would like to set as the tracing image. FrontPage will then place the image at the coordinates you set at the opacity you specify. In Figure 46.1, FrontPage has placed an artist's rendition of a Web page at 50% opacity. No content has been added to the page.

USING THE TRACING IMAGE DIALOG BOX

To add a tracing image to any open page, select <u>V</u>iew, Tracing I<u>m</u>age, <u>C</u>onfigure. This will open the Tracing Image dialog box, as seen in Figure 46.2.

> **NOTE**
>
> You can only use one tracing image on your screen at a time.

Once you have configured the image, you can toggle it on or off with the <u>V</u>iew, <u>S</u>how Image Tracing, I<u>m</u>age command.

 If you are having problems with opening your graphic for tracing in FrontPage, see "File Doesn't Show Up" in the "Troubleshooting" section at the end of this chapter.

Figure 46.1
The background image seen is not part of the Web page; it is a BMP file set as the tracing image at 50% opacity.

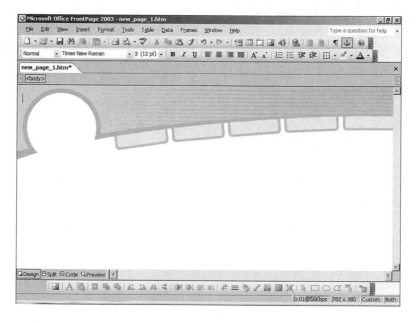

Figure 46.2
The tracing image dialog box lets you select the image file, the opacity, and the x,y location for the image.

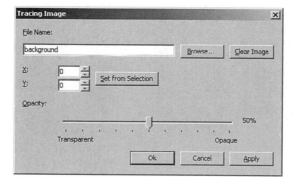

SETTING THE TRACING IMAGE LOCATION

The Tracing Image dialog box lets you set the x,y position for the image. If you set the image to an x,y location not currently available in your design, you will not be able to see the image until your design makes the location available.

SAVING A FILE WITH A TRACING IMAGE

If you save a Web page that contains a tracing image, you will be given the opportunity to save the tracing image as an embedded file, as seen in Figure 46.3.

The tracing image file will not be seen when viewed as a Web page. It can only be seen when the page is edited with FrontPage 2003.

46

Figure 46.3
Saving a Web page that contains a tracing image will result in FrontPage asking you to save the embedded file.

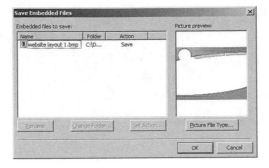

TIP

If you are doing a considerable amount of work with tracing images and expect to have several tracing images in your site, consider a naming convention for the files that reminds you of their purpose and lets you quickly identify them. In addition, consider placing them in a directory containing only tracing images so that the entire directory can be deleted at project completion.

TRANSFER A DESIGN WITH THE TRACING IMAGE TOOL

To transfer an existing graphic design image or picture to a Web layout, you simply set the tracing image, re-create the pieces on your site, and compare you work to the final design. These steps are described in detail next.

SET THE TRACING IMAGE

Initially, you will want to place the entire graphic on the site as your tracing image. You can then produce a page layout using the Layout Tables and Cells task pane.

→ For more on the Layout Tables and Cells task pane and its role in the design process, **see** "Using Tables," **p. 189**.

In Figure 46.4, a very simple table layout has been developed using a single graphic file as the background image.

PLACE THE PIECES

Once the site is laid out in terms of tables, the artist's rendition can be cut into pieces, greatly reducing the size of the initial site. The pieces can then be placed in the layout tables accordingly. You can cut up the images using any graphics program that you feel comfortable with and that can handle the file type you are working with. This method is referred to by many in the industry as "*slicing*."

TIP

A great tutorial for slicing images with ImageReady can be found at http://slicetutorial.frontpagelink.com.

Figure 46.4
By using the Layout Tables and Cells task pane, the user built a layout around the artist's rendition of the site.

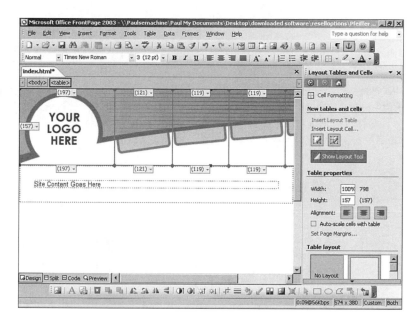

→ For more on using third-party graphics tools to edit your FrontPage images, **see** "FrontPage and Graphic Tools," **p. 887**.

46

TIP

> Don't attempt to cut up site images using FrontPage's cropping tool. Your requirements are too specific for this approach.

In Figure 46.5, the simple site graphic was cut in to a header and footer piece with a table in the middle for the insertion of content.

After the pieces have been placed, creative use of background colors or images can be used to provide a blend with the site elements. By cutting out the considerable amount of whitespace in the original site design in Figure 46.5, the graphic size is cut down considerably without the loss of any quality at all.

COMPARE YOUR WORK

After the site elements have been placed in the appropriate tables, the tracing image can be toggled off to assess if anything was forgotten or misplaced.

When the site passes the initial inspection within the FrontPage Design and Preview views, it should be tested in numerous browser and screen size types to ensure that the original design expectations are met.

 If you are having problems with your layout not looking exactly as you'd like it to, *see "Layout Is Off Just a Bit" in the "Troubleshooting" section at the end of this chapter.*

Figure 46.5
The original site design graphic was chopped in to three pieces. The white-space in the middle was discarded.

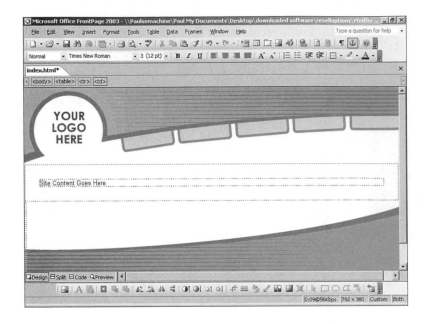

OTHER USES FOR THE IMAGE TRACING TOOL

You might want to consider using the image tracing tool for assisting you in the design of dynamic Web templates. Because dwts traditionally have very specific layout requirements, tracing against any previously designed layout could make great design sense. You can also use the tool to learn better Web design skills.

We examine both of these issues in this section.

USING IMAGE TRACING TO DESIGN DYNAMIC WEB TEMPLATES

Dynamic Web Templates are a means for developers to create multiple Web pages that share the same layout. They also allow the "locking" of areas of pages from editing by others within the Web design team. Dynamic Web templates are easily designed through the use of the image tracing tool.

They are by their very nature cut up in to tables. Certain cells are made available for editing, whereas others are locked. This prevents information workers from making considerable layout or markup mistakes.

→ For more on the Layout Tables and Cells task pane and its role in the design process, **see** "Dynamic Web Templates," **p. 411**.

Image tracing can be an ideal tool for designing Dynamic Web Templates. The inspiration for such templates often comes from a mock-up image that can be used in their design.

→ For more on the development and use of dynamic Web templates, **see** "Dynamic Web Templates," **p. 411**.

USING IMAGE TRACING TO LEARN DESIGN

FrontPage has always provided a means for the developer to experiment and learn the Web design process directly in the FrontPage interface. Deconstructing the HTML code of another site or learning HTML by watching how FrontPage authors it are examples of the possibilities FrontPage allows for.

One of the more powerful features of the image tracing tool is the ability to take a screenshot of a site or design you want to learn from. Place the screenshot within your Design view and begin creating your own site, emulating and learning from the design.

How many tables did they use to accomplish the design? Would you have done things differently? Can you figure out where the tables are?

CAUTION

> This is a feature for learning design, not copying the designs of others. Web designs can be copyrighted, and FrontPage is not a tool to steal the work of others.

The proper use of designing via tables takes a considerable amount of practice and experience. Grabbing a quick screenshot, placing it the background, and designing around it is a quick, easy, and effective way to learn (and perfect) this art.

TROUBLESHOOTING

FILE DOESN'T SHOW UP

My artist designed a site for me in PhotoShop and sent me the file. I want to trace it in FrontPage, but it won't appear as an option. What should I do?

The PhotoShop file extension (.psd) is not supported by the image tracing feature. Simply have your artist resave the file as a GIF, JPG, TIF, of BMP file. If your designer is worried about loss of file quality, remember that this image is only used for tracing and is never seen in the final site.

LAYOUT IS OFF JUST A BIT

The layout I designed from a traced image is off just a few pixels. I can't figure out how to make the images fit together without any spacing.

Any cells created through the Layout Tables and Cells task pane are exactly sized down to the pixel. If the cells that hold your images in layout tables designed for this use aren't the exact size of the images, space will appear in the cell areas not used by the image. Make sure that cells are the exact size of the images they contain.

FRONT AND CENTER: A FEW THINGS TO CONSIDER

The impact and importance of the image tracing tool can't be denied. Being able to develop and manipulate a page design around the images that will be included in the page is a popular feature seen in other Web design products. This is a powerful addition to FrontPage and, like many of the features added in this release, part of the feature set that makes FrontPage 2003 a tool equal in power to the competition. It is great to see it included. There are, however, a few dangers to using the tracing tool and the general approach of making Web pages as you would produce content traditionally printed. (These dangers are true of any Web design product that uses this paradigm for design.)

If you use the tool to produce Web designs that do little more than mimic an artist's rendition of what your site "should look like," you face a lot of potential problems. The simple fact that your artist designed your site in another graphics program instead of a Web design product shows that he doesn't understand Web design. Why would he develop on another platform if he did? (I'm sure I'll get some email because of that last comment, but I stand by it.)

There are variables in Web design outside of your control, such as font selection, font size, screen size, screen resolution, color quality, and the like. If you forget these issues in Web design and take a more "page layout" approach to development, you will find your pages are ineffective on other configurations and completely unusable on any nontraditional browser. With the hundreds of browsers and platforms surfing the Net, you can't assume anything and shouldn't design anything based on such an assumption. For example, some browsers resize images based on screen real estate. You are not guaranteed that they will manipulate your layout proportionally—or that they are even capable of doing so.

I'm not saying that you can't bring good layout to effective Web design; I'm saying that you need to make sure that your page includes both.

Artists are powerful (and necessary) in effective Web design, but they often don't understand *your design medium*. Stay on top of this important issue.

In addition, accessibility issues also come to play here. Every time extensive design is done with tables and graphics, the chances of producing a truly accessible site become less and less.

→ For more on accessibility, FrontPage, and Web design, **see** "FrontPage's Accessibility Features," **p. 235**.

The image tracing tool is not without merit when developing a solid Web design. Making sure that text is positioned well around a graphic or that text doesn't fall into a menu image is a solid idea. In addition, if you know the platform your audience will be viewing your site on, you obviously have more leeway in developing your site to specific design conditions.

And, as always, you can develop different sites for different browsers, but unless your budget is in the tens of millions, I suggest that there are better places to spend your money.

46

FRONTPAGE AND GRAPHICS TOOLS

In this chapter

AN OVERVIEW OF GRAPHIC OPTIONS

In the world of Web development, there is no doubt that content is king, but without high-quality graphics to round out the site, your content is nothing more than a king without clothes. Quality graphics are vital to a quality Web site.

FrontPage has some limited graphic capabilities. For example, you can use Clip Art or AutoShapes or a combination of the two. Using FrontPage's Pictures toolbar, you can manipulate the image somewhat, but no matter how much you massage Clip Art and AutoShapes, you still end up with Clip Art and AutoShapes. Few Web developers are willing to use Clip Art for all of their graphic needs.

→ For more information on Clip Art, **see** "Working with Clip Art," **p. 115**.

→ For more information on using AutoShapes, **see** "Drawings, AutoShapes, and WordArt," **p. 115**.

→ For more information on using the Pictures toolbar, **see** "Manipulating Clip Art Using the Pictures Toolbar," **p. 119**.

Most Web developers rely on an external graphics program for their graphics needs. Many packages are available on the market today that range from the professional-level tool with an appropriately high price tag to the open-source solution with no price tag. Any of these tools are a better choice than relying on FrontPage's limited graphics capabilities.

Two of the most widely used tools for Web graphics are Adobe Photoshop and Ulead PhotoImpact. Photoshop represents the professional-level segment and has the strongest feature set and highest price tag. PhotoImpact is geared toward the casual user, but it has some powerful features that rival just about anything else available.

NOTE

> Another tool commonly used for Web graphics is Jasc Software's Paint Shop Pro. This chapter covers Ulead's PhotoImpact 8.0 instead of Paint Shop Pro because of PhotoImpact's better graphic optimization toolset for Web graphics, but you might want to check out Paint Shop Pro on your own by visiting `http://www.jasc.com`.
>
> Adobe also offers a scaled-down version of Photoshop called Photoshop Elements. Although Photoshop Elements doesn't have the same capabilities as the full version of Photoshop, it does offer a substantial number of great features at a significantly reduced price. Check it out at `http://www.adobe.com`.

Through the course of this chapter, you will be using the `farmpond.jpg` file located in the CH47 folder on the CD accompanying this book.

ADOBE PHOTOSHOP

In the world of graphics applications, Photoshop (shown in Figure 47.1) is the boss. No application on the market today has the power that Photoshop wields. You will hear plenty of people talk about other less expensive graphics applications and how they can do everything that Photoshop can do. Don't believe them. Photoshop does more than other graphics tools, and it does them better. Such advanced functionality carries a high price: about $600.

Figure 47.1
Photoshop is the premiere graphic design package.

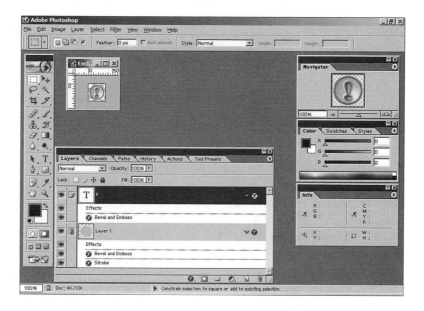

Photoshop includes ImageReady, Adobe's tool for designing Web graphics and optimizing graphics for the Internet. ImageReady (shown in Figure 47.2) includes all the tools you need for getting your graphics ready for the Internet, including tools for making rollover buttons, image maps, and slicing images.

Figure 47.2
ImageReady has all the tools you need for developing Web-specific graphics.

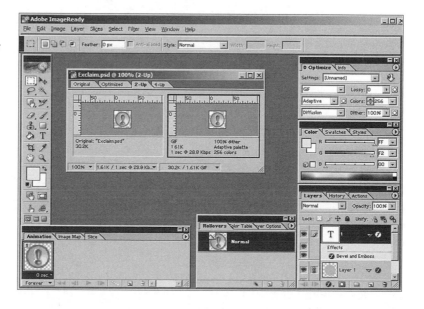

47

A trial version of Photoshop is available from Adobe. Visit http://www.adobe.com for more information.

NOTE

For more information on using Photoshop and ImageReady, read *Special Edition Using Adobe Photoshop 8* from Que Publishing.

ULEAD PHOTOIMPACT 8.0

Ulead's PhotoImpact (shown in Figure 47.3) has been around for a long time. It is a quality tool with an extended feature-set, and it's put out by one of the leaders in graphics and multimedia. PhotoImpact has tools to enable you to create graphics and enhance existing graphics such as pictures from your digital camera or scanner. PhotoImpact doesn't have all the same high-end capabilities of Photoshop, but it has the advantage of a lower price tag: about $90. For that $90, you get quite a lot.

Figure 47.3
Ulead's PhotoImpact 8 has a lot of power for the price.

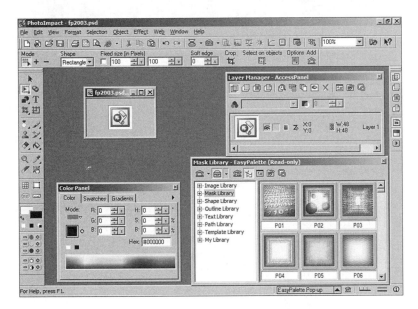

PhotoImpact has one of the best image optimization toolsets available as shown in Figure 47.4. PhotoImpact uses the same image optimization engine used in Ulead SmartSaver Pro, the standalone image optimization tool from Ulead that is widely considered the best image optimization tool available. This feature alone is worth the price of the software.

Ulead offers both a boxed and downloadable version of PhotoImpact. The downloadable version uses a tool that Ulead calls Smart Download to install features into PhotoImpact. When you download PhotoImpact, you get the primary program without the hundreds of megabytes of additional tools. You can then decide what libraries you want to add as you work and download only what you need when you need it. This is a great approach, especially if you want to optimize hard drive space.

A trial version of PhotoImpact is available from Ulead. Visit http://www.ulead.com for more information.

Figure 47.4
PhotoImpact's image optimizing features are as good as or better than anything available.

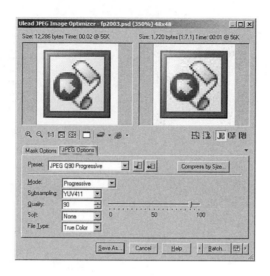

➔ For more information on using PhotoImpact, check out Stephanie's PhotoImpact Tutorials at http://www.eastofthesun.com.

CONFIGURING FRONTPAGE FOR YOUR GRAPHICS APPLICATION

FrontPage is configured by default to use the Microsoft Office Picture Manager (shown in Figure 47.5) when you open an image file. The Microsoft Office Picture Manager is suitable for editing photos taken with a digital camera or scanned in from a scanner. It has features such as red eye removal and other tools that are designed to be used on photos. However, for designing graphics or editing existing Web graphics, the Microsoft Office Picture Manager is not your best choice. You will be much better off configuring FrontPage to automatically use your image editing application.

To reconfigure FrontPage to use your chosen image editor, use the Options dialog box in FrontPage:

1. Select Tools, Options.
2. Click the Configure Editors tab.
3. In the Extensions list, select jpg jpeg gif png.
4. Click the New Editor button as shown in Figure 47.6.
5. In the Open With dialog box, select your image editing application as shown in Figure 47.7. If it's not listed, click the Browse for More button and browse to the executable file for your image editing application.

47

Figure 47.5
The Microsoft Office Picture Manager is the default graphics editor in FrontPage. You will almost certainly want to change it.

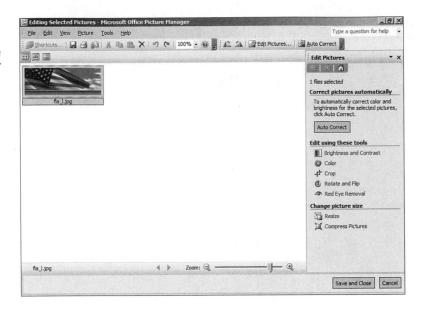

Figure 47.6
The Configure Editors tab in the Options dialog box lets you configure your image application as the default image editor.

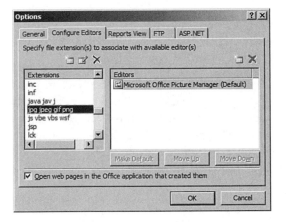

Figure 47.7
Select your image application in the dialog box or click the Browse for More button to select it.

TIP

If you're using PhotoImpact as your image editor, the executable filename is Iedit.exe and is located in the folder in which you installed PhotoImpact.

6. Click OK to return to the Options dialog box.

7. Select your newly added image editing application in the Editors list and click the Make Default button.

8. Click OK to apply your change.

Now that your image editing application is configured, it will be used to open images automatically from within FrontPage.

 If you get the Picture Properties dialog box instead of your image editing application when trying to edit an image, *see "Picture Properties Instead of Graphics Application" in the "Troubleshooting" section of this chapter.*

RESIZING IMAGES

When editing images for use in a Web site, one of the most common tasks is resizing them so that they will download more quickly. You can get fair results using FrontPage's built-in image editing capabilities, however, FrontPage is not always the best choice for this procedure.

File size is one of the most important considerations when saving images for use on the Web. Large file sizes mean long download times, and long download times mean fewer site visitors. Paying careful attention to image optimization is the key to keeping image sizes small.

FrontPage's built-in tools don't offer a lot of control over how an image is saved. You can choose the file format and the amount of image compression used. However, if you're really going to optimize your images as they should be, FrontPage just doesn't provide the necessary tools.

→ For more information on the options available when saving graphic files in FrontPage, **see** "Inserting Graphics Files," **p. 117**.

Import the farmpond.jpg file (from your CD) in to a FrontPage Web site and insert it onto a page. The first thing you will notice about this file (see Figure 47.8) is that it is large. You wouldn't want to use this file on a Web page because it would take more than 1.5 minutes to download over a 56K modem connection.

TIP

Even though the images you are using from the CD are in JPEG format, when editing images for your Web site, you should not use JPEG images. JPEG is a lossy format, which means that most editing on them causes a loss in quality that can never be retrieved. The more times the image is edited, the poorer the quality gets.

You should always save original copies of your images in a lossless format such as BMP or—better yet—the original file format of your graphics application.

47

Figure 47.8
The `farmpond.jpg` image after being inserted into a Web page. The image definitely needs to be resized.

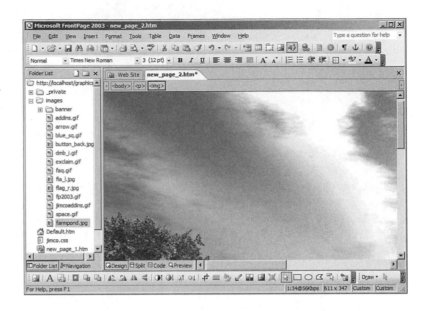

To resize the image, open it in your image editing program by double-clicking it in the folder list in FrontPage, or by right-clicking it and selecting Open With and the application you would like to use to open it.

Figure 47.9 shows the Image Size dialog box in Adobe ImageReady. Notice that the Quality dropdown is set to Smooth (Bicubic).

Figure 47.9
Adobe ImageReady's Image Size dialog box.

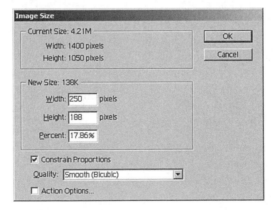

47

TIP

> Bicubic resizing is your best choice if you are making an image smaller. However, if you are increasing the size of the image, bicupic resampling will often cause unwanted blurring. You should experiment to find the best results for the image you are resizing.
>
> When you choose the Resample Picture to Match Size option on FrontPage's Picture Actions menu, FrontPage uses bicupic resampling to increase the quality of the image.

Figure 47.10 shows PhotoImpact's Image Size dialog box. PhotoImpact offers the same basic functions as ImageReady, but it adds some nice features, such as a preview that can be set to specific screen sizes so that you can see the relative size of the image when compared with common screen resolutions. In Figure 47.10, the farmpond.jpg image has been resized, and the preview shows its relative size to a 640x480 monitor resolution.

Figure 47.10
PhotoImpact's Image Size dialog box. The screen size setting in the Preview window is very convenient for Web developers.

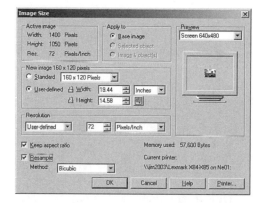

After you've resized your image, you will need to save the image back into your FrontPage Web site. In most cases, you can simply save the image in your image editing application and it will save your change directly into the Web site. However, if you need to, you can also save the image into the physical directory (that is, c:\inetpub\wwwroot\mywebsite) where your Web site resides. If your change is not visible in FrontPage after saving the image, refresh the page or close and reopen the page.

Figure 47.11 shows the farmpond.jpg image after being resized. Note that the download time is now 4 seconds over a 56K connection. That's quite an improvement.

 If you don't see your changes in FrontPage after saving your image, see *"Changes Not Visible in FrontPage"* in the *"Troubleshooting"* section of this chapter.

Figure 47.11
The `farmpond.jpg` image after being resized to a more suitable size.

DESIGNING GRAPHICS FOR YOUR WEB SITE

In addition to making changes to existing graphics, you will often need to create new graphics completely from scratch. This is often the case when you are redesigning your Web site or designing a new Web site. It's often easiest to design a page inside your graphics software and then slice up the graphics for use in your Web site.

Figure 47.12 shows an image mock-up of a Web site design. This image was created at a size of 1500 pixels wide and 500 pixels in height. The banner at the top was then created inside a 3D graphics package and pasted into the image.

To make the image a bit more appealing, a gradient bar will be added below the banner. Gradients are visually appealing graphical elements that are easy to create and add a sense of depth to a graphic.

Creating the gradient bar is very easy in Photoshop using the Gradient Editor shown in Figure 47.13. The gradient is configured to move from a dark blue to a lighter blue. The gradient is then applied to a selection as shown in Figure 47.14 to make the bar.

After adding the gradient bar, the only remaining item is a text logo for the site. Both Photoshop and PhotoImpact have excellent text tools to make adding professional looking text to an image easy. Figure 47.15 shows the mock-up with text added.

Figure 47.12
A Web page mock-up
created in Adobe
Photoshop.

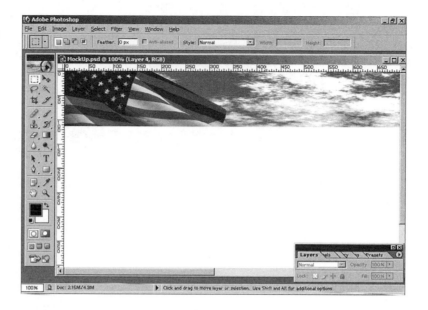

Figure 47.13
The Gradient Editor in
Photoshop. Gradients
are great for adding
depth to Web
graphics.

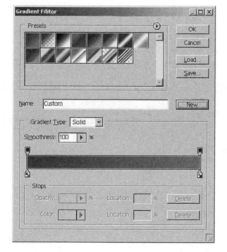

SLICING GRAPHICS

The Web page mock-up was created as a single large file in order to make it easier to lay
out the graphics in the proper proportion. Now that the graphic creation is complete, the
graphics need to be prepared for the Web page.

Figure 47.14
The gradient applied to a large rectangular selection.

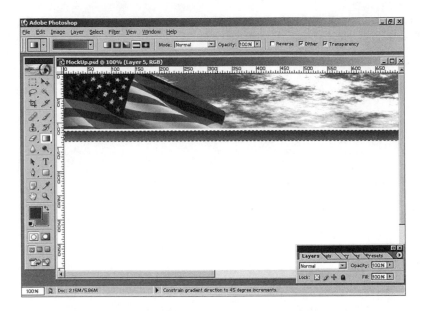

Figure 47.15
The graphics are now complete and ready to be prepared for the Web page.

47

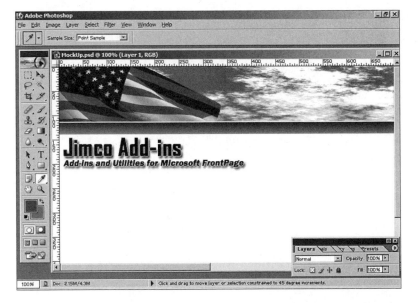

Obviously, the graphics need to be as small as necessary. Therefore, all the extra whitespace around them needs to be removed. Because the Web page will have a white background, you can remove any empty white areas of the mock-up graphic.

Both PhotoImpact and Photoshop make it very easy to slice up an image. They also allow you to easily specify image optimization settings for individual slices. This is especially handy because not all slices in an image are created equal. Figure 47.16 shows the Web page mock-up with slices applied in PhotoImpact. Notice that the Jimco Add-ins logo is in its own slice and the flag in the banner is in its own slice. The flag should be saved as a JPEG image, but GIF is the best format for text. Both PhotoImpact and ImageReady make it easy to save each slice in the format you choose.

Figure 47.16
The Web page mock-up with slices applied in PhotoImpact. Notice that the Slice Panel dialog box allows for optimizer settings for each slice.

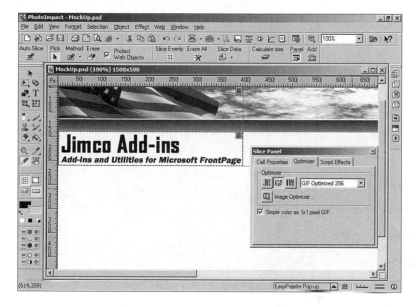

This Web page will consist of three different images. One will be the flag in the upper-left corner, another will be the Jimco Add-ins logo text, and the third will be the remainder of the banner to the right of the flag. The rest of the whitespace in the graphic will be discarded. Slices are created for each of the three graphics as shown in Figure 47.16.

SAVING SLICES

Adobe ImageReady is a bit more flexible than PhotoImpact when it comes to saving your slices. Figure 47.17 shows the Output Settings dialog box in ImageReady. These settings are used when you want ImageReady to generate the HTML file to contain your graphics. Although you can use FrontPage's Layout Tools to configure your Web page, it's often easier to let your graphics program do the work for you.

→ For more information on Layout Tools, **see** "Using Layout Tables," **p. 201**.

ImageReady allows you to choose whether you want it to create the HTML page for your images. In Figure 47.18, ImageReady is configured to save the HTML page and the images as indicated in the Save As Type dropdown. If you select Images Only, ImageReady will save only the images and no HTML. PhotoImpact does not offer this option. When you save slices using PhotoImpact, you must save the HTML page as well. Figure 47.19 shows the completed HTML page generated by ImageReady.

47

Figure 47.17
ImageReady makes quick work out of generating the HTML necessary to build your Web page.

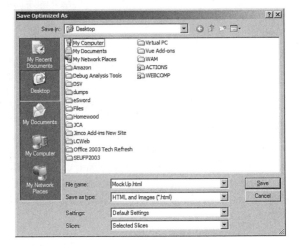

Figure 47.18
ImageReady offers more options than PhotoImpact when it comes to saving slices.

Once the Web page has been saved by the graphics editing software, the images are ready to be imported into your Web site. You can then save the generated page as a Dynamic Web Template, and you're ready to add content for your new Web site.

 If your images show up as broken links after importing your new HTML file, *see "Images Broken After Saving" in the "Troubleshooting" section of this chapter.*

→ For more information on Dynamic Web Templates, **see** "Creating Dynamic Web Templates," **p. 412**.

Figure 47.19
The ImageReady-generated Web page opened in FrontPage. All that's left is adding content.

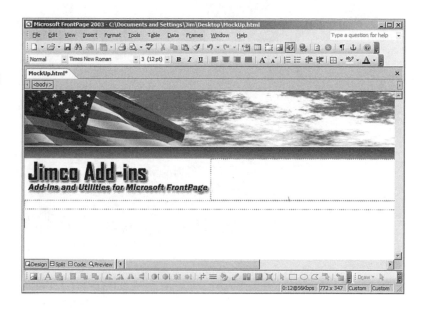

CREATING WEB BANNERS

Another very common use of graphics on Web sites today is Web banners. Because most Web sites that use Web banners rotate the graphics, it's important that any Web banners you create are the correct size. The standard size for a Web banner is 468 pixels wide and 60 pixels high.

NOTE

> The Web banner size of 468×60 was chosen because it takes up a full page width on a 640×480 display. Most people run at a resolution of at least 800×600 these days, but the standard size of Web banners remains 468×60.

47

Both PhotoImpact and Photoshop provide preset settings for creating Web banners. Figure 47.20 shows PhotoImpact's New Image dialog box configured for a Web banner. Figure 47.21 shows the same configuration in Photoshop.

Let's create a new Web banner for FrontPageCart.com, a new e-commerce Web site. If you look at its logo at http://www.frontpagecart.com, you will notice a beveled circle and the site name on a black background, as shown in Figure 47.22. Reproducing this in an attractive Web banner should be fairly simple with the powerful toolset provided by Photoshop or PhotoImpact.

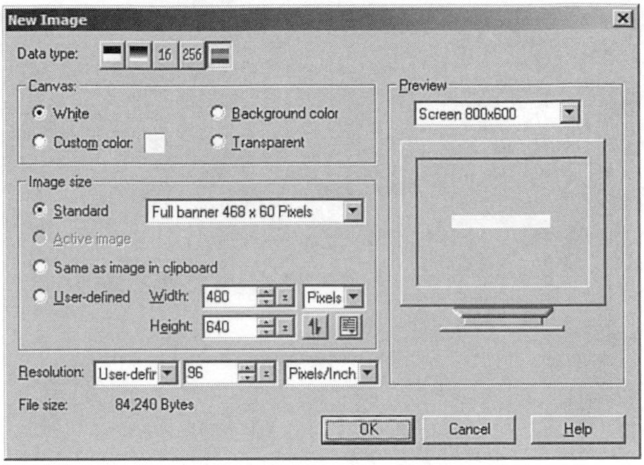

Figure 47.20
The New Image dialog box in PhotoImpact configured for a new Web banner.

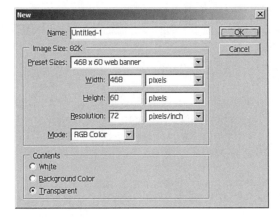

Figure 47.21
The New dialog box in Photoshop configured for a new Web banner.

You will want to start with the red circle. Notice that the edge is slightly beveled. Using a bevel is an easy way to make an image appear three-dimensional. As shown in Figure 47.23, PhotoImpact uses the Button Designer dialog box to apply a bevel. Figure 47.24 shows the Photoshop's Layer Style dialog box with the Bevel and Emboss option selected. PhotoImpact offers more flexibility in this area because it allows for the easy configuration of multiple light sources, which light the object from the top and the bottom.

Figure 47.22
FrontPageCart.com is a new e-commerce site for FrontPage and shows a great idea for a Web banner.

Figure 47.23
PhotoImpact's Button Designer allows for up to four light sources.

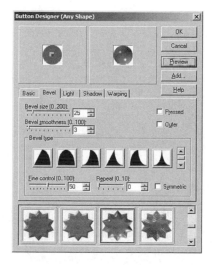

47

Figure 47.24
Photoshop's Bevel and
Emboss options pro-
vide high quality out-
put, but with only one
light source.

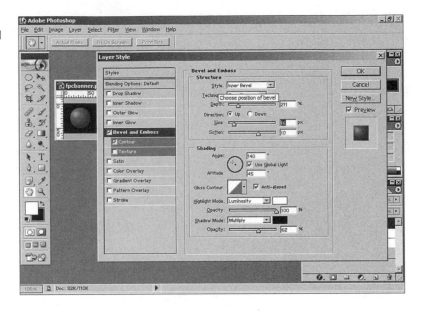

To complete the banner, text needs to be added. Verdana was chosen as the font to use for
the banner because it is the same font used in the original logo. Both PhotoImpact and
Photoshop allow you to enter and format text directly on to the image. This is a great
advantage because it lets you see what your text looks like in real-time. Figure 47.25 shows
the Text Panel in PhotoImpact and the FrontPageCart.COM text entered in to the banner.
Figure 47.26 shows the Photoshop equivalent.

Figure 47.25
PhotoImpact's Text
Panel makes config-
uring text simple.

47

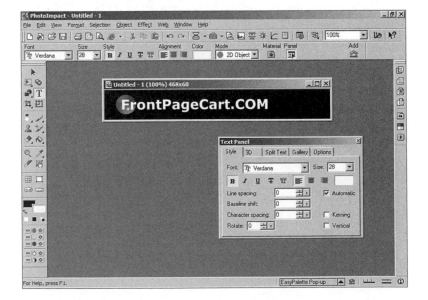

Figure 47.26
Photoshop's text tools are very similar to PhotoImpact's.

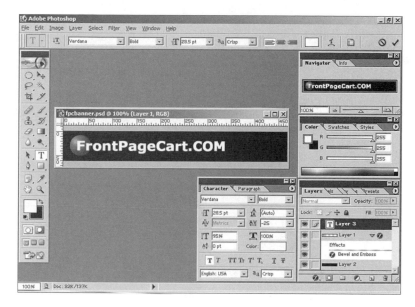

To finish out adding text, the COM part of the logo needs to be changed slightly. FrontPageCart uses Trebuchet MS as the font for the COM, and the size on those three letters is slightly reduced. PhotoImpact and Photoshop make it easy to change part of your text by simply selecting the text just as you would in a word processing program and changing the properties on it. Figure 47.27 shows the updated banner with the font corrected.

Figure 47.27
The text entry is complete and matches the look on the FrontPageCart Web site.

47

The last step in reproducing the FrontPageCart logo is to add a shadow to the text. PhotoImpact and Photoshop both offer comprehensive tools for configuring shadows. PhotoImpact's Shadow dialog box is shown in Figure 47.28. Figure 47.29 shows Photoshop's Drop Shadow options. Photoshop's capabilities far surpass PhotoImpact's in this area.

TIP

> One thing I don't like about PhotoImpact is that an object must be selected prior to adding effects. When you select an object, a dotted line marches around the object and that can make it hard to clearly see the effects of your edits. Photoshop does not select layers in this way when you are applying effects.

Figure 47.28
PhotoImpact configures shadows using the Shadow dialog box. This dialog box is more frustrating than Photoshop's Drop Shadow options.

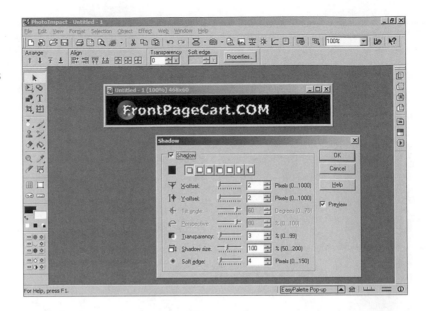

Figure 47.29
Photoshop's Drop Shadow options are much easier to use than PhotoImpact's Shadow dialog box.

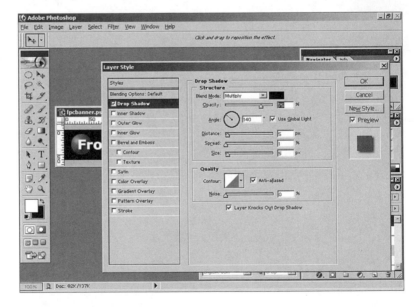

PhotoImpact and Photoshop also provide tools that allow you to add shapes to an image to make it more interesting. By adding shapes to simple graphics, you can make them appear much more professional and interesting, and callouts are a great approach when you want to draw attention to something in particular.

The final touch for the banner is to add a description of what FrontPageCart is as well as a thin white border, and it's ready for adding to your Web site. Figure 47.30 shows the finished banner displayed on the Jimco Add-ins Web site.

Figure 47.30
The completed Web banner proudly displayed on the Jimco Add-ins Web site.

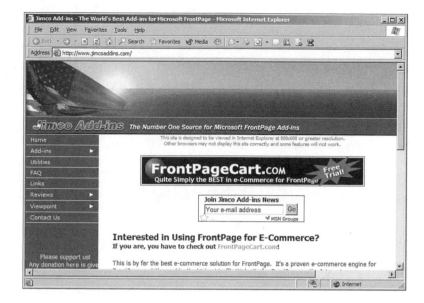

TROUBLESHOOTING

PICTURE PROPERTIES INSTEAD OF GRAPHICS APPLICATION

I've configured by graphics application as the editor for graphics files, but when I double-click an image, it just brings up the Picture Properties dialog box.

If you double-click on an image inside Design view in FrontPage, you will get the Picture Properties dialog box instead of your image editing program. If you want to edit the image in your graphics application, you can do it in several ways:

- Double-click the image file in the Folder List.
- Double-click the image file in any file list in FrontPage.
- Right-click the image file and select Open With and then select your graphics application.
- Open the Picture Properties dialog, click the General tab, and then click the Edit button.

CHANGES NOT VISIBLE IN FRONTPAGE

I've made changes to an image and saved it, but my changes are not visible in FrontPage even after refreshing the page view.

When you edit an image directly from FrontPage, it is saved into a temporary folder and then opened from there. FrontPage should take care of moving the file back to your Web site when you save it, but sometimes it doesn't.

It you find that your changes are not visible in FrontPage after refreshing the view using **View, Refresh**, try saving your file to another folder (such as your Desktop) and then importing it into your Web site. If you are working on a local Web site, you can also save the file directly into the Web site's disk drive location.

IMAGES BROKEN AFTER SAVING

I've just sliced up an image and saved the HTML file from my graphics software. After I imported the HTML file into my Web site, all the images are broken and don't display.

Most image editing software, including PhotoImpact and ImageReady, save sliced graphics into a folder by default. If you import the HTML file that these application create into your Web site, make sure that you also import the folder containing the images that were sliced. After you import all the files into FrontPage, you can move the image files into the folder of your choice and FrontPage will update your links.

FRONT AND CENTER: GRAPHICS FOR THE ARTISTICALLY CHALLENGED

This chapter has shown you some techniques for developing graphics that can be used by both artists and non-artists. However, any amount of graphic design takes some investment in time and money. Even if you opt for PhotoImpact's $90 price tag as opposed to Photoshop's whopping $600 price, you will still have to invest a significant amount of hours into learning the product you choose. Many users of Photoshop have been using it for years and still don't understand more than half of its features. These applications are not easy to learn.

You might be better off going another direction. Many options are available for those who are artistically challenged or for those who simply don't have the time to invest in purchasing and learning a graphics application.

One option is to hire a graphic designer. If you have one specific need for some graphics, this might be a viable option. When you choose this route, you are paying for someone else's expertise and time, so the costs could be more than you're willing to pay. You will likely end up paying much more than the cost of a copy of Photoshop, but you will not have to invest in the time to learn anything.

Another option, and perhaps a better one, is to purchase stock graphics. Graphics can be purchased in collections containing tens of thousands of graphics, or they can be purchased individually online. A quick Internet search for "stock graphics" or "stock images" should turn up more sources than you can possibly imagine. Most of the collections that include tens of thousands of images offer graphics similar to Clip Art, but they also tend to include many photographs and Web-specific graphics as well.

One other option available to Web developers is to take your own photos to be used for your graphics. A digital camera can go a long way toward building a collection of high-quality and unique graphics. Most digital cameras offer a macro mode, which will allow you to take photographs at very close distances. Try using the macro mode on your digital camera and take extreme close-ups of simple objects around the house. You'd be amazed at how quickly you can build up a collection of great looking images.

APPENDIXES

FRONTPAGE RESOURCES ONLINE

In this appendix

FRONTPAGE INFORMATION ONLINE

A tremendous wealth of information is available online regarding FrontPage and Web design. Some of these resources come from Microsoft, whereas others are produced by avid FrontPage enthusiasts and organizations that provide FrontPage related products and services. Options are not just limited to the Web—there are message board and newsgroup options for data as well. We highlight many of these resources in this appendix.

NOTE

> The very nature of the Web is change. By the time this book is published, a number of the sites and resources mentioned in this appendix will change their URLs. As a result, we provide all links in this chapter in the format `http://sitename.frontpagelink.com`. The link will forward you to the correct URL and will be updated if or when the sites change location. If you find that any of these links no longer work, notify `support@frontpagelink.com` and someone will update the link accordingly.

In addition to FrontPage-specific sites and information, we end this appendix with a series of links regarding additional topics such as scripting, Internet marketing, and more.

MICROSOFT'S OFFERINGS

Microsoft has spent a great deal of time and money bringing much of its information and offerings online so that users can access product-related information quickly and easily.

FRONTPAGE'S AREA AT MICROSOFT.COM

FrontPage's area at Microsoft is largely and commonly a marketing effort but contains regularly updated information on FrontPage related issues deemed important by Microsoft. It should not be your only FrontPage reference online, but it should be monitored on a regular basis.

```
http://frontpageatmicrosoft.frontpagelink.com
```

THE FRONTPAGE COMMUNITY PAGE

Microsoft is currently heavily promoting the concept of "community" surrounding each of its products. Although this approach is yet unproven and constantly changing, the FrontPage Community site offers great links to FrontPage sites, solid information, and great product support. It also serves as a great jumping off point for other members and sites in the FrontPage Community.

```
http://frontpagecommunity.frontpagelink.com
```

THE FRONTPAGE ADD-IN CENTER

The Add-in Center was designed as a place for developers to submit add-ins for FrontPage to be shared with the larger FrontPage Community. It is by no means an exhaustive resource and contains as many demos as fully functional products, but it remains a great place to find ways to extend FrontPage.

```
http://addincenter.frontpagelink.com
```

THE FRONTPAGE FANZINE

The FrontPage Fanzine is Microsoft's free monthly email newsletter that highlights information available at Microsoft and third-party Web sites. This link also provides and archive of previous issues.

```
http://frontpagefanzine.frontpagelink.com
```

THE WEB PRESENCE PROVIDER PROGRAM

Web Presence Providers (WPPs) provide Web site hosting services for FrontPage or SharePoint Team Services. They are certified by Microsoft to fully support the products. If you are not sure where to host your FrontPage Web site, this would be a great place to look.

```
http://wppprogram.frontpagelink.com
```

THE FRONTPAGE MVPS

Microsoft has an MVP (Most Valuable Professional) program that highlights the efforts of non-Microsoft employees to promote and support their products in the marketplace. The FrontPage MVPs represent a tremendous amount of FrontPage learning and experience outside of the Microsoft bubble.

```
http://frontpagemvps.frontpagelink.com
```

NOTE

> Author Paul Colligan is a FrontPage MVP.

THE FRONTPAGE AREA AT MSDN

MSDN (Microsoft Developer Network) is a resource for the more technically minded user of Microsoft products. The FrontPage area of MSDN is updated on a regular basis with developer-specific FrontPage related information.

```
http://msdnfrontpage.frontpagelink.com
```

A

OTHER FRONTPAGE RELATED WEB SITES

Microsoft is not the only source for great FrontPage related content on the Internet. In addition to what Microsoft has to offer, a number of great resources are online from FrontPage enthusiasts and companies alike.

FRONTPAGE WORLD

FrontPage World is the Internet's most visited FrontPage related Web site not located at Microsoft. It has been part of the FrontPage community since FrontPage 97 and offers solid information and provides a jumping off point for numerous sites on the topic. FrontPage World also provides a number of free and highly recommended email newsletters with a specific emphasis on doing business online with FrontPage. Paul Colligan (the author of this appendix) is the Webmaster for FrontPage World.

        http://frontpageworld.frontpagelink.com

ACCESS FRONTPAGE

Access FrontPage proudly claims to find "*FrontPage Resources so you don't have to*" and does a tremendous job of doing just that. This *exhaustive* resource provides links and information on all aspects of FrontPage, including all previous versions of the product.

        http://accessfp.frontpagelink.com

ANY FRONTPAGE

Any FrontPage is the combined effort of a number of popular FrontPage related Web sites that have pulled their talents together to provide a solid resource for FrontPage. Their newsletter is also very popular in the FrontPage community and highly recommended.

        http://anyfrontpage.frontpagelink.com

AT FRONTPAGE

At FrontPage provides FrontPage information, tips, tutorials, tools, templates & themes, add ins, and free goodies. The site is run by a FrontPage MVP and worth a regular visit.

        http://atfrontpage.frontpagelink.com

FRONTPAGE HOWTO

FrontPage HowTo teaches users how to integrate databases and scripting to produce dynamic content with FrontPage. The site is filled with a lot of examples and applications for those who like to learn by example.

        http://frontpagehowto.frontpagelink.com

OUTFRONT

OutFront is another standard on the Web for FrontPage related information. The site's emphasis is on the integration of FrontPage with the specifics of Webmastering.

        http://outfront.frontpagelink.com

EXTREME FRONTPAGE

"Surfer Frank" keeps his mantra of "Surf HARD" by reporting on the FrontPage and Web Development scene with this unique blog. If you want to keep up-to-date with the latest in the politics of FrontPage, Microsoft, and the other players in the industry, you will do well to bookmark this site.

```
http://extremefrontpage.frontpagelink.com
```

NEWSGROUPS AND DISCUSSION BOARDS

Web sites are not the only option for finding great FrontPage related information. In this section, we highlight a resource on FrontPage related newsgroups and examine two popular FrontPage message boards.

THE MICROSOFT PUBLIC NEWSGROUPS

Microsoft continues to provide a great deal of support for its products through its public newsgroups—available through most Internet service providers. In addition, the public newsgroups are a tremendous source for peer-to-peer support that is hard to find elsewhere.

TIP

> The world of newsgroups can seem a bit overwhelming to many people, but it is well worth the effort once you get over the initial hurdle. Although Outlook Express continues to get better as a newsreader, there are also a number of ways to access newsgroups through a Web interface. One is offered through the link that follows this tip and another can be found through `http://googlegroups.frontpagelink.com`.

The following link takes you to a reference at Microsoft regarding the latest news on the newsgroups and provides additional information and options on how to access them.

```
http://frontpagenewsgroups.frontpagelink.com
```

FRONTPAGE TALK

FrontPage Talk is the Web message board to thousands of active users who have made tens of thousands of FrontPage related postings to this very popular Internet destination for talking about FrontPage.

```
http://frontpagetalk.frontpagelink.com
```

OUTFRONT WEBMASTERS

OutFront Webmasters is another popular Web board focusing on both FrontPage and Webmastering.

```
http://outfrontwebmaster.frontpagelink.com
```

A

FRONTPAGE STORIES

This new site provides a place for FrontPage users to post their "FrontPage Stories" related to the sites they built, the problems they faced, and the lessons they learned. The site allows for other users to comment on the stories in a traditional Web portal format that encourages a tremendous amount of user interactivity. Although this site was brand new at publication, the potential for this project deserves a visit from (and the participation of) every reader of this book.

```
http://frontpagestories.frontpagelink.com
```

WEB SOURCES FOR FRONTPAGE ADD ONS

In addition to the FrontPage Add-in Center described previously, a number of sites are on the Internet that highlight and provide FrontPage Add Ons. Although many are freely available, others can be purchased online, and often provide for an instant download.

JIMCO ADD-INS

Jimco Add-ins offers add-ins and utilities for FrontPage that are not found anywhere else; best of all, they're all free! Many of the add-ins available on the Jimco Add-ins Web site are the direct result of requests from FrontPage users, and Jim has always been willing to enhance existing add-ins to meet people's needs. The co-author of this book, Jim Cheshire, is the Webmaster for Jimco Add-ins.

```
http://jimcoaddins.frontpagelink.com
```

FRONTPAGE TOOLS

FrontPage Tools is the largest online retailer of FrontPage related templates, tools, and training, and it sells add-ins from numerous vendors around the Internet. The site is updated on a regular basis with new products and specials and is worth frequenting often.

```
http://frontpagetools.frontpagelink.com
```

ASP AND .NET RESOURCES

If you are going to extend FrontPage by integrating scripting and database capabilities, a quick view of the Internet's offering on these technologies would be well worth your time and effort.

15 SECONDS

15 Seconds is part of the Internet.com Web network. Site keeps you up-to-date with the latest Active Server issues with articles, news, downloads, and code examples.

```
http://15seconds.frontpagelink.com
```

DevX

DevX provides comprehensive information on software development for corporate applications. Its sections specific to Microsoft technologies will be an asset for anyone looking to do higher end programming with FrontPage.

```
http://devx.frontpagelink.com
```

ASP.NET Web

ASP.NET is the Official Microsoft ASP.NET Web site and keeps great information on books, community sites, recently released code. Site also provides a comprehensive article library that is updated daily.

```
http://aspdotnet.frontpagelink.com
```

The ASP.NET Area at MSDN

MSDN, Microsoft Developer Network, is a resource for the more technically minded user of Microsoft products. The ASP.NET area of MSDN is updated on a regular basis with developer-specific FrontPage related information.

```
http://msdnaspdotnet.frontpagelink.com
```

Visual Studio

If you will be doing considerable work with ASP.NET and other Microsoft related technologies, an examination of the Visual Studio Product is certainly in order.

```
http://visualstudio.frontpagelink.com
```

WINDOWS SHAREPOINT SERVICES RESOURCES

As Windows SharePoint Team Services integrates so tightly with FrontPage, links and information related to the product will benefit any user attempting to bring these two technologies together.

TIP

> It is important to point out that SharePoint is a less matured technology than FrontPage, and Microsoft is still figuring out the market positioning, naming, and conventions for the product. As a result, there are sure to be additional sites and information not located here. Keep your eye on Microsoft site's listed after this tip as a means to keep up with this rapidly changing segment of Microsoft's ever-maturing business model.

A

WINDOWS SHAREPOINT SERVICES AT MICROSOFT

This is the home for Windows SharePoint Services at Microsoft.com. Contains downloads, articles, and support specifically for the SharePoint Windows Services product line.

```
http://sharepointatmicrosoft.frontpagelink.com
```

THE SHAREPOINT FAMILY

A lot of different products and technologies have the SharePoint name. To get a better idea of what the different products are and how they all link together, visit this link for the latest, as Microsoft sees, thing.

```
http://sharepointfamily.frontpagelink.com
```

THE SHAREPOINT AREA AT MSDN

MSDN, Microsoft Developer Network, is a resource for the more technically minded user of Microsoft products. The SharePoint area of MSDN is updated on a regular basis with developer-specific SharePoint related information.

```
http://msdnsharepoint.frontpagelink.com
```

THE SHAREPOINT COMMUNITY

Microsoft is attempting to build a strong community associated with the SharePoint Family of products. Use this link as a strong jumping off point to see what others are doing with the product.

```
http://sharepointcommunity.frontpagelink.com
```

SHAREPOINT UNIVERSITY

SharePoint University is a large third-party community dedicated to all SharePoint Technologies. The site provides expert level advice, a chat room and discussion forums, training, and professional service.

```
http://sharepointuniversity.frontpagelink.com
```

OTHER SITES WORTH NOTING

Because the Internet connects a number of technologies and practices together, it is important to understand the relationships between different technologies and disciplines. The following sites will give you a better understanding of FrontPage, the technologies it interacts with, and the industry it is part of.

OFFICE ONLINE

Office Online is currently positioned to provide assistance to all Microsoft Office users. The site offers links to training and support assistance from Microsoft and third-party providers. In addition, the site offers links for additional peer-to-peer support opportunities.

```
http://officeonline.frontpagelink.com
```

NOTE

> With the release of the Microsoft Office System, Microsoft is exploring a number of new options for communication and support. At the time of writing, Office Online was seeing tremendous support and growth, so we mention it here. It would be pointless to assume that Microsoft will not be continually developing additional efforts, so don't consider this section to be the last word on Microsoft's offerings.

OFFICE MARKETPLACE

Web services (especially paid ones) are becoming more prevalent in the marketplace as are third-party providers with products and services that support FrontPage (and the other Office products). The Office Marketplace is a (new to Office 2003) Microsoft-sanctioned area where approved vendors can market their wares to the larger Office Community. The following link takes you directly to the FrontPage area of the Office Marketplace, but links within will take you to other content regarding products for the entire Microsoft Office System.

```
http://officemarketplace.frontpagelink.com
```

INFOPATH AT MICROSOFT

This link takes you to the main page at Microsoft for InfoPath (previously entitled XDocs). If you are interested in integrating information shared via XML Forms with FrontPage, this site will provide a solid starting point for your efforts.

```
http://infopath.frontpagelink.com
```

BUILDER.COM

Builder.com is the developer channel of CNET's collection of technology related Web sites. It continues to maintain a strong collection of resources and articles that should be visited regularly by anyone wanting to keep up-to-date on the bigger picture of site building.

```
http://builder.frontpagelink.com
```

WEB SITE ACCESSIBILITY RESOURCE CENTER

This regularly updated site contains important links and information regarding the latest issues in Web site accessibility issues. Because it is run by a FrontPage MVP, you know the content will remain FrontPage friendly.

```
http://wsarc.frontpagelink.com
```

A

THE REAL START PAGE

Internet marketing guru Marlon Sanders assembled this collection of links as an alternative "Start Page" for users interested in Web design and Internet marketing. The page contains links to great resources all over the Internet, including HTML resources, merchant account information, Web site tools, and sources for free content online. Consider making it your home page as well.

```
http://therealstartpage.frontpagelink.com
```

123WEBTEMPLATESANDMORE.COM

If you are looking for a cheap resource for Web templates, ebooks, and other training options, you might want to look here. The templates aren't specifically designed for FrontPage, but they can be easily integrated into a FrontPage Web site; and the site offers a membership plan much cheaper than the traditional purchase per use model offered by others.

```
http://123webtemplates.frontpagelink.com
```

INTERNET MARKETING RESOURCE LIST

This page maintains an up-to-date link of popular Internet Marketing resources highlighting resources and information popular in the industry.

```
http://internetmarketing.frontpagelink.com
```

NOTE

E-commerce specific links will be highlighted in Appendix B, "FrontPage and E-Commerce."

A

FRONTPAGE AND E-COMMERCE

In this appendix

A BRIEF LOOK AT E-COMMERCE

The purpose of this appendix is not to give you everything you need to know about FrontPage and e-commerce—it is to provide you with a simple understanding of the essential elements of FrontPage and suggest possibilities and solutions for how some products can help you develop an e-commerce solution for your Web site. You will need to do your homework to find which products and solutions are ideal for your situation.

A lot of great information exists in this appendix, as well as links to many of the top e-commerce providers on the Internet today. It is a big Internet filled with a lot of great information, so make sure to do your homework before you step into this exciting world.

Many people go online for the very purpose of conducting commerce on the Internet. Being the "next Amazon" seems to be the dream of many, and FrontPage can help you in your quest.

There are products and services for e-commerce that integrate directly with FrontPage, and there is also a wealth of e-commerce products that could easily integrate with any FrontPage Web site. Because of FrontPage's easy integration with existing sites and technologies, the entire world of e-commerce is open to the FrontPage user.

NOTE

> The e-commerce landscape is always changing players and pricing. Although the links used in this chapter are dynamic and will be updated when needed, pricing and package elements are obviously subject to change without notice.

E-Commerce is, simply, the act of conducting some element of commerce online. It could be something as simple as a local deli providing a faxable menu from its Web site to the completely integrated online-only store with millions of product in its inventory.

TIP

> I've seen too many overly enthusiastic Internet entrepreneurs purchase expensive e-commerce systems before they understood the complexity (online and off) of integrating e-commerce with their Web sites.
>
> Doing your homework before starting this process is even more important when dealing in the world of e-commerce because the money to be lost on a bad mistake is considerable and can affect such issues as your company's standing with your bank and credit rating.

Companies have popped up to provide e-commerce assistance to the small and large business, and many established institutions that seemingly swore off the Internet years ago are now providing tools for their client base to conduct commerce online.

THE ELEMENTS OF E-COMMERCE

- **Product**: To sell online, you need something to sell. This can be anything from services, to information and groceries, to plane tickets.

- **Forms Processing:** You are going to need a way for the customer to express which products he desires and where to send them to. Data is entered online and needs to be processed in such a way that you know what to do with it. This could be anything from taking his credit card information to taking a phone number so that you can call to finalize an order.

- **Payment Processing:** If you are conducting e-commerce, you need some way for the customer to pay you. This can be anything from having him send you a check to you taking his credit card or checking information online.

TIP

> The funds transfer element of the e-commerce equation has attracted everyone from the most respectable banks to the most cunning of thieves. Be careful when you figure out who you want to handle your money and how much they charge you for the honor.
>
> I've personally gone through three e-commerce vendors before I realized why my bank, Wells Fargo, has been around for so long.

- **Security:** If you are going to take sensitive information over the Internet such as a credit card or checking account number, the customer is going to want assurance that no one other than your company will have access to that information.

- **Privacy Policies:** If you take sensitive information online, it will not only be important to the customer that you don't give his information to the wrong person, but he will also want to know what you'll be doing with the information within your own company.

SHOPPING CARTS

The most popular paradigm for e-commerce is the shopping cart method. Shopping cart software helps bridge the gap between shopping online with a model the traditional customer can relate to. In this approach, users work through a Web site as they would any store, "placing" items in their carts until they are ready to check out. At that point, delivery and contact information is collected.

Shopping carts are seen on the most popular e-commerce sites such as Amazon.com.

Because of the nature of online shopping, shopping cart software resides on the server. Several Web design products can interact with the shopping cart software—many of which integrate directly with FrontPage. At the end of this appendix, we discuss several such solutions.

B

No Shopping Carts Here

Shopping carts are not the only option for e-commerce. If you sell a single product, there is no need to over-whelm your audience with information that doesn't matter or an unnecessary shopping cart. In addition, it might not be which products and at what price your customer is looking for but information on quantity and availability. Shopping carts traditionally can't meet these needs and requirements.

Numerous extremely successful online merchants don't have a shopping cart system—they find that a simple order page meets all their needs.

Take a look at the site for Audio Generator (`http://audiogenerator.frontpagelink.com`). Because he sells a single popular service, his order process is a single Web page order form. Imagine how much more complicated things would be if you had to put the service in your cart and then "check out" to purchase it.

Another example is at FrontPage Cart (`http://frontpagecart.frontpagelink.com`). The site sells a shopping cart system design for FrontPage users, but if you purchase the product, you are taken to a simple order page.

I should point out that FrontPage Cart provides the means to sell online via both a shopping cart and an order form.

PAYMENT PROCESSING

The final part of any shopping experience is the means by which funds are transferred from the buyer to the seller.

It is not necessary for this process to take place online. Some e-commerce engines end the process by giving the customer an order number and the address to send the check to or provide a toll free number to call to finalize the order. Others provide information on who to contact to make payment.

For those wanting to receive payment online, a payment processing service is required. This service might work in conjunction with your e-commerce solution or independently at your Web site. The level of automation in payment processing can be considerably different from one site to another.

Several payment processing services are mentioned at the end of this appendix.

CHOOSING THE RIGHT E-COMMERCE SOLUTION FOR YOU

In choosing the "right" e-commerce solution for you, you need to understand each of the e-commerce elements mentioned previously, how they interact and integrate with FrontPage, and what the best solution for that element is for you and your situation.

In some cases, the right solution will be a publicly available product. We'll discuss many of them in the rest of this appendix. In other instances, you might have to modify an existing product or create a solution of your own.

For some, total automation from start to finish is the only possible option for an e-commerce solution. Where would Amazon be today if its employees were entering orders into their fulfillment system by hand? For others, the complexity of their product and client would make such automation impossible.

B

Some budding entrepreneurs uncover the simple realization that it is too much to handle. Others realize that the technology available makes possible and creates new entities that simply wouldn't have been possible a few years back.

No one-size-fits-all simple solution exists to e-commerce issues, whether they integrate with FrontPage or not.

INTEGRATING FRONTPAGE WITH E-COMMERCE ELEMENTS

The following sections examine the five elements of e-commerce mentioned previously and how the element does or doesn't integrate with FrontPage.

PRODUCT

Obviously, FrontPage has very little to do with the product you are selling—unless you are selling a software or information product.

Product has to be considered in many aspects of the e-commerce process—not only in elements of pricing, but also inventory and availability. Usually these issues are handled on the server side.

FrontPage's comprehensive coding capabilities could easily be used to write code to check an inventory database for availability and present such information to an interested customer. Such an inventory database could be created only for online use or the same database used by the rest of the business with the Web acting as another client.

→ For more on FrontPage's capability to interact with other data sources, **see** Part VIII, "Accessing Data with FrontPage 2003," **p. 661**.

FORMS PROCESSING

FrontPage's form capabilities make it a natural partner in the coding and development of the form related elements of any e-commerce solution. Whether you are writing a solution from scratch or integrating a third-party choice, there is no reason why you should not use the form capabilities of FrontPage in your implementation (see Figure B.1).

When you create a form in FrontPage, the form is surrounded by a dotted line in the Design view. To edit what happens to the form fields, right-click anywhere in the dotted line and select Form Properties from the option.

→ For more on FrontPage's capability to interact with other data sources, **see** "Using Forms," **p. 359**.

B

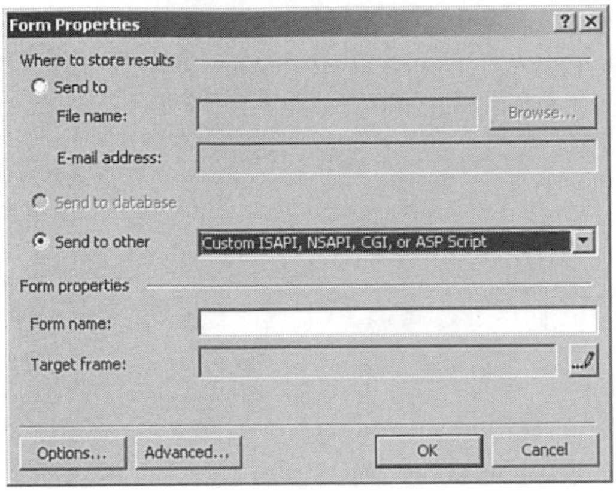

Figure B.1
The Form Properties dialog box allows you to integrate your form information with any custom script or data-base—FrontPage friendly, or not.

PAYMENT PROCESSING

Nothing in FrontPage directly controls or affects the transfer of funds from the customer to you (or vice versa). FrontPage is a product for Web design, not financial manipulation.

You can, however, use a FrontPage form to gather information that will lead to a funds transfer.

> **CAUTION**
>
> Remember, when you collect this kind information (credit card numbers, and so on) it is *extremely sensitive* in nature and should be treated with a tremendous amount of respect and caution. Always collect this type of information behind a secure connection to prevent snoops from grabbing your customers' private data.

There is nothing built in to FrontPage that would be suitable for this kind of information collection. You could build a form to take all the information, but as discussed in the previous caution, make sure to collect the information behind a strong level of Internet security.

> **TIP**
>
> FrontPage Cart (`http://www.frontpagecart.com`) provides a tool to collect simple payment processing information and does so behind its secure servers—only giving you the information via a secure connection. This keeps you from having to invest in a secure environment of your own.

SECURITY

If you are going to collect sensitive information in your FrontPage Web site such as credit card numbers or checking account data, you'll want to make sure that the numbers are secured and can't be lifted online by those sniffing data packets for this very information. The standard for such a connection is via SSL.

SSL?

SSL stands for *Secured Sockets Layer* and is a protocol (originally developed by Netscape) for the purpose of sending private information over the Internet. Netscape developed the protocol for the specific purpose of e-commerce, and it has been the standard online since it's introduction.

The Netscape specification for SSL can be found online at `http://ssl.frontpagelink.com`.

When a Web page is viewed online via SSL, the browser will show the Web address at *https://www. sitename.com* instead of *http:www.sitename.com,* where the *s* after *http* stands for "Secure." Different browsers indicate a secure connection in different ways, such as a key in Netscape or a lock in Internet Explorer.

Making an SSL connection is not as simple as adding an *s* after the *http* in your Web address. Secure Web server technology is needed as is a digital certificate that "proves" your online identity before the secure connection is made. Contact your ISP directly if you'd like to add the ability to add SSL to your Web site.

Although security and SSL is a server-side issue not controlled by FrontPage, FrontPage can connect to a site via SSL (via FrontPage Extensions) if the server is set up accordingly and has a valid digital certificate. In Figure B.2, I've connected to Colligan.com via SSL and FrontPage 2003 and can use the connection to transfer secure data to and from my server.

Figure B.2
You can open a Web site with FrontPage Server Extensions via SSL, keeping the information transferred between your computer and your Web server completely secured.

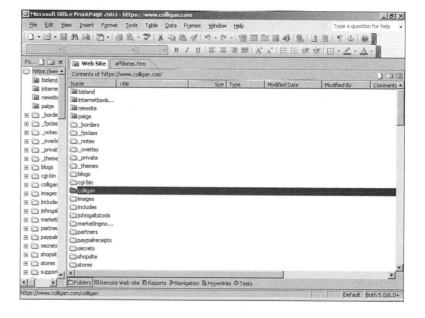

Security is not just an issue of the data transferred between the Web site and the customer. Issues of data stored and the site need to be considered as well. The news continues to report stories of hackers who break into a server with tens of thousands of credit card numbers, and you don't want to be one of the statistics.

B

TIP

> Hackers can't steal information that isn't available at your Web server. There is little reason to keep personal data stored on a server connected to the Internet for long periods of time. Back up your data on a regular basis to offline sources to minimize potential impact should your server be compromised.

Secured Shared Servers?

Even if your server is 100% secured from the outside, if anyone else has access to your server, it is important to determine if they have access to your data as well. This could be as obvious as locking your system every time you leave your desk to auditing the list of people who have access to the server your Web site is hosted on.

Many businesses host their e-commerce solutions in a shared hosting environment that holds the data of not just your customers but the customers of your "neighbor" as well. If you are "sharing a box" with anyone else and doing e-commerce online, take great care to make sure that your data is secure.

You also might want to consider placing your e-commerce solution on a server that only you have access to.

PRIVACY POLICIES

A privacy policy is a statement made by a Web site regarding what the company and organization behind the Web site is going to do with content collected and contained at a Web site. Smart shoppers are trained to look for a site privacy policy before they shop online and give away sensitive information that they don't want falling into the wrong hands.

TIP

> Privacy policies aren't limited to financial account information. They also should contain data on how the site will handle customer information submitted via email, over the phone, and so on.
>
> More and more "smart shoppers" are looking for a solid privacy policy at a site they visit before they'll give any information or make a purchase online.

The interesting thing about a privacy policy is that it is, just that, a policy. Although the Federal Trade Commission is still working out the specific laws of Internet Commerce, it is still a vastly uncharted territory.

TIP

> A great tool to help you develop your Privacy Policies can be found at
> `http://autoweblaw.frontpagelink.com`.

Once you have presented a privacy policy at your site, you are obligated to follow it. As a result, make sure to get your policy right the first time. Do your homework on this one. A great resource on privacy policies can be found online at `http://privacypolicy.frontpagelink.com`.

Privacy Policies for Third-Party Providers

If you are using a third-party provider for any element of your e-commerce process, do you know what their privacy policies are? Have you communicated these issues on your Web site's privacy policies?

E-Commerce Products that Integrate Directly with FrontPage

Now that we have examined the different elements of e-commerce, we'll take a look at products that integrate directly with FrontPage.

NOTE

> As mentioned previously, you are not limited to only e-commerce products that integrate directly with FrontPage. These options just make the process easier and have a better understanding of their audience.

bCentral Commerce Manager

bCentral is a popular Web portal for the small to medium business user. It is owned by Microsoft and sure to be and ongoing part of Microsoft's Web services strategies in the future. In addition to offering Web hosting (with FrontPage Extensions) and online sales and marketing products, the company also offers an option for online commerce that integrates tightly with FrontPage.

One of the many elements of bCentral is the Commerce Manager product (see Figure B.3). It provides the combined functionality of a Web-based sales engine with the ability to edit pages and layout from within FrontPage. Because many Web stores can suffer from the problem of everything looking the same, the ability to edit templates and content from a familiar interface is very attractive.

In addition to providing e-commerce capabilities, the bCentral Commerce Manager also provides additional features and capabilities because it can help push product content to other Web sites, including eBay and the MSN Marketplace.

Fans of the product point to the low price, ease of integration, and capability to get up and running quickly. Criticism of the product includes lack of customization options in the ordering process and the need to run all product information through a Web interface instead of a custom database.

B

Figure B.3
The Commerce Manager product/service of Microsoft's bCentral Web site offers optional FrontPage integration.

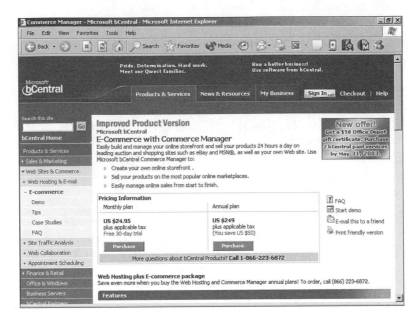

The bCentral Commerce Manager product can be found at `http://commercemanager.frontpagelink.com`. The current price for the product is $24.95 a month.

LaGarde's StoreFront

LaGarde has been a player in FrontPage integrated e-commerce since 1996. Its products have received great reviews from the user base, and the company has always worked closely with Microsoft to ensure as smooth an integration as possible.

In November 2002, LaGarde released version 6.0 of its StoreFront product. The product continued the tradition of tight integration with FrontPage but added the bonus of an ASP.NET backend that provided for the best Microsoft has to offer on the server end of things.

LaGarde has three different versions of its product providing the same core functionality but with more deluxe offerings based on user need (see Figure B.4).

LaGarde can be found online at `http://lagarde.frontpagelink.com`. The pricing model for its product can be found at on the Web site.

B

Figure B.4
LaGarde's site offers a
considerable resource
for e-commerce
options.

OTHER OPTIONS TO CONSIDER

The paradigm for e-commerce is constantly changing, and many players are added to the game on a weekly basis.

Because FrontPage integrates so tightly with any third-party product or system, the entire world of e-commerce is in fact open to the FrontPage user.

NOTE

> Exploit this fact to your fullest possible advantage. You are not stuck with a single supplier for all e-commerce tools—nor must you only work with a product with a FrontPage plug-in. Pick a "best of breed" approach that provides the options you need at the price that is right for you.

MICROSOFT COMMERCE SOLUTIONS

As discussed earlier, Microsoft is encouraging the use of the bCentral toolset for the small business. For larger businesses and industry requirements, Microsoft Commerce Server is the recommended Microsoft platform for e-commerce.

Although the product provides no plug-in for it, FrontPage 2003 can be directly used in the development process as the product is built on the Windows platform. Sites can be accessed and edited directly through FrontPage or products in the Visual Studio suite.

B

Microsoft Commerce Server 2002 provides most of the high-end features you'd expect from a professional e-commerce system. In addition to personalization options and customer-specific catalogs, it also provides levels of e-commerce intelligence to refine your shopping process and integrates tightly with Visual Studio and the entire Microsoft .NET platform push.

NOTE

More information about Microsoft Commerce Server can be found online at `http://commerceserver.frontpagelink.com`. At the time of publication, the retail prices for Microsoft Commerce Server 2002 (standard) was $6,999.

FRONTPAGE CART

FrontPage Cart is a unique e-commerce solution because it provides only the commerce-side of the e-commerce equation, allowing you to develop your site any way you want by sending the customer to the FrontPage Cart service only if he is ready to buy. You can customize the FrontPage Cart interface to model the look and feel of your site as you desire, as seen in Figure B.5.

Figure B.5
Customize your shopping cart interface with FrontPage Cart.

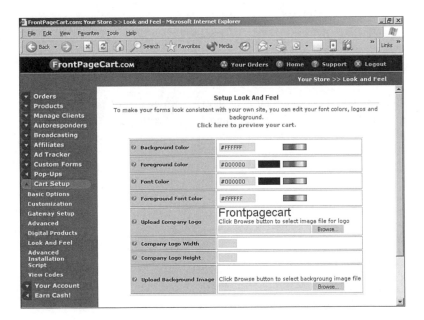

It is also unique in that it not only provides e-commerce capabilities, but it also provides an entire suite of services that complete the e-commerce process including a solid affiliate program (two-tiered), unlimited personalized sequential auto responders, e-couponing, ad tracking, digital delivery, and more.

The FrontPage Cart servers provide all the necessary security services, such as SSL connections and encrypted communications between their service and other payment processors. There is no need to purchase any digital certificates or security software if you are going to use this product.

NOTE

> FrontPage Cart is a version of the popular 1ShoppingCart product specifically updated with information and documentation for FrontPage users. The service is the same price and engine as 1ShoppingCart but provides focus for the FrontPage user.

Because the FrontPage Cart service only handles the e-commerce end of the Web transaction, it is one of the easiest solutions to integrate into any FrontPage Web site. It also provides the most flexibility because it requires little integration with your Web site short of a Click Here to Purchase link, as seen in Figure B.6.

Figure B.6
Each product in FrontPage Cart gets a Buy Me link that ads it to the shopping cart or a One Click link that takes you right to an order page.

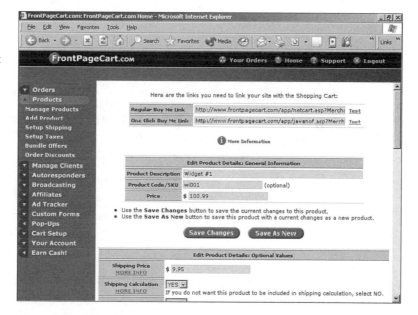

Who Uses This Service?

I have used FrontPage Cart as the e-commerce provider for all of my e-commerce endeavors (including http://frontpagetools.frontpagelink.com) for the past two years and have found its approach to be exactly what I needed for my e-commerce and marketing efforts. I can't recommend it highly enough.

I've sent a lot of money through FrontPage Cart and have done considerable research on the competition. I've found their unique approach to providing both e-commerce and marketing tools in the same package as the very tool I need to do business online.

Take a look around the site. With the free trial, you can't go wrong.

B

> **N O T E**
>
> FrontPage Cart can be found at `http://frontpagecart.frontpagelink.com`. Prices for the product range from $19 to $69 monthly based on the user's requirements. It currently offers a free month of service to anyone interested.

VeriSign Commerce Site Services

VeriSign recently purchased Network Solutions, the original source for all domain name registrations, and has been slowly putting together a series of products and services for businesses.

> **N O T E**
>
> At publication time, VeriSign's product offerings are in flux but more information can be found at `http://verisign.frontpagelink.com`.

Site Build It

Site Build It is a unique all-in-one approach to Web site marketing and sales that provides considerably much more than the traditional Web hosting package. It is truly a one-of-a-kind company and system that is worth seriously looking at.

Included in this unique service is a series of automated marketing tools and traffic building features that are too numerous to list here. Site Build It is the only service of its kind and should be examined by anyone looking at Web strategy options.

> **N O T E**
>
> At publication time, Site Build It had not launched its e-commerce initiative, but will do so shortly. When it does launch, it will quickly become a major force in e-commerce.
>
> How big is it in scope? It recently passed bCentral in customer traffic.

Site Build It allows the user to develop his site in any HTML design product and upload the pages into his system. There are a few tricks to using Site Build It with FrontPage, but you will find that they are well worth your effort. A great resource on adapting your FrontPage Web Site for Site Build It can be found at `http://sbifrontpage.frontpagelink.com`.

Soon, Site Build It will support both the sale of electronic goods through its product and a charge for services element that will help service providers eliminate that common "check is in the mail" problem. A full merchant account will be included in the service offering.

> **N O T E**
>
> Site Build It can be found at `http://sitebuildit.frontpagelink.com`. The service is currently $299 a year.

PAYPAL

PayPal made a name for itself in the early days of the Internet for providing a simple way for users on the Internet to transfer money safely between each other without the need for a credit card merchant account. PayPal's unique approach to an Internet escrow service brought it customers by the millions. It has since been purchased by auction giant eBay and rivals some banks in its size and impact on the Internet.

The role and impact of PayPal in e-commerce should not be underestimated. It has more than 25 million customers online (how is that for a market) and continues to grow at an astounding rate. Although a PayPal account is a little harder to get than it was in the past, it remains a powerful tool for people doing online commerce.

PayPal can be integrated into your FrontPage enabled e-commerce Web site in the following ways:

- On the most basic level, you can use PayPal to sell products on a single basis. A walk through the PayPal site will show you how to quickly create a "Buy Now" button for your Web site. By answering a few simple questions, PayPal will give you the HTML to insert into your site to make not only the button, but also provide the functionality that will give you the ability to sell online through PayPal.

- The PayPal Developer Network recently released a plug-in for FrontPage that makes developing "Buy Now" buttons easier than ever before (see Figure B.7). You can find the plug-in at `http://paypalplugin.frontpagelink.com`.

Figure B.7
The PayPal plug-in for FrontPage makes it easy to create "Buy Now" buttons for your FrontPage Web site that let you sell product online using PayPal as your payment processor.

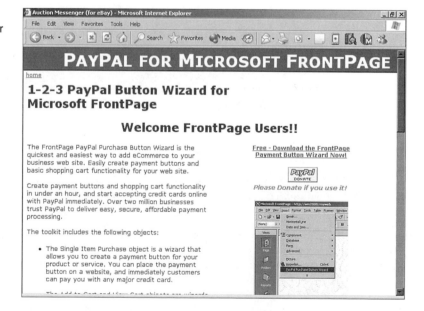

- On a slightly more complicated level, a few shopping cart scripts can use PayPal as a payment processor. One such script that integrates tightly with FrontPage can be found at http://fpcartpal.frontpagelink.com.

- The rise of PayPal's popularity has encouraged many shopping cart and e-commerce service providers to offer PayPal as a payment gateway option. In addition to many others, LaGarde and 1ShoppingCart, both mentioned in this chapter, provide for this option.

TIP

> Do go through the effort of getting a PayPal account and do spend some time in the PayPal Developer Network Area of the site. PayPal is doing some amazing things with e-commerce that should at least be examined by anyone pondering business online.

NOTE

> PayPal can be found online at http://paypal.frontpagelink.com. There is no charge to sign up for an account: Fees are assessed only when money is received.

Web Stores

Companies such as LaGarde, Yahoo!, and eBay provide Web store solutions—entire sites hosted on a third-party Web server that provide both the store and the process for building it.

There are two benefits to using an approach like this when developing an e-commerce strategy: 1) the entire e-commerce process is handled by another entity, and 2) the leverage these big names can bring to the process can potentially help you get more customers for your products.

Many find the ideal e-commerce solution is to build their corporate Web site with FrontPage and host it with a traditional host. The corporate site then links to the Web store enabling each site the capability to do what it does best.

eBay Stores

Very little needs to be said about eBay. Its impact on the Internet and the world of e-commerce is without compare. Its entry into the Web store universe brings both the stability of its name with the ability to promote store offerings within its e-commerce giant.

eBay Stores can be found at http://ebaystores.frontpagelink.com. The service has options as low as $9.95 a month with additional fees for product insertion, transactions, revenue sharing, and so on.

StoreFrontNow

LaGarde's StoreFrontNow program is the most recent entry into this field, but provides a unique angle because the program code used for the product is the same server code

LaGarde sells under the StoreFront name. As a result, the product is built on a well proven entity and supports additional feature sets, such as the ability to push your products to popular online auction sites such as eBay and Yahoo!Auctions.

LaGarde's StoreFrontNow program can be found at `http://lagarde.frontpagelink.com`. Prices start at $39 per month.

YAHOO! STORE

Yahoo! Store is the oldest entry in this space. It provides a solid product, can help with the acquisition of a merchant account, and gives you the ability to cross promote your product to the entire Yahoo! Shopping portal.

Yahoo! Store can be found at `http://yahoostore.frontpagelink.com`. The base for the service is $49.95 a month with additional fees for product insertion, transactions, revenue sharing, and so on.

NOTE

> Yahoo! recently announced that it would be producing a FrontPage plug-in for Yahoo! Stores, but no other information was available at publication time.
>
> When more information about this is made available, we'll update the `http://yahoostore.frontpagelink.com` dynamic link to send you directly to that information.

ONLINE PAYMENT PROCESSING OPTIONS

Only few e-commerce initiatives can exist without a means to process payment immediately after purchase. In order to succeed online, 99.99% of the people who read this are going to need to find an online payment processing option that takes traditional credit cards as payment.

TIP

> Anyone who buys online has heard the online horror stories and already comes to you with a built-in hesitance to buy online. If the payment processing element of your e-commerce system was obviously integrated to save money or put in place because you are "not sure yet," this will come through loud and clear to your customer and result in lost sales.

Although it is the most popular avenue for most e-commerce efforts, this does not immediately mean a traditional merchant account. There are other options for taking payment online as unique as the Internet, and we'll examine a number of them here.

B

MERCHANT ACCOUNTS

The most popular form of online sales is e-commerce by credit card sales. Merchant accounts are accounts with banking establishments that enable you to take credit cards at your place of business. We list a few options in the following sections.

WELLS FARGO

Wells Fargo provides merchant account services to many U.S.–based businesses and has quickly positioned itself as a leader in this industry. Its online toolset is considerable, but the capability to deal with people face to face by walking into a local branch is also powerful.

More information can be found at `http://wellsfargo.frontpagelink.com`.

INTERNET MARKETING CENTER

The Internet Marketing Center has provided Webmasters with numerous Internet related tools and services for years. It has helped many Webmasters get merchant accounts through their connections online.

More information on its recommendations for merchant account services can be found at `http://imcmerchantaccounts.frontpagelink.com`.

PAYPAL

As mentioned previously, PayPal provides an option for traditional credit card sales, but also allows for users to take credit cards through their Premier and Business Accounts. As a result, many business users utilize their PayPal relationship as a merchant account alternative.

PayPal Good and Bad

By the very nature of what PayPal is and the system developed around it, paying by credit card through PayPal will never be as "easy" as paying through a traditional merchant account connection. Some customers won't feel that the extra effort is worth it.

I strongly recommend a two-step approach to PayPal in any e-commerce efforts: 1) sign up for a PayPal business account immediately because the capability to "take PayPal" will increase your market share among the service's fans, and 2) find a traditional merchant account provider to handle the bulk of your transactions.

In addition, PayPal can provide an "alternative" merchant account option for whatever problems arise from you existing account. This could include anything from users who can't figure out your existing system to users with credit cards (such as American Express) that you can't accept through your current merchant account.

FrontPage Cart, mentioned earlier, lets you take both credit cards and PayPal payments through the same interface.

CLICKBANK

Clickbank has quickly positioned itself on the Internet as a service that provides Webmasters with the ability to take credit cards (and echecks) at their Web sites without the costs and hassles associated with a traditional merchant account.

Clickbank's service is limited only to electronic goods and services, but it provides a solid alternative for people in that market. In addition to this alternative merchant account solution, Clickbank also integrates an automatic affiliate program into its sales process.

More information can be found online at `http://clickbank.frontpagelink.com`.

PAYMENT GATEWAYS

A merchant account is merely an account with a bank that enables you to take credit cards. In a brick and mortar store, you connect to your bank to take credit cards through a terminal. Online, this is done through a payment gateway service.

The most common of these gateways is Authorize.net. Your merchant account provider will tell you which payment gateways it works with. Payment gateways almost always carry an additional service charge.

More information about Authorize.net can be found at `http://an.frontpagelink.com`.

ALTERNATIVES TO MERCHANT ACCOUNTS

Merchant accounts can be costly. Signup and monthly fees can quickly add up in price. In addition, many merchant accounts contracts require term lengths of a year or more. For those wanting to only do a small amount of sales online, there are companies and services that provide alternatives to traditional merchant account contracts and stipulations.

TIP

> If you do more than just a few sales online, the merchant account "alternatives" are seldom cheaper than a traditional merchant account. These companies make their revenue stream from the per-transaction charges, and when they stack up, you seldom benefit.

B

These companies usually charge a single sign-up fee and then a per transaction fee—usually higher than a traditional credit card discount fee, but without merchant account requirements.

Two options are examined in the following sections, but be aware that there are others. As always, do your homework and run the numbers when investigating these options.

Serious About E-Commerce?

If you expect anyone to give you his hard earned money through e-commerce (or any other endeavor), you've got to convince him that you are serious about what you are doing.

Whereas it might seem a little scary to spend money on a merchant account, you need to realize that smart shoppers know the difference between you taking their money and working with another service to do the same. They know when you are using a third party, and they know that that means.

Get serious about e-commerce; it is a serious business.

2CheckOut

2CheckOut provides a way to take credit cards online without any long term contracts or monthly fees. It also provides a free basic shopping cart program.

More information about 2Checkout can be found at `http://2checkout.frontpagelink.com`. At the time of publication, 2Checkout requires a $49 setup fee and charges 45 cents and 5.5% of transaction per sale.

PayPal

As mentioned previously, PayPal provides a way to accept credit cards with no up-front fees at all. Its process is a bit cumbersome, but you can't beat its availability and startup prices.

Where to Go for More Information

A search for the term e-commerce or merchant account on any search engine will result in a potential lifetime of reading. Information is available on every topic with every possible angle on this topic.

Understand that most of these information providers are looking to sell their services to you. Also remember that because they are online, it doesn't necessarily mean that they are reputable.

"Traditional" sources of information such as your bank, the Better Business Bureau, and local trusted establishments might be great sources as well.

A great resource for selling online can be found at `http://ycso.frontpagelink.com`.

CREDIT CARD FRAUD

With the rise of e-commerce comes the parallel rise of credit card fraud. Because online sales can't require the ability to see the customer face to face, the potential for fraud is extensive and is considerably exploited. This is an industry-wide problem with significant efforts associated with combating it.

Work with your shopping cart and merchant services provider to work on a solid strategy for fraud protection in your e-commerce efforts.

FINDING THE RIGHT HOST

If you are going to participate in the world of e-commerce, you want to make sure that you are working with the right host. If your Web site *is your store*, every second your site has problems is *lost money*.

The right Web host is vital.

Run the Numbers/Read the Fine Print

If your Web host promises to be up 99% of the time, that's a good thing, right? A 30 day month has 720 hours. *1%* of 720 hours is more than 7 hours of downtime. Oops!

How about a site with a 99.9% uptime guarantee? *.1%* of 720 hours is more than 30 minutes of downtime a month.

30 minutes of downtime at 2 a.m. for a site that only works with local customers is fine. Every e-commerce site owner knows that there are times in the day when 30 minutes of downtime can result in a considerable amount of lost sales and damaged reputation. Just ask the manager of your local grocery store how he'd feel if the store were shut down for a random 30 minutes every month.

What happens if your Web host does go down? Does it give you a free month or does it pro-rate your service loss? I once had a host who was down for 24 hours and gave me 1/31 of my month service fee back in exchange for more than a thousand dollars in lost sales. I didn't read the fine print in the contract.

Needless to say, I'm no longer with that host.

In the Web hosting world, it isn't a question of *if you'll go down*—it is a question of *what happens when you go down*. Find out what happens when your host has problems and ask for references of successful e-commerce clients. Check on the references.

And, obviously, run the numbers and read the fine print.

How many times (in the "real world") have you not purchased something because of a long line at the store? How many times have you given up because you couldn't find an employee to help make a decision? How many times did something in the store prevent you from doing the very thing the store wanted you to do?

If your site runs slowly, it has the same effect as a slow employee—it does nothing more than irritate the very customer you are hoping will buy from you. If your site is down, your customer won't wait until you open; he'll go someplace that is open and give it the very money you were looking for.

B

Don't save a few bucks to lose hundreds.

Pick and work with a Web host that has other customers who are using their sites for e-commerce as well. There is power in numbers.

If you are looking for a reputable discount hosting service, I have used and can recommend `http://discounthosting.frontpagelink.com`. As always, mileage may vary, but we will update this link if we hear any horror stories from our readers.

For managed hosting services, I have worked with several people who recommend `http://managedhosting.frontpagelink.com`. As with the other link, I'll change it to another company should I hear of any problems.

FRONT AND CENTER: DESIGNING FOR SALES

There is a great thrill in selling online. Setting up a Web site and having a customer visit and then buy something from you is a thrill well worth experiencing. When commerce is no longer limited to local geography, something amazing happens.

It can also be a great headache. Shipping a product that was purchased with a stolen credit card number not only makes no profit for you, but also ends with lost product, assorted fees from the bank, and a great deal of your time spent on a process of nothing more than providing a paper trail for a thief who ripped you off.

This chapter should not serve as your complete training on the wonderful world of e-commerce. You will face many issues and problems that having nothing to do with FrontPage, and handling them quickly and efficiently can only come from experience.

In short, do you homework before you start on this adventure.

The treatment Hollywood and the evening news has given to the rise of e-commerce makes it sound like all you have to do is put something for sale online and the world will beat a path to your door.

Remember this simple fact: *Just because you sell online, it does mean that people are going to buy from you.*

It is *your job and your duty* to produce the type of site that people would want to buy from. This obviously includes an attractive and functional layout, but it also demands a site that "feels" trustworthy (buyers are going to give you their credit card numbers after all) and looks like it is being run by complete and total professionals, regardless of whether it is being run from a garage.

Designing a Web site for sales is just that, designing a Web site for sales. The e-commerce elements briefly touched on in this appendix will help you find your necessary functionality, but the design process is still up to you.

So, make it a good one.

B

APPENDIX C

WINDOWS SHAREPOINT SERVICES 2.0

In this appendix

USING A WINDOWS SHAREPOINT SERVICES WEB SITE

A Windows SharePoint Services Web site provides a convenient way for the Web site users to share information with one another. Users of the Web site can be given different levels of access that span from simply being able to browse the site without changing any content to being able to redesign the pages themselves right within the Web browser.

Windows SharePoint Services Web sites work in a completely different way than Web sites you are probably familiar with. Instead of storing the content in a disk location (such as c:\inetpub\wwwroot), the content is stored in Microsoft SQL Server. This means that you won't be able to see your Web site's files using Windows Explorer. You will have no access to the files that make up your Web site unless you use FrontPage or Windows SharePoint Services running inside a browser. If you're one of those developers who makes changes to your Web site using an editor other than FrontPage, you need to be aware that such changes are not possible with a Windows SharePoint Services Web site.

How Windows SharePoint Services Works with IIS

Windows SharePoint Services Web sites store all their content in SQL Server. Therefore, there are no virtual directories in IIS that you can configure. All Windows SharePoint Services Web sites inherit their IIS-specific settings from the Default Web Site or the root-level provisioned site.

If you look in the Internet Information Services Manager, you will notice that none of your content appears there. So just how is it that Windows SharePoint Services is able to access server content via HTTP on the Web server?

When a request is made for a Web page on a virtual server that is running Windows SharePoint Services, the request is first processed through a special file running in IIS called an *ISAPI filter*. That ISAPI filter sits at a very low-level in the request process, and its job is to grab that request and process it through the Windows SharePoint Services content database. It then sends that content back to IIS, and IIS then serves it to the Web browser. To IIS, it looks like the content is in the regular content directory, but it isn't. It all comes from SQL Server.

UNDERSTANDING WEB PARTS

At this point, your Default Web Site should be provisioned as a Windows SharePoint Services Web site. Open the Default Web Site in your Web browser by browsing to http://localhost on the Web server, and you will see the Home page for your Windows SharePoint Services Web site.

A Windows SharePoint Services Web site consists of Web Parts, sections of the Web page that contain specific types of information. The Web site shown in Figure C.1 contains several Web Parts that can be edited from within the Web browser if you have sufficient permissions.

Look at the Announcements section of the page. The Announcements section is a Web Part. You can add a new announcement to this section by clicking on the Add New Announcement link. Clicking that link takes you to the Announcements—New Item page (shown in Figure C.1), where you can add new announcements to display on the page. The

Expires text box allows you to specify a date when the announcement automatically disappears.

Figure C.1
Adding new items to a Windows SharePoint Services Web page is done from within the browser.

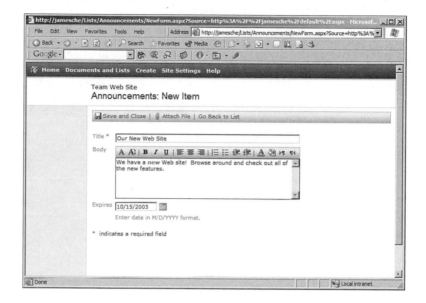

 If you don't have an Add New Announcement link, see "Cannot Add New Announcements" in the "Troubleshooting" section of this appendix.

To enter a new announcement:

1. Click the Add New Announcement link.

2. Enter a title for your announcement.

3. In the Body text area, enter the text you want to appear below your announcement. Use the formatting toolbar to format your text as you'd like it to appear.

4. Enter a date for the announcement's expiration or click the calendar button to select an expiration date for the announcement. The announcement will automatically be removed from the site on the expiration date.

5. If you'd like to attach a file to your announcement, click the Attach File link and browse to the file.

6. Click the Save and Close link to save your announcement.

Once your announcement has been added to the page, you can click its title to display its details, as seen in Figure C.2. By clicking the Edit Item link, you can make changes to your item. You can also specify that you would like email notification when changes are made to the item by clicking the Alert Me link.

NOTE

In order for alerts to work, the virtual server email settings must be configured in the SharePoint Central Administration page. See the Windows SharePoint Services documentation for more information.

Figure C.2
Editing a previously entered announcement is accomplished by clicking the item and then clicking Edit Item.

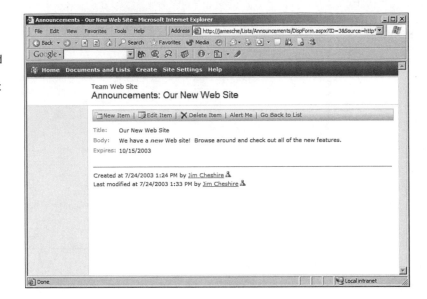

MODIFYING AND ADDING WEB PARTS

If you have sufficient rights to the Windows SharePoint Services Web site, you can also modify the configuration and layout of the Web Part itself. To configure the Web Part, click the Web Part menu, as shown in Figure C.3.

 If you don't have a Web Part menu, see "Web Part Menu Not Visible" in the "Troubleshooting" section of this appendix.

To edit a Web Part, click the Web Part menu button and then select Modify Shared Web Part from the menu to display the tool pane as shown in Figure C.4. Using the tool pane, you can configure the appearance and behavior of the Web Part.

The FrontPage client also provides the ability to configure Web Part properties in an interface very similar to the Web Part tool pane using the Web Part Options menu.

→ For more information on using the Web Part Options menu in FrontPage to configure a Web Part, **see** "Configuring a Data View and Web Parts," **p. 743**.

Figure C.3
The Web Part menu allows you to edit Web Parts within the browser.

Web Root menu

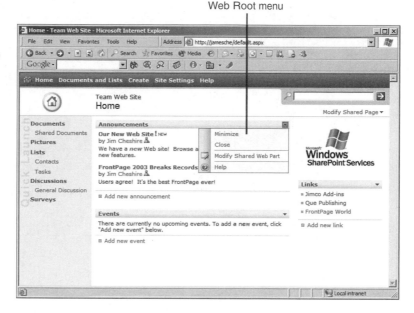

Figure C.4
The Web Part's tool pane allows for advanced configuration.

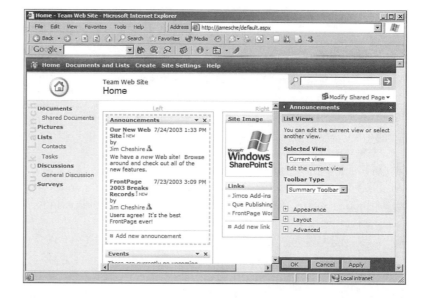

In addition to modifying a particular Web Part's appearance using the tool pane, you can also easily modify the layout of the entire page and where each Web Part appears on that page using the Web Part Page menu as shown in Figure C.5. When you click this button, you will see the Web Part zones that exist on the page. A *Web Part zone* is a compartment for Web Parts, and they appear as areas around a dark border with a text label at the top.

Figure C.5
The Web Part Page menu provides access to tools that allow you to modify the Web page.

Web Part Page menu

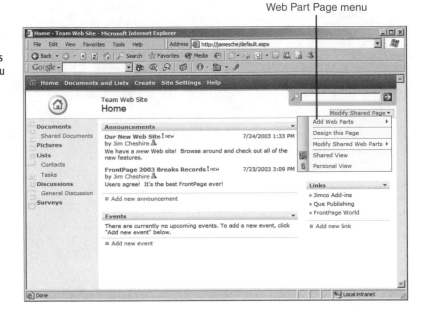

 If you don't have a Web Part Page menu, see "Web Part Menu Not Visible" in the "Troubleshooting" section of this appendix.

To modify a page

1. Click the Web Part Page menu and select Design This Page. The page will switch to Design mode.

2. Move your mouse pointer over the title bar of a Web Part so that the pointer changes to a four-way arrow. For example, in the page shown in Figure C.6, the mouse pointer is over the title bar for the Links Web Part.

3. While holding the mouse button down, drag the Web Part to a new location. In Figure C.7, the Links Web Part is being repositioned so that it appears underneath the Announcements Web Part. Figure C.8 shows the Web Part in its new location. A Web Part can only be moved into a Web Part zone.

4. From the Web Part menu, select Design this Page from the Web Part Page menu again to turn off design mode.

SHARED VIEW AND PERSONAL VIEW

When the Web Part Page menu says Modify Shared Page, you are editing in *shared view*, and changes you make to the Web page are visible to all visitors to the site. Windows SharePoint Services can also display Web pages in *personal view*, where pages are specific to the user browsing the site. Any changes made in personal view are visible only to the user who makes those changes.

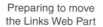

Preparing to move
the Links Web Part

Figure C.6
A page in design
mode. Note the mouse
pointer on the Links
Web Part is positioned
in preparation for
moving the Web Part.

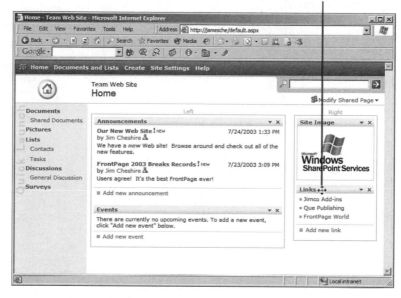

Figure C.7
The Links Web Part is
being moved to a new
location as indicated
by the translucent rec-
tangle.

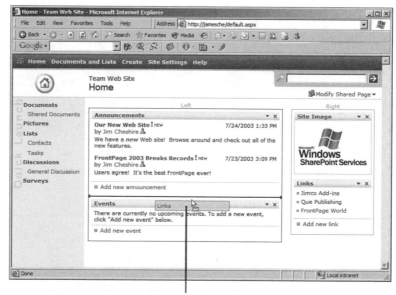

The Links Web Part being dragged to a new location

New location for
Links Web Part

Figure C.8
The Links Web Part in
its new location.

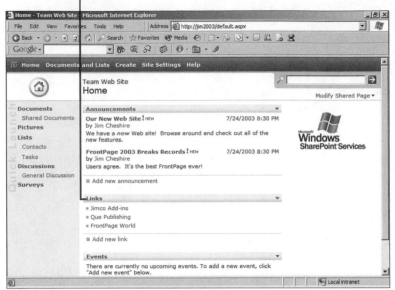

Windows SharePoint Services will display the Web page in personal view by default under the following circumstances:

- You have previously modified the page in personal view.
- You do not have sufficient rights to modify a shared page.
- A meta tag with a `name` attribute of `WebPartPageDefaultViewPersonal` meta tag exists in the page.

To manually switch to personal view, click the Web Part Page menu and select Personal View from the menu. If you then click the Web Part Page menu and select Design This Page, any changes made will only be visible by you and subsequent visits to the page will load in personal view by default.

CREATING A NEW WEB PART

In addition to editing existing Web Parts, Windows SharePoint Services users with sufficient rights can also add new Web Parts to a Web page.

To add a new Web Part to a Web page

1. Click the Web Part Page menu and select Add Web Parts, Browse to display the Add Web Parts tool pane, as shown in Figure C.9.
2. Select a Web Part from the Web Part List and drag its icon on to the page.
3. Drop the Web Part on to a Web Part zone on the page.

Figure C.9
The Add Web Parts tool pane makes adding new content easy.

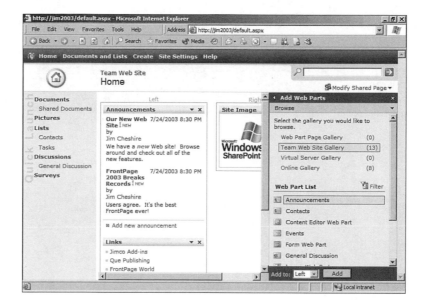

WORKING WITH WEB PART DATA

Windows SharePoint Services provides some very powerful tools for working with data collected in your Web site. For example, Windows SharePoint Services is a great place to keep contact information for a team of people. If someone's contact information changes, they just update it on the Windows SharePoint Services Web site. However, you might find yourself needing to do more with that data than just display it on a Web page.

Suppose that you wanted to take the list of contacts from your Windows SharePoint Services Web site and create a Microsoft Access database with the data so that it can be used in other applications. Another scenario might be that your team is getting ready to move to another part of your building, and the administrative assistant needs to update office numbers and email a diagram of the new assignments. It might be beneficial to have a Microsoft Excel spreadsheet containing all the team members that can be updated quickly and easily. Windows SharePoint Services makes it easy to take the data from your site and use it in many powerful ways.

1. Add a Contacts Web Part to your page and add some contacts to it.
2. Click on Contacts in the title bar of the Contacts Web Part to display the Contacts list.
3. Click the Edit in Datasheet link on the toolbar to display the Datasheet view, as shown in Figure C.10.

The Datasheet view provides a spreadsheet view of your data. The Datasheet view is very much like Microsoft Excel in that you can filter data, run calculations on data, move data around, and so on. By clicking on the Task Pane link in the toolbar, you can access links (shown in Figure C.11) that allow you to work on your data in Microsoft Excel or Microsoft

Access. You can export your data to Excel or create graphs and PivotTables. You can also generate reports in Access or export your data to Access.

Figure C.10
The Datasheet view is very similar to Microsoft Excel.

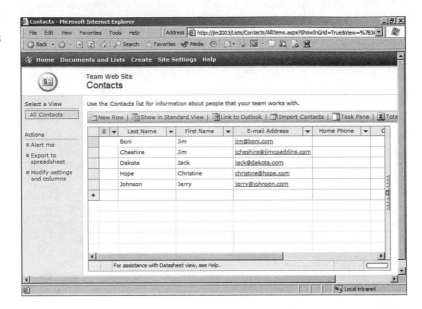

Task Pane button

Figure C.11
The Task Pane contains links that allow for tight integration with Office and Windows SharePoint Services.

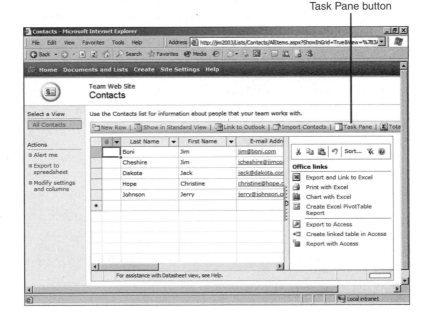

TIP

> You will naturally need to have Office products installed in order to be able to utilize them in conjunction with your Windows SharePoint Services Web site.

AN OVERVIEW OF WINDOWS SHAREPOINT SERVICES 2.0

Windows SharePoint Services 2.0 is the next release for what was previously called SharePoint Team Services. You will hear some people refer to it as SharePoint Team Services 2.0, but Windows SharePoint Services is a dramatic departure from SharePoint Team Services, as you will soon see.

Windows SharePoint Services can only be installed on Windows Server 2003. When installed, Windows SharePoint Services provides the following services:

- **Windows SharePoint Services Web Sites**—Web sites that provide a highly customizable solution for sharing data among a group of people. The Web site shown in Figure C.12 is a Windows SharePoint Services Web site. When Windows SharePoint Services is installed, the root Web site on the Web server is converted into a Windows SharePoint Services Web site.

Figure C.12
A Windows
SharePoint Services
Web site.

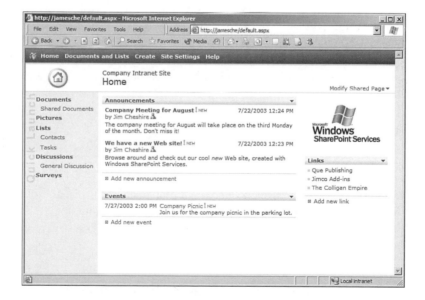

- **Web Parts**—Web Parts are compartmentalized components that can be used in a Web page to add dynamic functionality such as data from a database or a dynamic calendar of events. Web Parts can be added from within the Windows SharePoint Services Web site running in the browser or from within FrontPage 2003. Earlier versions of FrontPage do not support adding or editing Web Parts.

- **Data Views**—Data Views are specialized Web Parts that are designed to connect to many kinds of data. Data Views can connect to databases, XML Web services, XML files, and many other types of data. A Data View is inserted from within FrontPage 2003. Earlier versions of FrontPage do not support Data Views.

- **FrontPage Support**—After installing Windows SharePoint Services on your Web server, you will be able to open your Web sites with FrontPage just as you do with the FrontPage Server Extensions. You can also use FrontPage Web components such as the Hit Counter component and other runtime components on your pages. The FrontPage Database Results and Database Interface Wizards are not supported and are replaced with Data Views.

→ For more information on Data Views, **see** "The Data Source Catalog," **p. 736**.

→ For more information on the Database Results and Database Interface Wizard, **see** "FrontPage and Databases," **p. 705**.

> **NOTE**
>
> For more information on XML, read *Special Edition Using XML*. For more information on XML Web services, read *XML and ASP.NET* from Que Publishing.

Windows SharePoint Services Web sites store all their content on Microsoft SQL Server, which means that your content is not saved to a disk location. In other words, you can't get to your content by browsing to C:\inetpub\wwwroot because it isn't there. Windows SharePoint Services also does not create virtual directories for your Web sites in the Internet Information Services snap-in. If you want to administer a Windows SharePoint Services Web site, use the Windows SharePoint Services Administration tool that will be discussed in detail later.

→ For more information on Microsoft SQL Server, read *SQL Server System Administration* from Que Publishing.

INSTALLING WINDOWS SHAREPOINT SERVICES

Installing Windows SharePoint Services is not as simple as installing FrontPage. You can't just take the defaults and expect everything to go off without a hitch. In fact, Windows SharePoint Services is unique in that in some respects, it is easier to use it than it is to install it.

> **NOTE**
>
> Unless you are running your own Web server, Windows SharePoint Services needs to be installed by the administrator of the Web server.

To install Windows SharePoint Services, run SETUPSTS.EXE to start the installation process. After accepting the license agreement, you are asked to choose between a Typical installation or a Server Farm installation, as shown in Figure C.13. A *server farm* refers to a group of Web servers that each share a certain amount of the load for a busy Web site. It's easy to choose a Typical install believing that the Server Farm install is not appropriate for a stand-alone Web server, but that might not be your best option.

Figure C.13
Be careful which installation option you choose. The choice might not be as obvious as it seems.

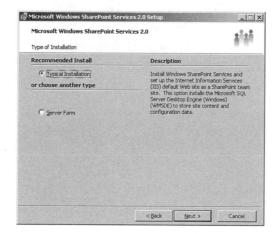

The Typical install option will install Microsoft SQL Server Desktop Engine (a scaled-down version of Microsoft SQL Server) without prompting you, even if you already have Microsoft SQL Server installed. If you choose the Server Farm option, you will have to point Windows SharePoint Services to a Microsoft SQL Server instance after you have installed it. In most cases, if you already have SQL Server installed and you would like to use it instead of MSDE, choose the Server Farm option, even if you are installing on a standalone server.

After selecting your desired install option, click <u>N</u>ext and then click <u>I</u>nstall to install Windows SharePoint Services.

After the installation is successful, Windows SharePoint Services will configure your Default Web Site as a Windows SharePoint Services Web site if you chose the Typical install. If you chose Server Farm as your installation type, Windows SharePoint Services will display the Configure Administrative Virtual Server page.

NOTE

If you chose a Typical install, you can skip the rest of this section.

CONFIGURING THE SHAREPOINT CENTRAL ADMINISTRATION VIRTUAL SERVER

The Configure Administrative Virtual Server page is where you configure the SharePoint Central Administration virtual server, as shown in Figure C.14. This virtual server is used to manage the configuration of your Windows SharePoint Services Web sites. To configure the SharePoint Central Administration virtual server, choose an existing application pool or specify a new application pool name.

Figure C.14
The Configure
Administrative Virtual
Server page appears
after a Server Farm
install.

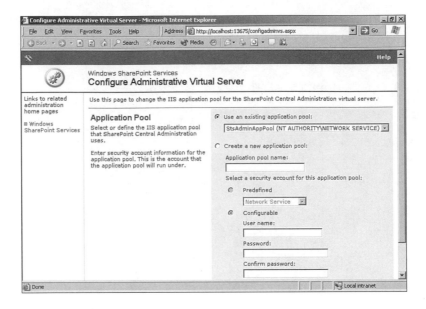

An *application pool* is an IIS 6.0 container in which you can run a Web application. You can specify configuration settings for each application pool, such as the identity that the application pool runs under and how it manages memory. If a Web application running in that application pool crashes, it will not affect Web applications running in another application pool.

Choose an existing application pool or create a new one and click OK to continue. If you are unsure what to choose, select the Create a New Application Pool and the Predefined options and click OK.

After Windows SharePoint Services configures the application pool, you will be asked to restart IIS as shown in Figure C.15. Open a command prompt and enter **iisreset** to restart IIS and then click OK in the Application Pool Changed page.

CONFIGURING THE DATABASE SERVER

Your next step is to configure the database server that will be used for all the Windows SharePoint Services sites on the Web server. You do that from the Set Configuration Database Server page as shown in Figure C.16. This is the database server that will store the configuration information for your install of Windows SharePoint Services. Enter the database server name and specify a name for the database on that server. If the database doesn't exist, it will be created for you. If the database does already exist, check the Connect to Existing Configuration Database check box before proceeding.

If you are running your application pool under the NETWORK SERVICE account, you will either have to choose SQL authentication to connect to the database or set up an account with access to SQL Server and configure the application pool to run under that account.

Figure C.15
Once the application pool is configured, restart IIS to continue.

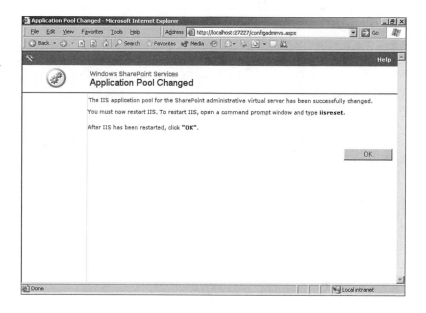

Figure C.16
The Set Configuration Database Server page configures your database for Windows SharePoint Services.

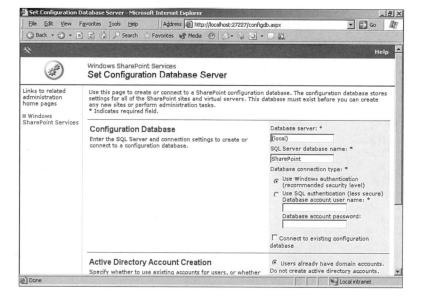

Choose the Active Directory options that are applicable to your environment and click OK. If you are unsure of what to enter for Active Directory configuration, ask your system administrator.

 If you receive an error telling you that the SQL Server does not exist or access is denied, see "SQL Server Doesn't Exist or Access Denied" in the "Troubleshooting" section of this appendix.

PROVISIONING THE WEB SITE

Once the configuration database has been successfully set up, you will be taken to the Central Administration page shown in Figure C.17. From here, you will need to install Windows SharePoint Services on your Default Web Site in a process known as *provisioning*. Click the Extend or upgrade virtual server link to display the Virtual Server List as shown in Figure C.18. Click the name of your Default Web Site to provision the site.

Figure C.17
The Central Administration page. No sites are configured, so you will need to do that first.

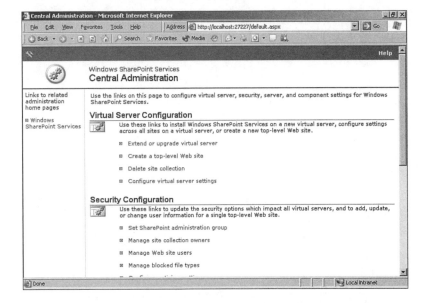

Figure C.18
The Virtual Server List lists the Default Web Site indicating that the Windows SharePoint Services is not installed.

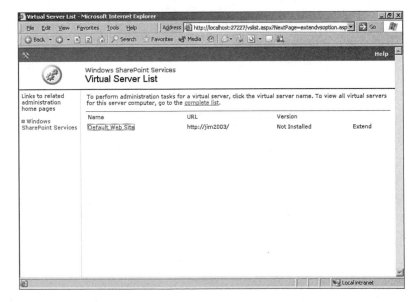

You are creating a new Windows SharePoint Services Web site, so in the Provisioning Options section, click Extend and Create a Content Database.

You will now see the Extend and Create Content Database page as shown in Figure C.19. The many sections available to you are as follows:

- **Current Virtual Server**—Displays the information for the current virtual server.
- **Application Pool**—Allows you to configure the application pool for the new site. The easiest option is to choose DefaultAppPool.
- **Site Owner**—The information for the owner of the Web site. The username is in DOMAIN/username format.
- **Database Information**—Configures the information for the content database. If you are unsure of how to configure this, check the Use Default Content Database Server.
- **Custom URL**—The URL for the new site. Because you are configuring the Default Web site, this will be /.
- **Quote Template**—There are currently no quote templates created, so No Quota is your only option. Quota templates will be covered later.
- **Site Language**—The language for the new Web site.

Once these options are set, click OK.

Figure C.19
The Extend and Create Content Database page.

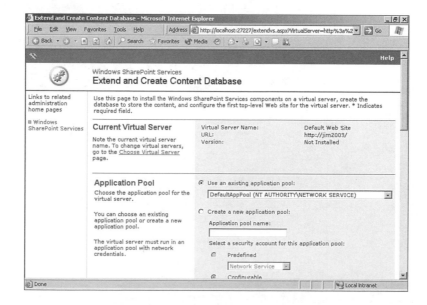

Windows SharePoint Services will now display moving gears while it configures your site. When the process is complete, you will be notified and a link will display that will take you to the next step. Click the link, and you will be asked to choose a template for your site, as shown in Figure C.20. Select a template and click OK to view your new Windows SharePoint Services Web site, as seen in Figure C.21.

TIP

Choose your template carefully. If you decide to change it later, you will have to delete the Web site and re-create it.

Figure C.20
You have many templates to choose from for your new site.

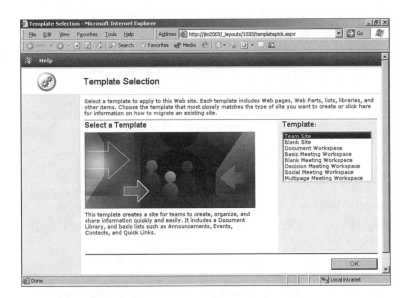

Figure C.21
Your new Windows SharePoint Services Web site. This one has the Team Web Site template applied.

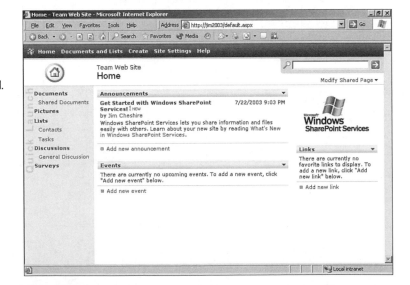

TROUBLESHOOTING

SQL SERVER DOESN'T EXIST OR ACCESS DENIED

I have entered a SQL Server name and chose Windows authentication. Even though I know I have access to the SQL Server, it still tells me that the SQL Server doesn't exist or that access is denied.

If the SQL Server is on a machine other than the Windows SharePoint Services site, you might have to use SQL Server authentication as opposed to Windows authentication. This is because Windows authentication will only work when there is only one hop between the Web browser and the SQL Server. If the SQL Server is on a computer other than the Windows SharePoint Services computer and you are browsing from a third machine, there is one hop from the browser to the Web server and then another hop from the Web server to the SQL Server. Windows authentication is designed to fail in these circumstances.

CANNOT ADD NEW ANNOUNCEMENTS

I have the site all set up, but I don't have an Add New Announcement list on my Announcements Web Part.

In order to add content to a Windows SharePoint Services Web site, you must have sufficient rights. There are four groups in a Windows SharePoint Services Web site:

- **Reader**—A Reader can browse the Web site, but cannot add any new content.
- **Contributor**—A Contributor can add documents to Windows SharePoint Services document libraries and can add new entries to Windows SharePoint Services Lists.
- **Web Designer**—A Web Designer can create Web Parts on the Windows SharePoint Services site and can also customize existing Web Parts and Web Part Pages.
- **Administrator**—An Administrator can do anything on the site he wants, as well as manage users and site configuration settings.

If you don't have the ability to add new announcements, it is almost certainly because your level of access is Reader.

WEB PART MENU NOT VISIBLE

I am trying to change the configuration of a Web Part, but the Web Part menu is not visible.

In order to customize a Web Part, you must be either a Web Designer or Administrator. If you are not, by default, you cannot change any page content.

FRONT AND CENTER: WINDOWS SHAREPOINT SERVICES SURVEYS

A popular feature of SharePoint Team Services 1.0 was the Surveys feature, the Windows SharePoint Services version of which is shown in Figure C.22. Using this feature, you can create a survey that appears on your Web site for people to fill out. You can tabulate and easily display the results to visitors to the site

Figure C.22
The Windows SharePoint Services Survey.

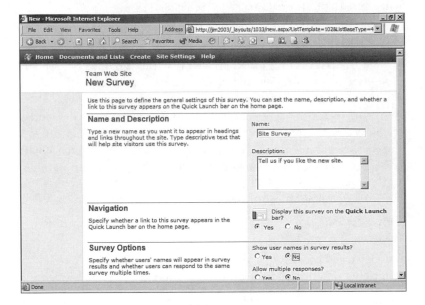

To create a new Survey, follow these steps:

1. Click the Create link at the top of a Windows SharePoint Services Web page.

2. In the Create Page Web page, click the Survey link in the Surveys section.

3. Enter a name for your survey and a description.

4. Select whether you would like the survey to appear on the Quick Launch bar on the home page by selecting either Yes or No in the Display This Survey in the Quick Launch Bar option.

5. Select whether respondents will see the names of those who have responded by selecting either Yes or No in the Show User Names in Survey Results option.

6. Choose whether to allow for multiple responses by selecting either Yes or No in the Allow Multiple Responses option.

7. Configure your questions by entering the question text and choosing the question type as shown in Figure C.23.

Figure C.23
Enter a question and choose between the many different types of answers available.

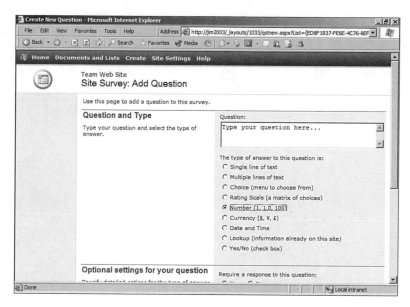

8. Set any custom settings for your question as shown in Figure C.24.

Figure C.24
Set optional settings for each question. These differ depending on the answer type.

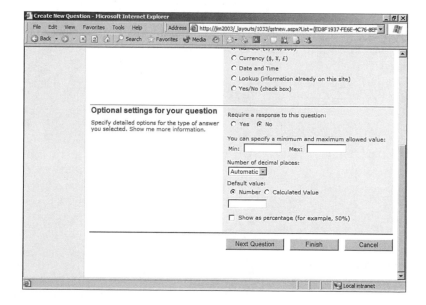

9. Make any settings changes you want from the Customize <Survey Name> page as shown in Figure C.25.

Figure C.25
After the survey has been created, feel free to tweak it and make settings changes.

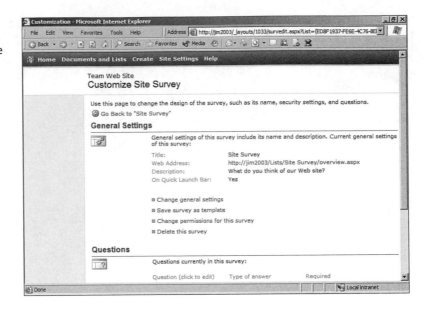

10. Click the Web Address link to see the survey in Windows SharePoint Services.

On the survey page, visitors can take the survey by clicking the Respond to This Survey link and can see responses by clicking either the Show a Graphical Summary of Responses or the Show All Responses links.

MAKING YOUR OWN WEB COMPONENTS

In this appendix

WHAT IS A WEB COMPONENT?

FrontPage includes many Web components that you can use to make your site more dynamic and interactive. This book gives you the information that you need to be very productive with the Web components included with FrontPage. Whether it's the FrontPage Photo Gallery or the Include Page component, they all have one thing in common. They have a dialog in which you configure settings, and they insert code into your Web page when you click OK. They also allow you to easily reconfigure them by double-clicking on them inside your page to bring up their dialog box again. That's a Web component.

FrontPage also ships with several special Web components such as the MSNBC Components, the Expedia Components, and the MSN Components. These are special components because they don't work exactly like the rest of FrontPage's components. All these components rely on information that changes frequently, and they also feed off Internet Web sites with URLs that might change over time. Take the Expedia Link to a map component shown in Figure D.1. This component allows you to create a link on your Web site that links to a map based on the address information you provide to the component. Now suppose that the URL that Expedia uses for maps changes. If this were a regular Web component, the only way for your component to continue working would be for Microsoft to release a patch to FrontPage to update the URL in the component. That's not a very efficient way to address the problem.

Figure D.1
The Expedia Link to a map component relies on the URL to the map link being up-to-date.

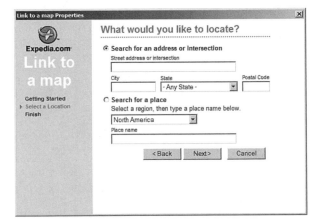

Microsoft realized this dilemma early on and built a new Web component system into FrontPage starting with FrontPage 2002, and fortunately for us, Microsoft built it so that users of FrontPage can take advantage of it to easily create their own Web components.

TIP

For sample Web components and documentation, download the FrontPage Software Developer's Kit from http://fpsdk.frontpagelink.com.

There are two types of Web components—those that display a dialog box to the user and insert code based on settings the user specifies in the dialog box, and those that simply insert code into the page without any dialog boxes. Microsoft calls components that rely on dialogs *interactive components* and those that don't rely on dialogs *noninteractive components*.

> **TIP**
>
> Web components are created completely at design-time. Therefore, unlike FrontPage's included browse-time components (such as the Hit Counter), they can be used on ASP and ASP.NET pages as well as HTML pages.

WEB COMPONENT ARCHITECTURE

A Web component is developed using a file called an *initialization file* (.ini) that specifies settings for the component, optional HTML files that contain scripting to add the functionality of an interactive component, and optional image files and other files to be included in the HTML file. The initialization file is saved to the following directory:

```
C:\<Office_Directory>\Office11\<LanguageID>\webcomp
```

> **NOTE**
>
> The Language ID is a numeric identifier for your version of Office. For example, the English version of Office uses 1033 as the Language ID.

HTML files and additional files required by the component are saved in a subfolder underneath the folder where the initialization file is saved. The name of that subfolder must be identical to the name of the Web component as specified in the initialization file.

UNDERSTANDING THE INITIALIZATION FILE

Web components all rely on an initialization file for their functionality. This file simply describes the component, specifies how it is to appear in FrontPage, and points to any other files that the component relies on. Let's have a look at a typical initialization file. Listing D.1 shows the initialization file from the JumpURL Web component that is included with the FrontPage 2002 Software Developer's Kit.

LISTING D.1   THE JUMPURL INITIALIZATION FILE

```
[Component]
Name="JumpURL"
Caption="Creates drop-down menu lists by automatically generating the
➡ JavaScript and HTML code"
Sorted=True
Type=Text

[Component.Options]
```

continues

LISTING D.1   CONTINUED

```
Option1=JumpURL with Go Button
Option2=Instant JumpURL

[JumpURL with Go Button]
Name="JumpURL with Go Button"
Description="Insert drop-down menu list with Go Button into your document."
URL="C:\Program Files\Microsoft Office\Office10\1033\webcomp\
➥jumpURL\jumpURL.htm"

[Instant JumpURL]
Name="Instant JumpURL"
Description="Insert drop-down menu list into your document."
URL="C:\Program Files\Microsoft Office\Office10\1033\webcomp\
➥jumpURL\jumpURL2.htm"
```

The initialization file is broken up into sections with each section header surrounded by square brackets. In the JumpURL file shown in Listing D.1, most of the sections for an initialization file are listed. The JumpURL component is added to the Insert Web Component dialog box in FrontPage using the settings specified in the initialization file as seen in Figure D.2.

Figure D.2
The JumpURL and its sub-options as seen in the Insert Web Component dialog box in FrontPage.

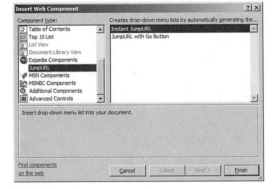

THE [Component] SECTION

The first section in the initialization file is the [Component] section. The [Component] section contains many different settings for the Web component, some of which are seen in Listing D.1.

The following settings are used in the [Component] section:

■ Name—This text appears in the FrontPage Insert Web Component dialog box. In the case of the JumpURL initialization file in Listing D.1, JumpURL is displayed in the Insert Web Component dialog box.

■ CommentText—Specifies the purple comment text that appears in FrontPage's Design view when the Web component is inserted on to a page. This setting is not included in the initialization file in Listing D.1 because the JumpURL component uses sub-options and the CommentText setting is not used if a component uses sub-options.

- Type—This optional setting specifies how the component appears in the Insert Web Component dialog box. Values for this setting are Text, IconAndText, and Image. If it is not specified, it defaults to Text.

- ImageFile—This optional setting specifies the name of the icon file that is used for the component in the Insert Web Component dialog box.

- Caption—This optional setting is only included if your component has sub-options. Sub-options appear in the right side of the Insert Web Components dialog box, and the text specified with the Caption setting appears directly above the list of sub-options.

- Sorted—This optional setting specifies whether sub-options are sorted by name. If the value is not equal to True or 1, sub-options will appear in the same order as they are listed in the initialization file.

> **TIP**
>
> To make your Web component stand out in the Web Component list, create an icon for it.

THE [Component.Options] SECTION

The next section of the initialization file is the [Component.Options] section. This section specifies any sub-options for the component. Sub-options appear in the right side of the Insert Web Component dialog box, as you saw in Figure D.2. The [Component.Options] section of the initialization file contains a list of sub-options for the component defined as Option1, Option2, and so on. The value of each setting in the [Component.Options] section specifies the section in the initialization file that contains settings for that particular sub-option.

In Listing D.1, you can see that the JumpURL component has two sub-options called JumpURL with Go Button and Instant JumpURL. Therefore, there will be a JumpURL with Go Button section and an Instant JumpURL section in the initialization file. Each one of these sections can have the following settings:

- Name—The name that is displayed in the right side of the Insert Web Components dialog in FrontPage.

- Description—This optional setting specifies the text displayed at the bottom of the Insert Web Component dialog box when the component is selected.

- URL—This URL is the path to the file that displays when the component is inserted. The URL can be an HTTP path on the Internet or Intranet, or it can be a file path to the user's local machine or a network share.

- ImageFile—This optional setting specifies the image file to be displayed next to the component's name in the Insert Web Component dialog box.

THE [<ComponentName>.HTML] SECTION

The last section of the initialization file, and one that is not present in Listing D.1, is an optional section used for noninteractive components called [<ComponentName>.HTML]. For example, if the Instant JumpURL sub-option of the JumpURL component were a noninteractive component, the section would be called [Instant JumpURL.HTML], and it would contain settings to specify the HTML to insert when the option is selected. This section is only used if a URL setting is not specified for the sub-option.

The [<ComponentName>.HTML] section has a setting called HTMLn, where n is equal to an incrementing numeric value. Suppose you were developing a noninteractive component called InsertJimcoLink that added a link to the Jimco Add-ins Web site when it was selected. In that case, the [<ComponentName>.HTML] section would appear as shown here:

```
[InsertJimcoLink.HTML]
HTML1="<a href='http://www.jimcoaddins.com'>Jimco Add-ins</a>"
```

When the component is selected and inserted, FrontPage would simply insert the HTML specified in the initialization file. If other lines of HTML were required, they could be specified as HTML2, HTML3, and so on.

UNDERSTANDING THE HTML FILE(S)

The HTML file for a Web component consists of the user interface for the component and script that is used to provide for the functionality of the component. For example, the JumpURL component allows you to build a dropdown list that will take you to a URL you specify depending on which option you select in the dropdown. Figure D.3 shows the jumpURL.htm page opened in FrontPage, and Figure D.4 shows the user interface for the JumpURL Web component. The size of the window that is displayed for the Web component is not configurable. It will always be 608x427 in size. However, the window is resizable by the user of your component by dragging the borders.

Figure D.3
The jumpURL.htm page provides the user interface for the JumpURL Web component.

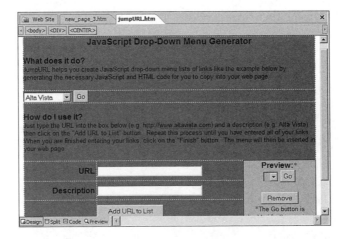

Figure D.4
The JumpURL Web component dialog box in FrontPage.

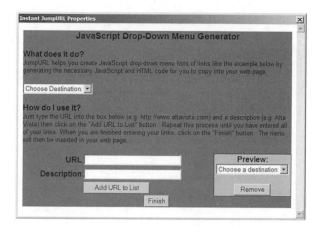

When you configure the Web component inside the dialog box, client-side JavaScript runs on the page that determines how the Web component behaves. In the case of the JumpURL component, the script is fairly complex, but it's much less complex than learning C++—a complicated and complex computer language that is used to write FrontPage Components.

> **TIP**
>
> A FrontPage Component (also called a FrontPage Web Component) is similar to a Web component, but the user interface of a FrontPage Component can be much more complex because they aren't made from HTML files.

Figure D.5 shows the JumpURL component after it has been inserted in a Web page. This component is a genuine FrontPage Web component, and if you look at the code of the page (seen in Figure D.6), you can see that FrontPage uses the `<webbot>` tag to store information about the component. This makes it very easy to edit the component by simply double-clicking on it inside of FrontPage to bring up the component's user interface.

In case you haven't yet realized it, this approach has an incredible benefit to Web component developers. You can keep the files that implement your Web component on a Web site or on a network share. If you need to fix a bug or add a feature, you simply make your change and then overwrite the existing files. The next time that a user of your component pulls up the component, she will automatically see the new version.

> **TIP**
>
> If you host your Web component on the Internet instead of on the user's local machine, the user of your component will have to be connected to the Internet whenever he is using your component. Otherwise, he will see an error message in the dialog box for your component. Keep that in mind when you are deciding on where to hose your component.

Figure D.5
The JumpURL component after being inserted on to a Web page.

```
<body>

<!--webbot bot="ExtWebComponent" S-Name="Instant JumpURL" U-Server="C:\Program Files\Microsoft Office XP
&lt;FORM ACTION=&quot;&quot;&gt;
&lt;select onChange=&quot;location=this.options[this.selectedIndex].value;&quot; value=&quot;GO&quot;&gt;
&lt;OPTION value=GoNowhere selected&gt;Choose a destination:&lt;/OPTION&gt;&lt;OPTION value=http://www.qu
&lt;/SELECT&gt;
&lt;/FORM&gt;
" ClientSide="TRUE" startspan -->
<FORM ACTION="">
<select onChange="location=this.options[this.selectedIndex].value;" value="GO">
<OPTION value=GoNowhere selected>Choose a destination:</OPTION><OPTION value=http://www.quepublishing.co
</SELECT>
</FORM>
<!--webbot bot="ExtWebComponent" endspan i-checksum="15913" -->
```

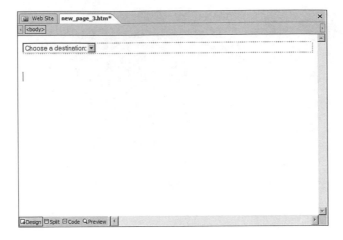

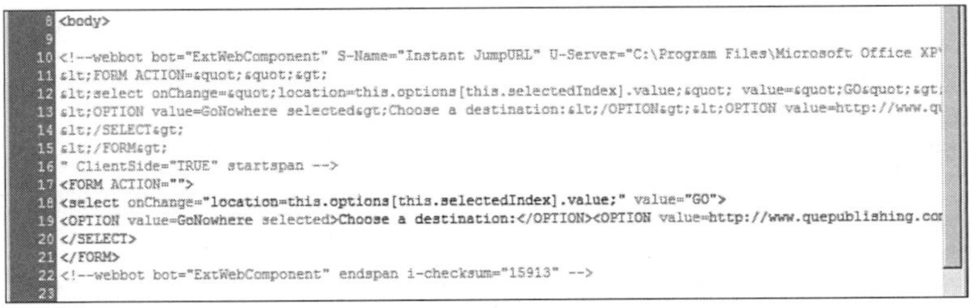

Figure D.6
The code for the JumpURL that was inserted shows the familiar `<webbot>` tag.

FRONT AND CENTER: BUILDING A WEB COMPONENT

NOTE

> The files that you create in this section are also found on the CD that accompanies this book.

I've always said that if you really want to learn how to do something, just do it. Let's build a Web component so that you can get a better understanding of exactly how they work.

Suppose you wanted to build a Web component that allows a user to insert an Add to Favorites link. You want to allow users to specify what text is used for the link. You also want to allow them to choose between a simple text link or a button. This is the perfect candidate for a Web component.

TIP

> Because Web technologies are always changing, Web components represent the perfect way to implement added functionality in FrontPage. As Web technologies improve, you can redesign your Web component and the new version will be automatically delivered to the users of your component.

CREATING AN INITIALIZATION FILE

The first thing you will need is an initialization file. Open Notepad or your favorite text editor and create a new text file. Save the file as **AddFavorite.ini** in the directory of your choice (you will move it to the correct location later) and add the following code to it:

```
[Component]
Name="Add to Favorites"
Caption="Adds a link or button to add to Favorites."

[Component.Options]
Option1=AddToFavoriteLink
Option2=AddToFavoriteButton

[AddToFavoriteLink]
Name="Add to Favorites Link"
Description="Adds a link to add the site to Favorites."
URL="C:\Program Files\Microsoft Office\Office11\1033\webcomp\
➡AddFavorite\AddFavoriteLink.htm"

[AddToFavoriteButton]
Name="Add to Favorites Button"
Description="Adds a button to add the site to Favorites."
URL="C:\Program Files\Microsoft Office\Office11\1033\webcomp\
➡AddFavorite\AddFavoriteButton.htm"
```

The initialization file will add a new Web component called Add to Favorites. It will have two sub-options—one called Add to Favorites Link, and the other called Add to Favorites Button. The user interface for the Add to Favorites Link component is the AddFavoriteLink.htm file, and the user interface for the Add to Favorites Button component is the AddFavoriteButton.htm file. These files contain the implementation of the component, the code that makes it all work.

CREATING THE HTML FILES

Create a new page in FrontPage, switch to Code view, and replace all HTML code in the file with the code from Listing D.2.

LISTING D.2   THE ADDFAVORITELINK.HTM FILE

```
<html>

<head>
<title>Add to Favorites</title>
<script language="JavaScript">
<!--

function insertHTML(url, caption)
  {
```

continues

D

```
    var code;
    var linkText;

    linkText = document.all.item("favText").value;

    // generate some JavaScript...
    code = '\n<SCRIPT LANGUAGE="JavaScript" type="text/javascript">\n';
    code = code + '<!--\n';
    code = code + 'function addFavLink(url, caption)\n';
    code = code + '{\n';
    code = code + '    if (document.all) {\n';
    code = code + '        window.external.AddFavorite(url, caption);\n';
    code = code + '    }\n';
    code = code + '    return true;\n';
    code = code + '};\n';
    code = code + '-->\n';
    code = code + '</'
    code = code + 'SCRIPT>\n';

    // generate HTML code...
    code = code + '<a href="javascript:void(0);"
      onclick="addFavLink(\'' + url + '\', \'' + caption + '\');">' +
      linkText + '</a>'

    window.external.WebComponent.PreviewHTML = code;
    window.external.WebComponent.HTML = code;
    window.external.WebComponent.Tag = "body";
    window.external.Close(true);

    return true;

    }

function defaultText()
  {
  document.all.item('favText').focus();
  return true;
  }

</script>
</head>

<body bgcolor="#FFFFFF" scroll=no onload="defaultText();">
<table border="0" cellpadding="3" style="border-collapse: collapse"
  bordercolor="#111111" width="532" height="358" bgcolor="#336699">
  <tr>
    <td valign=top height=300 width="532">
    <p><b><font face="Arial" color="#FFFFFF" size="4">Add to Favorites Web
    Component</font></b></p>
    <p><b><font face="Arial" color="#FFFFFF" size="2">
        Text for the Add to Favorites Link:</font></b><br>
    <input type="text" id="favText" size="50" name="favText"
        style="font-family: Arial; font-size: 10pt"></p>
    <p><font face="Arial" color="#FFFFFF" size="2"><b>Favorite URL:
    ➥</b></font><br>
```

```
    <input type="text" id="favURL" size="50" name="favURL"
        style="font-family: Arial; font-size: 10pt"></p>
    <p><b><font face="Arial" color="#FFFFFF" size="2">Favorite Caption:</font>
        </b><br>
    <input type="text" id="favCaption" size="50" name="favCaption"
        style="font-family: Arial; font-size: 10pt"></td>
  </tr>
  <tr>
    <td valign="top" align="right" width="532">
        <br>
<button class="button" style="width:70" accesskey="o"
onClick="insertHTML(document.all.item('favURL').value,
➥document.all.item('favCaption').value);">
<u>O</u>K
</button>  
<button class="button" accesskey="c" onClick="window.external.Close();">
<u>C</u>ancel
</button>
    </td>
  </tr>
</table>
</body>
</html>
```

The code in Listing D.2 consists primarily of the insertHTML JavaScript function. The function takes two parameters—one called url that will hold the URL for the favorite link, and one called caption that will hold the text to display in the browser window for the favorite link. The insertHTML function builds the JavaScript code that will be written to the page when the component is inserted and stores it in a variable called code.

At the end of the insertHTML function, some of the WebComponent properties are set with the following lines of code:

```
window.external.WebComponent.PreviewHTML = code;
window.external.WebComponent.HTML = code;
window.external.WebComponent.Tag = "body";
```

This code sets three different properties: PreviewHTML, HTML, and Tag. These are properties of FrontPage Web components that determine how the component is added to the page.

- PreviewHTML—This property sets the HTML code that is used to render the component in Design view in FrontPage.

- HTML—This property sets the HTML code that displays the component in the Web browser or in Preview view in FrontPage.

- Tag—This property sets the HTML tag into which the component is inserted.

These properties are written into the <webbot> tag that FrontPage generates. After your Web Component has been inserted, it can be edited by double-clicking on it to bring up your Web Component dialog box. The Web Component properties are available to you when the component is being edited, which means that you can write more JavaScript into the component so that the values entered are repopulated into the component when it is edited.

To create the Web Component that uses a button instead of a link, create another new file, switch to Code view, and replace all the existing HTML with the HTML from Listing D.3.

LISTING D.3   THE AddFavoriteButton.htm FILE

```
<html>

<head>
<title>Add to Favorites</title>
<script language="JavaScript">
<!--

function insertHTML(url, caption)
  {
  var code;
  var linkText;

  linkText = document.all.item("favText").value;

  // generate some JavaScript...
  code = '\n<SCRIPT LANGUAGE="JavaScript" type="text/javascript">\n';
  code = code + '<!--\n';
  code = code + 'function addFavLink(url, caption)\n';
  code = code + '{\n';
  code = code + '    if (document.all) {\n';
  code = code + '       window.external.AddFavorite(url, caption);\n';
  code = code + '    }\n';
  code = code + '    return true;\n';
  code = code + '};\n';
  code = code + '-->\n';
  code = code + '</'
  code = code + 'SCRIPT>\n';

  // generate HTML code...
  code = code + '<button class="button"
onclick="addFavLink(\'' + url + '\', \'' + caption + '\');">' +
➥linkText + '</button>';

  window.external.WebComponent.PreviewHTML = code;
  window.external.WebComponent.HTML = code;
  window.external.WebComponent.Tag = "body";
  window.external.Close(true);

  return true;

  }

function defaultText()
  {
  document.all.item('favText').focus();
  return true;
  }

</script>
</head>
```

```
<body bgcolor="#FFFFFF" scroll=no onload="defaultText();">
<table border="0" cellpadding="3" style="border-collapse: collapse"
 bordercolor="#111111" width="532" id="AutoNumber1" height="358"
 ➥bgcolor="#336699">
  <tr>
    <td valign=top height=300 width="532">
    <p><b><font face="Arial" color="#FFFFFF" size="4">Add to Favorites Web
    Component</font></b></p>
    <p><b><font face="Arial" color="#FFFFFF" size="2">
        Text for the Add to Favorites Button:</font></b><br>
    <input type="text" id="favText" size="50" name="favText"
        style="font-family: Arial; font-size: 10pt"></p>
    <p><font face="Arial" color="#FFFFFF" size="2"><b>
    ➥Favorite URL:</b></font><br>
    <input type="text" id="favURL" size="50" name="favURL"
        style="font-family: Arial; font-size: 10pt"></p>
    <p><b><font face="Arial" color="#FFFFFF" size="2">Favorite Caption:
        </font></b><br>
    <input type="text" id="favCaption" size="50" name="favCaption"
        style="font-family: Arial; font-size: 10pt"></td>
  </tr>
  <tr>
    <td valign="top" align="right" width="532">
        <br>
<button class="button" style="width:70" accesskey="o"
onClick="insertHTML(document.all.item('favURL').value,
➥document.all.item('favCaption').value);">
<u>O</u>K
</button>  
<button class="button" accesskey="c" onClick="window.external.Close();">
 <u>C</u>ancel
</button>
    </td>
  </tr>
</table>
</body>
</html>
```

Most of the code in these files consists of the HTML code necessary to render the user interface. As a power user of FrontPage, you should already be familiar with that code. The code in the insertHTML JavaScript function makes the Web component work. Going into the details of that JavaScript is outside of the scope of this chapter, but excellent resources are available on JavaScript if you need more information.

NOTE

For more information on JavaScript, read *Special Edition Using JavaScript* from Que Publishing.

INSTALLING YOUR COMPONENT

Now that all the files for your component are complete, you simply need to copy the files into the correct locations and your Web component is ready for use.

Copy the `AddFavorite.ini` file to the `C:\<Office_Folder>\Office11\<LanguageID>\Webcomp` folder on your machine. On my computer, that folder is `C:\Program Files\Microsoft Office\Office11\1033\Webcomp`. It might be different on your computer.

Next, create a new folder inside the folder you copied the `AddFavorite.ini` file into and name the new folder **AddFavorite**. Copy the `AddFavoriteLink.htm` and the `AddFavoriteButton.htm` files into the `AddFavorite` folder. Your Web component is now installed and ready to be used.

Open or create a Web page in FrontPage and select Insert, Web Component. Scroll down the Component Type list until you find your `Add to Favorites` component and select it. Select either the `Add to Favorites Link` or the `Add to Favorites Button` component and then click Finish. Enter the information for your component and click OK to insert it. Save your page and preview it in your browser to see your component in action.

If you want to extend this component, you can add code to the `defaultText` JavaScript function that will repopulate the component's user interface with the previous values when the component is being edited. Experiment with Web components and have some fun!

INDEX

C

G

GAC (Global Assembly Cache), 687

gateway services, e-commerce payment processing, 939

General Page Templates, 273-275

General tab, 79-80, 321
  Page Options dialog box, 526-527
  Picture Properties dialog box, 118
  Site Settings dialog box, 325-327
  View Styles dialog box, 744

Generator and ProgID tags (optimization setting), 313

Get Site List button, 579

getElementById function (JavaScript), 486

getElementById method (DOM document object), 482

getproperty command, 355

GetQuote method, 673

GetSubWebs function, 580

GetWebSites function, 582

GIF (Graphic Interchange Format), 848-849
  animations, 858-859
  guidelines for use, 849
  interlacing images, 855
  lossless compression, 848
  optimizing graphics, 853-854
  pronunciation, 849
  transparent graphics, 857

GIF Optimizer, 860

Global Assembly Cache. See GAC

Global Level option (navigation interface), 156

global.asa file, 691

global.asa files, 711, 782

Go To URL Behavior, 461

Gradient Editor (Photoshop), 896

Graphic Interchange Format. See GIF

graphics, 114, 888. See also images
  adjusting image properties, 117-119
  Adobe Photoshop, 888-890
  animations, 858-859
  audio files, 129-130
  AutoShapes tool, 115
  background images, 866
  bars and rules, 866
  clip art, 114
    accessing, 114-115
    Clip Art task pane, 115-117
    manipulation using the Pictures toolbar, 119-124
  configuring FrontPage, 891-893
  creating, 871
    background images, 871-873
    bars, 874-876
    header graphics, 872-873
    image maps, 125-126
    Navigational buttons, 874
    from PowerPoint slides, 803-804
    rules, 874-876
    spot art, 875-876
  cropping images, 867

designing, 896-898
Drawing tool, 115
Flash movies, 127-128
formats, 848
  converting between formats, 860-861
  GIF (Graphic Interchange Format), 848-849
  JPEG (Joint Photographic Experts Group), 849-850
  PNG (Portable Network Graphics), 851
  setting standards, 862-863
  troubleshooting, 862
  vector formats, 851-853
headers, 866
hiring designer, 908
inserting graphics files, 117
interlacing, 851
lo-res images, 859
moderation, 877-878
multimedia abuse of the Web, 131
Navigation buttons, 866
obtaining images, 866-869
  Microsoft Clip Organizer, 869-870
  Photo Gallery Web component, 870
  stock images, 870-871
optimization, 853, 859
  Debabelizer Pro, 860
  GIF images, 853-854
  GIF Optimizer, 860
  ImageReady tool, 860
  JPEG images, 854
  Ulead Systems SmartSaver, 860
Photo Galleries, 115
progressive rendering, 855-857

X-Y-Z

What's on the CD-ROM

- Jimco's SnipView (available exclusively with this book!)
- Trial versions of PageTools, Media Manager, CoolerEmail, and 123 Password Creator
- Book author examples
- Woody's Office POWER Pack (WOPR) 2003
- Web resources
- A graphics library

Windows Installation Instructions

1. Insert the disc into your CD-ROM drive.
2. From the Windows desktop, double-click the My Computer icon.
3. Double-click the icon representing your CD-ROM drive.
4. Double-click on start.exe. Follow the on-screen prompts to access the CD content.

NOTE

> If you have the AutoPlay feature enabled, start.exe will be launched automatically whenever you insert the disc into your CD-ROM drive.